THE LETTERS OF
ANTHONY TROLLOPE

The Letters of
ANTHONY TROLLOPE

EDITED BY N. JOHN HALL

With the Assistance of Nina Burgis

VOLUME ONE, 1835-1870

STANFORD UNIVERSITY PRESS   1983

Stanford, California

STANFORD UNIVERSITY PRESS
Stanford, California
© 1983 by the Board of Trustees of the
Leland Stanford Junior University
Printed in the United States of America
ISBN 0–8047–1076–7
LC 79–64213

15195

Published with the assistance of the
National Endowment for the Humanities

ACKNOWLEDGMENTS

MANY PEOPLE have assisted me in compiling this edition of Trollope's letters. I should like first to thank the officers of the libraries, collections, and publishing houses that have generously made letters available to me and given me permission to publish them. My largest debt in this regard is to the Morris L. Parrish Collection of Victorian Novelists, Princeton University Library, and to its Curator, Alexander D. Wainwright. The Parrish Collection has by far the most extensive holdings of Trollope letters in manuscript. Mr. Wainwright has patiently assisted me throughout and has continued to help me in securing copies of Trollope letters right through the last stages of proof. The Robert H. Taylor Collection, also housed in the Princeton University Library, has the second largest holdings of Trollope letters. Mr. Taylor, besides making these letters available, has frequently shared with me his broad knowledge of Trollope. Another major depository of Trollope letters is the National Library of Scotland, where Alan S. Bell's help was constant. I wish also to thank the following: American Antiquarian Society; Arents Collection, New York Public Library; Associated Book Publishers Ltd., London; Auckland Institute and Museum; Beinecke Library, Yale University; Berg Collection, New York Public Library; Berkshire County Record Office; Biblioteca Nazionale Centrale, Florence; Birmingham Oratory; William Blackwood & Sons, Ltd.; Bodleian Library, Oxford; Boston Public Library; Brandeis University Library; British Library; Brotherton Library, University of Leeds; Armstrong Browning Library, Baylor University; Buffalo and Erie County Public Library; University of California, Los Angeles; University of California Press; Chatto & Windus, Ltd.; Cheshire County Record Office; Colby College Library; Columbia University Library; *Contemporary Review*; Cornell University Library; Cremation Society of Great Britain; Dartmouth College Library; Milton S. Eisenhower Library, Johns Hopkins University; Fales Collection, New York University Library; Fitzwilliam Museum, Cambridge; Free Library of Philadelphia; Garrick Club; Glamorgan County Record Office; Guildhall Library; Harrow School; Harrowby Manuscripts Trust; Haverford College Library; John Hay Library, Brown University; Hereford and Worcester

County Record Office; Heritage Bookshop, Los Angeles; Hertfordshire County Record Office; Historical Society of Pennsylvania; Houghton Library, Harvard University; Humanities Research Center, University of Texas; Henry E. Huntington Library; University of Illinois Library; University of Iowa Libraries; Kent County Archives; University of Kentucky Library; Harold B. Lee Library, Brigham Young University; Leeds City Libraries; Library of Congress; University of Liverpool Library; University of London Library; Macmillan Press Ltd., London; Maryland Historical Society; Marylebone Library, City of Westminster; McGill University Library; Massachusetts Historical Society; University of Melbourne Archives; Mitchell Library, Library of New South Wales, Sydney; University of Michigan Library; Pierpont Morgan Library; John Murray, Ltd.; Natal Government Archives, Pietermaritzburg; National Library of Ireland; Newark Public Library; New York Historical Society; Newberry Library; Norfolk County Record Office; C. K. Ogden Library, University College, London; Oxford University Press; Carl H. Pforzheimer Library; Pickering & Chatto, Ltd., London; Pitman Publishing, Ltd., London; Post Office Records, Postal Headquarters, London; Princeton University Library; *Punch* Office, London; University of Rochester Library; Rhode Island Historical Society; Royal Literary Fund; St. Regis Newspapers, Ltd., Bolton; Somerville College, Oxford; South African Library, Cape Town; State Library of Victoria, Melbourne; State University of New York, Buffalo; *The Times*, London; Trinity College Library, Cambridge; Trinity College Library, University of Dublin; Trinity College Library, University of Melbourne; Alexander Turnbull Library, Wellington; Victoria and Albert Museum; Victoria University of Wellington; University of Virginia Library; and Virtue & Company, Ltd.

The following people have generously provided copies of letters and permission to publish them: D. R. Bentham, Robert A. Cecil, Desmond Corcoran, Peter Giffard, Major Richard G. Gregory, Sir Thomas Ingilby, Bart., Bernard Jackson, André LeCesne, Mrs. C. L. Mock, Ray Rawlins, Gordon N. Ray, Jacques T. Schlenger, Mrs. Seton Gordon, David Stivender, Chester W. Topp, and Sylvia Trollope.

For copyright permission to publish Trollope's letters I thank the Cheltenham Trust Bank of Lloyds Bank Limited, trustees of the estate of the late Muriel Rose Trollope.

The following people have provided valuable assistance: Gregory and Janet Abels, Reginald Allen, Hugh Amory, Catherine Barnes, Barry A. Bartrum, Scott Bennett, Margaret Berg, Clyde Binfield, J.E.H. Blackie, Victor Bonham-Carter, John Brett-Smith, Herbert Cahoon, Mary Ceibert, Laura L. Chace, Charles Chadwyck-Healey, Morton N. Cohen, Brenda Colloms, John Corbett, Marsha Cummins, R. L. Davids, James H. Davidson, Rodney Dennis, the late Rev. Charles Stephen Dessain, Janet E. Dunleavy, Jean Dyce, J. P. N. Ellis, Elizabeth Epperly, Lady Faber, K. J. Fielding, Mortimer H. Frank, William E. Fredeman,

Robert Frey, Jill Furlong, K. C. Gay, Judith Gelmon, Stephen Gill, Elizabeth Gotch, Rosemary Graham, Charles Green, Ann S. Gwyn, Gordon S. Haight, John Halperin, Mary Hamer, David Mike Hamilton, Christina M. Hanson, K. C. Harrison, Helen Heineman, Jack W. Herring, Sara S. Hodson, Gordon Hollis, Walter E. Houghton, Rita S. Humphrey, Susan L. Humphreys, William Ingoldsby, Harriet C. Jameson, Brian Johnson, E. D. H. Johnson, William R. Johnson, Roger B. Joyce, Alan Jutzi, Philip Kelley, James R. Kincaid, Thomas V. Lange, Coral Lansbury, Kenneth A. Lohf, Katharine M. Longley, Daniel K. Lowenthal, Victor Luftig, Mrs. C. McNamara, K. A. Manley, Michael Y. Mason, Mario and Millicent Materassi, Glenise Matheson, J. C. Maxwell, F. R. Miles, Walter James Miller, Rita Lloyd Moroney, the late A. N. L. Munby, Selma Muresianu, Winifred A. Myers, John Nicoll, Ellen M. Oldham, William O'Sullivan, Constance-Anne Parker, Gordon Phillips, Gerald Pindar, K. G. C. Prevette, Richard L. Purdy, Margery C. Ramsey, Victor B. Reed, Hinta Rose, Dennis Rowley, Suzanne L. Rutter, Alice Schreyer, Evelyn Schweidel, Peter Shillingsburg, Nathaniel N. Shipton, David Skilton, Norah Smallwood, W. A. Spowers, Patricia Thomas Srebrnik, June Starke, Donald D. Stone, Graham Storey, John Sutherland, Lola L. Szladits, Saundra Taylor, James E. Tierney, Kathleen Tillotson, Robert Tracy, Patrick L. Waddington, Colonel and Mrs. W. A. Wakefield, Malcolm Warner, Alexander Welsh, Pamela White, Brooke Whiting, John Wilson, Andrew Wright, Marjorie G. Wynne, Helen M. Young, and William Zalkin.

I wish to thank the following for their special help. Gordon N. Ray, for encouragement and advice from the beginning of the project. Robert H. Super, for his careful reading of the manuscript and numerous helpful suggestions, and for permitting me to see in typescript and to draw extensively on his book *Trollope in the Post Office*. Robert S. Call, for assistance in the early stages of transcription. P. D. Edwards, for assistance in matters Australian. Mary Rusden, for assistance with the G. W. Rusden letters. Nancy N. Coffin, for assistance in the Taylor Collection. Theodore G. Grieder, for making available to me the resources of the Fales Collection, New York University Library. John Sutherland, for facilitating my research at University College, London. Nigel Cross, for assistance with the archives of the Royal Literary Fund. Pamela Lumsden, for answering queries respecting the Garrick Club. Mrs. I. M. Roseveare, for answering queries respecting the Athenaeum Club. Ruth apRoberts, for her valuable reading of the manuscript for the publisher. At Stanford University Press, J. G. Bell, for helpful and generous editorial decisions, and Norris Pope, for scrupulous editing and an attention to detail that led him to library work on my behalf. Dolores DeLuise, for assistance with proofreading. Nina Burgis, for assistance in various phases of the project, including library research, proofreading, and indexing, assistance I am pleased to acknowledge on the title page. And my wife, Marianne, for help throughout.

I am grateful to Karl Miller and the authorities of University College, London, for affording me the status of honorary research fellow.

I acknowledge gratefully three Faculty Research Awards from the City University of New York, a year's fellowship leave from Bronx Community College, a Grant-in-Aid from the State University of New York, and a fellowship from the John Simon Guggenheim Memorial Foundation.

New York City, 1982   N. J. H.

CONTENTS

ILLUSTRATIONS

INTRODUCTION

THE LETTERS OF Anthony Trollope, collected here in an edition as complete as possible at the present time, chronicle the everyday life of Victorian England's busiest man of letters. But they do more than provide a vantage point for considering his literary achievement. In a manner that is straightforward and less consciously literary than that of most writers, the letters, though touching only obliquely on the inner life, reveal in their sum the man himself. Although it is probable that Trollope, who was notably reticent about his private life, would have been confounded at the publication of his letters, he wrote an autobiography containing much that was personal while purporting to be almost exclusively an account of his literary career. The *Autobiography* is evidence that Trollope had a sense of the relevance of his private life to his published work. These letters clarify, supplement, and correct the crafted view of his life, both professional and private, as given in the *Autobiography*.

The handful of preserved letters from his early years, beginning in 1835 when Trollope was twenty, give no more than a glimpse of the young postal clerk in London. Chiefly, they show him acting as his mother's agent with publishers. The letters are still sparse after his removal to Ireland in 1841 as a postal surveyor's clerk. Negotiations for his first novel, *The Macdermots of Ballycloran*, are documented, for example, only in letters from the publisher, Newby, to Trollope. Most of the surviving letters through the mid-1850's are to his mother and brother, and these letters unfortunately exist only in fragmentary form in F. E. Trollope's *Memoir of Frances Trollope*. More substantial correspondence survives, including readers' reports, in connection with the publication of *The Warden* and *Barchester Towers*, brought out by Longman in 1855 and 1857 respectively. Still, the letters are relatively few until 1860, when the publication of *Framley Parsonage* made Trollope a truly popular novelist. Now 45, he finally had a name, and people kept his letters. The record is detailed from this year onward. Not only did the appearance of *Framley Parsonage* in the spectacularly successful *Cornhill Magazine* make Trollope a premier serial novelist, but the *Cornhill* connection introduced him to literary and social London. The

outsider who had resided seventeen years in Ireland became the friend
and correspondent of writers, painters, politicians, and publishers; his
intimates included Thackeray, Millais, G. H. Lewes, George Eliot, and
Richard Monckton Milnes. Club life, which took almost as strong a
hold on him as novel writing and hunting, broadened his acquaintance.
In 1860 he formed a romantic attachment to Kate Field and began the
long and well-known series of letters to her. Many other activities served
to generate correspondence: his work for the Post Office until his resignation in 1867; his service to the Royal Literary Fund, a charity for which
he worked assiduously for more than twenty years; the editorship of his
own magazine, *St. Paul's*; and extended trips abroad, two to the United
States, two to Australia, one to South Africa. Yet all the while he worked
incessantly at writing, producing some seventy books, including 47
novels—more good novels than any other writer in English.

It is not surprising for a writer of Trollope's prodigious output that
many of his letters are addressed to publishers. More than anything else
this collection is a record of author-publisher relations. The list of Trollope's publishers is imposing, even bewildering: it is a roll call of the
great and less-than-great Victorian publishing houses: Newby, Colburn,
Longman, Bentley, Chapman & Hall, Smith Elder, Blackwood, Strahan,
Virtue, Bradbury & Evans, Hurst & Blackett, Tinsley, Sampson Low,
Macmillan, Isbister, Chatto & Windus, and numerous publishers of
magazines. What strikes one from the outset is Trollope's confidence in
his work, not only in its artistic worth, but in its value in pounds and
shillings. In a letter to Richard Bentley concerning his second novel,
The Kellys and the O'Kellys, Trollope took a firm line, albeit unsuccessfully (16 October 1847): "I will *not part with the Mss* on *any other terms
than that of payment for it*. I mean, that I will not publish it myself—or
have it published on half profits—or have the payment for it conditional
on the sale. It is, & must be, much more the publishers interest to push
a work when it is his own property."

From this, his first preserved letter to a publisher, through many
hundreds more, Trollope's correspondence is forthright and forceful.
Nevertheless, it was not until ten years and four novels later that Trollope won his point. He wrote to William Longman with respect to *Barchester Towers* (10 January 1857): "It appears that you think £100 too
high a sum to pay in advance for the book. It seems to me that if a three
vol. novel be worth anything it must be worth that. . . . If therefore you
are of opinion that you cannot afford to pay in advance so moderate a
price as £100 I think it will be better for me to withdraw my MS." Longman paid the £100. For his next novel, *The Three Clerks*, Trollope told
Longman (29 August 1857): "I certainly did mean you to understand by
my last letter that I should want a better price for another novel. Indeed I may say at once that I would not under any circumstances take
less than double what I received before." This time Longman declined,
and Trollope took the novel to Bentley, who paid £250. For his next,

Doctor Thorne, he received £400, from still another publisher, Chapman & Hall. Even of Thackeray, whom he had not yet met but whom he most admired of all English novelists, he asked boldly that his series of short stories be included in the projected *Cornhill Magazine* (23 October 1859): "I will tell you exactly what would be my views, and you will as frankly tell me whether they would suit you. . . . Harper gives me £20 for each story—or £2 a page for 10 pages." The response was beyond his fondest hopes: £1,000 for a three-volume novel, to be serialized in the place of honor in the new magazine. Thereafter he did not have to haggle with publishers, and his prices rose quickly and steadily until in 1867 he could command £3,200 from James Virtue for *Phineas Finn*.

But if Trollope could drive a bargain, he knew the market and did not, even at the time he was in most demand, overreach himself. To the same James Virtue, reporting prospects for the *St. Paul's Magazine*, of which Trollope was editor and Virtue proprietor, he wrote (14 December 1868):

I could begin [a novel] in Saint Pauls 1. January 1870; if you wish it. If you would prefer that I should apply to George Elliot [*sic*], I will do so. I think she would charge you double what I should. No doubt it would be worth much more than mine. It will be for you to judge what it would be worth your while to give her. Do not for a moment suppose that there will be any feeling of rivalry between her & me.

Trollope's decline in popularity through the 1870's and into the 1880's can be traced graphically in terms of payments received. He seems to have accepted this lessening of earning power with grace. Once, while offering the serial rights to a three-volume novel to Blackwood for £600, he remarked, completely without bitterness, "I have never had less but will listen to reason" (24 May 1877). Moreover, Trollope was not mercenary. One should keep in mind his almost quixotic honesty and fairness in dealing with publishers. When difficulties arose about the time of commencement of *John Caldigate* in *Blackwood's Magazine*, Trollope offered to reduce the agreed-upon price from £600 to £450 (14 January 1878). When he discovered that Chapman & Hall, of which he was at the time a director, had suffered a loss on *The Duke's Children*, he addressed to the firm's chairman a letter probably unique in publishing annals (13 August 1880): "I cannot allow that. It is the first account I have ever seen of one of my own books. The bargain was made as far back as June 1878. I will repay to the Company the amount lost, viz £120." Similarly, he insisted on giving the public its money's worth. When Alexander Macmillan, in whose magazine *Sir Harry Hotspur* had appeared, sold the book rights to Hurst & Blackett on the understanding that the small work would be stretched to two volumes, Trollope wrote (18 October 1870): "I am sorry that any thing to do with my tale should be less advantageous to you than you had expected. But the fact is that as one pound of tea wont make two by any variance in packing the article,—so neither will a one-volumed tale make two volumes." The publishers relented. So did Alexander Strahan, who earlier had gone as far as to have a small collection of short stories set in type in two volumes. Trollope expostulated (10 March 1867):

I must ask you to understand that I altogether refuse my sanction to such an arrangement— I have always endeavored to give good measure to the public— The pages, as you propose to publish them, are so thin and desolated . . . as to make me ashamed of the idea of putting my name to the book. . . . I am grieved that the expense of second printing should be thrown upon you. Tho' I have not been in any way the cause of this, I will share the expense of this printing with you on condition that you break up the type and print the stories afresh—

Trollope's most sustained connection with a publisher was with Chapman & Hall, an association that began in 1858 and continued until Trollope's death in 1882. But during the 1860's a more cordial connection was with George Smith of Smith, Elder, the publisher of the *Cornhill Magazine*. To Smith there survive 160 letters. They range in tone from playful good humor such as that in regard to a February or March starting date for a novel—"as you know, I always submit in all things" (25 November 1865)—to the obstinacy that on one occasion nearly led to a falling out. In a letter that hitherto has been a mystery, Trollope wrote: "I should have been unhappy to feel myself severed from the most popular periodical publication of the day" (5 January 1861). It is now clear that Trollope was answering a letter from Smith, who said he had seen Thackeray and was "authorized by him to say that 'Jones Brown & Robinson' [*sic*] shall be inserted in the 'Cornhill Magazine' without any editorial revision" (4 January 1861). Evidently Trollope was prepared to leave the *Cornhill*, which had all but made his reputation, rather than permit his novel to be edited, even by the revered Thackeray. Trollope's patience and flexibility are wonderfully in evidence in his dealings with Smith over *The Last Chronicle of Barset*, a novel Smith wanted written for serialization, first in 20, later in 30, and finally in 32 parts. At one stage in the proceedings Trollope wrote (6 February 1866):

But it is essential, in reference to the proposed 30 numbers, to be prepared for such a division if it be contemplated. It would not be practicable to divide 20 numbers into 30 equal parts, unless the work be specially done with this intent. . . . If you wish the work to be so arranged as to run either to 20 or to 30 numbers, I must work each of the 20 numbers by 6 chapters, taking care that the chapters run so equally, two and two, as to make each four into one equal part or each 6 into one equal part— There will be some trouble in this, but having a mechanical mind I think I can do it.

Trollope's closest friend among publishers was John Blackwood. On one occasion Trollope made Blackwood a gift of the copyright of a book (*The Commentaries of Caesar*), although, characteristically, a few months later Trollope could bring himself to tell the second Lord Brougham that if Blackwood did not come up with better terms for the autobiography of his brother (the first Lord Brougham) he ought to take the work to another publisher (24 November 1870). The Trollope-Blackwood letters are the nearest we come to possessing a complete two-way correspondence, largely because the Blackwood firm kept scrupulous letter books. (Trollope customarily destroyed letters he received, except those pertaining to business.) That Blackwood was his own reader enlivened the exchange. Blackwood could be fussy, and Trollope was not given to making revisions. When the publisher wrote (13 September 1867) that he had read *Linda Tressel* in its entirety and feared "you have made a blunder and so have I," one of the opinions he gave was that "Linda herself is excellent if she had a man to give her heart to. Ludovic is too much of a myth except in that frantic kissing scene. The descriptions throughout are vivid & good & I daresay the want of somebody like a man is the main defect." Trollope's first reaction was (16 September 1867): "I write a line at once to say that you are quite at liberty to give up the story if you do not mind the expense of having put it into type. Do not consider yourself to be in the least bound by your offer . . . and feel quite sure that your returning [the manuscript] to me will moult no feather between you & me." When Blackwood assured him he had no intention of not publishing the novel, Trollope addressed himself to Blackwood's objection (19 September 1867):

It is hardly possible for a novelist who depends more on character than on incident for his interest always to make the chief personages of his stories pleasant acquaintances. His object is to shew what is the effect of such and such qualities on the happiness of those on whom they act; and in doing this he can hardly contrive that a nice young man should always be there to be married to the nice young woman.

The exchange is typical. As he grew older Trollope became somewhat more willing to heed Blackwood's suggestions. When Blackwood complained that the hero of *John Caldigate* was unsympathetic, Trollope answered (14 January 1878):

In almost all that you say about John Caldigate I agree fully. . . . The fault of the book is that the reader cannot sympathise with the man. In such matters I generally know my own fault though I may have failed to avoid it. But to induce the circumstances it was almost necessary to make him poor;—I at least, as I wrote the book, did not see my way to avoid the necessity. I threw myself into her character, too negligent of him. . . . I think that in correcting the press I may add something of tenderness to him,—of tenderness in regard to her, and I will do my best as time is short. I fear I should not do any good by attempting to alter the conduct of the story.

Other letters show Trollope in an opposite role, not indeed that of publisher, but of editor. One letter (9 September 1863), previously incompletely transcribed, reveals that Chapman & Hall were planning for 1864 a new weekly, "conducted by Anthony Trollope." They had gone so far as a discussion of page size and whether to print in columns. The scheme fell through, but one can see in it the seeds of the *Fortnightly Review*, which Trollope and Frederic Chapman were foremost in establishing the following year. By the end of 1866 James Virtue and Trollope were in consultation, amply recorded here, over the establishment of *St. Paul's Magazine*, which Trollope edited from 1867 to 1870. He was a conscientious but not overbearing editor. He asked Austen Henry Layard to "soften" the scorn and "assured threat of destruction held out against the 'Tory' order & class" in an article on politics (7 November 1867). He told Mrs. Cudlip (6 March 1868) that her short story was set in print but could not be used without "a considerable change in the event or ending of the tale. . . . Your finale wounds all our ideas of probability." He cajoled George MacDonald (7 August 1868): "Let [your story] not be sensible;—but weird rather, and of a Christmas-ghostly flavour, if such be possible. I don't know whether Pudding and Hades can be brought together;—but if any man can do it, you can." He edited poetry very carefully, line by line. To Austin Dobson, his leading contributor of verse, he wrote (8 October 1868): "I dislike the word 'weigh' . . . the simple change to 'play' would be an improvement. . . . Blessed as the blind &c . . . I may be stupid, but I see no idea in this. The blind, if they bless, bless without seeing. But the blind are not specially given to the conferring of blessings." Also (2 October 1869): "*Above* the merry mouth—eyes are of course above the mouth. Is there any real meaning or description in the word. . . . 'Misconstrue' is harsh for such playful lines. In either praise or blame is a thought tame." And (13 February 1870): " 'Shew'—for declare is not happy. . . . Chill is a bad epithet for locks. Whoever, even in fiction, had said he was slender?" He did not demand compliance from Dobson and others, but they usually accepted his suggestions, which, as a glance at the text shows, were eminently sensible.

As for his own works, Trollope was not much given to discussing them in his letters other than in correspondence with publishers. With Mary Holmes, who seems to have been an indefatigable correspondent of authors, he is drawn into some comment on his novels. For example (1 May 1874): "The Macdermots had its merits,—truth, freshness, and a certain tragic earnestness being the list of them. The execution was *very bad*. The best novel I ever wrote was the Last Chronicle of Barset." Or, in connection with characters in *The Way We Live Now* (8 July 1875): Paul Montague "is badly done throughout, and fails in interest. Hetta [Carbury] also is bad, and you are quite right in saying that Mrs. Hurtle, (who is well done) is kept too long on the stage. But she was wanted to give an interest to the last chapters, as Hetta &c were uninteresting. . . . Melmotte however is good, and the Longestaffes, and Nidderdale & all the 'rowdy' lot." Occasionally Trollope will explain or defend, while at the same time playing down his accomplishment. To an unidentified correspondent who pointed out certain "errors" in the *Last Chronicle of Barset*, Trollope wrote (15 June 1867):

Many thanks for your kind letter. . . . I forget now how I got over the final difficulty of discharging Crawley,—not having the sheets by me, & the whole thing being with me a task long over & almost forgotten. The first great lapse of examining the wife was very great. But I console myself with thinking that a novelist, in dealing as he must do, almost necessarily, with many affairs of life, with many professions & with various trades may be excused, perhaps, the blunders if his pictures are generally true. Not to be false in sentiment, not [to] be untrue to nature, not to be dull, not to be grandiloquent, not to be injurious in his teaching, not to be immoral in his pictures,—these I think should be his attempts. Do not suppose that I think myself to have been successful in all, or always in any.

Writing to Millais from Australia (it is often when corresponding with people at a great distance that Trollope becomes more personal), he insisted (30 June 1875): "I like a man to be honest enough to say that he is proud of his own work and contented with what he has been able to do for himself. I hate the namby pamby humility of a man who thinks it necessary to belittle himself and his efforts." These words, though primarily intended for Millais' benefit, clearly refer also to Trollope himself. And yet he frequently does precisely what he here deplores, namely belittle himself and his own works. Only rarely, and to close friends, did he reveal his pride in accomplishment, although even in these instances some self-irony always intruded. To Arthur Tilley he wrote (5 December 1881):

"Barchester Towers" was written before you were born. Of course I forget every word of it! But I dont. There is not a passage in it I do not remember. I always have to pretend to forget when people talk to me about my own old books. It looks modest;—and to do the other things looks the reverse. But the writer never forgets. And when after 30 years he is told by some one that he has been pathetic, or witty, or even funny, he always feels like lending a five-pound note to that fellow.

From Baden, Trollope wrote to G. W. Rusden in Australia (26 September 1878): "Yesterday I completed my 80th tale;—not all what you would call novels, but of very various lengths— I doubt whether a greater mass of prose fiction ever came from one pen— I have never consciously drawn a character or a plot from the writings of another author." In the same letter, urging Rusden to attempt a pleasing style in his histories of Australia and New Zealand, Trollope remarked: "Anything lighter than my books on the Colonies cannot be imagined,—or indeed more inaccurate. But large numbers of each of them have been sold because I know the knack of writing a book."

Trollope's letters touch his strictly personal life infrequently. Little

has been added to the celebrated letters to Kate Field, first published by
Michael Sadleir in 1927. But Trollope's innocent susceptibility to feminine charm is to be seen frequently enough, as for example when he
writes (19 December 1875) to Miss Jane Dulany, whom he met aboard
ship:

I was very glad to get your letter. No;—the photograph is not good; but it is the
best that I have or ever had. . . . People are thrown together [during ocean
crossings] in absolute intimacy for a few days, till they have time for loves and
quarrels, for sympathies & heart burnings, sometimes for tears & embracings,
and then they part,—never to see each other again! You I hope I may see again,
as I think I may probably be in Paris for a day or two in the spring. . . . In the
mean time I shall expect to hear from you, as you will certainly send me your
photograph.

One of Trollope's most personal statements comes in a letter to Rusden (8 June 1876):

As to that leisure evening of life, I must say that I do not want it. I can conceive of no contentment of which toil is not to be the immediate parent. As
the time for passing away comes near me I have no fear as to the future— I
am ready to go. I dread nothing but physical inability and that mental lethargy
which is apt to accompany it. Since I saw you I have written a memoir of my
own life,—not as regards its activity but solely in reference to its literary bearing, as to what I have done in literature and what I have thought about it,—
and now I feel as though every thing were finished and I was ready to go. No
man enjoys life more than I do, but no man dreads more than I do the time
when life may not be enjoyable.

Then, provoked by Rusden's defense of what he considered religious
cant in Macready's *Reminiscences*, Trollope is led to express his own
religious sentiments, in a way he does in no other surviving letter:

You tell me of his beautiful humility before God! I do not prize humility before
God. I can understand that a man should be humble before his brother men
the smallness of whose vision requires self-abasement in others;—but not that
any one should be humble before God. To my God I can be but true, and if
I think myself to have done well I cannot but say so. To you, if I speak of my
own work, I must belittle myself. I must say that it is naught. But if I speak of
it to my God, I say, "Thou knowest that it is honest;—that I strove to do good;—
that if ever there came to me the choice between success and truth, I stuck to
truth." And I own that I feel that it is impossible that the Lord should damn
me, and how can I be humble before God when I tell him that I expect from
him eternal bliss as the reward of my life here on earth.

Aside from this unusual emphasis on religion, the letter, in its frankness
and its love of work, is quintessential Trollope; he even goes on to make
his oft-repeated comparison of the novelist and the shoemaker, admitting that this was a doctrine "I have always found it difficult to explain
as I would have it explained."

The same letter to Rusden contained early evidence of Trollope's growing concern about his own death. Writing to his brother to announce his move to Harting in Sussex, he said (? May 1880): "It will sometimes take a man more than 5 years to die. I thought I was going to die in Montagu Square when I came here." In 1881 he closed a letter to former Governor Howard of Rhode Island with the words, "I am now an old man, 66, and shall soon come to the end of my tether" (26 February 1881). Six months later he began a letter to the same correspondent, who had urged him to continue the Barsetshire series, "I am nearly seventy years of age, and cannot hope to do what you propose in reference to bringing back our old friends" (29 August 1881). And in an undated letter, probably written in his last year, he said to his brother, "The time has come upon me of which I have often spoken to you, in which I should know that it were better that I were dead." What he feared most was a lingering and incapacitating illness, which, in the event, he was spared.

The style of Trollope's letters will add little to his literary reputation. Many of the letters are, as Bradford Booth noted about the first edition of Trollope's letters, "perforce strictly functional, often indeed perfunctory." But others are far from strictly functional and can be by turn light or serious, friendly or angry, gentle or impatient, succinct or repetitious. Simplicity and intelligibility characterize them throughout. Intelligibility was the quality of prose that Trollope, writing in his *Autobiography*, called most essential in a novelist: "It is not sufficient that there be a meaning that may be hammered out of the sentence, but that the language should be so pellucid that the meaning should be rendered without an effort to the reader;—and not only some proportion of meaning, but the very sense, no more and no less, which the writer has intended to put into his words."

The letters also exhibit a constant effortlessness. Trollope seems utterly careless, never on his guard, never watching his words, even when he hits upon a particularly apt phrase, or when he is loving or erudite. This is surely the case when he writes to someone as important to him as Kate Field (8 July 1868): "Give my kindest love to your mother. The same to yourself dear Kate—if I do not see you again,—with a kiss that shall be semi-paternal—one third brotherly, and as regards the small remainder, as loving as you please." A curious letter to Gladstone (2 May 1880) exhibits the same ease, coupled with characteristic directness. It begins: "Dear Sir. May I venture to ask whether I have in aught offended you? For some years I have thought that you had, not unnaturally, forgotten me. But latterly,—and again yesterday,—I have been made to suppose that you purposely shunned me." Sometimes the businesslike lapidary style can be humorous, or cutting, as it is in this letter to G. N. Richardson (7 October 1882): "Dear Sir, The Fraser's Magazine is I believe dead. At any rate I am not going to write a story for it. Yours truly Anthony Trollope." Occasionally the simple style rises to quiet heights, as when Trollope writes with notable succinctness to Annie Thackeray on the death of her sister, Mrs. Leslie Stephen (4 December 1875): "Dear Annie. I do not know how to write to you, or how to be silent. I will send one word to say that we have thought of your grief, and of his, with many tears. God bless you, Your affectionate friend Anthony Trollope."

Making a draft of a letter, no matter how sensitive or critical the subject, would have been all but unthinkable to Trollope. In fact, he seems to have thought a first draft of anything as somehow dishonest, or at least unhelpful. In the _Autobiography_ he said of his Post Office reports (of which he wrote thousands and in which he took considerable pride) that he wrote them "in the form in which they should be sent,—without a copy. . . . A rough copy, or what is called a draft, is written in order that it may be touched and altered and put on stilts. . . . If a man knows his craft with his pen, he will have learned to write without the necessity of changing his words or the form of his sentences." He wrote his books the same way: the manuscripts that have survived, the manuscripts he sent to the printer, are not second drafts or even fair copies; they are the pages he began to work on at 5:30 every morning. For good or ill, he was simply not given to revising any text—of a novel, a report, or a letter.

The importance Trollope attached to postal reports and the importance of the Post Office in Trollope's life required the inclusion in this collection of a representative sample of postal reports, of a number of letters concerning everyday matters of the post, and of the sequence of letters connected with his angry reaction at having been passed over in 1864 for the number-two position in the Post Office. For Trollope, the Post Office was not just a job. It is true he came to it in 1834 because it was something to do. But after the first unhappy years as a junior clerk in London's postal headquarters, Trollope fell in love with his work. It became a vocation, almost a passion, and he brought to it the same incredible energy he brought to novel writing. We have no cause to doubt the sincerity of his professed melancholy at leaving the service in 1867 to devote himself full-time to literature. As he said in the _Autobiography_: "I was attached to the department, had imbued myself with a thorough love of letters,—I mean the letters which are carried by the post,—and was anxious for their welfare as though they were all my own." Till the end he had an intense professional concern with postal efficiency. When a letter to him from Tom Taylor was delayed 48 hours, he indignantly sent the envelope to the Secretary of the Post Office (10 April 1874).

But with regard to the writing of his own letters Trollope made little fuss. They were an important but not essential part of his writing day. Doubtless he did them after his serious early morning writing, or dashed them off on the run (he carried stationery around with him). Many letters are addressed from the Garrick Club or the Athenaeum Club. He did not make his letters a literary exercise; they contrast markedly with the marvelous letters he inserted in his novels. If only his letters were like *that*, one says. But with the Old Testament-like pronouncements of Mr. Crawley or the clever wheedling letters of Arabella Trefoil, Trollope was illuminating character, which of course was not his intent in his own letters. Nonetheless, his letters indirectly but constantly reveal the kind of person Trollope was: honest, frank, blunt, crusty, gallant, playful, quick to take offense and quick to be reconciled, kind, generous, intelligent, self-deprecating but with a strong belief in his own ability and worth. Lovers of his fiction will be grateful for the portrait the letters provide. For no matter how often we are urged to trust the tale and not the teller, there remains the natural and valid curiosity about the man. Trollope is to be found in his letters. Like life itself they do not always entertain, and they have dull stretches. But they bring Trollope into sharp focus.

THE PRESENT EDITION

This edition of Trollope's letters makes available more than twice the material printed in Bradford Allen Booth's *The Letters of Anthony Trollope*, published in 1951. It is nonetheless indebted to that work. Booth, together with Michael Sadleir, provided the impetus for scholarly Trollope studies during this century. Booth published extensively on nearly every aspect of Trollope and founded *The Trollopian*, the journal that while still under his editorship became *Nineteenth-Century Fiction*. His edition of the *Letters*, the first collection of Trollope's correspondence, not only reflected Trollope's growing importance but contributed much to it.

The major difference in method between the present edition and Booth's is that Booth summarized many letters that he considered unimportant, whereas I have transcribed in their entirety all available letters. Quite simply, Trollope's stature today calls for a complete and inclusive edition. The present edition has 1,826 entries, Booth's 932. But since Booth's total included summaries, 318 of which I have been able to print in full, this edition considerably more than doubles the contents of the earlier one.

All the letters for which a manuscript could be traced have been transcribed from the manuscript or from a photocopy. The letters published by Booth have been transcribed afresh, with the following exceptions: 12 letters printed in full in Booth, for which he saw manuscripts that are now unavailable, and 39 summaries for which his sources have disappeared (prominent among missing sources are Sadleir's transcripts, made while he prepared his *Trollope: A Commentary*, published in 1927).

Included here are 85 letters to Trollope and 16 about him that either complement or supplement his own letters. As noted, Trollope usually destroyed the letters he received. Exceptions were business letters, and many of these are preserved among Trollope's papers at the Bodleian. Publishers' letter books, most notably those of Blackwood, now kept in the National Library of Scotland, make available copies and drafts of letters to Trollope. In the Taylor Collection at Princeton is a portfolio, apparently assembled by Trollope's wife, of some thirty letters addressed to Trollope and to her by well-known contemporaries, including Thackeray, Dickens, Wilkie Collins, Bulwer Lytton, George Eliot, and Cardinal Newman. And among the Trollope family papers now in the University of Illinois Library, there survive additional letters of interest to Trollope including some from his son Frederic. Letters to Trollope have been incorporated into the text only selectively; many have been used in footnotes.

Trollope usually dated his letters. To the relatively small number of undated letters, however, must be added fragments, which often do not include dates. A whole series of letters to T. A. Trollope has been torn in half, with only the bottom half surviving. Undated letters for which exact or approximate dates could be supplied are placed in the chronological sequence. Letters that could be dated only approximately are placed at the end of the nearest appropriate year. Other undated letters are gathered together at the end of the edition, but even there I have attempted an approximate chronological order on the evidence of Trollope's hand, his printed stationery, and the content. Watermarks have been helpful in dating letters because Trollope's private stationery was almost never watermarked more than a year before its use. Surprisingly few envelopes for Trollope's letters survive, and they are referred to (in footnotes) only when they assist in dating a letter or in identifying a recipient or his address.

Fuller annotation is supplied here than in Booth's edition. For annotating the letters in Booth's edition, however, I am of course indebted to his investigations. Where I have had to rely on a Booth note as the sole source of my own note, or where Booth provided a particularly telling insight, I have indicated this with "(B)." But the annotation of the letters published by Booth, like the transcription of these letters, has been done afresh. Two other books were a constant source of assistance: Michael Sadleir's *Trollope: A Commentary* (1927) and his *Trollope: A Bibliography* (1928).

Unless otherwise noted, the place of publication for all books cited is London. Cross-references to letters included in this edition (and these have been liberally supplied) are generally given in the form "See Trollope to Smith, 31 March 1865." The manuscript source or earliest available source for each letter is given first in the headnote; this is followed by a chronological listing of subsequent appearances of the letter or extracts from it in print. Headnote references to Booth's edition of the letters are by letter number, not by page number.

Trollope's handwriting, never very easy to decipher, became increasingly illegible over the years. Examples of his hand can be seen in the plates that reproduce the letters of 25 May 1839, 18 October 1863, 2 February 1874, and 26 February 1881. (The 1874 example includes the leaping stag—from the Trollope family coat of arms—that Trollope frequently had printed on his stationery.)

EDITORIAL PRINCIPLES

I have transcribed Trollope's letters literally for the sake of basic fidelity to the originals and in the interest of preserving their varying and particular flavor. Thus:

1. Misspellings and grammatical errors are reproduced, sometimes followed by *"sic"* in square brackets.
2. Ampersands and abbreviations, including Trollope's frequent use of "Mss" for "MS," are retained.
3. Trollope's signature is reproduced in its various forms: Anthony, Anthy, Anty, Any, A. T.
4. Words or dates supplied editorially are given in square brackets.
5. Important cancellations are given in angle brackets.
6. Conjectural readings of illegible words are preceded by question marks in square brackets.

The following normalizations have been made:

1. Periods are supplied at the ends of sentences in the few instances where Trollope omitted them.
2. Raised letters in Trollope's abbreviations are lowered and followed by periods, whether or not the raised letters were underlined.
3. Double quotation marks are used throughout, following Trollope's nearly invariable practice, and periods and commas at the ends of quotations are placed inside the quotation marks, again following Trollope's usual practice.
4. Inadvertent duplications are not reproduced.
5. All dates of letters are placed at the upper left, following Trollope's usual practice, and all return addresses are placed at the upper right, again following Trollope's usual practice.
6. Printed letterheads are reproduced in small capitals. Lengthy letterheads of publishers are sometimes shortened. When Trollope used stationery with a printed letterhead but added a different address by hand, the printed letterhead is disregarded unless it is of particular interest.
7. In letters taken from published sources, dates, addresses, salutations, and closings are given in the forms most often found in manuscript sources; the texts proper, including all ellipsis points, follow the published sources, except for the normalizations already cited.

Letters that can be traced only to summaries in Booth's edition or to descriptions in booksellers' catalogues are given in essentially the published form, though in a smaller typeface than the usual one. Quotations from such sources are given as published. Three asterisks are used to indicate gaps in the text of letters. In letters to Trollope and in material quoted in footnotes, ellipses are supplied editorially and indicated by spaced periods.

SHORT TITLES

Autobiography	Anthony Trollope, *An Autobiography*, ed. by Frederick Page (1950).
B	Bradford Allen Booth, ed., *The Letters of Anthony Trollope* (1951).
Bibliography	Michael Sadleir, *Trollope: A Bibliography* (1928).
Bradhurst	Minna Evangeline Bradhurst, ed., *A Century of Letters* (1929).
Commentary	Michael Sadleir, *Trollope: A Commentary* [1927] (3d ed., 1961).
Escott	T. H. S. Escott, *Anthony Trollope: His Work, Associates, and Literary Originals* (1913).
Hamer	Mary Hamer, "Forty Letters of Anthony Trollope," *Yearbook of English Studies*, 3 (1973), 206–15.
Illustrators	N. John Hall, *Trollope and His Illustrators* (1980).
"Isbister"	Bradford A. Booth, "Author to Publisher: Anthony Trollope and William Isbister," *Princeton University Library Chronicle*, 24 (Autumn 1962), 51–67.
Meetkerke	Cecilia Meetkerke, "Last Reminiscences of Anthony Trollope," *Temple Bar*, 70 (January 1884), 129–34.
Memoir	Frances Eleanor Trollope, *A Memoir of Frances Trollope* [*Frances Trollope: Her Life and Literary Work*] (2 vols, 1895).
Parker	W. M. Parker, "Anthony Trollope and 'Maga,'" *Blackwood's Magazine*, 257 (January 1945), 57–64.
Parrish Collection	The Morris L. Parrish Collection of Victorian Novelists, Princeton University Library.
Porter	Mrs. Gerald Porter, *Annals of a Publishing House: John Blackwood*, Vol. III of *William Blackwood and His Sons* (1898).

SB	Bradford Allen Booth, ed., *The Letters of Anthony Trollope* (used for letters given in summary form by Booth).
Smalley	Donald Smalley, ed., *Trollope: The Critical Heritage* (1969).
Taylor, "Bentley"	Robert H. Taylor, "The Trollopes Write to Bentley," *The Trollopian*, 3 (September and December 1948), 83–98, 201–14.
Taylor, "Letters"	Robert H. Taylor, "Letters to Trollope," *The Trollopian*, 1 (September 1946), 5–9.
Taylor Collection	Robert H. Taylor Collection, Princeton University Library.
What I Remember	Thomas Adolphus Trollope, *What I Remember* (New York, 1888).

CHRONOLOGY, 1815-1870

1815	24 April	Born at 16 Keppel Street, Bloomsbury, London.
	? late in year	Family moves to Harrow.
1823	Summer	Sent as day-boy to Harrow School.
1825	early in year	Transferred to Arthur Drury's private school at Sunbury.
1827	April	Sent to Winchester College.
1830	Summer	Removed from Winchester.
1831	January	Sent again to Harrow School.
1834	April	Leaves Harrow in consequence of family's flight to Bruges.
	Summer	Becomes for six weeks a classical usher at William Drury's school at Brussels.
1834	4 November	Appointed a junior clerk in the Secretary's Office in the General Post Office, London; settles in London lodgings.
1840	Spring-Summer	Has serious illness.
1841	29 July	Appointed Surveyor's Clerk in Central District of Ireland.
	15 September	Arrives at Dublin, en route to Banagher, postal headquarters of the Central District.
1843	mid-September	Begins *The Macdermots of Ballycloran*.
1844	11 June	Marries Rose Heseltine, at Rotherham, Yorkshire.
	27 August	Transferred to Southern District of Ireland.
	September	Moves to Cork.
1845	March	Moves to Clonmel, Co. Tipperary.

	?July	Completes *The Macdermots of Ballycloran* (published by Newby, March 1847).
1846	13 March	Henry Merivale Trollope born.
?1846–47		Writes *The Kellys and the O'Kellys* (published by Colburn, June 1848).
1847	27 September	Frederic James Anthony Trollope born.
1848	Autumn	Moves to Mallow, Co. Cork.
1848–49		Writes *La Vendée* (published by Colburn, June 1850).
1850		Writes *The Noble Jilt*.
1851	1 August	Sent to the west of England and Channel Islands on special postal mission.
	21 December	Returns to Ireland on postal work.
1852	11 March	Continues postal mission in west of England and Wales.
	late May	Conceives, at Salisbury, the story of *The Warden*.
1853	19 April–31 May	On leave; goes abroad with Rose and John Tilley, spending May in Florence with T. A. Trollope.
	29 July	Begins *The Warden*.
	29 August	Moves to Belfast, having been appointed acting Surveyor of Northern District of Ireland.
1854	?Autumn	Completes *The Warden*, sending manuscript to Longman on 8 October (published by Longman, January 1855).
	9 October	Officially appointed Surveyor of Northern District.
1855	?January	Begins *Barchester Towers*.
	February–March	Writes *The New Zealander*.
	2 April	Longman's reader advises against publication of *The New Zealander*; Trollope reworks text through May 1856.
	3 May–13 June	On leave; goes abroad with Rose, meeting Frances Trollope and T. A. Trollope in Venice.
	June	Moves to Donnybrook, near Dublin.
1856	12 May	Resumes *Barchester Towers*.

	9 August– 7 September	On leave; goes abroad with Rose and John Tilley.
	9 November	Completes *Barchester Towers* (published by Longman, May 1857).
1857	15 February	Begins *The Three Clerks.*
	18 August	Completes *The Three Clerks* (published by Bentley, November 1857).
	24 August	Begins *The Struggles of Brown, Jones, and Robinson* (breaks off, 7 September).
	5 September– 18 October	On leave; goes abroad with Rose, spending three weeks in Florence with T. A. Trollope.
	20 October	Begins *Doctor Thorne.*
1858	30 January	Leaves from London on postal mission to Suez.
	10 February	Arrives at Alexandria.
	31 March	Completes *Doctor Thorne* (published by Chapman & Hall, May 1858).
	1 April	Begins *The Bertrams.*
	4 April– 10 May	Travels home via Malta, Gibraltar, and Spain.
	late May– September	Various postal visits in Scotland and in north of England.
	16 November	Leaves from London on postal mission to the West Indies.
	2 December	Arrives at St. Thomas; travels extensively in Caribbean and Central America.
1859	17 January	Completes *The Bertrams* (published by Chapman & Hall, March 1859).
	25 January– June	Writes *The West Indies and the Spanish Main* (published by Chapman & Hall, October 1859).
	16 May	Travels home via Bermuda and New York, arriving at Liverpool on 3 July.
	?July	Writes two short stories later collected in *Tales of All Countries* (published by Chapman & Hall, November 1861).
	4 August	Begins *Castle Richmond.*
	7 September– 21 October	On leave; goes to Pyrenees with Rose, T. A. Trollope, and John Tilley; writes

		five short stories later collected in *Tales of All Countries*.
	23 October	Writes to Thackeray, offering series of short stories for *Cornhill Magazine*.
	26 October	Commissioned to write serial novel for *Cornhill*.
	2 November	Begins *Framley Parsonage*.
	21 November	Takes up duties as Surveyor of Eastern District of England (appointment official on 10 January); settles at Waltham Cross, Hertfordshire.
1860	1 January	*Framley Parsonage* begins serialization in *Cornhill* (continued until April 1861; book publication by Smith, Elder, April 1861).
	2 January	Resumes *Castle Richmond*.
	? 31 March	Completes *Castle Richmond* (published by Chapman & Hall, May 1860).
	3 April	Resumes *Framley Parsonage*.
	27 June	Completes *Framley Parsonage*.
	4 July	Begins *Orley Farm*.
	24 September– 4 November	On leave; goes abroad with Rose, visiting T. A. Trollope in Florence; meets Kate Field.
1861	March	*Orley Farm* begins appearing in monthly numbers (published by Chapman & Hall, continuing until October 1862; book publication, Vol. I, December 1861, and Vol. II, September 1862).
	24 April	Told of election the previous week to Cosmopolitan Club.
	22 June	Completes *Orley Farm*.
	24 June	Resumes *The Struggles of Brown, Jones, and Robinson*.
	1 August	*Brown, Jones, and Robinson* begins serialization in *Cornhill* (continued until March 1862; book publication by Smith, Elder, November 1870).
	3 August	Completes *Brown, Jones, and Robinson*.
	24 August	Leaves from Liverpool for the United States with Rose to collect material for a

		travel book (Rose returns to England on 27 November).
	5 September	Arrives at Boston.
	16 September	Begins *North America*.
1862	12 March	Leaves New York for England, arriving at Liverpool on 25 March.
	5 April	Elected to Garrick Club.
	? 27 April	Completes *North America* (published by Chapman & Hall, May 1862).
	20 May	Begins *The Small House at Allington*.
	1 September	*The Small House at Allington* begins serialization in *Cornhill* (continued until April 1864; book publication by Smith, Elder, March 1864).
	13–23 September	On leave; goes to Holland.
1863	11 February	Completes *The Small House at Allington*.
	February	*Tales of All Countries: Second Series* published (by Chapman & Hall; a collection of stories published in periodicals during 1861).
	3 March	Begins *Rachel Ray*.
	March	Florence Bland becomes a member of the Trollope household.
	29 June	Completes *Rachel Ray* (published by Chapman & Hall, October 1863).
	20 July– 15 August	On leave; goes abroad to Switzerland with Rose, Henry, and Fred.
	16 August	Begins *Can You Forgive Her?*
	10 September	Takes Henry to Florence; returns on 28 September.
	6 October	Death of Frances Trollope.
1864	1 January	*Can You Forgive Her?* begins appearing in monthly numbers (published by Chapman & Hall, continuing until August 1865; book publication, Vol. I, September 1864, and Vol. II, July 1865).
	9 March	Becomes member of General Committee of the Royal Literary Fund.
	12 April	Elected to Athenaeum Club.
	28 April	Completes *Can You Forgive Her?*

22 May	Begins *Miss Mackenzie.*
18 August	Completes *Miss Mackenzie* (published by Chapman & Hall, February 1865).
24 August	Begins *The Claverings.*
3–12 October	On leave; goes to Paris with Henry, then to Isle of Wight with Rose.
early December	Beginning of discussions about starting *Fortnightly Review.*
31 December	Completes *The Claverings* (serialized in *Cornhill,* February 1866–May 1867; book publication by Smith, Elder, April 1867).
1865 mid-January	Begins writing articles for *Pall Mall Gazette.*
30 January	Begins *The Belton Estate.*
7 February	*Pall Mall Gazette* starts publication.
9 February	First Hunting Sketch published in *Pall Mall Gazette* (series completed 20 March; collected and issued in book form by Chapman & Hall, May 1865).
15–29 April	On leave; goes to Florence, following the death of Theodosia Trollope; brings Beatrice Trollope to England.
15 May	First number of *Fortnightly Review* published, containing first installment of *The Belton Estate* (continuing until 1 January 1866; book publication by Chapman & Hall, December 1865).
23 May–13 June	On postal business in Scotland and Ireland.
3 August	First Travelling Sketch published in *Pall Mall Gazette* (series completed 6 September; collected and issued in book form by Chapman & Hall, February 1866).
4 September	Completes *The Belton Estate.*
17 September–29 October	On leave; goes abroad with Rose and Fred, meeting Harry at Coblentz; Fred continues to Australia.
3 November	Begins *Nina Balatka.*
20 November	First Clerical Sketch published in *Pall Mall Gazette* (series completed 25 January 1866; collected and issued in book

		form by Chapman & Hall under the title *Clergymen of the Church of England,* March 1866).
	31 December	Completes *Nina Balatka* (serialized in *Blackwood's,* July 1866–January 1867; book publication by Blackwood, January 1867).
1866	21 January	Begins *The Last Chronicle of Barset.*
	15 September	Completes *The Last Chronicle* (published by Smith, Elder in weekly numbers, 1 December 1866–6 July 1867; book publication, Vol. I, March 1867, and Vol. II, July 1867).
	late September	Goes to Ireland.
	October	On leave; goes to Italy and to Paris, where Rose and Henry meet him, for T. A. Trollope's marriage to Frances Ternan.
	15 November	Asked by James Virtue to undertake editorship of projected monthly magazine (eventually called *St. Paul's Magazine*).
	17 November	Begins *Phineas Finn.*
1867	15 May	Completes *Phineas Finn* (serialized in *St. Paul's,* October 1867–May 1869; book publication by Virtue, March 1869).
	2 June	Begins *Linda Tressel.*
	10 July	Completes *Linda Tressel* (serialized in *Blackwood's,* October 1867–May 1868; book publication by Blackwood, May 1868).
	18 July– 20 August	On leave; goes abroad, Rose joining him in Paris; visits Switzerland.
	August	*Lotta Schmidt* published (by Strahan; a collection of short stories published during the past six years).
	1 September	Begins *The Golden Lion of Granpere.*
	1 October	*St. Paul's Magazine* starts publication.
	9 October	Post Office accepts his resignation, effective 31 October, when he is given a farewell dinner.
	22 October	Completes *The Golden Lion* (serialized in *Good Words,* January–August 1872; book publication by Tinsley, May 1872).

	13 November	Begins *He Knew He Was Right*.
1868	17 March	Presented at Court.
	11 April	Leaves Liverpool for the United States on postal mission, arriving in New York on 22 April and Washington on 24 April.
	12 June	Completes *He Knew He Was Right* (published by Virtue in weekly numbers, 17 October 1868–22 May 1869; book publication by Strahan, May 1869).
	15 June	Begins *The Vicar of Bullhampton*.
	15 July	Leaves the United States, arriving home on 26 July.
	1 November	Completes *The Vicar of Bullhampton* (published by Bradbury & Evans in monthly numbers, July 1869–May 1870; book publication, April 1870).
	17 November	Defeated in effort to be elected to the House of Commons for the Borough of Beverley.
	27 December	Begins *Sir Harry Hotspur of Humblethwaite*.
	December	Fred comes home from Australia for a visit.
1869	30 January	Completes *Sir Harry Hotspur* (serialized in *Macmillan's Magazine*, May–December 1870; book publication by Hurst & Blackett, November 1870).
	?March	Dramatizes *The Last Chronicle* under title *Did He Steal It?* (never performed).
	4 April	Begins *Ralph the Heir*.
	26 April	Fred returns to Australia.
	7 August	Completes *Ralph the Heir* (published by Strahan in monthly numbers and simultaneously as supplement to *St. Paul's*, January 1870–July 1871; book publication by Hurst & Blackett, April 1871).
	September	Travels in France with Rose.
	4 December	Begins *The Eustace Diamonds*.
1870	29 January	Begins *The Commentaries of Caesar*.
	January	Eased out of *St. Paul's*, agreeing to give up editorship after the June issue (in fact July).

25 April	Completes *The Commentaries of Caesar* (published by Blackwood, June 1870).
June	*An Editor's Tales* published (by Strahan; a collection of stories published in *St. Paul's*, 1869–70).
25 August	Completes *The Eustace Diamonds* (serialized in *Fortnightly*, July 1871–February 1873; book publication by Chapman & Hall, October 1872).
13 September	Begins *An Eye for an Eye*.
10 October	Completes *An Eye for an Eye* (serialized in *Whitehall Review*, 24 August 1878–1 February 1879; book publication by Chapman & Hall, January 1879).
23 October	Begins *Phineas Redux*.

The Chronology for 1871–1882 is given in Volume Two, pp. xi–xv.

LETTERS, 1835-1870

1835

To Richard Bentley[1]

MS Taylor Collection. Taylor, "Bentley," p. 85; B 1.

24 May 1835.
Sunday
My dear Sir   22—Northumberland St.[2]

I called on you the other day at the request of the lady who is correcting the sheets of my mothers work—[3] The Printers send the sheets very irregularly; in fact for the last month I believe they have not sent any— Of course you are the only judge of the time when the book is to appear, but perhaps you may not be aware of the dilatoriness of the Printers.

I now ask to trouble you on my own less important score— Is it in your power to lend me any assistance in procuring the insertion of lucubrations of my own in any of the numerous periodical magazines &c which come out in such monthly swarms— I am not aware whether you are yourself the Proprietor of any such—[4] My object of course is that of turning my time to any account that I am able, and if you would put me into the way of doing so, & excuse the liberty I am taking you would much oblige[5]

My dear Sir
Yours truly
Anthony Trollope

[1] Richard Bentley (1794–1871), well-known publisher. In 1858 Bentley published Trollope's *The Three Clerks*, and in 1876–77 his successor serialized Trollope's *The American Senator* in the firm's monthly magazine, *Temple Bar*.

[2] Trollope wrote of this residence: "That was Northumberland Street by the Marylebone Workhouse, on to the back-door of which establishment my room looked out—a most dreary abode, at which I fancy I must have almost ruined the goodnatured lodging-house keeper by my continued inability to pay her what I owed." (*Autobiography*, p. 53.) Trollope was at this time a junior clerk in the General Post Office, London, an appointment obtained for him in November 1834 with a beginning salary of £90 a year. During his seven years in London, most of the time alone in lodgings, he was never out of debt. Northumberland Street is now Luxborough Street, and the Marylebone Workhouse has been torn down to make room for the new buildings of the London Polytechnic.

[3] Frances Trollope (1779–1863), daughter of the Reverend William Milton, Vicar of Heckfield. In 1809 she married Thomas Anthony Trollope (1774–1835), a barrister and later an unsuccessful gentleman farmer. Late in life she became a prolific and popular writer. *Domestic Manners of the Americans* (1832) was her first and most successful work. The book referred to here is probably *Tremordyn Cliff*, published by Bentley in 1835.

[4] *Bentley's Miscellany*, edited by Dickens, did not begin publication until 1837.

[5] It is fitting that Trollope's earliest extant letter should reveal literary aspirations; for more on his youthful ambitions in literature, see Appendixes A and B.

1836

To Thomas Adolphus Trollope[6]
Memoir, I, 248. B 2.

[January 1836]   [London]

      *   *   *

Mamma will, I feel confident, have a second thousand of the Paris.[7] No work of hers was ever abused so much—or sold so fast—or praised in the periodicals so little,—especially by her own party.

      *   *   *

To Thomas Adolphus Trollope
Memoir, I, 259. B 3.

[12 February 1836]   [Hadley[8]]
My dear Tom.

It is all over! Poor Emily[9] breathed her last this morning. She died without any pain, and without a struggle. Her little strength had been gradually declining, and her breath left her without the slightest convulsion, or making any change in her features or face. Were it not for the ashy colour, I should think she was sleeping. I never saw anything more beautifully placid and composed. . . . It is much better that it is now, than that her life should have been prolonged only to undergo the agonies which Henry suffered. Cecilia was at Pinner[1] when it happened, and she has not heard of it yet. I shall go for her to-morrow. You went to the same house to fetch her when Henry died.

      *   *   *

[6] Thomas Adolphus Trollope (1810–92), Trollope's elder brother, a novelist, newspaper correspondent, and prolific writer on Italian history. For the last twenty-five years of his mother's life, he was her inseparable companion. After 1843 they lived in Italy, where Thomas Adolphus was one of the lights of the Anglo-Florentine set.

[7] Mrs. Trollope's *Paris and the Parisians in 1835* (1836), a second thousand of which was sold. The book was attacked for its praise of King Louis Philippe's government (see *Memoir*, I, 248–50).

[8] Trollope's mother had taken a small house in Hadley, a village twelve miles north of London, shortly after her husband's death in 1835.

[9] Emily Trollope (1818–36), Trollope's sister. Besides Emily, three other Trollope children died from tuberculosis: Arthur William (1812–24), Henry (1811–34), and Cecilia (1818–49).

[1] Pinner, near Harrow, was the home of Lady Milman, widow of Sir Francis Milman (1746–1821), physician to George III. Lady Milman was a longtime friend of Mrs. Trollope, and Cecilia had gone to stay at Pinner when Emily's disease made it necessary for her to leave Hadley.

1837

To John Murray[2]

MS John Murray. B 4.

2 Feb 1837   Genl Post Office
My dear Sir
  I believe my Brother saw you before he left Town on the subject of
the "Belgium"[3] and the account between yourself and my Mother, and
that you either gave him or promised to give him a cheque for £25— My
Mother has mentioned the subject in a letter I received this morning,
and as it [is] so much the quickest way of learning what has been done,
I have ventured to write to you about it— Would you have the kindness
to send me a line, I shall be writing to my Mother tomorrow, or next
day, and excuse the trouble I am giving you—
                              Dear Sir
                              Yours very truly
                              Anthony Trollope

To Richard Bentley

MS Taylor Collection. B 5.

20 Feb. 1837   Genl Post Office
My dear Sir
  I called this morning in the hope of seeing you on the subject of a
message from my mother.
  She has written to me saying that she has found her expenses so high,
that she is pressed for money, and she wishes to know if you would object
to advance her £100 as you have a part of the MS of her Austrian book[4]
in your hands—and as the rest is almost completed— It would [be] a
great accomodation [sic] to her—and would not make you incur any risk.
If you would be kind enough to send me a line at your *earliest* conve-

---

[2] John Murray (1778–1843), the celebrated publisher; best remembered for his
connection with Byron and for starting the *Quarterly Review*. On 20 January 1835,
Mrs. Trollope had written to Murray of Anthony: "He would gladly occupy the
hours of his evening in some profitable employment [to augment the small income
from his Post Office clerkship]. He is a good scholar, and, as I believe your friend
Henry Drury [Trollope's tutor at Harrow School] will allow, has very good abilities.
It has been suggested to him that he might possibly find employment either by correcting the press, or in some other occupation of the kind, and I should be very
grateful if you could help him in obtaining such." (MS John Murray.) Nothing came
of the request.
[3] *Belgium and Western Germany in 1833* (1834).
[4] *Vienna and the Austrians* (1838).

nience— I would call on you any evening that you would name and speak to you on the subject. I wish to settle it as soon as possible, as my mother writes pressingly on the subject.

Yours very truly

Anthony Trollope

To Richard Bentley

MS British Library.

20. March 1837   General Post Office
Dear Sir

I acknowledge to have received at your hands this day your promissory note for £100 at 6 months date to the order of Mrs. F Trollope as part of the consideration agreed to be paid to her for the copyright of her forthcoming work on Austria.

As this Bill, which is given at Mrs. Trollopes particular request, is drawn earlier than the time required by the agreement, which requires that the bills are to be dated from the delivery of the MS—I hereby agree that the payment of a similar sum shall be extended to a period equivalent to the time anticipated by the present Bill.

I am dear Sir

yours very faithfully

Anthony Trollope

R. Bentley Esq
New Burlington Street

To Richard Bentley

MS Taylor Collection. Taylor, "Bentley," pp. 85–86; SB 6.

16 Sept 37   G. P. O.
My dear Sir

I enclose a note from the lady on whose behalf I spoke to you the other day—to whom my mother has entrusted the translation of her work on Austria into French—

If you will kindly read the accompanying letter [you][5] will perceive what she desires; can anything be done in the matter you would much oblige me, & confer a great obligation on Madame de Montalk[6]— She wishes an assurance from you which she might shew to Sournier [? Fournier] that no one else would be enabled by you to translate the

---

[5] MS damaged; word supplied.

[6] Probably Judith de Montalk, who is mentioned in a letter from T. A. Trollope to Trollope, 27 July 1860 (MS University of Illinois). She was perhaps the "Madame de M." of the *Memoir*: "A friend of Mrs. Trollope's—English by parentage, Italian by education, and French by marriage and a protracted residence in Paris" (II, 102). No translation of *Vienna and the Austrians* by Madame de Montalk has been traced; a translation by Achille Morisseau was published by Fournier in 1838.

Mss—this is the chief thing—the next is that she might have the sheets of at le[ast]⁷ the 1st. vol as they are printed—in the latter point if you are of opinion that it would be injurious, I would not of course press you, but I would answer for their safety—

ever yours truly
Anthony Trollope

Will you have the goodness to return the enclosed—

1838

To Miss Dancers

MS Parrish Collection. *N&Q*, n.s. 21 (December 1974), 446–47.

16 August 1838.   General Post Office
My dear Miss Dancers.

Like a man of honor I send you what I owe—that horrid white and pink which ought never to have won the race!! If the gloves do not fit pray let me know—& I will procure another pair.

Pray tell Ellen with my best thanks for her kindness—that I have her flowers blooming on my desk the envy of all the Clerks in the Office—tell her also that I have still the pin which she wanted, but was not able to purloin—

I trust your "cousin Emma" is consoled for the loss of the gingerbread man—tell her that she should never allow grief for anyone to prey upon her spirits so long. It is very bad for the complexion— She should learn to bear it with Christian meekness & patience—

I think Mr. G. T. must have been hid in that cupboard yesterday evening—else Emma would not have been so *very* angry with me— Poor man if he was—he must have been very much confined—⁸

Yours very faithfully
Anthony Trollope

---

⁷ MS damaged; letters supplied.

⁸ This letter is the only surviving evidence of Trollope's "hobbledehoyhood" while a junior clerk in the General Post Office in the late 1830's (*Autobiography*, chap. iii). The tone of the letter unmistakably recalls the two characters generally regarded as autobiographical: Charley Tudor of *The Three Clerks* and Johnny Eames of *The Small House at Allington*.

1839

To Alexander Donnadieu[9]
MS Parrish Collection. SB 7.

20 York Street
Portman Square[1]

12 March 1839
My dear Sir,

Will you me do me [*sic*] the pleasure of dining with me in York Street on Thursday the 28th. Inst at 6 o.Clock, when I shall have much pleasure in introducing you to my mother— I send this note to Campbell as I forget your number. I have asked him to join our party so I trust you will accompany him.

Yours very truly
Anthony Trollope

To Alexander Donnadieu
MS Parrish Collection. SB 8.

23 March 1839   20 York *Street* (not Place)
My dear Sir,

I much fear that between us we have made some mistake— I meant to have said in my note, *Thursday the 21st.*— I hope I did, as in that case the mistake will be on your shoulders. On the 26th. we all dine out, but I trust that before long we shall be more fortunate— I shall call with this note in the hopes of seeing you—if I do not, I trust this will explain the mistake.

Yours very truly
Anthony Trollope

To Alexander Donnadieu
MS Parrish Collection. SB 9.

[? March 1839]
My dear Donnadieu.

I could not understand the Servants message this morning—as to whether you would or would not come— I am now going out of town; would you send a line by the bearer, which my mother will open—

yours very truly
Anthony Trollope

---

[9] Alexander Donnadieu (*d.* 1861), musician and autograph dealer. Donnadieu had served under Napoleon and had come to England ca. 1829.

[1] Trollope's mother had taken a house at this address in the summer of 1838.

To Thomas Adolphus Trollope

MS Parrish Collection.

25th. May 1839.
Saturday   General Post Office
Dear Tom

I have today paid £50—into Herries to your credit at Messrs. Flock—Brest—of which advice will leave town on Monday—you will therefore be able to receive your money the day but one after you get this.

I have but little news of any kind. I do not think that Awdry[2] will join you, as he says he shall have no money, but he is so uncertain and capricious that there is no guessing what he means to do.

I trust you get on well in your tour, & your book.[3] Give my love to Hervieu—[4]

yours affectionately
Anthony Trollope

Sydney Smith[5] says that Lord Normanby[6] has returned from Ireland covered with laurels, all gathered in the groves of Blarney.

[2] Walter Herbert Awdry (1812–?69), educated at Winchester College and later at Exeter College and Magdalen Hall, Oxford. Awdry took Holy Orders late in life and held curacies between 1861 and 1869 in Shropshire and on the Isle of Man. The recorded facts of his career make it obvious that he was the "W— A—" of Trollope's *Autobiography*, "whose misfortunes in life will not permit me to give his full name, but whom I dearly loved" (p. 54).

[3] T. A. Trollope's *A Summer in Brittany* (1840).

[4] Auguste Jean Jacques Hervieu (?1794–1880), painter and illustrator; French exile. A close friend of Trollope's mother, Hervieu had accompanied her to the United States in 1827; he later supplied illustrations for six of her books.

[5] Sydney Smith (1771–1845), clergyman, essayist, and celebrated wit. Escott claimed that Trollope, while still a young man, had met Smith in the company of William Gregory (Escott, pp. 139–40), but his account is at variance with that given by Gregory. Both tell of Smith being mistaken for the family chaplain at Carlton House Terrace, but Gregory does not mention Trollope as present (Lady Gregory, ed., *Sir William Gregory: An Autobiography* [1894], pp. 116–17).

[6] Constantine Henry Phipps (1797–1863), 1st Marquis of Normanby, was Lord Lieutenant of Ireland from 1835 to 1839.

General Post Office
Saturday 25th May, 1839.

Dear Tom

I have to day paid £50. into Dovries to your credit at Messrs Block. Brest. of which advice will leave town on Monday. you will therefore be able to receive your money the day but one after you get this.

I have but little news of any kind. I do not think that Awdry will join you, as he says he shall have no money, but he is so uncertain and capricious that there is no guessing what he means to do.

I trust you get on well in your town, & your book. Give my love to Hervieu—

Yours affectionately
Anthony Trollope

Sydney Smith says that Lord Normanby, has returned from Ireland covered with laurels, all gathered in the groves of Blarney.

Letter to Thomas Adolphus Trollope, 25 May 1839

1840

Mrs. Frances Trollope to Lady Bulwer[7]

Louisa Devey, *Life of Rosina, Lady Lytton, with Numerous Extracts from Her MS Autobiography and Other Original Documents* (1887), pp. 195–96.

[? June or July 1840]   3, Wyndham Street, Bryanston Square.

＊   ＊   ＊

I have no heart to write to you, dear friend, and yet I could not see my son[8] sending off a letter without one word from me. Oh! how your kind warm heart would pity me could you witness the anxious misery I am enduring! My poor darling lies in a state that defies the views of his physicians as effectually as it puzzles my ignorance.[9] It is asthma from which he chiefly suffers now; but they say this can only be a symptom, and not the disease. He is frightfully reduced in size and strength; sure am I that could you see him, you would not find even a distant resemblance to the being who, exactly three months ago, left us in all the pride of youth, health, and strength. Day by day I lose hope, and so, I am quite sure, do his physicians; we have had three consultations, but nothing prescribed relieves him, nor has any light been thrown on the nature of his complaint.[1] . . .

Ever affectionately yours,
F. Trollope

[7] Rosina Bulwer (1802–82), née Wheeler, the estranged and eccentric wife of Sir Edward Bulwer (Bulwer Lytton after 1843). Mrs. Trollope had befriended Lady Bulwer in Paris in 1839.

[8] T. A. Trollope was assisting Lady Bulwer settle with a publisher for her novel *The Budget of the Bubble Family* (1840), a work that contained a fulsome dedication to Mrs. Trollope.

[9] Trollope was at this time suffering from a mysterious and nearly fatal illness. T. A. Trollope recalled how the Okey sisters, the young subjects of public mesmeric experiments by Dr. John Elliotson (a friend of Mrs. Trollope), seemed able to predict the deaths of hospital patients when they "saw Jack" nearby. "The Okey girls, especially one of them (Jane, I think, her name was), were very frequently in the lodgings occupied by my brother at the time, during the period of his greatest danger, and used constantly to say that they 'saw Jack by his side, but only up to his knee,' and therefore they thought he would recover—as he did! I am almost ashamed to write what seems such childish absurdity. But the facts are certain, and . . . are very curious." (*What I Remember*, pp. 257–58.) In 1838 Elliotson had resigned his post at University College Hospital, which he had been instrumental in founding, following the *Lancet*'s denunciation of the Okeys as imposters and the Hospital's ban on the use of mesmerism.

[1] On 3 July 1840 Mrs. Trollope wrote to Lady Bulwer that "my poor Anthony is . . . very nearly in the same state as when I last wrote." On 9 July she wrote that "Anthony goes on decidedly improving, but so slowly as to make every morning's inquiry one of fear and trembling. Still I DO hope and believe that we shall be able to leave England early in September." (*Life of Rosina, Lady Lytton*, pp. 197, 201.)

To Henry Colburn[2]

MS Gordon N. Ray.

16th. December [1840]   Wyndham Street
Dear Sir
   I forward you the corrected proof sheets of Charles Chesterfield[3]—not knowing the Printer's name—which I wish you would have the goodness to inform me of.

                                             Yours truly
H. Colburn Esqre.   Anthony Trollope

1841

W. L. Maberly[4] to the Postmaster General[5]

MS (copy) General Post Office, London.

29th. July. 1841
The Postmaster General
Your Lordship will please to decide whether you will comply with Mr. Trollope's request in the event of your removing Mr. Turner fr Mr. Drought's district.[6]

                                             W L M

   [2] Henry Colburn (d. 1855), London publisher. Like Bentley, with whom he had once been in partnership, Colburn published numerous works by Mrs. Trollope. He later published two of Trollope's novels (see Trollope to Colburn, 27 March 1848; Colburn to Trollope, 11 November 1848; and Trollope to Mrs. Frances Trollope, ? 5 February 1850).
   [3] Mrs. Trollope's *Charles Chesterfield: or the Adventures of a Youth of Genius* (1841).
   [4] William Leader Maberly (1798–1885), Secretary of the Post Office, 1836–54. In his *Autobiography* Trollope said he was on poor terms with Maberly, claiming that when he volunteered for Ireland Maberly "was glad to be so rid of me" and that Maberly had sent a very bad letter of recommendation to the Secretary of the Irish Post Office (pp. 58, 65). But see Trollope to Hardwicke, 25 November 1852.
   [5] Thomas William Anson (1795–1854), 1st Earl of Lichfield.
   [6] After seven unhappy years in London as a junior clerk in the Secretary's Office of the General Post Office, Trollope applied for the position of surveyor's clerk for Ireland's Central District, under Surveyor James Drought. (Report had it that Drought's first clerk, George L. Turner, was "absurdly incapable" [*Autobiography*, p. 58]; in any event, Turner was transferred to the Money Order Office in Dublin.) The Postmaster General approved Trollope's appointment shortly after receiving Maberly's note of 29 July, and Trollope arrived in Dublin on 15 September. Ireland

1844

Mrs. Frances Trollope to Rose Trollope[7]

MS Taylor Collection.

7 August 1844   Teignmouth[8]

I cannot say in the usual phrase my dear Rose, that "I hasten to answer your letter" for truly I have been a very long time about it— But as I have my hands just now very full of writing I thought it would be wisest to wait till our movements Southwards were fixed. . . . I am very glad, dearest Rose, that the library subscription is paid, and I hope you carry with you to Banagher a good package, to comfort you in your retreat. I do not yet give up all hopes of Dublin for you, but as yet we have nothing in the way of information on the subject. This delay is very vexatious and must be *very* vexatious to you—for suspence is always more tormenting than any certainty.[9] I rejoice to hear that Anthonys M.S. is

---

had three Post Office surveyors, Scotland two, and England seven. The surveyors lived in their districts to superintend all aspects of postal services, work that involved traveling around investigating complaints, examining accounts, and arranging deliveries to isolated houses. Much of the salary of the surveyor and his clerk was made up of allowances for time spent away from home. Trollope received 15s. per day and 6d. per mile while away. In his *Autobiography* he claimed that this additional income, on top of his initial annual salary of £100, brought his salary after expenses "at once" up to £400; in fact, his travel account books (Parrish Collection) show that his net income was £313.4s. 2d. for his first year in Ireland, and £326.19s. 2½d. for his second year. During his first three years in Ireland, Trollope lived in Banagher, Co. Kings (now Co. Offaly); in this period he began his first novel and married (see next letter). Trollope called his appointment to Ireland "the first good fortune of my life" (see *Autobiography*, pp. 57–58, and chap. iv).

[7] Rose Trollope (?1821–1917), née Heseltine, was the daughter of Edward John Heseltine, of Rotherham, Yorkshire. (Rose's mother, Martha Heseltine, died in 1840 as a result of a railway accident. Her father remarried in December 1842; his second wife was Charlotte Platts, daughter of John Platts, a Unitarian divine.) Heseltine was manager of the Rotherham office of the Sheffield and Rotherham Joint Stock Company; he retired in ill health at the close of 1853, and in 1854 evidence came to light that he had been tampering with the books for some twenty years (his defalcations were eventually estimated to be between £4,000 and £5,000). Heseltine refused to explain the irregularities, and was forced to flee to France early in 1855 to avoid criminal proceedings. He died at Le Havre on 15 September 1855. Trollope met Rose Heseltine in 1842 at Kingstown, Ireland; they were married at Rotherham on 11 June 1844.

[8] A seaside town in Devon.

[9] Trollope had asked to be transferred to Ireland's Southern District, and his request was granted on 27 August 1844. There he was clerk to Surveyor James Kendrick. From September 1844 through February 1845 he was at Cork; and in March 1845 he and Rose settled at Clonmel, Co. Tipperary (though he often had to be away from home). It was at Clonmel that his two sons were born.

found, and I trust he will lose no *idle* time, but give all he can, without breaking in upon his professional labours, to finish it.[1] . . .

Your affectionate friend
and mother
Frances Trollope

1845

T. C. Newby[2] to Trollope

MS Bodleian.

Sep 15/45
Dear Sir

I regret not having been able to send you the usual agreement ere this.— I propose printing 400 copies & it will require about 190 copies to cover the expences—& the profit from copies sold beyond that number will be 20/3.[3]

If you have no objections to the agreement if you will copy it & sign your copy & send to me, the one I now enclose you can keep & the affair will be settled.

I presume that you would wish to revise the proof sheets.

Believe me Dr. Sir in haste
Yrs. truly
T C Newby

[1] In August and September 1843 Trollope had been sent to investigate money shortages at the village post office in Drumsna, Co. Leitrim. While walking in the neighborhood with his friend John Merivale, he came upon a ruined country house and conceived the plot of his first novel, *The Macdermots of Ballycloran*. Trollope, who had long entertained ambitions of becoming a novelist, began the story in mid-September 1843 and had completed the first of its three volumes by the time of his marriage. (*Autobiography*, pp. 70–71.)

[2] Thomas Cautley Newby (?1798–1882), a minor London publisher who, at the urging of Trollope's mother, had undertaken to publish Trollope's first novel, *The Macdermots of Ballycloran*. Newby developed a reputation for false advertising, and in some of the advertisements he issued for *The Macdermots*, he made it appear that the novel was by Mrs. Trollope (see Lance Tingay, "The Publication of Trollope's First Novel," *TLS*, 30 March 1956, p. 200). J. A. Sutherland argues convincingly that Newby was a publisher too small, too niggardly, and too slow to have launched Trollope successfully (*Victorian Novelists and Publishers* [1976], pp. 44–49).

[3] The agreement for *The Macdermots*, signed 15 September 1845, stipulated half profits after expenses. (Like almost all three-volume novels published during Trollope's lifetime, *The Macdermots* sold for 31s. 6d.) Trollope, however, received no money from Newby; see *Autobiography*, pp. 74–75.

T. C. Newby to Trollope
MS Bodleian.

Sep 24/45   72 Mortimer St
My dear Sir,

I return a duplicate of the agreement copied verbatim from the one you sent.

1st. With regard to the time of publication. I should propose having the work ready for February.

2nd. I shall be happy to send you 8 copies of the work.

3rd. The proof sheets shall be sent to you for revision.

I would have appointed an earlier time for publication, but my engagements stand so heavily for October, Novr. & Decr. that I see but little chance of being able to hope for an earlier time. That will, however, be as good a season as it can possibly appear in.[4]

Believe me my dear Sir
Yrs. sincerely
T C Newby

1847

To Richard Bentley
MS Taylor Collection. Taylor, "Bentley," p. 86; B 10.

16 October 1847   Clonmel Co. Tipperary
My dear Sir.

When in London in May last I spoke to you respecting a novel[5] which I was then writing, and which I told you I should probably have finished in October. You said that if you published it, you would like to do so in November.

It is now all but completed—and I would wish to know at what time you would wish to publish it, if you do publish it.

I will *not part with the Mss* on *any other terms than that of payment for it.* I mean, that I will not publish it myself—or have it published on

---

[4] Newby procrastinated. In August 1846, Mrs. Trollope wrote to her daughter Cecilia: "I have seen Newby about Anthony's book. He, like everybody else, gives a most wretched account of the novel-market. . . . He says that he thinks it very cleverly written, but that Irish stories are very unpopular." (*Commentary*, p. 148.) *The Macdermots of Ballycloran* was not published until 1847, probably in March.

[5] *The Kellys and the O'Kellys.*

THE MACDERMOTS

OF

BALLYCLORAN,

BY

Mr. A. TROLLOPE.

IN THREE VOLUMES.

VOL. I.

LONDON:
THOMAS CAUTLEY NEWBY, PUBLISHER
72, MORTIMER St., CAVENDISH Sq.

1847.

Title page of *The Macdermots of Ballycloran*

half profits—or have the payment for it conditional on the sale. It is, & must be, much more the publishers interest to push a work when it is his own property.[6]

If you wish it under these circumstances, I will send you the Mss— But I should be glad to know at what time you would think of publishing it. I could immediately send the Mss of the whole wanting about 60 pages— It may however be a month before I am able to complete it, as the opening of the Irish Railways take up all my time.

very faithfully yours
Anthony Trollope

Richard Bentley Esq
Publisher
New Burlington Street

To Richard Bentley

MS Taylor Collection. Taylor, "Bentley," p. 87; SB 11.

October 30—1847   Clonmel
My dear Sir
I have sent the MS of my novel to you—by the hands of Mr. Milton,[7] who will deliver it to you. It wants four chapters of being complete, but I imagine you can judge of it now as well as if it were complete. I had an opportunity of sending it which I did not wish to pass over. The remainder will be ready at any time at which it may be wanted—

faithfully yours
Anthony Trollope

R Bentley Esq

To Richard Bentley

MS Parrish Collection. SB 12.

21 Nov. 1847   Tralee.[8]
My dear Sir
I shall feel much obliged if you will send my Mss. to
John Milton Esq
War Office
Whitehall.

Very faithfully yours
Anthony Trollope

R. Bentley Esq

[6] Bentley eventually declined to take the novel on Trollope's terms; Colburn later published it at half profits (see Trollope to Colburn, 27 March 1848).

[7] John Milton (1820–80), later Sir John, son of Trollope's uncle Henry Milton. John Milton entered the War Office in 1840 and had a distinguished career as a civil servant (he was appointed Assistant Accountant-General of the Army in 1860, and Accountant-General in 1871).

[8] A town in Co. Kerry. It was here that Trollope caught out, by means of a marked sovereign, a young assistant postmistress who was stealing from the mails. During her

1848

To James Kendrick

MS University of Illinois.

8 March 1848   Tarbert.[9]
My dear Sir.
    I leave this tomorrow—and shall be in Clonmel on Friday after-
noon—& stand then ready to obey your further directions in the *South*.
                                          very faithfully yours
J Kendrick Esq   Anthony Trollope

To Henry Colburn

MS Parrish Collection. B 13.

27 March 1848.   Killarney
My dear Sir.
    I have heard from my friend Mrs. Merivale[1] that you have expressed
yourself willing to publish my novel on the half profit system—but have
declined to make any offer of a price for it. I dislike the half profit, as
all writers do; but as I should wish to have the novel published by you,
I will accede to your proposal. I shall be glad of course to have a draft
of an agreement signed by yourself, which I will copy and sign for you,
if I approve it. I must however stipulate that the proof sheets be sent to
myself for correction. I shall be glad to know when you propose that the
work shall appear.
    It is now finished, and I will take an early opportunity of sending you
the second portion of the 3rd. volume.[2]
                                          very faithfully yours
H Colburn Esq   Anthony Trollope

---

trial at the Kerry summer assizes in July 1849, Trollope was vigorously and humorously cross-examined by Isaac Butt, who even quoted from the court scenes in *The
Macdermots of Ballycloran*; but Trollope answered with equal vigor and humor, and
as Justin McCarthy recalled, had the better of the contest (Kerry *Evening Post*, 28 July
1849; Justin McCarthy, *Reminiscences* [New York, 1900], pp. 369–72).
    [9] A port and post town in Co. Kerry, Ireland.
    [1] Presumably Louisa (1787–1873), widow of John Herman Merivale and sister of
Henry Drury, Trollope's tutor at Harrow and his father's old friend.
    [2] Colburn replied on 30 March, enclosing a memorandum of agreement and adding
that as the work was "illustrative of Irish Society, it should appear as soon as it could
be printed" (MS Bodleian). Colburn was as good as his word: *The Kellys and the
O'Kellys* was published on 27 June 1848.

To Mrs. Frances Trollope

Memoir, II, 123–24. B 14.

[Spring 1848]   [Ireland]

*   *   *

Everybody now magnifies the rows at a distance from him. You write of tranquillity in Tuscany, where we expected to hear of revolt, provisional governments, and military occupation. And I get letters from England, asking me whether I am not afraid to have my wife and children[3] in this country, whereas all I hear or see of Irish rows is in the columns of the *Times* newspaper. . . . Here in Ireland the meaning of the word Communism—or even social revolution—is not understood. The people have not the remotest notion of attempting to improve their worldly condition by making the difference between the employer and the employed less marked. Revolution here means a row. Some like a row, having little or nothing to lose. These are revolutionists, and call for pikes. Others are anti-revolutionists, having something to lose and dreading a row. These condemn the pikes, and demand more soldiers and police. There is no notion of anything beyond this;—no conception of any theory such as that of Louis Blanc.[4] My own idea is that there is no ground to fear any general rising either in England or Ireland. I think there is too much intelligence in England for any large body of men to look for any sudden improvement; and not enough intelligence in Ireland for any body of men at all to conceive the possibility of social improvement.

*   *   *

Henry Colburn to Trollope

MS Bodleian. *Autobiography*, pp. 78–79.

Novr. 11. 1848   13 Great Marlborough St.
My dear Sir.

I am sorry that absence from town and other circumstances have prevented me from earlier examining into the results of the sale of the "Kellys and OKellys," with which the greatest efforts have been used, but in vain. The sale has been, I regret to state, so small that the loss upon the publication is very considerable and it appears clear to me that although in consequence of the great number of novels that are published, the sale of each, with some few exceptions, must be small, yet, it is evident that readers do not like novels on Irish subjects so well as

[3] Henry Merivale Trollope (1846–1926) and Frederic James Anthony Trollope (1847–1910).
[4] Louis Blanc (1811–82), French socialist and historian who played an important role in the February Revolution of 1848.

on others. Thus you will perceive, it is impossible for me to give any encouragement to you to proceed in novel writing—

As however I understand you have nearly finished the novel of La Vendee,[5] perhaps you will favor me with a sight of it when convenient.

I remain

My dear Sir

Yours truly

H Colburn

PS. I enclose you a Copy of the account of the O'Kellys made up some-time ago and I assure you that the remainder will not fetch a price to nearly cover the loss, the regular sale being entirely over.[6]

1849

To John Tilley[7]

MS (photocopy) UCLA. B 15.

7 April 1849   Mallow.[8]

My dear John

I cannot say that I have been sorry to get your last letter— I have felt so certain since Cecilia's last relapse, that she could never recover, that I have almost wished that her sufferings should end. I know, that altho you have expected her death, it will still come to you as a great blow— but you are not the man to give way to sorrow— You will be absent from your office, I suppose, for a month or six weeks—bring mama over here[9]—

---

[5] See Trollope to Mrs. Frances Trollope, ? 5 February 1850.

[6] The account Colburn sent Trollope showed that out of 375 copies of the novel printed, only 140 copies had sold, leaving Colburn with a loss of £63 10s. 1½d. (MS Bodleian). Though Trollope "never for a moment doubted" the truth of the account, he also "never thought of obeying" Colburn's discouraging advice (*Autobiography*, p. 78).

[7] John Tilley (1813–98), later Sir John, Post Office official. Five years Trollope's senior in the service, Tilley had been a junior clerk with Trollope in London until he was named a surveyor in 1838. He became Assistant Secretary of the Post Office in 1848 (besting, among other candidates, Thackeray), and then Secretary in 1864. Trollope had introduced Tilley, one of his closest friends, to his sister Cecilia, and they were married on 11 February 1839. Cecilia died on 4 April 1849.

[8] The Trollopes had moved to Mallow, a town in Co. Cork, in the fall of 1848.

[9] The visit was paid in July and gave Trollope's mother great pleasure. On 15 August 1849 she wrote from Charmouth, Dorset, to Rose Trollope: "I most really and truly do feel thankful for the great enjoyment in all ways which this dear visit has given me—and as much as one may venture at my age to look forward to any thing, I

it will be infinitely better for you—for you both—than remaining alone in the house which must for a time be so sad a place to you. I greatly grieve that I cannot at once start so as to be with you on Tuesday—but I could not do without crippling myself with regard to money, in [a] way which not even that object would justify—and I am sure you would think me wrong to do so—it is a great comfort to me to have seen her so shortly before her death.[1]

I will write to mama either tomorrow or on Monday.

God bless you my dear John— I sometimes feel that I led you into more sorrow than happiness in taking you to Hadley.

Very affectionately yours
Anthony Trollope

To Thomas Adolphus Trollope

Memoir, II, 175. B 16.

[Autumn 1849]   [Mallow]

*   *   *

I cannot pretend to condole with you on Mrs. Garrow's[2] death, for it is impossible that it should be a subject of sorrow to you. But of course Theodosia[3] must feel it. I am sorry to hear that she required such a prescription as that of Dr. Latham.[4] Where do you mean to go? It is well for you that some of the continental republican bubbles have burst. This

---

shall indulge myself by looking forward to a repetition of it— Truly rail-roads are a blessing. . . . I glided on by Birmingham, Gloucester, Bristol and Taunton positively without any fatigue at all, and only suffering a little from want of a due supply at fitting intervals of new-laid eggs, salmon curry, Irish potatoes (1849) and bread and butter, together with a little honey and a little coffee and a little porter from the same green land—not to mention a few other trifles all singularly beneficial . . . since we left your hospitable domicile." (MS Taylor Collection.)

[1] Mrs. Trollope wrote to Rose on 20 April 1849: "Sad as the scene [of Cecilia's death] was I almost wish you could have witnessed her departure— It was like an angel falling asleep in happy certainty of awakening in Heaven— I am *very* glad that my dear Anthony saw her on her death bed— The impression left on his mind, however painful at the moment of receiving it, will remain with him for ever more as consolation, than sorrow." (MS Taylor Collection.)

[2] Theodosia Fisher Garrow (1766–1849), née Abrams, said to be the mother of T. A. Trollope's first wife (also named Theodosia). Mrs. Garrow, however, was 23 years older than her second husband, Joseph Garrow (1789–1857), and would have been at least 58 when the younger Theodosia was born in 1825. The Stebbinses conjecture that the younger Theodosia was in fact the daughter of Harriet Fisher, Mrs. Garrow's daughter by her first marriage (Lucy Poate Stebbins and Richard Poate Stebbins, *The Trollopes: The Chronicle of a Writing Family* [1947], p. 122).

[3] Theodosia Trollope (1825–65), the gifted poet whom T. A. Trollope had married in 1848.

[4] Latham advised leaving England for the south of Europe. It was finally decided that T. A. Trollope, his wife Theodosia, his mother, and Mr. Garrow should make a permanent home in Florence.

time last year you would hardly have known where to pitch yourself. I suppose you can now go to Florence for the winter, if you so please. I hope at any rate that you will both be with us next summer. Ireland is sloppy—the south especially so—but it is as warm as it is sloppy. We have hardly any snow or frost, and generally no really cold weather till March.

*   *   *

1850

To Mrs. Frances Trollope
Memoir, II, 178. B 17.

January 29th. 1850.   Tipperary
Dearest Mother.

You will have been very much shocked to hear of your brother's[5] death, for I am afraid the previous accounts which you have received had not made you expect it—at least not so suddenly. Till the last week I had no idea that he was in immediate danger. It appears that latterly he entirely wanted the spirit and hope which might have given him strength to rally. It seems that it was not the actual disease, but the consequent weakness which caused his death; and that for some time previous to it he was in a state almost of lethargy. His death will be a most severe blow for you and my aunt Mary;[6] for he was a most affectionate, fond brother.

*   *   *

To Mrs. Frances Trollope
Memoir, II, 179. B 18.

[? 5 February 1850][7]   [Ireland]
                          *   *   *
We are very sorry. But we have no right to complain. Indeed, the incurring the chance of losing her at any moment after we had become

---

[5] Henry Milton (?1784–1850), senior official at the War Office. He had died on 16 January.

[6] Mary Milton Clyde (1776–1870).

[7] Perhaps this date, since Trollope refers to "Tuesday—*i.e.* this day week," but certainly earlier than 15 February, when Colburn accepted *La Vendée*. However, it is impossible to tell from the *Memoir* whether this excerpt was from a separate letter or was part of the letter of 29 January, also a Tuesday.

Frances Trollope. Portrait by Auguste Hervieu, ca. 1832.

fond of her, was the only drawback to the pleasure of taking her.[8] . . .

My uncle's death has put a stop to my hand-book for the present. I am, however, not inclined to give it over. I mean to go to London and see Murray.[9] I shall be there and back within a week. I hope to go next Tuesday—*i.e.* this day week. Of course I shall be with Tilley. Tell Tom that I finished "La Vendée" and sent it to Colburn.[1]

* * *

To Mrs. Frances Trollope
Memoir, II, 203–4. B 19.

[May 1850]   [Ireland]

* * *

I am very glad you are suited with a house. I hope we may live to see it! At any rate I hope nothing will prevent our all meeting under the shadow of some huge, newly invented machine in the Exhibition of 1851. I mean to exhibit four 3 vol. novels—all failures!—which I look on as a great proof of industry at any rate. I want you and Tom to make out six lists each containing thirteen names, modern or ancient (Biblical characters excluded), of the following persons:—

1. Great men;—*i.e.* men who have moved the world, not literary or scientific merely. 2. Great women. 3. Men of genius. 4. Great Captains. 5. Great Rebels. 6. Statesmen. Ask Theodosia to make a list also. I have got different people to do so, and then I [? shall] see how they all tally together.

* * *

[8] In July 1849 the Trollopes had taken into their home at Mallow Edith Diana Mary Tilley, one of John Tilley's five children by Cecilia. They may have offered to take her soon after her mother's death, for on 20 April Mrs. Trollope wrote to Rose: "John Tilley is not a demonstrative man—as Anthony knows—but his eyes filled with tears when he read your mention of his poor little Edith." (MS Taylor Collection.) In 1850 Edith returned to her father shortly after he married Mary Anne Partington, a cousin of Cecilia.

[9] Trollope wrote that the manuscript of about a quarter of his proposed guidebook on Ireland languished unopened at Murray's for nine months, after which "it was returned without a word, in answer to a very angry letter from myself. . . . In all honesty I think that had he been less dilatory, John Murray would have got a very good Irish Guide at a cheap rate." (*Autobiography*, p. 87.)

[1] Colburn accepted *La Vendée*: according to an agreement of 15 February 1850, Trollope was to receive £20 down for the novel, with the prospect of an additional £30 when the sales reached 350 copies, or a further £50 if the sales reached 450 copies within six months. This was surprising in view of Colburn's pessimistic remarks of November 1848 (see Colburn to Trollope, 11 November 1848). *La Vendée* was published in June 1850, and since it was unsuccessful, Trollope received nothing beyond the £20 (see *Autobiography*, pp. 80–81).

To Thomas Adolphus Trollope

Memoir, II, 205. B 20.

[Summer 1850]   [Ireland]
Dear Tom.

I send the lists with the number of votes, including yours and Theodosia's. You pay a poor compliment to women, by having recourse to
fiction to fill a female list. You have no man of genius for the first four
thousand years, and only one man who influenced the world; only one
rebel, and one great woman. Theodosia is equally fond of the moderns.
She admits no great man or statesman before Christ, and only Eschylus
as a man of genius. I believe Metternich is the only living man mentioned
in the lists as I send them,—yes; Wellington. Tell Theodosia I cannot
allow Cathelineau[2] to be called a rebel, as he took up arms for his king.
We certainly should have had Masaniello, John of Procida, and Huss.
Only seven names have been *unanimously* voted: Shakespeare, Mahomet, Joan of Arc, Napoleon, Richelieu, Pitt, and Wolsey;—all of them
moderns. And yet I should be inclined to say that Caesar was the greatest man who ever lived. So much for the lists.

I don't think there is any obstacle to our coming to Florence in the
summer—say May or June—of 1852. And there is nothing on earth we
should like better.

*   *   *

To Mrs. Frances Trollope

Memoir, II, 186. B 21.

[Summer 1850]   [Ireland]

*   *   *

God send that we may all meet in 1851, when I mean to put three
or four works into the Exhibition. They will, at any rate, give me as
much encouragement as Colburn does!

*   *   *

To Mrs. Frances Trollope

Memoir, II, 186–87. B 21.

[Summer 1850]   [Ireland]

*   *   *

Strangely enough, until I got your letter, I had seen nothing of the
case in the Dublin papers. I shall not fail to send you all particulars of
the trial,—if she is tried.[3]

*   *   *

---

[2] Jacques Cathelineau (1759–93), a leader in the Catholic royalist insurrection of
1793 in La Vendée; hence Trollope's interest.

[3] A clergyman's wife was to stand trial on a charge of murdering her husband in a

To Thomas Adolphus Trollope

Memoir, II, 213. B 22.

[July or August 1850]   [Ireland]

*   *   *

To be sure there are certain very palpable delights in being *expeditus*;
—in living in other people's houses, being served by other people's servants, eating other men's roast and boiled, and having one's *gendarmerie*
paid for by other men's taxes! But still there is a comfort, a solidity, a
nescio quid decori [? *decoris*],⁴ in one's own arm-chair by one's own fireside, which after all I should not wish to want.⁵

*   *   *

1851

To Thomas Adolphus Trollope

Memoir, II, 217. B 23.

March [1851]   [Ireland]

*   *   *

I grieve to find that you and Theodosia do not intend coming to London next summer. Your stay in Italy will, I presume, occasion my
mother's. And there is our pleasant party broken up! I cannot tell you
how I grieve at this. . . . *We* intend going to see the *furriners* in June. I
think it will be great fun seeing such a crowd. As for the Exhibition itself, I would not give a straw for it,—except the building itself, and my
wife's piece of work which is in it.⁶ I suppose you have nearly completed
your decorations and improvements. I hope I shall live to see them. I
have just finished an article on Charles Merivale's⁷ "Rome," and sent it

---

particularly brutal manner. Frances Eleanor Trollope, T. A. Trollope's second wife,
wrote that Trollope made "many allusions" to the case in subsequent letters (*Memoir*,
II, 186).

⁴ "An I-know-not-what of fittingness."

⁵ Trollope congratulates his brother on having completed the additions to the
house in Florence bought earlier in the year. The "Villino Trollope," in what was
later called Piazza dell' Indipendenza, became an important haunt of the British
colony in Florence.

⁶ An embroidered screen, which won a bronze prize.

⁷ Charles Merivale (1808–93), historian and later Dean of Ely. Merivale was a son
of the John Herman Merivales, friends of Trollope's parents since the early years of
the Trollopes' marriage (when they lived in Keppel Street, London).

to the Dublin University Mag. But I doubt their printing it. It is too late, and they don't know me.

* * *

To Mrs. Frances Trollope
Memoir, II, 218–19. B 24.

[7 May 1851]   [Limerick]

* * *

It is May by the calendar, but February by one's feelings as affected by rain, winds, and cold air. The oldest inhabitant knows nothing like it. . . . I regret more and more every day that Tom is not to see the Exhibition. I am sure it is a thing a man ought to see. John Tilley is enthusiastic, and knew all about it before it was opened; corresponds with all the Secretaries and Commissioners, and has regularly made a study of it! I think he is right. It is a great thing to get a new pleasure. . . . Will there be no such thing as a cheap trip from Florence by which a man could come to London and go back within a fortnight or so? Touching the "Papal Aggression,"[8] my opinion is that nothing at all should have been done. I would have let the whole thing sink by its own weight. . . . We set up *very much* the idea of going to Italy in the summer of 1852. I hope we may live to do it. At present we are all agog about going to London. Rose is looking up her silk dresses, and I am meditating a new hat!

* * *

To Thomas Adolphus Trollope
Memoir, II, 217. B 25.

[May 1851]   [Ireland]

* * *

My article on Charles Merivale's "Rome" is in the May No. of the Dublin University Magazine:[9]—a periodical which, I presume, has not a large sale in Florence! Charles Merivale sent me word that it was the best

[8] The so-called Papal Aggression of 1850 (the creation of a Roman Catholic hierarchy in England by Pius IX) caused a great stir of resentment in the press, in Parliament, and throughout the land.

[9] "Merivale's History of the Romans," *Dublin University Magazine*, 37 (May 1851), 611–24. Here Trollope reviewed the first two volumes of Merivale's *The History of the Romans Under the Empire* (1850, 1851), which dealt with Julius Caesar's rise to power and his achievements as a ruler and general. The writing of this article occasioned extensive study and led to Trollope's interest in the character of Caesar (which later prompted him to write his work on Caesar's *Commentaries*) and to a "taste generally for Latin literature, which has been one of the chief delights of my later life" (*Autobiography*, pp. 101–2). Trollope subsequently reviewed the third, fourth, and fifth volumes of Merivale's work; see the *Dublin University Magazine*, 48 (July 1856), 30–47.

review of the work which had appeared. Certainly it is by no means the most laudatory. I wrote it for the purpose of differing from him on a certain point.[1]

*　　　　*　　　　*

George Bartley[2] to Trollope

MS Taylor Collection. Michael Sadleir, "Preface," *The Noble Jilt* (1923), pp. xiv–xv.

18th. June 1851　　　　　　　　　　　11 Woburn Square. London
My dear Mr. A Trollope

I am sorry I did not see you on Monday but as I was obliged to remain in Town until this afternoon, I occupied myself yesterday in carefully perusing your M.S. and feel myself bound, as you ask for my opinion, to give it candidly. And it is this.

When I commenced I had great hopes of your production— I did not think it opened dramatically, but that might have been remedied, and the dialogue, both serious & comic, promised admirably, but as the plot proceeded, I found the serious parts deficient in interest, and the comic ones overlaid with repetitions. There is not one character serious or comic to challenge the sympathy of the audience—and without that, all the good writing in the world will not assure success on the stage. We are *told* the Count Upsel is a most amiable and quiet man, but you have given him no scope to assert or form his good qualities—he has really nothing to do. Mark Steinberg[3] is merely a republican and why he makes his base proposal to Margaret, except to carry on the plot of the play, I cannot understand. As far as it is explained in his own person, it is wholly gratuitous—nor, if you mean him for a villain (with this fatal exception) he has nothing of villainy in him. Nor is his character prominently brought out, indeed such little lead does he or the Count take in the business of the drama—that you have a five act play without a hero!

---

[1] Although praising Merivale's style, narrative power, and extensive knowledge, Trollope contended that Merivale had written a life of Caesar rather than a history of Rome and, in particular, that his perspective had made him undervalue Pompeius.

[2] George Bartley (?1782–1858), comic actor and theater manager. In his *Autobiography* Trollope explains how, after writing three unsuccessful novels, he decided to write a comedy (partly in blank verse) entitled *The Noble Jilt*. He then asked Bartley for his opinion of the play: "I have now before me the letter which he wrote to me,—a letter which I have read a score of times. It was altogether condemnatory. . . . But I accepted the judgement loyally. . . . In later days I have more than once read the play, and I know that he was right. The dialogue, however, I think to be good, and I doubt whether some of the scenes be not the brightest and best work I ever did." (*Autobiography*, pp. 85–86.) Trollope later used the plot of *The Noble Jilt* in *Can You Forgive Her?*, where the following character parallels can be discerned: John Grey and Count Upsel; George Vavasor and Steinmark; Alice Vavasor and Margaret; Kate Vavasor and Helen; and Mrs. Greenow and Madame Brudo. See also Trollope to Dallas, 1 September 1868. The play first appeared in print in Sadleir's 1923 edition.

[3] A slip for "Steinmark."

The Comic scenes are good, but too long, and all so much alike, that one is merely a repetition of the other. Helen's character is well and boldly written, and (to me) the least objectionable personage in the play, though I am not in love with her, or her ready inter-meddling. As to the character of Margaret, I felt at a loss how to describe it, and my objections to it—but you have done it for me in the last speech of Made. Brudo: "Margaret my child—never play the jilt again. *Tis a most un-becoming character. Play it with what skill you will, it meets but little sympathy!"* [4]—and this be assured would be its effect upon an audience. So that, I must reluctantly add—that had I been still a manager, "The Noble Jilt"—is not a play I could have recommended for production. I qualify all this, by honestly stating, I have often been mistaken in my opinions, and may be wrong in this—but you ask me for my honest impressions—and I have too much regard & respect for your excellent & highly gifted mother, and all her family, not to give them candidly as they are—and am most truly sorry they are not more favorable.

> I am my dear Mr. A Trollope
> respectfully & sincerely
> Yours
> Geo Bartley

To Thomas Adolphus Trollope

Memoir, II, 223. B 26.

[September 1851]   [Exeter] [5]

*   *   *

If you cannot come to Mahomet, Mahomet shall go to you, but I should greatly prefer your coming here, as I have such very heavy work on hand. You would, moreover, see Rose and Harry, who are with me. I should much like you to see little Harry.

*   *   *

[4] Underlined twice.

[5] Because of the energy and efficiency Trollope had shown in reorganizing and extending rural deliveries in the Southern District of Ireland, the Post Office sent him in August 1851 on temporary special assignment to perform the same services in the southwest of England. Trollope spent what he described as two of the happiest years of his life at this task: "I had an opportunity of seeing a considerable portion of Great Britain, with a minuteness which few have enjoyed. And I did my business after a fashion in which no other official man has worked, at least for many years. I went almost everywhere on horseback." (*Autobiography*, pp. 87–88.) See Trollope to Hardwicke, 25 November 1852.

To G. H. Creswell[6]

MS General Post Office, London. B 28.

21 November 1851   Guernsey
Sir.

... There is at present no receiving office in St. Heliers [*sic*], and persons living in the distant parts of the town have to send nearly a mile to the principal office. I believe that a plan has obtained in France of fitting up letter boxes in posts fixed at the road side, and it may perhaps be thought adviseable to try the operation of this system in St. Heliers— postage stamps are sold in every street, and therefore all that is wanted is a safe receptacle for letters, which shall be cleared on the morning of the despatch of the London Mails, and at such other times as may be requisite. Iron posts suited for the purpose may be erected at the corners of streets in such situations as may be desirable, or probably it may be found to be more serviceable to fix iron letter boxes about five feet from the ground, wherever permanently built walls, fit for the purpose can be found, and I think that the public may safely be invited to use such boxes for depositing their letters.

Should the Postmr Genl be willing to sanction this experiment, I would recommend the four sites which I have marked with red ink on the enclosed small map of the town, the site of the principal office being marked with a black cross. In this event no expense need be incurred for clearing the letters from the boxes, as this duty on post mornings would be performed by the person who brings in the rural receiving house bags, and at the other times by the town Letter Carriers.

I can give no estimate of the cost of erecting such letter boxes as those proposed.[7] It would probably be necessary to consult the town authorities, before the different localities were absolutely fixed. . . .

To G. H. Creswell

MS General Post Office, London.

19th. December 1851   Exeter
Sir.

With reference to the Secretary's letter to you of the 17th. Instant conveying the authority of the Postmaster General for the adoption of road side letter boxes at St. Heliers Jersey, and to the confidential

[6] George H. Creswell, Post Office Surveyor for the Western District of England and Trollope's superior during his temporary assignment in the southwest. The text printed here is an excerpt from a lengthy official report.

[7] Various people, including Rowland Hill, had suggested pillar letter boxes, but "Anthony Trollope surely deserves full credit for their eventual introduction to this country, for it was his energy and persistence, and his alone, that finally resulted in their adoption in 1852." (Jean Young Farrugia, *The Letter Box: A History of Post Office Pillar and Wall Boxes* [Fontwell, Sussex, 1969], p. 122.)

report lately made on the Guernsey office in which the want of town receiving offices is alluded [to], I beg to recommend that similar road side letter boxes may also be tried at St. Peters Port [*sic*], in that island.

I enclose a map of the town and environs in which I have marked the sites I would propose for these letter boxes, 3 in number. They would be cleared on the mornings of the despatch to London, by the persons employed to bring in the bags from the country receiving offices, and on the other 3 mornings by the town letter Carriers, previously to the arrival of the London Mail.

I am
Sir,
Your most obedient Servant

G H Creswell Esq　　　　　　　　　　　Anthony Trollope

To Mrs. Frances Trollope

Memoir, II, 218. B 30.

[1851][8]

*　　　*　　　*

I have read—nay, I have bought!—Carlyle's *"Latter Day Pamphlets,"* and look on my eight shillings as very much thrown away. To me it appears that the grain of sense is so smothered up in a sack of the sheerest trash, that the former is valueless. He does not himself know what he wants. He has one idea,—a hatred of spoken and acted falsehood; and on that he harps through the whole eight pamphlets. I look on him as a man who was always in danger of going mad in literature, and who has now done so. I used to swear by some of his earlier works. But to my taste his writings have lost their pith and humour, while they have become stranger, and more uncouth, than ever.[9]

*　　　*　　　*

[8] The *Memoir* places this letter in 1851, although the reference to the eight-shilling cost of the *Latter-Day Pamphlets*, which originally appeared in parts between February and August 1850, suggests 1850. It is possible, however, that Trollope purchased a set of parts rather than the volume edition.

[9] In *The Warden* (chap. xv), Trollope caricatured Carlyle as "Dr. Pessimist Anticant," who "constituted himself censor of things in general, and began the great task of reprobating everything and everybody. . . . [His] monthly pamphlet on the decay of the world did not receive so much attention as his earlier works." However, Trollope's own concern with Carlylean themes, especially public honesty, led him to write *The New Zealander* (see Trollope to Longman, 27 March 1855; and Cauvin to Longman, 2 April 1855). For a discussion of Trollope's attitude toward Carlyle, see N. John Hall, "Trollope and Carlyle," *NCF*, 27 (September 1972), 197–205; and Ruth apRoberts, "Carlyle and Trollope," in John Clubbe, ed., *Carlyle and His Contemporaries* (Durham, North Carolina, 1976), pp. 204–26.

1852

To Thomas Adolphus Trollope
Memoir, II, 231–32. B 31.

[March 1852]

*   *   *

I am delighted not to find myself scolded for having changed our purposed plans. I trust, when 1853 does come, I may find myself repaid for my patience by the *greenth* of your lawn. A twelvemonth does not seem so long to wait now as it did ten years ago. It ought to seem longer, for as one has fewer months to come one should make more of them. But somehow, the months and years so jostle one another, that I seem to be living away at a perpetual gallop. I wish I could make the pace a little slower. . . . Whom should I meet in Exeter the other day but our old acquaintance S. J. I brought her to dine with us. She is not in the least changed. She still tells wonderful romances about herself and all the rest of the family; says ill-natured things about other people; laughs, talks, and eats, and makes herself sufficiently agreeable for a short time. I was glad to see her for the sake of old times. . . . She, S. J., has written three books; and if Mama were only in England, she, S. J., would get her, Mama, to *have them published for her*, as she, S. J., sadly wants to make some money! Perhaps you had better not tell Mama. It would make her so bitterly lament not being in England! I do hope to take six weeks next year,—about May, as you suggest,—and trust that nothing may again prevent our getting to Italy.

*   *   *

To Mrs. Frances Trollope
Memoir, II, 241–42. B 32.

[September 1852][1]   [Haverfordwest][2]

*   *   *

We have heard a rumour (some one told John Tilley in Kensington Gardens!) that Theodosia is about to make Tom a father.[3] If so, why has not Tom told us what we should have been so glad to learn from him? If it be true, I heartily wish Theodosia well through her trouble.

---

[1] The text of this letter suggests that it was written sometime between Wellington's death, on 14 September 1852, and his burial four days later.

[2] A town in southwest Wales.

[3] Beatrice (Bice) Trollope (1853–81) was born the following March. There were some rumors, evidently unfounded, that T. A. Trollope was not her father: see Trollope to Houghton, 15 April 1865.

... I have been expecting, dearest mother, to hear either from you or Tom these two months. I hope you have not both forgotten me!

We are now living, or staying for a while rather, in South Wales. Rose and the bairns are at a place on the sea-side called Llanstephen [*sic*], where there is plenty of air and bathing. We shall stay in Carmarthen during November, and then go to Gloucester for the winter. Harry and Freddy are quite well, and are very nice boys:—very different in disposition, but neither with anything that I could wish altered. ... We are all here getting dreadfully sick of the Duke of Wellington. He is administered at all hours, and in every shape. The papers have no other subject, and people write, speak, and think, of nothing else. Oh, that he was well buried, and there an end! I have heard fifty anecdotes of him in the last five days,—all equally applicable to any one else.

I had a couple of civil letters from Sir John Trollope[4] recently, about using his interest for me at the G.P.O. And I believe he has done what he could do.[5] But I ought not to want any private interest. The more I see the way in which the post-office work is done, the more aggrieved I feel at not receiving the promotion I have a right to expect. However, this does not really annoy me. I can't fancy any one being much happier than I am,—or having less in the world to complain of. It often strikes me how wonderfully well I have fallen on my feet. ... My kindest love to Tom and Theodosia. I will write to him soon; and I hope he will do the same to me.

* * *

To Thomas Adolphus Trollope
Memoir, II, 242–43. B 33.

Oct. 5th. 1852.   Haverfordwest
My dear Tom.

Though I wrote to my mother only last week, I must send a line to acknowledge your letter. ... I am glad you are to have a child. One wants some one to exercise unlimited authority over, as one gets old and cross. If one blows up one's servants too much, they turn round, give warning, and repay one with interest. One's wife may be too much for one, and is not always a safe recipient for one's wrath. But one's children can be blown up to any amount without damage,—at any rate, for a considerable number of years. The pleasures of paternity have been considerably

---

[4] Sir John Trollope (1800–1874), later Baron Kesteven, was a well-to-do landowner and MP for Lincoln. His grandfather was Thomas Middleton Trollope, a brother of Trollope's grandfather.

[5] On 25 November Sir John wrote to Lord Hardwicke, Postmaster General, that Trollope had been "employed in the *Gen. Post Office for 20 years* with great credit to himself, as I have every reason to believe he is one of your most able officers." Hardwicke replied that he would "weigh Mr Trollope's claims & abilities with those of others." (MSS British Library.)

abridged, since the good old Roman privilege of slaying their offspring at pleasure, has been taken from fathers. But the delights of flagellation, though less keen, are more enduring. One can kill but once; but one may flog daily, and always quote Scripture to prove that it is a duty. And then the gratification of disinheriting a disobedient son, and sending him adrift, with the determination that no calf shall be killed on his return!

A daughter, I fear, does not offer so much innocent enjoyment. But some fathers do manage to torment their daughters with a great degree of very evident and enviable satisfaction. I have none, and therefore have not turned my attention to that branch of the subject.

You don't at all say when you expect to see your child, but from Mama's letter to Rose I presume it will be early in the Spring. I shall be very anxious to hear that Theo and her baby are well and out of danger. Alas, alas, the Duke of Wellington is dead, or of course you would have had him for a godfather.

Joking apart, I am heartily glad to hear the news, and assure you that, to my thinking, nothing that could happen to you would be so likely to add to your happiness as this.—(You know all about the fox who lost his tail!).

*   *   *

To the Earl of Hardwicke[6]

MS British Library. B 34.

25th Nov 1852.   Gloucester
My Lord

I understand that it is probable that your Lordship will soon have to appoint a new Superintendent of Mail Coaches, and I hope you will not consider that I am taking an undue liberty in soliciting the appointment.

I have been 18 years in the service, and I believe I may confidently refer your Lordship to any of the officers under whom I have served, and especially to Col Maberly, as to my fitness for the situation.[7]

[6] Charles Philip Yorke (1799–1873), 4th Earl of Hardwicke; Postmaster General in Derby's 1852 ministry.

[7] The Hardwicke correspondence contains no recommendation from Maberly. But a letter of 2 November 1852 from Maberly to Hardwicke, urging the continuance of Trollope's temporary duty in England, was most favorable: "Mr. Trollope having completed the revision of the rural Posts [in southern Ireland] in a very prompt & satisfactory manner, it was considered by yr. Predecessor desirable to afford the advantage of his assistance to one or more of the English Surveyors . . . first to the Western district in which he has completed the duty . . . & thence to the South Wales district where he is now engaged in revising rural Posts." Trollope was returned to Ireland briefly (21 December 1851 to 11 March 1852) after "urgent representation" from his district, where his old duties were being performed "in an unsatisfactory manner, owing principally to the loss of his services," in spite of an officer having been sent as a replacement. Trollope's work in England and Wales "has been & would be

Should your Lordship find it expedient to entrust to me the duties of the office in question, I will not fail to devote to them my best energies and attention.

I have the honor to be,

My Lord,

Your Lordship's most obedient Servant

The Right Honble   Anthony Trollope

The Earl of Hardwicke

To T. T. Walton[8]

MS Parrish Collection. B 35.

27 Nov. 1852   Llandilo.[9]

My dear Sir.

May I trouble you with a very troublesome commission.

Mrs. Trollope wishes to have the lumber which at present burdens you at Bristol, sent by luggage train to her present address. No. 5 Paragon buildings Cheltenham—. I dont know how many articles there are, but if you could have the address as above put on them, & the articles forwarded, she & I would be your debtors— There will necessarily be a large outlay in porters &c, but you are used to large advancements for official purposes, & if you will make this on my account, & let me know the tot of the whole, I pledge myself to reimburse you at any rate with as much punctuality as the money order office does.

There are I believe some maps—a case of maps— That had better be sent by post, addressed to me—"to be kept at the post office till Mr. Trollope's arrival—"

You are not, I hope, my enemy—but if you were, & if I could not bring myself to wish you well in a charitable christian manner, but were excited by the Devil to wish you all evil, I could wish you nothing worse than a residence in South Wales for the rest of your life—

Pray give my compliments to Mrs. Walton. I trust neither she, nor either of your boys have been washed away in the floods— Clifton tho' has probably escaped— I have very frequently had to swim for it— The people here are mostly swimming at present—those at least who are not sinking—[1]

Yours always very truly

T. T. Walton Esq   Anthony Trollope

---

most useful." (MS General Post Office, London.) The appointment of Superintendent of Mail Coaches went to W. T. Wedderburn, whose letter of application to Hardwicke cited 26 years of service in the mail coach department (MS British Library).

[8] Thomas Todd Walton, Jr., Postmaster of Bristol.

[9] A small town north of Swansea.

[1] Very heavy rain for more than two months had caused widespread destruction.

1854

To Mrs. Frances Trollope

MS Taylor Collection. B 38.

28 June 1854   Coleraine.[2]
Dearest Mother—

I have received from London today, not my appointment as Surveyor—but what is tantamount to a direct promise of it. Urquharts[3] pension was settled—whereon Tilley asked Lord C[4] to appoint me at once. His answer was—"He must wait till July— I will then appoint Beaufort[5] & Trollope at the same time—" Now I don't at all understand this, except he chose from some cause that Beaufort shall be my senior—nor do I think that I shall get my appointment in July, as the vacancy to which Beaufort is to succeed will not then yet exist—but I do look on my appointment now as a certainty—and therefore I write at once to you to tell you—[6] As to the income—it is not fixed—but I presume it will not be less than £600—and mine has been that for the last nine months— I think it will be about £650— This I mean in Ireland, which is worth £750 in England— Should I go to England I do not think it would exceed £700—if it came to that—at least not for some years—[7] Should I however get the chance of going to England I should take it.

Now you know all about my official prospects— I do feel myself certain of my district and I know you will rejoice with me— I would much sooner however have to communicate the fait accompli—, as we all know that there are slips.

I write to Tom about our route—but I still have this doubt—if Lord Canning wont fill up the district before September I may very probably not get away—& of course I must let you know early in August— His Lordship said July—but one can't bind Lords down to what they say always—

Then comes the important question of residence— Where shall we live? We both dislike the north—& the districts may all be changed—

[2] A town in Co. Londonderry, Ireland. In August 1853, after two years in England, Trollope had been sent to Ireland's Northern District as acting Surveyor.

[3] Patrick Urquhart, Surveyor for Ireland's Southern Counties.

[4] Charles John Canning (1812–62), Earl Canning, was Postmaster General from 1853 to 1855; he was later Governor General of India.

[5] John St. Lawrence Beaufort, who was about to become Surveyor for Birmingham.

[6] It was not until 9 October 1854 that Trollope was appointed Surveyor for Ireland's Northern District.

[7] By 1855 Trollope's annual salary was £700, top for his rank. He received an additional £30 per year in office rent, since he used his home for his office, as well as 20s. per day for days away from his office, and reimbursement for official travel.

but this also we must discuss on a gondola. We wont buy our furniture at any rate till we have discussed with you the color of the drawing room curtains—[8]

Harry came home from Cork today—with such a Cork brogue—& such a pair of cheeks—& no shoes to his feet— They must both go to some school here in the North after midsummer— We are all now going to the sea side for a month. Fred is somewhat delicate—he is so miserably thin— he is like a skeleton—but full of life & spirits—a horse threw him last week and trod on his hand—how he escaped is marvellous—but he only had one nail squeezed off—

Tilley's coming also is dubious—more so than mine, for I do believe we shall get away—but he can't or won't leave till all these changes are over—nor R. Hill[9] either—& then when the changes are complete, of course Hill, will have the first choice.

God bless you dearest mother
ever your own little boy
A. T.

On reading over my letter I find it to be most wretchedly disconnected, and all but unintelligible—but I am writing at 3 AM—& I want to write at once—so pray try to make it out—

To Thomas Adolphus Trollope

MS Taylor Collection. B 37.

28 June 1854   Coleraine
My dear Tom—

Tilley to whom I sent your last letter anent the routes begins his answer thus "Tom is a tyrant—to hear is to obey"—to the which I say ditto—specially as to obeying. Our route out shall be—Paris, Geneva— Simplon–Como–Milan–Venice. Our route home will be afterwards dis-

[8] Trollope obtained permission to make Dublin his headquarters, and was able to leave Belfast on 2 May 1855. In June he took a house in the Dublin suburb of Donnybrook, at 5 Seaview Terrace, where he and his family remained until the end of 1859.

[9] Rowland Hill (1795–1879), later Sir Rowland, originator (as an officer of the Treasury) of the penny post. In 1846 Hill was given the anomalous position of "Secretary to the Postmaster General," while Col. Maberly continued as "Secretary to the Post Office," and the two engaged in a power struggle until Maberly retired in 1854, whereupon Hill became Secretary (on 22 April). Hill respected Trollope's abilities and had been largely responsible for having Trollope sent on special assignment to the southwest of England. Nonetheless, he distrusted Trollope. In the fall of 1852, for example, he suspected that there might have been "an understanding between the two brothers [-in-law] that Tilley would succeed M[aberly]" (MS General Post Office, London). Trollope, for his part, seemed to relish his "delicious feuds" with Hill until the latter's retirement in 1864. See *Autobiography*, pp. 133–34, 162, 283. See also Trollope to Smith, 8 May 1860, n. 8, 8 January 1861, n. 6, and 26 June 1861, n. 5; Trollope to Tilley, 13 June 1860, n. 6; Trollope to Lowell, 2 September 1862, n. 6; and Trollope to Hill, 2 March 1864.

cussed—but we shall be found to be babes in your hands. On one point
only can you not have your way—5 weeks—i e. 35 days must be our widest
limit. Suppose we leave London—night of 4th. September could we not
do the proposed route—reach Venice 15 Sept—stay our full 12 days—
leave 27th. & get home by 6th. October? This would give us 9 days out—
and 9 home—but if this would hurry both journeys too much we could
take 11 out & gallop back—though we long to see something of the
Tyrol—

We suggest going back Innsbruck–Munich–Frankford [*sic*]–Cologne–
Ostend which is one of your routes— Now when a man leaves Kensington which train does he take to Geneva? I presume Paris–Chalons– and—
not Lyons I suppose—probably Besancon—however tell us the quickest
route from Paris to Geneva.

From Geneva over the Simplon—queries—What time by Vet[1]–? &
what time by diligence?[2] are there diligences? if Tilley does not come
would not a vet be very dear for two—? & should places be taken, if by
diligence, beforehand—? & where should one stop between Geneva &
Milan—? In fact just give me a concise Murray[3]—the bits we want— You
know all about it of course to the very houses at which every vehicle
starts—

You will hear from my mother all about my Surveyorship— I trust my
state of vassalage is over— So the Turks have come out strong—and the
Czar has gone back—not in the least because he is beaten, but merely to
oblige his friend the Emperor of Austria! If peace be made without extracting some plumage out of his tail, there will be a row in the house—
Lord Aberdeen undoubtedly would consent to such a peace, if he dared.[4]

Give my kindest love to Theo— Rose would write, but she does not
know I am writing— You say nothing of my lady Bimba—[5]

> ever yours
> A. T.

Our object will be to spend as much of our time in coming as we can
near the Alps—but Rose stipulates that she must have one night to sleep
in 4—

What is the time from Milan to Venice—?

T. A. Trollope Esq

[1] An Italian four-wheeled coach.
[2] A public stagecoach.
[3] John Murray's celebrated guidebooks for travelers.
[4] George Hamilton Gordon (1784–1860), 4th Earl of Aberdeen, headed a coalition
ministry from 1852 to 1855. Public opinion considered him too conciliatory toward
Russia, and his ministry did not survive the Crimean War.
[5] Beatrice Trollope ("Bimba" is Italian for "baby").

Mrs. Frances Trollope to Trollope
MS Taylor Collection.

July 24 1854   Baths of Lucca

Most truly can I assure you, my dearest Anthony, that each and all of us are considered by all and each of us as being really and truly not worth a thought in comparison to you and dear Rose. You have been so shamefully tormented that the loss of this one dear little interval of enjoyment was *necessary* to you both, and that you should lose it is most deeply felt by us all. Were it not for this feeling I think we should all be disposed to say that *May* would be better than Septr. The heat in Italy is more fearful— It would be passed a joke, even for Tilley, as Septr. after such a summer would not give us fragrant gales from the Venitian canals. Perhaps *I* bear this present disappointment better in consequence of the manner in which it reached me. Your thin-paper letter was enclosed in a very thick page from Tom, which opening itself widely before me displayed these words . . . "You will not only sympathize in his vexation, but you will feel as I do most bitterly the indignation which such treatment calls forth. How can we trust to any promises or representations made by such people? It is *too* shameful!" Whereupon I immediately took it for granted that the hopes, *all* hopes, of the Surveyorship had melted into air, and there I sat, resting my head upon my hands as if on purpose to prevent my reading any farther, as miserable a poor soul as you can paint to yourself, let your fancy be as dolorous as it will.

You may therefore easily understand how much less the real evil when I came to comprehend it, appeared. It was *really* small in comparison. I hope and trust, my dear children, that you will get out of *town* somehow— At any rate you can get to the sea, and one that shall smell sweeter in September than the Lagoon. Why will not somebody do a little mischief to some other body? I am worn out with looking for news —important slash and cut news— But none such seems likely. It seems very like marching up the hill and then marching down again. Emperors can do that as well as Kings. This place is very beautiful, and, compared to Florence, cool; but I cannot get Theodosia to come here. What is John Tilley going to do? If he cared for scenery as much as you do I would ask him to come *here*— But we have nothing but our chesnut-covered mountains to shew him. Most assuredly I do not recommend his coming to *Florence*, and we must wait for you and Rose for Venice. I too, dearest Anthony mean to keep my Venice money safe & your unpaid *ten*. God bless you and yours— Bear your plagues, as you have always done—*philosophically* and not as I was doing just now! Ever your affectionate mother

                                                F. T.

[Postscript by T. A. Trollope]
I have just received this, from Baths of Lucca my dear Anthony, to be forwarded. I waited for it—or should have answered yours before. The conduct, shabby, *unjust*, and insolently tyrannical of your superiors, makes me feel *very* radically inclined. I think any opening of opportunity would convert me into a Post-office Guy Office [Fawkes]. And I have no belief in your promotion, till you get it. Damn them all! Amen. As for us I can only say ditto to all my mother has said. There is no doubt that May is a better month for Venice than Septr.—⁶ And for various reasons it will suit *me* better to leave home then than in Septr. Besides six weeks is 20 per cent better than five. . . . Best love to Rose & you from self & Theo.

T. A. T.

Joseph Cauvin⁷ to William Longman⁸
Sadleir's transcript, Bodleian. *Commentary*, p. 166.

Oct. 13 1854   20 Porchester Terrace.
In re *The Precentor*

This story takes its rise from the recent exposé of the abuses that have crept into Cathedral and Hospital Trusts. Not a very promising subject, one might infer at first sight! But such is the skill of the author that he has contrived to weave out of his materials a very interesting and amusing tale. The scene is laid in a cathedral town; and the chief characters consist of the precentor, a good-natured conscientious clergyman who is at the same time warden of an adjoining hospital; his son-in-law, the archdeacon, a keen and ardent churchman; the Bishop—easy indolent and benevolent; and an eager reformer of Church abuses who is in love with the warden's younger daughter and in whose internal conflict between love and duty lies the main interest of the story.

How the story ends I will not tell you, as I hope you will read it for

---

⁶ The visit to Italy had to be postponed until the following year. In 1854 Trollope was able to take only two brief leaves: from 10 to 12 July in London, and from 1 to 5 August in Scotland (account books, Parrish Collection).

⁷ Joseph Cauvin (*d.* 1875), author and translator, served as reader for the publisher William Longman. The holder of an LL.D. from the University of Gottingen, Cauvin had been assistant editor of W. T. Brande's *Dictionary of Science, Literature, and Art* (1842), and was a member of the Corporation of the Royal Literary Fund from 1852.

⁸ William Longman (1813–77), a partner since 1839 in the well-known publishing house founded by Thomas Longman in 1724. Trollope met Longman through his friend John Merivale. On 8 October Trollope mailed Longman the manuscript of *The Precentor* (the title was soon changed to *The Warden*), a novel he had begun in July 1853 (Trollope wrote 1852 in his *Autobiography*; the mistake was corrected in the first edition, but 1852 was restored in later editions). Reprinted here is the reader's report on the work that would bring Trollope his first modest popularity. Longman's agreement to publish the novel on half profits was dated 24 October, and the novel was published on 5 January 1855.

yourself. The characters are well drawn and happily distinguished; and the whole story is pervaded by a vein of quiet humour and (good-natured) satire, which will make the work acceptable to all Low Churchmen and dissenters.

The description of the *Times*, under the nom de guerre of *Mount Olympus*, I will back against anything of the kind that was ever written for geniality and truth. In one word, the work ought to have a large sale. *Roderick Random* has made me cautious, and therefore I think it right to say that there is a passage at page 23 which might be too strong for men and women of strong imaginations. To me it is quite fair.

Joseph Cauvin

To T. T. Walton
MS Parrish Collection. B 39.

23 Nov. 1854. Strabane[9]
My dear Sir

I am very much obliged for your kind note— Yes—I should prefer to be employed in England, but we cant get all we want—& failing that I should prefer the South to the North of Ireland, preferring on the whole papistical to presbyterian tendencies— I shall hope to leave this district some day, but till then shall endeavor to make myself contented.

Bristol is unfortunately not the thoroughfare from the North of Ireland to any place—unless it might be Pile[1] or Portishead[2]—but still I shall hope to see you and Mrs. Walton again some day before we are too old to remember each other. When I do so I shall endeavor to come in summer, remembering the very pleasant febrifuge which you prescribed & supplied.

In the mean time, tho' the North of Ireland is not the choicest permanent residence, it has some charms for the tourist—& should you take my advise & visit there, I beg to offer myself as your host & guide.

My present residence is Belfast, but I hope to be enabled to move to Dublin which is a nice city enough.

always faithfully yours
Any Trollope

Do you find your troubles less, now that the Poster Genl no longer deluges you with all the blood of all the Howards & such like other incapables?

[9] A town near Londonderry in Northern Ireland.
[1] Pile March, Gloucestershire, near Bristol.
[2] A watering place on the estuary of the Severn near Bristol.

1855

To William Longman
B 40 (Sadleir's transcript).[3]

17 Feb. 1855   Dublin.
My dear Sir.

I should feel much obliged to you if you would tell me whether sale of *The Warden* has been so far satisfactory. My object in asking you is this. When the book was written, I intended to write a second part[4] for publication in the event of the first part taking and the tale was framed on this intention. I have written about one third of the second part and if I should hear from you that the sale of the first part has hitherto been fairly successful I will make an effort to finish the second before I go abroad on 1st May.

Very faithfully yours
Anthony Trollope

To William Longman
Commentary, p. 168. SB 41.

27 March 1855   Dublin

*   *   *

I send you the MS. of which I spoke to you when in London and will be obliged if you will see if it will suit you and let me know as soon as you conveniently can. There are some reasons incident to the MS. itself which will make it desirable that it should be published soon. It is called *The New Zealander*.[5]

*   *   *

[3] Trollope's letters to Longman were destroyed in the London fire of 29 December 1940. These and a number of others no longer extant are now available only as they appear in the Booth edition, since Michael Sadleir's transcriptions, which Booth copied or summarized, have also been lost (though the Bodleian manuscript of Sadleir's *Commentary* in some instances provides fuller texts than any in print).

[4] *Barchester Towers*, of which Trollope had written some 85 manuscript pages. Longman's report on the sales of *The Warden* was discouraging, and Trollope interrupted work on the sequel to write a book of social criticism, *The New Zealander*. He resumed *Barchester Towers* on 12 May 1856, at about which time he adopted his system of writing while traveling: "I . . . found after a few days' exercise that I could write as quickly in a railway-carriage as I could at my desk." (*Autobiography*, p. 103.) He also began to keep a working diary in which he entered each day the number of pages he had written, "so that if at any time I have slipped into idleness for a day or two, the record of that idleness has been there, staring me in the face" (*Autobiography*, p. 119).

[5] For the report of Longman's reader, see next letter.

Trollope, at about age forty

Joseph Cauvin to William Longman

Sadleir's transcript, Bodleian. *Commentary*, pp. 168–69.

2 April 1855

*　　*　　*

If you had not told me that this work was by the author of *The Warden* I could not have believed it. Such a contrast between two works by the same pen was hardly ever before witnessed. The object of the work is to show how England may be saved from the ruin that now threatens her!! And how the realisation of Macaulay's famous prophecy of the "New Zealander standing on the ruins of London Bridge" may be indefinitely postponed.[6]

With this view the author goes through all the leading influences and institutions of the State and pours out the vial of his wrath upon them. This he does in such a loose, illogical and rhapsodical way that I regret to say I would advise you not to publish the work on any terms.[7]

All the good points in the work have already been treated of by Mr. Carlyle, of whose *Latter-Day Pamphlets* this work, *both in style and matter*, is a most feeble imitation.

*　　*　　*

To ?

MS Parrish Collection.

[? early 1855]

*　　*　　*

post)— I shall be in London—and Tom will also be there—for two or three days in May—about the 18th.[8] If you & yours are to be there at that time pray let me know, & know also where— If it be but for five minutes I will beg your mothers pardon for the three maligned bishops[9]—and yours for not answering your former letter—which sin the length of this may perhaps be supposed to aggravate.

Yours very sincerely
Anthy Trollope

[6] Macaulay's "prophecy" appeared in his article "Ranke's *History of the Popes*," *Edinburgh Review*, 72 (October 1840), 228.

[7] *The New Zealander* first appeared in print in N. John Hall's 1972 edition (Oxford).

[8] On 3 May Trollope began a six-week leave during which time he traveled to the Continent with Rose and met up with T. A. Trollope and his mother at Venice. Thereafter he returned briefly to southern Ireland to refamiliarize himself with the district prior to giving testimony in London in late July before the Select Committee on Postal Arrangements (*Parl. Papers 1854–55*, XI [445], 127–228). His testimony drew a commendation, composed by Tilley, from the Postmaster General (MS General Post Office, London).

[9] In chap. viii of *The Warden*, Trollope had used Archdeacon Grantly's sons to satirize three contemporary bishops: the temporizing Blomfield of London, the pug-

My address is Dublin.

Pray know that when a man begins writing a book he never gives over. The evil with which he is beset is as inveterate as drinking—as exciting as gambling.

To Charles Bianconi[1]

MS Parrish Collection. SB 42.

15 Oct 1855   Gwedore[2]

My dear Sir.

I send you a notice to quit the Strabane & Sligo car,[3] and I add this private note to let you know that we do not intend to keep up the line at all.—We shall advertise for two separate cars, one from Sligo to Bally-shannon which will be in Mr Smiths territory—the other from Strabane to Donegal which will be under my jurisdiction.

I hope I shall not lose you altogether from under my clutches.

                                                                                    very faithfully yours
C Bianconi Esq   Anthony Trollope

1856

To the Editor of the *Athenaeum*[4]

MS Richard Purdy. SB 43.

5 Feby. 1856   Dublin.

Mr. Anthony Trollope presents his compliments to the Editor of the Athenaeum, & takes the liberty to forward an article on the 3rd. No. of Little Dorrit.[5]

---

nacious Phillpotts of Exeter, and the overdiplomatic and charming Wilberforce of Oxford.

[1] Charles Bianconi (1786–1875), inventor of the celebrated Irish car that bore his name. Trollope knew Bianconi well, and in his nine-page "History of the Post Office in Ireland" wrote: "It may, perhaps, be said that no living man has worked more than [Bianconi] has for the benefit of the sister kingdom." (*Parl. Papers 1857*, IV [2195], 62: Third Report of the Postmaster General; Appendix J.) See also Trollope to Henry Merivale Trollope, 2 July 1877.

[2] Trollope means Gweedore, a town in Co. Donegal.

[3] Previously, Bianconi had held a monopoly on the mail car service between Strabane and Sligo.

[4] William Hepworth Dixon (1821–79), biographer and historian, was editor of the *Athenaeum* from 1853 to 1869.

[5] Trollope's article, doubtless a challenge to Dickens's "Circumlocution Office," was rejected by Dixon and has not survived. (The third number of *Little Dorrit* included

Should the article not suit the paper, the Editor will perhaps have the kindness to return it in the cover now enclosed.

The Editor of the Athenaeum.

Mrs. Frances Trollope to Trollope

MS Taylor Collection.

8th. July 1856   Villino Trollope

Age eighty, (minus not quite three) thermometer eighty, (plus rather more than four) must be accepted as an excuse my very dear Anthony both by you and my highly valued correspondent[6] for not having acknowledged your very precious *packet* earlier. I am in truth grown most woefully idle, and, worse still, most woefully *lazy*, and this symptom is both new and disagreeable to *me*. But the degree of activity of which I have been wont to boast, and on which I have so often been complimented might have been accounted in my very best days as positive *idleness* when compared to what you manifest. Tom and I agree in thinking that you exceed in this respect any individual that we have ever known or heard of—and I am proud of being your mother—as well for this reason as for sundry others. I rejoice to think that you have considerably more than the third of a century to gallop through yet before reaching the age at which I first felt inclined to cry halta la![7] I believe I gave Tom a great many troublesome commissions, and as he has for the most part executed them very well I must not be too fierce—although he forgot one which I certainly wished should be carefully executed—namely the repaying you what you have expended for the fitting up the Naples chess table— But the worst part of this *forget* is that he has lost the mem. of the sum expended. Nor can I find it among my papers though I have sought for it most carefully— In fact having given the commission to him, I thought the business *done*. Now again then, dearest Anthony I must submit to being your debtor, and *you must* as certainly submit to trusting me, little as I seem to have deserved your confidence. *Moreover* I must borrow of you in addition the sum of one golden sovereign which I have told dear Harry in the inclosed is to assist his reserve fund of pocket money when he goes to his foreign school. I hope you will

---

chap. x, "Containing the Whole Science of Government.") Dixon was not likely to welcome Trollope's criticisms: he was an admirer of Dickens, a contributor to *Household Words*, and, as an authority on prisons, especially partial to *Little Dorrit*. See Bradford Booth, "Trollope and *Little Dorrit*," *Trollopian*, 2 (March 1948), 237–40.

[6] Mrs. Trollope enclosed a letter for Trollope's son Henry (MS Taylor Collection).

[7] Mrs. Trollope's last novel, *Fashionable Life: or Paris and London*, appeared in August 1856. Her literary industry had been prodigious: in all she had written 41 books, and her first, *Domestic Manners of the Americans* (1832), had been published when she was 53.

perform this commission for me better than Tom did his.—I will give you your choice of transmitting to *John Milton* the amount of my chess table debt *plus* the sovereign to Harry *or* of asking John Tilley to pay it to you— In which case he must apply to John Milton for payment. If I live long enough to *realize* the delight of having you all here next year (Edith[8] included) I shall feel that age is worth something. My journeyings last year were too fatiguing to leave me energy enough for enjoyment—but quietly sitting up here to receive you in state will be a very different thing. I long for you all to know Beatrice. I think she will amuse you. Give my very very kind love to Rose and believe me my own very dear Anthony most truly your loving mother

Frances Trollope

[Postscript by T. A. Trollope]
Dear Anthony, I add a line to my mother's letter to tell you that I have nothing to say. You live in the centre of the civilized world's system—I at the extremity of it;—there is therefore always plenty to be told by you to me—but little or nothing vice versa. . . . My mother mistakes about the chess table commission given to me. My instructions were limited to asking you what was the amount. I think you told me about £3. My mother is pretty well, though weak, and it is impossible not to see that the last year has made a greater change in her than ever any one year did before. She does not suffer in any way but from inability to exert herself.[9] Best love to Rose.

Yrs always
T. A. T.

Joseph Cauvin to William Longman

Commentary, pp. 169–70.

Dec. 8 1856.

It is very difficult for me to convey to you a distinct impression of my opinion of this work,[1] since my own impressions of it are themselves very indistinct. And no wonder; for the execution is so unequal, that while there are parts of it that I would be disposed to place on a level with the best morsels by contemporary novelists, there are others—and unfortunately these preponderate—the vulgarity and exaggeration of which, if they do not unfit them for publication, are at least likely to be repulsive to the reader.

Viewed as a whole the work is inferior to *The Warden*, to which it is

---

[8] Edith Tilley; see Trollope to Mrs. Frances Trollope, ? 5 February 1850.
[9] See Mrs. Frances Trollope to Trollope, undated, following Trollope's letter to her of 27 January 1859.
[1] *Barchester Towers.* For Trollope's response, see the following letter.

a sequel. You have the old characters again in action, with the addition of a weak bishop and his managing wife, Mr. Slope, the bishop's chaplain (a low-minded Low Churchman), an Oxford don, some rural grandees and their dependents, besides the dean and chapter and all the other odds and ends of a Cathedral town, in which High and Low Church are struggling for mastery.

Plot there is none, the main part of the story turning upon the [? filling][2] up of the office of Warden and the intrigues arising out of it. These give full scope for a display of the author's best powers and his subtle analysis of the motives that actuate his dramatis personae, while the style is easy and natural and correct (not so the orthography). The grand defect of the work, I think, as a work of art is the low-mindedness and vulgarity of the chief actors. There is hardly a "lady" or "gentleman" among them. Such a bishop and his wife as Dr. and Mrs. Proudie have certainly not appeared in our time, and prebendary doctor Stanhope's lovely daughter, who is separated from her husband—an Italian brute who has crippled her for life—is a most repulsive, exaggerated and unnatural character. A good deal of the progress of the tale depends upon this lady, whose beauteous countenance makes sad havoc of the virtuous feelings of the clergymen and others who come in contact with her. The character is a great blot on the work.

But in noticing these defects I am far from saying that it is uninteresting. On the contrary, there is a fatal facility in the execution that makes you fancy that the author is playing with his reader, showing how easy it is for him to write a novel in three volumes, very much in the same way as [Aytoun] proved how easy it was to [? rival] the "spasmodic poets."[3] It would be quite possible to compress the three volumes into one without much detriment to the whole. If you will read Vol. 2, chapters 1, 2 and 3, you will discover specimens of the author's merits, and if you wish to have a notion of what I consider his defects you will find a specimen in Vol. 1, page 177 seq.—"Mrs. Proudie's Reception"—and Vol. 2, page 173 seq.—"A Love Scene."

To William Longman

B 44 (Sadleir's transcript). *Commentary*, p. 171.

Dec. 20. 1856   Derry

I am sorry that I am such a distance from you. Were I in London we might more easily settle as to what you would wish to have withdrawn

---

[2] Printed text has [? giving].

[3] William Edmondstoune Aytoun's dramatic poem *Firmilian: or, the Student of Badajoz. A Spasmodic Tragedy* (1854) parodied the extravagant styles and themes of the poets Philip James Bailey, Sydney Thompson Dobell, and Alexander Smith so effectively that its satire was sometimes missed.

from *Barchester Towers* and as to what I would not object to withdraw.
I beg at any rate to assure you that nothing would be more painful to
me than to be considered an indecent writer.

I shall have no objection to altering any scene open to objection on
this score but I do object to reducing the book to two volumes—not because I am particularly wedded to three but from a conviction that no
book originally written in three can be judiciously so reduced. . . . But I
do not think that I can in utter ignorance have committed a volume of
indecencies. I do not now remember what can be the sin of the special
scene to which you allude. Of course the woman is intended to [? appear][4]
as indifferent to all moralities and decent behaviour—but such a character may I think be drawn without offence if her vice be made not
attractive.

But I do not now write in my own defence. I propose to get my friend
Mr. Tilley to call on you. You will find him a sufficiently rigid censor.
If you can explain to him to what you object or can show him the passages marked they will either be altered or else the MS. withdrawn. I
do not think I should be disposed to make other changes than those suggested on the score of delicacy. Mr. Tilley will however have carte
blanche to act for me in any way.

Very faithfully yours,
Anthony Trollope

To John Merivale[5]

MS Parrish Collection. B 45.

21 Decr. 1856—   Derry.
My dear John.

I am much ashamed of myself that I have not sooner given up my
time and attention to the affairs of the G— & G—[6] But in truth I was
unwilling to turn to such a matter till I could do so with a clear mind &
full attention—& that time has not even yet arrived. However I can wait
no longer.

And first as to the great question of the motto—with which I must confess I have bothered my brain not to sufficient purpose— Brother Moles-

---

[4] Manuscript damaged by fire; word supplied conjecturally by Sadleir.

[5] John Lewis Merivale (1815–86), the youngest son of John Herman Merivale, was
Trollope's "earliest friend in life" (*Autobiography*, p. 54), having known Trollope
since his school days at Sunbury and Harrow. A barrister and later a Commissioner
in Bankruptcy, Merivale is portrayed by his nephew Herman Charles Merivale as a
convivial man with many friends and as something of an eccentric (*Bar, Stage, and
Platform* [1902], p. 96).

[6] Goose and Glee. Trollope later introduced a Goose and Glee Club into *The Last
Chronicle of Barset* (chap. xlii), and a Goose and Gridiron Club into *Brown, Jones,
and Robinson* (chap. xviii).

worth[7] offers many which have in them a savor of wit—but they hardly hit the point with full swing— One may say that in any motto for a G— & G— Club, the goose and glee must each be brought forward as bearing on each other—and as little else as possible must be in it— It must refer also to the goose as comestible (not sibillant [*sic*]—and here let me say that the crest should be a couchant goose—impennatus et coctus— plucked & roasted—& on a field lanceal—viz a dish—this I look on as *very* material to the true spirit of the matter). It must refer, I say, to the goose as comestible—and to the glee as following on, & in some sort consequential on, the goose— I utterly deprecate any allusion to Cann—as host—it would be unworthy of the club— The motto hardly admits of canting heraldry—which requires some special name—if for instance you chose to specify solely your great present V— P— you might have a pair of moleskin breeches for your crest—& Moles worth—(or value) for your motto— That I take it would be canting heraldry. What would suit the club best would be Macaronic heraldry— A motto that would run in English and Latin— Such for instance as the following (*only* it does *not* run in English)

> Can't a tory bus answer—

It might be

> "Can't a tory answer."

The goose is for the singers—& so give an idea of politics beautifully misleading to the novices.

The motto should be so written—and to the un[in]itiated would so remain a mystery, but to those who had sat these full five years below the goose (respecting which proposed rule anon) it would, with many injunctions as to secrecy, be explained that the true motto was

> "Cantatoribus anser"

The goose is for the singers.

I cannot however get over the "bus"—
The following might suit—

> "Cantabit vacuus?"[8]
> (goose)
> "Hic hic Cantantibus answer"

"Can an empty man sing? Here—here is a reply to those who will sing"— The goose being of course tipified in the "answer"—

This however does not satisfy me— I must however remark that the caesura, and the intervening goose, will make the us in vaccuus, quite as long as you please—[9]

---

[7] Almost certainly Walter Hele Molesworth (1823–85), a grandson of Sir William Molesworth, 6th Bart., of Pencarrow, Cornwall.

[8] *Cantabit vacuus coram latrone viator*: "The traveler with an empty purse will sing in the presence of the robber." (Juvenal, *Satires*, x, 22.) Trollope's motto is a play on this line and on the Latin words for singers (*cantantes*) and goose (*anser*).

[9] In Latin prosody, *-us* is lengthened only if a consonant follows (B).

I think very little true reason has been adduced by brother Moles-worth for admitting recitations— There is an almost Indian love of the scalping knife in his wish for bores that the throes of the bored might be the source of gratification to others— The milk of human kindness runs too freely in my veins to allow me to participate [in] his views.

But my dear President let me above all things counsel you against what I cannot but regard as a most insidious proposition on the part of the V— P—. What forsooth! take to yourself powers to suspend the law in exceptional cases—!

Let me descend to a lower arena to shew you to what this would lead.

The Speaker of the H of Commons rules the debates of that section of Parliament. Members have a right to speak— What would be his position were he called on, mero motu—out of his own will & judge-ment, to suspend this law in exceptional cases— Fancy him forbidding a Spooner to speak, while he listened to Disreali [*sic*]— Would the house hold him?

No—if you once admit recitations—farewell then to all quiet harmony —farewell the genial song, the easy pipe, the hot tumbler— Men will not come from North & South, from distant London & remote mines of Cornwall to hear long stories tamely drawn out— Each "mutus frater" (let me call your attention to the name) would be desirous of being honored by a recitation— Let such *be* fratres muti— Maintain the spirit of your club— Let it be the G. & G— Be true to your colors whatever you do— Nor can I more cordially agree with that proposed elimination from the Statutes of the rule De non mingendo in poculis peuteribus—[1] Who would wish to see removed from the Cambridge code that law which forbids students to play at marbles in the high street? It is good to maintain these remembrances of olden days— Had not some one once sinned such a rule would not have existed— Can it be that the V. P. was the sinner, & thus wishes to expunge the record of his own disgrace?

I quite agree that no flunky should be admitted— No member should have a flunky within 5 miles at the time of sitting— I would suggest— "Ne famulus adesse liceat infra quinque millia passuum"—

I would also suggest that at table the goose should be in the middle— (or geese on both sides)— That new members should sit below the goose— That the "Cantantes" should rise to higher seats after eating three geese —the "Muti" after 5—

And now with much solemn reserve I would also propose one further statute— I fear the club is going from its holding, stranding from its moorings, becoming the plaything of radicals— I am terrified by that dreadful innovation of your V. P. respecting recitations— Even you can-not live forever— That you will preside for the next 40 years let no man doubt—but what if 41 years hence a recitating president should suggest

[1] "Concerning not urinating in pewter goblets," *peuteribus* being a joking coinage.

that singing should be forbidden! How would your ghost lie in its grave at Barton!² The rule I would propose is—Ne mutus frater sit praeses—
Yours ever
Anthony Trollope

The V. P.s letters have been very welcome—but why "Emma Nesseaus" note about the brandy?³

To John Merivale
MS Parrish Collection.

[1856–57]
My dear John
   The enclosed is most capital fooling—and what would your world be worth if your fooling were not good? Who is Bere, your sentimental tenor. Who the unfortunate Magg, whom history does but mention. Would I had been there—would I could even hope to [be] there on future occasions—tho' by the mass I will keep myself away till those two slender props so admirably touched upon have been duly attended to by the qualified local carpenter— I am fast becoming a 15 stone man & two slight—& may we not also suggest rotten props,—what could they be to intervene between the open street of Morden & me in the undress peculiar to Cloacina's⁴ worship? I think the president should require a report from some local member before the next October meeting.
   —But I must object to that new fangled proposition of yours No. 4— are you not a goose & glee club? & the Goose being done with, should you not in your after dinner moments be all Glee? Believe me those recitations will be condemnable bores— Why because you have some one man who professes to give you pieces out of Shakespear should you open a door to one of the greatest nuisances of the age.—Experto crede— I know a man what recites— You met for the purposes of harmony, & if a non-chaunting & very delinquent member may speak his mind, it is by sticking to harmony that you will continue to meet—renew that good old rule—"De recitationibus—"
   And pray be firm about the beer—not only for the clubs sake, but for

² Barton Place, near Exeter, the family home of the John Herman Merivales.
³ At the foot of the letter there are several notes in other hands, notably the following from Molesworth:
Dear Paul
   Will you kindly give a perusal to this letter. You see the Presidents wishes respecting the motto— You may send it to Hugo, but he must send it back to me, as Trollope is the talented author of the "Warden" &c& when he becomes Ch Dickens or Thackreay [sic] this letter will be valuable
Yours fraternally W H M—
⁴ From *cloaca*, the artificial canal in Rome that carried sewage into the Tiber.

Englands. Will it not soon come to this, that you shall not get a good glass of ale in all merry(?) England, unless you will drink Bass or Alsopp?—[5]

* * *

1857

To William Longman
B 46 (Sadleir's transcript). *Commentary*, pp. 171–72.

Jan. 10. 1857   Dublin.
My dear Sir.

I have just heard from Mr. Tilley that he has seen you respecting *Barchester Towers*, and I am led by what he says to fear that you do not think well enough of the MS. to publish it on terms to which I could agree. If this be so, it will be useless for me to give you further trouble by making arrangements as to any alterations.

It appears that you think £100 too high a sum to pay in advance for the book. It seems to me that if a three vol. novel be worth anything it must be worth that; and that it is vain for an author to publish such a work with any view to profit if he is to consider such a sum as this excessive. Indeed were it to be regarded as full payment of the work it would be wholly inadequate.

Of course there is no reason why you should pay so much or half so much if you do not judge the article to be worth so much of your money. But it is a reason why we should not deal. You allege very truly and with great kindness that a change of publisher will be prejudicial to my interests as an author. I feel that this is true. But I also feel that if a novel of mine in three vol. is not worth to a publisher £100 I have no interest to prejudice and that I cannot depreciate in value that which is already so valueless.

If therefore you are of opinion that you cannot afford to pay in advance so moderate a price as £100 I think it will be better for me to withdraw my MS. In such case I shall be very sorry to be deprived of the value of your name on my title-page. I think your form of agreement with your authors too vague as to the period of your interest in their

[5] Beer from the Burton-on-Trent breweries of Bass (founded 1777) and Allsopp (founded 1707). The trend throughout the century was toward large breweries such as these, and away from small local breweries.

work. Unless you buy a copyright surely a term could be put to your
[? interest].[6] Otherwise the author is left without the power of republishing in an after time when your interest in the work shall have ceased.

A. T.

To William Longman

Sadleir's transcript, Bodleian. SB 47.

18 Jan. 1857   Donnybrook

*   *   *

I will consent to your terms[7] . . . provided that you specify some time for
the publication—say not later than 1st of May next. As I am not in a position that will justify me in insisting on my views in other particulars I
will enter into your terms as to you having the continued right of publication. I think, however, that in justice some term should be put in such
an agreement between an author and a publisher. When a publisher
does not buy a copyright the right of republication should, I think, revert to an author at some fixed period. I am, however, aware that I must
at present give way on this.

*   *   *

To William Longman

B 48 (Sadleir's transcript). *Commentary*, pp. 172–73.

Feb. 1. 1857.   Donnybrook.

*   *   *

I now send your reader's list with my observations and I feel inclined
to think that you will be contented with what I have done. I have complied completely with by far the greater number of his suggestions and
have done so in part with all but three. I have de bon coeur changed all
the passages marked as being too warm. And I believe in every case
have struck out the whole of what was considered objectionable. I have
complied with all the objections to short passages whether I agreed or
no in the [? validity][8] of the objections, being willing to give way wherever I could do so. In the longer passages marked as ineffective I have
with two exceptions either omitted or re-written them. In these two cases
objection is made to two whole chapters that they are tedious. I will not
praise myself by saying that they are not so, but I must profess that I
cannot make them less so. I am sure you do not expect a perfect novel
from me and must . . .[9] Were I to withdraw these chapters I must write

[6] Word omitted in Sadleir's transcript and supplied conjecturally by Booth.
[7] Half profits against an advance of £100. The agreement was dated 5 February
1857, and *Barchester Towers* was published in May.
[8] Manuscript damaged by fire; word supplied conjecturally by Booth.
[9] Sadleir's omission.

5 Seaview Terrace, Donnybrook, Ireland

others and I am quite sure that such patch work would not be an improvement on the original composition.[1]

* * *

To William Longman
B 49 (Sadleir's transcript). *Commentary*, p. 174.

March 3. 1857.

* * *

At page 93 by all means put out "foul breathing" and page 97 alter "fat stomach" to "deep chest," if the printing will now allow it. But I should have thought the sheets had been taken off long ago. I do not like a second title nor the one you name. I do not wish the bishop male or female to be considered the chief character in the book. I was puzzled for a title but the one I took at last is at least inoffensive and easy of pronunciation.

I write in a great hurry in boots and breeches, just as I am going to hunt but I don't like to delay answering your very kind letter. I am very thankful to Longmans for the interest they feel in the book.

* * *

To G. C. Cornwall[2]
MS (photostat) Parrish Collection. B 50.

April 18. 1857   Trim[3]
Sir.

In returning these papers on the subject of a house to house delivery,[4] I beg to say that I consider the subject one of so much difficulty that I hesitate to express a decided opinion as to its feasibility without more information than I possess.

A house to house delivery is I believe effected in France; but I imagine that the appetite for letters is, in the rural districts of France, less craving than with us; and that more time can be consumed in their distribution

---

[1] On 3 February Cauvin wrote Longman that "the MS was satisfactorily altered"; it was accordingly sent to the printer (Sadleir's transcript, Bodleian).

[2] Gustavus C. Cornwall, Secretary of the Dublin Post Office, 1850–85.

[3] A town in Co. Meath about 25 miles northwest of Dublin.

[4] The extensive reorganization of the rural posts in England and Ireland, work in which Trollope was heavily relied upon, was designed to secure mail deliveries to every house while making the Post Office self-supporting. In rural areas the full penny of postage went for delivery (sorting, railway transportation, etc. were paid for by savings from mail deliveries in more populous areas). The question here is whether the penny postage of letters addressed to a country house but customarily picked up at a post office could be used to offset the cost of delivery of other letters in the same area. By the time Trollope wrote this report, he was of course a full surveyor and no longer doing the legwork of setting up deliveries in rural areas; but his opinion was clearly sought because of his experience in such work.

than could be possible in England as regards the bulk of letters. Presuming that a delivery were arranged which would effect a distribution of all rural letters at, say as an average hour, 10 am on every other morning, there can I think be little doubt that individual energy, would, as regards nine tenths of the correspondence, be brought to bear in such a way as to forestall the official delivery, and leave but a tithe to be counted as absolutely benefitted by the official arrangement.

This difficulty has already been felt in carrying out the existing rural posts. It has been vain to compute the revenue arising from a gentlemans letters, or those of a commercial establishment, unless, when they were to be delivered, either at the beginning of a walk or else by a man going out in a tolerably direct line. Such persons will not esteem it a boon to have their letters carried to them over a circuit.

In arranging a house to house delivery in England the letters found actually available towards affording the revenue required for the increased expense, will be pretty nearly confined to those for the poor and for farmers.

But I feel myself, with much hesitation, compelled to differ from the English Surveyors in the opinion expressed by them, through Mr. Godby[5] on the 12th. Ultimo, that it would be delusive to take as the basis for the proposition of a post correspondence which would not in effect be invariably, or perhaps not usually, delivered by that post. My impression is that such a correspondence may fairly be taken as giving the revenue required for the delivery, whether in fact it be officially delivered or not. For instance; if the Squire of a parish, A, get his letters by his own postboy, I think that the halfpenny each on his correspondence, which by the existing rate is applicable to the delivery of rural letters, may in each case be fairly applied to the delivery of those of his less opulent neighbors, farmers, B. C. and D. In such case we afford him a delivery if at any time he chose to avail himself of it. Had not this theory been already adopted to a considerable extent I imagine that the rural delivery now carried out would not have been so far extended as it has been.

Should a house to house delivery be decided on, and any sum per letter be fixed on as that applicable to the purpose,—say a sum not to exceed 1d. per letter—I think it should be allowed to the Surveyor so to count *all* letters distributed in the rural districts—i e all letters distributed beyond the free delivery of principal post towns, or of sub offices established in places which may fairly be termed towns. A limit should be fixed—all letters might be excluded when delivered to the number of, say 250 a week, by free delivery in the street—

Should it be found that under such a computation a house to house delivery could be effected under any post town, at a rate not (say 1d.) exceeding the amount allowed per letter for all the rural letters, I think

[5] William J. Godby, chairman of the Post Office surveyors.

that such proposed delivery should be regarded as satisfactory, altho' the letters actually carried out might cost 2d. per letter.

It would probably be desirable in testing this to make some occasional subdivision of districts less in area than that now served by some of our post towns. The reduction of offices has made this very arbitrary. It would, perhaps, be absurd to take the pence derived from the letters of a gentleman living near Exeter or Crediton,[6] and expend them on delivering the letters of farmers in the north of Cornwall. In such extreme cases however it would be easy to revert to the area of the reduced offices.

It would perhaps hardly be judicious to direct the establishment of a house to house delivery throughout the country irrespective of expense. When some sum has been decided on, it may perhaps be expedient that the Surveyors should from time to time report at what offices they consider that the house to house delivery will under such a restriction be feasible. They have it seems been requested, to report each as to two offices. They will know with tolerable accuracy where facilities for such a measure exist; and where there are great obstacles in the way. The localities offering the facilities may pretty [? certainly] be considered as having prior claims to those which offer only obstacles. From my remembrance of the places I should say that a house to house delivery might be easily effected under Stroud[7] where there is an extensive rural post district, but that it could hardly be done at any reasonable cost under Crediton where there is also an extensive rural post district.

In this manner the house to house delivery could I think gradually extend itself till it covered the kingdom. By the time that the thinner populated districts were reached experience would have been gained as to the best manner of overcoming the difficulties of such deliveries, and various relaxations of the rule would have probably crept in, both as to the occasional expenditure of a higher sum than that named, and an occasional delivery less frequent than thrice a week.

My impression is that the house to house delivery should in all cases be an addition to and engrafted on the present rural post system, and that it can only be carried out by one means—viz by allowances to Sub Postmasters for the work to be done. The present rural posts may of course be extended; walks may be lengthened or new walks established, but I doubt whether anything could be done in this way towards the house to house delivery now suggested. Anything so to be done would probably be done irrespective of that measure.

The allowance to be made to the Sub Postmasters should not, I think, be regulated so much by the distance from house to house over which the persons employed might have to walk, as by the probable time which would be expended daily in the deliveries. It would of course be desirable that a three day delivery should not all take place on the same three

---

[6] A market town seven miles northwest of Exeter.
[7] A town ten miles south of Gloucester.

days— A Sub Post[mast]er should be enabled to deliver—say to the right on Mondays, Wednesday, and Fridays, and to the left on the alternate days.

The arrangements made would be as it were a kind of contract; the Sub Poster would bind himself for the sum allowed to deliver free all letters left at his office for his district—those within a specified boundary on Mondays, Wednesdays and Fridays, and those within another specified boundary on the other days.

There would of course be much difficulty in the fast carrying out of such an arrangement. Not the least would be that of enforcing this contract or agreement— Letters for poor people would be left, not at their houses, but at houses more or less near to them. The poorer classes would however gradually learn their rights in this particular, and a fairly adequate performance of the duty might be ultimately looked for.

It will probably be remembered that the carrying out of such an arrangement thro' any district must be a work of time, and would add very much to a Surveyors labors— A house to house delivery for any district cannot, I imagine, be well suggested originally, or afterwards well carried out without any minute local knowledge.

I have presumed that in reporting on this subject I am not wished to allude in any special way to Ireland. A house to house delivery in Ireland would, I imagine, be more expensive than in England altho labor is less costly, the distances being so much greater over which single letters would have to be conveyed.

I am
Sir,
Your most obedient Servant
Anthony Trollope

To William Longman

SB 51 (Sadleir's transcript).

24 April 1857   Dublin

In the proof of the title page of *Barchester Towers*, Trollope struck out "Author of *The Warden*": "I think an author should proclaim nothing of himself." Longman protested, and on this date Trollope finally yields. He also acknowledges his £100 cheque and asks for copies of reviews to be sent him.

To T. T. Walton

MS Parrish Collection.

May 18. 1857   Dublin

My dear Sir.

May I trouble you to call on the gentleman to whom the enclosed note is addressed, having first closed it, and obtain his execution of the enclosed guarantee, if he be willing to execute it.

The form and the letter will I believe explain the matter to you—

I hope the various post offices changes from day to day have left you scathless, if not in a happier condition than when I last had the pleasure of seeing you. I hardly know who is the suzerain to whom at present you owe homage—for there have been such upheavings & earthquakes in the post office matters that all ancient land marks seem to have been removed—

Should you & Mrs. Walton, to whom I beg to be kindly remembered ever venture your necks in Ireland, I and Mrs. Trollope would be happy to make you as safe as the nature of so turbulent a country would allow.

very faithfully yours

T. T. Walton Esq   Anthony Trollope

To William Longman

Sadleir's transcript, Bodleian. *Commentary*, p. 177; SB 52.

15 July 1857   Derry

I have all but finished a novel in 3 volumes.[8] . . .

I shall be glad to know whether you would approve of publishing at Christmas one volume—say about two-thirds the size of *The Warden*—to be called *The Struggles of Brown, Jones and Robinson; by one of the Firm*. It will be intended as a hit at the present system of advertising, but will, of course, be in the guise of a tale. Publisher's advertisements are not reflected on.[9]

To William Longman

B 53 (Sadleir's transcript). *Commentary*, pp. 180–81.

21 Aug. 1857   Dublin

*   *   *

I have finished the three vol. novel. Though it is ready I do not want it to be published now or sooner than you approve. What I do want is to know on what terms you would be willing to publish it. While you were from town I got a letter from your firm not saying much about the sale of *Barchester Towers*, while your letter just received though it gives no bad news gives none that are good. From this I suppose I may imagine that you do not consider the sale satisfactory. If this be so to such a degree as to make your firm unwilling to deal with me on such terms as are usual for works of fiction of fair success, perhaps I may be giving

---

[8] *The Three Clerks*.

[9] Longman declined to consider *Brown, Jones, and Robinson*. In the following year, Edward Chapman also decided against it (see Chapman to Trollope, 16 June 1858). Eventually, George Smith accepted it for serialization in the *Cornhill Magazine*, where it appeared in 1861–62 (see Trollope to Smith, 4 July 1860 and 6 July 1860).

you useless trouble by sending you my MS. I am strongly advised not to publish without getting a price that may be regarded as in some way remunerative. If therefore you think your firm will decline to purchase from me at some such price perhaps you will say so.

My project of a tale in one vol. still holds good but it is not written.

*   *   *

To William Longman

B 54 (Sadleir's transcript). *Commentary*, p. 181.

29 Aug. 1857   Dublin.

*   *   *

I certainly did mean you to understand by my last letter that I should want a better price for another novel. Indeed I may say at once that I would not under any circumstances take less than double what I received before, viz: two hundred pounds in advance and as you seem to think that your firm will not give more than £100 I fear it will hardly be worth while for you to have the MS. read.

I am sure you do not regard £100 as adequate payment for a 3 vol. novel. Of course an unsuccessful novel may be worth much less—worth indeed less than nothing. And it may very likely be that I cannot write a successful novel, but if I cannot obtain moderate success I will give over, and leave the business alone. I certainly will not willingly go on working at such a rate of pay.[1]

*   *   *

To Richard Bentley

B 55.

10 Octr. 1857   Florence
My dear Sir:—

I hope to be in London on this day week, the 17th Saturday—and to call on you with reference to the MS I left in your hands at about 12. The boats however along the coast have become irregular thro' bad weather so that it is possible I may not be able to reach London till Sunday morning. It would I presume be impossible for me to see you on that day—but I shall feel obliged if you will let me have a line addressed to the London Bridge Hotel, written on Saturday, should I not see you on that day:—so that I may get it there on the Sunday morning, & that

---

[1] Trollope recounted how Longman tried to dissuade him from taking *The Three Clerks* to another publisher: " 'It is for you,' said he, 'to think whether our names on your title-page are not worth more to you than the increased payment.' . . . I did think much of Messrs. Longman's name, but I liked it best at the bottom of a cheque." (*Autobiography*, p. 109.)

you will send the MS to that address should you determine to decline it,
so that I may also find that at the hotel on the Sunday morning—[2]

Very faithfully yours

Anthony Trollope

To William Longman

Sadleir's transcript, Bodleian. *Commentary*, p. 181; B 56.

18 Oct. 1857.   Dublin.

*   *   *

I promised to let you know what I did about the MS. of my new novel.
I disposed of it yesterday to Mr. Bentley who acceded to my own terms.
The sum I asked was indeed higher than that I suggested to you. I know,
however, that this will not break any bones between you and me.

*   *   *

To Richard Bentley

MS British Library.

31. Oct. 1857   Dublin.

My dear Sir.

When I was in New Burlington Street on 19 ultimo I told your son
that I would wait till 16 December, the day named in your agreement,
& then take £250 by your cheque. It will however suit me better to have
your note of hand payable on that day, as suggested in your agreement—
Perhaps you will do me the favor to send me your note drawn accordingly, made payable at your bankers.

very faithfully yours

R Bentley Esq   Anthony Trollope

To Richard Bentley

MS Taylor Collection. Taylor, "Bentley," p. 87; SB 57.

GENERAL POST OFFICE

Nov 3. 1857   Dublin.

My dear Sir

I have received your note of hand & am obliged—amount £250.

I did *not* dispose of the copy right of B. Towers to Messrs Longman—
I do & will return the sheets to Messrs Woodfall & Kinder[3] without delay of a post— I think there must be some mistake for they have sent me

___

[2] Bentley wrote Trollope from Brighton on 13 October, acceding to "the terms proposed by you to me viz £250 for the copyright" (MS Bodleian). Trollope's negotiations with Longman and Bentley over *The Three Clerks* are discussed in his *Autobiography*, pp. 109–11, and in Sadleir's *Commentary*, pp. 180–82.

[3] Woodfall and Kinder (of Angel Court, Skinner Street, London) were printing *The
Three Clerks*.

back today a lot of sheets, which I had corrected—or rather they sent me duplicate sheets, these duplicates *not* containing the corrections made by me.

I cannot imagine why this has been done.

Yours very truly

R. Bentley Esq   Any Trollope

To Richard Bentley

MS Parrish Collection. SB 58.

21. Nov. 57   GENERAL POST OFFICE

My dear Sir.

I send back today the last sheets of the Three Clerks. You have got it through very quickly. I have not seen the proofs of the title page, & the page of headings, but I dare say they will be sent. I hope you will make money of it.

You will, I presume, give me six copies. Will you send them for me addressed as on the accompanying slip of paper. That is five copies—& will you keep one till my brother T. A. Trollope, shall either call or send for it.⁴

May I also ask you as a favor to send me any notices you may see of the work. I see here no London papers but what I take—& I take only the Times and Atheneeum [*sic*]. If you will procure & send me any you see or hear of, I will settle with you for the price of them when I see you—

very faithfully yours

Anthony Trollope

To James Pycroft⁵

Escott, pp. 114–15. B 925.

[?1857]

*   *   *

Before you put her⁶ down as a freak of fancy, let me ask you one question. Review the spiritual lords and their better halves such as you have known, and tell me whether it is the bishop or the bishop's wife who always takes the lead in magnifying the episcopal office? If you and I live long enough, we shall see an indefinite extension of the movement

---

⁴ T. A. Trollope lent his copy of *The Three Clerks* to the Brownings, who agreed that it was the best of Trollope's three recent novels: Elizabeth was "wrung to tears by the third volume" and reported that her husband, "who can seldom get a novel to hold him, has been held by all three, and by this the strongest" (*What I Remember*, p. 402).

⁵ James Pycroft (1813–95), clergyman and author; known for his writings on cricket and later for his *Oxford Memories* (1886).

⁶ Trollope is discussing Mrs. Proudie. According to Escott, this is in reference to *Barchester Towers* rather than to the later Barsetshire novels.

that has already created new sees in Manchester and Ripon. In the larger and older sees there will be a cry that the diocesan work is too heavy for one man; then will come the demand for the revival of suffragan bishops. You now speak about the higher and lower order of the clergy; you will then have a superior and inferior class of prelates. If at some great country-house gathering there happen to be a full-grown wearer of the mitre and his episcopal assistant, you may expect to hear the hostess debating whether the suffragan should have his seat at the dinner-table when the guests sit down, or whether his chief might not prefer that he should come in afterwards with the children and the governess to dessert. He, good easy man, may take it all meekly enough, but not so his lady. When the suffragans are multiplied, human nature will undergo some great revolution if the suffraganesses do not contain a good many who are as fussy, as officious, as domineering, and ill-bred as my chatelaine of the Barchester palace.

*   *   *

1858

Richard Bentley to Trollope
MS Bodleian.

Jany 25. 1858   New Burlington [Street]
Dear Sir

   To my regret I find I miscalculated the extent of sale of *Three Clerks.* The sale of that work will not enable me to give more than £300 for the new story.[7] To give more would leave me wholly without profit. I send this off at once that you should be informed of this without delay.[8]
                                                            Yours faithfully
Anthony Trollope Esq   Richard Bentley

---

   [7] *Doctor Thorne.*
   [8] On 27 January Bentley again wrote Trollope, offering "for the copyright of your new work of fiction Dr Korner [*sic*] in 3 vols the sum of Four Hundred & Fifty Pounds in manner following:—£300 on going to press with an edition of 1250 copies[,] £50 more on sale of this edition, and £100 more on going to press with another edition" (MS Bodleian). See Trollope to Bentley, 28 April 1858.

To Rose Trollope

MS Taylor Collection. B 59.

31 Jany 1858   Paris[9] Sunday night
Dearest Love.

Here I am, & here also is Tom—& Grenlata[?]—& that other Italian fellow who used to be hanging about when they were selling their pots & pans. They have got a whole heap of their things here—& a great many more are coming—but the sale will not be for three weeks. Tom is sanguine as to the result— I fervently wish however that he were out of italy.

My mother it seems is very well—& their fear now is that she should eat too much. It appears that the modicum of wine has now become quite an affair of routine.

It seems that Tom will get nearly £3000 by Garrows death,[10] and as this £3000 is all over & above what he expected, it ought to relieve him from all his embarrassments—he has also had a very good offer for his house—so good that were I he I should certainly take it.

I have not got to work yet tho' I had meant to do so today— It has been a nasty wet muddy day & I have been slopping about with Tom & doing nothing—except smoking a cigar in order to prepare myself for the Turkish nargileh of which I must of course take a few whiffs—just to prove that I am in a Mohammedan country—

I was with Judith[1] today for an hour or so— She is just the same as ever—vegetating up 5 pair of stairs—& talking of politics as if she understood all about them—

I had an awful passage from Dover to Calais, & was very sick— I thought I was going to be turned to peices [*sic*], & indeed even now I am hardly all right—in spite of having eaten a very good dinner at the hotel des Princes—when we dined with Judith— Tomorrow we talk of going to Chartres to look at the painted glass— The next morning I believe I start for Marseilles. I will if possible write again before I go.

God bless you my own dearest love.

Ever your own
A. T.

My best love to Fred—to Mary & Ella.

---

[9] Trollope was en route to the Mediterranean on a special mission for the Post Office that included negotiating a treaty for the conveyance of mail from Alexandria to Suez by rail (see Trollope to R. Hill, 16 February 1858 and 23 February 1858, and Trollope to F. Hill, 19 June 1858 and 1 July 1858), investigating the question of substituting bags for boxes for mails sent through Egypt to India and Australia (see Trollope to F. Hill, 14 February 1858), and inspecting the postal services at Malta (see Trollope to R. Hill, 16 April 1858).

[10] Joseph Garrow, father of Theodosia Trollope, had died in 1857.

[1] Almost certainly Judith de Montalk; see Trollope to Bentley, 16 September 1837.

To Rose Trollope

MS Taylor Collection. B 60.

2. Feb. 1858   Paris

Dearest love.

Thanks for your nice letter which I got this morning. I have hardly a minute now. The two latin words were "toga virilis"²—

I do not know of what chapters you want the headings— In vol 2. Chap 7—Mr Moffat falls into trouble
        8—Sir Roger is unseated
        9—Retrospective—
        10—Louis Scatcherd.
        11—Sir Roger dies.

I now send you Chap 12—"War"— This I think will be good for 18 of your pages. You will of course let me know— The slips are long. I think I have made it intelligible how it goes— You must of course be careful about the reading, and also alter any words which seem to be too often repeated.

If Harry has subscribed 5/ to the library out of his own pocket of course you will repay him & charge me. All the other points in your letter will I think have been already explained— I will write a line if I can from Marseilles, I shall however be but a few hours there. Yesterday we went to Chartres, where you & I will go some day to see the painted glass— It is the finest in the world—& is magnificent!

I have not been idle to get so much done in Paris, with Tom by my side, & all the comparative provocations to sightseeing, even of Paris, around me. I have not been inside the Louvre— It is now one, and I have been writing all day— I must do 5 of my pages daily, or I cannot accomplish my task—

Do not be dismal if you can help it— I feel a little that way inclined, but hard work will I know keep it off.

God bless you dearest love— My best love to the boys—& love to Mary— I am glad Ella succeeds.

Ever dearest love
Your own
A. T.

² In the first edition of *Doctor Thorne*, the words were printed as *toga virile*. Trollope's handwriting was probably at fault, though Frederic Harrison cited the error as an example of Trollope's hasty mode of composition (*Early Victorian Literature* [1895], p. 224). This error and many others were corrected in the second edition: see p. 2 of "Addenda and Corrigenda" (1934), *Bibliography*.

To Frederic Hill[3]
MS General Post Office, London.

14th. February. 1858   Alexandria
Sir.

In answer to your letter of the 29th. Ultimo—No. 1222 containing copy of a letter from Capt Johnson[4] as to the expediency of substituting bags for closed boxes in forwarding the overland Indian Mails, and also to the 9th. paragraph of your further letter of that date referring to the same subject, I beg to express my opinion that the proposed change should not be made immediately as regards any part of the Mails.

I have not yet been over the line from hence to Suez, but I purpose doing so between this and the 17th. Instant, in company with the Consul here and Nubar Bey,[5] the head of the Transit administration. The road is open and conveying passengers, mails, &c, to [a] point distant about 25 miles from Suez. It will be open for passengers, Mails &c in about 12 days, to a point said to be 20 miles from Suez. With reference to the remaining portion different statements have been made to me, but I think that it may be open at any rate before the 30th. June.

I should hesitate very much to recommend that the bags be used in lieu of boxes as long as they may be subject to be carried on camels. In the first place they would be liable to very great friction; and in the second place their contents would not be safe from pillage. Eighty or ninety camels are I am informed often used at the same time. And where so many Arabs are employed—one namely to each camel—it is impossible to answer for the conduct of them all. As the boxes are on hand, it will I submit be inexpedient to send the Mails in bags which can be ripped by any knife— This objection will of course fall to the ground, when they can be sent the whole way by Railway.

The latter reason for the present continuance of the boxes has been suggested to me by Mr Green,[6] the consul here.

I am however of opinion that bags may be used in lieu of boxes for a great portion if not the whole of the Indian and Australian Mails— I am at present inclined to think that they may be used for the whole—as

---

[3] Frederic Hill (1803–96), brother of Rowland Hill; Assistant Secretary of the Post Office, 1851–75.

[4] Captain H. Johnson, Postmaster at Alexandria.

[5] Nubar Bey (1825–99), later Nubar Pasha, Armenian-born Egyptian diplomat; subsequently premier of Egypt (on three occasions). For Trollope's account of his successful negotiations with Nubar Bey, see *Autobiography*, pp. 122–24. Nubar Bey later said that Trollope's method as a negotiator "had about it less of the diplomatist than of the author who might have meditated scolding his publisher if he did not come round to his terms, and of carrying his literary wares elsewhere" (Escott, pp. 123–24).

[6] John Green (?1808–77), later Sir John, Acting British Consul-General and postal agent at Alexandria.

soon as the Railway is completed. I shall however have a further opportunity of reporting on the matter.[T]

It is not, I fear, possible that the Mails should be sent in vans, over
the Suez end of the line, as is done with the passengers. The Transit
Administration is not, I am told, in possession of vans for the purpose,
and could not be expected to supply them for so short a period.

I am

Sir

Your most obedient Servant

F. Hill Esqre.   Anthony Trollope

To Rowland Hill

MS General Post Office, London.

Feb. 16. 1858   Cairo.
My dear Sir.

I arrived at Alexandria on Wednesday evening the 10th.—and have
been engaged since chiefly with Mr. Green, the Consul, on the subject of
the new treaty of which he had the draft prepared, and which he has
altered in accordance with any suggestion I have thought myself justified in making.

I must first explain that this proposed treaty is now worded on the
presumption that the Southampton Mail shall arrive at Alexandria a
day before that viâ Marseilles, and leave a day after that viâ Marseilles.
This I understood from your brother to be the projected plan, and the
one which he wishes to see carried out. It is also the plan which has been
suggested here. Mr. Green before reading to me the draft of the treaty
shewed me a letter from Nubar Bey, the present head of the Transit
Administration, in which he demanded 50 hours for the transit each
way—providing the Mails from Southampton & Marseilles arrived together—50 hours as I understood from sea to sea, tho this was not plainly
put.—And 18 hours for the transit from Station to Station—i e Alexandria to Suez & back—providing the Southampton boat was in 36 hours
before that from Marseilles. The sum named for the service by Nubar
Bey was £12000. Mr. Green in his draft of the treaty had left all these
points blank—and I found no allusion to the time to be taken from *sea
to sea*, should the point as to the earlier arrival of the Southampton boat
be conceded.

These points have now been filled up as follows. The time named is
16 hours from station to station, and 24 hours from sea to sea, providing
the Southampton packet be in *20* hours before that from Marseilles, and
start 20 hours after it. (I said 20 instead of 24 so that an occasional slight

[T] In further reports Trollope repeatedly argued that after completion of the railway the change from boxes to bags would save time, labor, and expense. Bags gradually became universal.

irregularity in the Southampton packet should not be made an excuse for corresponding irregularity in carrying thro the Marseilles Mails. The intention however would be that the despatch from Suez should be one full day after the arrival at Alexandria from Marseilles & two after that from Southampton). To this timetable Mr. Green now tells me that Nubar Bey has assented. I have had some conversation with Nubar Bey— with Mr. Greens cognizance—and tho he speaks of the demand for time as being pressing, he says he can do it, if he can only be sure that the treaty in the proposed form will be adhered to in England. His doubt is as to the earlier arrival of the Marseilles packets. He seems to think it unreasonable that he should be asked to consent to these terms till he absolutely knows that the packets will be so worked. I have told him that I believe the packets will be so worked, and that his assent to the proposed hours will make it more probable.

I do not think that the time allowed could be further curtailed. It is impossible that we should make the Mails wholly independent of either passengers or baggage. But by the proposed plan the Mails viâ France will pass thro Egypt at a rate nearly as quick as they could be expected to do, even were they independent of passengers.

The time table assumes that the railway will be open to Suez before 30 June. I believe this will be the case. But it has seemed to me better not to put any special clause into the treaty providing for extra time if the line be not fully completed, as by doing so justification would be afforded for loss of time, even if only a mile or so were uncompleted.

You will of course observe that the 24 hours named is for the transit from *sea to sea*—whereas the time now allowed, 75 hours one way & 65 the other, is from the periods at which the mails are handed over to the Transit Administration.

I have not made any remarks as to the sum demanded, other than this; that it should certainly be a lump sum, not in any way dependent on the encreased weight or encreased frequency of the Mails. Mr. Green tells me that he has submitted the question of the amount to the Foreign Office, from which doubtless the Postr. Genl will receive a copy of the proposed treaty.

You will perceive that in the event of the proposed arrangement as to the early arrival of the Southampton boat not being carried out, the time for the transit will stand at 44 hours—and a day will be lost by each mail each way.

I shall be glad of instructions on the following point. The treaty is now between the Viceroy of Egypt & the Hon. E. I. Company. It is to be between the Viceroy & the Foreign Office. The messengers who accompany the Mails are now paid by the E. I. Company. By what office will they be paid when the new treaty shall come into operation? Will the Foreign Office pay them thro the Consul, or the Hnb. E. I. Company thro it's [sic] Agent—or the Post Office thro' it's agent. The latter seems to me the more rational. In such case I should, I presume, report as to the number of men necessary, & the amount of cost.

I am obliged to write some days before the post goes out as I am up here with the view of going on to Suez with Mr. Green & Nubar Bey.

> I am My dear Sir
> Very faithfully yours
> Anthony Trollope.

To Rowland Hill
MS General Post Office, London.

23. Feby. 1858   Suez.

Sir.

With reference to the 8th. paragraph of your letter of the 29th. Ultimo I beg to say that Mr. Green the acting Consul General in Egypt has drawn out a draft treaty for the conveyance of the Mail thro' Egypt on and from 1st. July next, the terms of which have now received the approbation of the Viceroy.

This treaty in its third clause stipulates that the outward Mails arriving viâ Marseilles shall be conveyed thro' Egypt in 18 hours, providing that they arrive 20 full hours before that from Southampton, and that the homeward mails viâ Marseilles shall be also conveyed thro' Egypt in 18 hours providing that the packet for Marseilles shall be fixed to start 20 full hours before that from Southampton. The hours to be computed from the time the Mail is handed over to the officers of the Transit Administration in Egypt, and up to the delivery of the said Mails to the Post office agents at Suez or Alexandria.

By this you will see that it is intended that 18 hours shall be the time for the Marseilles Mails, and 38 hours for that viâ Southampton, and that if the Marseilles Mail shall not be in the full 20 hours before the other, so much additional time will be allowed for its transit; if, for instance it should be in only 10 hours before that arriving from Southampton, then 28 hours would be allowed for its transit.

A copy of the contract or treaty will of course be sent to you; and I beg to say that I suggested the following clause to be inserted as clause 4—

"The time to be employed in carrying the Mails from the packets at Alexandria and Suez to the Railway Stations, and from the Railway Stations at Alexandria and Suez to the packets shall not exceed 8 hours per trip: so that the whole time to be taken in the transit from the packet at Alexandria to the packet at Suez, and from the packet at Suez to the packet at Alexandria shall not exceed 24 hours."[8]

---

[8] Hill replied on 10 March that the need for this clause would be fully considered, and he asked Trollope for a further report on the time required at the British Packet offices at Alexandria and Suez for the duties connected with forward correspondence.

It was then proposed to do the thro' service in 16 hours instead of 18.

Mr Green fully concurred in the expediency of this clause, and has pressed its adoption. It has however been strongly objected to by Nubar Bey, the Viceroys officer; and Mr Green has felt himself obliged to omit it from the draft treaty as now made out. It appears however to me that it is very material, and I think that it, or something tantamount to it, should be inserted. Hitherto whatever ground there may have been for complaint has not been with reference to the absolute working of the railway, but has been attributable to delay at either end; and I think I may say that such delay has furthered the ends of the Peninsular and Oriental Company. While we wish celerity in the transit, they are urging on Nubar Bey, what he calls "tranquillity" in the transit: that is, they are anxious to ensure the certain despatch of any merchandise they may have to carry, at the same pace and hours as the Mails.

My own impression is that they will always achieve this, even at the hours now proposed, and it is of course desirable that they should do so. But their Agent at Alexandria is not I think anxious for a very quick transit, and hence I believe is the strong opposition which Nubar Bey is making to the hours as suggested by Mr Green & myself. The Company pay £8 a ton for goods sent with the Mails, and £4 a ton for goods sent at a slower pace, and they are therefore able to urge their views strongly on the Administration.

Such being the case I think that a clause is very desirable which shall fix a time from sea to sea. The whole duty of conveyance, from the moment the mails are put over the side of the vessel in the one sea till they are put on board the packet in the other sea, is performed by the Egyptian Transit administration, and is arranged for in the treaty. I think therefore the whole time should be specified, even tho' an hour or two more be named that [*sic*] may be absolutely necessary.

Perhaps the PosterGeneral may think fit when the draft treaty shall be submitted to him, to propose to the Foreign office that Mr Green should be instructed to urge the matter further. I should not urge the point if I found that Mr Green differed from me; as it is we fully agree on the matter.

Nubar Bey's objection is that there is no such clause in the now existing treaty, and that he cannot make himself responsible for such work. These objections do not seem to me to be worth much. The omission in the treaty with Honble. E. I. Company should I think be remedied; and as the work in question is done, by the Egyptian Transit Administration, that administration should, I imagine, be responsible.

You will see that a clause has been inserted in which it is stated that

(Trollope answered this request with a lengthy report dated 25 March.) In the end, Trollope's precise language was not inserted in the treaty, but its intention was achieved: the treaty specified 24 hours as the maximum time allowed for transporting the mail from boat to boat.

if the number of monthly mails be encreased, such encrease shall be made matter of further agreement. I have pointed out to Mr Green that this clause might become troublesome; but it has been insisted on, and I cannot say that it is unreasonable. In wording this I have taken care that the full number of Indian Mails from Southampton and Marseilles, as well as an equal number from Calcutta & Bombay if desired, shall be included; as well as the Australian, even should the Australian monthly arrival & despatch be at any future time divided, as are those to & from India.

£1200 is the sum named for the service. I do not know that it is necessary that I should make any observations on this point.

I am
Sir
Your most obedient Servant
Anthony Trollope

R. Hill Esq

To Edmund Yates[9]

MS University of Kentucky. Edmund Yates, *Edmund Yates: His Recollections and Experiences* (1884), I, 113–14; *Commentary*, p. 198; B 61.

11 March [1858]   Alexandria
My dear Yates.

It is a matter of great regret to me that I should miss you— But were I to stay now I should lose my only opportunity of going to Jerusalem. I had hoped to have got there & back before you came out, & it has been impossible for me to start till today. I shall probably still see you on the 22nd.

At Cairo. See (above all) the newly opened catacombs at Sakkara—by taking a horse & mounted guide you may see that & the Pyramids at Ghizeh in one day.

Hear the howling dervishes at Cairo—at 1—on Friday. They howl but once a week. Go to the citadel at Cairo—& mosque of Sultan Hassan. See also the tombs of the Caliphs—

Heliopolis is a humbug—so also is the petrified forest—

At Alexandria see the new Greek church they have just excavated.

Go to the Oriental hotel at Alexandria.

And Shepherds at Cairo.[1]

Yours ever
Any Trollope

[9] Edmund Hodgson Yates (1831–94), minor novelist, miscellaneous writer, and editor. Trollope and Yates were colleagues at the Post Office. They later fell out (see Trollope to Smith, 21 July 1860, n. 2), and Yates's comments on Trollope in his *Recollections* and elsewhere should be read with this in mind.

[1] Trollope incorporated much material from his travels to Egypt and the Holy Land into *The Bertrams*; see, for example, his lengthy description of the dervishes at Cairo in chap. xxxviii.

To Rowland Hill

MS General Post Office, London.

16 April 1858   Malta—
Sir.

I beg to say that in obedience to instructions contained in your letter of 29 January last I have inspected the office here.

On the whole the duties are I think efficiently performed. There have been some points as to which I have called Mr. Coxons[2] attention; but I have found no neglect or omission of a nature to make it necessary that I should bring it under the notice of the Postr. General.

The first idea as to the Malta office that strikes an officer used to the working of English offices is that the force is excessive for the services to be performed. It is probably the case that a Maltese, or even an Englishman in a climate so hot as that of this island, will not work so quickly or perhaps so effectively as our clerks at home; but even with this allowance I can not think that six clerks with a stamper and Messenger can be required for the duties.

It appears that at the time of the Russian war two clerks were added to the establishment—I believe very much at the instance of the Governor—with the view mainly of preventing delay in the delivery of letters from the office windows. The war had added much to the correspondence of the island, and the delay felt was at that time peculiarly inconvenient. But that cause has now ceased; and moreover the number of Mails from England to Malta has encreased; which fact, tho' it may add to the total work of the office, must of course diminish the number of letters arriving by each mail; and therefore diminish also the delay in question.

A money order business has been added, but this is not heavy in its operations; and I am inclined to think that one clerk and the stamper could be dispensed with. As regards the clerk I would propose that the next vacancy should not be filled up; as it would probably be considered a hardship to deprive the man of his situation. The salaries of the clerks are not high; nor is there any encrease to be looked for by any of them, except what may be obtained by vacancies. I do not think that the total sum allowed should be decreased; but that the salary of the Junior—viz £60 per ann:—should in the event of a vacancy be distributed in the way of encrease to the other five—viz £20 to the Senior, and £10 each to the other four— Their total incomes would then be £150 —£125—£90—£70 and £70. The amount paid is made up of £395 allowed by the Poster General, and £110 by the Island office. Some modification in the arrangement of these payments will hereafter be necessary; but this must depend on the duration in office of the second clerk, who has a salary of £60, and is entitled to [a] pension, from the Island Govern-

---

[2] John Coxon, Postmaster at Malta.

ment. I enclose a statement of the Postmaster's estimated income and of that of the clerks, together with the income I have suggested for the latter.

The above proposition is made under the idea that the two men who were temporarily employed during the war are now to be considered as being on the establishment. Mr. Coxon states that he received a sanction for their permanent employment. If the two Juniors are still considered as temporary assistants, the removal of one might take place at once.

As regards the Stamper, I think that his services are not required in that capacity, and that the duty may be adequately done between the Messenger and the Letter Carriers. I intend to forward a report as to the expediency of extending the free delivery of Valetta; but before doing so I must have returns which are not yet complete. Should I be enabled to make such a proposition, I shall suggest that the present stamper be employed as a Letter Carrier, as was heretofore the case. Mr. Coxon concurs with me as to the expediency of these propositions.

While on the subject of the clerks in this office I may mention that I found their hours of attendance to be unnecessarily long—more especially as in consequence of the uncertainty of the mail arrivals a portion of it must be given, not only at unseasonable hours, but at hours not regularly fixed. The average has been about eight hours a day, Sundays included. I found that half of the force of the office might, without detriment to the service, be off duty every day from 1 PM—in the event of no mail arriving or being despatched— This will give about three hours to each man twice a week. As Mr. Coxon agrees with me as to the expediency of the measure it has been carried out.

The greater portion of the revenue now received at Malta is collected by the sale of stamps; the amount of stamps on hand must therefore necessarily be always considerable. In making up his weekly account the Postmaster enters the amount on hand. I think it would be expedient for various reasons, but specially with reference to the security to be given by the present and future Postmasters, that the amount so entered should be checked by the senior clerk. I believe such a check would be taken in all banking operations. I would suggest that a list of the stamps on hand, such as that made by Surveyors in England should be sent monthly, signed by the Senior clerk as counted by him, and countersigned by the Postmaster.

This suggestion is not made at all with reference to the present management of the Malta office. I have no ground whatever for imagining that the entries have not been correct. Indeed I have very good ground to believe that they have been so. I checked the balances of revenue and money order cash, and found the amount due in the Postmasters hands. I have observed however that in making the monthly remittances the Postmr. has customarily kept back by far too large a balance. This has amounted to about £80. There can be no reason why it should exceed £25 or £30. I have suggested this to Mr Coxon, and he has said that he will comply with my suggestion.

I think that some of the forms of accounts now used at Malta might be made more simple, so as to save some time, and cost in paper and printing. I imagine also that many of the copies of bills &c now kept in the Malta office are useless, and create unnecessary labor. But I purpose speaking on this matter to the Accountant General in London, before I venture on any suggestion.[3]

I am
Sir
Your most obedient Servant
Anthony Trollope

To Richard Bentley

MS Taylor Collection. Taylor, "Bentley," p. 87; SB 62.

28 April 1858   Cadiz

My dear Sir

The day after I last saw you, I sold the Mss of Dr. Thorne to Mr. Chapman.[4] It will be published I believe in May.

I shall be in London soon, & I will then call on you.

faithfully yours

R. Bentley Esq   Anthony Trollope
New Burlington Street
London

Edward Chapman to Trollope

MS Bodleian. Excerpt, *Commentary*, p. 178.

June 16. 1858   193, PICCADILLY. LONDON.

Dear Sir,

I have been serving my country as a Grand Juryman for the last two days, so could not reply to you sooner.

I think on the whole that I had better hold to my resolve to decline B. J. & R.—[5] I should not like to do it without your name & at the same

---

[3] All Trollope's recommendations were approved by the Postmaster General (on 15 and 16 June 1858).

[4] Edward Chapman (1804–80), co-founder of Chapman & Hall in 1830. Chapman agreed to pay £400 for *Doctor Thorne*, which was published at the end of May (for Trollope's colorful account of rushing from Bentley to Chapman, see *Autobiography*, pp. 116–17). Trollope's connection with Chapman & Hall, who published works of Dickens, Carlyle, and the Brownings, lasted throughout his life. (In 1869, he purchased a partnership in the firm for his son Henry; in 1880, when the firm was registered as a limited company, he became one of the original directors.)

[5] *Brown, Jones, and Robinson*. See Addenda, Trollope to Chapman, 13 June 1858.

time I feel convinced that it is better that your name should be withheld, for there is a strong impression abroad that you are writing too rapidly for your permanent fame.

The Doctor has sold about 700. I do not know how long the sale of your book continues after the first burst, but I should think I might print 250 more, if I can sell these I will be satisfied.

I am Dear Sir
Yours truly
A. Trollope Esqr   E Chapman

To Frederic Hill
MS General Post Office, London.

June 19. 1858   Glasgow.[6]
My dear Sir.

I send you a note I have just received from Mr Green our Consul at Alexandria.

I must observe that Nubar Beys objection to the 24 hour clause—namely that of the sea risk—is moonshine. The sea risk is encountered now & will in no way be encreased; and as to the interference of the weather he is precluded from any liability in that respect by a section in the clause which provides for the impediments over which he has no control. His real objection is that afterwards named by Mr Green—viz. that "the agent of a Company to whom the Viceroy owes from seventy to eighty thousand pounds, & who is alway [sic] ready with cash, is very likely to have influence!!" Very likely.

As to the Agent—Mr Holtons objection—I think it should not be allowed to have weight. Families with children, one may say always, go by Southampton. Those who can not stand fast travelling should do so. If there were no isthmus to cross over, people would not require a night on shore, but would be content with their berths. I cannot see that there is any hardship in their having to make a journey of 220 miles by railway in one day.[7]

I made no mistake about the pace of the camels— I was informed by those of whom I enquired, our own agents & the agents of the Railway,

---

[6] On his return from Egypt, Trollope was sent to Glasgow for two months to reorganize the Glasgow Post Office. He commented: "I walked all over the city with the letter-carriers, going up to the top flats of the houses. . . . It was midsummer, and wearier work I never performed. The men would grumble, and then I would think how it would be with them if they had to go home afterwards and write a love-scene. But the love-scenes written in Glasgow, all belonging to *The Bertrams*, are not good." (*Autobiography*, pp. 127–28.)

[7] John Green's note of 10 June 1858 reported: "Mr. Holton laughs at the idea of the mails being carried from ship to ship in 24 hours, and urges me to impress on HM's Govt. the utter impossibility of passing women & children through Egypt without allowing them a night's rest at Cairo." (MS General Post Office, London.)

that when laden they travelled 3 miles an hour. Mr Green may very probably be right in saying that they only go 2½ miles—viz 20 miles in eight hours. He has however probably got his information from Nubar Bey, & Nubar Beys officers, when talking the matter over; and they would doubtless claim ample time— You will probably not object to give the eight hours for the Camels—in addition to the time given for loading, if they ask it.

I quite agree with Mr. Green that any discussion as to the passengers—if any be necessary—should take place in London & not in Alexandria.

You will observe what Mr Green says about the progress of the railway—which you were assured would certainly be opened throughout in last February.[8]

very faithfully yours
Anthony Trollope

F. Hill Esq

To Frederic Hill
MS General Post Office, London.

1 July 1858   Dublin
Private
My dear Sir.

I send you a further note from Mr. Green received this morning, which I hope you will think satisfactory. To the new wording of the clause allowing additional time till the line be completed you will probably not object.[9]

I believe that one should never give way in any thing to an Oriental. Nubar Bey, who now that the treaty is signed declares that there will be no difficulty in carrying it out, assured me at least a dozen times, that if the Viceroy insisted on his signing such an agreement he would at once abandon his office, seeing that the work to which he would be bound would be absolutely impracticable! That was the method he took to carry out the views of the Steampacket Company's Agent!

---

[8] Green wrote: "A huge number of Fellahs are at work on the Railway, but the incapacity of the French Engineer is perfectly sickening, and the progress making so slow, that however unpleasant it may be in my position to complain of a Frenchman, I feel I shall be compelled to do so." (MS General Post Office, London.)

[9] Green's note of 21 June 1858 said: "The Postal Agreement goes home by this mail, signed without the alteration of a word except the 6c. Article, a change in which was unavoidable [to provide for the use of camels for the unopened portion of the railway from Cairo to Suez]. . . . It would be a long story to tell you how I got over the difficulties as to signing; suffice it to say Nubar Bey now declares that as regards the *Administration* there is not the slightest difficulty in performing the transit in the time stipulated. The 'Alma' anchored at Suez yesterday at 2.30 am & the mails &c were down here at 9 am this morning." (MS General Post Office, London.) The treaty was signed in London on 16 July; the Fifth Report of the Postmaster General commended Trollope on his accomplishment (*Parl. Papers 1859*, VIII [2493], 19).

I now only hope that such arrangements may be made with the company as will enable us to use the power we shall have of passing the mails via Marseilles through in 24 hours—

I think that the Post Office is much indebted to Mr. Green.

very faithfully yours

F. Hill Esq   Anthony Trollope

To Charles Banning[1]

MS Parrish Collection.

August 9. 1858   Glasgow.
My dear Banning.

I send back your own sheet with thanks. I have kept it too long. I also send proof copies of those I have had printed—from your model—as regards Glasgow in & out. I only got them yesterday. I hope to be able to reduce them in size.

Yours ever

C Banning Esq   Any Trollope

To Richard Bentley

MS Parrish Collection. SB 63.

12 Augt 1858   Glasgow
My dear Sir

I send back the Three Clerks. I have cut out as much as I could—[2]

I was in a hurry to do it, as I may be going abroad this autumn—& if so shall not be back for some months.

Yours very truly

R Bentley Esq   Anthony Trollope

To J. B. Blake[3]

MS Parrish Collection. B 64.

POST OFFICE
1 October 1858   Dublin
My dear Blake

I was very glad to get your letter, and glad to hear that you were out, as it would break the monotony of your life at Edinbro.

Your own bond is certainly not yet executed as the papers have been

[1] Charles Barber Banning, Postmaster at Liverpool.
[2] In January 1859 Bentley issued a five-shilling, one-volume edition; the cuts included an entire chapter, "The Civil Service."
[3] James B. Blake, second-class postal clerk, Scotland.

delayed here. They desired Fitzgibbon[4] to get a magistrates certificate as to my sufficiency—and I would not let him do it—and so the paper has been to & fro. It was absurd asking for a magistrates certificate in my case as the men in the office know better as to my means than any magistrate can do— However, to prevent further delay I did get a magistrate—& the paper went in only to day.

Do not lose any opportunity when you are at country offices of getting up the rural posts. Make a point of walking them all with the men whether you are employed to do so, or no. You will learn by doing so the system of rural posts, and it will soon be known that you have learnt it— And this will lead to your being employed as a Surveyors clerk, when there is need for such employment. You should do all you can to learn a Surveyors business when you are travelling. It will be sure to be useful to you.

Let me know when you have executed your own bond. I suppose there will be no further delay.

Yours very faithfully
Anthy Trollope

I think the lad I have got, will do for a stationery clerk. His name is Irvine.[5] He comes from the Queens Dublin office—

To Edward Chapman
MS Parrish Collection. SB 65.

20. Oct 1858.   Dublin.
Dear Sir

Will you send me here by book post your last number of the National Review—[6] I see that I am handled in it— I must know whether for good or bad. I shall be in London before long—& will settle with you for that & I hope for something else—

Yours very truly

E. Chapman Esq   Anthony Trollope

---

[4] R. Fitzgibbon, first-class surveyor's clerk: Trollope's immediate subordinate.

[5] J. Irvine, stationery clerk under Trollope and Fitzgibbon.

[6] "Mr. Trollope's Novels," *National Review*, 7 (October 1858), 416–35, long excerpts of which are reprinted in Smalley, pp. 80–89. The article discussed Trollope's fiction from *The Warden* through *Doctor Thorne* with very high praise, regretting only that Trollope "should be guilty of the bad taste of counting quantity before quality." Smalley raises the possibility that the article was by Richard Holt Hutton, the most discerning of Trollope's contemporary critics and Trollope's own favorite (see *Autobiography*, p. 205).

To J. B. Blake

MS (photocopy) Parrish Collection. SB 66.

Nov 11. 1858
Private   London.
My dear Blake.

I am glad to find you still at Thwaites[7]—it is better than being at Edinbro— I am glad also that your bond is completed.

There is a chance that you may be called up to London before I am back—with reference to changing you to some place in the London office. If so, my advice is to comply with any such suggestion made to you.

I write in very great haste.

Write me a letter in two or three months to say how you are & what you are doing—& put it under cover to J. Tilley Esq G.PO. London.

Yours ever very faithfully
Anthy Trollope

T. C. Haliburton[8] to Trollope

MS University of Illinois.

                                                      Gordonhouse
12th. Novr. 58   Isleworth
My dear Trollope—

I have just received your letter of the 10th, and I assure you it has given me very great satisfaction to hear *directly* from you, indirectly I often hear of you from our mutual friend Bentley upon whom, poor fellow, sorrow & years have made unmistakable traces— Have also had the gratification of reading your singularly clever works, and congratulate you with all my heart, upon attaining the enviable distinction of being by far the best delineator of female character of the present day— If I were capable of entertaining a feeling of envy, it would be of that masterly & delicate hand that so truly & so skilfully portrays the feelings, impulses and instincts of the fair sex— Go and prosper—

I look back with great pleasure and great gratitude, to the days & they are not a few, spent in your mothers hospitable house, in bygone times, when you write to her next, pray remember me most affectionately to her— How glad I should be to renew our acquaintance.[9] . . .

                                                Yours always
Anthony Trollope Esqre.   T C Haliburton

---

[7] A village in Cumberland.

[8] Thomas Chandler Haliburton (1796–1865), author of *Sam Slick*. Haliburton left his native Nova Scotia in 1856 and settled in England; he served as MP for Launceston, 1859–65.

[9] Haliburton met Mrs. Trollope through Bentley, the English publisher of *Sam Slick*, during his first visit to England in 1838 (*Memoir*, I, 296–98). T. A. Trollope found his mother's friend "exactly like his books—extremely amusing reading if taken in rather small doses" (*What I Remember*, p. 250).

To Edward Chapman

MS Parrish Collection. SB 67.

2 December. 1858.   St. Thomas. West Indies.[1]
My dear Sir.

I send the 7 first chapters of the third volume of the Bertrams.[2] This will reach you I think on the 17 of this month. Can you have these printed so that the proofs shall be with Mr Tilley by 1st. of January—say by one on that day. If so, I shall get them out in time to return them to you by the middle of February—and then the remainder can be corrected by Mr Tilley in London.

You will remember his address.

> J. Tilley Esq.
> G.P.O.
> London.

You had better address to me to his care—

very faithfully yours

E. Chapman Esq   Anthy Trollope

To J. B. Blake

MS Parrish Collection. B 68.

Decr 25. 1858   Kingston Jamaica.
My dear Blake.

I have been very happy to hear that you have been selected to go to Mr. Warren's[3] district as acting Surveyors clerk in room of Mr. Hobson,[4] who takes charge of my district. If you succeed there, as I do not doubt you will, it will be a very great step for you, and coming so soon after your recent appointment it ought to put you in good spirits. A Surveyors clerkship is by far the nicest appointment which a young man can have in the post office service; and I know none so desirable in any other branch of the Civil Service. Make yourself useful where you are now, and you will be sure of such an appointment permanently before long.

I am getting on with my work here, but it will I fear be very long be-

---

[1] On 16 November Trollope had left England on a postal mission to the West Indies to "cleanse the Augean stables of our Post Office system there" (*Autobiography*, p. 128). His most important task was to propose new routes for mail service acceptable to the Royal Mail Steam Packet Company (see Trollope to Hill, 6 September 1859); he was also to advise on the transfer of the Kingston Post Office to local control and to negotiate a reduction in the tax levied by New Grenada on British mail crossing the Isthmus of Panama. The Sixth Report of the Postmaster General highly praised Trollope's work (*Parl. Papers 1860*, XXIII [2657], 27–28).

[2] Chapman & Hall had contracted (in an undated agreement) to pay Trollope £400 for a three-year copyright to *The Bertrams*. The novel was published in March 1859.

[3] J. Warren, Surveyor for Scotland's Northern District (Aberdeen).

[4] R. Hobson, first-class surveyor's clerk.

fore I get home. I am terribly bothered by the musquitoes. Let me have a line to say how you get on.

I hear that Mr. R. R. Smith[5] who was in Central district in Ireland, goes to the South Scotland district, and that Mr. Barnard[6] goes to his.

> very faithfully yours
> Anthy Trollope

Let me have a line to say how you get on. Send it to the care of Mr. Tilley.

You will have 15/ a day while travelling as a Surveyors clerk. Do not be too economical. You should always live at the hotels as a gentleman. It will pay best in the long run.

1859

To Edward Chapman
MS Parrish Collection. B 69.

Jany. 11. 1859.   Kingston. Jamaica.
My dear Sir

I send you in two parcels, the two first vols of The Bertrams corrected —& the second portion of the 3 vol. up to page 260—of Mss. There will be 35—or 40 more—which will give it ample length. You shall have them by the next mail. This will give it you by 16th. February—as the copy has not to come out to me, but will be corrected by Mr. Tilley, this will give you ample time. The proof of what I now send will also be corrected by Mr. Tilley.

And now, as I have always a prudent eye to the future, I shall be glad to know whether you will think well of a volume of travels on these parts— As I dont yet know how far a field I shall wander, I cannot say what will be comprised—Jamaica, Cuba—British Guiana—Panama—& God knows what other latitudes or longitudes.

My idea is about 450 pages of the Dr. Thorne size—i e so much matter —to be put into one goodly volume—in such shape as you may prefer; to come out before Xmas. Mss—to be with you by 31 October—(most probably a good deal earlier.) Price £250 for three years.

Whether this would suit you—or whether no—be kind enough to let

---

[5] R. R. Smith, Surveyor for Scotland's Southern District (Edinburgh).
[6] W. W. Barnard, Inspector of Mails.

me have an answer. Send it to Mr. Tilley. I suppose the cheap edition of
Dr. Thorne is by this time in existence.

Ah—I wish Providence had made me a publisher.[7]

Yours very truly

E Chapman Esq   Anthony Trollope

To Mrs. Frances Trollope

Memoir, II, 283–84. B 70.

January 27. 1859.   Brig *Linwood*

Dearest Mother.

I must write you a line to tell you how I am going on in my travels,
tho' my present position is not very favourable for doing so.

I finished my business in Jamaica last Monday, and then, by way of
making a short cut across to Cuba, I got into this wretched sailing vessel.
But we have been becalmed half the time since, and I shall lose more
time than I shall gain. I believe that in these days a man should never be
tempted to leave the steam-boats.[8]

I am now on my way to the Havana, and shall have to travel across
Cuba to reach it. When I have done there, I go viâ St. Thomas to De-
merara,—thence to Panama,—thence I hope to the States, where I have
some idea that Rose may meet me.[9] In this way it will be 1860 before I
can see you or Florence. But what could I do? When I had accepted the
shorter journey which was first proposed, I could not well refuse it when
it became longer, and the scheme larger.

I liked Jamaica very much, but did not like Kingston, the chief town,
at all. I met with very great hospitality in the island, and found the
country to be very, very lovely. I went over the whole island, and saw
as much of it, I flatter myself, as any man ever did in the time. I think I
shall save the Post Office £1300 a year by my journey there. I like to feel
that the expense has not been for nothing.

[7] On 8 February Edward Chapman answered: "I quite recognize the truth of your
having a 'prudent eye to the future' but I wish it was not quite such a piercer, it goes
quite through my heart and out at the bottom of my pocket. . . . Let it be £250 for a
gaudy 8vo. of about 550 or 600 pps of Dr Thorne—a hundred pages more or less is
nothing to you when you are writing. Let it be also for three years. . . . Providence
has too good a regard for you to make you a publisher, it was a very fine business
some 20 years ago but authors are too knowing now-a-days for Paternoster Row to
become a California." (MS Bodleian.) T. A. Trollope agreed to these terms on his
brother's behalf on 9 April 1859. Frederic Chapman signed a more formal copy on
14 July, and *The West Indies and the Spanish Main*, the first of Trollope's travel
books, was published in late October 1859. In his *Autobiography* (p. 129), Trollope
made the extravagant claim that he regarded *The West Indies* "on the whole . . . as
the best book that has come from my pen."

[8] Trollope began his book on the West Indies with a colorful and detailed account
of his slow voyage aboard the frequently becalmed *Linwood*.

[9] Trollope's wife did not go to the United States on this occasion.

Tom will be in England, I presume, when this reaches you, looking after the family literature. John Tilley says that he has done all that he can. His house is now quite full, and he *cannot* stow away any more Trollope books. This is since the cheap editions have set in upon him! . . .

I found your novels advertised with quite new names,—one by that horrid blackguard R.[1] Should not this be stopped? And then there's "The Days of the Regency, by Mrs. Trollope,"[2] brought out by Thomas Hodgson in his Parlour Library. Surely you never wrote a "Days of the Regency"? The worst is that it makes an appearance as tho' you were in league with the publishers in palming off old novels. . . .

Tom and I both come out in March,[3] and both under the same auspices, namely those of the Messrs. Chapman. . . . Do not be angry at the bad writing, for the ship tosses.

My best love to Theo and Bimba. I had hoped to have been with you all about the time you will get this letter.

Your own affectionate son
Anthony Trollope

Mrs. Frances Trollope to Trollope[4]

MS Taylor Collection.

My dear Anthony

You ask me to write— I and my pen have been so long divorced that I hardly know how to set about it— But you ask me to write and therefore write I will—though I have no news to tell you more fresh than that I love you dearly— I should like to see you again, but can hardly hope it! God bless you my dear dear Son!

Your loving mother
Frances Trollope

To J. B. Blake

MS Parrish Collection. B 71.

10 July. 1859.   Dublin
My dear Blake.

I got home last Tuesday, & I go up to London next Tuesday. Your first letter telling me that you had got the place in the Sec's office has not

---

[1] Probably George Routledge, who had issued Mrs. Trollope's *The Ward of Thorpe Combe* (1841) as a Routledge Railway Novel under the title *The Ward*.

[2] Hodgson reissued Mrs. Trollope's *Town and Country* (1848) under this title in 1857.

[3] T. A. Trollope's *A Decade of Italian Women* and Trollope's *The Bertrams*.

[4] This barely legible letter, which may have been among the last things that Mrs. Trollope wrote, is impossible to date; it is accordingly reprinted here following Trollope's last surviving letter to her. (By this date, Mrs. Trollope's mind or at least memory had begun to fail: see *Memoir*, II, 297.)

reached me. One parcel of letters is travelling after me somewhere—Your subsequent letter of 3 June I received at New York.

I *am* sorry you have gone into the Secretary's office— I think you were somewhat impatient— It is true your salary was low, but you were receiving 15/– a day for every day—& therefore your position at the moment was not bad. You would probably have remained there for a considerable time, and would I think have got the permanent appointment.

However I do not at all find fault with you. As you did try it was well to get it, & the appointment is certainly an eligible one. I believe the salary rises by £10 per an. & that you can look forward to another, better class, above you.

Still, were I you, I would look forward to a Surveyors desk. Your chance is not shut up by your going into the Secretary's office, tho' it certainly is not so good as it would have been in the other position. Let me know if you would still wish for that change.

If I remember rightly you did not lose your leave of absence last year by my absence, but by the fact of your own promotion. When a man is changing from office to office in the process of furthering his own interests, as you are doing—and as young men should certainly strive to do—they must thereby lose the privilege of leave of absence. A man going fresh into an office cannot expect his leave as regularly as a man who has been sometime fixed. In a large office too the juniors must put up with the winter months.

If you write address
    G. P. O.
    London.

                ever very faithfully yours
                Any Trollope

To Rose Trollope

MS Taylor Collection. B 72.

[2 August 1859]
To ye. ladie of Waltham House[5] in ye. Countie of Herts. These—
Deareste Madame

Havinge withe infinite trouble & pain inspected & surveyed and pokèd manie and diverse holes in ye aforesaid mansion, I have at ye laste hiréd and taken it for yr. moste excellente ladieship—to have and to hold from ye term of St. Michaels mass next comynge. The whiche Waltham House

---

[5] Trollope makes arrangements for his move in November to Waltham Cross in Hertfordshire (on the boundaries of Essex and Middlesex), about twelve miles northeast of London, where he had just taken a residence "somewhat too grandly called Waltham House" (*Autobiography*, p. 147). The Post Office had appointed him Surveyor for the Eastern District of England, and his territory included Essex, Suffolk, Norfolk, Cambridgeshire, Huntingdonshire, and the eastern parts of Bedfordshire and Hertfordshire.

Waltham House, Waltham Cross

is now the property of one Mistress Wilkins, who has let it to your lovynge lord & husband for 7—14—or 21 yeares, with manie and diverse clauses which shall hereafter as time may serve be explained to your excellente ladieship—

In ye. mean time I am with all true love and affection your ladieships devoted servant and husband

Anthony Trollope

The second daye of this monthe of Auguste in the yeare of our Lord 1859

Frederic Chapman to Trollope

MS Bodleian.

Aug. 2nd. 1859   193, PICCADILLY. LONDON. W.
My dear Sir,

I have seen Mr. Forster[6] about the "Kellys of O'Kelly" [*sic*] and he gives his consent to the publication with the greatest pleasure—[7] As soon as you send a copy corrected, I will put it into hand.

Enclosed is the agreement for Castle Richmond—[8]

Yrs. most truly
Anthony Trollope Esq.   Fred: Chapman

To Richard Bentley

MS Taylor Collection. Taylor, "Bentley," pp. 87–88; B 73.

8 Augt 1859.   Dublin.
My dear Sir.

Your letter of the 4th. Inst has followed me here.

When you were about to bring out your 5/- edition of *The Three Clerks*, I reduced the book by about 60 pages, and I fear I should find it impossible to put out 100 more. It gives more trouble to strike out pages, than to write new ones, as the whole sequence of a story, hangs page on

[6] Doubtless John Forster (1812–76), biographer, historian, critic, and editor; literary adviser to Chapman & Hall, 1837–60. As editor of the *Examiner*, Forster had accepted Trollope's series of seven letters on the distressed state of Ireland (published in the *Examiner* between August 1849 and June 1850). Trollope later commented: "The world in Ireland did not declare that the Government had at last been adequately defended, nor did the treasurer of the *Examiner* send me a cheque in return." (*Autobiography*, p. 84.)

[7] In November 1859 Chapman & Hall issued a one-volume, five-shilling edition of *The Kellys and the O'Kellys*. Forster was involved with the negotiation because he had married the widow of Colburn, the original publisher of the novel.

[8] According to the agreement, Trollope was to receive £600 on the publication of *Castle Richmond* in return for allowing Chapman & Hall full copyright for three years and a half share in the copyright thereafter. The novel was published on 10 May 1860. Almost immediately (13 July 1860) Trollope bought back his half share for £100.

page— There is an episode—a story of some 40 pages in the three vol edit., which I would put out if that would suit you— But even that wd. require some care as it is alluded to in different places.[9]

I should not at all object to your midwifery for a new book. But as long as Mr. Chapman will give me what I ask him for my goods, of course I shall continue to sell them to him.

very faithfully yours

R Bentley Esq Anthony Trollope

To [? Fletcher Harper][1]

MS Taylor Collection. B 74.

London.
(address,

1st. September. 1859.   General Post Office, London.[2]

My dear Sir.

Thank you for your letter & the order for £40—which it covered. That sum has been paid to me by Mr. Low.[3]

I think of writing a series of tales, of which the two which I have sent you will be the two first—to be called when completed, "Tales of all Countries." Each would refer to some different nation or people; and in each case to some country which I have visited. They would run to from 24 to 28 in number, & would average in length 10 of your monthly magazine pages.

My intention would be to republish them in two series, as they should be finished, certainly here in England, and I should hope in the States, with your assistance.

What I now wish to know is whether it would suit you to publish one such tale monthly. If not brought out monthly, the project would run over too long a period. About 12 would make one volume for republication.

I have already given you stories about the Italy[4] and Belgium.[5] You should have a story of the Pyrenees[6] about the end of October if the

---

[9] These negotiations concerned the 1860 publication of the novel in a new series entitled Bentley's Standard Novels. See *Bibliography*, p. 23.

[1] Probably Fletcher Harper (1806–77), of the publishing house of Harper & Brothers, New York.

[2] Parentheses left open.

[3] Sampson Low (1797–1886), the London publisher, was Harper's agent in England.

[4] A slip of the pen for "the States." The story was "The Courtship of Susan Bell," *Harper's New Monthly Magazine*, 21 (August 1860), 366–78; reprinted in *Tales of All Countries* (1861).

[5] "Relics of General Chassé," *Harper's*, 20 (February 1860), 363–70; reprinted in *Tales of All Countries*.

[6] "La Mère Bauche," included in *Tales of All Countries*. Though sold to *Harper's*, the story was not published by *Harper's*.

project would suit you—& then the series regularly as fast as you would want them.

very faithfully yours
Anthony Trollope

Of course it would be understood that I should have the power of re-publication in England as soon [as] a series of 12 (say) had appeared in your Magazine.[7]

To Frederic Hill

MS General Post Office, London. B 75.

6 September 1859   G. P. O. London.
My dear Sir.

The papers referring to the projected changes in the routes of the West Indian packets have again been referred to me, together with the scheme as proposed by the Company[8] and the objections made by the Company to my scheme.

As I go out of town today I shall not see you; and it is probable that the matter may be settled before my return; I therefore think it well to say a few words to you on the matter which I can hardly put into an official report.

The Company, in objecting to the proposition for making Jamaica our headquarters, shew that they can not bring back the vessels to Southampton under my plan, so as to give an interval of even an entire day, whereas an interval of 3 days is required. But in shewing this they go on the presumption that the vessel which runs to Colon must return on the return journey, i e the same vessel. But there is no necessity for this. *Such is not the case now—* The vessel which now goes down to Colon passes the up vessel on the St. Thomas side of Colon, between Carthagena & Colon— And such should still be the case. The vessel from Jamaica to Colon should not return at once; but on the next trip.

Of course it is for the advantage of the Company to encrease the number of miles & diminish the number of vessels— But the interests of the Crown are exactly opposite to this. Providing there be two vessels from Jamaica to Colon & back, the Colon route need offer no impediment to our proposition.

It is absurd for the Company to allege that a first class ship cannot work from Colon to Jamaica or from Jamaica to St. Thomas at above 9 miles. The former journey is a very fair one for ordinary work, being opposed by no wind— And as to the latter, tho it be in the teeth of the

---

[7] The only other story published in *Harper's* was "The O'Conors of Castle Conor, County Mayo," 20 (May 1860), 799–806. This was also reprinted in *Tales of All Countries*.

[8] The Royal Mail Steam Packet Company.

trade wind & therefore a difficult route for a small ship, it should offer no impediment to 10 miles an hour with a first class vessel.

The route to Cuba & the Mexican ports offers the only real difficulty. This difficulty will cease when we are able to land our mails on the southern side of the island;—say at Cien Fuegos; but I cannot recommend that this should be done till the railway between that port and the Havana be completed. In the mean time one of three things should be done: Either the Company should work from Jamaica to Tampico at a quicker pace than 9 miles—say 10—which would not be difficult on the route *to* Tampico; & thus save time—or else they should keep a small vessel to run from Tampico to Vera Cruz & back, making Vera Cruz the end of their main line; or they should have two vessels on the Station, so that the same vessel which goes to Tampico need not return on the same trip.

I think that one of these three things should be done, till the necessity of running round to the Havana be prevented; and that the service to such a port as Tampico should not stand in the way of a change which would in other respects be so beneficial to British interests.

I have made some observations officially on the Company's objections; but as you may probably see Mr. Clifton on the matter before it is decided, I have thought it best to explain this to you privately. *Of course* the Company do not desire a diminution of mileage; but they do desire a diminution in the number of vessels employed, in comparison with the mileage—

But we desire a diminution of mileage—in order that the distances may be available elsewhere; and we feel that we have a right to demand a fair number of ships for the service, seeing the enormous amount of the Crown Subsidy.

I am very anxious that the point should be carried, as I am certain it would greatly benefit our own interests.[9]

Very faithfully yours

F. Hill Esq   Anthony Trollope

[9] The West Indies mails were transferred from the large transatlantic vessel to smaller vessels at the Danish port of St. Thomas (in the Virgin Islands). Since three of the four local vessels followed almost parallel courses westward from St. Thomas, Trollope proposed that the transatlantic vessel drop only its bags for the eastern Caribbean at St. Thomas and then proceed to Jamaica to transfer the rest of its bags to local steamers. The transatlantic vessel was faster than the local vessels; and there would be substantial savings in costs since the Packet Company was paid by the ship-mile. Trollope's point was supported by the Admiralty, but it was not carried because of the resistance of the Packet Company. The threat of the new arrangement, however, was held over the Company's head in an effort to make their services more efficient.

To W. M. Thackeray[1]
MS (Trollope's copy) Bodleian. B 76.

Donnybrook.

October 23—1859.   Dublin.

Dear Sir.

I do not know how far the staff of your new periodical[2] may be complete. Perhaps you will excuse my taking the liberty of offering to make one of the number if it be not so.

I will tell you exactly what would be my views, and you will as frankly tell me whether they would suit you.

I am writing a series of stories to be called—unless I change the name, Tales of all countries. I began them last summer with the view of publishing them first in Harpers magazine, & then of republishing them here. He has two of them already in his hands.

My idea is to publish one a month, & to republish the 12 in a single vol at the end of a year. They wd. run on in this way for two years. They would occupy, each, from 8 to 13 pages of a big-paged magazine—such as yours may probably be.

If it suited you to take one each alternate month, I would send one for each alternate month to Harpers. It does not suit him to have to take one monthly—or I would send them all to you, if you so wished.

If this idea would suit you, you would probably let me know your rate of pay. Harper gives me £20 for each story—or £2 a page for 10 pages. Of course I have the right of republication whenever it may suit me.

I have five of these stories now by me. Each refers to or is intended to be redolent of some different country—but they apply only to localities with which I am myself conversant.

You will I hope at any rate excuse my writing to you in this manner.

Yours faithfully

Anthony Trollope

As I have before me a letter from Harper respecting these stories which I must answer, perhaps you will let me have a reply as soon as may be convenient to you.

[1] Trollope regarded Thackeray, whom he had not yet met, as the foremost novelist of his day; see *Autobiography*, pp. 243-45.

[2] The *Cornhill Magazine*. The plan for this new shilling magazine originated with its publisher, George Smith, who wanted to provide a moderately priced monthly that combined serial fiction and critical and factual articles, together with poetry and illustrations. Thackeray was engaged in February 1859 to write the opening serial; later, he agreed to accept the editorship, though with Smith shouldering much of the responsibility. Then, as Smith recalled, "I set to work with the utmost energy to make the undertaking a success. We secured the most brilliant contributions in every quarter. Our terms were lavish almost to the point of recklessness. No pains were spared to make the new magazine the best periodical yet known to English literature." Thackeray suggested that the magazine take its name from its place of publication

Smith, Elder & Co.[3] to Trollope

MS Bodleian.

26th. October 1859
Anthony Trollope Esqre.
Donnybrook
Dublin.   65, CORNHILL, LONDON, E.C.
Dear Sir,

Mr. Thackeray having informed us that we might hope for your co-operation in our new Magazine if we could make satisfactory business arrangements with you, we have the pleasure of addressing you on the subject.[4]

We understand from Mr. Thackeray that you have proposed to contribute a series of short stories to be published every alternate month, and for the entire copyright of these we should be happy to pay you at the rate of Two pounds per page of our Magazine a specimen page of which we now enclose. You will perceive that it contains rather less than half the quantity of a page of Harpers Magazine, and we trust you will therefore consider the rate of remuneration a liberal one.

We should however much prefer a continuous story to extend through twenty four sheets of the Magazine, which would be equivalent to the bulk of an ordinary three volume novel, and for the entire copyright of which we should be happy to pay you One Thousand pounds.

Being desirous that any papers reprinted from our Magazine should be published by ourselves, we have made this proposal to you on that basis, and we anxiously hope that we may have the gratification of including your name in the list of contributors, in one form or other.

We beg to remain
Dear Sir
Yours very faithfully
Smith Elder & Co

PS. We may mention that we have arranged for the re-publication of our Magazine in America.

(an idea initially laughed at, then imitated), and Godfrey Sykes, an art student, designed its cover. See Leonard Huxley, *The House of Smith Elder* (1923), pp. 89–96.

[3] This letter is in the hand of George Smith (1824–1901), head of Smith, Elder & Co. since 1846. Under Smith's direction, the firm's banking business and commercial interests abroad (especially in India) prospered, allowing Smith to take risks as a publisher. He loved books and the company of writers, and he became the friend as well as the publisher of Ruskin, Charlotte Brontë, Thackeray, and Mrs. Gaskell. The *Cornhill Magazine* proved spectacularly popular. In 1865, Smith started a highly successful evening newspaper, the *Pall Mall Gazette*; and in 1882, he began publication of the *Dictionary of National Biography*. A cordial friendship developed between Smith and Trollope.

[4] Thackeray had sent a note to Smith: "I will write to Trollope saying how we want to have him—you on your side please write offering the cash." (J. A. Sutherland, *Victorian Novelists and Publishers* [1976], p. 142.)

W. M. Thackeray to Trollope[5]

MS Taylor Collection. *Autobiography*, pp. 137–38; *Letters of W. M. Thackeray*, IV, 158–59; B 77.

October 28 [1859]   36 Onslow Sqr. S.W.
My dear Mr. Trollope
   Smith & Elder have sent you their proposals: and the business part done, let me come to the pleasure, and say how very glad indeed I shall be to have you as a Cooperator in our New Magazine. And, looking over the annexed programme, you will see whether you can't help us in many other ways besides tale-telling. Whatever a man knows about life and its doings that let us hear about. You must have tossed a deal about the world, and have countless sketches in your memory and your portfolio. Please to think if you can furbish up any of these besides the novel. When events occur on wh. you can have a good lively talk, bear us in mind. One of our chief objects in this magazine is the getting out of novel spinning, and back into the world. Don't understand me to disparage our craft, especially *your* wares. I often say I am like the pastry cook, and don't care for tarts, but prefer bread and cheese—but the public loves the tarts (luckily for us), and we must bake & sell them. There was quite an excitement in my family one evening when Paterfamilias (who goes to sleep over a novel almost always when he tries it after dinner) came up stairs to the Drawing Room wide awake and calling for the second volume of The Three Clerks. I hope the Cornhill Magazine will have as pleasant a story; and the Chapmans, if they are the honest men I take them to be, I've no doubt have told you with what sincere liking your works have been read by yours very faithfully.
                                                W. M. Thackeray.[6]

---

[5] Trollope's delighted response to this letter and to the preceding letter is recounted in his *Autobiography*, pp. 136–41. *Framley Parsonage*, the novel Trollope supplied for the *Cornhill*, proved to be the most important of his career since it made him a widely popular novelist; moreover, as Trollope later said, "my connection with the *Cornhill* . . . was the means of introducing me very quickly to that literary world from which I had hitherto been severed by the fact of my residence in Ireland." (*Autobiography*, pp. 146–47.) *Framley Parsonage* was serialized in the *Cornhill* from January 1860 through April 1861, and was published in three volumes in April 1861.

[6] Closing and signature cut away; supplied from printed versions.

To George Smith
MS Bodleian.

11. November 1859.   Dublin
My dear Sir.

Thanks for your last letter. I shall be in town myself on the 22nd. Instant, and I will then hand you the Mss of the first Number; and you
shall have the second as soon afterwards as you may please. The name of
the story will be "Framley parsonage."

                                              very faithfully yours
G Smith esq   Anthony Trollope

To John Hambley
MS Taylor Collection.

14. November 1859.   Dublin.
John Hambley.

I think you had better order in as much coal as will fill, or nearly fill,
the larger coal hole. I should say about eight or perhaps ten ton. You
mentioned some man to me, who lives I believe near the railway station.
I hope he will give me the best household coal; otherwise of course I
cannot get more from him. Tell him to let me know his price. I will pay
him immediately.

I want to get as much as the place will hold, so as to avoid having the
dirt again sooner than can be helped. They should bring it through
your gate. You must then lock the place up, as I will not have these coals
touched till we are there.

I shall be in London on the 22nd. of this month, & hope I may be at
Waltham on the 23rd.

You have not told me whether you have got a laborer.

If they have cut the oil cloth for the hall, do not let them put it down
permanently before the furniture is in.

                                              Yours truly
                                              Anthony Trollope

To George Smith
MS John Murray. B 78.

                                              Maldon.[7]
25 Nov. 1859.   address. G.P.O. London
My dear Sir.

I return the proof of the article—[8] I *have* cut out a page—but it was as
tho you asked for my hearts blood.[9]

---

[7] A small river port ten miles east of Chelmsford in Essex.

[8] The first number of *Framley Parsonage*, published in the *Cornhill* in January.

[9] It is impossible to determine what Trollope cut because the manuscript of *Framley Parsonage* (Harrow School Library) lacks chaps. i–xviii.

And the fault must have been your own in giving me too long a page as a sample— I had even the words counted, so that I might give you exactly what I had undertaken to give & no more.

I should like to have the Mss with the proofs. A man sometimes is at a loss for his own meaning till he sees his own Mss. It can all be sent by book post.

As I must send back these sheets—I hence attend the press; but I should like to have a revise *in duplicate*—so that I might keep one.

Yours very truly

G Smith Esq Anthony Trollope

Were I to lessen the number of paragraphs it would make it read heavy.

To George Smith

MS Bodleian. SB 79.

25–Decr.–1859 Waltham X.

My dear Sir.

The other day you handed me a check for the 2n. part of my novel for your magazine. I did not look at the check, but paid it into my bank. In my bank book today I see the amount is entered as £65.10. The payment should have been £62.10/ only. Will you look to your check book & see if you did overpay me £3–. If so it can be deducted next month.

I congratulate you warmly on your first number.

Would you oblige me by having a number always sent when it comes out to

J. Tilley Esq
G. P. O.

& charged to me. Perhaps you will now direct the first number to be so sent—& oblige me.

very faithfully yours
Anthony Trollope

To W. M. Thackeray

MS Parrish Collection. B 80.

28 December 1859 Waltham Cross.

My dear Sir.

Allow me to congratulate you on the first number of the magazine. Putting aside my own contribution, as to which I am of course bound to say nothing laudatory whatever I may think, I certainly do conceive that nothing equal to it of its kind was ever hitherto put forth—[10]

---

[10] Trollope was given the place of honor. Other contributors to the *Cornhill's* first number included Thackeray (with the first installment of *Lovel the Widower* and the first of the "Roundabout Papers"), G. H. Lewes, Sir John Bowring, Thornton Leigh Hunt, and General Sir John Burgoyne. The number sold 120,000 copies, a record for

The Cornhill Magazine

The great aim in such a work should be, I think, to make it readable, an aim which has been so constantly lost sight of in a great portion of the pages of all magazines. In your first number there is nothing that is not readable,—with the single exception above mentioned;—and very little that is not thoroughly worth reading.

very faithfully yours

W M Thackeray Esq   Anthony Trollope

To Mrs. Harriet Knower[11]

MS Parrish Collection.

[1859–60][12]

Wednesday night—

My dear Mrs. Knower.

I have seen Mr. Pardee[13] and he says that he and Mrs. Pardee will meet us at the Station at 4.45 pm, on Friday, & join our party to Richmond. I will therefore call for you at about 4—or a few minutes after—

I am glad the Pardees should join us, but even had they not I think we could have had a very pleasant evening together. I don't know that we ever found each other stupid yet,—& I flatter myself we should not have been more so at Richmond than on board the Africa.

However I am very glad that you & Miss Knower[1] can manage to come. —for after all the only way for people to see each other is for them to eat and drink together. There is no other sort of society now a days.

very truly yours

Anthony Trollope

---

an English periodical, and had an estimated half-million readers. "It is almost too good," R. M. Milnes wrote, "for the public it is written for and the money it has to earn." (Gordon N. Ray, *Thackeray: The Age of Wisdom* [1958], p. 296.)

[11] Harriet Knower, née Strong (a Mayflower family), widow of Edmund Knower of Albany, New York. Trollope met Mrs. Knower and her daughter aboard the R.M.S. *Africa* during the crossing from New York to Liverpool (22 June to 4 July 1859). Mrs. Knower settled in New York City, where Trollope later visited her. He remained a warm friend of both Knowers, as subsequent letters show.

[12] This letter was certainly written sometime between the arrival of the *Africa* and Trollope's writing to Mary Knower on 6 March 1860. It may have been written shortly after 12 July 1859, when Trollope went to London after a brief visit to his home in Donnybrook.

[13] Probably D. W. Pardee of Hartford, Connecticut, who was among Trollope's fellow passengers on the *Africa* (*New York Times*, 23 June 1859, p. 8).

[1] Mary Knower (?1840–1931), of whom Trollope seems to have been especially fond. In 1866 she married Samuel J. Penniman (?1833–1876), an oil merchant and widower who had also been aboard the *Africa*, with his two small children, along with Trollope and the Knowers. After her husband's early death, Mary Penniman continued to reside in New York City until her own death at the age of 90. Her estate was estimated at nearly a million dollars. She left large sums to charities and a bequest of $25,000 to her "faithful maid," this last occasioning a headline in the *New York Times* (10 March 1931, p. 16).

1860

To George Smith

MS Bodleian. *Commentary*, p. 211; B 81.

20 Jan. 1860   Waltham X.
My dear Sir.

I think the scene most suited to an illustration in part 3 of Framley parsonage would be a little interview between Lord Boanerges & Miss Dunstable. The lord is teaching the lady the philosophy of soap bubbles, & the lady is quoting to the lord certain popular verses of a virtuous nature. The lord should be made very old, & the lady not very young.[2] I am afraid the artist would have to take the description of the lady from another novel I wrote, called Dr. Thorne.

As this occurred to me I mention it, but I still me [*sic*] leave the matter to your better judgement,—or to anyone else who may have a better judgement.

> Yours always
> Anthony Trollope

I leave home on the morning of the 27th. Let me have a copy by post of 26th. if you can—

Nathaniel Hawthorne to James T. Fields[3]

MS (copy in Trollope's hand) Taylor Collection. *Autobiography*, pp. 144–45.

11 February 1860

*   *   *

It is odd enough, moreover, that my own individual taste is for quite another class of works than those which I myself am able to write— If

---

[2] Trollope refers to a scene from chap. viii, but Millais chose a scene from chap. xi ("Lord Lufton and Lucy Robarts"); the illustration appeared in the fourth number, not the third number.

[3] James Thomas Fields (1817–81), partner in the Boston publishing house Ticknor & Fields; editor of the *Atlantic Monthly*, 1861–70. Several months after receiving this letter, Fields, a friend of Thackeray, met Trollope at a *Cornhill* dinner. On 20 May 1860, he wrote to Hawthorne: "Do come up to London. Among others who wish to meet you is Trollope the novelist whom I met at a dinner yesterday. I told him you were a reader of his books and he seemed really delighted that you praised his novels." (James C. Austin, *Fields of 'The Atlantic Monthly': Letters to an Editor, 1861–1870* [San Marino, Calif., 1953], p. 212.) Fields, who became a close friend of Trollope, published an extract from Hawthorne's letter, first in "Our Whispering Gallery," *Atlantic Monthly*, February 1871, p. 257, then in his Hawthorne chapter in *Yesterdays with*

I were to meet with such books as mine by another writer, I don't believe I should be able to get through them. Have you ever read the novels of Anthony Trollope? They precisely suit my taste; solid and substantial, written on the strength of beef and through the inspiration of ale, and just as real as if some giant had hewn a great lump out of the earth and put it under a glass case, with all its inhabitants going about their daily business and not suspecting that they were made a show of. And these books are just as English as a beefstake [*sic*]— Have they ever been tried in America? It needs an English residence to make them thoroughly comprehensible, but still I should think that human nature would give them success anywhere—

*   *   *

To George Smith

MS Bodleian. SB 82.

Feb. 12—1860   Cambridge.
My dear Sir.

I shall be home on Thursday, & will send you up No. 4. of F. P. by that days post—& you can have No. 5—as soon as you like afterwards,—or up to No. 8 if you wanted them.

Should I live to see my story illustrated by Millais[4] no body would be able to hold me.

yours very faithfully
G Smith Esq   Anthony Trollope

Authors (1872), p. 63. Hawthorne did not meet Trollope until the following year: see Lowell to ?, 20 September 1861.

[4] John Everett Millais (1829–96), later Sir John, well-known painter; one of the original Pre-Raphaelites. He became Trollope's principal illustrator, supplying illustrations for four novels and frontispieces for two more. For Trollope's high opinion of this work, see *Autobiography*, pp. 148–50, where, amid other praise, Trollope says "I have carried on some of those characters from book to book, and have had my own early ideas impressed indelibly on my memory by the excellence of his delineations." See *Illustrators*, pp. 10–12. Millais became one of Trollope's closest friends.

To George Smith

MS Bodleian.

Feb—17—1860   Waltham Cross.
Dear Sir.

I send No. 4 of Framley parsonage by post registered. You will perhaps cause the per contra—£62–10/—to be paid to my credit at the London – Joint Stock Bank.

Yours very truly
G Smith Esq   Anthy Trollope

To George Smith

MS John Murray. B 83.

3 March 1860   Waltham House
My dear Sir.

I have to thank you for your liberally premature payments—but I had not anticipated that I should have drawn upon your funds so much before the legal time.

But I do feel that a few months sooner or later can be nothing to the happy possessor of an established literary property such as the Cornhill Mag. commanding a *fixed* sale of a

100,000 copies!!
Yours very truly
Anthony Trollope

To Mary Knower

MS Parrish Collection.

Waltham house
March 6. 1860   Waltham Cross.
My dear Miss Knower.

I have been much pleased at getting a letter from your mother— Among other things she tells me that she has left you behind among the Frenchmen but that she expects you will be coming home in June or July. i e. as I understand leaving London for the States in one of those months.

I shall be returning from Italy to London so as to be home at the address above given on June 15th.[5] and I and Mrs. Trollope will be so delighted to have you if you will come to us on your route. After June 15th. I will be your humble slave, & come & fetch you at any time or point. I suppose you will not return by Paris or I might pick you up there. My present house is 14 miles from London—by railway, & if you would let me know when you would be at the London Bridge Station—i e the

[5] Trollope in fact postponed his departure for Italy until September.

Station at which you would arrive in London from Aix, I would come & meet you, or my wife would. Only it must be after 15 June. The 16th. or any day after would do. I would afterwards have you shipped off to the States, if at the last moment you do make up your mind to do such a stupid thing as go home.

Let me have a line to say what are your plans.

Yours most sincerely
Anthony Trollope

To ?

MS Parrish Collection. SB 84.

March 21. 1860   Huntingdon[6]

My dear Sir.

I have just got here & have only one moment to say that I shall not be home myself till—tomorrow Thursday at 6. PM. I shall be home all Friday & Saturday, unless specially summoned to London.

very truly yours
Anthy Trollope

To George Smith

MS John Murray. *Commentary*, p. 215; B 85.

2 April 1860.   Waltham.

My dear Sir.

I send back the revises of Chapters 13, 14, 15, 16, 17, 18, & the corrected sheets of Chapters 19, 20, 21, 22, 23, & 24.

Look at page 18—& chapter 15, in the revise, & see what the printer has done for me by changing a word in one line instead of in the one below. Utterly destroyed the whole character of my own [? most] interesting personage. If he dont put the word back I shall resign.

Yours very truly
Anty Trollope

Thomas Adolphus Trollope to Trollope

MS University of Illinois.

6th. April 1860   Florence

My dear Anthony

. . . Theo says my 2 Paul book is the best I have written. I can form no idea. You said, the Strozzi was the best. I thought it very inferior to the Decade.[7]

---

[6] The county town of Huntingdonshire, 60 miles north of London.

[7] Three of T. A. Trollope's books on Italian and especially Florentine history: *A Decade of Italian Women* had been published the previous year; *Filippo Strozzi: A History of the Last Days of the Old Italian Liberty* was about to appear; and *Paul*

She also thinks Framley, your best. I am inclined, to think it is. All the folk here speak very highly of it. My mother has kept Castle Richmond ever since it arrived. So I have not looked at it yet. . . .

Of course I presume your start from London stands fixed for 20th. Septr. I can form no idea;—not being able to guess how long your Dutch excrescence[8] may take. . . .

With best love to Rose, yours always

T. A. T.

To Mrs. Catherine Gould[9]

MS Parrish Collection. B 86.

April 13 1860.   Waltham Cross.
My dear Catherine.

I have no more doubt than you have,—and probably in truth much less, that a man like Gould[10] with good education & good intellect may make money by writing. I believe that the profession requires much less of what is extraordinary either in genius or knowledge that most outsiders presume to be necessary. But it requires that which all other professions require,—but which outsiders do not in general presume to be necessary in the profession of literature,—considerable training, and much hard grinding industry— My belief of book writing is much the same as my belief as to shoemaking.[1] The man who will work the hardest at it, and will work with the most honest purpose, will work the best.

---

the Pope and Paul the Friar was to be published in December 1860 (1861 on the title page). In *What I Remember*, T. A. Trollope commented that though *Filippo Strozzi* was the best received, he thought most highly of *Paul the Pope and Paul the Friar*, the story of the quarrel between the Papacy and Venice (p. 417).

[8] Rose Trollope's chronological list of events (probably prepared to assist Trollope in writing his *Autobiography*) has a scored-through entry for 1860: "You go to Holland with John Tilley(?)." For 1862, the list has "Went to Holland." (MS University of Illinois.) Trollope subsequently wrote "My Tour in Holland," *Cornhill*, 6 (November 1862), 616–22.

[9] Catherine Gould (Mrs. Nutcombe Gould), daughter of Colonel and Mrs. James Grant. The Grants were neighbors and friends of the Trollopes at Harrow, and Catherine was a favorite with Anthony's sisters. See *Autobiography*, pp. 16, 27.

[10] John Nutcombe Gould (?1806–78), Rector of Stokeinteignhead, South Devon, from 1847 until his death; BA Wadham College, Oxford, 1827. There is no evidence of his having contributed to periodicals.

[1] Trollope's habit of comparing novel writing to shoemaking was lifelong: see Lowell to ?, 20 September 1861; Trollope to Rusden, 8 June 1876; and *Autobiography*, pp. 121, 323–24. On at least one occasion, however, the comparison was used as an argument against Trollope. Trollope had arrived, the *Saturday Review* claimed in an 1860 notice of *Castle Richmond*, "at the point when he makes a novel just as he might make a pair of shoes, with a certain workmanlike satisfaction in turning out a good article, but with little of the freshness and zest which marked his earlier productions" (19 May 1860, pp. 643–44). The *Saturday Review's* notice is reprinted in Smalley, p. 113, though its shoemaking analogy was first discussed by P. D. Edwards, *N&Q*, n.s. 15 (November 1968), 419–20.

All trades are now uphill work, & require a man to suffer much disappointment, and this trade more almost than any other. I was at it for years & wrote ten volumes before I made a shilling—, I say all this, which is very much in the guise of a sermon, because I must endeavor to make you understand that a man or woman must learn the tricks of his trade before he can *make money* by writing.

As regards the Cornhill magazine, hitherto nothing has been published but articles from persons on the staff—i e bespoken articles from persons known as writers to the Editor or proprietor. If Gould likes to send up an article, I will ensure that it shall be read. That is all that I can do— I have myself nothing to do with any part but my own story— But I can secure so much for you, & will do so very willingly. The Manager of the magazine told me the other day that he had 2,000 articles lying by him from persons not on the staff—i e, outsiders. Of course it is not possible that a quarter of them should be read.

I have been very sorry to hear that Mrs. Grant[2] suffered so much. I heard from Perry[3] that you were with her the other day, and I was very anxious to go down to Hillingdon;[4] but I was forced to go out of town, and you had gone before I returned. Peregrine seems to feel confident that it is only an affair of time & that she will recover in a month or two. Peregrine was to have been with me this week, but he could not leave Anna, whom he thought was weak. His boy Wyrley is with my boys here.

I do hope I may before long have an opportunity of seeing you & Gould here. I can safely say that there is no one I would sooner have under my own roof than yourself— I am 14 miles out of town on the Norwich line of railway. My house is Waltham house Waltham X.

My wife would send her love but she is not here at this moment.

always yours most sincerely
Any Trollope

To Herbert Watkins[5]

MS Parrish Collection. SB 87.

13 April 1860   Waltham House
My dear Sir.

I think the portrait as it now stands will do very well. It looks uncommon feirce [*sic*], as that of a dog about to bite; but that I fear is the nature of the animal portrayed.

---

[2] Mrs. Gould's mother, Mary Penelope Grant (1795–1861), widow of Colonel Grant (*d.* 1852).

[3] Peregrine Birch (1817–98), a clerk in the House of Lords; his wife Anna was a sister of Mrs. Gould.

[4] A town in Middlesex, west of London, where Mrs. Grant lived.

[5] Herbert Watkins, photographer, Regent Street.

The lighter colored copy on the back ground of which there is a smudge, seemed to us to be the better of the two.

Will you let me have two colored copies and one plain, with frames— the frames not to be very fine— And if you will oblige me by letting me know the price I will send you a check.

Yours faithfully

H Watkins Esq   Anthony Trollope

To ?

MS Parrish Collection.

25 April 1860   Waltham
My dear Sir.

I have asked Mrs. & Miss Coulton[6] to dine with me on Tuesday next. My brother also will be with me. He comes to London on Tuesday morning. Will you come down on that day, of course I can give you a bed? 5–10 pm is a good train, & I shall probably go down by it myself. Your train up is at 10—am. My house is less than half a mile from the Waltham Station.

Yours ever
Any Trollope

To George Smith

MS Bodleian. *Commentary*, p. 216; B 88.

Garlants hotel[7]

8 May 1860   Suffolk Street.
My dear Sir.

Touching the story for the C. M. wanted for six numbers, I think I could do one that would not be known as mine by intrinsic evidence. I have the story, that is to say the plot, but the scene is laid in Italy. In such case it would be indispensable that I should know at once, as I shall myself be going to Florence this month, if this Committee be brought to an end.[8] I fancy the Italian story would be less easily recognized than

---

[6] Miss Sophia Coulton (*b.* 1806), an author whom Trollope later recommended to the Royal Literary Fund for assistance (see Trollope to the Committee of the Royal Literary Fund, 2 November 1863, and Trollope to Blewitt, 11 May 1866). The Mrs. Coulton referred to is probably the widow of Sophia Coulton's brother David.

[7] Trollope frequently made Garlant's Hotel (later Garland's Hotel) his London residence for brief stays. (He was staying at Garlant's for the winter months when he suffered his paralytic seizure in November 1882; see Appendix D.)

[8] On 2 April Trollope had been named to a Post Office committee that was appointed after *The Times* (on 29 and 30 March) had criticized the apparent overwork, inadequate pay, and poor working conditions of postal employees in the so-called minor establishment (letter carriers, sorters, and messengers). By the end of April

Jones Brown & R.⁹ My belief however is that these things always get wind. If you really think of either let me know at once, & I will come to the city on Thursday, or perhaps in such case you could hit me here on your way to Cornhill. In such case name your hour on that day. This would save me a journey—

Yours very truly
Anthony Trollope

To George Smith

MS John Murray. SB 89.

May. 10—1860
My dear Mr. Smith.

When the mountains would not go to Mahomet, Mahomet went to the mountains. However in this case that horrid affair at the P. O. made Mahomet perform the greater part of the journey.

I called mainly to know if you could come down to Waltham on Saturday— Field[1] will be there & my brother. Field goes back (with his wife) the same evening. I will keep you over the Sunday if Mrs. Smith[2] will spare you—if not you can go back on Sunday morning, or in short do any thing else you may please.

Let me have a line to Garlant's hotel.

Suffolk Street
Pall Mall,

where I hang out till Saturday morning—

On that other matter I will speak when I see you—but get Rd. King if you can.

Yours ever
faithfully
Any Trollope

Rowland Hill had suspended the committee, which he regarded as an intrigue against him, pending the appointment of a new Postmaster General. This was the Duke of Argyll, who created a second committee, with Trollope again a member, which heard evidence from 19 May to 2 July and reported on 21 July. Its recommendations for improving pay and conditions for the lower grades of postal employees included ending the recent system of classification, and returning to promotion by seniority (since promotion by merit deprived many efficient workers of advancement). Trollope and Tilley felt strongly on the question of promotion, as they did on the unsuitability of Civil Service examinations for entrants to the minor establishment, a subject on which they had given evidence to the Select Committee on Civil Service Appointments on 26 April 1860 (*Parl. Papers 1860*, IX [440], 122–44). In regard to promotion by seniority at the lower levels, Trollope and Tilley prevailed: see Trollope to Tilley, 13 June 1860; also see Trollope to Lowell, 2 September 1862, n. 6.

[9] Trollope never wrote the Italian novel. Smith serialized *Brown, Jones, and Robinson* in the *Cornhill*; see Trollope to Smith, 6 July 1860.

[1] Clearly a slip for "Fields": James T. Fields was in London at the time.

[2] Elizabeth Smith (1831–1914), née Blakeway; she married George Smith in 1854.

To George Smith

MS John Murray. SB 90.

16 May. 1860
"Was it not a lie?"   Waltham
My dear Sir.

The above, taking the words from the text, is I should say the best legend for the picture. I am glad that Millais found a subject in Chap. 16, but the plate will illustrate the last line in the volume![3]

Yours always
Anthony Trollope

To George Smith

MS John Murray. B 91.

23 May 1860   Waltham house
My dear Mr. Smith.

I can hardly tell you what my feeling is about the illustration to the June No. of F. parsonage. It would be much better to omit it altogether if it be still possible,—tho I fear it is not—as the copies will have been sent out. The picture is simply ludicrous, & will be thought by most people to have been made so intentionally. It is such a burlesque on such a situation as might do for Punch, only that the execution is too bad to have passed muster for that publication.

I presume the fact to be that Mr. Millais has not time to devote to these illustrations, & if so, will it not be better to give them up? In the present instance I certainly think that you & Mr. Thackeray & I have ground for complaint.

very truly yours
Anthony Trollope

Even the face does not at all tell the story, for she seems to be sleeping— I wish it could be omitted.[4]

---

[3] Trollope was looking ahead to the publication of *Framley Parsonage* in three volumes; the first volume closed with this illustration.

[4] Millais' illustration depicts a scene at the close of chap. xvi, where Lucy Robarts, having told Lord Lufton that she cannot love him, throws herself on her bed in despair. Two contemporary reviewers commented on the appropriateness of the illustration: see *Sharpe's London Magazine*, n.s. 19 (July 1861), reprinted in Smalley, p. 130; and the *Saturday Review*, 4 May 1861, reprinted in Smalley, p. 122. See *Illustrators*, pp. 14–18.

"Was it not a lie?"

Illustration for *Framley Parsonage*, by J. E. Millais

To George Smith

Sadleir's transcript, Bodleian. SB 92.

6 June 1860.   Waltham.

My dear Mr. Smith

In the enclosed page you will see that the word "successfully" has been turned into "unsuccessfully." I wish the word to remain as first printed— i.e. "*not* altogether successfully." I don't know whether you will understand the point with reference to the paper duties.

If you carry out your queer idea about the East Indies⁵—say thro' any other writer—why not have the MS. home from time to time and bring it out in the Mag. You would have the book afterwards. Think of this.

* * *

To John Tilley

MS General Post Office, London. B 93.

June 13. 1860

I think that promotion by seniority should be the rule throughout the service, excepting always Staff appointments.⁶

Under the head of Staff appointments I intend to include all those situations to which are attached special duties of superintendence, and they may usually be defined as positions to the holders of which some special name is attached,—such as chief clerk, superintendent, inspector, or the like.

With these exceptions I think that all promotion should go by seniority, *and as a matter of right*, a certificate of general competence being only required.

I myself hold a very strong opinion that the good of the service would be best forwarded by such a rule and that the largest aggregate amount of good work would be thus secured. I presume however that it is not intended that I should argue the matter at length on the present occasion.

                                                      Anthony Trollope

⁵ Smith was contemplating a book on India: see Trollope to Smith, 3 July 1860 and 5 July 1860, n. 8, and T. A. Trollope to Trollope, 27 July 1860.

⁶ On 11 June, Tilley had requested, for the Postmaster General, Trollope's opinion "whether in regulating promotion from Class to Class, Seniority, provided the Candidate be fully competent, should, so far as your District is concerned, be the rule throughout the Service—or only in the lower classes." This inquiry, sent to heads of departments, was the result of a memorial circulated among postal clerks protesting the promotion of two clerks over the heads of men senior to them. Tilley's eventual report to the Postmaster General led to a policy (counter to Hill's position) stipulating that promotion at the lower levels would be by seniority (MSS General Post Office, London). See Trollope to Tilley, 24 May 1863.

To George Smith

Commentary, p. 216. SB 94.

28 June 1860.   Waltham.

*   *   *

I will be at the Post Office at any time at which you will say that you will call. Let me have a line to say when— Make your man ring at the private door (? private!)—nearest to the gates at the South end, *i.e.* the end of Newgate Street. I hang out within that door.

*   *   *

To George Smith

MS John Murray. *Commentary*, pp. 216–17; B 95.

3 July. 1860
Private.   G. P. O.
My dear Mr. Smith.

C & H have accepted all my terms as to the serial.[1] I therefore am not in a position to accept your proposal on that head.

On the other two matters,—the India question and the short story for the Magazine I would accede to your propositions—if it would suit you to carry them out without the serial. I.E. I would write the book on India, 2 vols, octavo say 400 pages in each volume, with three papers in the magazine for £3000—the book to come out in October 1861, and the papers in the magazine as soon as may be.

I would also give you the short story for the magazine—8 numbers 16 pages for each, to be inserted in any eight continuous months between October 1861 and October 1862—for £600—i e £75—a number.

I should certainly like to do the India book, but will not break my heart if the plan falls to the ground. Per se going to India is a bore,—but it would suit me professionally.

Even should you accede, the matter must still remain partly undecided till I hear whether or no I get the leave. I do not think I should have any difficulty.

I shall not be in town again till Friday. Shall I come to you then or you to me. I shall be here at 11.30 am, if that would suit you, or would be with you at 11am in Cornhill. I will then have with me the 8 remaining numbers of the Framley P.—that is to say the whole *"womb of time."*

Yours always
Anthony Trollope

[1] On 3 July, Chapman & Hall agreed to pay Trollope £2,500 (£125 for each of twenty monthly parts) for part and book rights to *Orley Farm*; after the first 10,000 copies, half interest in the copyright and half of all further proceeds were to go to Trollope, an arrangement that eventually netted him £3,135. The novel, Trollope's first venture in the shilling-part format so much associated with Dickens, ran from

To George Smith

MS Bodleian.

July 4 [5]. 1860　　　　　　　　　　　　　　　　　Waltham
My dear Mr. Smith.

I will leave the Mss as I go by tomorrow, Friday, morning. I shall, I fear, be too early to see you. There is no inconvenience at all in my calling, & if I sd. find you at 11. tant mieux.

If not, I shall be at the P.O. at any time up to 4.

As regards B. J. & R. I did intend the whole copyright for the £600— but I confess your desires in this respect detract from the otherwise pleasant prospects which you hold out.[8]

　　　　　　　　　　　　　　　　　Yours always
　　　　　　　　　　　　　　　　　Any Trollope

To George Smith

MS Bodleian. Excerpt, Hamer, p. 212.

July 6. 1860　　　　　　　　　　　　　　　　　Waltham
My dear Sir.

I send you back the agreement signed as to Brown Jones & Robinson. It is all right.[9]

I also send you a receipt for the £1000 for Framley, & thank you for your more than prompt payment.

In giving you the Mss. I had not intended to dun you for the money.

　　　　　　　　　　　　　　　very faithfully yours
G. Smith Esq　　　　　　　　　　　Anthony Trollope

If the receipt be not sufficient, word another in any way that may be so.

March 1861 through October 1862. Sadleir notes that "Smith had clearly expressed an interest in *Orley Farm*, inquiring whether Chapman & Hall were able to give the story the serial publicity that the *Cornhill* could offer" (*Commentary*, p. 217).

[8] Smith replied the same day: "We must make up our mind to abandon the Indian Project—but we shall be glad to make arrangements with you for the publication of 'Jones Brown & Robinson' in the Magazine—on the terms stated in your note." (MS Bodleian.)

[9] In sending Trollope the agreement giving him £600 for the absolute copyright, Smith had added, "if you desire any alteration it shall be made" (MS Bodleian). The novel, serialized in the *Cornhill* from August 1861 through March 1862, was a failure, and Smith delayed publication in book form until 1870. Trollope later wrote: "I think that *Brown, Jones, and Robinson* was the hardest bargain I ever sold to a publisher." (*Autobiography*, p. 161.)

To G. H. Lewes[1]

MS Yale. B 96.

July 9. 1860   Waltham Cross
My dear Sir.

I have asked the Duke of Argyll[2] for a nomination for your son[3] to the situation of supplementary clerk in the Secretary's office in the G.P.O. This is by far the best position in which a lad can enter our office & the only one,—putting aside one or two positions which are exceptional—which I would recommend a friend to seek for a youth.

I should not, naturally, have mentioned this to you till I had received the Dukes answer,—were it not for this reason. There are now two existing vacancies, & he may give me a recommendation for one. It is no great favor as there are always 3 or 4 nominated, between whom there is a competitive examination. I tell you this now, as if you think well of the matter, it may be expedient that your son should employ himself with reference to it. The subjects of examination are Handwriting Dictation in English—which means spelling. Ordinary arithmetic including the rule of three, & Composition. A young man may volunteer on other things—but that which is essential is a fair knowledge of figures, and a fair knowledge of English. The subject on which most men break down is spelling.

Should the Duke give me the nomination I will explain to you what is the nature of the situation. The office is the one in which I entered the service.

You will I am sure understand that I am by no means certain of the nomination, & that I only mention the circumstance to you in the present stage, as the time may be of value.[4]

Yours very truly
G H Lewes Esq   Anty Trollope

---

[1] George Henry Lewes (1817–78), the distinguished literary critic and student of philosophy; author of *The Life of Goethe* (1855); consort of George Eliot, with whom he had been living since 1854, three years after the collapse of his marriage. He wrote on science for the *Cornhill* and helped edit the journal for a time after Thackeray's retirement. Lewes and Trollope became intimate friends.

[2] George Douglas Campbell (1823–1900), 8th Duke of Argyll; Postmaster General from 1855 to 1858, and again in 1860; Secretary of State for India, 1868–74.

[3] Charles Lee Lewes (1842–91), the eldest of the three surviving sons of Lewes's marriage.

[4] Lewes noted in his journal for 23 July 1860: "Among the two or three people I spoke to about [Charles] was Anthony Trollope, and of him I only asked information, yet he most kindly interested himself and wrote to the Duke of Argyll for a nomination to compete for a vacancy in the Post Office." (*George Eliot Letters*, III, 326.)

To Richard Monckton Milnes[5]

MS Trinity College, Cambridge.

July 15—1860   Waltham Cross
My dear Sir.
Should I be asking you to do me too great a favor, in begging you to
put my name down for the Cosmopolitan?[6] If you will do so, I will ask
Tom Taylor[7] to second me—
                              very faithfully yours
                              Anthony Trollope

To George Smith

MS Taylor Collection.

July 19 1860   Waltham
My dear Mr Smith.
I send back the proof of the September number. I shall be very
anxious to see the proof of Mr Millais' illustration.
                              Yours always
                              Anthony Trollope

To G. H. Lewes

MS Yale. B 97.

July 20. 1860   Waltham X
My dear Mr. Lewes.
The tide in the affairs of your young man has so far come— May it lead
on to fortune!
You will see that the D of Argyll has given him a nomination for the
Secretary's office. He will either have to compete with 3 or 4 for one
situation or with 6 or 7 for two.
When I asked for the nomination I did not wish to tell you, & put his
name down—G—at a shot. If, as the chances are, it be not G, let me have
a line saying what it is.
You shall either here [sic] from me or from Mr. Barlow[8] on what day
he should present himself at the G.P.O.
The danger to young men educated on the continent is in spelling &
in ordinary English idioms.

---

[5] Richard Monckton Milnes (1809–85), later 1st Baron Houghton; miscellaneous
writer and politician; editor of Keats and early champion of Swinburne; patron and
intimate of many distinguished men of letters. Milnes was a friend of George Smith
and a contributor to the *Cornhill*.

[6] The Cosmopolitan Club; see Milnes to Trollope, 24 April 1861.

[7] Tom Taylor (1817–80), popular dramatist; editor of *Punch*, 1874–80.

[8] Oldham Thomas Barlow, private secretary to the Postmaster General.

My belief is that if you took the 12 most popular authors in England they would all be beaten.

For myself I should not dream of passing. I sd. break down in figures & spelling too, not to talk of handwriting.

I regard a situation in the Civil Service—if it be a decent situation, as those in the Secretary's office G.P.O. are—to be valuable in this respect. It neither necessitates nor tends to create dishonesty, and it leaves ample time for other work. The law, if strictly followed, does tend to create dishonesty & leaves no time for other work. The church, if this pill can be swallowed, incapacitates a man for most other work. And medicine requires all a man can possibly give. I know no basis for a literary career, so good as an appointment in the C Service—always presuming the man to be one who must live by the sweat of his brow.

Yours always
Any Trollope

To George Smith
MS Bodleian. Commentary, pp. 217–18; B 98.

July 21. 1860   Waltham.
My dear Mr Smith—

Many thanks for the Magazine. The Crawley family is very good,[9] & I will now consent to forget the flounced dress. I saw the *very pattern of that dress* some time after the picture came out.

There is a scene which would do well for an illustration. It is a meeting between Lady Lufton & the Duke of Omnium at the top of Miss Dunstable's staircase.[1] I can not say the number or chapter as you have all the Mss. But I think it would come into the second vol. If Mr. Millais would look at it I think he would find that it would answer. If so I would send him the vol. of Dr. Thorne in which there is a personal description of the Duke of O.

Yours very truly
Any Trollope

The R. Paper[2] is not so severe as I thought it would be—but it is better so.

[9] Millais' illustration for *Framley Parsonage* in the August number of the *Cornhill*.

[1] The illustration appeared in the October number; for Trollope's belief that authors should select the subjects for illustrations, see Trollope to Smith, 3 November 1862.

[2] Thackeray's Roundabout Paper, "On Screens in Dining-Rooms," *Cornhill*, 2 (August 1860), 252–56. This rebuked the *Saturday Review* for the hypocrisy of its 23 June 1860 piece entitled "Newspaper Gossip," which denounced, and by its denunciation gave wide circulation to, an offensive article by Edmund Yates in the *New York Times* of 26 May, 1860, containing an attack on Smith and Thackeray and a second-hand account of one of Smith's dinners for *Cornhill* contributors. This flare-up was a prolongation of the celebrated "Garrick Club Affair," which pitted Thackeray against

To G. H. Lewes

MS Yale. B 99.

July 23. 1860.   Waltham Cross
My dear Lewes.

I have written to have the name altered from George to Charles.

I do not know exactly when the examination will take place, but it will not be long [? after the] first. I will let you know as soon as I can, or else your son shall hear from Mr. Barlow.

Rejected candidates are not as a rule allowed to present themselves again, tho' there is no reason why a rejected candidate should not have another nomination to that or any other office. The reason why they cannot come forward again is this. If they were allowed to do so; they would constantly present themselves, & the patronage book of the Postmaster General would always be encumbered with the same names. Indeed men would hold on till they did get in, and the competitive system would become clogged. I can explain this to you more fully when I see you.

Yours very faithfully
Anthony Trollope

To Mr. Gibbon[3]

MS Yale.

July 24. 1860   Waltham
My dear Mr Gibbon

I & my wife are very happy in the thought that Mrs. Gibbon & Emily are coming to us on Saturday.

I dont know whether any thing has been said about it, but *as a matter of course* you come with them. I called in Half acre street yesterday but found no one at home.

Yours always affectionately
Anthony Trollope

Yates and, more importantly, against Dickens, who championed Yates. Trollope had innocently given rise to this further exacerbation of ill-feelings by his indiscreet talk with Yates. For details, see *Commentary*, pp. 213–14; and Gordon N. Ray, *Thackeray: The Age of Wisdom*, pp. 305–8.

[3] Unidentified; perhaps the same Gibbon to whom Trollope wrote on 12 February 1866.

To ?

MS Parrish Collection. B 100.

July 25—1860   Waltham House
Dear Sir.

Many thanks for the book you have sent me, which I have just received & will read.

As regards the negroes, I in writing of them have written of them as free men; you in pleading for them, plead for them in their condition as slaves. I am quite as eager for their freedom as you can be, abhorring slavery on all accounts. But I have not therefore felt myself debarred for [? from] describing in what I believe to be true language the condition in which they now exist in our West Indies.[4]

Yours faithfully
Anthony Trollope

Thomas Adolphus Trollope to Trollope

MS University of Illinois.

27. July. 1860.   Florence.
My dear Anthony,

Many thanks for your letter, and for your promise of another in a few days, when you should have seen Mr. Pike;—for whose reply, I am anxious, as I need the £100 which I suppose he has by this time paid.[5]

I cannot help regretting that the Indian scheme is given up;—and I cannot well see, from what you write to me, that there was—on those grounds—sufficient reason to give it up. Why not have agreed to give Smith all he wanted, arranging for the long serial to begin when that agreed for with Chapman should come to a close? Did not Smith, at the time of making to you the threefold proposition, know that you had signed with Chapman for a serial? I am sorry for the Indian scheme; I feel confident that the book would have improved your literary position, and given you a standing among government men, and such like, which the most successful novel-writing will not do. . . .

Yrs. always
T. A. T.

---

[4] See *The West Indies and the Spanish Main*, chaps. iv and v.

[5] Probably a payment due on money invested in England. (Trollope sometimes acted for his brother in business matters.)

To George Smith

MS John Murray. *Commentary*, p. 218; B 101.

29 July 1860
Sunday   Waltham.
My dear Mr. Smith.

I will sign a dozen such receipts if your accountant wishes it—altho I was told in London last week that a lady denies that I wrote F. P. claiming to be the author herself.[6] I don't know what better compliment she could pay to the book.

I will send back Chaps 28–29–30—corrected tomorrow. I suppose I did correct 25–26–& 27, but I dont remember.

Yours always
Any Trollope

I have a story, written within the last ten days, about the Holy Land— I suppose it would not be wanted by you for the magazine. It would run 30 pages & have to be divided in two,—or three if you preferred. But, as I said, I do not presume it would be wanted, & therefore ask the question almost idly.

The name is
The Banks of Jordan.[7]

If you see it or hear of it elsewhere dont mention it as being mine. Not that I have any idea of publishing it immediately.

To [? Edward] Chapman

MS Parrish Collection.

July 31. 1860   Waltham
My dear Chapman.

Would you oblige me by sending a copy of the West Indies to
Mrs. Milton[8]
Care of John Milton Esq
War Office.
Whitehall.

I think you said some time since that you had sent one so addressed.

---

[6] "A young lady in the West Country posed to her friends and relatives as the anonymous authoress of [*Framley Parsonage*]! . . . The upshot was an interview, the most painful, George Smith declared, he ever had, when he was compelled to tell the girl's father that she had deceived him." (Leonard Huxley, *The House of Smith Elder*, pp. 112–13.)

[7] See Trollope to Smith, 1 August 1860 and 9 August 1860.

[8] Either Blanche Milton (daughter of Thomas Meyrick Field, and the wife of Trollope's cousin John Milton since 1850) or the widow of Henry Milton.

She however says that she did not get it. She is going abroad in a day or two, & wishes to take it with her.

Yours always very truly
Anthony Trollope

To Thomas Adolphus Trollope
What I Remember, pp. 394–95. B 126.

[? July 1860]

*   *   *

The lines[9] are very beautiful, and the working out of the idea is delicious. But I am inclined to think that she is illustrating an allegory by a thought, rather than a thought by an allegory. The idea of the god destroying the reed in making the instrument has, I imagine, given her occasion to declare that in the sublimation of the poet the man is lost for the ordinary purposes of man's life. It has been thus instead of being the reverse; and I can hardly believe that she herself believes in the doctrine which her fancy has led her to illustrate. A man that can be a poet is so much the more a man in becoming such, and is the more fitted for a man's best work. Nothing is destroyed, and in preparing the instrument for the touch of the musician the gods do nothing for which they need weep. The idea, however, is beautiful, and it is beautifully worked. ... In the third line of it [the seventh stanza], she loses her antithesis. She must spoil her man, as well as make a poet out of him—spoil him as the reed is spoiled. Should we not read the lines thus:

> "Yet one half beast is the great god Pan
> Or he would not have laughed by the river.
> Making a poet he mars a man;
> The true gods sigh," etc.?[1]

*   *   *

[9] Elizabeth Barrett Browning's "A Musical Instrument," *Cornhill*, 2 (July 1860), 84–85.

[1] The original reads:
> Yet half a beast is the great god Pan
> To laugh, as he sits by the river,
> Making a poet out of a man.
> The true gods sigh for the cost and pain,—
> For the reed that grows nevermore again
> As a reed with the reeds in the river.

Trollope quoted the concluding lines twice near the close of Phineas Finn's trial (*Phineas Redux*, chap. lxvii). T. A. Trollope gave Anthony's letter to Isa Blagden, who showed it to Mrs. Browning; for Mrs. Browning's lengthy reply (addressed to Miss Blagden), see *What I Remember*, pp. 395–96.

To George Smith

MS Bodleian. SB 102.

1. August. 1860   Waltham.
My dear Mr Smith.

I send you the story—if it should suit you, keep it; if not return it without scruple.[2]

If you keep it & divide in [*sic*] into two, you will find the place marked by a cross on the margin in pencil at page 26— That will be the better division.

If you divide it into three, the places will be at pages 20 (quite at the top)—and 23 marked thus ⇛ on the margin.

In either case a word or two of addition to make the recommencement less bald will be expedient.

                                        Yours always
G Smith Esq   Anthy Trollope

You will find that the whole story will run 30 pages of the Magazine. If you print it in two divisions the present name will be the best.

If you prefer three, I must change it to
                    A Ride across Palestine.

To Sampson Low

MS Parrish Collection. SB 103.

4 Augt 1860   Cambridge
My dear Sir.

I shall not be in London for the next week, but when I am I will call on you.

                                        Yours very faithfully
Sampson Low Esq   Anthony Trollope

To George Smith

MS John Murray. B 104.

9. August. 1860.   Ipswich.
My dear Mr Smith.

There shall be no rap on the knuckles. I do nothing in that line unless I am purposely rubbed against the hair. But you city publishers are so uncommonly delicate,[3] whereas anything passes at the West End! I shall

---

[2] "The Banks of the Jordan"; see Trollope to Smith, 9 August 1860.

[3] Smith rejected "The Banks of the Jordan" for its indelicacies. The story was subsequently published in the *London Review* (on 5, 12, and 19 January 1861) and later reprinted under the title "A Ride Across Palestine" in *Tales of All Countries*, Second Series (1863). See Oliphant to Trollope, ? February 1861, for the difficulties the story caused the *London Review*; and see Trollope to Thackeray, 15 November 1860, for Trollope's spirited defense of yet another story declined by the *Cornhill*.

never forget a terrible & killing correspondence which I had with W. Longman because I would make a clergyman kiss a lady whom he proposed to marry— He, the clergyman I mean; not he W Longman. But in that instance William Longman's church principles were perhaps in stake.

The affair of the saddle, and that other affair of the leg—(I think I said leg—) could be arranged; but I fear the proposal won't suit in other respects. Did you ever buy your own meat? That cutting down of 30 pages to 20, is what you proposed to the butcher when you asked him to take off the bony bit at this end, & the skinny bit at the other. You must remember that the butcher told you that nature had produced the joint bone & skin as you saw it, & that it behoved him to sell what nature had thus produced. Besides one cannot shorten a story. Little passages are sure to hang on to what is taken out— Words occur which are unintelligible because of the withdrawal of other words, & the labor of rearrangement is worse than the original task.

And then, I can by no means part with the copyright. It is one of many stories written or to be written which will come out in subsequent shapes —I trust to my profit. I have, indeed, already arranged for the republication of one such volume.

As to the sum named, had you taken the story, leaving me the copyright and sent me 50 guineas, I should have been satisfied & said nothing— But I am doing better than that with the others. Much better than double that, including the republication & copyright.

As to the smoothness of skin, beard &. I had thought of that—but I should have declared my mystery at once, had I described those feminine appearances. Besides it behoved me not to make my man out to be too much of a fool in not having made the discovery himself.

Do not tell of me if you hear of my story in the "Birmingham Halfpenny Cyclopedia" or the "London Laborers Social Friend."[4]

You can return the Mss at your leisure to Waltham Cross, which is my present address.

Yours always
Anthony Trollope

To G. H. Lewes

MS Yale. B 105; *George Eliot Letters*, VIII, 269.

Augt 9. 1860   Waltham
My dear Lewes.

I hear that C. L. Lewes was at the head of the Poll at that Civil Service examination, & I suppose I may congratulate him in being a Queens ser-

---

[4] Invented titles. Trollope is alluding humorously to the cheap periodicals associated with mechanics' institutes and other agencies promoting working-class education and self-help.

vant. I hope I shall soon shake hands with him over his desk at the Post Office.

Do not let him begin life with any idea that his profession is inferior to others. Men may live as vegetables, or worse again as dead sticks, in the Civil Service. But so they may, & so many do, in the church & as lawyers. But in the Civil Service, now a days, exertion will give a man a decent gentleman's income not late in life, if it be accompanied by intellects not below par. I do not know that more can be said of any profession except that in others there are great prizes. To compensate this the Civil Service allows a man, who has in him the capacity for getting prizes, to look for them elsewhere. A government clerk, who is not wedded to pleasure, may follow any pursuit without detriment to his public utility. One such man in our days edits the Edinbro, a great gun in his own way;[5] another has written the best poem of these days;[6] a third supplies all our theatres with their new plays;[7] and a fourth plies a small literary trade as a poor novellist.[8] We boast also of artists, philosophers, newspaper politicians, & what not.

Do not therefore let him think that six hours a day at the shop is to be the Be all & End all of his life.

Yours always
Any Trollope

To G. H. Lewes

MS Yale. B 106; George Eliot Letters, VIII, 270.

August. 14 1860
My dear Lewes.

There are two men just appointed to the Secretarys office, your son being one. The man who first comes to duty stands senior. Let your son present himself at once to Mr. Parkhurst[9]—at whose table I am now writing. If he then wants a few days leave of absence he can get it, but it may [give] him one step in seniority.

I hear that he passed quite a first rate examination. He got the full numbers for general intelligence which is *very* unusual.

very faithfully yours
Anthony Trollope

[5] Henry Reeve (1813–95), editor of the *Edinburgh Review* from 1855 to 1895, was Registrar to the Judicial Committee of the Privy Council from 1843 to 1887.

[6] Henry Taylor (1800–1886), later Sir Henry, author of verse dramas and miscellaneous prose, worked in the Colonial Office from 1824 to 1872. Trollope thought very highly of Taylor's verse and listed Taylor among his eighteen "giants" of English literature, giving special praise to *Philip Van Artevelde* (1834), to which reference is made here (*The New Zealander*, pp. 174–75). See Trollope to Taylor, 3 February 1865.

[7] Tom Taylor was Secretary to the Board of Health and subsequently to the Sanitary Department.

[8] Trollope himself.

[9] Rodie Parkhurst, chief clerk of the Secretary's Office, General Post Office.

To Edward Chapman

MS John Rylands Library. B 107.

Augt 23—1860   Waltham
My dear Chapman.
I send back No. 1—which you may now consider quite complete as far
as I am concerned.[1] You shall not have so much trouble with the others.
Can I take the 8 Commandment to Florence?[2] That is can you spare
it till the end of October? Not that I think it worth carrying so far, but
Tom may like to see it. It is —— to my way of thinking.

Yours always
Any Trollope

The boys are very much obliged to you, & declare they'll call on you
again next holydays.

To George Smith

MS Leeds City Public Library.

[1860][3]
My dear Mr Smith.
Do you know where your Editor[4] is—& whether [he] is get-at-able. I
want if possible to get you & him down here before every body has miz-
zled.[5] Say some day in the last week in the month— Can you come if I get
him? can he come if I get you? We will have a seance and a medium. I
have a table uncommonly good at sneezing—

Yours very truly
Anthy Trollope

To George Smith

MS (photocopy) UCLA. B 108.

Sept. 15—1860.   Cambridge.
My dear Smith.
Many thanks for the copy of Millais' illustration which I like very
much.[6] The scene makes a better picture than the ladies bustle—however

[1] Proof of *Orley Farm* (though the first of the shilling parts did not appear until
March 1861).

[2] *The Eighth Commandment* (1860), a discussion of literary property and copyright
for drama by the novelist and dramatist Charles Reade (1814–84).

[3] Probably written before September 1860 (when Trollope dropped the "Mr." from
his salutation to Smith).

[4] Thackeray.

[5] Slang for disappeared suddenly, decamped.

[6] "Lady Lufton and the Duke of Omnium" (chap. xxix), for the October number of
Framley Parsonage.

I shall not mean to say a word more about that. Thanks also for the spectacles. I will call & pay the first time I am in London. I go, I think, 22 Inst, could you let me have a copy of the Mag by that time? If so I can take it out with me.

I wrote to my brother saying that you were to have a second Italian article by 12 October, & you will have it without fail.[1] What about any beyond that? I do not mean for the next consecutive numbers, because that would be giving you too much of our Italian colony.—But as to other similar articles after a month or two? I should like to know whether you will think more desirable as my brother would probably write them for others, if you do not want them. I do not want an instant or decisive answer to this; but should be glad to let him know what are your or Thackerays ideas about it, as soon as you have an idea—or he.

Yours always
Any Trollope

To George Smith

MS John Murray. B 109.

22 September 1860   Waltham house
My dear Smith.

Yesterday as I was sitting with my wife over the "damp" number of the last,—rather next—Cornhill, a large parcel arrived from the railway. One attains by experience an intuitive perception whether or no a parcel is or is not agreeable; whether it should be opened on one's study table, or sent down to the butlers pantry. This parcel I myself opened at the moment, & took from it fold after fold of packing paper—varying from the strongest brown to a delicate tissue of silver shade—till I reached,—a travelling bag.

"I never ordered it" said I angrily.

"It's a present," said my wife.

"Gammon— It's a commission to take to Florence for some dandy and I'll be ——"

For a moment I fancy she imagined it was intended for her, but we came at once on a brandy flask & a case of razors, and that illusion was dispelled.

"It's the lady who said she wrote your book intending to make you some amends," she suggested.

And so we went on but never got near the truth.

No one is more accessible to a present than I am. I gloat over it like a child, and comfort myself in school hours by thinking how nice it will be to go back to it in play time. In that respect I have by no means outgrown my round jacket, & boy's appurtenances.

Whether or no I shall ever become a proficient in using all those toilet

---

[1] "Italy's Rival Liberators," *Cornhill*, 2 (November 1860), 591–96.

elegancies with which I now find myself supplied,—gold pins, silver soap-dishes, & cut glass, I cannot say. I feel a little like a hog in armour, but will do my best.

However let me thank you sincerely for your kind remembrance. I argue from your good nature that you are satisfied with the work I have done for you, & that after all is better than any present. I also feel that I owe you some cadeau of worth, seeing that you have brought me in contact with readers to [be] counted by hundreds of thousands, instead of by hundreds.

Thanks also for the Deux Mondes.[8] I should not have seen it, but for your kindness. That number I am glad to have, but, as a rule, for dull, hard reading, with nothing in it, recommend me to the deux mondes.

I will tell my brother what you say. You may be sure of the six pages exactly. The first time I am in London I will call in to see the drawings on wood. I am now just starting for Italy.

Yours very faithfully
Anthony Trollope

To William Little[9]

MS Historical Society of Pennsylvania. B 110.

Waltham House
Waltham Cross.

22 Sept 1860

Sir.

I am not able to write a continuous story or romance for the London Review, as my hands are full in respect to work of that description.

I am writing a set of stories of which the first series will be republished in May next, called,—or then to be called, "Tales of all Countries"— I intend to complete a second series, eight in number, and if they would suit Dr. Mackay[1] I could make terms with him for bringing them out in his periodical from the beginning of next year. None of the second series have been as yet published or disposed of. Indeed one only is as yet written.

The stories would average in length 20 pages of the Cornhill Maga-

---

[8] Smith was calling Trollope's attention to E. D. Forgues's article on *The Bertrams* and *Castle Richmond*, "Une Thèse sur le mariage en deux romans," *Revue des Deux Mondes*, 29 (15 September 1860), 369–98. Forgues praised Trollope's almost scientific detachment in presenting his characters and their moral dilemmas.

[9] William Little, business manager and one of the owners of the *London Review and Weekly Journal*, a new periodical that had begun publication on 7 July 1860.

[1] Charles Mackay (1814–99), editor of the *London Review*; previously editor of the *Glasgow Argus* and the *Illustrated London News*. Mackay did not think that Little was a very good manager of the *London Review*, since Little spent three-fifths of the journal's subscribed capital on a huge advertising campaign, putting large placards "on all the vacant walls and hoardings of the metropolis," including those of "the un-literary slums of the populous East End" (Charles Mackay, *Through the Long Day* [1887], II, 208).

zine; or at any rate should not be less than that. My price would be £50 for each story, the right of republishing being mine, after, say six months. My intention would be to republish them in May 1862.[2]

I am
Sir
Your obedient Servant
Anthony Trollope

W. Little Esq
"London Review" Office

To [? O. T.] Barlow

Bell, Book, & Radmall Catalogue, No. 2 (1975).

September 1860.   Post Office
Trollope writes concerning the appointment of a Mr. John Knowles, presumably to a Post Office position.

To George Smith

MS John Murray. B 111.

October 1. 1860   Florence
My dear Smith.

I—and the travelling bag—are here all safe. And *we*, with my brother are thinking of going to Naples, in about ten days. I need hardly tell you that Naples is at the present moment the centre of all that is most interesting in Italy. I write to you now especially, to know whether you would like to have an article on the state of affairs at Naples—and between Garibaldi and Rome,—from my brother. It would be dated from Naples, and as he would have the means of knowing what is being done there from those who are really engaged in settling or endeavouring to settle the affairs of Italy I think he would give you an interesting paper. In this case I would bring it back with me in ample time for you to put it into type for your December number. i e. the number printed & published in November. You must answer me at once as we propose to start on 10th. of this month. Address to Florence. As there would be but one article on Naples I would suggest that the length should exceed the six pages, as it would be very difficult to tell the story in that space—say 8— or if possible 10. But your orders in this respect should be obeyed. The other article on Tuscan politics will leave this on 6th. of this month, & will be with you by or before the 12th.

Yours always
Anthony Trollope

[2] By an agreement dated 22 December 1860, the *London Review* purchased serial rights to eight stories at £50 each; it published, however, only three of these stories, disposing of the others elsewhere (see Trollope to Chapman, 1 January 1862). All eight were reprinted in *Tales of All Countries*, Second Series (1863).

To George Smith

MS John Murray. B 112.

October 27. 1860.   Florence
My dear Smith.

Your letter of the 8th. did not reach us,—i e me & my brother till our return from Rome. I had calculated that I might have got your reply before we started on the 12th., but it did not arrive till we had gone. On reaching Rome we found that we could not get on to Naples without running more risk than the occasion warranted. There was between us & it a Scylla & Charybdis of Garibaldian & Neapolitan armies which made any such attempt very imprudent; and consequently we remained at Rome.

With reference to your proposed article my brother will write the ten pages for the December Number—to be ready, in your hands, by 12 November—*dated from Rome* & giving you the state of things as existing there; but *quite understanding* that you are not in any way bound to take it unless you please to do so.[3] That you will doubtless think the best thing he can now do. You will get this letter about 1 November, & could not receive it in time to say yes or no. If you do not wish the article on Rome, you can send it to me in England.

I shall be home about the 5th. or 6th. & will see you soon after that. I shall be glad to hear your opinion of the "Temple Bar."[4]

If you will kindly pay into Coutts' to the account of T. Adolphus Trollope what money is due to my brother, he will be much obliged.

very truly yours
Anthony Trollope

After all it seems probable that Rome will become the capital of the united Italia.

To George Smith

MS John Murray. B 113.

6 Nov. 1860   Waltham
My dear Smith.

The story[5] shall be done, & shall be with you without fail by 11 am Tuesday 13th. Instant—18 pages exact. I say 18 that you may be able to make sure, & thinking that that number may be most suitable—being the mean of 16 & 20— If 20 (twenty) will suit you better, & if you will say so by return, you shall have 20 *exact*[6]— If I don't hear again from you it will be 18—

[3] "The Pope's City and the Pope's Protectors," *Cornhill*, 2 (December 1860), 719–28.
[4] The *Temple Bar* had just begun publication. For efforts to persuade Trollope to become its nominal editor, see de Fauche to Trollope, 5 August 1861.
[5] "Mrs. General Talboys"; see Trollope to Thackeray, 15 November 1860.
[6] Underlined twice.

It shall be among the most inward of my inward things—no one being privy to it but my wife—

Yours always
Anty Trollope

Have no scruple in saying 20—if that amount will be most convenient—

I quite understand & agree to your terms as to the use of the copyright of the story—

To George Smith
MS John Murray. SB 114.

6. November. 1860.   Waltham X.

My dear Smith.

I saw Fred Chapman[7] to day after I saw you. And singularly enough— looking to the remark you made as to the date at which my serial[8] was to commence—he asked me to allow it to come out for 1 March instead of 1 May— I told [him] I would if you had no objection, but would not if you had. If you think it would not do your magazine any harm I should be glad to commence on 1 March, but will not press it against your wish. Let me have a line in reply.

Yours very faithfully
Anthony Trollope

George Smith to Trollope
MS Bodleian.

November 7th. 1860   65, CORNHILL, E.C.

My dear Mr. Trollope

I have no objection to the commencement of the serial in March— If all authors were as frank as you are, and all Publishers were as considerate as Mr Chapman (you will remember that he let us have "Framley Parsonage")[9] and as some one else, what a happy family we should be! Many thanks for the promise of 18 pages—that quantity will fit in exactly as we stand at present.

believe me
Yours sincerely

Anthony Trollope Esqre   G Smith

---

[7] Frederic Chapman (1823–95), a cousin of Edward Chapman, had entered Chapman & Hall in 1841 and had become a partner in 1847; he became head of the firm in 1864 on Edward's retirement. Trollope was closely associated with Frederic Chapman and this publishing house until his death. From the reference to Frederic here, and because Frederic signed agreements with Trollope for "self and partner," it appears that Trollope was dealing primarily with Frederic even before Edward's retirement.

[8] *Orley Farm*.

[9] In 1859 Edward Chapman had agreed to release Trollope from his contract for *Castle Richmond*, a story set in Ireland, if the novel suited the *Cornhill*; Smith, how-

To George Smith

MS Bodleian. *Commentary*, p. 221; B 115.

Novr. 10. 1860.   Waltham.
My dear Smith.

I shall be in London on Tuesday & will call to settle the important question as to the young lady's copy of the A. Nights.[1] Will you kindly send in to Milroy, telling him not to pack the box till I call.

Thanks for the letter about Miss Blagdens book.[2] I do not suppose you will make a fortune by it;—nor, I suppose, will she. Can you say when it will be published; and also can I tell her that she may have the sum which the American publisher will give for sheets? Do not forget that she wants to describe the novel as by

Ivory Beryl.[3]

I have completed Mrs. Talboys. My wife, criticising it, says that it is ill-natured. I would propose you should call it

Mrs. General Talboys.[4]

—I hope & trust that there is not & never has been any real General of that name. If so we must alter it. I shall hereafter call it "Mrs. Talboys at Rome"—but you will probably choose to sink the Rome, as you have an article in the same number about the eternal city.

Mr. Tilley will leave the Mss at the paper on Monday morning. It is addressed to you privately. I suppose you can let me [have] a proof *in duplicate.*

Yours always
Anty Trollope

To George Smith

MS John Murray. B 116.

13. Nov. 1860.   Piccadilly.
My dear Smith.

I have just been with Mrs. Stirling[5] who wishes to get from me permission to dramatise some scenes out of Framley parsonage— She wishes to have it brought out at Drury Lane before Xmas. Have you any ob-

---

ever, preferred "an English tale . . . with a clerical flavour," and Trollope interrupted his writing of the Irish novel to take up *Framley Parsonage* (*Autobiography*, pp. 141–42).

[1] See Trollope to Field, 15 November 1860.

[2] *Agnes Tremorne* (1861). Isa Blagden (?1818–73) had lived in Florence from 1849, where she had developed a wide circle of friends including the Brownings and the T. A. Trollopes (she tended Theodosia Trollope during Theodosia's last illness).

[3] The pseudonym was not used.

[4] See Trollope to Thackeray, 15 November 1860.

[5] Mrs. Fanny Stirling (1813–95), the actress. The scheme for a dramatic version of *Framley Parsonage* came to nothing.

jection? The difficulty seems to be that they will have to guess at the ending, but I do not think this could possibly do the magazine any harm—
Will you let me have a line. If you write tomorrow address to Stafford. If
on Thursday—to the Secretary's office, G. P. O. to be forwarded. I have
promised to see her & give her an answer on Friday.

Yours very truly
Anthy Trollope

To George Smith

MS Bodleian. SB 119.

Nov. 15. 1860   Lichfield[6]
My dear Smith.

Mrs Stirling wd. of course guess my ending. Indeed she had guessed it,
for she told it me. I will therefore make her understand that you wd. not
wish it to be done till the whole thing has been published. I left it entirely dependent on your will.

Could you send me back the Mss of Mrs. Talboys. And of course there
will be no printed copy of it left in your hands or Thackerays. I am
sorry you put yourself to the Expense of printing it— I need hardly say
that you will owe me nothing.

very faithfully
Anthony Trollope

To Kate Field[7]

MS Boston Public Library. *Commentary*, pp. 221–22; B 117.

November 15. 1860.   Waltham Cross.
My dear Miss Field.

I have fulfilled my promise as far as the Arabian Nights[8] are concerned, having seen a copy put into the box which is to take out to

---

[6] A town in Staffordshire ten miles north of Birmingham.

[7] Mary Katherine Keemle Field (1838–96), American journalist, actress, lecturer,
and advocate of women's rights. Trollope developed a long-standing romantic attachment to Kate Field, whom he had met in October 1860 at his brother's home in
Florence. Trollope later wrote: "There is an American woman, of whom not to
speak in a work purporting to [be] a memoir of my own life would be to omit all
allusion to one of the chief pleasures which has graced my later years. In the last
fifteen years she has been, out of my own family, my most chosen friend. She is a ray
of light to me, from which I can always strike a spark by thinking of her." (*Autobiography*, p. 316.)

[8] Kate Field wrote to a friend: "Anthony Trollope is a very delightful companion.
I see a great deal of him. He has promised to send me a copy of the 'Arabian Nights'
(which I have never read) in which he intends to write 'Kate Field, from the Author,'
and to write me a four-page letter on condition that I answer it." (Lilian Whiting,
Kate Field: A Record [Boston, 1899], p. 123.)

Beatrice her saddle. I hope it will do you good mentally & morally. (I saw yesterday over a little school this announcement put up—"In this establishment morals and mentals are inculcated"; and if your education be not completed, I would recommend you to try a term or two. The mentals may be unnecessary, but the morals might do you good.) Don't attempt to read them,—the An. Nts.—through at a burst, but take them slowly & with deliberation & you will find them salutary.

I am beginning to feel towards you & your whereabouts as did your high-flown American correspondent. Undying art, Italian skies, the warmth of southern, sunny love, the poetry of the Arno and the cloud clapt Apennines, are beginning again to have all the charms which distance gives. I enjoy these delicacies in England—when I am in Italy in the flesh, my mind runs chiefly on grapes, roast chesnuts, cigars, and lemonade. Nevertheless let me council [*sic*] you in earnest not to throw away time that is precious. If in some five years time you shall hear & read of precious things in Florence which then you do not know, you will not readily forgive yourself in that you did not learn to know them when the opportunity was at your hand.

Give my love to Miss Blagden. I shall write to her as soon as I can answer her letter. And tell . . .[9] triumph at Florence.

Remember me most kindly to Cleopatra—to whom by the bye I propose to send a very highly bred asp, warranted of unadulterated poison. Recommend her to that picture of Guido's with reference to the elegant use of the animal.[1] Tell her also and tell yourself that I shall be delighted to see you both here when homesickness takes you away from Florence. Not that it is homesickness with you in the least. . . .

I do not in the least know your address—so send this to the care of my brother. Kate Field, near the Pitti might not reach you.

*   *   *

To W. M. Thackeray

MS Parrish Collection. *New York Times Book Review*, 13 July 1941, p. 18; *Letters of W. M. Thackeray*, IV, 206–7; B 118.

November 15. 1860   Waltham Cross.
My dear Thackeray.

I trust you to believe me when I assure you that I feel no annoyance as against you at the rejection of my story.[2] An impartial Editor must do

---

[9] Four lines are cut away from the manuscript; several more lines are similarly cut away at the end of the next paragraph.

[1] Guido Reni's *Death of Cleopatra*, in the Pitti Palace, Florence.

[2] "Mrs. General Talboys." The story was subsequently published in the *London Review* (2 February 1861), and reprinted in *Tales of All Countries*, Second Series (1863). See Oliphant to Trollope, ? February 1861, for the stir the story provoked when it first appeared.

his duty. Pure morals must be supplied. And the owner of the responsible name must be the Judge of the purity. A writer for a periodical
makes himself subject to this judgement by undertaking such work; and
a man who allows himself to be irritated because judgement goes against
himself is an ass. So much I say, that I may not be set down by you as
disgusted, or angry, or malevolent. But a few words I must say also in
defence of my own muse.

I will not allow that I am indecent, and profess that squeamishness—
in so far as it is squeamishness and not delicacy—should be disregarded
by a writer. I of course look back for examples to justify myself in alluding to a man with illegitimate children, and to the existence of a woman
not as pure as she should be. I think first of Effie Deans.[3] Then coming
down to our second modern great gun— Observe how civil I am to you
after the injury you have done me— I reflect upon the naughtinesses of
Miss Beatrice,[4] all the more naughty in that they are told only by hints;
—and also of the very wicked woman at Tunbridge Wells who was so
surprised because young Warrington did not "do as others use" with
her—[5] I forget whether it was her daughter, or her niece or her protegeè.
Then there is that illegitimate brat in Jane Eyre with the whole story of
her birth; and Hetty Sorrel[6] with almost the whole story of how the child
was gotten. I could think of no pure English novelist, pure up to the
Cornhill standard, except Dickens; but then I remembered Oliver Twist
and blushed for what my mother & sisters read in that very fie-fie story.[7]
I have mentioned our five greatest names & feel that I do not approach
them in naughtiness any more than I do in genius.

But in such cases, you will say, the impurities rest on the heads of the
individual authors,—and that you must especially guard the Cornhill.
Well. But how have we stood there? History perhaps should be told even
to the squeamish, and therefore the improprieties of the improper
Georges must be endured.[8] But how about the innuendoes as to the
opera dancers which made the children of Terpsichore so mad thro' the
three Kingdoms?[9]

You speak of the squeamishness of "our people." Are you not mag-

[3] From Scott's *The Heart of Midlothian.*
[4] Beatrix Esmond, from Thackeray's *Henry Esmond.*
[5] From Thackeray's *The Virginians,* chap. xix; the quotation is from *Lycidas,* l. 67.
[6] From George Eliot's *Adam Bede.*
[7] Doubtless a reference to Bill Sikes and Nancy.
[8] A reference to Thackeray's "The Four Georges: Sketches of Manners, Morals,
Court, and Town Life," published in four parts in the *Cornhill,* July through October
1860.
[9] In the first chapter of *Lovel the Widower,* which appeared in the *Cornhill* for
January 1860, Thackeray described a dancing girl kept in "an elegant little cottage in
Regent's Park," a description that provoked a spate of letters accusing him of libeling
all dancing girls. He discussed these letters (reprinting two of them) in "Thorns in
the Cushion," Roundabout Paper No. 5, *Cornhill,* 2 (July 1860).

nanimous enough to feel that you write urbi et orbi;[1]—for the best &
wisest of English readers; and not mainly for the weakest?

I of course look forward to bringing out my own story in a magazine
of my own— It will be called "The Marble Arch," and I trust to confound you by the popularity of Mrs. Talboys.

Joking apart I must declare that I disagree with your criticism. But
at the same time I assure you that I am quite satisfied that you have used
your own judgement impartially & with thoroughly good intention.

always yours
Anthony Trollope

W. M. Thackeray to Trollope

MS Parrish Collection. *Letters of W. M. Thackeray*, IV, 208; B 120.

Novr 17. 1860.   36 O. Square
My dear Trollope.

I am just out of bed after one of my attacks, wh. leave me very nervous
and incapable of letter writing or almost reading for a day or two. So,
as your letter came, and upon a delicate subject too—I told one of the
girls to read it.

I give you her very words—I can't help it if they are not more respectful. She says after reading the letter "He is an old dear and you
should write him an affectionate letter."

Then I had courage to have your letter read. I am another, am I? I
always said so.

"The Marble Arch" is such a good name that I have a months mind to
take it for my own story.

Always yours
W M T.

To George Smith

MS John Murray. B 121.

25. Nov. 1860.   Norwich.
My dear Smith.

Remember I have not corrected any further in F. P. I fear I must ask
your people for a revise, which I have not had for the last few numbers,
as I think I trace a little independent punctuation—no doubt better
than my own,—but still not my own. I am not clear also that I have not
come across a slight omission or two, which I could not verify not having the Mss; and which I do not care to verify not being bellicose about
trifles.

[1] The Pope gives his blessing *urbi et orbi*: "to the city and the world."

I congratulate you on two thoroughly good articles. That by Pater-familias,[2] & "behind the curtain."[3] Is the latter by Tom Taylor? What became of Hollingsheads paper about the publishers?[4]

Yours always
A. T.
address Waltham

Ariadne[5] begins finely, but waxes sloppy & common place towards the end. Maria has watched for her lover with red eyes, almost once too often. Who is the poet? & who the artist? The latter has a fine idea of a frame, but why has he feared to produce a face?

To T. T. Walton

MS Parrish Collection. B 122.

POST OFFICE
Norwich.

26 November 1860   address Waltham Cross.
My dear Sir.

Do you know what is a tontine?[6] I do not. But I have an interest in a tontine—whatever that is—established in Bristol heaven knows how many years ago— I know nothing more about it than that this interest is derived from a share in such undertaking originally the property of the Revd. Wm. Milton[7] who then lived at, or in the neighborhood of, Bristol. And that the life (still living) which he put into the concern was that of his daughter, then Mary Milton, now Mrs. Clyde. Have you, without giving yourself any trouble, the means of learning whereabouts in Bristol, or from whom, I could learn anything as to this tontine? I believe it,

[2] "A Second Letter to the Editor of the 'Cornhill Magazine' from Paterfamilias," *Cornhill*, 2 (December 1860), 641–49. The author was Matthew James Higgins (1810–68), generally known to the public as "Jacob Omnium," one of the foremost journalists of the day. Higgins's article was one of a number of articles that exposed abuses at Eton and eventually led to reforms.

[3] "Behind the Curtain," *Cornhill*, 2 (December 1860), 742–51. The author was John Hollingshead (1827–1904), a journalist and the longtime manager of the Gaiety Theatre.

[4] No such paper was published in the *Cornhill*.

[5] "Ariadne at Naxos," *Cornhill*, 2 (December 1860), 674–76. The author and illustrator was Joseph Noël Paton (1821–1901), later Sir Joseph, Queen Victoria's Limner for Scotland. A revised version was published in Paton's *Poems by a Painter* (1861) as "Ariadne: Four Sketches from the Antique."

[6] A tontine is "a financial scheme by which the subscribers to a loan or common fund receive each an annuity during his life, which increases as their number is diminished by death, till the last survivor enjoys the whole income" (OED).

[7] William Milton (1743–1824), for many years the Vicar of Heckfield, was Trollope's maternal grandfather.

or they, or he, or she, as the case may be, owns house property in Bristol.

Hoping you will excuse my troubling you on such a matter I am yours always[8]

                                                    Anthony Trollope

T. T. Walton Esq
Bristol—

To George Smith

MS John Murray. B 123.

Nov 30—1860.   Waltham.
My dear Smith.

I send the proof of No. 13— When do you illustrate again. You have four to give to 13–14–15–& 16.

I make the amende honorable about the omitted passage or passages. I thought that a certain line & a half was in No. 12, but I have found it in No. 13— I always think a revise is well if it be not troublesome. I have cut out five or six lines to bring in that last bit of a page.

I have read Ariadne again. Your modest poet has got it in him—or her, but sd. have chosen a less hackneyed subject.

                                                    Yours always
                                                    A. T.

To Charles Merivale

MS Taylor Collection.

[December 1860]
My dear Mr Merivale.

You remember how the friendly bear drove away the flies from his friends face—& the injury he did. Whenever we try, in the post office, to do a good & beneficent turn to any favored portion of the public, we always turn out to be bears. In driving away the flies we utterly destroy the comfort & good looks of our friends.

I thought that Bergholt day mail delivery would have been so convenient to all concerned. Of course you or any others who may feel yourselves injured by it can put yourselves in the former position, & have your letters left at Manningtree. If you wish me I will so instruct the people in the Manningtree office. Whether the post can be turned round

---

[8] Walton noted on back of this letter: "Mary Milton* 7 years old in 1 Augt. 1783 now at Exeter, and on Monday the general meeting will take place when she will get about £30. 200 shares on 190 Lives—now only 12 remain, and the Property will eventually be divided among 5 survivors / Answered to above effect / T.T.W. / 3. Dec., 60 / *widow of Capt: Clyde in Army." Commander Charles Clyde (d. 1853) was a naval officer. Mary Milton Clyde died in 1870.

in the way you propose, I will see. I can not give an immediate answer, as I must first learn the number of letters for different localities. I will however enquire & let you know.

The next time I am in the neighborhood of Lawford I will call. As it [is] 35 years since I saw you, I did not feel myself at liberty to look you up as an old friend.[9]

Yours very faithfully
Anthony Trollope

To Charles Merivale

MS Parrish Collection.

POST OFFICE
Waltham Cross.

December 7. 1860.

My dear Mr. Merivale

I find that the letters which the man will carry out of Manningtree by the day mail would be in numbers about as follows.

per week.

Railway Stat. & the Mill beyond it———————————	48 letters.
East Bergholt———————————————	92 —
Shalford———————————————————	45.
Dedham———————————————————	151
Lawford———————————————————	22.

I should therefore hardly be justified in turning the messengers route —leaving out the Station, & putting Bergholt last—more especially as the Bergholt people were those who moved in the matter. In fact I should have about 20 complaints as indignant as yours and added to this the complaints would be just—

The truth is that it is hardly possible to give a second delivery to rural deliveries, & is very seldom attempted. In this case the intention was to serve Bergholt & Dedham which are towns—& a struggle was made to give Lawford a little advantage by a side wind. I regret the good idea has so failed.

I have just got a most indignant letter from your brother John, in

[9] Merivale was the Rector of Lawford, near Manningtree in Essex, 1848–69. He had renewed his acquaintance with Trollope by 7 March 1861, when he wrote to his sister Louisa: "Mr. Trollope is to come here on Monday to look after his letters. I offer him a bed and invite Zincke [Rev. Foster Barham Zincke, author of travel books] to meet him." And on 11 November 1861, Merivale wrote to his mother: "The P. O. is constantly blundering, notwithstanding the whitewashing it gets in the *Times*, and the numerous complaints I make myself to Trollope about it." (Judith Anna Merivale, ed., *Autobiography and Letters of Charles Merivale* [Oxford, 1898], pp. 319, 331.) In 1866 Trollope persuaded Merivale to join him as a member of the Committee of the Royal Literary Fund. For Merivale's opinion of Trollope's *The Commentaries of Caesar* (1870), see Trollope to Blackwood, 7 May 1870, n. 2.

which he tells me of Hengist and Horsa and says that for the future, or at any rate till my official demise, any communication will be impossible with Essex by way of Post— But, nevertheless, do not you have a regular delivery of all your letters before breakfast? I have just got back from Rome, where I learned that the Pope has but one delivery daily—his letters reaching the Vatican at 11—all too early and all too often as he thinks. So at least it is whispered among the Cardinals. The archbishop at Rheims does not get his letters till near ten. The bishop of St. Davids has but one delivery a day. (!!!) The bishop of Jerusalem has none at all. And the letters of the canons at Seville are read before they get them. These are facts, ecclesiastical and historical, which should have been considered before John talked of Hengist & Horsa with reference to the Eastern Counties.

Of course you can have your letters from the Manningtree office if it will suit you. In that case you will only have to let the Postmaster know your wishes.

very truly yours
Anthony Trollope

To Mrs. Mary Christie[1]

MS Columbia. SB 124.

Decr. 9. 1860
Sunday   Waltham
My dear Mary

I fear I cannot get to Hillingdon next week by any possibility—unless Sunday next, can by stress of imagination be supposed to be in next week. Will you be at Hillingdon on next Sunday.

Yours always
Any Trollope

To [? Frederic] Chapman

MS Parrish Collection.

11th. Decr. 1860.   Waltham
My dear Chapman.

Read the enclosed & let me have it back again. I suppose you could see Dickenson[2] the photographer. But for anything I know the house may be altered. However he might as well go down & see it. I presume the people would let it [sic] do it.

[1] Mary Grant (?1819–1908), the eldest daughter of Trollope's Harrow neighbors Colonel and Mrs. Grant, had married William Dougal Christie (1816–74), a diplomat and barrister, in 1841. She remained a close friend of Trollope. For Trollope's review of a work by her husband, see Trollope to Smith, 18 January 1865.

[2] Possibly Dickinson Bros., Artists, 114 New Bond Street.

The house is at Sunbury[3]—on the London side of Harrow. There are two houses which did belong to my father, & were then called "Julians"— I doubt whether the name has been kept— In one, the larger, Mr Cunningham[4] the rector of Harrow still I believe lives. The other which is a little lower down the hill, and a little further from the high road, is the house in question.[5] I will however write to Harrow & learn the name of the occupier.[6]

> very truly yours
> Anthony Trollope

G. H. Lewes to Trollope
MS Brigham Young University.

15 Decr 1860   16 Blandford Square N.W.
My dear Trollope
The 15 Feby will suit me perfectly, and I think your title a capital one—much better than my own.[7]

[3] A slip for "Sudbury," perhaps from Trollope's memory of his school days at Sunbury (see *Autobiography*, pp. 5–6).

[4] John William Cunningham (1780–1861), Vicar of St. Mary's, Harrow-on-the-Hill, 1811–61. Julians, the house Cunningham occupied, was built by Trollope's father in 1818 but then vacated by the Trollopes for financial reasons in 1820, after little more than a year's occupancy. (The house still stands.) Cunningham, a leading Evangelical and for many years the target of Mrs. Trollope's satire, was quickly recognized as the original for the hypocritical Rev. W. J. Cartwright in Mrs. Trollope's popular *Vicar of Wrexhill* (1837). See N. John Hall, *Salmagundi: Byron, Allegra, and the Trollope Family* (Pittsburgh, Penn., 1975), pp. 22–54.

[5] Trollope had used Julians Hill, the other Harrow residence of the Trollope family, as the original for Orley Farm in the novel of that name. The house was originally Ilotts (or Illots) farm house, purchased by Trollope's father in 1813, into which he moved his family in 1815. When money problems forced him to lease the newly built Julians, he returned his family to the farm house, enlarged it greatly, and renamed it Julians Hill. It was this house that the bailiffs seized for debt in April 1834 and whence the family fled to Bruges. (See Helen Heineman, *Mrs. Trollope: The Triumphant Feminine in the Nineteenth Century* [Athens, Ohio, 1979], pp. 19–24.) The reference in this letter is apparently to Millais' illustration of the house for the novel's first number (March 1861), an illustration that was used also as the frontispiece for the first volume of the book edition (December 1861). According to his son, Millais "took flying visits to the country" for the backgrounds of his illustrations (John Guille Millais, *The Life and Letters of Sir John Everett Millais* [1899], II, 493). But in this instance Millais may have worked from a photograph: an old photograph of uncertain date but strikingly similar to the illustration survives at Orley Farm School.

[6] At this time Julians Hill was owned by Edward Ridley Hastings, who used it for his preparatory school. Shortly after *Orley Farm* was published, Hastings obtained Trollope's permission to name his school Orley Farm School. The school is still known by this name, although it moved into new quarters nearby in 1901. The old house was pulled down about 1905.

[7] Trollope had enlisted Lewes's participation in a series of lectures for postal employees given by men of letters. (Other speakers included Trollope, Edmund Yates, and Thomas Hughes.) Lewes spoke on "Life from the Simple Cell to Man," and he

ORLEY FARM.

Illustration for *Orley Farm*, by J. E. Millais

I presume you have long ago had your umbrella?

Enclosed is a letter from Dr. Müller of Hofwyl—at least that part of it which concerns the school. I have been promised details about Geneva but they havent come yet.[8]

Ever yours truly

G. H. Lewes

W. M. Thackeray to Trollope

MS Berg Collection. *Letters of W. M. Thackeray*, IV, 363.

[? December 1860]

My dear Trollope.

I haven't a lecture by me except that stale old Humour & Charity wh. I give for literary men in distress *not* for Societies— Otherwise there wd. be no end to the calls on me.[9]

So with the greatest desire to do what you ask—you see I cant. And as for writing a lecture just now I am much too busy preparing my friend Philip.[1]

Yours ever

W M T.

Have you mind to dine here on Monday at 7 . 30?

---

described the lecture as "immensely successful" in his journal entry for 15 February 1861 (*George Eliot Letters*, III, 378).

[8] Trollope was considering sending his sons to school abroad. Lewes's sons attended Müller's school at Hofwyl, Switzerland. In regard to Geneva schools, George Eliot had written on 6 December to François D'Albert-Durade: "Mr. Lewes begs me to thank you for your kind attention to his request about the schools. Mr. Trollope is a friend of ours who has exerted himself so obligingly on behalf of our son Charles, that we should be glad to be able to procure him any useful information." (*George Eliot Letters*, III, 362.) Trollope's sons attended Bradfield College, near Reading, which they had both entered early in 1860; Henry left the school in 1863, Frederic in 1865.

[9] Doubtless a reference to the series of lectures by literary men for postal employees. Thackeray first delivered "Charity and Humour" (also called "Weekday Preachers") in New York in 1853; he subsequently gave it at various benefit readings.

[1] *Philip* was serialized in the *Cornhill* from January 1861 through August 1862. On 15 October 1860, Thackeray had written to Charles Lever that he was determined to make *Philip* "as strong as I can to fetch up the ground wh. I have—not lost, I trust, but only barely kept. I sang purposely small [in *Lovel the Widower*]; wishing to keep my strongest for a later day, and give Trollope the honors of *Violono* [*sic*] *primo* [with *Framley Parsonage*]. Now I must go to work with a vengeance." (MS Huntington Library; quoted by Gordon N. Ray, *Thackeray: The Age of Wisdom*, pp. 303–4.) *Framley Parsonage* and *Philip* overlapped in the *Cornhill* from January through April 1861. On 24 May 1861, Thackeray wrote to Mrs. Baxter: "I think Trollope is much more popular with the Cornhill Magazine readers than I am: and doubt whether I am not going down hill considerably in public favor." (*Letters of W. M. Thackeray*, IV, 236.)

To F. I. Scudamore[2]

MS Parrish Collection. B 125.

18 Decr 1860.   POST OFFICE

My dear Scudamore.

I have sent on your suggestion to Tom Hughes.[3]

Your prospectus is very good—only ugly. Could you not make it out, giving the days, & names, & titles—? I suppose all your men can now give you your titles. And then men are fixed. Lewes, whom I saw last night at Mudies great flare up,[4] wants chalk and a diagram board. He is very hot about his board. I have promised— Have I done wrong? He wants to know about locale, hour, &c &c. Could you not write him a line.

16 Blandford Square.

Yours ever

Any Trollope

1861

George Smith to Trollope

MS Bodleian.

January 4th. 1861   65, CORNHILL. E.C.

My dear Mr Trollope

I should have written to you before now on the subject of our recent conversation had I been able to learn Mr Thackeray's view there anent, but he has been ill and unable to attend to any business. I am now however authorized by him to say that "Jones Brown & Robinson" [*sic*] shall be inserted in the "Cornhill Magazine" without any editorial revision.

I remain

Yours very faithfully

Anthony Trollope Esqre   G Smith

---

[2] Frank Ives Scudamore (1823–84), Post Office administrator. Scudamore was promoted to Assistant Secretary over Trollope's head in 1864 (see Trollope et al. to Tilley, 8 April 1864, n. 8).

[3] Thomas Hughes (1822–96), novelist, biographer, educator, Christian Socialist; author of *Tom Brown's School Days* (1857). Hughes was scheduled to give one of the lectures to postal employees.

[4] On 17 December a large hall and library were opened at the Oxford Street premises of Charles Edward Mudie (1818–90), founder of Mudie's Lending Library. The opening was attended by "a company of authors, artists, naturalists, and publishers . . . including nearly all the best names in literature and the trade" (*Athenaeum*, 22 December 1860, p. 877).

To George Smith

MS John Murray. B 127.

Jany 5. 1861   Waltham Cross.
My dear Smith.

I have been very glad to get your letter. I should have been unhappy
to feel myself severed from the most popular periodical publication of
the day, & assure you that I will do the best I can for you with B. J. & R.[5]
I purpose that you shall have the entire Mss some time in July.

always yours

G Smith Esq   Anthony Trollope

To George Smith

MS John Murray. *Commentary*, p. 224; B 128.

8 Jany 61
Wednesday night.   Suffolk Street.
My dear Smith.

I have only just got your note. The Civil Service Gazette I think I may
say did not report the lecture. The Morning Post, Daily News & Telegraph did. I send you the Telegraph as being the fullest.[6]

I shall probably call tomorrow between one & two, but you are always
eating little plates of cold meat or pork pies at that time.

Yours always

Anthony Trollope

[5] Evidently Trollope had determined to break with the *Cornhill* if his story had to
undergo editorial revision, even at the hands of Thackeray, whom Trollope ranked
first among English novelists.

[6] The *Daily Telegraph* (5 January 1861, p. 3) was enthusiastic about Trollope's
lecture, the first in the series for postal employees (see Lewes to Trollope, 15 December 1860). Delivered on 4 January at the Post Office headquarters in St. Martin's-le-
Grand, the lecture advocated more independence (including the right to vote) for
civil servants and also the abolition of promotion by merit; the latter system (Hill's),
Trollope claimed, enabled a senior officer to "put unfairly forward his special friends."
Hill was all the more offended when Trollope had a shortened version of the lecture,
with some of the more personal elements removed, published in the *Cornhill*, 3
(February 1861), 214–28, and he asked the Postmaster General, Lord Stanley (Edward
John Stanley [1802–69], 2d Baron Stanley of Alderley; Postmaster General, 1860–66),
to censure Trollope. (Hill apparently did not, as the *Autobiography* claims, ask for
Trollope's dismissal [p. 134].) But Stanley, who was on good terms with Trollope, refused to comment on the publication officially (Trollope had in fact shown him the
article in proof). Trollope had the full lecture, entitled "The Civil Service as a Profession," privately printed; it is included in Morris L. Parrish, ed., *Four Lectures*
(1938).

To George Smith

MS John Murray. *Commentary*, p. 224; B 129.

26 Jany. 1861 Waltham X.
My dear Smith.
Thanks for your check for £26.5/. You wd. have been quite welcome to the article.[7] For such a subject the payment is more than liberal.
Indeed I consider it so high for—"padding" that I ought to make it known to the Saturday.[8]

Yours always
Anty Trollope

You have three! novels this time—which must be very depressing to the padding trade.

To ?

MS Historical Society of Pennsylvania. SB 130.

January 29. 1861 Waltham Cross
Dear Sir.
I have this moment received the volume of poems you have been so good as to send me. I know that the book has been at Chapmans for some time, but owing to an accident it was delayed there. I mention this as you may have thought me uncourteous in not acknowledging your kindness.
I hope I may some day have an opportunity of telling you my opinion.

Yours very faithfully
Anthony Trollope

To Mrs. Mary Christie

MS Parrish Collection. B 131.

Feb. 16. 1861 Waltham X.
My dear Mary.
I have received your note & one from Perry, and am very much distressed to hear what you tell me about your mother. And yet, if it be impossible that she should recover I do not know how one can wish that

---

[7] The *Cornhill* version of "The Civil Service as a Profession."

[8] The *Saturday Review* had just contended that serials were the real attraction of magazines, the articles being "merely looked at as the stuffing which give the stories bulk enough to appear with decency." It added: "The prices of padding are continually rising. The judicious liberality of the *Cornhill* has given quite an impetus to this species of traffic, and few things produced with so little trouble are so well paid for." ("Padding," *Saturday Review*, 19 January 1861, pp. 63–64.) The *Saturday Review* and the *Cornhill* were for some years on unfriendly terms.

she should linger on in suffering. I do so wish I could have seen her again. Not that to her it could have been any pleasure, & to me, tho I delighted to see her & was always happy to see that the expression of her face & the tone of her voice was the same that it was in old days, yet it was very painful to feel that she would never be herself again. Of all friends that I have ever had out of my own family she has been the dearest.

I would send her my best & kindest love but that probably she may be too weak to be told of any one but those who are nearest to her. I am sure that she has known that I have loved her well.

It will be a great blank when she has gone. I shall have a line from some of you when the day does come. I wish I knew how I could be of service to you—[9]

> Dear Mary
> Always yours affectionately
> Anthony Trollope

Laurence Oliphant[1] to Trollope

MS University of Illinois.

[? February 1861]
Saturday   4 Mount Street
My dear Sir

As I was the person who recommended to the Proprs. of the London Review the publication of your tales in that Journal,[2] I am sure you will excuse my taking upon myself the unpleasant task of expressing to you their feeling of disappointment at the disapprobation with wh. the public has received them, and which has been communicated to us in a number of letters. I only enclose an extract from the one written in the mildest tone of condemnation— "For my own part I shall immediately destroy the supplements containing the two tales that have as yet come out and if they are continued I shall be compelled to give up the paper— anyone who wants stuff of that description will find it in plenty in the 'London Journal'—[3] You must make your election whether you will

---

[9] Mary Penelope Grant died on 18 February 1861.

[1] Laurence Oliphant (1829–88), war correspondent and miscellaneous writer; one of the proprietors of the *London Review*. Trollope endorsed this letter "From Laurence Oliphant / A wonderful letter."

[2] The *London Review* published "The Banks of the Jordan" on 5, 12, and 19 January 1861, and "Mrs. General Talboys" on 2 February 1861. Although it owned the rights to eight stories by Trollope (see Trollope to Little, 22 September 1860), it published only one more, "The Parson's Daughter of Oxney Colne" (2 March 1861), and sold the remaining five to *Public Opinion* (see Trollope to Chapman, 1 January 1862).

[3] The *London Journal* was a penny weekly started in 1845 by George Stiff. During the 1840's its serials were considered strong, but by the 1860's it had become more respectable. The serials running in February 1861 were Pierce Egan's *The Wonder of Kingswood Chace* and Mrs. Gordon Smithies' *'Our Mary'; or, Murder Will Out.*

adapt your paper to the taste of men of intelligence & high moral feeling *or* to that of persons of morbid imagination & *a low tone of morals.*" I feel that I owe you an apology for not having read the tales before publication, but I felt such perfect confidence that anything from your pen would have defied any such criticism as the above that I had not looked at it until I saw it in the paper—

I still believe that tales of a high moral tendency and possessing the literary merit which I know it is in your power to impart to them wd. have exercised a most beneficial influence not only on the circulation but on the character of the paper, and I cannot express to you how deeply I regret that this does not seem to have been the case— I trust you will take these remarks in the friendly spirit in which they are written— as your name is attached to the tales I feel it is due to you to be informed of an impression wh. seems to be so universal while I felt myself bound to be the medium of conveying to you that impression—

> Believe me
> My dear Sir
> Yours very truly
> L Oliphant

Lord Carlisle⁴ to Trollope

MS Taylor Collection. Taylor, "Letters," p. 5.

Feb 28./61   Dublin Castle
Sir.

... I have been induced to address this letter to yourself, because it gives me an opportunity of expressing my very sincere regret & compunction, that it so fell out that I missed the opportunity of making acquaintance with the Author of the Kellys & O Kellys & Castle Richmond, when he resided in that country he has so admirably portrayed. I hope that if you ever find yourself within my reach again you will allow me to repair my loss.

> I have the honor to be, Sir,
> Your Servant & Admirer
> Carlisle

I am quite curious to know what effect the Essays & Reviews may produce upon the Barchester Society.⁵

---

⁴ George William Frederick Howard (1802–64), Viscount Morpeth, later the 7th Earl of Carlisle; Irish Secretary, 1835–41; Viceroy of Ireland, 1855–58 and 1859–64.

⁵ *Essays and Reviews* was published in 1860 in the wake of the upheaval caused by Darwin's *Origin of Species* (1859). Written by a group of seven Anglicans (among them, Benjamin Jowett, Mark Pattison, and Frederick Temple), the book created enormous controversy by counseling Christians to accept the new discoveries of science. Trollope kept the controversy out of Barsetshire, though in "The Clergyman Who Subscribes for Colenso" (*Pall Mall Gazette*, 25 January 1866; reprinted in *Clergymen of the Church of England* [1866]), Trollope offered his own condemnation of Biblical literalism.

To George Smith

MS John Murray. SB 132.

March 1—1861   Waltham
My dear Smith.

I am not too proud to receive the Cornhill at your hands, but I feel
rather about the postage. Of course you will stop the copies sent to my
brother & brother-in-law when my own novel is done. I hope you will
continue to send me one as I shall still consider myself on the staff.

I do not care to correct the sheets of F. P. again, unless you wish it.
I dare say I shall see you before it comes out in its new shape.

I enclose a check for the amount of your bill & am much obliged.

                                              Yours very truly
                                              Anthony Trollope

To ?

MS Parrish Collection. SB 133.

March 13—1861   Chelmsford
My dear Sir

I am very much obliged to you for your kind invitation— I must however reach Ongar viâ Chelmsford⁶ as I shall come up from Lowestoff in
Suffolk on the Friday, & could not therefore get to you in time for dinner.
Otherwise I should have been very happy. We had a wretched day of it
today—ploughing about thro the mud & rain—all day in the woods—our
great success was the digging out of one fox. The run was 10 minutes—
The digging out 50—

                                              Yours very truly
                                              Anthony Trollope

To [? Frederic] Chapman

MS Parrish Collection.

13 March 1861
My dear Chapman—

What shall I say in answer to the Frenchman's letter. He is the man
who came to me at your shop the other day.

My brother must be in London on May 10—but will *not* as I think be
there much before that. I take it he will be in London nearly all May.

                                              Yours always
                                              Anthony Trollope

You tell me of dozens of Orley Farm, but I want to hear of hundreds &
thousands—

Have you sent La Beata⁷ to my brother.

⁶ Chelmsford and Ongar are both in Essex.
⁷ Chapman & Hall published T. A. Trollope's novel *La Beata* in May 1861.

To Major John Bent[8]

MS Parrish Collection.

Waltham House
March 19. 1861   Waltham Cross
My dear Major.

I was very much pleased with your affectionate letter. I should have answered it at once but I could not fix with certainty any day for going to Exeter. Nor can I yet. I will however certainly run down one day in April & back the next, & will give you at any rate a weeks notice. What with the post office & what with publishers, I find it very difficult to call any time my own. I write a line by this post to my aunt.

Always dear Major
As ever yours affectionately
Anthony Trollope

To George Smith

MS Bodleian. SB 134; excerpt, Hamer, p. 208.

March 24. 1861   Waltham Cross.
My dear Smith.

When does the 3 vol Edition of F. P. come out? I presume you will accord to me a few copies. If so will you send 3—to me here. One to John Tilley Esq—G. P. O. London. One to John Merivale Esq. 5 Norfolk Square Paddington—and one to the Post Office Library—care of F. I. Scudamore Esq Post office. How many are you printing of it? Thanks for the copy of Doyles party.[9] He has I think crowded it too much.

very faithfully yours
Anty Trollope

Now that you have two houses[1] seeing you is out of the question. You are always just gone to the other place, or at any rate just going.

---

[8] Major John Bent (?1791–1873), a first cousin of Frances Trollope and the brother of her beloved Fanny Bent (*d.* 1860). T. A. Trollope recalled Fanny Bent as he knew her in the 1820's, though his statements about her parentage are confused and inaccurate (*What I Remember*, pp. 23, 26–27). John and Fanny Bent were among the children of the Reverend George Bent (?1741–1814) of Sandford Crediton (at his death Rector of High Bray and Jacobstow, and Chaplain of Sandford) by his first wife, Mary, the sister of William Milton, Frances Trollope's father. Fanny Bent lived at 8 York Buildings, Exeter, and was the original for Aunt Stanbury in *He Knew He Was Right*.

[9] Richard "Dicky" Doyle (1824–83), cartoonist and illustrator, closely associated with *Punch* during its early years. Doyle drew a series of sixteen satirical sketches for the *Cornhill* under the general title "Bird's Eye Views of Society" (running, with interruptions, from April 1861 through October 1862). Trollope probably refers to No. 2, "A Juvenile Party," or to No. 3, "A Morning Party" (May and June 1861). Smith published the series in volume form in 1864.

[1] The expansion of Smith, Elder had led to the opening of an additional office in the West End, at 45 Pall Mall.

To Dorothea Sankey[2]

MS (photocopy) Parrish Collection. B 135.

Waltham House
March 24. 1861   Waltham Cross
My dearest Miss Dorothea Sankey

My affectionate & most excellent wife is as you are aware still living—
and I am proud to say her health is good. Nevertheless it is always well
to take time by the forelock and be prepared for all events. Should anything happen to her, will you supply her place,—as soon as the proper
period for decent mourning is over.

Till then I am your devoted Servant

Anthony Trollope

To George Smith

MS John Murray. Excerpt, *Commentary*, p. 224; SB 136.

31 March 1861   Waltham
My dear Smith

The cover[3] seems very nice. I hope you may have a good sale & make
lots of money.

It is not your holydays that makes you so difficult of access, but that
double counting house—at each of which you spend 10 minutes ten
times a day, living the best part of your life in cabs.

always yours
Any Trollope

[2] Trollope's correspondent may have been Dorothea Sankey, third of the four
daughters of Matthew Villiers Sankey of Coolmore House, Co. Tipperary. Since her
father died in 1815, she was (unless a twin) clearly older than Trollope. She remained
unmarried (Clement Sankey Best-Gardner, *Memorials of the Family of Sankey* [1880]).
Coolmore is near Clonmel, the place where Trollope lived for the first several years
after his marriage, and where both his sons were born. Rose Trollope's chronological
memorandum indicates, under 1846, "To Glengariff and Killarney in Sept. with the
Sankeys" (MS University of Illinois). Or, the recipient may have been a member of
another branch of the Sankey family, perhaps a child. Every informed student of
Trollope considers the letter a joke; but in 1942 Sotheby's Catalogue called it "one
of the most extraordinary letters ever offered for sale," and it provoked heated controversy in the press. See the *New York Times*, 12 August 1942, p. 17; 13 August 1942,
p. 18; 16 August 1942, p. E9; and 18 August 1942, p. 20. See also Michael Sadleir,
"Trollope's Proposals," *TLS*, 10 August 1946; and Alban F. L. Bacon, "Friend of Trollope's," *Spectator*, 6 December 1946, p. 613, with discussion, *Spectator*, 13 and 20
December 1946, pp. 644, 676. (Bacon quotes from a letter sent to him by Lady Carnock,
the niece of Captain Sankey's wife, who recalled that when she was staying with the
Sankeys as a child in 1870 she was taken to visit Captain Sankey's sister Dorothy, "a
cheerful, stout lady of middle age.")
[3] For the three-volume edition of *Framley Parsonage*, published April 1861.

To Mrs. S. C. Hall[4]

MS Parrish Collection. B 137.

Waltham house

7 April 1861   Waltham Cross.

My dear Mrs. Hall.

I am much flattered by your kind offer to join your staff. As you say, my Cornhill tale has at last come to an end; but I have already begun another which is coming out monthly in a separate form. I have also two other engagements with publishers, and the three together[5] would prevent my doing you justice, if I were to accede to your tempting proposal at present. The time may however come when, if you are of the same mind, I may join your establishment for a while.[6]

very faithfully yours

Anthony Trollope

To G. H. Lewes

MS Yale. B 138; *George Eliot Letters*, VIII, 279.

April 7. 1861   Waltham Cross.

My dear Lewes.

I must consider your letter as in some degree special, and give it a special answer.

You take me too closely au pied de la lettre as touching husbands & lovers. As to myself personally, I have daily to wonder at the continued run of domestic & worldly happiness which has been granted me;—to wonder at it as well as to be thankful for it. I do so, fearing that my day, also, of misery must come;—for we are told by so many teachers of all doctrines that pain of some sort is mans lot. But no pain or misery has as yet come to me since the day I married; & if any man should speak well of the married state, I should do so.

But I deny that I have done other. There is a sweet young blushing joy about the first acknowledged reciprocal love, which is like the bouquet of the first glass of wine from the bottle— It goes when it has

---

[4] Anna Maria Hall (1800–1881), wife of Samuel Carter Hall and a prolific writer; editor of the *St. James's Magazine,* to which reference is made here.

[5] *Orley Farm* was appearing in monthly numbers for Chapman & Hall; *Brown, Jones, and Robinson* was scheduled to appear in the *Cornhill* for Smith; and Trollope had signed an agreement with Chapman & Hall for a two-volume work on North America. Moreover, Trollope had been in contact with the *Illustrated London News,* which on 12 April 1861 (MS Bodleian) agreed to pay him £50 for a Christmas story ("The Mistletoe Bough," *Illustrated London News,* 21 December 1861; reprinted in *Tales of All Countries,* Second Series [1863]).

[6] Trollope contributed one article to the *St. James's:* see Trollope to Hall, 3 July 1861.

been tasted. But for all that who will compare the momentary aroma with the lasting joys of the still flowing bowl? May the bowl still flow for both of us, and leave no touch of head ache.[7]

When do you go Alpwards? & what do you do before that. I shall be here from Sunday 14th. to Friday (morning) 19th.—but with no one in the house but wife & boys. Again from Tuesday 23rd. to Sunday 28th. & then shall have friends—who will like to meet you. Can you name a day for either period? Of course a man who comes here sleeps here.[8]

Yours always
Anthony Trollope

To Blanchard Jerrold[9]
MS Parrish Collection.

Waltham House
Waltham Cross

April 8—1861

Dear Sir.

I am extremely sorry your letter about the book union[1] should have remained unanswered so long. I was away from home all last week moving from place to place, & it so escaped me.

I shall be most happy to assist the Book Union in any way, and shall be proud to see my name on the list of patrons. My name I fear will do you but little good. If I can serve you in any other way I shall be very glad.

your faithful Servant
Anthony Trollope

B Jerrold Esq

---

[7] Lewes had doubtless referred to the final chapter of *Framley Parsonage* where Trollope says that anticipation is the greatest happiness in marriage. The passage closes: "When the husband walks back from the altar, he has already swallowed the choicest dainties of his banquet. The beef and pudding of married life are then in store for him;—or perhaps only the bread and cheese. Let him take care lest hardly a crust remain,—or perhaps not a crust."

[8] Lewes wrote in his journal for 15 April: "Went down to Waltham to dine and sleep at Trollope's. He has a charming house and grounds, and I like him very much, so wholesome and straightforward a man. Mrs. Trollope did not make any decided impression on me, one way or the other." (*George Eliot Letters*, VIII, 279.)

[9] William Blanchard Jerrold (1826–84), journalist and miscellaneous writer; son of Douglas Jerrold.

[1] The National Book Union, of which Jerrold was Secretary, was a short-lived scheme (on the model of the Art Union) for making books available to the working classes; subscribers were to pay for books by shilling installments and were to be eligible for prizes. In May, A. H. Layard introduced a bill in the House of Commons to legalize book unions, but in July the House of Lords rejected the bill.

Richard Monckton Milnes to Trollope
MS Taylor Collection. Taylor, "Letters," p. 6.

April 24/61   16. Upper Brook St.
My dear Sir.
You were elected this week a member of the Cosmopolitan Club. I
hope we shall see you there sometimes on Wednesday and Sunday evenings. You will pay yr. entrance & subscription to Mr. Philipps,[2] the Sec.
& the painter.

I am, yrs truly
R. M. Milnes.

To Richard Monckton Milnes
MS Trinity College, Cambridge.

25 Ap. 1861   Waltham House
My dear Sir.
Many thanks for your kindness touching the Cosmopolitan. I had received a line from Mr Phillips. I hope I may meet you there on Sunday
week.

Yours very faithfully
R. M. Milnes Esq   Anthony Trollope
MP.

To Anna Drury[3]
MS University of Virginia. B 139.

May 10—1861   Suffolk Street
My dear Anna—
Yes; I understand it all, & have gone thro' it all myself. But of the first
book of mine that was published in a cheap form I did cut out over 64

[2] Henry Wyndham Phillips (1820–68), portrait painter, of Hollow Combe, Sydenham. J. L. Motley described the Cosmopolitan as "a club which meets late in the
evenings twice a week, Sundays and Wednesdays, in a large room which is the studio
of the painter Phillips, in Charles Street, leading from Berkeley Square. The object
seems to be to collect noted people and smoke very bad cigars." (George William
Curtis, ed., *The Correspondence of John Lothrop Motley* [1889], I, 227.) A number
of Trollope's friends were members; in addition to Milnes, these included A. H.
Layard, Thackeray, M. J. Higgins, William Stirling, and Arthur Russell. The Cosmopolitan was the original for the "Universe," a club prominent in *Phineas Redux*.

[3] Anna Harriet Drury, a minor novelist and the granddaughter of Mark Drury.
(Mark Drury was the second master at Harrow when Trollope was a pupil and also
a close friend of the Trollope family.) Trollope frequently negotiated with publishers
on Miss Drury's behalf. The reference here is to Chapman & Hall's 1861 edition of
Miss Drury's novel *Misrepresentation* (1859).

pages,—working very painfully in the doing of it. Since that I have been careful so to reduce myself in the first writing, that I have had nothing to cut out.

If it be impossible, or very disagreeable with you, you shall not be asked; but before I see Chapman I think it well to write to you & explain. The 32 pages—(he does not ask 64—) need not be elided in one place, nor even in 30 places, but it may be possible that by going thro' the work you might find passages the omission of which would not do material damage.

Now as to Chapman & his reasons;—which are reasonable. In the first place he sent word to you proposing to call upon you but found you gone;—& therefore had no alternative but writing.

Of course in all cheap editions the margin of profit is comparatively small and depends upon a large sale. But if the expense be much greater than that generally incurred, the small margin of profit suffers much. Now the paper for an extra two sheets—viz 32 pages, and the extra setting up, of course costs money—and in a 5/ volume this cannot be remedied by closer printing, as it can in the 2- or 3 vol-edition. Again one of those volumes if too thick & fat loses in attractiveness of appearance, & all that tells on the sale. So much I say that you may know that your own interests as well as Chapmans would be served by your reducing the matter.

Of course to an author all these material considerations are vile bonds, repressing the divine afflatus— But the divine afflatus has to suffer, when pecuniary views force themselves forward. Remember that I & a dozen better than I am have to tuck ourselves into contracted limits every month.

However you shall not be compelled if it goes utterly against the grain with you. Think it over again & then let me have another line—to Waltham.

Yours always
Anty Trollope

At any rate you must not blame Chapman who spoke to me first. He is decidedly right to ask—for your interest as well as his own.

To Octavian Blewitt[4]

MS Royal Literary Fund.

12 May. 1861   Waltham X.

Dear Sir.

I regret that I shall be unable to attend your meeting[5] tomorrow. I have written to Mr Bell[6] to this effect— I shall wish to have two seats for myself, but Mr Bell will be aware of this.

Yours very truly

O Blewitt Esq   Anthony Trollope

To J. E. Millais

MS Parrish Collection. B 140.

June 1. 1861   Cambridge

My dear Millais.

It strikes me I said I would send you an order for my lecture[7]—and therefore do so— Do not conceive that I suppose you to be bound to

[4] Octavian Blewitt (1810–84), miscellaneous writer and editor; author of topographical and travel works; Secretary of the Royal Literary Fund, 1839–84.

[5] A meeting (held on 13 May) of the stewards for the Royal Literary Fund's Anniversary Dinner (held on 15 May). The Royal Literary Fund, founded in 1790 to assist needy authors and their families, became Trollope's favorite charity. In 1861, he became a life member (after a donation of ten guineas); in 1864, he became a member of the General Committee (which managed the Fund and allocated grants); and in 1869, he became one of the Fund's three treasurers. He remained one of the treasurers and a member of the General Committee until his death. As many subsequent letters show, Trollope worked actively promoting the Fund's annual dinners; he also spoke at many of these (in 1861, 1863, 1864, 1866, 1867, 1869, and 1871), and during the 1870's expended considerable energy seeking out stewards and arranging for notables to take the chair. On 14 December 1882 (after Trollope's death), the Committee passed a resolution commending his many years of service to the Fund and calling special attention to his "constant attendance at the Meetings of the General Committee [and] . . . his valuable advice and assistance in the administration of the Fund" (MS Royal Literary Fund). See also Bradford Booth, "Trollope and the Royal Literary Fund," *Nineteenth-Century Fiction*, 7 (December 1952), 208–16, and Robert H. Super, "Trollope at the Royal Literary Fund," forthcoming in the Trollope centenary issue of *Nineteenth-Century Fiction* (1982).

[6] Robert Bell (1800–1867), prominent journalist and editor of English poets; an intimate of Thackeray and contributor to the *Cornhill*. Bell, who became one of Trollope's closest friends and literary associates, had recruited Trollope on behalf of the Royal Literary Fund.

[7] Trollope's lecture, "The National Gallery," was never given, though it was eventually published; its subject would account for Millais' interest. An art fancier and inveterate museum-goer, Trollope wrote three fairly elaborate statements on art: chap. xii of *The New Zealander* (written in 1856); the lecture mentioned here; and "The Art Tourist," *Pall Mall Gazette*, 22 August 1865 (reprinted in *Travelling Sketches* [1866]). The two later articles exhibit attitudes toward Raphael that Trollope may well have taken from Millais.

come. It will be a horrid bore;—tho perhaps not so bad as dining at the M House.[8]

Yours always
Anthony Trollope

I quite forget all your legitimate addresses—

To George Smith

Sadleir's transcript, Bodleian. SB 141.

11 June 1861.   Waltham

*   *   *

I send the lecture—unlectured— I have reduced it as much as I well can. It will I think certainly be within 16 pages.[9] I suppose I cannot have it to correct. Will your printers object to having it done in pencil?

*   *   *

To William Little[1]

MS Parrish Collection.

June 12—1861   WALTHAM HOUSE, WALTHAM CROSS.
My dear Sir.

I am very much obliged to you for your kindness about the stories. I should not have liked to ask any one to copy them for £1 – 11/.! If I am not in Southampton Street myself in a day or two, I will ask a friend to call & settle with you.

Yours very truly
I. Little Esq   Anthony Trollope

To [? Frederic] Chapman

MS Parrish Collection.

June 16—1861   WALTHAM HOUSE, WALTHAM CROSS.
My dear Chapman.

All right about the money—say £200 on July 10.

You are very good about the articles; but I hope you understand that I did not wish you to give your consent against your will.[2]

Yours very truly
Anthony Trollope

[8] Mansion House, the residence of the Lord Mayor of London and the scene of numerous banquets.

[9] Trollope had apparently asked Smith to print copies of his lecture on the National Gallery, though it is possible that he was in fact submitting it (unsuccessfully) to the *Cornhill*. The lecture was published in *St. James's Magazine*; see Trollope to Hall, 3 July 1861.

[1] Trollope addressed this letter to "I. Little," but this was doubtless an error for "W. Little." (William Little was business manager of the *London Review*.)

[2] This letter and the following letter to Smith suggest that Trollope planned to write a series of articles on America for the *Cornhill*, though a book on this subject

To George Smith

MS John Murray. SB 142.

16 June 1861   WALTHAM HOUSE, WALTHAM CROSS.
My dear Smith

There has been some positive villainy about that glass— We—your wife & myself—were at great trouble in getting the proper glasses into the proper cases on our way home. However I shall be in town tomorrow or Tuesday & will do as you say.

All right about the 3 articles—say 16 pages each. You wont put the name of course. I dont want to be tarred & feathered before my time.

Yours always
Anthony Trollope

To Octavian Blewitt

MS Royal Literary Fund.

June 22—1861   WALTHAM HOUSE, WALTHAM CROSS.
My dear Sir.

Many thanks. I believe the enclosed is as good as it can be made— which is saying very little for it.[3]

Yours very truly

Octavian Blewitt Esq   Anthony Trollope

To George Smith

MS Bodleian. Excerpt, *Commentary*, p. 224; B 143 (incomplete).

June 26—1861   WALTHAM HOUSE, WALTHAM CROSS.
My dear Smith.

I should like to have a little chat with you about your proposition.[4] There are two drawbacks to your offer. In the first place you want the copyright. And in the next place you will, I presume, wish to extend the publication over a considerable time.

---

had been promised to Chapman (the agreement, dated 20 March 1861, provided for a payment of £1,250 for the right to print 2,500 copies of a two-volume work on North America). The articles were never written; see Trollope to Chapman, 1 January 1862. Trollope reckoned his earnings on *North America* at £660, after adding £35 from Tauchnitz to the £1,250 from Chapman & Hall, then subtracting £625 in expenses (Trollope's account books, Parrish Collection).

[3] The text of Trollope's speech at the Royal Literary Fund's Anniversary Dinner. The speech was printed in the Fund's 1861 *Annual Report*, p. 27.

[4] On 24 June Smith had written to Trollope about a proposed novel (*The Small House at Allington*): "There are some stipulations to add respecting the period of publication, and with reference to my venture not being jostled by another novel or serial from your pen; but I do not apprehend your considering anything that I have to ask, unreasonable." (MS Bodleian.) Smith, Elder offered £3,500 for absolute copyright; for the final arrangement, see Trollope to Smith, 9 July 1861.

Presuming the novel to be intended for the magazine—which would be the manner of publication which I should prefer— It would extend over 20 months. The money stretched over that time, with an interdict against other writing of a similar class, would as you will see, not come to so much as it looks.

Therefore before I give a definite answer I should like to see a little more of your plans.

Of course you would not bring the novel out separately. It must either be for the magazine or as a separate serial. As the latter it would run over 16 months; but in that case could not commence till November or October 1862—

I could not of course give it you, binding myself down against other similar writing, till I knew something more as to your wishes as to time &c.

I shall probably be in town this day week—i e next Wednesday. Will it be city or West End on that day?

I will send you on Sunday next the first No. of B.J.&R.—& the other numbers shall follow quickly thro July & be completed the first week in August. I shall like to have the proofs of these as speedily as possible, because I look to sail on 17 August.[5]

You will thus get your quid piecemeal— But I will have my quo in a lump when it is finished.

Yours always

G Smith Esq   Anthony Trollope

[5] Trollope's seven months' leave of absence from the Post Office to visit and write a book about America was another occasion for an altercation with Rowland Hill. On 9 April Hill had forwarded Trollope's request to the Postmaster General, Lord Stanley, saying that he knew of no precedent for such a lengthy leave, which was "in many respects objectionable." Hill suggested that the leave be granted "with the distinct understanding that the indulgence be considered a full compensation for the special services [including Trollope's missions to Egypt and the West Indies] on which he rests his claim." Stanley then suggested that Trollope be asked to help in negotiating postal arrangements in America. Hill demurred, and Stanley granted the leave. But Trollope objected to the "special services" clause, which Stanley had apparently not intended to endorse. Finally, on 23 April Stanley strongly rebuked Hill: "I consider that the valuable services rendered by Mr. Trollope to the Department, justified me in granting the leave requested, though somewhat out of the ordinary course. I never thought that Mr. Trollope made any claim for compensation, nor did I intend that the Leave now granted should be considered as such. Mr. Trollope's services discharged with Zeal Diligence & Ability will always give him that claim to consideration which the exhibition of such Qualities must entitle any officer to expect from the PMG, and the leave now granted can in no respect be considered as diminishing such claims on the part of Mr. Trollope." (MSS General Post Office, London.) Trollope, who was on good terms with Stanley, had gone directly to him beforehand (*Autobiography*, pp. 162–63). The rebuff continued to annoy Hill; see Trollope to Lowell, 2 September 1862, n. 6. On "special services," see Trollope to Tilley, 8 July 1864.

To George Smith

MS John Murray. SB 144.

June 30—1861   WALTHAM HOUSE, WALTHAM CROSS.
My dear Smith
    I shall not be in town on Thursday, but can go up on Tuesday. If that day wd. suit you I would be with you at 2. PM. either at Cornhill or Pall Mall. If that will not, I will turn up on Friday.
    I send perpost 1st. No. of B. J. & R.
Yours always

G Smith Esq   Anthony Trollope

Will you come down Friday—dine & sleep— Mrs. Trollope bids me say that if Mrs. Smith would come it wd. give her the greatest pleasure. I suppose she ought to call first, but then Upton Park[6] is so far!

To George Smith

MS Bodleian.

2 July. 1861   WALTHAM HOUSE, WALTHAM CROSS.
My dear Smith.
    I forgot to ask you what you thought about my brothers story.[7]
    My wife is very keen to have that receipt for melted butter.[8]
    Who sells good champaigne? Could you get a dozen sent down to my address here, so that I should have it on Saturday. If I liked it I would get more. I care as much as any body about price, but I care almost more about quality— It is very impertinent in me to ask you to do this, but you kept me so long today I had not time to go anywhere.
Yours very truly
Anthony Trollope

To G. H. Lewes

MS Parrish Collection.

July 2—1861   WALTHAM HOUSE, WALTHAM CROSS.
My dear Lewes—
    I must hear what you have to say. If I call about 5. PM on Friday next shall I find you, *and Mrs. Lewes*, at home.
Yours always faithfully
Anthony Trollope

---

[6] The Upton Park Estate, laid out and built in 1842, in the village of Upton, near Slough, Buckinghamshire.
[7] Perhaps *La Beata* or some unidentified short fiction.
[8] Probably *beurre blanc*.

We start on 24 August. We haven't eaten our pudding. We have our pudding all before us.[9]

To G. H. Lewes

MS Yale. B 146.

July 3—1861
Wednesday   WALTHAM HOUSE, WALTHAM CROSS.
My dear Lewes.

I cannot resist the triple temptation you offer me, & will be with you tomorrow at 5 PM, to dinner. I confess I should very much like to meet Carlyle, but imagine he is a man who does not like being entered in upon by every body— Mihi cura non mediocris inest fontes ut adire remotos atq haurire queam vitae praecepta[1]—, on you however be the responsibility if in such a matter you do what you should not. I suppose I can get down from our station by train at 11.30 pm.[2]

                                        Yours always
                                        Anthony Trollope

To Mrs. S. C. Hall

MS Parrish Collection. SB 145.

July 3—1861   WALTHAM HOUSE, WALTHAM CROSS.
My dear Mrs. Hall.

I send my lecture.[3] I have made the necessary alterations in the first 12 or 14 pages. What changes will be necessary in the remainder are few, & I will make them in the press. The best name will be "Our National Gallery."

I go away next month. Perhaps you will cause your Chancellor of the Exchequer to send me his check before I do so—say in the first or second week of August.

                                        very faithfully yours
                                        Anthony Trollope

If I am wrong in sending this to your private address pray excuse me.

[9] Apparently a reference to the discussion of marriage in *Framley Parsonage*; see Trollope to Lewes, 7 April 1861.

[1] "I have no slight longing to be able to draw near to the sequestered fountains and to drink in the rules for living." (Horace, *Satires*, II, vi, 94.)

[2] On 5 July Lewes reported the meeting to T. A. Trollope: "As [Anthony] had never seen Carlyle, he was glad to go down with us to tea at Chelsea. Carlyle had read, and *agreed* with the West Indian book, and the two got on very well together; both Carlyle and Mrs. Carlyle liking Anthony—and I suppose it was reciprocal, though I didn't see him afterwards to hear what he thought." (*George Eliot Letters*, VIII, 287.)

[3] "The National Gallery," *St. James's Magazine*, 2 (September 1861), 163–76.

To Mary [? Christie][4]

MS Parrish Collection.

July 3. 1861   WALTHAM HOUSE, WALTHAM CROSS.
My dear Mary.

I find I must be in town tomorrow Thursday. I will call about 2—or a little after. Do not wait lunch as I am going to dine early. Tell your mother with my love to have no compunction as to refusing me admittance, if she had rather not see me— I shall understand it.

Yours always affectionately[5]

To [? Thomas Colley] Grattan[6]

MS Taylor Collection.

July 3. Wednesday night [1861][7]   WALTHAM HOUSE, WALTHAM CROSS.
My dear Grattan

I am very sorry you cant come to us—but perhaps we may arrange for another day.

I write now to say, that together with your letter I have got another making it necessary that I should go up to London on Thursday, tomorrow. I will therefore be at the Athenaeum at 3.30 tomorrow. If, as is probable, I do not find you, I shall go up again on Friday— If I do find you tant mieux. You will understand all this as well as tho' I wrote a volume. Any way I will not miss you one day or the other.

Can you come to me Thursday 11th.

Yours always
Any Trollope

To John Tilley

MS General Post Office, London. B 147.

July 4. 1861
For the Secretary

I agree altogether with Mr. Good,[8] and think that the moveable indicator is not required in places for which these boxes are intended, and would be too complicated for the class of persons by whom they would be worked.

[4] Possibly Mary Elizabeth Christie (1847–1906), daughter of William Dougal and Mary Grant Christie; later a worker for the Art for Schools Association and a contributor to the *Pall Mall Gazette, Spectator,* and other publications.

[5] Signature cut away.

[6] Probably Thomas Colley Grattan (1792–1864), travel writer and historical novelist, who for many years had been a friend of Trollope's mother.

[7] Watermark 1861; also, 3 July 1861 was a Wednesday.

[8] John Patten Good, Surveyor for the Gloucester District.

An attempt of such a kind, if a failure, places the Office in great difficulty, and I think that the cases of failure would be very numerous.[9]

Anthony Trollope

To George Smith

MS John Murray. B 148.

July 9. 1861   WALTHAM HOUSE, WALTHAM CROSS.

My dear Smith.

To save you trouble I have had your agreement copied, & have signed
& now send the copy. If you wish to have it in your own writing I will
sign another.

The agreement as drawn out is in accordance with what passed between us; but there are points I dont quite like. You have I believe a 2/6
set of novels. I trust it will not suit your views to put it into that, as your
doing so would go far to prevent any after publication at a higher rate—[1]

I find I have given uncommon short measure for the first number of
B. J. & R—barely over 15 pages. I hate short measure as I do poison; but
I hate inserting little bits to lengthen a chapter. Will it suit if I make
some other number somewhat longer? If the exigencies of the magazine
require 16 in the next number, I will do you another page. Let me know
this at once.

Yours always

G Smith Esq   Anthony Trollope

---

[9] Pillar boxes, which Trollope himself had introduced into England (see Trollope
to Creswell, 21 November 1851), listed collection times, but a person depositing mail
had no way of knowing whether he had just missed a collection. Trollope objected to
a movable indicator. Eventually, however, collection boxes were equipped with
indicators.

[1] Having rejected Smith's offer of £3,500 for absolute copyright in *The Small House
at Allington*, Trollope settled (by an agreement of 6 July 1861) for Smith's offer of
£2,500 for serial rights and an eighteen months' license to issue two kinds of book
editions; thereafter, Trollope had an option to buy out the current stock of the cheap
edition and resume ownership of the copyright. Trollope did not exercise his option,
nor did he ever again seek this particular arrangement with a publisher (see *Bibliography*, p. 279). *The Small House at Allington* was serialized in the *Cornhill* from
September 1862 through April 1864, and published in two volumes in March 1864.

M. de Fauche[2] to Trollope

MS Bodleian. *Commentary*, p. 205.

5 August. 1861
Sir—

Mr. Maxwell[3] the proprietor of the "Temple Bar" has asked me to offer you £1000 a year for three or five years, with the ostensible Editorship of the Magazine if you will undertake to supply a novel and fill the position that Mr Sala[4] now occupies in "Temple Bar."

All the real work of Editorship will be performed as heretofore by Mr Edmund Yates, who would act with you as Subeditor.

It is requested that the offer may be kept a secret, in the event of your being unable to accept it.[5]

M. D. F.

To Kate Field

MS Boston Public Library. *Commentary*, p. 226; B 149.

Augt 9. 1861   Waltham Cross
My dear Kate.

The great distance added to my bald head may perhaps justify me in so writing to you. I thank you heartily for your letters, one of which I

---

[2] M. de Fauche was probably connected with the Fauche who served as British Consul at Ostend in the early 1830's and whose wife was an old acquaintance of Trollope's mother (*Memoir*, I, 186, 195). This conjecture is based on a note from de Fauche to Trollope accompanying this letter: "Mr. Maxwell being an old friend of my father and knowing the intimacy that once existed between our two families, has written to beg I will make the enclosed communication to you." (MS Bodleian.)

[3] John Maxwell (1824–95), publisher; founded *Town Talk* in 1858, *Temple Bar* in 1860, *St. James's Magazine* in 1861, and *Belgravia* in 1866. He married the novelist M. E. Braddon in 1874.

[4] George Augustus Henry Sala (1828–96), well-known journalist and miscellaneous writer. Sala later claimed that he had started and named *Temple Bar*, though he acknowledged that the idea of establishing a rival to the *Cornhill* was Maxwell's: see Sala's *Life and Adventures* (New York, 1895), I, 358. Sala wrote an account of Trollope at the first *Cornhill* dinner, describing him as "very much to the fore, contradicting everybody; afterwards saying kind things to everybody, and occasionally going to sleep on sofas or chairs; or leaning against sideboards, and even somnolent while standing erect on the hearthrug. . . . [Trollope] had nothing of the bear but his skin, but [his] ursine envelope was assuredly of the most grisly texture." (*Things I Have Seen and People I Have Known* [1894], I, 30–31.)

[5] Trollope endorsed this letter "Ansd. 6 Augt 1861 / Hands full. / Would not undertake a mock Editorship." In addition to the affront to his honesty, the news that Edmund Yates was to do the real work must have been especially distasteful (see Trollope to Smith, 21 July 1860, n. 2). This offer of a nominal editorship is the subject of Gay to Trollope, 28 May 1863, and Trollope to Gay, 29 May 1863. For Yates's account of his subeditorship, see his *Edmund Yates: His Recollections and Experiences* (1884), I, 57–64.

have already sent off in a note from myself begging that rooms may be kept for us in the Tremont house.[6]

Has not this battle been terrible?[7] The worst of it is, that by no event could a stronger presage of long bloodshed be given. Had the Southerns [*sic*] been thrashed it might have led to some compromise; but victory on the part of the Southerns can lead to none. It is very sad, and one cannot but feel that the beginning of the end has not yet come.

You were thinking of returning.[8] But as you say nothing about it, and as I hear nothing of it from others, I suppose your plans are altered. I can not but think that Florence is at present the better residence for you.

Remember me most kindly to Cleopatra—if the sacrifice be still incomplete.

> Yours always most sincerely
> Anthony Trollope

To Mrs. S. C. Hall

MS New York University.

15 August—1861   WALTHAM HOUSE, WALTHAM CROSS.
My dear Mrs. Hall.

I go away in a weeks time for 7 or 8 months. Shall I be considered a dun if I ask you to have a check for £15 sent to me before I go—[9] It will save trouble. If I knew to whom else I might apply, I wd. not trouble you on so mundane a matter.

> Yours very truly
> Anthony Trollope

James Russell Lowell[1] to ?

Horace Elisha Scudder, *James Russell Lowell: A Biography* (Boston, 1901), II, 82–84.

20 September 1861

*   *   *

I dined the other day with Anthony Trollope, a big, red-faced, rather underbred Englishman of the bald-with-spectacles type. A good roaring positive fellow who deafened me (sitting on his right) till I thought of

---

[6] A well-known Boston hotel. On 24 August Trollope and his wife left for the United States.

[7] The first Battle of Bull Run, 21 July 1861; first major engagement of the Civil War.

[8] The Fields returned to Boston in October.

[9] Payment for "The National Gallery," *St. James's Magazine*, 2 (September 1861), 163–76.

[1] James Russell Lowell (1819–91), American poet, essayist, and diplomat.

Dante's Cerberus. He says he goes to work on a novel "just like a shoe-maker on a shoe, only taking care to make honest stitches." Gets up at 5 every day, does all his writing before breakfast, and always writes just so many pages a day. He and Dr. Holmes were very entertaining. The Autocrat started one or two hobbies, and charged, paradox in rest—but it was pelting a rhinoceros with seed-pearl.

"*Dr.* You don't know what Madeira is in England?

"*T.* I'm not so sure it's worth knowing.

"*Dr.* Connoisseurship in it with us is a fine art. There are men who will tell you a dozen kinds, as Dr. Waagen would know a Carlo Dolci from a Guido.

"*T.* They might be better employed!

"*Dr.* Whatever is worth doing is worth doing well.

"*T.* Ay, but that's begging the whole question. I don't admit it's *worse* doing at all. If they earn their bread by it, it may be *worse* doing (roaring).

"*Dr.* But you may be assured—

"*T.* No, but I may n't be asshŏrred. I *won't* be asshŏred. I don't intend to be asshŏred (roaring louder)!

And so they went it. It was very funny. Trollope wouldn't give him any chance. Meanwhile, Emerson and I, who sat between them, crouched down out of range and had some very good talk, with the shot hurtling overhead. I had one little passage at arms with T. *apropos* of English peaches. T. ended by roaring that England was the only country where such a thing as a peach or a grape was known. I appealed to Haw-thorne,[2] who sat opposite. His face mantled and trembled for a moment with some droll fancy, as one sees bubbles rise and send off rings in still water when a turtle stirs at the bottom, and then he said, "I asked an Englishman once who was praising their peaches to describe to me exactly what he meant by a peach, and he described something very like a cucumber." I rather liked Trollope.

*   *   *

[2] Trollope's impression of Hawthorne, whom he met on this occasion, is recorded by James T. Fields: "Trollope fell in love with you at first sight and went off moaning that he could not see you again. He swears you are the handsomest Yankee that ever walked this planet." (James C. Austin, *Fields of 'The Atlantic Monthly'*, p. 215.)

To H. T. Tuckerman[3]

Anderson Galleries Catalogue, Edwin T. Coggeshall sale, 25–27 April 1916, item 597. B 150.

1 November 1861

*   *   *

We are alarmed at the idea of an Embargo. I hope it is only a maneuvre [*sic*] of the Administration. . . . No man can have [a] greater or better object than that of making Englishmen understand Americans & Americans English.

*   *   *

To James T. Fields

MS Harvard.

November 3. 1861   Clarendon. New York

My dear Fields.

We are settled here for some week or ten days having returned from St Paul by Chicago— I will tell you all our adventures when I see you. We purpose being in Boston—tomorrow,—(Monday)—week, i e 10th. November,[4] or perhaps on Tuesday. I wrote to Mr Emerson some time since writing to him to your address, telling him that I hoped he would allow me to dine with him at his club on the last Saturday of November instead of the last of October. I hope he got my letter. Write me a line and tell me. I have desired Mr Gregory here to send me, to your address at Boston, his edition of all Coopers novels—32 volumes. He will have them delivered at your house of business. Will you give them house room till we reach Boston? I have seen F Harper and I will tell you what passed between us when I see you. Do you know anything of Miss Field. She was to have to [*sic*] let me know her address when I reached New York, but I have not heard of her. I am very anxious to know her address if I can find it. Probably however you do not know,—write me a line like a good fellow.

Yours always
Anthy Trollope

---

[3] Henry Theodore Tuckerman (1813–71), American critic, essayist, and poet. In his *America and Her Commentators* (New York, 1864), pp. 232–44, Tuckerman reviewed Trollope's *North America*, praising the book in general but censuring Trollope's inadequate preparation.

[4] Presumably Trollope's slip for "11th."

To Kate Field

MS Boston Public Library. *Commentary*, pp. 226–27; B 152.

November 5. 1861   New York
My dear Kate.

I am amused by the audacity of your letter. Ever since we have been here we have been abusing you for not keeping your word. You told us that we should find you in the neighbourhood of New York. That you would let us know your address there or thereabouts. And that we were to trust to you to meeting—not at Boston but New York. Now you turn upon us as tho' we were to blame.

However we will forgive you on condition that you remain at the address named till next Tuesday—this day week. We shall reach Boston that evening, & will make you out very soon. I suppose you could not come up to us that evening.

You write about sending my wife home as tho' she were as free from impediments in the world as your happy self. She has a house, and children & cows & horses and dogs & pigs—and all the stern necessities of an English home. Nor could a woman knock about in winter as we have both done during the autumn. But we shall be a fortnight in Boston, & I do hope we may have a good time of it. I can assure you that in looking forward to it, I do not count a little on you. I have been real angry with you this week for not turning up.

Yours always
Anthony Trollope

To R. H. Dana[5]

MS Massachusetts Historical Society. B 153.

22 Novr. 1861   Tremont House
My dear Mr. Dana.

Mrs. Trollope and I are very sorry that we are prevented from going to you on Monday evening. We dine that day with Mr. Sturgis.[6] Mrs. Trollope leaves, and returns home on Wednesday by the Cunard packet. She will however go out to Cambridge on Monday morning and will call on Mrs. Dana. I am very sorry that we have been so unlucky in missing you—

very faithfully yours
Anthony Trollope

[5] Richard Henry Dana (1815–82), lawyer and writer; author of *Two Years Before the Mast* (1840).

[6] Perhaps William Sturgis (1782–1863), a wealthy Boston merchant; formerly a Massachusetts state legislator.

To ?

MS Haverford College. SB 154.

26 November 1861   Boston
Dear Sir.

I have pleasure in sending you below that for which you ask, attaching very small value to the present.

Your faithful Servant
Anthony Trollope

You must excuse me if I have found it beyond my power to decipher your name aright—

To Charles Eliot Norton[7]

MS Harvard. SB 155.

[26 November 1861][8]
Tuesday night   Tremont House
My dear Sir.

I hardly remember how we stand about your kind invitation to me. Was I to write to you or you to me?

If you are still disengaged I shall be happy to go to you on Friday. If so let me know the hour. If however you sd. have changed your plans *pray* do not hesitate to say so—

very faithfully yours
Anthony Trollope

To James T. Fields

MS Berg Collection. SB 918.

[28 November 1861][9]
Thursday morning
My dear Fields

The box contains books *written by myself* and published in England —nothing else. They are for a present to a lady here.

I am just off to Concord. If you or Mr Ticknor[1] can get the box on by the C. House,[2] I should be much obliged. In that case keep it till you see me.—tomorrow.

Yours very truly
Any Trollope

[7] Charles Eliot Norton (1827–1908), well-known editor, author, and professor of fine arts at Harvard.

[8] Envelope postmarked 27 November, a Wednesday.

[9] Trollope's account books (Parrish Collection) show that he went to Concord on Thursday, 28 November.

[1] William Davis Ticknor (1810–64), publisher; partner in the Boston publishing firm of Ticknor & Fields.

[2] The Boston Custom House.

Kate Field

To William Barlow Lee

MS Columbia. SB 156.

7. Decr.—1861   Philadelphia. Continental
My dear Sir.

I have just received a letter from Dr. Lothrop[3]—containing yours to him. But as he does not give me your address, and as it is not in your letter I fear this may not reach you.

I am very much obliged by the trouble taken by you on my behalf, & shall be very happy to take the rooms you speak of at $5 a day. You do not give their address & therefore I must ask you—to take the trouble to let me have a line addressed to the Utah House Baltimore. I purpose to take them from the 14 of this month. I shall probably be in Washington on that day, but if not will of course pay for them from that time. I might be detained till Monday.

Again thanking you much for your trouble

                         I am Dear Sir
                     Your very faithful Servant
W B Lee Esq   Anthony Trollope

To Kate Field

MS Boston Public Library. *Commentary*, pp. 227–28; B 157.

                               305. I Street
Decr. 17. 1861   Washington.
My dear Kate.

You will be surprised to hear from me again so soon, but I want to know whether that lecture which we heard from Everett[4] at Roxbury has been published; and if so I want to get it. Can you let me know?

I am in a lamentable position. I have an anthrax on my forehead & can not get out of the house. I have been to see no one since I came here & am all alone in my lodgings. A doctor has chopped it across twice, as you see in the following picture.

---

[3] Dr. Samuel Kirkland Lothrop (1804–86), minister of the Brattle Square Unitarian Church, Boston. Trollope's account books (Parrish Collection) show that Trollope dined with Charles Sumner and Lothrop at Lothrop's home on 6 September 1861, the evening after his arrival in Boston.

[4] Edward Everett (1794–1864), statesman, orator, Unitarian minister, Harvard professor, and editor of the *North American Review* (also a friend of Trollope's mother). He delivered his famous speech "The Causes and Conduct of the Civil War" 62 times. Trollope heard the speech on 22 November, at Roxbury, Massachusetts, and later wrote of Everett: "I did not like what he said, or the seeming spirit in which it was framed. But I am bound to admit that his power of oratory is very wonderful." (*North America*, I, 349.) For the text of Everett's speech, see his *Orations and Speeches on Various Occasions* (Boston, 1868), IV, 464–89.

 my forehead

The cross means the two chops. But the chops will keep healing and the thing which has collected itself inside will not come out. Tomorrow it is to be chopped again and the chops cauterized to prevent their healing. All this is pleasant especially as I am anxious to get out and see the people before war is declared. I wish you were here to condole with me and get yourself scolded.

There will be war if those two horrid men are not given up. I wish Wilkes with his whole cargo had gone to the bottom.[5] I am no lawyer, but I felt from the first that England would not submit to have her ships stopped and her passengers hauled about & taken off. The common sense of the thing is plain, let all the wigged fogies of the Admiralty courts say what they will. Because you quarrel with your wife nobody else is to be allowed to walk the streets quietly! I expect we shall be in Boston before long, shaking hands with you & embracing and crying, as I get on board the Cunard boat with my head tied up in a huge linseed poultice,— as it is now.

Tell me about the lecture.

Yours ever
A. T.

[5] Captain Charles Wilkes, commander of the U.S.S. *San Jacinto*, had boarded the British ship *Trent* on 8 November to remove James Murray Mason and John Slidell, Confederate diplomats on their way to London and Paris, respectively. The British issued a demand for the release of the prisoners, who were detained in Boston, and there was fear that war might ensue. Trollope wrote: "It was understood that Mr. Sumner was opposed to the rendition of the men, and Mr. Seward in favour of it. Mr. Seward's counsels at last prevailed with the President, and England's declaration of war was prevented. I dined with Mr. Seward on the day of the decision [27 December 1861], meeting Mr. Sumner at his house, and was told as I left the dining-room what the decision had been." (*Autobiography*, pp. 165–66.) In *North America* Trollope was frequently critical of Seward. See also Trollope to Knower, 18 February 1866.

To Salmon P. Chase[6]

MS Historical Society of Pennsylvania. SB 158.

31. Decr. 1861   305 I Street—
Tuesday
Mr Anthony Trollope presents his compliments to Mr Chase. He got Mr
Chase's card after 10 am this morning. Mr Trollope will be out of
Washington from tomorrow till Friday—but will be very glad to have
the honor of waiting on Mr Chase after that.

1862

To Mr. Russell

MS (photostat) Parrish Collection. SB 166.

[? January 1862][7]
Sunday   305 I Street.
My dear Mr Russell.
    I must beg ten thousand pardons for my stupidity in not having read
& inwardly digested your note before I rushed up with an answer. I see
that your dinner does not come off in presence of your own Lares, & you
must therefore allow me to beg off.
    In any way I should be fidgetty as to getting back—at your own place
I should have felt easy that you would not have waited. But as it is I
shall be more comfortable in my mind without an engagement.
                                                    Yours very truly
                                                    Anthony Trollope

    [6] Salmon Portland Chase (1808–73), Senator for Ohio, 1849–55, 1860; Governor of
Ohio, 1855–59; Secretary of the Treasury, 1861–64; Chief Justice of the Supreme
Court, 1864–73.
    [7] Trollope's account books (Parrish Collection) show that he dined several times
with a Mr. Russell during his stay in Washington (from 14 December to 13 January).

To Frederic Chapman

MS Parrish Collection. Excerpt, *Commentary*, pp. 240–41; B 159.

1 Jany 1861 [1862]   Washington.
My dear Chapman.

Thanks for your letter. I did recommend marriage to you, and am glad you have been so docile.[8] I hope you got my letter of congratulation.

I know nothing of the "Public Opinion"—never to the best of my belief having heard the name. Little wrote to me asking leave to put the stories into some paper.[9] He may have named that. I sent his letter to R Bell; and as I had before acted in the matter on Mr. Bell's opinion, I gave him authority either to give or refuse the permission which Little requested. My impression is that the stories have been published without any permission.

I have sent no articles to the Cornhill, and have told Geo Smith that I could not send any. I found that my doing so would interfere with other work.[1]

You sent me an article on "Mr Trollope," cut out of some paper.[2] From what paper was it cut? The author of it criticizes my writings, pointing out their weakness, and in doing so follows the proper line of his profession. But he goes beyond that when he takes upon himself to analize my motives in writing. His charge is that I write for money. Of course I do;—as does he also— It is for money that we all work, lawyers, publishers, authors and the rest of us. If we do bad work we shall not get paid for it,—and I like others must feel myself to be governed by that law or else shall fall to the ground. If my work be bad let him so tell his readers and there his work should end.

But I have worse to say of this critic than that. He insinuates that I have published under my name the writings of other people. He does not dare to say this; but he says that which is intended to make his readers

---

[8] Frederic Chapman married Clara Woodin, a wealthy heiress, on 21 November 1861.

[9] The *London Review*, managed by William Little, had purchased the serial rights to eight stories by Trollope (see Trollope to Little, 22 September 1860); five of these stories were in turn sold to the London weekly *Public Opinion*. See *Bibliography*, pp. 49–50, 276.

[1] See Trollope to Chapman, 16 June 1861, and Trollope to Smith, 16 June 1861.

[2] "Mr. Trollope," *The Literary Budget*, 1 December 1861, pp. 61–62. The article contended: "In these days of economical science it has been discovered that literature is governed, just like other things, by the laws of supply and demand. . . . The first object of a writer is to get a reputation with the least possible waste of trouble; the next, to traffic upon the capital which he has acquired, and to make a well-known name guarantee the washiest effusions of his own, or, perhaps, of another's brain." Of Trollope's accelerated output, the writer remarked: "Such extraordinary fecundity can only result in a brood of rickety children: it would be hardly excusable were it Mr. Trollope's only resource for earning his bread; but surely it is utterly without justification in the case of a well-paid government official." See P. D. Edwards, "Trollope and the Reviewers: Three Notes," *N&Q*, n.s. 15 (November 1968), 418–19.

so believe. This is in every way unfair & cowardly. No man should insinuate such a charge, unless he has strong ground to believe it to be true. This man can have no such ground. To those who know me I need make no assurance that such a charge is false.

So we are to have no war. I for one am very glad— The Americans just at present are rather quiet on the subject; but they will not forget to tell us about it, when their present troubles are over.

I am greatly shocked at the Princes death.[3] The effect on the Queen will be terrible.

always faithfully yours
Anthony Trollope

I am very sorry to hear of Edward Chapman's accident. Pray remember me to him. Keep the cigars for me—like a true man. I shall have none if not them. Thanks for paying. If you wish you shall have some when I arrive. How many are there?

To Kate Field

MS Boston Public Library. *Commentary,* pp. 230–31; B 160 (incomplete).

4. Jany 1862.   Washington
My dear Kate.

All manner of happy new years to you and to your mother.

Why no story? I fear you are idle;—that you spend your time in running after false gods,—Wendall Philips,[4] woman Doten[5] & so on, seeking the excitement of ultra ideas and theoretical progress, while you begrudge the work of your brain, and the harder work of your fingers and backbone. Those lectures are but an intellectual idleness, an apology for sitting without a book to read or a skirt to hem or a shirt to fell[6] instead of with them. You want to go ahead of other folk,—you know you do; but you wish to do it lazily;—or rather you are lazy in your mode of wishing it. You would whistle for a storm like a witch; but storms now a days will not come for whistling. You must sit down with a trumpet and blow at it till your cheeks would split. If you'll do that, something of a puff of wind will come at last. Now I hope you will find yourself well rated, & will send me your story off hand.

---

[3] Prince Albert died on 14 December 1861.

[4] Wendell Phillips (1811–84), prominent Boston abolitionist. Trollope had heard Phillips speak in Boston and was very critical of him in *North America*: "To me it seemed the doctrine he preached was one of rapine, bloodshed, and social destruction." (I, 354.)

[5] Elizabeth Doten (*b.* 1829), poet and short-story writer who claimed to receive inspiration by communicating with the spirits of Shakespeare, Poe, Burns, and others. Her *Poems from the Inner Life* (1863) went through many editions (the seventh was published in 1869). Kate Field's interest in spiritualism led to her interest in Doten. See Trollope to Field, 6 January 1862 and 3 June 1868.

[6] To sew or hem.

So Slidell & Mason are gone. I will not argue with you about them in a letter. To do so fairly would take hours and pages. Cobden[7] is no statesman;—never even tried his hand at state craft. As for Bright[8]—of course, if he or any other man will re-echo American ideas & American desires, Americans, and you as one, will return the echo again. But he has been alone in England. He did not even dare to make that speech in a large city.[9] But the men are gone, & thank God we shall have no war. Do not think that I triumph because they are gone. I only triumph because I need not quarrel with you and yours.

The blaze on my forehead has gone out, & I have been starring it about with all my accustomed personal attractions. I have seen most of the bigwigs here except the President, but have not as yet been to the White House. I spent four days in the camp, (without washing) and had quite enough of it. I think of leaving this for Harrisburg & Cincinnati on the 12th. or 14th.

Yours always dear Kate—
Very affectionately
Any Trollope

My love to your mother—

I presume you will have heard from Rose. She was very unhappy in her voyage, having resolved that she would be so— But now is at peace with her cows & pigs. Write to her.

To James T. Fields

MS Massachusetts Historical Society. B 161.

305 I Street.
Washington.

Jany 4. 1861 [1862].
My dear Fields.

You were to have given me Longfellows[1] autograph—for my wife (She has just sent me the enclosed). Pray do— She had but a sorry passage home, but is now settled peaceably among her pigs and poultry.

---

[7] Richard Cobden (1804–65), liberal statesman; leader of the Anti-Corn Law League. Cobden had visited America twice, and (like Bright) supported the Northern cause in the Civil War.

[8] John Bright (1811–89), liberal statesman; extremely able speaker for many liberal causes; a leading representative (along with Cobden) of the emerging manufacturing class as a political force. Trollope was justly accused of caricaturing Bright as Mr. Turnbull in *Phineas Finn*: see Trollope to the Editor of the *Daily Telegraph*, 31 March 1869.

[9] A reference to Bright's speech at Rochdale on 4 December 1861, defending the seizure of Slidell and Mason from the *Trent*. Privately, however, Bright had recommended to Charles Sumner that the issue be submitted to unconditional arbitration.

[1] Trollope had met Longfellow in Cambridge on 29 November (account books, Parrish Collection). He greatly admired Longfellow's poetry and called Longfellow "the poet-laureat of the West" (*North America*, I, 380).

I go hence to Cincinnati on 12th. Inst. That at least is my programme.
I shall beat you up about 15 of March on my way home. Heavens, how
quickly the time goes.

I have been over in the lines spending some days. It was dull enough—
& awfully cold!! I am not given greatly to military pursuits. I went down
to Mount Vernon, where we might all have gone easily enough, & shed
a metaphorical tear over the Great Mans grave. Ah me! that they should
now be fighting over the spot.

Ch Sumner[2] told me to day that Dana is in town but I have not seen
him. I shall try to do so— I am dining out & *teaing*[3] out, & doing a deal of
talk, but somehow the place is dull to me. I dont care for such conviviali-
ties if the people are merely strangers.

Yours always
Anty Trollope

If you do not write before 12th. address to Cincinnati. Fred Chapman
writes in sombre strains as to trade— But that is the way with all you
publishers when you write to us slaveys.

To Kate Field

MS Boston Public Library. *Commentary*, pp. 231–32; B 162.

Jany 6. 1861 [1862]   Washington.
Dearest Kate.

I am afraid my verdict about the enclosed will pain you. The lines are
not manipulated,—not cared for and worked out with patience and long
thought as should I think be done with poetry. Fine poetry is not I think
written by flashes. Take the ode to Liberty. "Smile on," and "Union"
surely form no rhyme. Nor do "Freemen" and "gleethen." But the
thought and imagery of a poem is more important than the rhyme. Take
the Susannah. "Watch lady watch. Glow worms the night illume; Pulsating fire;—" So far, good, at any rate the idea is true if not new. But
the fourth line upsets the metaphor altogether. The glow worm con-
sumes nothing, & its fire is altogether innocent.

Watch lady watch. Glow worms illume the night
Pulsating fire. Your watching is as bright.

Then the image would have been entire throughout; tho the stanza
would be not perhaps worth much.[4]

---

[2] Charles Sumner (1811–74), prominent Massachusetts Senator, 1851–74; a leading
opponent of slavery in the years preceding the Civil War.

[3] Underlined twice. Dana records in a scrap of diary that he breakfasted with
Trollope on Thursday, 9 January; he found Trollope "intolerable, no manners, but
means well, & would do a good deal to serve you, but says the most offensive things—
not a gentleman" (MS Massachusetts Historical Society).

[4] These poems have not been traced; presumably, they were never published.

Jokes in poetry should be clear as crystal—& should be clear to all readers. But how many would catch the joke of the "pragmatic sanction"? Besides the joke is untrue to itself, for the word pragmatic means nothing apart from the joke.

Poetry should be very slow work—slow, patient, and careless of quick result. That is not your character. Philanthropical ratiocination is your line, not philandering amatory poetising. I will not say that poetry will not come. As you grow older and calmer and as you learn to think slower and with less of individual blood in your thought, the gift of poetry may come to you. But I doubt that it is to be desired. Who but the very highest do anything as poets? What is the reputation of Poe or Holmes,[5] or [our] own L.E.L.?[6] What good have they done? It is a mistake to suppose that prose is grander than poetry per se.[7] It may be so; and has been so. But it has been so in the hands of a few people on whom God has set a very special mark. Scott will be known by his novels & not by his poetry. As is Johnson also, by his prose. And also Irving. And also Landor.

Ah me. It gives me such pain to write this. I still believe in you as strongly as ever. I still think that if you will work, you will succeed. But I should have said, a priori, that you would do better as a writer of prose than of poetry. I still think so—and advise you accordingly.

I know how bitter this is. You'll say that it isn't, and you'll be good; and then you'll go about for a day or two with a heavy feeling of illtreatment at your heart;—illtreatment not from me, but from the world. I know from *much* experience how bitter are the sapient criticisms of one's elders on the effusions of one's youth! I too have written verses, & have been told that they were nought. I am very fond of you, and it grieves me to pain you. But that will be no consolation!

You will have understood that my late "jobation" letter was written before yours came with the pieces of poetry. Take courage dear Kate, & stick to the story. If you don't like it, do it again— It is a great profession that of writing; but you must spoil much paper, & undergo many doubting, weary, wretched, hours. But I do think that you can write good nervous readable prose;—and I know that you have a mind capable of putting something into that vehicle.

Tom says. "I *have* written to Kate Field." There was no special Florence news. I presume you will by this have heard from Rose. She said she should write to you. She had a bad time going over:—but then she had made up her mind to have a bad time.

---

[5] Oliver Wendell Holmes (1809–94), distinguished man of letters. For James Russell Lowell's account of Trollope playfully shouting Holmes down at a dinner, see Lowell to ?, 20 September 1861.

[6] Letitia Elizabeth Landon (1802–38), popular poet and novelist; a friend of Trollope's mother in the early 1830's.

[7] Doubtless a slip for "poetry is grander than prose."

My kind love to your mother. Do not let her be ill. I am trying to manage to get South, but believe I shall fail.

Your affectionate friend[8]

Thanks for the woman Doten's effusion. It is not bad, but not so good to read as it was to hear.

A. T.

To Salmon P. Chase

MS Historical Society of Pennsylvania. B 163.

8 January 1862
Private.   305 I Street
Dear Sir.

Will you excuse me if I take up your time for a minute. Our press in England has among other charges brought this accusation against you,—that you—(I do not mean the Secretary of the Treasury but the United States people) are not willing to take on yourselves any portion of the present cost of the war—but are staving it off onto the shoulders of those who will follow you. On my return to England I shall probably publish some remarks referring more or less to the present state of the Country, and according to my views as at present taken, I shall endeavor to shew that this charge is not true. I do not myself think that your present financial crisis will lead to any tremendous future financial embarrassment;—but as far as I am at present informed it seems that some change in your constitution must be made before you can arrange the stock of your debt satisfactorily.

I venture to say this, not as supposing that my opinion can be of any possible weight to you, but in order that you may be aware of the subject on which I am very anxious to have an opportunity of hearing you for five minutes. Should you however tell me that you do not wish to speak to me on the matter, I shall not take it the least in dudgeon; and shall quite understand that coming from you such an answer will be in no way uncourteous. I can assure you that my views as regards your war in general are probably in accordance with your own.

Your faithful Servant
Anthony Trollope

I shall do myself the honor of waiting on you on Saturday in accordance with your permission.

[8] First signature cut away.

To Kate Field

MS Boston Public Library. *Commentary*, pp. 232–33; B 164.

12 Jany 1861 [1862]   Washington
My dear Kate.

I have just got your letter & have only one moment to tell you that my address will be St. Louis. I shall be there 23 of this month, but shall not remain there. You had better now keep your story as I shall be in a state of turmoil, and heaven knows where in regard to post offices. You speak of causes which prevent your working. Do you mean, your health? But you may have troubles and sorrows by the score of which I know nothing. It is so with our dearest friends. But God has been good to me and gives me no grievance of which I can not speak—unless it might be thought unmannerly to say that I have another horrible carbuncle on the small of my back—(If my back has a small).

Your letter to me was written after receipt of my first, but before the receipt of my last. I fear I shall have pained you— The upshot of my criticism was meant to be this—that good work will require hard toil.

Rose writes in most lachrymose spirits, all my letters from the west having gone astray. I hope they have amused the Post office officials.

Yours always—just now in great trouble of haste.

A. T.

To James T. Fields

MS Huntington Library. B 165.

January 20—1862   Cincinnati.
My dear Fields.

Many thanks for your note—and very many to Longfellow for his poem which Mrs. Trollope will value much.

Who is the author of the enclosed? I want to know—also whether it is new or an old song? Did it appear in the Atlantic? Did Whittier write it?[9]

So you are going the whole hog for abolition.[10] Well, it is consistent. But by Jove you are bold fellows to do it now. I think it is a mistake. Abolition drove the South to Secession, & will make a return to Union impracticable. You know I am no Southern or I should not venture to say so.

Fred Chapman is always in the dumps. If he do not make money hand over hand he thinks the world is coming to an end. Perhaps it is.

---

[9] Trollope enclosed a copy of Whittier's immediately popular "Song of the Negro Boatmen" (apparently clipped from a Pittsburgh newspaper [B]). The poem was later published in the *Atlantic Monthly*, 9 (February 1862), 244–46.

[10] Probably a reference to A. D. White's "Jefferson and Slavery," *Atlantic Monthly*, 9 (January 1862), 29–40.

I am just now going—God knows where. If you answer this at once address to St. Louis. If not keep your answer till you hear again. But remember I want an answer about the nigger song;—which if new, I will—"borrow."

My kindest regards to your wife. I never saw a woman so ill used as she was that Sunday when you made her go down to dinner giving her only 30 seconds to brush her hair & do her fixings,—nor any woman who bore such ill usage so well.

Thanks greatly for your kind hospitality. I will write to you in full when I find myself returning,—if ever I return. I was not raised in New England, & had no high schools &c in my diggings. So it is well that I can write at all,—let alone so unwriteable a name as my own.

Yours always
Anthony Trollope[1]

Should any letter come to you for me, keep it.

To Kate Field

MS Boston Public Library. *Commentary*, pp. 233–34; B 167.

4. Febry. 1862   Cairo.[2]
My dear Kate.

I was very glad to get your letter—and your pardon for my criticisms. As I hope to be in Boston by the end of this month, or quite early in March, I will not now say any more about the story. Miss Crow[3] says that you are not well. Is this so? I know that you are not a female Hercules. None but Englishwomen are. But I hope you are not really ill,—or, which is almost worse,—really ailing. If so I will not bully you again about writing—

Mr. Crow was very civil to me at St. Louis & also to a friend who was with me. Dr. Elliot[4] I also saw, but he was in affliction for the death of a child. I do not like the West. It is well to say it out at once. Boston I do like; and New York. I do not dislike the people at Washington, tho' the town itself is bad. At Philadelphia I could get on very well. But I do not love the Westerns. They are dry, dirty, and unamusing. Till I came here I thought St Louis the dirtiest place in the world; but this place certainly bears the palm. The discussion of my military adventures I must put off till I see you. I am great in guns, bombs, shells, mortars, and questions of gunpowder generally. Oh, what thieving, swindling, and lying

---

[1] Unusually large and legible signature. In his next letter to Fields, written on 12 March 1862, Trollope printed his signature in large capital letters.

[2] A town in southern Illinois.

[3] Emma Crow, a childhood friend of Kate Field (whom Trollope had met in Florence).

[4] William Greenleaf Eliot (1811–87), Unitarian minister; founder and later Chancellor of Washington University, St. Louis; grandfather of T. S. Eliot.

there has been in the management of this war! How your unfortunate country has been plundered! Gunpowder that wont explode— Shells that won't burst. Blankets rotten as tinder. Water put up in oil casks. Ships sent to sea that can hardly hold their planks together! There have been crimes in the North worse even than the sin of Buchanan & Floyd.[5]

If you only want money to go to St Louis I will not pity your poverty. You are better at Boston. But if it was wanted to carry you to England, I would negotiate a loan for you under Mr. Chase's wing among the Croesus's of Wall Street.

Write me a line saying how you are, to Niagara Falls Postoffice. My kind love to your mother.

Yours affectionately.
A. T.

I had some talk with Eliot about you. "Let her marry a husband," said he. "It is the best career for a woman." I agreed with him—and therefore bid you in his name as well as my own, to go & marry a husband.

To Frederic Chapman

MS Berg Collection. B 168.

13. February. 1862   Cincinnati.
My dear Chapman.

Mrs. Trollope has written to me, asking me whether I would like to have a portion of my book on America printed on slips,[6] ready for me when I return. I will tell you exactly how I stand about it, and leave you to decide as to the printing. I have finished two thirds of the whole, & shall have the MS completed by the middle of April. I propose that it shall be published by the middle of May.[7] You can have Vol I, ready for the printers, by April 3rd. or 4th.—and the second volume by instalments as quick as you may wish them. If under these circumstances, you think well to print, say half the first volume, on slips, you can write to Mrs. Trollope for the first ten chapters. If you think you will have time after the 3rd. or 4th. April for the whole, so as to get it out by 15—or 20 May, you need not put yourself to the expense. I do not anticipate that there will be much change in the first chapters; tho there will doubtless be some.

---

[5] James Buchanan (1791–1868), President of the United States from 1856 to 1860 and an ardent advocate of states' rights, had appointed a number of secessionists to office, including John B. Floyd (1806–63), former Governor of Virginia. Floyd resigned from office (as Secretary of War) and eventually became a major-general in the Confederate Army. In *North America* Trollope repeatedly accused Buchanan of treason for "allowing the germ of secession to make any growth" and for sending arms out of the North to Southern arsenals (I, 10, 22–23, 434–35; II, 71).

[6] Galley proofs.

[7] *North America* was published in May.

Mrs. Trollope says you are disappointed about the 1st. vol of Orley Farm. Who the deuce buys the first volume of a book? As far as I can hear the novel is as well spoken of as any I ever wrote. I fear we made a mistake about the shilling.[8]

For heavens sake pay my money in from month to month. If you do not I shall be overdrawing my account some fine morning.

I hope matrimony suits you. I shall be home by the 24 March.

Yours always

F Chapman Esq Anthony Trollope

To A. N. Zevely[9]

MS Jacques T. Schlenger.

16 Feb—1862. Baltimore.
Dear Sir.

The enclosed which I have received from London will answer your question as to the number of letters returned daily by each clerk in the London Post Office.

I shall be in Washington in a day or two when I will do myself the pleasure of calling on you.

Yours very faithfully

A. N. Zevely Esq Anthony Trollope

To [? William] Sturgis

MS American Antiquarian Society.

[6 March 1862][1]
Thursday night
My dear Mr. Sturgis—

I shall be most happy to dine with you on Saturday at 5, if you will allow me to leave early after dinner. I have a previous engagement to go to Cambridge with some ladies at 8.

very faithfully
Anthony Trollope

---

[8] *Orley Farm* was published in two volumes at eleven shillings per volume instead of the usual ten shillings; the first volume was published on 3 December 1861, the second on 25 September 1862. (The novel was also being issued in monthly parts; these ran from March 1861 through October 1862.)

[9] A. N. Zevely, Third Assistant Postmaster at the Washington postal headquarters.

[1] Trollope's account books (Parrish Collection) show that the arrangements described in this letter were for Saturday, 8 March 1862.

To Mrs. Sturgis

MS American Antiquarian Society.

[9 March 1862]
Sunday morning   Boston.
My dear Mrs. Sturgis.
    I send you all that I have in the world to comfort me. The offering may not seem much to you, but you must confess that it is a great deal for me to give. If however you will do me the kindness of placing the tribute on your drawing room table, I shall feel more than satisfied altho the value of the article to me personally is so great.

always very sincerely
Yours
Anthony Trollope

To James T. Fields

MS Yale.

12 March [1862]
10. am.   N. Y.
I have the books for your wife's sister all right.
Nothing has reached me for Landor.
If you have sent Landor's Mss² to the Clarendon, it will be dealt with there as you may direct. Only in such case you must write to them.
    Now I'm off.
    God bless you

A TROLLOPE

Norman Macleod³ to Trollope

MS Bodleian. *Commentary*, pp. 243.

[? March or April 1862]   ADELAIDE PLACE
Friday   GLASGOW
My dear Sir,
    As the Editor of a humble sixpenny monthly—"Good Words"—I approach you with the respect & reverence becoming a beggar seeking crumbs from a rich mans table. But as Chaplain of the Gaiters, I knock

---

² Fields had agreed in 1860 to publish the definitive American edition of W. S. Landor's works. In the event, Landor was unable to supervise the editing, and the Civil War offered Fields an excuse for abandoning the project.

³ Dr. Norman Macleod (1812–72), Scottish divine; chaplain to Queen Victoria, 1857–72; editor of *Good Words*, 1860–72. This letter began the troubled publication history of *Rachel Ray*: see Trollope to Millais, 4 June 1863; Trollope to Strahan, 10 June 1863; Macleod to Trollope, 11 June 1863; and *Commentary*, pp. 242–52. On "Chaplain of the Gaiters," see Trollope to Burns, 12 July 1878.

at your door with the boldness of one having authority. Be so good my son as [to] hear your Revd. Father!

You will be waited upon by my publisher Mr Strahan[4] as sensible a fellow as I know—truthful, honorable, generous—and with enterprise fit to cement again the American Union.

He wants a story i.e. a Novel from you for Good Words for 1863. Now please read on & don't pitch this into the fire.

You never perhaps heard of Good Words? But Strahan will tell you all about it. Enough, that our circulation is now 70,000—& that *I* am Editor!

You fancy we wont pay up to the mark? Well, name your price to Strahan & hear what he says—as to matters of detail we have time enough to consider them.

Seriously, you & Kingsley[5] are the only two men whom I should like to have a story from—and I should feel proud to have you—& one of your best—in my pages. I think you could let out the *best* side of your soul in Good Words—better far than even in Cornhill—

Strahan is in London & is to call for you—[6]

I remain yours sincerely
N. Macleod

To R. H. Dana

MS Massachusetts Historical Society. B 169; William Coyle, "The Friendship of Anthony Trollope and Richard Henry Dana, Jr.," *New England Quarterly*, 25 (June 1952), 258–59.

Waltham House
Waltham Cross.

1 April 1862

My dear Mr Dana.

You know the old saying. Give an inch and you'll be asked for an ell. You have been so kind to me in that matter of judicial information that I am tempted to ask you to read two chapters of my book in order that any errors *in fact* may be corrected by your correct knowledge. They are

---

[4] Alexander Strahan (1833–1918), publisher of *Good Words, Argosy*, and the *Contemporary Review*. Strahan later published several of Trollope's works: *Lotta Schmidt and Other Stories* (1867), *He Knew He Was Right* (1869), *An Editor's Tales* (1870), and the part-issue and first illustrated edition of *Ralph the Heir* (1870–71). See Virtue to Trollope, 25 January 1870, for Strahan's involvement with *St. Paul's Magazine*.

[5] Charles Kingsley (1819–75), clergyman and novelist.

[6] Trollope noted on the letter: "Saw Strahan Monday 7 April 1862 agreed to write one volume novel, long as Lovel the Widower—for 6 numbers of Good Words—from July to Decr. 1863 for £600. Magazine to possess simply the use of the story— It being in my power to break the arrangement." A further note reads: "On Friday 5th. December 1862 saw Strahan again, & agreed with him that the novel should be twice the aforesaid size, still to come out in six numbers from 1 July to 1 Decr. 1863— the price to be £1,000. Decr. 7. 1862." (MS Bodleian.)

on the Constitution and Judicature of your country. I take the written Constitution; and the mixed practice of your law Courts. You will perceive that my object is, not that of writing learned treatises on either subjects [*sic*], but of making representations which shall put them before Englishmen in a familiar light.

As to my opinions, of course they will not find favor with you. There must be much as to which in opinion any two men of the two countries must differ. You will disagree with me entirely as to the suspension of the writ of H. C.[1] (Can you tell me what is that H. C.?)—and probably also on other political conclusions to which I have come. But perhaps your friendship will induce you to give me notice on the margin left for that purpose, of any *errors in facts* which I have made. You can write in ink as the MS sent to you will not go to the printer.

My book comes out on May 12—& you will therefore see that I want your corrections *at once*. Both chapters were written on my way home at sea—

It may be as well to divulge my political heresies & follies to none of my friends or enemies till I myself place myself in their power.

Oh—that my enemy would write a book.

With a grateful remembrance of your pleasant voice and a thoro' hope that I may soon hear it here I am

Dear Mr. Dana
always faithfully yours
Anthony Trollope

Do not prepay your parcel back to me. I have a few remaining privileges as a Post Office officer. Address. A Trollope

General Post Office
London.

I calculate the pages will come back by the Cunard of 23 April from N. York.

To George Smith

MS Bodleian. Excerpt, *Commentary*, p. 241; B 170.

May 2nd. 1862.   WALTHAM HOUSE, WALTHAM CROSS.
My dear Smith.

I called this morning but I was a little too early. I will change the name, tho' I cannot as yet say what the name shall be. I will change it, as you don't like it, as I myself do not feel strongly in its favor. But I must say that your reason against it as touching Mrs. B. Stowe's novel

---

[1] Trollope contended that Lincoln, in suspending the writ of habeas corpus without the authority of Congress, had "committed a breach of the constitution" (*North America*, II, 277). The constitutional problem is by no means settled even today. For further discussion, see Trollope to Dana, 10 May 1862.

would not have much weight with me. Am I to eschew pearls because she has got one?[8] Not if [I] know it.

Can you tell me what was our agreement—or rather our understanding for there was no agreement—as touching the period up to which I was not to write any other serial. If I remember rightly I did make some offer to you in a note,—saying that I would not do so for four, six, or eight months after the commencement of the Cornhill serial. But it has not been put into the agreement, & I should like to know to what I am supposed to be bound. I rather think you suggested six months, & I, with my usual liberality, offered eight— I am willing to make it ten. But I am thinking of publishing (or rather of having published) a short story in Scotland in the latter half of next year.[9]

Yours always

Anthony Trollope

To R. H. Dana

MS Massachusetts Historical Society. B 171; William Coyle, "The Friendship of Anthony Trollope and Richard Henry Dana, Jr.," *New England Historical Quarterly*, 25 (June 1952), 260–61.

May 10. 1862   WALTHAM HOUSE, WALTHAM CROSS.
My dear Mr. Dana.

I do not know how to thank you sufficiently for all that you have done for me. I only hope that you will believe me to estimate it not only as a valuable work but also as one of great friendship.

What you say as to keeping your name unmentioned in the matter is a thing of course. I should have been greatly gratified in owning all that I owe you; but in questions such as those under discussion, of course I cannot do so publicly, as in doing so I should seem to make you responsible for my heresies and also for my blunders.

As regards that one great question of the privilege of the writ of H. C. I must declare at once that you do not carry me with you. I have placed my own paragraphs, your notes, Storeys[1] commentaries, and Binneys[2]

---

[8] *The Small House at Allington* was to have been entitled *The Two Pearls of Allington*, but Smith objected because Harriet Beecher Stowe's *The Pearl of Orr's Island* was then appearing serially in England.

[9] *Rachel Ray.*

[1] Joseph Story (1779–1845), eminent American jurist; named to the Supreme Court in 1811 (at age 32); accepted a law professorship at Harvard (and in effect founded the Law School) in 1829; began writing his famous *Commentaries* (which he continued publishing until his death) in 1832. Trollope was no doubt referring to Story's three-volume *Commentaries on the Constitution of the United States* (1833).

[2] Horace Binney (1780–1875), distinguished member of the Philadelphia Bar. Binney wrote three pamphlets upholding Lincoln's right to suspend habeas corpus, of which only *The Privileges of the Writ of Habeas Corpus under the Constitution* was in print by May 1862. Trollope attacked Binney's arguments in *North America*, II, 277–79.

pamphlet in the hands of one of our best constitutional lawyers,—
Spencer Follett,[3] a brother of the late Wm. Follett,[4]—and he declares my
views to be in his judgement right, and also declares that such must have
been Storeys views had Storey been alive. Of course I will not now
trouble you with discussion on the matter. But I tell you so much in
order that you may know that I have followed your advice in going to
an English lawyer, and that I have not ventured to differ from you without support.

As regards other matters pointed out by you I think I have in every
respect either adopted your suggestions, or modified my statements in
accordance with your views. I have done this as to Madisons original
opinions. As to the instructions to Senators. As to the introduction into
Congress of Ministers. As to pledging (practical pledging) of Electors
even before the time of Van Buren.[5] As to the conduct of Massachusetts
with reference to the F. S. Law;[6] and in a certain respect as to my use of
the words "universal suffrage", explaining that I used them as they are
generally used in this country. I have also altered a few words to which
you have objected. "Foulmouthed." "Set" &cc.

But still there remains my great sin as regarding the H. C. (What is
that H. C?) And as to that you must put forth your energies and crush
me in the Atlantic.

I will send you over a copy by the next Cunard if it be possible. Otherwise by the succeeding packet. In the mean time pray accept my expression of gratitude.

> Most faithfully yours
> Anthony Trollope

To G. H. Lewes

MS Yale. B 172; *George Eliot Letters*, VIII, 300.

15 May. 1862   WALTHAM HOUSE, WALTHAM CROSS.
My dear Lewes.

I know my letter will grieve you, but still I think I had better write it.
They tell me at the Post Office that your boy is not doing well. Nothing
is said against his character,—i e against his character as to conduct or
good feeling; but they say that he utterly fails in making himself useful.
"He is careless & very slow; and will not exert himself." That is the report made to me, and I am moreover told that this has been so strongly

---

[3] Brent Spencer Follett (1810–87), barrister and chief registrar of the Land Office.
[4] Sir William Webb Follett (1798–1845), Solicitor-General under Sir Robert Peel,
1834–35, 1841; Attorney-General under Peel, 1844.
[5] Martin Van Buren (1782–1862), President of the United States, 1837–41.
[6] The Fugitive Slave Law of 1850 was designed to facilitate the return of escaped
slaves. The law was widely ignored in the North.

felt that for this reason he has been sent back to the missing letter branch. I learn that his name has been taken off the list of candidates for the next step above him.

I fear that you will think me harsh to write in this way— But I am only doing as I would be done by. I believe his defect to be this,—that he is more au fait in French or German than he is in English, and that he is awkward & slow in the use of his own language. If he wishes to remain in the office I would strongly counsel you to put him in the way of writing English quickly. I need not tell you how such lessons are to be learned. The Secretary's Office at the G.P.O is a very good office for a young man, if he can get his promotion in his turn. But it is anything but a good office, if a man is to be continually passed over.

You should make him work at English in his after hours.[7]

> very faithfully yours
> Anthony Trollope

To James T. Fields

MS Columbia.

May. 19. 1862   WALTHAM HOUSE, WALTHAM CROSS.
My dear Fields.

I send to your care five copies of my book.[8] Pray oblige me by sending them as they will be addressed. One to Longfellow. One to Mrs. Homans.[9] One to Dr. Lothrop— One to my friend Synge[1] which can be left at Dr. Lothrops; and for the other I would wish to obtain house room in Charles street, if so much favor can be extended to it. I fear that a certain lady whose feelings respecting abolition are strong will hardly al-

---

[7] On 17 May Lewes recorded in his journal that during the past week "Anthony Trollope came to lunch, and heard with surprise that Charley was back in his old office, not having any advancement. He inquired into the cause, and wrote me a kind, candid, but painful letter telling me that the boy was not doing well, was careless, slow, and inefficient. This completely upset me." (*George Eliot Letters*, IV, 34.) Charles Lewes remained in the Post Office until 1886, attaining the rank of Principal Clerk.

[8] *North America.*

[9] Dr. and Mrs. Charles Homans, 12 West Street, Boston; friends of Trollope.

[1] William Webb Follett Synge (1826–91), diplomat and author. In 1856 Synge was appointed secretary for Sir William Gore Ouseley's special mission to Central America; he was staying in San José, Costa Rica, when Trollope arrived there in 1859. Recalling their first meeting, Trollope described Synge as "a very prince of good fellows. At home he would be a denizen of the Foreign Office, and denizens of the Foreign Office are swells at home. But at San José, where he rode on a mule, and wore a straw hat, and slept in a linendraper's shop, he was as pleasant a companion as a man would wish to meet on the western, or indeed on any other side of the Atlantic." (*The West Indies and the Spanish Main*, p. 275.) Trollope and Thackeray later loaned Synge a large sum of money: see Trollope to Merivale, 13 January 1864.

low of this, seeing that her pet General is not well spoken of.[2] If so, you must leave it among some of the other rubbish in Washington Street. Nevertheless give my kindest regards to the same lady—

Yours always very
faithfully
Anthony Trollope

To ?

MS Parrish Collection. SB 173.

May 23—1862   Wisbeach[3]
Gentlemen.

As I am out of town, & shall probably remain so for some time it will not, I regret to say, be in my power to join you as to the within proposition.

very faithfully your servant
Anthony Trollope

To [? W. H.] Russell[4]

MS Parrish Collection.

31—May. 1862
My dear Russell.

Will you dine with me at the Garrick[5] on Wednesday, June 11 at 7 PM.[6] My brother will be with me.

Yours always
Anthony Trollope

I have no means here of getting at your address, & therefore

*   *   *

[2] Probably General John Adams Dix (1798–1879), whom Trollope criticized for holding Baltimore at gun point (*North America*, I, 462–63).

[3] Wisbeach or Wisbech: a river port and market town in Cambridgeshire.

[4] Perhaps William Howard ("Billy") Russell (1820–1907), later Sir William, correspondent for *The Times* and *Daily Telegraph*. Russell was a Garrick Club friend of Trollope: see *Autobiography*, pp. 152–53.

[5] Trollope had been elected to the Garrick Club on 5 April 1862 (MS Garrick Club), having been proposed by Robert Bell and seconded by Thackeray. (Trollope mistakenly says that this happened in 1861 in his *Autobiography*.) Club life, and especially that of the Garrick, meant much to Trollope; he called the Garrick "the first assemblage of men at which I felt myself to be popular" (*Autobiography*, p. 159). In 1864, with the assistance of Lord Stanhope, Trollope was elected under Rule II (i.e., by special invitation) to the Athenaeum Club. For Trollope's membership in the Cosmopolitan Club, see Milnes to Trollope, 24 April 1861.

[6] In fact Trollope dined with the Alpine Club on 11 June; see Trollope to King, 28 June 1862, n. 1.

To C. W. Giles-Puller[7]

MS Parrish Collection.

POST OFFICE

June 1. 1862.   Waltham Cross

Dear Sir.

I beg to acknowledge the receipt of your letter of 31 May enclosing a memorial respecting the hour at which the Ware & Bishop Stortford mail cart passes through Much Hadham & other villages lying between those towns.[8]

I should be most happy to give any postal accommodation that I could afford to the Gentlemen who have signed the memorial, but I am afraid that the Postmr General could not consent to subject the people of Bishop Stortford to the inconvenience of losing the early delivery of their Hertfordshire letters, seeing that no real postal grievance is inflicted by the present arrangement. The early delivery at B Stortford begins at 7. am. and certain country posts are despatched at 6. am. Letters for all these deliveries would be too late if the proposed change were made.—At present a letter from Hertford to Newport goes direct by one nights post. The proposed alteration would detain such a letter for 24 hours.

I have the honor to be
Your very faithful
Servant

C. W. Giles Puller Esq MP.   Anthony Trollope

To Miss Mowbrey

MS Parrish Collection.

1st. June 1862

My dear Miss Mowbrey.

I wish I could send you something of more value than my name. In sending it however I can assure you that I am yours

very faithfully
Anthony Trollope

[7] Christopher William Giles-Puller (1807–64), MP for Hertfordshire, 1857–64.

[8] Bishop's Stortford and Much Hadham are both in East Hertfordshire (about four miles apart).

To Mrs. Mary Christie

MS Parrish Collection. SB 174.

2 June 1862   Piccadilly 193.
My dear Mary.

I have just seen Owen[9]—who is coming to us on Saturday, & who can with the greatest ease bring you down after you have done at Wimbledon. He will write to you. There is a train from Shoreditch at 4.5 pm. another at 5.10 pm. another at 6.10 pm. We will make either in time for dinner. We shall be ever so happy to have you & William, & will settle about that on Saturday. The difficulty of getting to each other is always in the beginning. But Tom is very anxious to see you and I fear he may be engaged after the 11th. He is only here for a short time.

I am sure you will find you can manage it on Saturday. Tom will be in town & would go anywhere to meet you, only Owen seems to think you will be *safer*[1] with him. He must let me know which train so that we may send to meet you.

Yours always
Anthony Trollope

To ?

MS Parrish Collection.

7 June 1862   WALTHAM HOUSE, WALTHAM CROSS.
My dear . . . [2]

I should feel obliged if you could order to be sent to me a correct set of the Mail time bills applicable to the Eastern Counties;—also of the London & Edinburgh day mail Time bill, seeing that the towns as far as Huntingdon are served by that route.

very faithfully yours
Anthony Trollope

J. B. Lippincott & Co. to Trollope

MS Bodleian.

June 20, 1862   J. B. LIPPINCOTT & CO
Anthony Trollope Esq   PHILADELPHIA
Dear Sir,

We have the pleasure of sending you herewith a copy of our edition of your "North America"[3] in two Vols.—the style in which it was originally decided to issue it.

---

[9] Owen Edward Grant (1831–1921), a clerk in the Printed Paper Office of the House of Lords; a brother of Mrs. Christie and the third son of Colonel James Grant.
[1] Underlined twice.
[2] Name so crossed through as to be illegible.
[3] In a letter of 11 March 1862, Lippincott agreed to pay Trollope a royalty of 12½

The Mess. Harper have however printed the work upon us, in one cheap volume which they sell, at retail, at 60 cents pr. copy. This will of course compel us to reduce the price of ours to about the cost of manufacturing—and bind the two volumes in one.

We regret exceedingly that Mess. H. should have thus ignored, not only the courtesy due to us as members of the trade, but also to yourself as the Author of the work and interested in our edition.[4]

Trusting that the appearance of the Vols. will meet your approval we remain

> Very faithfully
> Your Obt. Servts.
> J B Lippincott Co.

To the Old Bailey Printing Establishment[5]
MS Parrish Collection.

June 27—1862
Mr Trollope will have much pleasure in dining with the Gentlemen of the Old Bailey Printing Establishment on Saturday 5 July.

To George Eliot
MS Yale. B 176; *George Eliot Letters*, VIII, 303-4.

June 28—1862   Waltham Cross
My dear Mrs. Lewes.

I have just read the first number of Romola[6] and I cannot refrain from congratulating you. If you can, or have, kept it up so to the end you will have done a great work. Adam Bede, Mrs. Poyser, & Marner have been very dear to me; but excellent as they are, I am now compelled to see that you can soar above even their heads. The descriptions of Florence, —little bits of Florence down to a door nail, and great facts of Florence up to the very fury of life among those full living nobles,—are wonderful in their energy and in their accuracy. The character of Romola is artistically beautiful,—a picture exceeded by none that I know of any girl in any novel. It is the perfection of pen painting;—and you have been

percent on all copies of its edition of *North America* sold after the first 2,000; in return, Trollope agreed to furnish Lippincott with early sheets (MS Bodleian).

    [4] For further details of this piracy, see Lippincott to Trollope, 24 July 1862. The episode provoked Trollope into writing his public letter on copyright to James Russell Lowell (2 September 1862). See also Addenda, Trollope to Fields, 11 March 1862.

    [5] Smith, Elder & Co. had its own printing office at 15 Old Bailey, Little Green Arbour Court.

    [6] In the *Cornhill*. The acquisition of *Romola* was a triumph for George Smith, whose campaign to get the work is described by Gordon S. Haight, *George Eliot* (Oxford, 1968), pp. 354-60.

nobly aided by your artist. I take it for granted that it is Leighton.[7] The father also of Romola is excellent.

Do not fire too much over the heads of your readers. You have to write to tens of thousands, & not to single thousands. I say this, not because I would have you alter ought of your purpose. That were not worth your while, even though the great numbers should find your words too hard— But because you may make your full purpose compatible with their taste—

I wonder at the toil you must have endured in getting up your work,[8]— wonder and envy. But I shall never envy your success, or the great appreciation of what you have done that will certainly come,—probably today, but if not, then tomorrow.[9]

Yours very heartily
Anthony Trollope

To S. W. King[1]

MS Parrish Collection. SB 175.

June 28—1862.   Norwich
My dear Mr King.

I forget exactly what passed between us at the Alpine dinner[2] as we parted. But I know you were kind enough to say you would let me come & see you when I was down here. If it quite suits you I will go out to you on Monday. If you can give me a bed I will get over to the London train at the Flordon Station on Tuesday morning. If not I will keep my trap & come back to Norwich.

---

[7] The artist was Frederick Leighton (1830–96), later Baron Leighton of Stretton, who was to become a distinguished painter and eventually President of the Royal Academy. Thackeray had suggested the young painter as a *Cornhill* illustrator, but it was not until *Romola* that Smith secured him; the choice proved a particularly good one because of Leighton's knowledge of Italy (Leonard Huxley, *House of Smith Elder*, p. 140).

[8] For a discussion of T. A. Trollope's assistance to George Eliot in her research on Florentine antiquities, see *What I Remember*, pp. 451–63.

[9] George Eliot recorded in her journal for 30 June: "This morning I had a delightful, generous letter from Mr. Anthony Trollope about Romola." (*George Eliot Letters*, IV, 45.)

[1] Samuel William King (1821–68), Rector of Saxlingham Nethergate, Norfolk.

[2] Sir William Hardman's diary for 12 June 1862 records: "Last night I dined at the Castle, Richmond, with the Alpine Club. We had a jolly party round William Longman . . . Anthony Trollope sitting next to him. . . . Trollope is also a good fellow, modelled on Silenus, with a large black beard. There was a call for Trollope, and Silenus made a funny speech. . . . He added that not very long since, in the city of Washington, a member of the U.S. Government asked him if it were true that a club of Englishmen existed who held their meetings on the summits of the Alps. 'In my anxiety,' he said, 'to support the credit of my country, I may have transgressed the strict limits of veracity, but I told him what he had heard was quite true.' (Great Cheers)." (S. M. Ellis, ed., *A Mid-Victorian Pepys* [New York, 1923], pp. 143–44.)

If this be in any way inconvenient you will not of course scruple to say so—

very faithfully yours

Rev S W King   Anthony Trollope

Henry Wadsworth Longfellow to Trollope
MS Taylor Collection. Taylor, "Letters," p. 6.

July 16. 1862   Nahant—
My dear Sir

Returning from a tour to Niagara and Canada, I find your two hand-some volumes[3] waiting for me "with the author's kind regards" and I hasten to thank you, not only for the book but for the friendly remem-brance which counted me among those by whom it would be welcomed and appreciated.

As yet I have not had time to read it, but have brought it with me to the seaside. I come, therefore, only to thank Caesar, not to praise him. But, like me, like my book! and as I do like you, the other will not fail. I am sure to find it frank, outspoken, and friendly; and you are sure, in return, to find in me a friendly reader, and not a captious critic. . . .

Begging you to present my compliments and regards to Mrs. Trollope,

I am, Dear Sir
Yours most truly
Henry W. Longfellow.

J. B. Lippincott to Trollope
MS Bodleian.

J. B. LIPPINCOTT & CO

July 24, 1862   PHILADELPHIA
My dear Sir,

Your favor of the 5th. inst has been received. I trust the copy of your work which we sent has ere this reached you.

I fully share your feeling of vexation at the course of the Mess Harper in publishing your book and must confess that I was a good deal sur-prised at the appearance of their edition after my explanation to them of the arrangement that existed between yourself and us. Ordinary courtesy should have prevented them from printing the book, but on the contrary they made the greatest efforts to forestall us in the market, stopping their other operations as I understand in order to bring out your book at the earliest possible moment. The current half year being then near its close, (a time when we are always compelled to withhold our new publications and await semiannual settlements) we were not

[3] *North America.*

able to distribute the book to our correspondents as promptly as would otherwise have been done. This gave the Harpers an opportunity to reach the public with their Edition quite as soon as ourselves. They fixed the price at about the cost of manufacture (40 cents wholesale) and as our edition was gotten up in a much more expensive style than theirs —we find ourselves in the position of *positive losers* in the enterprise. Still we shall endeavor to retain the field in the best way possible and by getting up future editions more cheaply we hope to recover our losses upon this. We believe we have the sympathy of the trade to a good degree.

It will be impossible for us to determine the number sold until the close of the year when we receive statements of accounts from our correspondents.

Of course I shall be quite willing to have an account of this matter given to the public.

With much respect I remain
Very faithfully yours

Anthony Trollope Esq. J B Lippincott

To [? Samuel] Lucas[4]

MS Bodleian. SB 342 (misdated).

ADELAIDE PLACE

24 July. 1862. GLASGOW

Mr. Anthony Trollope present [*sic*] his compliments to Mr Lucas.

Letters for Mr. Synge can be addressed to the care of
John Bidwell Esq[5]
Foreign Office
Whitehall.
or Mr Trollope would be happy to enclose any letter from Mr Lucas in his packet to Mr. Synge.

Mr Trollope's address is
Waltham Cross

To Thomas Adolphus Trollope

MS Parrish Collection.

August 3. 1862—Sunday Diss. Norfolk

My dear Tom

Instantly on receipt of your two letters, which came together, I wrote to Jones for Pike's address. In *six days* I got his answer. I instantly wrote

---

[4] Perhaps Samuel Lucas (1818–68), barrister and journalist; founder of the *Shilling Magazine*.

[5] John Bidwell, senior clerk at the Foreign Office.

to Pike (on Friday, August 1) begging for an answer by return of post, but I got none. Therefore I have to day sent to Coutts a check to your credit for £100—explaining that the money would be wanted on the 4th. (tomorrow). I have no doubt but that it will be all right.

You should have given me longer notice, seeing that I am not constantly at home. I have been away from home and from London since I wrote last.

I trust I may continue to have good accounts of Theo's progress.

Yours affectionately

Anthony Trollope

To Isa Blagden

MS David Stivender.

August 5. 1862.   WALTHAM HOUSE, WALTHAM CROSS.
My dear Miss Blagden.

I send you a note just received from Kate Field.

I have not answered your letter but you are not to suppose that I have neglected it. I fear however you will have to submit your Mss. to a publisher before it will be purchased. These men, as you are doubtless aware, are very dilatory in giving an answer.

—You do not give me your address in London, but I write to Dorset Place. I hope my letter will find you. You say that you remain in town for a fortnight. If you will let me know your whereabouts I will endeavor to see you.[6]

Yours very truly

Anthony Trollope

To Owen Grant

MS Parrish Collection. SB 177.

August 10. 1862   WALTHAM HOUSE, WALTHAM CROSS.
My dear Owen.

I heartily congratulate you, and hope we may know your wife in due time.[7] It's the thing to do, most assuredly. When you have settled down any where you'll let us know your whereabouts—

I need hardly say how truly I wish that you and she may be happy together for very many years.

Yours always

most sincerely

Anthony Trollope

I do not know your address & therefore write to the House of Lords.

---

[6] Miss Blagden's novel *The Cost of a Secret* was published by Chapman & Hall in 1863. See Trollope to Field, 23 August 1862.

[7] Owen Grant married Adelaide Higginson, youngest daughter of Lieutenant General and Lady Frances Higginson, on 28 August 1862.

To Smith, Elder & Co.

MS Yale.

Augt 13. 1862   WALTHAM HOUSE, WALTHAM CROSS.
Mr A Trollope presents his compts to Messrs Smith & Elder.

Mr Trollope has just received proofs of Numbers 3. 4. & 5. of his new novel.[8] He would be obliged if duplicates could be sent to him, as he must keep one copy by him.

Messrs Smith & Elder

To Kate Field

MS Boston Public Library. *Commentary*, pp. 234–37; B 178.

August 23—1862—   WALTHAM HOUSE, WALTHAM CROSS.
My very dear Kate—

I forget when I wrote to you last, but I know it was not very long ago, & that in writing now I display my own great merit rather than satisfy any just claim of yours. However I have a very nice long letter from you to answer, & therefore acknowledge that you are a fit *object* for my generosity.

You will be very glad to hear that Theo is improving very greatly and that Tom is becoming tranquil— At one time what with four doctors, & his determination to believe the worst, he was nearly crazed. He would bear her loss very badly. I begin to believe that he will not be called on to endure such sorrow.

You will not be glad to hear me declare that your dear friend (and my dear friend also) Miss Blagden is a plague. She has no idea of business, and in her shandiness[9] greatly perplexes those who want to befriend her. She got me to sell a Mss of hers—& then bargained about it with some one else, because she did not get from me a letter by return post,— she having given me no address! So I have to go back from my word with the publisher! Don't you tell her that I grumble, for I don't want to make her unhappy. But she is a plague.

Yes: I was mean not to give you my book. I wrote to you about it before you wrote to me,—blowing me up—which you did with a vengeance. I was mean. I had to buy all the copies I gave, and did not think your beaux—(I cannot remember how to spell the word) worth 24/—. There! I have owned the fact, you may make the most of it. But, dear Kate, I would give you ten times twenty four shillings ten times over in any more pleasant way, fitting for yourself. One gives presentation copies to old fogies & such like. When you write a book, you will of course give

[8] *The Small House at Allington*, which ran in the *Cornhill* from September 1862 through April 1864.

[9] Empty-headedness. Cf. Trollope's description of Mrs. Ray as "so inconsequent in her mental workings, so shandy-pated" (*Rachel Ray*, chap. xii; quoted in the *OED*).

one to me. You are a young lady.—A ring, a lock of my hair, or a rose-
bud would be the proper present for you; not two huge volumes weigh-
ing no end of pounds. Believe me, I would have been very wrong to send
it to you.

Your criticisms are in part just—in part unjust,—in great part biassed
by your personal (—may I say love?) for the author. The book is vague.
But remember, I had to write a book of travels, not a book of political
essays—and yet I was anxious so to write my travels, as to introduce, on
the sly, my political opinions. The attempt has not been altogether successful. The book is regarded as readable,—and that is saying as much
for it, as I can say honestly. Your injustice regards chiefly abolition
ideas, Freement [? Freedom] & such like; on which matters we are poles
asunder.

What am I to say about your present state? I am not myself so despon-
dent, as it seems to me are many of you Yankees. Things will go worse
before you gain your object than I thought they would;—but still you
will ultimately gain it. This proscription[1] is very bad. Was it absolutely
necessary? My feeling is that a man should die rather than be made a
soldier against his will. One's country has no right to demand everything.
There is much that is higher & better & greater than one's country. One
is patriotic only because one is too small & too weak to be cosmopolitan.
If a country can not get along without a military conscription, it had
better give up—& let its children seek other ties. But I do not on this account despair. It was not to be supposed that in doing so much all should
be done without a mistake.

Thanks for your newspapers. They are however very bad. I thank you
as a friend of mine once thanked his God. "I thanked God," said he, "for
a quiet night. But he did not give me one wink of sleep!" I say as much
to you for the newspapers; but I never can learn anything from them.

We are not going to Italy this autumn. But in the spring. We are
building a house,—or making ours larger, & it does not suit to be away.
The bricklayers would run away with the forks.

I am now writing a letter to be published about that beast Harper.
But as I write it I cannot but feel that this is no time for such matters.
Why don't they draught him & send him to New Orleans?

I was thinking today that nature intended me for an American rather
than an Englishman. I think I should have made a better American. Yet
I hold it higher to be a bad Englishman, as I am, than a good American,

---

[1] A slip for "conscription."

—as I am not. If that makes you angry, see if you would not say the reverse of yourself—

Tell me whom you see, socially, & what you are doing socially and as regards work. I didn't at all understand how you are living, where—with whom—or on what terms. But I don't know that it matters. How little we often know in such respects of those we love dearest. Of what I am at home, you can have no idea;—not that I mean to imply that I am of those you love dearest. And yet I hope I am.

I am not writing at home,—in spite of the great red words—²or Rose would send her love. I send mine to your mother & my kind regards to your aunt.³ To yourself—full assurance of true friendship & love.

A. T.

Write often.

To W. Hepworth Dixon
MS Parrish Collection. SB 179.

31—August 1862.   Cromer⁴
My dear Mr Dixon.

I ought probably to have named a date when I last wrote to you. I have found it necessary since that to wait for a letter from America. I will have my paper ready on Tuesday and will send it on that day to your office in London,—for insertion as soon as you may find convenient.⁵

I am very much obliged to you.

Yours very faithfully
Anthony Trollope

I have much better accounts from Florence. My sister in law is now at Como, and I trust doing better.

To James Russell Lowell
Athenaeum, 6 September 1862, pp. 306–7. B 180.

Sept. 2. 1862.   Waltham Cross
My dear Mr. Lowell.

I do not know that the present moment is very opportune for the discussion on your side of the water of such questions as that of Interna-

---

² The address on Trollope's personal stationery was invariably printed in red.

³ Cordelia Riddle Sanford (1824–94), only fourteen years older than Kate, was the wife of a Newport millionaire, Milton T. Sanford. The Sanfords had been especially kind to Kate after her father's death in 1856, and they had taken her to Florence in 1859. Kate and her aunt remained very devoted.

⁴ A seaside resort in Norfolk, 130 miles north of London.

⁵ See next letter.

tional Copyright. You have your hands rather full of other matters, and may probably lack time just now to attend to the niceties of civilization. But the subject is one of great importance to your countrymen, and, as nobody is more fully aware than yourself, is so esteemed by them. As regards myself, if I did not moot the matter now, I should probably never do so. I will therefore, in the teeth of the war, endeavour to enlist your attention and your sympathy on the subject.

To you and me, and to men, who, like us, earn our bread by writing,[6] the question is, of course, one of pounds, shillings and pence, or of dollars and cents; although there are those who affect to think that an author should disregard such matters, and that he should work for fame alone. For myself, I profess that I regard my profession as I see other men regard theirs: I wish to earn by it what I may honestly earn,—so doing my work that I may give fair and full measure for what remuneration I may receive. As to you, may I not presume that you also regard the literary labourer as worthy of his hire? I say so much at once, because I wish you to understand that I am pleading here for the honest payment for goods supplied by me to your countrymen; but I am pleading also for the honest payment for goods supplied by you to my countrymen. And in putting forward those pleas, I think I can show that such honesty on both sides will tend to the general advancement of literature for the two countries, and will injure none; or, at any rate, none whose interests are worthy of our care.

I must begin my argument by the story of personal injustice done to myself. Had I not suffered, or imagined that I had suffered, such injustice, I should not now trouble you with this letter. But I can assure you that in placing myself in my present position, I have thought more of the general justice of the question than of my own interests, and have been actuated in what I have done by an endeavour to prove, either that an English author may deal on fair and secure terms with an American publisher, or else that there exists good ground for international interference in the matter.

[6] Rowland Hill wrote in his diary for 6 September 1862: "*Trollope* is suspected of neglecting his official duties to attend to his literary labours— Engagement in connection with the Cornhill Magazine and another periodical whose name I do not recollect—numerous novels— Trip to the United States (1861-2) and work thereon— In confirmation see in Athenaeum of this day letter from Trollope in which he speaks of earning 'his bread by writing'—as though literature were his 'profession' &c." On 16 September Hill added: "Matthew [Hill] has had a correspondence with Trollope. T. takes the opportunity of speaking highly of me, and of defending his own conduct. Don't believe in T's sincerity—no man both clever and honest could be a party to the elaborate misrepresentations in the two Reports of the Committee on the Circulation office [see Trollope to Smith, 8 May 1860, n. 8], and as T. is undoubtedly clever, it follows in my opinion that he is dishonest— E[dward] Page to whom I mentioned the circumstance in confidence assures me, also in confidence, that T. has recently spoken of me in his presence, in a manner quite inconsistent with his present professions." (MS General Post Office, London.)

For some years past, the Messrs. Harper, of New York, have undertaken the speculation of reprinting my books. This they did without any reference to me; but they paid some small sum on, as I think, each work to my English publishers,—with which payment I, however, had then no concern. Nor had I any ground of complaint, seeing that I had sold all my immediate rights in those books to the publishers in London. In 1859 I was in New York; and I then offered to the Messrs. Harper the early sheets of a book I was writing on the West Indies. This they declined, saying the subject did not suit them. But they afterwards applied to my publisher in London as to that work, and paid them again a small sum for the privilege of reprinting. I had then parted with my immediate rights in the book, and perhaps had no ground for complaining that the Messrs. Harper had changed their mind. Soon afterwards I became engaged on a periodical novel called "Orley Farm," which is now being republished in *Harper's Magazine.* Having resolved to keep the privilege of the foreign market as regards this work in my own hands, I essayed to deal with the Messrs. Harper's agent in London; but when I came to mention my price, I was told that if I did not accede to Messrs. Harper's price, the Messrs. Harper could and would publish it without any terms. Thereupon I again made over my privilege to my London publishers, feeling that I was foiled, and that I myself in London had no mode of fighting the battle further. My publishers took Messrs. Harper's price, and we are dividing the proceeds. That was the first time that Messrs. Harper's republication of my works has produced for me a dollar. I was not contented with the bargain, I will confess; but I was specially discontented with the manner of the bargain. I was compelled to sell my wares to one man, and he had the power of naming his own price! I had it in contemplation, however, to visit the States again, and I still hoped to adjust these little matters of commerce to my satisfaction.

In the autumn of last year I did go to the States, and, among many other great pleasures, had that of making your acquaintance. I also renewed that which I before had made with Mr. Fletcher Harper. I called on him in New York, and explained to him, with what courtesy I could use, that I did not quite like his mode of republishing my books. He was civil enough to assure me that the transactions had been gratifying to him. I then asked him whether in the event of my making an engagement with any other American publisher as to the reprinting of a work of mine, he would take reprisal by reprinting it also. I did not mention any special work, or allude to my intention of writing about your country. He was again very civil, and told me that much as he should regret my doing so, he would not reprint any book under such circumstances.

You no doubt know the name of Mr. Lippincott, publisher and bookseller of Philadelphia. After my interview with Mr. Harper, I came to terms with him as to the republication of my then projected volumes on

North America, and in compliance with those terms I supplied him with the early sheets of the work. Mr. Lippincott has printed and published it; but the Messrs. Harper had out an edition, unauthorized by writer or publisher in England, four days before Mr. Lippincott had published his edition. This they are selling at a price—60 cents, or 2s. 6d.—which must, I believe, entail a loss upon themselves, increasing in amount in accordance with the magnitude of their sale. Either this, or else, by great commercial economy, they may be able to produce the article for the amount charged. I think I may say that any profit to them is out of the question.

May I not fairly call this literary piracy? It is piracy in the spirit, though it may not be so by law. No doubt, American publishers have legally the power of republishing all foreign works of literature, and need ask the leave of no one. But they have found it better to deal with the English authors. The Messrs. Harper have repeatedly assured the American public of the fact that they buy their English works from the English writers. But in this special case their *animus* is shown by the manner in which the thing was done. I have not learnt how the firm in New York was able to have out an edition, they having no copy supplied to them, before the firm in Philadelphia, to whom the early sheets were sent. As far as I can ascertain, the edition of the Messrs. Harper was out within three days of the arrival of the earliest steamer which could have brought them a copy of the English book. They undoubtedly have been very smart; but I think you will agree with me that such smartness is not creditable to their trade or their country.

The question, however, between me and the Messrs. Harper is not worth to you, or to the public of either country, the paper on which this is written. I have told the story because I could not otherwise illustrate the grievance under which authors lie in our two countries. It is not that tricks such as these are often played, but that the possibility of such tricks takes away all security both from the author and from the publisher. In the above case there was a determination on my part to escape from the trammels of the Messrs. Harper, and a determination on their part, better based, that I should not escape. There was also on their part a determination that their brothers in the trade should be taught that they were not to be touched with impunity. It is against the exercise of such power that I make my protest.

Between no other nations can a copyright law be of the importance that it is to you and us, because no other two great reading people speak the same language. A small class only in France read English books, and a small class only in England read French books. But almost every man and woman in the Northern States reads our authors; and your authors are known at any rate as well in our country as they are in your own; and this interchange of literature has increased twenty-fold in the last twenty years, and may increase again twenty-fold in the next twenty. You yourself have thousands of British customers; and having indeed been blessed with a special British editor of your own, may probably have experienced no individual hardship; but you will not on that account be less alive to the interests of your profession. A friend and countryman of yours, whose name is with us a household word, but which I cannot mention, as I have not his permission, told me that the pecuniary results of the republication of his works in England was to him very slight. He made no complaint, but seemed to regard the fact as the natural consequence of there being no law of international copyright. Had he possessed the privilege which such a law would have given him, that alone would have afforded him a large income. For aught I know, he may be as affluent as he desires; but there are but few of us who do not like to get the price of our wares. But perhaps the publishers are worse off in this matter than are even the authors. The republication of new English works is as important a branch of an American publisher's work as the publication of national literature. But at present he has no protection in this business. The firm which is most unscrupulous and most powerful in its commercial operations has advantages over others against which they cannot contend. Mr. Lippincott—who is, however, in a large way of business, and probably will not mind it—must have burnt his fingers by daring to publish my volumes. Various American publishers have assured me that they desired nothing so much as an international copyright with England, in order that they might undertake British works with some security. "You are Mr. Harper's property," has been said to me, "and we don't dare to touch you." It was in vain that I declared that I had not made myself over to the Messrs. Harper. "He has put his hand upon you," I was told, "and we cannot interfere." I should have but little doubt of obtaining an international copyright if the question could be carried by the votes of the publishers and booksellers in the States.

It has sometimes been argued that an international copyright would do a material injury, as it would raise the price of English books in the States. I will not now do more than notice the fact, that such an argument throws over all idea of honesty, and that it might as well be used against domestic copyright law in either of the two countries; but I will dispute the assertion. An international copyright law would not enhance the price of English books in the States, or of American books in England. The security given to those concerned in the trade would fully compensate the privilege which the trade now has, in each country, of republishing works without special permission from the authors or owners. The proof of this is very simple, and easy to be understood. New works by American authors are not now cheaper in England than new works by English authors; nor, in New York, are new works by English authors cheaper than those by native authors.

Then why is there not an international copyright law? I think you will admit that the difficulty is on your side of the water, and that such a law would be sanctioned here without doubt or dissent. I have heard no literary man in the States defend the present state of the question, though I have discussed it with many. The answer to me has been that such a law would not be popular. Should it not be the work of such men as you to make it popular? For myself, I believe that if you and your brethren in Boston would put your shoulders to the wheel, the thing would be done.

Yours very sincerely
Anthony Trollope

To ?

MS Taylor Collection.

4 Sept. 1862.   Cromer.
Dear Sir.

I have a note from Mr Dixon saying that my letter to Mr Lowell will appear in this weeks Athenaeum. I have addressed it to *W.* Russell Lowell. I think his name is *J.* (James) not W. Could you see to this. He is the author of the Biglow papers, which you have reviewed. He is known to his friends as Russell Lowell—if you do not ascertain the first name, omit the first initial.[1]

Could you oblige me by sending copies of this number of the Athenaeum postpaid to the addresses on the other side. The first time I am in the Strand I will call & pay the cost at your office—or will send postage stamps if you will kindly tell me how much.

faithfully yours
Anthony Trollope

Russell Lowell Esq
   Cambridge
   Massachusetts
R. H. Dana Esq Junior   Messrs. Lippincott
   Boston U.S.   Publishers
Mrs. Homans   Philadelphia. U.S.
   12 West Street.   Miss K. Field
   Boston U.S.   Care of M. Sandford Esq [*sic*]
Revd. S. K. Lothrop   Cordaville.
   12 Chesnut Street.   Massachusetts
   Boston U.S.   W. W. F. Synge Esq
J. T. Fields Esq   Care of J. Bidwell Esq Foreign Office.
   Washington Street   London
   Boston US

---

[1] Trollope's correction came too late. Harper noted the mistake in his answer to Trollope (in the *Athenaeum*); and in a rebuttal, Trollope said that the mistake was a "clerical error" (Trollope to the Editor of the *Athenaeum*, 22 October 1862).

To James Russell Lowell

MS Harvard.

Sept 5th. 1862   WALTHAM HOUSE, WALTHAM CROSS.

My dear Mr Lowell—

I have sent a letter to the Athenaeum, our literary paper of best repute here, touching the reprinting of my volumes in America, by Mr Harper, —and have addressed that letter to you. I hope I have not done wrong towards you in doing so. Strictly speaking I should have had your permission; but Fields gave me to understand that I might do so without risk of offending you. I have ordered the Athenaeum to be sent to you— also to Fields & Dana & one or two others,—and as it will go by the same post as this I do not trouble you with a MS copy of the letter. Nor will I argue the matter with you here, as I have said my say in that letter— I believe you will agree with me personally that an international copyright would be of service to both countries.

I trust that I may some day see you over here, & that we may soon hear that your national troubles are coming to an end.

very faithfully yours
Anthony Trollope

To Smith, Elder & Co.

MS Bodleian.

8th. Sept 1862   Cromer. Norfolk

Gentlemen.

I did answer Mr Williams[8] letter—to him—addressed to Cornhill as soon as I could. I was down here, & had to go thro the numbers of the work after Mr Williams letter reached me, which caused the delay.

I did not hear from Mr Smith who was designing the Initial letters, but I presumed that it was Millais. I see that that in the first number does *not* bear his mark.[9]

very truly yours

Messrs. Smith & Elder.   Anthony Trollope

[8] William Smith Williams (1800–1875), for many years reader for Smith, Elder. Williams was concerned with the graphic arts in book publication, though he is perhaps best remembered for his role in acquiring Charlotte Brontë's *Jane Eyre* for Smith.

[9] Millais did in fact illustrate the initial letters introducing each new installment of *The Small House at Allington*; his monogram appeared on his design for the third installment (November 1862) and on others thereafter.

To W. H. Blake

MS Parrish Collection. SB 181.

Sept 23—1862   Waltham Cross.
My dear Sir.

I have just received this and your own note on my return from abroad. I cannot tell when you may be summoned to compete, but you will hear from Mr Barlow. It will probably be very soon. You will see that you will have four chances of success among twelve competitors. Many of those nominated to compete are I believe very weak adversaries.

Yours truly—heartily wishing
for success—

W H Blake Esq   Anthy Trollope
Cashel

To Edward Gillett[1]

MS Parrish Collection.

POST OFFICE
Oct 10. 1862.   Waltham Cross.
Sir.

I beg to acknowledge the receipt of your letter of the 7th. Instant. I fear I can do nothing for you, but I will take the first opportunity I can find of going out from Norwich to your locality & of calling upon you. I cannot now name a day, but I will endeavor to do so with as little delay as possible.

Your very ob Servant
Revd. E. Gillett   Anthony Trollope

To the Editor of the *Athenaeum*

Athenaeum, 25 October 1862, pp. 529–30. B 182.

Oct. 22. 1862.

I must trouble you with a few words of rejoinder to Mr. Fletcher Harper's letter on the matter of American literary piracy.[2]

In his first-numbered paragraph, he simply repeats what I had asserted with reference to my early works. I made that statement as a necessary beginning to my story. In his second paragraph he re-tells what I had told as to "Orley Farm," adding the price given by him, and taunting me with having at last grumblingly accepted a crown for my wares, hav-

---

[1] The Reverend Edward Gillett (*d.* 1869), Vicar of Runham, Norfolk.

[2] Fletcher Harper had answered Trollope's letter on American literary piracy (Trollope to Lowell, 6 September 1862) on 26 September, and the answer was printed in the *Athenaeum*, 18 October 1862, p. 496. Trollope replied immediately.

ing first asked a sovereign. But here he altogether omits the point. When I attempted to make my bargain, I was met by the threat that if I did not take the price offered, my wares should be taken from me without any price. Such, at that moment, was the nature of my agreement with my English publishers, Messrs. Chapman & Hall, that though I had the power of refusing Messrs. Harper's offer, I could not do so without injury to them. I was so intent on refusing that offer, that I proposed to pay to Messrs. Chapman & Hall the moiety which would accrue to them —amounting to 100L—in order that I might rid myself of any dealings with the American house. This they generously declined; and I therefore felt myself constrained to allow them to deal with the Messrs. Harper, resolving that in future I would keep the foreign right entirely in my own hands. I have never pretended to say that the price named by me for the use of my novel in America indicated its real value more correctly than the offer made by the American publishers. I did not like the bargain, it is true; but, as I said before, it was the manner of the bargain that I specially disliked. The Messrs. Harper affect to deal with the English authors and publishers, but they do so with a threat in their mouth. "If you do not sell to us at our price," they say, "we will take your goods without any price." This is what we call piracy.

But it is on his third paragraph that I must now come to a distinct issue with Mr. Harper. I gave, in my letter to Mr. Lowell, the result of a conversation which I had with Mr. Harper, and he states that my recollection of that conversation is incorrect. My inaccuracy, if I have been inaccurate, amounts to a total misrepresentation of the purport of what passed between us. I called on Mr. Fletcher Harper with the express and single purpose of asking him whether, in the event of my dealing with another firm in America, he would reprint the work of which I would so dispose. "You can, of course, answer my question or decline to answer it," I said, thinking that in either case I should have his intention. He told me distinctly that in such a case he would not reprint my book. I repeat this assertion on my own personal credit, and I think that I shall be believed in England: I am very sure that I shall be believed in America. As Mr. Harper says, I made him no offer, seeing that I had determined not to deal with him on any terms.

In his fourth paragraph, Mr. Harper defends his general practice of dealing; and in doing so he explains the risk incurred by him in paying anything to English authors. His firm have no protection against piracy! —no protection except the comity of trade, which is, as he says, enforced by reprisals! By this he intends us to understand that the American publisher who first ventures upon the works of an English author,—even though he has done so, as the Harpers did in my case, without any consent from that author,—has a vested right in his man. The comity of the trade, to be enforced by reprisals, is to guarantee these vested rights! The comity of publishers is to insure to each of them among themselves the power and privilege of taking at their own price, or without price, the works of authors, without any of that protection which the competition of an open market gives to the seller! I think that the readers of America, as well as those of England, will acknowledge that no stronger argument than this can be put forward in favour of an International Copyright Law.

Mr. Harper twits me with being unwilling to name the terms on which the Messrs. Lippincott agreed to publish my work on "North America." I have no right to make them public without the permission of the Messrs. Lippincott. I can only say that those gentlemen are perfectly at liberty to publish them, if they please to do so; as is any publisher with whom I may have been concerned at liberty to make known the terms on which he has dealt with me. Such private matters are not generally considered as interesting to the public at large.

Mr. Harper has pointed out to me that I have called Russell Lowell by a wrong name. In your impression of September the 6th, he is unfortunately called William instead of James Russell Lowell. It was a clerical error, not of my own, for which I ask and confidently expect his pardon.

Anthony Trollope

To George Smith

MS John Murray. B 151 (misdated).

November 3—1862   WALTHAM HOUSE, WALTHAM CROSS.
My dear Smith.

Very many thanks for your thoughtful remembrance of a poor author's worldly wants.

I have not seen Mr. Millais since I don't know what distant time, & have said nothing to him about those five illustrations. Is he not still in Scotland?

As regards the last three numbers Mrs. Millais[3] wrote to "your" Mr. Williams for the subjects[4]—& I sent them thro Mr. Williams,—while you were gambling at Homburgh— Guided by this I have supposed he has wished to have his subjects closely marked out. I will go on doing so—& I wd. suggest that you sd. always send the paper to him. If he chooses to change the subject I shall not complain. I feel however that the author can select the subjects better than the artist—having all the feeling of the story at his fingers end.

Yours always
A. T.

[3] Euphemia Chalmers Gray (1828–97) had married Millais in 1855, one year after obtaining a decree of nullity ending her marriage to Ruskin.
[4] For Millais' illustrations for *The Small House at Allington.*

To Frederick Locker[5]

MS Harvard. SB 183.

November 9. 1862.   WALTHAM HOUSE, WALTHAM CROSS.
Sir.

I have to thank you heartily for your volume of poems. I have only now got them, and have not yet read them— But I have no doubt that in doing so I shall have much pleasure.

very faithfully yours

F Locker Esq   Anthony Trollope
St. James Palace
S.W.

To Alexander Strahan

MS Parrish Collection.

18 Nov. 1862.
9. AM   WALTHAM HOUSE, WALTHAM CROSS.
Dear Sir

I have this moment got your letter. I shall be very glad to write a Christmas story for you. But cannot you give me till December 10th? I find the 12th. or 14th. does with other monthlies. I never run myself to the last day—but here I have no choice from the lateness of the order. Let me know this by return of post.

"Out of Work" would be a very nice name for a story— But it wd. be needfull with such a name that the chief character should be an operative. I do not think I could manage this. But the line of the story shall be of the same nature—if possible.[6]

Yours always
in great haste
Anthony Trollope

[5] Frederick Locker (1821–95), later Locker-Lampson, author of *London Lyrics* (1857), which went through many revised and expanded editions (reference here is to the 1862 edition). Trollope and Locker became good friends. Late in life Trollope presented Locker, who was a well-known book collector, with the manuscript of *The Small House at Allington*, inscribing the flyleaf: "Frederic [*sic*] Locker, with the kind regards of these tediously written pages. March. 1882." (MS Huntington Library.)

[6] On 17 November Strahan wrote Trollope offering £100 for a "short christmas tale" of ten pages for the January number of *Good Words*. Strahan added: "Dr. Macleod thought 'Out of Work' would make a *seasonable* story [because of widespread unemployment in the textile industry, the result of the "cotton famine" during the American Civil War], but of course you will do what you consider best for the Magazine." (MS Bodleian.) On 8 December Trollope delivered "The Widow's Mite," which appeared in *Good Words* for January 1863; the story was reprinted in *Lotta Schmidt* (1867).

To George Smith

B 184 (Sadleir's transcript). Excerpt, *Commentary*, pp. 241–42.

21 November 1862

*   *   *

I have been very remiss in not sending back to you the three numbers
which you now have. I have been very busy. I have been trying to hunt
three days a week. I find it must be only two. Mortal man cannot write
novels, do the Post Office and go out three days.[7]

*   *   *

To George Smith

Commentary, p. 242. SB 185.

1 December 1862

*   *   *

I have just returned from a hunting campaign in Oxfordshire and have
five days to write a Christmas story for *Good Words*.

*   *   *

Rose Trollope to Kate Field

MS Boston Public Library. B 186.

3 Dec 1862
Dear Kate,

Why dont you write to me? We are both really unhappy— I because I
still think you are offended with me— My husband because he does not
know why— I therefore will not wait for another week, and that will be
certain to bring a letter—just as one takes out an umbrella & there will
be no rain—but leave the thing at home & down it pours— He—my husband—not the rain nor the umbrella—has gone to hunt and on such days
I always write heaps of letters because I dont like to be out of the way
never knowing at what hour he may be in— Well at any rate if you are
angry with me I am not going to care and shall torment you when the fit
comes on. . . .

Yours affly
R. T.

---

[7] Trollope's enduring passion for hunting began in Ireland; after moving to Waltham, he was able to hunt in Essex (see *Autobiography*, pp. 63–65, 170–72).

George Smith. Portrait by G. F. Watts.

To George Smith

MS John Murray. *Commentary*, p. 242; B 187.

4. December 1862.   WALTHAM HOUSE, WALTHAM CROSS.
My dear Smith.

Many thanks for the Cornhill. I did make your wife a promise to go down to Brighton,[8] & I am a beast not to keep a promise, the keeping of which would be so pleasurable; but the fact is I have become a slave to hunting;—as men who do hunt must do at this time of the year. It is not that I would not willingly give up my hunting for the Wednesday—or even the Wednesday & Saturday; but that engagements get themselves made which will not have themselves broken. And so I have people here on the Wednesday—& indeed up to I dont know what day—Xmas I believe, who are all more or less in the boots & breeches line.

Mrs. Trollope bids me say that no further persuasion than your own would have been necessary—had she been a free agent. But she is not. A good wife always does head groom on such occasions.

Pray tell your wife from me that I own myself a beast—& humbly beg pardon. As things have arranged themselves it is too late now to do more than beg pardon.

Yours always
Anthony Trollope

To George Smith

B 188 (Sadleir's transcript).

21 December 1862

*   *   *

Julia Cecilia Collinson,[9] whom I know to be a very nice person, she having been an intimate friend of my sister tho' I never saw her myself—writes to me saying that as I am editor of the Cornhill Magazine she humbly hopes I may have grace enough to return to her the MS. of a story which she sent to that magazine—for which she has since been bidden £20, but has no other copy. The perplexing woman wrote the name of the tale on a separate bit of paper which I have lost. It was "Don't you wish you may get it" or something like that. I know there was a "get it" in it. Can you help her or me? Of course I shall undeceive her as to the high pinnacle of literary eminence to which she has erroneously exalted me.

*   *   *

[8] Smith spent his winters at Brighton, traveling daily to London to conduct his business.

[9] Julia Cecilia Stretton (1812–78), née Collinson, minor novelist. Her parents, the Reverend John Collinson, Rector of Gateshead in Durham, and his wife Emily, were old friends of Trollope's mother (*Memoir*, II, 17). Julia's first husband, Walter de Winton, died young; in 1858 she married Richard William Stretton.

To [? Frederic] Chapman

MS Parrish Collection.

Decr. 21 1862   Waltham Cross.
My dear Chapman.

I do not quite understand your note about the books. I saw the books
to be nice copies & marked at B & B¹ at the prices I quoted. If you bought
them they wd let you have them at trade price, but wd not let me. I don't
like giving you trouble, but if you can get them I will be obliged to you.
I don't care two straws whence they come.

Yours always
Anthy Trollope

The books you named are right.
    Bancrofts America   7. vol —
    Encly of Biography.   3. vol.
    De Quincy—   14. vol.—²

To George Smith

SB 189 (Sadleir's transcript).

23 December 1862

Trollope asks Smith to print two dozen copies of his lecture "The Present
Condition of the Northern States of the American Union."³

To the Editor of the *Athenaeum*

Athenaeum, 27 December 1862, p. 848.

Dec. 23. 1862.   Waltham Cross.

Your Correspondent "C. W. H." instructs my brother that when speaking, in his "Lenten Journey," of the Pope's Swiss Guard, and of their
exploits at Perugia, he has fallen into a blunder and repeated a calumny
against the Swiss. The purport of the argument is to prove that the Pope
employs no Swiss among his soldiers. "C. W. H." is mistaken—certainly
as regards the Pope's soldiers who were at Perugia. They were under the
command of a Swiss general, and were themselves in part, if not all, Swiss.
Friends of mine, American ladies, the story of whose wonderful preserva-
tion in the hotel of Perugia when all others in the house were murdered
is well known, were saved by the humanity and gallantry of a Swiss

¹ Bickers and Bush, 1 Leicester Square.
² The first seven volumes of George Bancroft's *A History of the United States*
(1851–61); perhaps the three-volume edition of Charles Knight's *The Cyclopaedia of
Biography* (1862); the fourteen-volume edition of *De Quincey's Works* (1853–60).
³ Trollope gave the lecture in the provinces on 30 December 1862 (according to
Booth) and again in London on 13 January 1863. The text was published in *Four
Lectures*.

soldier. This man was then in the Pope's pay, and has since been made
happy in his own country by the gratitude of the ladies whom he saved.[4]

Yours, &c.,

Anthony Trollope

To ?

MS Parrish Collection.

December 26. 1862   WALTHAM HOUSE, WALTHAM CROSS.

Sir.

I ought to have sooner answered your letter of the 5th. Instant. But I
have been very much pressed for time.

The project of which you speak for publishing a volume of gratis contributions from authors on behalf of Lancashire[5] would not, I feel assured, meet with much approval among authors, because they would all
feel, as I do, that the value contributed by them in time & matter would
not be at all fairly represented by the profit arising from such a volume.
The thing has been often tried. Almost every living author of repute has
written for such publications. But the success never equals the amount
of work given. I could write nothing for such a publication that would
take me less than a week,—but the value to the Charity would be very
poor payment for that weeks work. I should do better to sell my story, &
give the money.

Your obt Servant

Anthony Trollope

To James T. Fields

MS (copy in Annie Fields's hand) Harvard. SB 917.

[?1862]

*   *   *

weak. It amounted to an admission that he[6] allowed the grass to grow
under his feet while he had the sheets, and while Harper who had no
such advantage was hard at work.

[4] C. W. H.'s letter had appeared in the *Athenaeum* on 20 December 1862 (p. 814).
He wrote again on the subject two weeks later (*Athenaeum*, 3 January 1863, p. 24),
though the last word was had by Edmund Waterton (*Athenaeum*, 10 January 1863, p.
60). The "well-known" story may be that of "an inoffensive family of American travellers [who] narrowly escaped being murdered by the Pope's troops in [Perugia] where
they witnessed the murder of the landlord, and were forced to be the spectators of
other horrors." (T. A. Trollope, *Lenten Journey in Umbria and the Marches* [1862],
p. 107.)

[5] Doubtless to relieve the distress caused by the American Civil War in the region's
cotton-manufacturing districts. The volume referred to may have been *An Offering
to Lancashire: Something New; or, Tales for the Times*; this was edited by Captain
Eustace W. Jacob and published by Emily Faithfull's Victoria Press in March 1863.
No well-known writers were among the contributors.

[6] J. B. Lippincott, in connection with the publication of *North America*.

Of course I suffer much; but I should not begrudge that in the least if I could bring about any better state of things.

Yours always most heartily
Anthony Trollope

To [? S. L.] Howard[7]

MS Parrish Collection.

[?1862–63][8]
Friday WALTHAM HOUSE, WALTHAM CROSS.
My dear Mr. Howard

I extremely regret that I have to send word to you that I cannot come. I have tumbled into the doctors hands & heaven knows when I shall be out again. I regret this the more because I must be absent tomorrow morning. I hope our old friend will stick to us. Better the Deil you do know than the Deil you don't. If more money be wanting,—as more money will be wanting—I will do anything in my little way;—up to doubling my subscribtion [*sic*] if that be needed. Say so for me.

Yours always
Any Trollope

Many thanks for the offer of the bed—unfortunately I am obliged to stick to my own.

1863

To James T. Fields

MS Parrish Collection. B 190.

Jany 8—1863. WALTHAM HOUSE, WALTHAM CROSS.
My dear Fields.

I send to you a lecture on the present condition of the Northern States which I have given once here in the provinces, & which I am to give again in London on next Tuesday. I think you will acknowledge that I am fighting your battles for you almost better than you are fighting them

---

[7] Probably Colonel Samuel Lloyd Howard (1827–1901), of Goldings, Loughton, Essex; a JP and Deputy-Lieutenant of the county. Howard and Trollope both rode with the Essex Hunt. In Richard Francis Ball and Tresham Gilbey's *The Essex Foxhounds: With Notes upon Hunting in Essex* (1896), Howard is described as an "intimate friend" of Trollope (p. 162).

[8] Watermark 1862.

yourselves. I wish you to publish the lecture in the *Atlantic*, if you think well of doing so.[9] The small country audience received it well—what a larger audience in London may do, I cannot say. If you do publish it, do it with my name, & with *no alterations*. I am very strong in it against slavery, but I must not be made to appear what you call an abolitionist.[1] If you do this take means to let me have a copy.

I send a few other copies for you to distribute by post or otherwise. We have no book post hence to the States or I would not trouble you. I fear I may put you to some expense in this;—if so I will honestly pay you if you will condescend to tell me. By the bye I always fear that I put you to some expense about those books I sent, tho' I did all in my power to prevent it.

Give my very kindest regards to your wife & pray let me hear from you.

I have had no word from Lippincott as to his sale—2500 have been sold here at 34/. At so high a price the sale is large. In the spring it will come out in a cheaper form,—or perhaps later.[2]

Yours always very truly
Anthony Trollope

To George Smith

MS Parrish Collection. Excerpt, *Commentary*, p. 242; B 191.

Feb—11—1863.   WALTHAM HOUSE, WALTHAM CROSS.
My dear Smith.

I wrote this morning telling you that I meant to see you to day. But the doctor came ordering me to bed—which was a bore as I was going to dine with our Poster General. So I didn't go to town.

This is to tell you that the S. H. of A. [*sic*] is now finished—and as I always fear having it burned while the MS remains with me, shall be conveyed to you, very shortly. If it quite suits you to let me have the quid pro quo, I shall be very much obliged.

I wish you had my liver just for to day.

Yours always
Anthy Trollope

---

[9] Fields did not publish the lecture.

[1] Trollope said: "I am no abolitionist, for abolition, as the term is now used, means the instant emancipation of four million helpless creatures who as free men—made free by instant edict—could only starve or live by rapine till they were extirpated. I am no abolitionist; but I would not own a slave for all the wealth of all the Indies." (*Four Lectures*, p. 36.)

[2] A "Fourth and Cheaper edition" of *North America* was published in February 1864 at sixteen shillings; a one-volume edition was published in 1866 at six shillings.

To George Smith

MS Bodleian. Excerpt, *Commentary*, p. 242; B 192.

Feb 18–63.   WALTHAM HOUSE, WALTHAM CROSS.
My dear Smith.

Many thanks. All *my* interest in the S. H of A. is now over.
Just at this moment you fellows are beginning. I hope the great man
Wilson has been in a good humour. Ah me! If I could only have one of
those spitted nests of oysters to remind me of what you are doing. For
myself, I had a bit of boiled mutton at three; & my wife remarked that
she didn't think half a glass of sherry wd. do me any harm.

Yours always

Anthony Trollope

To Emily Faithfull[3]

MS Parrish Collection.

19 Feb. [1863]
Thursday night.   WALTHAM HOUSE, WALTHAM CROSS.
My dear Miss Faithfull.

I am at your work, & write to tell you exactly how I & it are circum-
stanced. I can let you have the story by Tuesdays post,—Tuesday 24th.
but I fear not sooner. Will this do for you? If it will, tell me so. If it will
not, & you must go to press without me, tell me also, as in that case I
need not go on. In any case believe me that I got myself to your work
at the earliest possible hour.

Yours always faithfully

Anthony Trollope

The story can be delivered at your house on Tuesday evening.

---

[3] Emily Faithfull (1836–95), feminist, lecturer, and publisher. Especially interested
in women's employment, Miss Faithfull founded in 1860 the Victoria Press, a printing
firm with female compositors; her first volume, edited by Adelaide Ann Procter, was
entitled *Victoria Regia* (1861) and was dedicated, by permission, to the Queen. In
1862 the Queen appointed Miss Faithfull Printer and Publisher in Ordinary, and in
the same year Miss Faithfull opened a steam press printing office. In 1863 she published *A Welcome: Original Contributions in Poetry and Prose*, and she began publishing and editing the *Victoria Magazine*. Trollope had contributed a story entitled
"The Journey to Panama" to *Victoria Regia*, and here he arranges to donate another,
"Miss Ophelia Gledd," to *A Welcome*. Other contributors to these volumes included
Thackeray, Tennyson, Arnold, D. G. Rossetti, George Macdonald, Mrs. Oliphant,
Harriet Martineau, T. A. Trollope, and Charles Kingsley. Trollope's two stories were
reprinted in *Lotta Schmidt* (1867).

To [? Frederic] Chapman

MS Parrish Collection.

March 23–1863   WALTHAM HOUSE, WALTHAM CROSS.
My dear Chapman.

Miss Drury goes to Dresden on 9th. April, and is *very* anxious to correct her proofs[4] before that. Will you hurry the printer so as to enable her to do it.

I have told her about the three volumes and about the £25—

Yours always

Anty Trollope

To Mrs. Cecilia Meetkerke[5]

MS Yale.

19 April 63.   Yarmouth.
My dear Mrs. Meetkerke

I have gone thro' the enclosed with care. The pen and ink alterations, which apply solely to the stopping, you may take as correct,—I think. Those in pencil are for your consideration. The lines against which I have put a cross—thus X—you should I think alter. The last line of the first piece is hardly rythmical [*sic*]. At any rate it is too weak to end so pretty a thing.

In line 3 page 3 you have used the word "bereft" wrongly,—tempted by the rhyme. The man is bereft, not the thing. "If I am bereaved of my children, I am bereaved."

Thoughts of sorrow cannot be like phantoms of sleep. Sleep should come at the end of the last line.

Never use Italics. They are the struggles of imbecility. Strong nervous language will always shew itself.

Dolores. Lines sixth to tenth—you will see I have somewhat altered your version, but I think the change makes the passage clearer. "Altho' " is

---

[4] For *Deep Waters* (1863).

[5] Cecilia Elizabeth Meetkerke (?1823–1903), daughter of the Hon. Edward Gore and granddaughter of the 2d Earl of Arran; second wife of Adolphus Meetkerke (1819–79), a cousin of Trollope's father. (Adolphus's father, also named Adolphus [1753–1840], had been childless until his late second marriage; his son's birth disappointed the expectation of Trollope's father that he would succeed to the Meetkerke estate in Hertfordshire, as the son of the elder Adolphus's sister Penelope.) For many years Trollope assisted Mrs. Meetkerke in her efforts to publish her poetry.

ugly to the ear,—particularly when followed by "Though." And you had got a little aground in your construction.

It must be *"that* word"; otherwise the " 'twas," would be wrong. The "It", must refer to "word" in the singular. To my ear word is better than words.

Barbëd is bad. You must nowadays use words as they are pronounced. Those · · are not admissible.

—Your beautiful idea—"If human hearts are sealed &c" has been brought out obscurely. I think I have improved it. But still the line about Love on bended knee is obscure. You mean "While Love on bended knee strugles [*sic*] in vain to read them." See if you can improve it. I can't find the word. The "now" is decidedly bad, & the word sd. be "betwixt."

Immolate is fantastic. Put sacrifice.

"Such deeper in the wound &c—" is obscure. Put your nominative case before your verb when you can.

Of kindness that had knit our hearts of old. The repeated "of" is needed.

"Grew less alive"— "Grew to feel less" is surely bad.

The last three lines are very weak. Alter them or else put out the four.

Wearied to calm—is not expressive— I have tried my hand at another line.

Your very sweet idea in the following lines is marred by its obscurity. The reader is left in the dark as to what "him" means till the end—and the "mortal tongue" is weak. I send a slightly altered version on a separate slip.

Those two last lines about consolation must come out.

"Soulless" is bad. "Dying" is better, & issues in good antithesis to the final word.

"Their"—in the last line should certainly be "his."
[————]
Page 11. Line 5. The word "Each" is wrongly used, & the passage is obscure. And the word "divine" means nothing, there, of what you wish

to express. I have altered the three lines,—& leave them to your judgement.

Tears do not flow on "Marble cheeks."

Page 12. The six lines marked X. are weak. The last marked XX. very weak— It is the worst line in the whole— Eyes' averted looks!! You will see that it will not do.

Put a full stop at tenderness. I think I have made the two last lines on the page more clear.

"Stood in the valley of the shadow of death," is poetic prose but not rythmical [*sic*] poetry. I have made rhym [*sic*] of it. I will leave it to you to say whether your own scriptural views will be sufficiently carried out.

I think the 4 first lines in page 14. do not express your meaning. I have ventured to suggest four at the foot of the page.

Comforted is a weak word & a bad rhyme.

"Wrung" what? Wring must have an accusative.

You will now be imploring protection from your friends,—who are always the most remorseless of critics.

In the other sheets I will if you so like it better confine myself to the stopping.

Yours always faithfully
Anthony Trollope

My address is at home.

To George Smith

B 194 (Sadleir's transcript).

9 May 1863

Trollope invites Smith to Waltham House and will not allow the Derby[6] to interfere with their arrangements.

[6] Run on 20 May. Apparently none of the guests Trollope had invited for that day was able to come; see Trollope to Millais, 21 May 1863.

To M. J. O'Connell[7]

MS National Library of Ireland.

May—10—1863.   WALTHAM HOUSE, WALTHAM CROSS.
My dear M. J. O Connell.

Long postponed may yet come at last.

Can you come down to us on Monday 18th. & stay till 20th. There will be some people with us—but the eating will be poor. Our cook[8] has got drunk,—perpetually drunk. If there be nothing to eat we can do the same.

Yours very truly
Anthony Trollope

To Octavian Blewitt

MS Royal Literary Fund.

May 12th. 1863   73 St. Georges Square[9]
My dear Sir.

Bad as I am at it, I will do as you ask me tomorrow.[1] I only got your note this moment.

Yours very truly

O Blewitt Esq   Anthony Trollope

To J. E. Millais

MS Pierpont Morgan Library.

21 May 63   73 St. Georges Square
My dear Millais

We had a very melancholy day—which wd. have been less melancholy had you all come. But it could not be helped. My wife was awfully disgusted as women always are when nobody comes to eat their pastries and sweetmeats. As for me, I only hope you lost your money at the Derby. I

---

[7] Morgan John O'Connell (1811–75), barrister; popular MP for County Kerry, 1835–52; a friend of Thackeray and member of the Garrick Club. Trollope knew O'Connell's father-in-law, Charles Bianconi, well.

[8] The 1861 Census of Trollope's household at Waltham Cross listed Bernard Smith, groom, aged 63, born Ireland; Anne Smith, dairymaid, aged 48, born Ireland, married; Catherine Magnee, housemaid, aged 32, born Ireland, unmarried; Rachel Robins, cook, aged 43, born Westminster, Middlesex, unmarried; and Fanny Campbell, under cook, aged 12, born London, unmarried (Public Records Office). The name Bernard Smith further complicates the identification of Trollope's old Irish groom "Barney": see Trollope to Beatrice Trollope, 8 June 1865.

[9] John Tilley's address.

[1] Trollope made a brief speech at the Anniversary Dinner of the Royal Literary Fund, held on 13 May, in answer to a toast to the writers of fiction.

hardly know as yet when I am going to be at home, so we must put off the new day for a week or so.

> Yours always
> Any Trollope

I thought I might perhaps have seen you at the Cos. last night.

To ?

MS Taylor Collection.

May 24. 1863   WALTHAM HOUSE, WALTHAM CROSS.
My dear Madam.

I purpose to do myself the pleasure of calling on you, but I do not choose that you should suppose in the mean time that your letter is neglected.

With reference to Mr. Tyler I fear that it is beyond my power to do as you would have me. I have been in correspondence with Lady Stradbroke[2] who has made the same request; but the matter had gone too far, and another Postmaster had been appointed.

I may also assure you that Tyler does not deserve to be re-appointed. It is true that the office at Wangford has been in the hands of his family for many years, and the result has been one very common under such circumstances,—namely an absolute neglect of his duties. The office had been with him so long that he regarded it as his own by right & he would do nothing that he was told. Cautions & threats were thrown away upon him—till it had become necessary to vindicate the authority of the department by his removal.

Pray believe me that it would have given me most sincere pleasure to have obliged a person for whom I have so high an esteem as for yourself.

> Your very faithful Servant
> Anthony Trollope

To John Tilley

MS (unidentified hand; Trollope's signature) General Post Office, London. B 195.

24 May 1863.   Waltham Cross.
Sir.

I beg to acknowledge the receipt of your letter of the 8th. Instant asking me whether I think that Seniority coupled with full competency for the duties of a higher class should be the condition of promotion throughout the entire Post Office Service.[3]

[2] Augusta, Lady Stradbroke (*b.* 1830), wife of 2d Earl of Stradbroke, of Henham Hall, Wangford, Suffolk.

[3] Tilley was once again soliciting opinions on promotion by seniority, in this case to see whether department heads stood by their former views. (See Trollope to Tilley, 13 June 1860.)

I certainly do think so, as I have always thought; but my opinion has been much strengthened by watching the way in which the contrary system has worked. I feel very sure that the system of promotion by merit, as it is called, cannot in truth be carried out; and that it is injurious to the service and ever will be so, in so far as it can be or hereafter may be carried out.

It cannot be carried out, firstly because men will not commit the monstrous injustice which it enacts; and secondly because no weights and measures can be found by which merit can be weighed in the balance. The system demands that promotion shall be given to the best man, let the merits of those who are to be superseded be what they may,—and let the years of service and well-grounded expectations of the senior candidates be also what they may. A man may have worked his best for twenty years for the Crown; he may have amply deserved promotion; he may have married on the assured conviction that the merited reward would in due time be his; he may in all respects be fitted for the duties of the higher place; but by the system of promotion, now assumed to be carried out in the Civil Service, he is to lose it all if some better man than himself shall have come into the same class with him at the last moment! From the very wording of the rule it is apparent that no amount of excellence is safe, because a greater amount of excellence must always be possible. No extent of devotion to his duties will secure any man in his expectation of promotion, because some devotion, supposed to be more extended, may come after him. Such a system is so cruel in its nature that men will hardly attempt to work it.

The superior officer will certify that the senior man is the best man, —presuming always that he is a good and fitting man,—even tho' he be not the best or nearly the best. Such falsehood is very grievous to him; but it is not so grievous as the ruin which he would inflict on deserving men by the truth. But the attempt is sometimes made. It is made, I think, less frequently now than when the theory was in its first flush of triumph;—and it will, in course of time, cease to be carried out at all even tho' the rule should not be officially revoked,—for such rules die of their own accord. The attempt however is still made; but there is absolutely wanted to those who make it any measure by which excellence may be meted. The reporting officer who is zealously anxious to work the new system, and who is resolved to throw all other considerations to the wind in carrying out a theory that sounds so well, can at last only depend on his own judgement. To know whether a man be absolutely fit or unfit for certain duties is within the capacity of an observant and intelligent officer;—but it is frequently altogether beyond the capacity of any officer however intelligent and observant to say who is most fit. Zeal recommends itself to one man, intelligence to a second, alacrity to a third, punctuality to a fourth, and superficial pretense to a fifth. There can be no standard by which the excellence of men can be judged as is the weight of gold.

Nor can I understand why the service should require more than actual competency. Indeed no service can require more than that, or obtain better than that, let its duties be ever so exalted. If a man be in all respects fit to do the work he has engaged to perform, no better man can be had. It has always seemed to me that the Civil Service can obtain nothing by the odious comparisons which this system institutes. But it undoubtedly loses very much. It is my opinion that the selected man is deteriorated by the act of selection;—that he is taught to imagine himself to be too great and too good for the very ordinary work which, in spite of the glory of his selection, he is generally called upon to perform; but, be that as it may, there can be no doubt that the men who are passed over are deteriorated. Very little experience in the Civil Service, or, as I imagine, in any other service, will teach an observer as much as that. The unfit man becomes more unfit;—so much so that even unfitness should not be measured too closely; and the man who was perfectly fit is made to be unfit by the cruelty to which he has been subjected. As to this there can be no doubt. The man who is competent and has exerted himself and is yet passed over, cannot but be broken-hearted; and from a broken-hearted man no good work can be obtained.

The theory of promotion by merit,—that theory by which promotion is to be given not to the senior man who is fit, but to the man who is fittest, be he senior or junior—is thoroughly Utopian in its essence; but it has in it, as I think, this of special evil which is not inherent in most Utopian theories,—that it is susceptible of experimental action, and that the wider the action grows the greater is the evil done.

> I am,
> Sir,
> Your most obedient Servant
> Anthony Trollope

The Secretary
General Post Office

To W. H. Russell

Maggs Catalogue 988 (Spring 1978).

26 May 1863   GARRICK CLUB
My dear Russell
Will you come down to us on Friday June 12— Of course we give you bread as well as victuals. . . . Its a long day off, but other people are coming & therefore I name it. . . . Our house is Waltham House about ½ mile from Waltham Station—

*   *   *

William Gay[4] to Trollope

MS Parrish Collection.

May 28/63   POST OFFICE

> Mr. Anthony Trollope was offered 2,000*l*. a-year
> for five years, if he would lend his name as editor
> to a magazine, without having the labour of being
> the acting editor; but Mr. Trollope declined on
> account of his already having as much on his
> hands as he can well attend to.[5]

Tell the Publisher he shall have my name for £*100* per ann.

This is just the addition that should be conceded to the Salary of the Surveyor of the Manchester District.

W. Gay

To William Gay

MS Parrish Collection.

May 29. 1863

This is a fair sample of the truth of such rumours. I was offered £1000 a year to edit—(or rather be nominal Editor of—)—a magazine. I answered that I would put my name to nothing as to which I did not do what my name imported that I would do, & that I was too busy to undertake the work—

A. T.

I will of course make the offer on your behalf. But as it was 12 months ago the people have probably suited themselves.

[4] William Gay (1812–68), Post Office Surveyor for the Manchester District. Gay's daughter recalled Trollope as a house guest: "No more repose was left in the house when he awoke in the morning. Doors slammed, footsteps resounded, and a general whirlwind arose, as he came or returned from his bath, or walked out in the garden, and from that time until nightfall, he was as busy as a man could be. He had a scorn of everything in the way of pretensions—even of justice to time-honoured institutions —and slurred over his family history and belittled 'the service' right royally. 'Post Office' (he always omitted the 'General' or departmental style and title)—he would write with a little 'p' and a little 'o,' as though it were a village sub-office, retailing stamps with tobacco and onions." (Susan E. Gay, *Old Falmouth* [1903], p. 216.)

[5] Newspaper clipping pasted to the letter. Trollope's reply (the next letter) is written on the reverse of this letter. For the offer itself, see de Fauche to Trollope, 5 August 1861.

To W. H. Russell

MS Taylor Collection.

May 29. 63.   Waltham X.
Dear Russell.
Come down on Sunday—June 14th. Bell will be here, & Blumenthal[6]
the musical man—and that female Caxton of the Age E Faithfull.[7]
                                  Yours ever & always
                                  Any Trollope

I remembered me afterwards that asking you on Friday was adding an
insult to the original injury of Saturday. You sent no enclosure.

To J. E. Millais

John Guille Millais, *The Life and Letters of Sir John Everett Millais*
(1899), I, 283–84. Excerpt, *Commentary*, p. 246; excerpt, B 193.

June 4th. 1863.   WALTHAM HOUSE, WALTHAM CROSS.
My dear Millais.
Ten thousand thanks to you, and twenty to your wife, as touching
Ian. And now for business first and pleasure afterwards.
X. (a Sunday magazine)[8] has thrown me over. They write me word that
I am too wicked. I tell you at once because of the projected, and now not-
to-be-accomplished, drawings. They have tried to serve God and the
devil together, and finding that goodness pays best, have thrown over
me and the devil. I won't try to set you against them, because you can
do Parables[9] and other fish fit for their net; but I am altogether unsuited
to the regenerated! It is a pity they did not find it out before, but I think
they are right now. I *am* unfit for the regenerated, and trust I may remain so, wishing to preserve a character for honest intentions.
And now for pleasure. I get home the middle of next week, and we
are full up to the consumption of all our cream and strawberries till the
Monday—I believe I may say Tuesday, *i.e.*, Tuesday, June 16th. Do,
then, settle a day with the Thackerays and Collinses,[1] and especially with

---

[6] Jacques Blumenthal (1829–1908), composer; pianist to Queen Victoria; Garrick
Club friend of Trollope.

[7] Emily Faithfull; see Trollope to Faithfull, 19 February 1863.

[8] Obviously substituted by J. G. Millais for *Good Words.* See the next two letters.

[9] Throughout 1863 *Good Words* published twelve of Millais' illustrations of Biblical parables; these, together with eight more drawings, were published in a book
edition in 1864 (*The Parables of Our Lord*). The drawings are considered master-
works of Sixties-style wood engraving. As this letter indicates, Millais had also been
engaged to illustrate *Rachel Ray*; in the end, he supplied the frontispiece for Chapman & Hall's one-volume 1864 edition of the novel (the seventh), which sold for five
shillings.

[1] Charles Allston Collins (1828–73) and his wife Kate, née Dickens, the third child
of the novelist. Collins, the brother of Wilkie Collins and a former member of the
Pre-Raphaelite Brotherhood, had forsaken painting for literature.

Admiral Fitzroy,[2] to come off in that week. I shall be in town on Wednesday night. Look in at about 11.30.

Yours always
Anthony Trollope

Why have you not put down Leighton, as you promised?

To Alexander Strahan

MS (Trollope's copy) Bodleian. Commentary, p. 247; B 196.

June 10. 1863.   Waltham Cross.
Dear Sir.

I am sorry that you and Dr. McCleod have been forced to the conclusion at which you have arrived with reference to my story.[3] I claim for myself however to say that the fault in the matter is yours, & not mine. I have written for you such a story as you had a right to expect from me,—judging as you of course did judge by my former works. If that does not now suit your publication I can only be sorry that you should have been driven to change your views.

I have, as I take it, an undoubted right to claim from you the payment of £1,000 for the story. I do not however desire to call upon you for a greater sacrifice than must be made to place me in a position as good as that which would be mine if you performed your agreement & published my story during the next six months. If I publish that story in another form during the autumn,—as I shall do under the circumstances I am now contemplating,—I shall get for it £500 less than the sum which I should receive, when [? were] you to publish it in Good Words.[4] That sum of £500 I am willing to accept from you. But you will of course understand that in making this offer I reserve my legal right to demand the £1000, should you not accept the proposed compromise.[5]

A. T.

A. Strahan Esq

[2] Admiral Robert Fitzroy (1805–65), author with Darwin of *Narrative of the Surveying Voyages of H.M. Ships 'Adventure' and 'Beagle'* (1839).

[3] *Rachel Ray*. For Macleod's first overture to Trollope, see Macleod to Trollope, March or April 1862.

[4] By an agreement of 26 January 1863, Chapman & Hall were to pay Trollope £500 for the right to print 1,500 copies of a book edition of *Rachel Ray*; on 10 June 1863, they agreed to pay Trollope £1,000 for the right to print 3,000 copies of a book edition (MSS Bodleian). This second sum, plus the £500 from Strahan, gave Trollope the same total earnings that he would have received under the original arrangements with *Good Words* and Chapman & Hall.

[5] On 13 June Strahan replied: "I shall be quite prepared to do whatever you think right in the matter of the remuneration. If it is to be £500 I shall have much pleasure in paying this. . . . I am quite agreeable to your publishing the story in any magazine you like. It is presumptuous in me to speak in this way, as if I had any right to interfere with your arrangements, but you ask me for definite information." On 16 June Strahan again wrote: "I am much obliged to you for your note. I see and appreciate

Norman Macleod to Trollope
MS Bodleian. *Commentary*, pp. 248–51.

June 11 1863   Glasgow.
My dear Trollope.

I presume you and Strahan have to day met, settled accounts, and parted—friends?— I resolved, for many reasons, not to write to you until that part of the unpleasant business was over.

As it is now past 12 o'clock it is full time for me to settle, as far as possible, my accounts with you, should I be able to pay only 6d. in the pound.

Let me begin my letter by most cordially reciprocating the kind wish with which yours ends, that after this you and I may be as we were. Thank you, my boy, for that! It has removed a burthen from me.

And now a few (?) words in explanation of what induced me with so much reluctance to give up "Rachel Ray"— *You* are not wrong; nor have you wronged me or my publishers in any way. I frankly admit this. But neither am I wrong! This "by your leave" I deny, and will "stick to my bundle" if my bundle will stick to me. The fact is that I misunderstood you, and you me—tho' I more than you have been the cause of the misunderstanding.

What I tried to explain and wished you to see when we met here, was the peculiar place which Good Words *aimed* at occupying in the field of cheap Christian literature. I have always endeavoured to avoid on the one hand the exclusively narrow religious ground—narrow in its choice of subjects & in its manner of treating them—hitherto occupied by our "Religious" Periodicals; and on the other hand to avoid altogether whatever was either antagonistic to the truths or spirit of Christianity, and also as much as possible whatever was calculated to offend the prejudices, far more the sincere convictions and feelings of fair & reasonable Evangelical men. Within these extremes it seemed to me that a sufficiently extensive field existed in which any novelist might roam & find an endless variety of life & manners to describe with profit to all & without giving offence to any. This problem which I wished to solve did not & does not seem to me a very difficult one, unless for very one-sided "Evangelicals" or anti-evangelical writers. At all events, being a clergyman as well as an Editor, the one from deepest convictions, tho' the other, I fear is from the deepest mistake, I could not be else than sensitive lest anything should appear in Good Words out of harmony with my convictions & my Profession. Well then, was I wrong in assuming that you as a Christian worshipper were an honest believer in Revealed Christian truth? I was not! Was I wrong in believing & hoping that there were many truly Christian aspects of life as well as the

the reasonableness of what you say, and shall have much pleasure in remitting you the £500 as agreed." (MSS Bodleian.)

canting & *humbug* ones with which you heartily sympathised & which you were able and disposed to delineate? I was not! Was I wrong in thinking that Good Words was a periodical which from its aims & objects afforded you perhaps freer scope for this kind of writing than even Cornhill? Perhaps I was wrong in my judgment, & had no ground for hoping that you would give me a different *kind* of story than those you had hitherto published. If so, forgive me this wrong. Possibly the wish was father to the thought. But the thought did not imply that any of your former Novels had been false either to your own world within or to the big world without—false to truth or to nature—it assumed only that you could with your whole heart produce another novel which instead of showing up what was weak, false, disgusting in professing Christians might also bring out, as has never yet been done, that Christianity as a living power derived from faith in a living Saviour, working in and through living men & women, does, has done, & will do what no other known power can accomplish in the world for the good of the individual or of mankind. If no such power exists neither Christ nor Christianity exist—and if it does, I must confess that most of our great novelists are, to say the least of it, marvellously modest in acknowledging it. The weaknesses—shams—hyprocrisies—gloom—of some species of professing Christians are all described & magnified, but what of the genuine human born Christian element? Why, when one reads of the good men in most novels it can hardly be discovered where they got their goodness. But let a Parson, a Deacon, a church member be introduced, & at once we guess where they have had their badness from! They were *professing* Christians.

Now all this & much more was the substance of my sermon to you at Arran and here—& I thought you would either bring out more fully the positive good side of the Christian life than you had hitherto done, or avoid at least saying anything to pinch, fret, annoy, or pain those Evangelicals who are *not* Recordites.[6]

Now, my good Trollope, you have been, in my humble opinion, guilty of committing this fault—or, as you might say praiseworthy in doing this good—in Rachel Ray. You hit right & left—give a wipe here, a sneer there, & thrust a nasty *prong*[7] into another place, cast a gloom over Dorcas Societies, & a glory over balls till 4 in the morning,—in short, it is the old story—the shadow over the Church is broad & deep, & over every other quarter sunshine reigns—that is the *general impression*

---

[6] "Recordite" was a label commonly applied to members of the most extreme group of Anglican evangelicals, after this group's notoriously combative party newspaper, the *Record*. In the spring of 1863, the *Record* had furiously attacked Macleod and *Good Words* for mixing religious and nonreligious works, calling Trollope "this year's chief sensation writer" and claiming of *Good Words* that in some of its "trashy tales the most ungodly sentiments are uttered and left to work their evil effects on the young mind" (13 April 1863; reprinted in *Commentary*, p. 245).

[7] A play on the name Samuel Prong, a sanctimonious clergyman in *Rachel Ray*.

which the story gives, so far as it goes. There is nothing of course bad or vicious in it—that *could* not be, from you—but quite enough, & that without any necessity from your head or heart, to keep Good Words & its Editor in boiling water until either were boiled to death. I feel pretty certain that you either do not comprehend my difficulties, or laugh in pity at my bigotry. But I cannot help it.

You do me however wrong in thinking—as you seem to do—that apart from the structure of your story, merely because of your Name I have sacrificed you to the vile Record & to the cry it & its followers have raised against you, as well as against me. Before I read your story, I and Strahan had taken a decided stand against such "Evangelical" tyranny & bigotry. As some proof of this I send you a printed copy of a letter written weeks ago to Professor Balfour in Edinburgh—but sent only a few days since—my only pain is that the Record will suppose that its attack has bullied me into the rejection of your story!

What you mean by my attempt to serve God & Mammon, I do not understand—for I presume neither you nor the Record represent either Deity![8] I know well that my position is difficult, & that too because I do *not* wish to please both parties, but simply because I wish to produce if possible a Magazine which tho' too wide for the Evangelicals & too narrow for the anti evangelicals & therefore disliked by both cliques, may nevertheless rally round it in the long run the sympathies of all who occupy the middle ground of a decided, sincere, and manly Evangelical Christianity.

I wish I could *say* all this, with such comments as would prevent my words or my spirit being misinterpreted. Please *take* a kindly meaning out of it, and don't give a Recordite meaning to it. But you have had enough of this kind of extempore (out of season?) preaching, and I suppose my sermon like many others will leave preacher & hearer very much where they were.

I look forward with sincere pleasure to the Pipe & Baccy with "summ'at to cheer the heart"—for mine is rather sad and heavy after a hard winter's work. I intend probably going to Iceland with George in August. Will you come & light your pipe at Heckler [*sic*] or make your toddy from the Geysers? Let us dispute on the voyage. It will enliven it. There is no chance of your giving in to me. I'll be hanged if I give in to you! So farewell, and light your pipe with my epistle to make it legible & luminous.

Yours sincerely,
N. Macleod.

[8] The *Record* had written: "It would seem as if by means of high retaining fees . . . the spirited publishers had at last bridged over the impassable gulf . . . [and] that God and Mammon, God and the World, were all reconciled in the Utopian harmony of the genial gospel proclaimed in *Good Words*." (*Record*, 20 April 1863; reprinted in *Commentary*, pp. 245–46.)

P.S. This letter will keep cold till you are at peace with all the world with a pipe well filled & drawing well. Read it then—or a bit each day for a month.[9]

To ?

MS Parrish Collection.

June 12. 63   WALTHAM HOUSE, WALTHAM CROSS.
My dear Sir.
I shall be very happy to dine with you on Thursday 25th.
I never ventured on an archbishop yet. But who knows?
Yours always
Anthony Trollope

To G. E. Frere[1]

MS Parrish Collection. SB 197.

POST OFFICE

June 15. 1863   Waltham Cross.
Sir.
I have now before me a medical report posted at Diss on the 7th. inst; which, according to your letter of the 8th., reached Kenninghall in [due] course on that morning. This letter bears no Thetford stamp,—and that omission has been noticed; but it was not delayed in its transit.

I presume that the letter (or report) to which you alluded in your first application as not having been received at Kenninghall on June 1, was not posted on the previous day, or if posted was not posted in time. I

---

[9] This letter may be the one of which Trollope said "a letter more full of wailing and repentence no man ever wrote" (*Autobiography*, p. 188). If so, Trollope either failed to remember the letter's tone or wished to play down the author's attempts at self-justification. In any event, Trollope and Macleod remained close friends. Several years after Macleod's death, Trollope wrote to Macleod's biographer: "I need not say that Dr. Macleod's rejection of the story never for a moment interfered with our friendship. It certainly raised my opinion of the man." (Donald Macleod, *Memoir of Norman Macleod* [1876], II, 149.) Indeed, Trollope agreed to propose a toast to Macleod at a charitable dinner in 1865 (see Trollope to Moir, 17 November 1865), and he wrote a vigorous article for the *Fortnightly* in January 1866 in response to a sabbatarian attack on Macleod (see Trollope to Smith, 3 February 1866). Trollope also continued to write for *Good Words*: "Malachi's Cove" was published in December 1864 (reprinted in *Lotta Schmidt*); the novel *The Golden Lion of Granpere* ran from January through August 1872; and the novel *Kept in the Dark* ran from May through December 1882. For more on the *Rachel Ray* and *Good Words* difficulty, see Trollope to Isbister, 17 April 1877, n. 4.
[1] George Edward Frere (1807–87), barrister; brother of Sir Henry Bartle Edward Frere.

cannot however make any statement with reference to that unless I see the report on the cover of it.

Your faithful Servant
G. E. Frere Esq   Anthony Trollope
Roydon Hall
Diss

To Octavian Blewitt
MS Royal Literary Fund.

June 24. 1863   Cambridge
My dear Sir.
I have endeavoured to lick the enclosed into some shape.[2]
Yours always
O Blewitt Esq   Anthony Trollope

To Emily[3]
MS University of Rochester. SB 198.

July 2—1863.   WALTHAM HOUSE, WALTHAM CROSS.
My dear Emily.
I certainly will manage to see you before you go. You do not say how long you think of staying. We, at this moment, are expecting every day the arrival of Tom & his wife, who, I grieve to say, is coming here as an invalid, for change of air. Rose can go nowhere till they come. But she will probably be able to get to town either on Monday or Tuesday, but will write you word beforehand. She cannot possib[ly] get away this week. My motions must also depend on my brothers coming;—but I will certainly get to you some time next week.
affectionately yours
Anthony Trollope

To Lucette Barker[4]
SB 199.

8 July 1863   Waltham Cross
*   *   *
[Trollope sends his thanks for a drawing.] I had originally intended to call the story The Two pearls of Allington and your drawing makes me wish that I had adhered to my original name.
*   *   *

[2] Probably the text of Trollope's speech at the Royal Literary Fund's Anniversary Dinner: see the Fund's *Annual Report* for 1863, p. 30.
[3] Unidentified.
[4] Lucette E. Barker, a gifted amateur artist and the sister-in-law of Tom Taylor. Much admired by Mrs. Gatty, Miss Barker had furnished an illustration for Mrs. Gatty's first book of stories, *The Fairy Godmother* (1851).

To George Eliot

MS Parrish Collection. B 200; *George Eliot Letters*, VIII, 311.

July 10—1863.   WALTHAM HOUSE, WALTHAM CROSS.
My dear Mrs. Lewes.

Not for your sake but for my own I must write you one line to thank you for your present. I will say nothing further of the book but this;— that were you now departing from us, as I trust you may not till you have added many another leaf to your wreath,—you might go satisfied that you had written that which would live after you.[5]

I will get up to you as soon as I possibly can,—but you are regularly out (with a wise regularity) at the hour at which mortals call.

Yours most sincerely
Anthony Trollope

You will know what I mean when I say that Romola will live after you. It will be given to but very few latter day novels to have any such life. The very gifts which are most sure to secure present success are for the most part antagonistic to permanent vitality.

To George Smith

SB 201 (Sadleir's transcript).

19 July 1863

Trollope writes about making some slight changes in *The Small House at Allington*. He is just leaving for Switzerland.

To Altisidora Annesley[6]

MS Parrish Collection.

Grindelwalde
Switzerland

July 26. 1863.
My dear Miss Annesley

I received your note at the London Bridge Railway Station on Sunday evening last as I was in the agony of starting with all my belongings for a summer tour among the Alps. It happened that my brother in law[7] was with me, and I asked him to call on Mr. Murray & explain that I was on the wing when I got your letter. This, I hear from him, he did, and I also learn that he found Mr Murray to be a very pleasant gentleman. More than that I did not learn. I suppose he, Mr Murray, will have taken his departure before I shall have returned. If he has not, I will

[5] For Trollope's first impression of *Romola*, see Trollope to Eliot, 28 June 1862.
[6] The Hon. Altisidora Arthur Victoria Annesley (?1828–1922), youngest daughter of Sir Arthur Annesley, 10th Viscount Valentia.
[7] John Tilley.

find him out. We shall not be long here, as I have to go to Italy before the end of September.

Touching America, knowing your strong Southern predilections at Bletchington[8] I will say nothing as to the late Northern successes. I shall feel anxious to know how F. L. will speak of them. I was rash enough to venture on some prophesies, and like all prophets am of course anxious for the verification of my vaticinations. He will be quite as anxious—or probably much more so,—the other way, and therefore on that subject we must be poles asunder, till some future day when, after the end of all the bloodshed, we shall be able to talk over it all in cool philosophy. I trust that day may come soon;—for his sake, and for that of humanity.

Pray remember me to all at Bletchington who may remember me. I was to have seen Sir Hercules Robinson[9] again in town, but he did not keep his appointment at the club— Tell him from me, if he be with you, that I did.

> very faithfully yours
> Anthony Trollope

To Herbert Joyce[1]

MS Fitzwilliam Museum. SB 202.

POST OFFICE
August 22. 1863   Durham
My dear Joyce.

I return the enclosed with thanks. I fear the "correspondence" will not be of much utility,—except as enabling some one man in arguing the question to say that the general opinion of the superintending officers is against the new-fangled rule. There is too much of it, so that nobody will read it. And then some large part of it is hardly worth reading.

> Yours always
> Anty Trollope

---

[8] Bletchington Park, Oxfordshire, family seat of the Annesleys.

[9] Sir Hercules Robinson (1824–97), later 1st Baron Rosmead, at this time Governor of Hong Kong; subsequently Governor of Ceylon, Governor of New South Wales, Governor of New Zealand, and Governor of the Cape Colony. Sir Hercules, the husband of Miss Annesley's sister Nea, became a good friend of Trollope.

[1] Herbert Joyce (1831–97), head of the discipline branch of the Post Office, under the Post Office Secretary; Assistant Secretary of the Post Office, 1880; later Post Office librarian.

To W. W. F. Synge

MS Parrish Collection.

August 28—1863.　　　　　　　WALTHAM HOUSE, WALTHAM CROSS.
Dear Synge.

This is not a letter from me. Harry has just brought me the enclosed to put up under cover to you, and I cant do it without one line. But I don't doubt I shall write again by the same post. I am working awfully hard—I can hardly describe to you what at, for you know nothing now of my literary doings. I have a novel in 2 vols coming out in October[2] and a new serial commencing on 1 January—like Orley Farm—for which I am aground as to a name.[3] We came home from Switzerland two weeks since, and I go to Italy on 10 Sept, conveying back my brothers wife, her little girl, & Harry;—who has left school and who is going to begin life as a young man at Florence.

I got your letter which was all about money.[4] You'll remember which I mean. There was nothing in it especial to answer. There rarely is— I'm always writing novels. You're always patronizing Kings. Thats our mutual news. Your side is I dont doubt the easier, and, putting aside either's results, the pleasanter. It is awfully hard work spinning continual novels.

The last time I saw Thackeray he told me he had done 2 & ½ numbers of a new one.[5]

God bless you all—my love to your wife & bairns, whom may good angels protect.

Yours with my pen tumbling out of my fingers

Anty Trollope

To [? Frederic] Chapman

MS Parrish Collection.

6. Sept. 1863.
Sunday　　　　　　　　　　WALTHAM HOUSE, WALTHAM CROSS.
My dear Chapman.

I must be in town again tomorrow, Monday. If you can conveniently do so, wait for me till half past four, as I shall want to see you. I will be a little earlier if possible.

---

[2] *Rachel Ray.*

[3] *Can You Forgive Her?*

[4] Trollope and Thackeray had each lent Synge £900 (see Trollope to Merivale, 13 January 1864). Omitting Synge's name and his own, Trollope later told the story as an example of Thackeray's generosity (*Thackeray* [1879], chap. i).

[5] *Denis Duval*, the novel begun in May 1863 and left unfinished at Thackeray's death.

I send a cheque for £25—would you let Goddard get me napoleons for the amount & give them to me tomorrow.

I want to answer the enclosed letter from the French publisher. Do you know whether Orley Farm & Dr. Thorne have been translated? What should I ask & what should I get? We'll go halves if we do get anything. Mind that I get the note back when I call tomorrow.

Yours always
Anthy Trollope

To [? Frederic] Chapman

MS Columbia. B 203 (incomplete).

September 9. 1863.   WALTHAM HOUSE, WALTHAM CROSS.
My dear Chapman.

I had been thinking much about the novel[6] for the periodical before I got your letter and had intended to write to you. I dont think I can make my story shorter than I had intended;—that is I am not minded to do so— People will not have to wait longer, or so long, as for the monthly numbers. Indeed it may be question whether it should not all be included in one year. In that case I should lessen the price as against the paper, and of course charge you separately as publishers for the republication— I think the object should be to bring it out in two volumes— such as the Orley Farm volumes for 20/. A sale of 4,000 or 5,000 in that shape is better than 1,500 in 3 volumes. If we make the weekly to consist of 40 or 48 pages without columns (i e 36—or 44) could not the printing of the story be so arranged, that we could pull off from the same type the sheets for the subsequent volumes? Or we might have 32 pages on one sheet, and have the novel printed separately in similar type, and bring it out together, say 32 pages of the periodical and eight or twelve of the novel. You will understand what I mean. Consider it well before you answer me— But let me have an answer addressed to Florence as soon as you can.

As to name I think the "New Weekly"—would be the best. The new weekly conducted by Anthony Trollope. You can discuss that with Bell.

In discussing the question between columns and no columns, should you find the work would not bear 48 pages (and I think it would not)— and that 40 pages cannot be printed & folded in one sheet, it will then be a question whether the saving of the printing for the republication of the novel, (as above explained) would not make it worth while to have the extra sheet. I should like to avoid columns if possible, and I should like the thickness of the larger number of pages if the paper would not overweight us.

I should much wish the outside cover for the monthly numbers to be colored.

[6] *Can You Forgive Her?*

Of course you will enquire what would be the cost of weekly stitching. It would be very desirable.

You must remember in considering the publication of my own novel, that I cannot sacrifice that. I can not make it shorter than it should be, in order that it might suit the periodical. If the novel as now arranged will do for the periodical, (as I think it will,) let it come out in that shape on 1st. of January. If it will not it must come out alone, & the periodical be postponed.[7]

Yours always
Anthony Trollope

To [? Frederic] Chapman

MS Newark, New Jersey, Public Library.

Sept 19. 1863.
Saturday.   Florence.
My dear Chapman.

I got your note with the three pages this morning. I had expected that you would answer my proposition about the novel; but that must now stand over to be talked of when I return. I shall be in at home on the morning of Monday Sept 28th. Instant—& will be with you on the afternoon of that day between 4. & 5 PM.

I think we must take the middle one of the three enclosed pages which would contain about 700 words. The smaller page would not contain enough. My impression is that we should give 32 pages (i e 28 after taking out 4 for the covers,) and a supplemental sheet of 8 pages for the novel. The question is whether the paper with the supplemental sheet would be too costly. You can now make your calculations before I return. The 8 pages a week of the novel, at the sized page of which I now speak—viz No. 2—would take the whole novel in 12 months. At least I would make it fit to that. But then, I fear, the subsequent publication of the novel, must be in one volume instead of two.

I send back all the three sheets which of course you will keep.

We must be prepared to decide what we shall do during the three days after my return, if we intend to go on with it on 1 January.

Yours always
Anthy Trollope

---

[7] It is evident from this and the following letter that Chapman & Hall were planning a new weekly periodical under Trollope's editorship. The venture, however, never got off the ground. *Can You Forgive Her?* was serialized in twenty monthly parts, from January 1864 through August 1865; the first volume of the book edition was published in September 1864, the second volume at the end of July 1865. A year later Trollope and Frederic Chapman were foremost among the group that launched the *Fortnightly Review* (see Trollope to Lewes, 24 December 1864).

I should purpose to sell the novel afterwards in one volume for 15/—.
You were to ascertain whether 40 pages could be taken off at once. You
do not say whether or no you have done so.

If you prefer the smaller page, which is certainly the prettier, the
novel must run thro 10 pages a week, or alternate 8 & 12 pages. Could
you not calculate the expense of each.

To [? Frederic] Chapman
MS Parrish Collection.

Sept 30. 1863.   Waltham Cross.
My dear Chapman.

You have the letters sent to me about the wine from Germany. It
strikes me that I ought probably to send to the shipping office therein
named, & give orders as to what should be done with the wine.

Could you have this done. Of course I will pay any expense. I feel no
doubt the wine is laying somewhere in London.

Do find out for me if you can what is being done about Beppo in the
Once a Week. As you are to publish in January, I cannot see how they
are to get it thro before then, seeing that they have not as yet commenced to send the proofs.[8] Or are they publishing it without sending
any proofs?

Yours always
Anthony Trollope

To C. W. Jones[9]
MS Taylor Collection.

Sept 30. 1863.   WALTHAM HOUSE, WALTHAM CROSS.
Sir.

I have just returned from Italy—and have therefore only now received
your letter of the 10th. Instant. I shall be very hard at work during the
winter months, and should not have time to prepare a lecture. The only
one I have by me that I could give at Bury is on the state of the American war;—and as my views are not now popular, being strongly Northern,
such a lecture would not probably be well received at Bury.[1]

Your faithful Servant
C W Jones Esq   Anthony Trollope

---

[8] T. A. Trollope's *Beppo the Conscript* was published in two volumes by Chapman
& Hall on 23 February 1864; serialization in *Once A Week* was not completed until 19
March.

[9] C. W. Jones, Secretary of the Athenaeum, Bury St. Edmunds.

[1] After giving Jones a second indecisive answer on 7 October, Trollope did lecture
on this subject to the Bury Athenaeum on 26 January 1864.

To ?[2]

MS Parrish Collection.

Sept 30—1863.   WALTHAM HOUSE, WALTHAM CROSS.
My dear Sir.

I was sorry to miss you when I called at Skeyton— Perhaps I may meet you on some other occasion when I am in Norfolk.

I will see whether we can do anything as to putting up a pillar box or wall box in your parish; but I fear not. The difficulty is the expense of sending a messenger to collect the letters, which would cost about £6 per annum. I fear it will be found that we already give as much accommodation to the parish as the letters will afford.

very faithfully
Anthony Trollope

To W. Hepworth Dixon

MS Newberry Library.

Oct 7—1863.   73—St. Georges Square
My dear Mr. Dixon.

My mother died at Florence yesterday morning. She would have been 85 had she lived till February, having been born in 1779.[3] I trouble you with this statement because you will perhaps put a short notice into the Athenaeum.[4] She wrote her first work when she was 50.[5] My father's circumstances were then very bad & she commenced her work simply for an income. She wrote for 25 years—publishing her last work in 1856— when she was 77 years old.[6] Her only remaining children are my brother & myself.

Yours faithfully
Anthony Trollope

---

[2] The reference to "your parish" suggests the addressee may have been the Rector of Skeyton, William Stracey. Skeyton is a village in East Norfolk.

[3] Trollope's mother was born on 10 March 1779 (the *Memoir* mistakenly gives 1780, the year T. A. Trollope had inscribed on Mrs. Trollope's tombstone at Florence [I, 8; II, 301–2]).

[4] See Trollope to Doran, 10 October 1863.

[5] *Domestic Manners of the Americans*, published in 1832, a work that brought Mrs. Trollope instant and lasting renown.

[6] *Fashionable Life: or Paris and London* (1856).

To Frederic Chapman

B 204 (Sadleir's transcript). *Commentary*, p. 109.

October 7. 1863   WALTHAM HOUSE, WALTHAM CROSS.
My dear Chapman.

My mother died at Florence yesterday morning. I tell you this, that if you are intending to go to Florence, you may delay your journey for a few days.[7]

Yours always
Anthony Trollope

To C. W. Jones

MS Historical Society of Pennsylvania. SB 205.

October 7—1863.   WALTHAM HOUSE, WALTHAM CROSS.
Sir.

I have been prevented by my mothers death from answering your letter sooner.

I fear you have gone a little too fast in taking my last letter as a promise to lecture;—as, if you look at it, you will see. I doubt the suitableness of the only subject on which I have an unpublished lecture by me. I will however make some further enquiry & let you know at the earliest possible date—say in three or four days. I could not certainly lecture so early as the day you name from circumstances of business which have lately occurred.

Your very obt. Servant
Anthony Trollope

C W Jones Esq
Athenaeum
Bury St. Edmunds

---

[7] Sadleir coupled this letter with an excerpt from a letter of Trollope to Mrs. Mary Christie (29 February 1864) and suggested that their "brevity, their practical good sense, their strict avoidance of all facile mournfulness are of the essence of the writer's character" (*Commentary*, p. 109).

To John Doran[8]
MS Parrish Collection. B 206.

Oct 10—1863   Waltham House
My dear Doctor Doran.

I cannot but thank you again for the kindliness, heartiness, as well as excellent taste of your article on my mother.[9] And moreover there was no word that contained a mistake.

very faithfully
Anthony Trollope

To Frederic Chapman
MS Parrish Collection.

October 14. 1863   Waltham Cross.
My dear Chapman.

I specially want to see your artist[1] before he goes to work. When can I meet him? He should have read the work first. Could I see him at your house on Friday afternoon,—say at 4. or 4.15—PM? If so I would go up on purpose that day.

Thanks for the books, also for the revises, which I return for the first No. I am anxious to know whether the second number will go into the 32 pages.

Have you paid for the wine—& if so how much?

Have you paid in the money for me? If not pray do.

Yours always
A. T.

We shall be very glad to see you either Monday or Tuesday next week— Which day will suit you?

If I meet your artist on Friday, pray arrange that he shall have read the numbers first—

---

[8] Dr. John Doran (1807–78), miscellaneous writer and writer on stage history; frequent contributor to and substitute editor of the *Athenaeum*; editor of *Notes and Queries*, 1872–78.

[9] Doran wrote that Mrs. Trollope's "literary career . . . made her one of the most remarkable women of her period. . . . The venerable lady has passed tranquilly out of life, leaving a name in English Literature, and a memory to be honoured by her two surviving sons." (*Athenaeum*, 10 October 1863, p. 469.)

[1] The illustrations for the first ten monthly numbers (the first volume) of *Can You Forgive Her?* were by Hablot Knight Browne (1815–82), usually known as "Phiz," the popular illustrator best remembered for his collaboration with Dickens. For Trollope's dismissal of Browne, see Trollope to Chapman, 10 June 1864, n. 8. See also *Illustrators*, pp. 89–98.

Waltham House.
Waltham Cross.

October 18. 1863,

My dear Mrs Lewes,

            Will you accept a copy
of Rachel Ray, a little story which
I have just published in two volumes.
I have desired Chapman to send it
you.

            You know that my novels are
not sensational. In Rachel Ray
I have attempted to confine myself
absolutely to the commonest details
of commonplace life among the
most ordinary people, allowing
myself no incident that would be
even remarkable in any day
life. I have shorn my fiction of all
romance. I do not know what you
who have dared to handle great

Letter to George Eliot, 18 October 1863

names & historic times will
think of this. But you must
not suppose that I think the
little people are equal or
second to the great names. Do you,
who can do it, go on. I know you
will not be deterred by the criticism
of people who cannot understand.
Neither should you be deterred by
internal criticism. That which
you have in you flesh you are
bound to pour forth.

Yours always most truly
Arthur P. Stanley

To George Eliot

MS University of Virginia. B 207; *George Eliot Letters*, VIII, 313.

October 18. 1863.   WALTHAM HOUSE, WALTHAM CROSS.
My dear Mrs. Lewes.

Will you accept a copy of Rachel Ray, a little story which I have just published in two volumes. I have desired Chapman to send it you.

You know that my novels are not sensational. In Rachel Ray I have attempted to confine myself absolutely to the commonest details of commonplace life among the most ordinary people, allowing myself no incident that would be even remarkable in every day life. I have shorn my fiction of all romance.

I do not know what you who have dared to handle great names & historic times will think of this. But you must not suppose that I think the little people are equal as subjects to the great names. Do you, who can do it, go on— I know you will not be deterred by the criticisms of people who cannot understand. Neither should you be deterred by internal criticism. That which you have in your flask you are bound to pour forth.

Yours always most truly
Anthony Trollope

George Eliot to Trollope

MS Parrish Collection. *George Eliot Letters*, IV, 110–11.

Oct 23. 63.   16 Blandford Sq.
Dear Mr. Trollope

I received your kind letter some days before I received Rachel Ray. But now I have read the book & can thank you both for your remembrance & for the gift. I value both.

Rachel has a formidable rival in The Small House, which seems peculiarly felicitous in its conception & good for all souls to read. But I am much struck in Rachel with the skill with which you have organized thoroughly natural everyday incidents into a strictly related well proportioned whole, natty & complete as a nut on its stem. Such construction is among those subtleties of art which can hardly be appreciated except by those who have striven after the same result with conscious failure. Rachel herself is a sweet maidenly figure & her poor mother's spiritual confusions are excellently observed. But there is something else I care yet more about, which has impressed me very happily in all those writings of yours that I know—it is that people are breathing good bracing air in reading them—it is that they, the books are filled with belief in goodness without the slightest tinge of maudlin. They are like pleasant public gardens, where people go for amusement, & whether they think of it or not, get health as well.

It seems rather preachy and assuming in one way that, out of all the other things I might say. But it is what I feel strongly & I can't help thinking that it is what you care about also, though such things are rather a result of what an author is than of what he intends.

We shall soon be in the agony of moving,[2] & after that I hope we shall continue to see you by planning.

Always yours very truly
M. E. Lewes

To George Smith

MS John Murray. B 208.

October 29—1863.   WALTHAM HOUSE, WALTHAM CROSS.
My dear Smith.

My wife bids me say that she will like nothing better than to run down to Brighton for a couple of nights,—if you will take us in for so long, & if you can make it within the first ten days of December. If so, will Mrs. Smith fix the time within those ten days?

You spoke the other day to me about the Cornhill. Did you mean anything? I'll tell you why I ask, and you must not suppose that I mean to press you. A proposition has been made to me since I saw you, which very likely will come to nothing in any case, but which would certainly come to nothing if I were to write another novel for the Cornhill so early as 1865.[3]

I should not have thought of naming the matter had you not spoken, believing you to have enough on your hands with Thackeray and Wilkie Collins—[4] But if you think you should like to have another of mine to commence about April 1865, and if you made me an offer which I could accept, I should then certainly decline the other proposition.

This is looking very far ahead and if you say it is too far ahead for you, I shall be satisfied.

Yours always
Anthony Trollope

To the Committee of the Royal Literary Fund

MS Royal Literary Fund.

November 2. 1863.   WALTHAM HOUSE, WALTHAM CROSS.
My Lords & Gentlemen.

I have been much grieved to learn that Miss Sophia Coulton, the author of The Farm of Four Acres and other literary works, has been

---

[2] See Trollope to Lewes, 16 November 1863, n. 3.

[3] Thus begin Trollope's negotiations with Smith for *The Claverings*, Trollope's fourth and last novel for the *Cornhill*. It was serialized from February 1866 through May 1867. (See Trollope to Smith, 5 November 1863.)

[4] William Wilkie Collins (1824–89), the novelist. George Smith had met Collins through Ruskin, and in 1860 narrowly missed the chance of publishing the book edi-

driven by the stress of hard circumstances to apply to the Literary Fund for aid. Miss Coulton is a friend of mine, and I am able to say that she in every way is entitled to your kindest consideration; nor can I imagine that any one can come before you with claims for assistance superior to hers. Of her own literary claims I do not know that I need say anything here. I suppose that they will be considered by you more than sufficient to entitle her to a place on your list, if in other respects you may judge her to be a fit recipient of the benevolence of your subscribers. But as a woman of very great worth I can vouch for her. She is possessed of a moderate income,—thought by her friends to have been secure as is so often the case,—but which has been absolutely stopped by certain law proceedings with reference to the property from which it was drawn. There has been no fault of her own. I may add that her brother[5] was also one who drew his daily bread from literature,—a man widely known, much loved, & much respected. Some five years since he died, leaving children wholly destitute. These children his sister took under care & has since educated & clothed,—that same sister on whose behalf I am now asking your consideration. And I may safely say that she would have sufficiently provided for any such time of trouble as has now come upon herself, had she not expended her means in giving a home to the orphan children of her brother.[6] I am, my Lords & Gentlemen,

Your very faithful Servant

To the Committee   Anthony Trollope
  of the Literary Fund

To George Smith

SB 209 (Sadleir's transcript).

5 November 1863

    Trollope advises Smith that he is tempted by an offer from another publisher and would like to know Smith's decision about another novel fifteen months hence.[7]

---

tion of *The Woman in White*. Collins's *Armadale* began serialization in the *Cornhill* in November 1864, and Smith published all his later books. For Trollope on Collins's fiction, see *Autobiography*, pp. 256–57. After Trollope's death, Collins wrote: "His immeasurable energies had a bewildering effect on my invalid constitution. To me, he was an incarnate gale of wind. He blew off my hat; he turned my umbrella inside out. Joking apart, as good and staunch a friend as ever lived—and, to my mind, a great loss to novel-readers." (Robert Ashley, *Wilkie Collins* [New York, 1952], p. 105.)

    [5] David Trevena Coulton (1810–57), miscellaneous writer, editor of periodicals.

    [6] Sophia Coulton, who had been a neighbor of Trollope at Waltham Cross, received on this occasion a grant of £50 from the Royal Literary Fund. See also Trollope to Blewitt, 11 May 1866.

    [7] By an agreement dated 13 November, Smith agreed to pay £1,800 for serial rights to *The Claverings*, with the provision that he could purchase, if he so wished, the entire copyright for an additional sum. In the end, Smith exercised his option, and Trollope was paid £2,800 for the novel. Because Trollope conceived of (and sold) his

To [? Frederic] Chapman

MS Parrish Collection. B 210.

9. Nov. 1863.   WALTHAM HOUSE, WALTHAM CROSS.

My dear Chapman—

I'm sorry to hear of your rheumatics— I had no business when I called the other day— I only came for a parcel of Mss from Tom for the Victoria, which was lying at your place.[8]

I am glad to hear you are doing so well with R.R. After all the old fashioned mode of publishing does very well now and then as a change.[9]

I quite agree about the Editions. Dont let them print at the same time Nos 5—& 6— Whatever is printed at once let them call it one & the same edition.[1] When anything is to be gained by dishonesty there may be an excuse; but why be dishonest when we don't want it?

Yours always
Anthony Trollope

To W. W. Glenn[2]

MS Parrish Collection.

10 Nov. 1863.   WALTHAM HOUSE, WALTHAM CROSS.

My dear Mr. Glenn.

I supposed that you had not got back. If you do stay in town, (—and do if you can,—) of course you will come to us on Saturday. But if you would like to see a days hunting, I will mount you very safely on the Saturday, and in that case come on the Friday to dinner. You will find others here & you should have a little party out to the hunt on Saturday morning. Perhaps you might like to see so thoroughly British an institution as a fox hunt.

Yours always
Anthony Trollope

---

novels in terms of units roughly the length of a volume of a traditional "three decker," this figure for the three-unit *Claverings* represented "the highest rate of pay that was ever accorded me" (*Autobiography*, p. 197). See Trollope to Virtue & Co., 24 January 1867.

[8] T. A. Trollope's *Lindisfarn Chase*, published in the *Victoria Magazine* from May 1863 through August 1864.

[9] Having been rejected by *Good Words*, *Rachel Ray* was never serialized. Instead, it was published in October 1863 in a two-volume edition.

[1] Despite this letter, Sadleir finds evidence that the many early two-volume editions of *Rachel Ray* (six between October 1863 and 30 April 1864) may represent nothing more than a deliberate splitting up of the originally agreed upon 3,000 copies into six "editions" of 500 copies each. See *Bibliography*, pp. 277–79.

[2] William Wilkins Glenn (1824–76), American journalist; part owner of the Baltimore *Daily Exchange*.

To G. H. Lewes

MS Yale. *George Eliot Letters*, VIII, 315.

Nov 16 1863   WALTHAM HOUSE, WALTHAM CROSS.
My dear Lewes.
I think I can be with you on the 24th.[3] I will do my very best.

                       Yours always
                       Anthy Trollope

To Captain Byng[4]

MS Parrish Collection.

Nov 22—1863.   WALTHAM HOUSE, WALTHAM CROSS.
Sir
    In answer to your letter about Cook the mail cart contractor I had better explain to you,—as I have done to some others who have written to me about him,—that he has not been, as he & they suppose, dismissed. Never having been a servant of the department, the department could not dismiss him. He is a Contractor, and has received notice to quit, and can put in a new tender. If his new tender be lower than any other eligible tender I will recommend that it be accepted.

    The fact is that no contract for a mail cart should run on so long as his old contract has been allowed to do. There is a rule that they should be terminated after 7 or 8 years. His present Contract is now 11 years old. The men after a while become indifferent, get into slow paces, & when they have received twenty or thirty cautions without any actual evil result, come to think that seven miles an hour will do as well as eight.

    In this case I did not act without ascertaining to a certainty that the man was going slower than he should go,—and that I could not make him go his proper pace. You need not therefore think that he has been punished for fault on the part of the Postr. of B Stortford. If he get the contract again you will find that the whole thing will have brightened him up. If he do not, the fault will have been his own. I am, Sir,

                     Your very faithful Servant
The Honbl Capt. Byng   Anthony Trollope

---

    [3] On that date Trollope attended a housewarming combined with Charles Lee Lewes's coming of age party at the Priory, Regent's Park, where G. H. Lewes and George Eliot had moved on 5 November.

    [4] Perhaps Captain Henry Byng (1811–81), R.N., of Quendon Hall, Essex, grandson of the 5th Viscount Torrington.

To Christopher Hodgson[5]

MS Parrish Collection.

Nov 28—1863   WALTHAM HOUSE, WALTHAM CROSS.
My dear Greek Professor
(So Benthall[6] says you are) I send below what you ask with greatest pleasure.

                              Yours always
C Hodgson Esq   Anthony Trollope

To W. W. Glenn

MS Parrish Collection.

Decr. 2—1863.   WALTHAM HOUSE, WALTHAM CROSS.
My dear Glenn.
If you have nothing better to do will you spend Christmas day with us, as you like the fox hounds. I'll give you another morning on the Saturday after Xmas day. Mrs. Trollope bids me say that she hopes you'll come. If so come on the Thursday to dinner.

                              Yours always
                              Anthony Trollope

Fred[7] has got a second edition of his toggery now, so you needn't scruple to borrow.

To G. H. Lewes

MS Yale. B 212; *George Eliot Letters,* VIII, 315.

Decr 13. 1863.   WALTHAM HOUSE, WALTHAM CROSS.
My dear Lewes.
On returning home I have found your life of Goethe,[8] for which, I presume, I have to thank you. I do thank you heartily. I must get your name in it some day. I shame to say I never read the former edition. I have already been at work at this, and am charmed with it. Alas, me—for 11 years I learned Latin & Greek—nothing else—& know it now, you, who understand our English schooling, will know how superficially. Of German of course I know nothing. Shall I hereafter have an action against my pastors & masters?

                              Yours dear Lewes
                              always yours
                              Anthony Trollope

[5] Christopher Hodgson, Post Office Surveyor for the Northern District.
[6] A. Benthall, first-class clerk in the office of the Post Office Secretary.
[7] Frederic, Trollope's younger son.
[8] The second edition of Lewes's *The Life and Works of Goethe* (1855), published in 1864.

How excellent is your outside got up. Calico—we call it cloth when we want to be grand,—has thereon achieved its greatest biblical triumph.[9]

To George Smith
MS John Murray. B 214.

December 25. 1863. WALTHAM HOUSE, WALTHAM CROSS.
My dear Smith.

I was going to write to you on another matter,—but I have been stopped in that, as in every thing, by Mr. Thackeray's death.[10] I felt it as a very heavy blow.

You will of course insert in the next Cornhill some short notice of him. Who will do it for you? If you have no one better, I will do it gladly.[1] Lewes, or Bell, or Russell would do it better. I only make the offer in the event of your having no one better—

If you hear that anything is fixed about the funeral, pray let me know. I have not the heart to wish any one a merry Christmas.

Yours always
Anthy Trollope

Of course you will know that what I offer is a work of love.

To [? Frederic] Chapman
MS Parrish Collection. SB 213.

25. Decr. 1863. WALTHAM HOUSE, WALTHAM CROSS.
My dear Chapman.

I send back the revise of No. 3—corrected—and also the Illustrations, of No. 2, with the lettering of one of them corrected. What a fellow you are! You ask me for the subjects for the Illustrations of No. 3, and, I gave them into your own hand when I last saw you.

Many happy Christmases to you
Yours always
Anthony Trollope

[9] The book was elaborately bound with brown cloth, a leather label, gold lettering and rules, and beveled edges.

[10] Although Thackeray had not been in good health, his sudden death on 24 December came as a surprise.

[1] In the notice, "W. M. Thackeray," *Cornhill*, 9 (February 1864), 134–37, Trollope claimed *Esmond* to be "the first and finest novel in the English language" and Colonel Newcome (from *The Newcomes*) "the finest single character in English fiction." Of Thackeray himself, Trollope wrote: "One loved him almost as one loves a woman, tenderly and with thoughtfulness,—thinking of him when away from him as a source of joy which cannot be analysed, but is full of comfort." See also *Autobiography*, pp. 185–86.

I have been greatly cut up by Thackerays death, which I only learned in the Times. It has not been a merry Christmas with us. I loved him dearly.

To W. W. Glenn

MS Parrish Collection.

December 31. 1863.   WALTHAM HOUSE, WALTHAM CROSS.
My dear Glenn.

I should have been delighted to dine with you, on Monday, but we have a large party of young folk coming here for the week,—& indeed of folk who are not so very young,—and I cannot be spared away from home. I should be very glad to have met Gallenga,[2] whom I know by reputation of course, tho' not personally.

Yesterday we buried poor Thackeray.[3] His death was a great blow to me and to many others.

You seem to make no stay in London so that I shall hardly see you. If you are back from France before the end of the Season I'll mount you when you come.

I hope you are getting better.

Yours always
Anthony Trollope

To W. W. F. Synge

Herman Merivale and Frank T. Marzials, *Life of W. M. Thackeray* (1891), p. 215. B 215.

[? December 1863]
Dear old fellow—

I saw him for the last time about ten days before his death, and sat with him for half an hour talking about himself. I never knew him pleasanter or more at ease as to his bodily ailments. How I seem to have loved that dear head of his now that he has gone.

I had better tell the story all through. It is bad to have to write it, but you will expect to be told. He had suffered very much on the Wednesday (23rd), but had got out in the afternoon. He was home early, and was so ill when going to bed that his servant suggested he had better stay. He was suffering from spasms and retching, having been for some months more free from this complaint than for a long time previously. He would not have the servant, and was supposed to go to bed. He was heard moving in the night. . . . It is believed that he must have gone off between two and three, and I fear his last hours were painful. His arms and face

---

[2] Antonio Carlo Napoleone Gallenga (1810–95), Italian refugee, author, and journalist.

[3] Thackeray was buried in All Souls' Cemetery, Kensal Green, on 30 December. For an account of the funeral, which attracted a crowd of upwards of 1,500 people, see Gordon N. Ray, *Thackeray: The Age of Wisdom*, pp. 417–18.

were very rigid—as I was told by Leech⁴ who saw him in the morning afterwards.

*   *   *

To Emily Faithfull
MS Parrish Collection.

[?1863]   73. St Georges Square
Wednesday morning.   Pimlico
My dear Miss Faithful [*sic*].
    I am engaged tomorrow or I sd. have been so happy to have gone to you tomorrow. I have only just got your card.
Yours very faithfully
Anthony Trollope

To George Smith
MS Bodleian.

[1863 or 1864]   WALTHAM HOUSE, WALTHAM CROSS.
My dear Smith.
    Many thanks for Doyles sketches.⁵
Yours always
Anthony Trollope

You shall have the paper you wot of on Tuesday or Wednesday at furthest.

1864

To E. J. Smith⁶
MS Parrish Collection.

January 10. 1864.   WALTHAM HOUSE, WALTHAM CROSS.
My dear Sir.
    Many thanks for your kindness, of which,—in the matter of your hospitality,—I shall be delighted to avail myself should I come to Leeds.

---

   ⁴ John Leech (1817–64), comic artist; friend of many literary men, including Thackeray, Dickens, and Trollope; *Punch*'s chief cartoonist from 1843 until his death. Leech loved hunting, the subject of many of his well-known sporting sketches.
   ⁵ Doyle's *Bird's Eye Views of Society* (1864) were issued by Smith in book form on 12 December 1863 (sixteen sketches together with the texts that had accompanied them in the *Cornhill*).
   ⁶ Perhaps Edward James Smith, Postmaster of Leeds.

I will lecture on Friday 19th. February if it is thought desirable. Thursday would suit me better as I always hunt on Saturday— But that shall not stand in the way if Friday be thought better— If, however, all these regular nights are full, might it not be better to put it off to next Session? But all this I will leave you to settle for me. I will lecture Thursday 18 Feb—or Friday 19—or promise to lecture next winter as you may arrange.[7]

Yours always
Anthony Trollope

E J Smith Esq

To John Leech
MS Parrish Collection. SB 216.

Jany 11. 64
Monday.   WALTHAM HOUSE, WALTHAM CROSS.
My dear Leech.

Millais was here yesterday, and promised to come down on Tuesday week so as to hunt on Wednesday—on condition that you would do so also. I hope you can make it convenient— Mrs. Trollope bids me say that she will be delighted to see you. A train leaving Shoreditch at 5.10 pm will bring you down in time for dinner.

It will be best to put off any arrangement about your horse till I know where the meet will be. If you find it impracticable to send your own nag across, I will contrive to mount you.

Yours always faithfully
Anthony Trollope

To Herman Merivale[8]
MS Berg Collection. B 217.

January 13. 1864.   WALTHAM HOUSE, WALTHAM CROSS.
My dear Merivale.

John[1] asks me to let you know the particulars of a debt due from W. W. F. Synge to poor Thackeray.

Synge, who is now Consul at Honolulu, borrowed, before he went in May 1862, £900 from Thackeray & £900 from me. It was agreed that £100 should be paid off quarterly. The first quarter to Thackeray & the second to me,—& so on. We each received the first £100, but then there was a

---

[7] Trollope gave a lecture entitled "Politics as a Daily Study for Common People" to the Leeds Mechanics' Institution and Literary Society on Thursday, 18 February 1864. A lengthy summary of the lecture (one of the points of which was the suitability of politics as a study for women) was given in the *Leeds Mercury*, 19 February 1864.

[8] Herman Merivale (1806–74), Under-Secretary for India; political economist and writer; elder brother of Trollope's friend John Merivale. Along with Matthew Higgins, Fitzjames Stephen, and George Smith, Merivale had taken charge of Thackeray's estate.

[1] John Merivale.

stop. Last year, in the spring, I think, Synge's father died, & there were some proceeds out of which Thackeray received £400 & I £400— It was then agreed that the remainder should be repaid by quarterly payments of £50 instead of £100. Whether Thackeray has had any such payment I cannot say. I have not. They were to be made by Messrs Bidwell & Alston the clerks of the F.O.[2] who pay moneys for the consuls &c. They can tell you whether Thackeray has had any further instalment.[3]

The debts were to bear interest at 5 per cent. Thackeray had a bond, prepared by Mr. Gregory M. Wheeler in Bedford Row.

Yours faithfully

Anthony Trollope

To George Smith

MS John Murray. Excerpt, *Commentary*, p. 253; B 218.

January 17. 1864.   WALTHAM HOUSE, WALTHAM CROSS.
My dear Smith.

I received together at Norwich on Friday your letters of the 13—& 14!! In the former you propose to insert my paper with papers & verses from Dickens & Lord Houghton,[4] and in the latter you suggest a longer memoir for the March number.

I prefer the former plan. I do not feel up to writing a memoir. And I do not personally know enough, and tho' I might possibly borrow all that can be said from Hannays excellent article I do not care to borrow in that way.[5] More of criticism that [than] what I have attempted would I think be almost out of place. I have said nothing that I do not think and believe, but if I were to say more I should perhaps run into rhodomontade or else cool down into ordinary eulogy.

You will see what alterations I have made. If you do not like what I have said,—a mere word—as to Hannays paper (which he sent me printed with his name) put it out.

I should be glad to see a revise—& let them print Anthony instead of "A." My brother is commonly called Adolphus.

Yours always

Anthony Trollope

I have destroyed C.D.'s paper—i e the copy you sent me.

Why not put the name in the front—as with Dickens,—& so also with the other paper.

[2] John Bidwell and Francis Beilby Alston of the Foreign Office.

[3] Trollope later wrote, with more kindness than truth, that "the money was quickly repaid" (*Thackeray*, p. 60).

[4] Dickens's tribute to Thackeray, "In Memoriam," and Houghton's poem "Historical Contrast. May, 1701: December, 1863." Both appeared in the *Cornhill*, 9 (February 1864), 129–32, 133.

[5] In his article Trollope called attention to James Hannay's *A Brief Memoir of the late Mr. Thackeray*, first published in the *Edinburgh Evening Courant*.

To Charles Burney[6]

MS Gordon N. Ray.

January. 21—1864   WALTHAM HOUSE, WALTHAM CROSS.
My dear Sir.

Do you remember the hospitality you proffered to me when I met you with all those parcels in Trafalgar Square? If so,—& in case it be in every other way convenient, will you take me in on Thursday next for a night—? I shall be in Halstead on Thursday.

very faithfully
Yours
Anthony Trollope

To ?.

MS University of Michigan. SB 220 (misdated).

January 24. 1864.   WALTHAM HOUSE, WALTHAM CROSS.
Sir.

Perhaps you could, without inconvenience, call on me at the Suffolk Hotel Bury St. Edmunds on Tuesday morning between 9 – & 10 – am. I shall be going out of Bury again in the day or I would not name so early an hour.

very faithfully yours
Anthony Trollope

To Frederic Chapman

MS Parrish Collection. SB 219.

Jan 26. 1864   Cambridge.
My dear Chapman.

I send back the corrections and revises of Numbers 4. & 5. I fear I must have another revise of two of the sheets which I have marked;—one because of a blunder of the printers & the other because of a blunder of my own.

I also send a copy for Mr Brown, with the subjects marked—and herewith I send you, for him, a statement of the proposed subjects for these two numbers with the lettering.

Will you be good enough to let him have it.

Yours always
Anthony Trollope

---

[6] The Reverend Charles Burney, Vicar of Halstead, Essex.

To George Smith

MS Bodleian. Excerpt, Hamer, p. 212.

Jany 29. 64   Chelmsford
My dear Smith.

Certainly. I should say, print in the headings of the chapters.

Your men I have no doubt will see the book properly thro' the press without my correcting it. I have put one error right in the portion I have returned.[7]

Yours always
Anthony Trollope

To G. H. Lewes

MS Yale. B 221.

January 31. 1864.   WALTHAM HOUSE, WALTHAM CROSS.
My dear Lewes.

If I come to you at 5. pm on Thursday (or is it 5 . 30?), will you give me my dinner?

My lecture at Bury went off magnificently. I went there in a carriage with a marquis, who talked to me all the way about the state of his stomach—which was very grand; and the room was quite full, and the people applauded with thorough good nature, only they did so in the wrong places;—and two or three Lady Janes told me afterwards that it was quite nice;—so that I was, as you see, quite in a little paradise of terrestrial Gods & Goddesses.

As you and your wife wouldn't come to see the wonders of Bury with me, I went off the next morning to hunt, 30 miles away, at 6. am.

Yours
Anthony Trollope

To Charles Burney

MS Taylor Collection.

Feb 3. 1864   WALTHAM HOUSE, WALTHAM CROSS.
My dear Burney.

I will do it[8] only on condition that Mr Overton[9] sits in the front bench —& pledges himself to sit it out, without shirking.

You have not said when your annual meeting takes place. If I find I

---

[7] Trollope is referring to the book edition of *The Small House at Allington*, published in March 1864.

[8] Give a lecture at Halstead (see Trollope to Burney, 11 February 1864).

[9] The Reverend Thomas Overton (1804–93), Rector of Black Notley, a parish near Halstead.

can do as you ask with reference to these engagements, I will;—but I
have other lectures on hand in different places.

Yours always faithfully

Anthony Trollope

To George Smith

SB 252 (Sadleir's transcript).

[February 1864][10]

Trollope is lecturing in Leeds soon but has not yet finished writing. Can
Smith print a few copies for him in twenty-four hours?

To George Smith

MS John Murray. B 222.

Feb. 10. 1864.   WALTHAM HOUSE, WALTHAM CROSS.
My dear Smith.

Touching the article on our dear old friend[1] my wife is mercenary, and
requires payment. She wants you to give her a copy of Esmond,—the
1-vol. Edit. of 1858. The book in that shape is a great favorite with her,
and we have used up our copy among ourselves & friends.

There is a shop in the Rue St. Honore devoted to Eau de Cologne,
and in which as my wife thinks is the only true fountain. Will you bring
her home the biggest bottle you can conveniently do. I think they are
about 12 francs. Tell your wife also that that Eau de Cologne if kept for
a year or two, (as we always keep it,) is certainly the best I ever met. The
shop used to be 333, but the numbers have been changed. It is on the
Rue Rivoli side, about half way between the Palais Royal, and the street
up to the Place Vendôme.

Thanks as to the printing.

My kindest remembrances to your wife. I hope your honeymooning
will be all fresh and nice,—just as it was the first time.

Yours always

Anthony Trollope

What is it the disciples of Banks[2] do? They eat every good thing going,
and then add two dry biscuits, and expect to be saved by them. That is
what I heard yesterday.

---

[10] Trollope's working diary indicates that he interrupted work on *Can You Forgive
Her?* from 4 to 20 February 1864 to prepare a "Lecture on politics."

[1] Thackeray.

[2] George Linnaeus Banks (1821–81), miscellaneous writer and journalist; advocate
of franchise extension and other social advances; promoter and organizer of mechanics'
institutes.

To Charles Burney

MS Gordon N. Ray.

February 11. 1864   WALTHAM HOUSE, WALTHAM CROSS.
My dear Burney.

Since I wrote to you & got your letter I have been ill with sore throat & have repented me. I am terribly teased with sore throat— It comes just when the lectures come, & tho' I have never absolutely broken down I am always fearing it. I lecture at Leeds on Thursday 18th. & am now in an awful funk. I shall not be home till Saturday night, & shant want to turn out again so soon as the next Tuesday if I can help it.—would Thursday 25 do for you?[3] If you must have me Tuesday you shall—i e 23rd. Only I shall say naughty words to myself about you. —But if my throat fails me, & I am dumb, you are not to let Mr Overton get up & have his fling.

Yours always
Anthony Trollope

To Mrs. J. M. Neale[4]

MS Berg Collection.

Feb—12. 1864   WALTHAM HOUSE, WALTHAM CROSS.
Madam.

Mrs. Dale did send for the extra 3 yards of brown silk,—it was plain & not flowered,—but in the hurry of going to press I omitted to mention the circumstance.[5]

Your very faithful Servant
Anthony Trollope

---

[3] Trollope delivered his lecture on the American Civil War to the Halstead Literary and Mechanics' Institution on 25 February. The *Halstead Times* (27 February 1864) gave a favorable and full account, describing the audience, which included "members of most of the principal families of the town," as "large and influential."

[4] Sarah Neale, wife of the High Churchman John Mason Neale (1818–66). A writer and noted hymnologist, Neale was the Warden of Sackville College, East Grinstead.

[5] On 9 February Mrs. Neale had written to Trollope, saying that Mrs. Dale "could not have been the good manager she is represented, and yet be ignorant of a very simple way of remedying the misfortune, viz: by sending a pattern by post to town, and procuring the additional quantity. . . . We have no reason to suppose it was a figured silk, so that she could have had no difficulty in matching it." The reference is to the first number (chap. iii) of *The Small House at Allington*. Mrs. Neale closed by saying "how much Dr. Neale and myself hope that you will give Archdeacon Grantly a bishopric before you end" (Sadleir's transcript, Bodleian).

To George Smith

SB 223 (Sadleir's transcript).

12 February 1864

*   *   *

I think Mrs. Smith should be asked for her opinion on this matter⁶ before any large number of the new edition are issued. My wife refuses to have any opinion, alleging that she has no pecuniary interest in the matter. I feel that my future literary reputation is at stake.

*   *   *

To W. W. Glenn

MS Maryland Historical Society.

Feb 12—1864.   WALTHAM HOUSE, WALTHAM CROSS.
My dear Glenn.

I shall be at the Garrick tomorrow, somewhere from 3 till 4.30 or thereabouts. Come & tell me about Lawley⁷ and settle about some hunting. I am full of horses & can mount you easily.

Yours—in a horrid rush of hurry
Anthony Trollope

That small print, after so much large print, is very trying. Its those d—— Danes⁸ that have done it for you.

To Frederic Chapman

MS Parrish Collection.

Feb. 20. 1864   WALTHAM HOUSE, WALTHAM CROSS.
My dear Chapman.

Thanks for the £150—as [to] the number of the North America, I must leave it altogether to you. I hardly know what are your arrangements about stereotyping—or keeping up the type of those cheap editions.

Yours always
Anthony Trollope

Was not the 18th. the day for the balance on Rachel Ray?

⁶ Mrs. Neale's objection about the silk dresses.
⁷ Francis Charles Lawley (1825–1901), journalist and sportsman; special American correspondent for *The Times*, 1856–65. Lawley later became a contributor to *St. Paul's Magazine*.
⁸ Perhaps a joking reference to the Schleswig-Holstein question and the Austro-Prussian occupation of Schleswig on 1 February.

To W. W. Glenn

MS Maryland Historical Society.

20 February 1864[9]
8.30 am—Saturday.   WALTHAM HOUSE, WALTHAM CROSS.
My dear Glenn.

We got your telegraph last night at 7. PM. As you say, it is too cold to hunt; but it was not too cold to dine, & we should have been glad to see you at dinner.

Will you come now by the 5 – 10 PM train today— I shall come back from town by the same. That is I shall do so, if I go up. We dine at 6.30.

Yours always
Anthony Trollope

To Charles Burney

MS Parrish Collection.

22 Feb. 1864.   WALTHAM HOUSE, WALTHAM CROSS.
My dear Burney.

I shall not be at Halstead on Thursday till 3—or 3.20—by gig across from Braintree. I trouble you with this lest you should think I had deserted you when you did not find me to have come by the train.

Yours always
Anthony Trollope

To Mrs. Mary Christie

MS Parrish Collection. B 224 (misdated).

Feb 29. 1864.   WALTHAM HOUSE, WALTHAM CROSS.
My dear Mary.

You know how the men answer the charges brought against them in the courts. I didn't take the man's money, or if I did I paid it back again, or if I did not pay it back again, I had very good reasons for keeping it. So I say to you, I got no letter from you. Or if I got one I answered it. Or if I didn't answer it, there must have been some good reason. I am, in an ordinary way, so good a correspondent, that I can never allow anyone like you to say that I have left a letter unanswered.

My dear mother died full of years and without anything of the suffering of old age. For two years her memory had gone. But she ate & slept & drank, till the lamp went altogether out; but there was nothing of the usual struggle of death. I think that no one ever suffered less in dying.

Of Charlie's[1] want of success, or of his success, we at present know nothing. It is not decided. But I greatly hope that if he be unsuccessful

---

[9] Date added in another hand.
[1] Charles Gould, son of Catherine Grant Gould.

we can induce the Poster General to employ him temporarily for—say—a year, and then give him another chance. I am writing to Kate today to tell her this.

The big looking glass has been put up, and we are very grand in our new room. Pray come & see it, & bring the girls so that they may ride. Tell Mary[2] that Miss Vesey[3] can go as quiet as ever.

Very[4] nice houses are scarce, but nice houses may be got. I wish we could get you to come & settle near us. I think we could find a place not dear; but it is so hard to find places that are perfect in every respect. My kind regards to Christie. Would he & you come to us here? We should be so delighted. My wife sends her love.

Yours always
Anthy Trollope

To Frederick Enoch[5]

MS John Murray. SB 226.

2 March 64   WALTHAM HOUSE, WALTHAM CROSS.
Sir

I return the title page.[6] I should prefer to having the words erased through which I have put my pen. They are perfectly worthless— It is an old habit, but it disfigures the page.[7]

Yours faithfully

Mr Enoch   Any Trollope

To Sir Rowland Hill

The Times, 1 December 1883, p. 7. B 225.

March 2. 1864.   WALTHAM HOUSE, WALTHAM CROSS.
My dear Sir Rowland.

I have to thank you for your paper on the results of postal reform, the amended copy of which has just reached me.[8] I yesterday heard of your resignation. I hope that this has been caused rather by the fear that pro-longed exertion might be dangerous than by existing ill-health, and that comparative leisure may restore your strength. As there is no longer any official connexion between us, I may perhaps say a few words which I could not have said while you were our secretary. I cannot but have felt for the last year or two since I was called upon to make one of a com-

---

[2] Mary Christie's daughter.
[3] A small riding horse belonging to Trollope (B).
[4] Underlined twice.
[5] Frederick Enoch, George Smith's secretary.
[6] Of *The Small House at Allington*.
[7] Doubtless the words "Author of . . ."
[8] *Results of Postal Reform* (1864).

mittee of inquiry during your illness, that you have regarded me as being in some sort unfriendly to your plans of postal reform.[9] I am not going to trouble you with any discussion on that matter, but I cannot let your resignation from office pass without assuring you of my thorough admiration for the great work of your life. I have regarded you for many years as one of the essential benefactors, not only of your own country, but of all the civilized world. I think that the thing you have down [? done] has had in it more of general utility than any other measure which has been achieved in my time. And there has been a completeness about it which must, I should think, make you thoroughly contented with your career, as far as it has gone. There are national services, for which a man can receive no adequate reward, either in rank or money, and it has been your lot to render such a service to the world at large. I hope that you may live long to enjoy the recognition of your own success.[1]

Believe me, my dear Sir Rowland,

Very faithfully yours
Anthony Trollope

To George Smith

MS John Murray. B 227.

4 March 64   WALTHAM HOUSE, WALTHAM CROSS.
My dear Smith.

The bearer of this letter of introduction is a distinguished rebel from Maryland and my particular friend. I believe he has done more in assisting Englishmen to get into rebeldom during the war, than any other American out— And if he have not sent South any contraband articles less innocent than Englishmen he is a much libelled man.

He wants an introduction to an English publisher, and I have much pleasure in giving him a line to you.

very faithfully yours
Anthony Trollope

My friends name is Mr. W. W. Glenn.[2]

---

[9] See Trollope to Smith, 8 May 1860, n. 8.

[1] Hill wrote in his journal: "Among the numerous letters of congratulation are . . . some even from men whom I have had too much reason to believe unfriendly. There is an excellent letter, among others, from Trollope." (MS General Post Office, London.) After the October 1883 publication of Trollope's *Autobiography*, with its very unflattering comments about Hill, the *Postal, Telegraphic, and Telephonic Gazette* published this letter (30 November 1883, p. 274) as evidence that Trollope's public and private opinions of Hill differed. *The Times* reprinted Trollope's letter the next day. For further developments following Hill's retirement, see Trollope et al. to Tilley, 8 April 1864, n. 8.

[2] Glenn was arrested and imprisoned in Fort McHenry for allegedly treasonable activities on behalf of the Southern cause (B).

To Miss Fredemann

MS Taylor Collection.

March 10—1864.   WALTHAM HOUSE, WALTHAM CROSS.

Mr. Anthony Trollope presents his compliments to Miss Fredemann. If Miss Fredemann would call on Mr. F. Chapman 193 Piccadilly—the publisher of Can You Forgive Her, Mr Chapman will be able to make any arrangements as to the translation. Mr. Chapman is to be found any day after 11—& before 5—except on Saturdays. Mr Trollope has spoken to Mr. Chapman on the subject. He finds however that it is generally better to have such

*   *   *

To Octavian Blewitt

MS Royal Literary Fund.

March 14. 1864   WALTHAM HOUSE, WALTHAM CROSS.
My dear Sir.
I beg to acknowledge the receipt of your obliging letter of 11th. Instant, & to say that I shall be most happy to act on the Committee of the Royal Literary Fund.[3]

very faithfully yours
Octavian Blewitt Esq   Anthony Trollope

To J. E. Millais

Transcript (in an unidentified hand) UCLA. SB 228.

March 20 1864   Waltham House, Waltham Cross.
My dear Millais
I shall be happy to dine with your painters on the 16th. April.[4] I'll give you something. How much ought it to be—in a moderate way? I've spent all my money in buying a dish at poor Thackeray's sale.[5]

Yours always
Anthony Trollope

[3] The General Committee decides cases and allocates grants to needy authors and their families. Trollope served on the Committee conscientiously until his death.
[4] The Anniversary Festival of the Artists' General Benevolent Institution, held at Freemasons' Hall, with the Bishop of Oxford in the chair.
[5] A sale of Thackeray's furnishings and books had netted his estate more than £3,000.

To G. H. Lewes

MS Yale. B 229; *George Eliot Letters*, VIII, 317.

March 21. 1864   WALTHAM HOUSE, WALTHAM CROSS.
My dear Lewes.

On Sunday I got your Aristotle[6] & went at it at once. It is wonderfully and deliciously lucid. Indeed I know no one so lucid—and at the same time so graphic—as you are. Your Goethe was charming to me as combining those two qualifications.

I shall get to you before long. I went to see Carlyle last week. Oh, heavens;—what a mixture of wisdom & folly flows from him!

Yours always—

A. T.

I have told Geo Smith to send to your wife the Small House of Allington. Ask her to receive it from me with my kindest regards.

To Frederic Chapman

MS Parrish Collection. SB 230.

March 31—1864   WALTHAM HOUSE, WALTHAM CROSS.
My dear Chapman.

I send a cheque for the bill—with many thanks for the trouble. I suppose I must still owe for the carriage of the articles.

I yesterday left No. 6—corrected with Mr March (you ask for Number 5, but that was returned long since and the drawings made, as I believe—). This morning I sent back No. 7. with the subjects. Now I send No. 8—also with the subjects for illustration. No more have been printed.

Toms story will be completed in the August number of the Victoria— You can hardly bring the book out till October.[7]

I am very sorry to hear about your wife. I hope she will recover as the weather becomes milder.

always yours

Anthony Trollope

[6] *Aristotle: A Chapter from the History of Science* (1864).
[7] T. A. Trollope's *Lindisfarn Chase* (1864).

To John Tilley[8]

MS General Post Office, London.

8th. April 1864   Bedford

Sir.

During our meeting at this place we have taken an opportunity of discussing the scale of Salaries by which we are ourselves paid, and are desirous of asking you to recommend the Postmaster General to revise it. The Surveyors are now appointed at Salaries of £500 a year which rise by increments of £25 a year to £700, and we believe that his Lordship may think, if his attention be called to the matter, that the remuneration thus allotted to us is not equal to that which our position in the department should give us. When the present scale was fixed, our maximum of Salary was made to be £100 per annum less than that paid to the Heads of the Department in London, and £300 a year less than that of the Assistant Secretaries. But since that time it has been found expedient to encrease by special allowances the Salaries of all these officers. It has, we believe, been felt that, owing to the change in the value of money, which has taken place since the Salaries were fixed, the services of men fit to hold such positions could not be regarded as being adequately paid for by the stipends given by the existing scale; and tho' we do not at all mean to question the special value of the services of any one of the gentlemen whose cases have been so considered, we think when we observe that these special cases have become so general that it must be acknowledged that the Surveyors have a claim to similar consideration.

We are Sir
your most obedient Servants
Wm. J. Godby
Chairman

G. H. Creswell   J. H. Newman
J P Good   Christ Hodgson
Anthony Trollope   E Milliken
William Gay   A. M. Cunynghame

We also request permission to bring under the special notice of the Postmaster General the services rendered to the department by our

[8] On 15 March John Tilley, Trollope's brother-in-law, was promoted from Assistant Secretary of the Post Office to Secretary, filling the post created by Rowland Hill's retirement. Trollope then applied for the post vacated by Tilley, but on 17 March the appointment went to the highly qualified Frank Ives Scudamore, six years Trollope's junior in Post Office service. It is debatable whether this memorial (in Trollope's hand and signed by all the surveyors) was the direct result of Trollope's being passed over (since there was a history dating back to 1855 of surveyors asking for the same pay as London department heads); but Trollope was the only surveyor to challenge the memorial's rejection officially. See Tilley to Trollope et al., 21 April 1864; Trollope to Gay, 24 April 1864; Trollope to Tilley, 8 July 1864; Trollope to Stanley, 9 July 1864 and 18 July 1864; and Tilley to Trollope, 13 July 1864.

Chairman. His Lordship is aware that the gentleman holding that position is called upon to perform a large amount of work which by no means belongs to his district, and which is always work of a high class, requiring much ability and discretion. If that be acknowledged to be the case we think that the Postmaster General will be disposed to allot some special scale of Salary to that Officer.

G. H. Creswell
J P Good
Anthony Trollope
William Gay
J. H. Newman
Christ Hodgson
E Milliken
A. M. Cunynghame

John Tilley Esqre.

To Lord Houghton

MS Trinity College, Cambridge.

April 19. 1864.   WALTHAM HOUSE, WALTHAM CROSS.
My dear Lord Houghton.

Is anything being done about a bust for Thackeray in Westminster Abbey? Some time since a circular was sent to me, bearing your name among others,—but I do not hear that anything has been done since.[9] I know you have been away, and, as I fear, ill; but now that you are back again surely it can be managed.

I address this to the House of Lords as I do not know whether or no you have yet left Brooke Street.

very faithfully yours
Anthony Trollope

John Tilley to Trollope and other Surveyors

MS (copy) General Post Office, London.

April 21. 1864   General Post Office
Gentlemen,

I have submitted to the Postmaster General your application of the 8th. instant, requesting, 1st. a revision of your salaries as Surveyors, 2nd. a special scale of Salary for your Chairman, Mr. Godby.

His Lordship refrains from offering any opinion whether your own Salaries or those of the Heads of Departments, whose case you contrast with your own, are sufficient or otherwise; but he desires me to observe

---

[9] See Trollope to Smith, 6 July 1864.

that in no case in which allowances have been granted to Heads of Departments in addition to their Established Salaries, has this been done in consequence of the assumed insufficiency of those Salaries, but for special Services rendered by the Individual, that the allowance is accordingly personal to the present possessor in each case and will not be continued to the gentleman who may succeed him.

Lord Stanley feels that a compliance with your request in this particular would involve a general revision of the Salaries of what may be termed the "Staff appointments" throughout the Department; and this, he desires me to add, is a step which he is not prepared to take at present.

As regards the second part of your application, I am to state that, while fully recognizing the good service rendered by Mr Godby as chairman at your meetings, His Lordship conceives that these, from their rare occurrence, cannot entail any very great additional labour upon that gentleman and he regrets that neither in this particular would he be justified at present in complying with your application, especially as Mr Godby's salary is already in excess of the scale.[1]

I am,

Gentlemen, &c

J. Tilley

To W. H. B.[2]

MS Parrish Collection. B 231.

April 22—1864   WALTHAM HOUSE, WALTHAM CROSS.
My dear Sir.

I do not quite understand who you are;—whether the son or son in law of John Tyler;—but in either position I should be very glad to shake hands with you;—and again to do the same with you as a brother Wykamist.

I remember John Tyler very well. I never in my life heard him called Mr. Tyler. I remember his marrying,—so you must be very young. I remember going to see his wife, as a boy,—when they were living at the junction of Davies Street and Mount Street, and thinking that she was very beautiful, and had as fine a taste in pound cake as I had ever met— And well I remember Aunt Charlotte. It is as good as 30 years ago,—nay, I suppose more, since I have heard of their whereabouts, and therefore

---

[1] For Trollope's rejoinder, an official "remonstrance," see Trollope to Tilley, 8 July 1864.

[2] A note at the bottom of the letter in another hand identifies the correspondent as "W. H. B." The letter shows that the correspondent was a Wykehamist, and the *Winchester College Register* lists William Henry Bennett (*b.* 1827), who had married Helen Shebbeare in 1860. But this does not square with the correspondent being the son or son-in-law of John Tyler.

you will excuse me for not understanding your exact connexion with our old & dearly loved friends.[3]

My mother, whose death last year caused the black fringes around this paper, loved John & Charlotte Tyler very dearly.

Yours faithfully
Anthony Trollope

To William Gay

MS D. R. Bentham.

Ap 24. 1864   Norwich.

My dear Gay

My feelings of indignation are, I am quite sure, as sharp as yours are. The letter was false as well as insolent. If we meet this next month I think we should[4]

*   *   *

my house for a day. What does Hodgson think about it? I wrote a line to Godby, & shall write a line to Creswell.

Yours always
Anthony Trollope

Let me hear again.

To Lord Houghton

MS Trinity College, Cambridge.

April. 24. 1864   WALTHAM HOUSE, WALTHAM CROSS.

My dear Lord Houghton.

I shall be very happy to dine with you on 6th. May.

Mrs. Trollope will be in London after 10th. May and will use Lady Houghton's kind permission to call upon her.

I should think there could be no impediment about Thackerays bust, but unless somebody like yourself will stir himself it will not be put up. When you have done with Othello,[5] perhaps you will lend a hand to that.

You give no address, so I address again to the House of Lords, having some idea that somebody has told me that your Lordship has left Brooke Street.

very faithfully yours
Anthony Trollope

---

[3] Perhaps John Chatfield Tyler (1787–1851) and his sister Charlotte (1784–1831), members of the Tyler family of Gloucestershire and Bristol. (Mrs. Trollope had family connections with Bristol.) John Tyler was living in Chesterfield Street, near Mount Street, at the time of his marriage to Amelia Whately (in 1826).

[4] Page of letter missing.

[5] Perhaps a reference to Houghton's attending the Shakespeare tercentenary celebrations at Stratford on 23 April.

To Owen Grant

MS Parrish Collection. B 232.

May 1. 1864.   WALTHAM HOUSE, WALTHAM CROSS.
My dear Owen.

I ought to have written to you before about Charlie Gould— You know his position now. He is employed in the Post office, but is not on the establishment. The position is not a desirable one except so far as it affords him present employment & may make it easier for him to get a second nomination, or chance of competing. I have little doubt but that such other nomination may be had;—say in the course of the winter; but it would be of no avail, unless he can coach himself up in *arithmetic* and the writing of English. He should have lessons in that, & also in *writing*. Now I fear that Charlie, tho the best young fellow in the world, does not like the learning of lessons,—or indeed hard work of any kind. The question is whether you can and will keep his nose to the grindstone & make him do what is necessary. If he will work he will succeed, & then Tilley would see that in the office things were made for him as pleasant as they could be. I have not written to Kate since Charlie left us as I have not liked to say that her boy was idle— I saw no other fault in him at all. He is quite a gentleman. Indeed how could her boy be anything else.

When you write to her tell her that I have written to you.

I hope she [? we] shall meet soon.

          Yours always
          Anthony Trollope

To Tom Taylor

MS Parrish Collection. B 233.

May 5—1864   Waltham Cross
My dear Taylor.

There has come up a violent dispute which for the sake of a very pretty woman, you must take the trouble to decide. I have no doubt on the subject; but your decision must be had. Did Hawkshaw when shewing the handcuffs to the Tiger know that the Tiger was the Tiger?[6]

          Yours always
          Anthony Trollope

[6] The reference is to Act III, Scene 3, of *The Ticket-of-Leave Man* (1863), Taylor's best-known play.

To Mrs. Henry Wood[7]

MS Parrish Collection.

7. May. 1864. WALTHAM HOUSE, WALTHAM CROSS.
My dear Madam.

I have already at the request of M Marzials sent a parcel of my books with my name in them for the bazaar.[8] You will probably think, as I do, that enough is quite as good as a feast of a thing so very indifferently good; but still, if you wish it I will, of course, sign the markers for you.

I hate these bazaars as methods of charity, believing the tendency of them to be altogether bad.[9] I cannot refrain from saying as much as that; as otherwise that which I would, (& will if required) do for you, would go as a testimony of my approving the thing in general.

very faithfully yours
Anthony Trollope

To Mrs. Henry Wood

MS Parrish Collection.

May 13. 1864 WALTHAM HOUSE, WALTHAM CROSS.
My dear Mrs. Wood

I send back the markers signed;—as I said I would do, if they were sent to me. I could not refuse so slight a request to such a fellow work-man as you are,—nor one that were less slight if any such were in my power. But, if I am ever fortunate enough to know you personally, I shall be bold enough to explain to you that I hate all these bazaars.

Yours very faithfully
Anthony Trollope

To Miss E. B. Rowe[1]

MS Parrish Collection. B 234.

May 16. 1864. WALTHAM HOUSE, WALTHAM CROSS.
My dear girls.

I have got your letter, but I do not know that I can tell you anything about Lily Dale & her fortunes that will be satisfactory to you. You are

---

[7] Mrs. Henry Wood (1814–87), prolific novelist; author of the very popular *East Lynne* (1861).

[8] Mrs. Wood had a stall in a bazaar held in St. James's Hall, 19 and 20 May, to benefit London's French Protestant Free Schools. According to a prospectus for the bazaar, the schools "arose from a mission set on foot by Pastor Marzials on behalf of his compatriots in London" (*Queen*, 30 April 1864).

[9] Trollope wrote a stinging attack on this mode of charity: see "Bazaars for Charity," *Pall Mall Gazette*, 21 April 1866, p. 12.

[1] Miss Rowe wrote on behalf of herself and her sisters (B).

angry with me because I did not make my pet happy with a husband, but you would have been more angry if I had made it all smooth, & supposed her capable of loving a second man while the wound of her first love was still so fresh. Indeed the object of the story was to shew that a girl under such circumstances should bear the effects of her own imprudence, and not rid herself of her sorrow too easily. I hope none of you will ever come to such misfortune as hers;—but should such a fate be yours do not teach yourself to believe that any other man will do as well.[2]

Yours with much good will
Anthony Trollope

To ?

MS Parrish Collection.

May 23. 186[4]
Monday.   WALTHAM HOUSE, WALTHAM CROSS.
Sir.
Did you send the books I bought last Thursday—
    Beaumont & Fletcher.
    Smollett— &
    Fielding. ? They have not as yet reached me.

yours truly
Anthony Trollope

To Mrs. George Trollope[3]

MS University of Michigan. B 235.

May 24. 1864.   WALTHAM HOUSE, WALTHAM CROSS.
Dear Madam.
For our names sake and I believe for some distant cousinship may I be forgiven in asking you to interest yourself for Miss Curwood, as to whom I send a paper. You I believe are a subscriber, & Miss Curwood's friends are very desirous of obtaining for her some annuity from the Governesses' benevolent institution. I see that Mrs. Trollope of Christs Hospital[4] also has a vote. Perhaps you might also interest her in the

[2] "I have been continually honoured with letters, the purport of which has always been to beg me to marry Lily Dale to Johnny Eames. . . . It was because she could not get over her troubles that they loved her." (*Autobiography*, p. 179.)

[3] The name of the addressee has been penciled at the top of the letter by another hand. Reports of the Governesses' Benevolent Institution show her to have been Mary Trollope (*d.* 1876), wife of George Trollope (1792–1871) of the Westminster Trollopes.

[4] Alicia Trollope, widow of George Trollope (1802–64) of the Casewick Trollopes. This George Trollope, who was chief clerk of Christ's Hospital, was the son of the Reverend William Arthur Trollope, a distinguished scholar and for 30 years the headmaster of Christ's Hospital.

matter. If you or she could send a Proxy, would you send it to Mrs. George Burns— Again asking you to excuse I am very faithfully yours

Anthony Trollope

To Major John Bent

MS Parrish Collection. B 236.

May 26. 1864   WALTHAM HOUSE, WALTHAM CROSS.
Dear Major.

Do I understand that you'll be up in London on June 6th? Of course I do. The fusiliers can't go to Exeter to eat their dinner. If it be so of course you will come to us. *Tom will be with us*—as also my boy Harry whom I should so like you to see;—a lad of 18 whom you will not be ashamed to call your cousin, I think. We have lots of beds for you,—that is if one will not suffice;—or if any of your young folk come with you.

Let me know what time would suit you best? I dine in London on June 4—Saturday, but come home that night; and my wife will dine at home. We shall be at home on the Sunday;—and as far as we are yet advised on the Tuesday following. We live 11 miles out of town on the Great Eastern line of railway,—and a good deal nearer to our station than you are to yours. I wish I could think the strawberries would be ripe, but I fear all our summer is over.

Give my love to all my cousins and to aunt Mary when you see her.

Yours affectionately
Anthony Trollope

To Lord Houghton

MS Trinity College, Cambridge.

May 26. 1864.   Waltham Cross
My dear Lord Houghton

I am anxious to get a nomination for a boy of mine to the Foreign Office for next year.[5] Can you in any way assist me? I do not know Lord Russell[6] & I hesitate to write to him asking the favour. Indeed I do not like writing to you as I am averse to asking people to trouble themselves on my behalf. Perhaps however, if you are on terms which admit of your doing so, you would not object to speak to Lord Russell, telling him that if it be in his power to oblige me, I should receive his kindness as a great favour.

[5] Henry Merivale Trollope. Nothing came of Trollope's efforts to place him in the Foreign Office.

[6] Lord John Russell (1792–1878), 1st Earl Russell of Kingston Russell; Prime Minister, 1846–52 and 1865–66; Foreign Secretary under Palmerston, 1859–65.

My son is now 18. He has been for the last eight months in Italy, with masters there. He will have a private tutor here for the next three months, and will spend the autumn & winter in Paris.

Yours very faithfully
Anthony Trollope

To Mr. Anderson[7]

MS Parrish Collection.

June 4. [1864]
Saturday.   Garrick.
My dear Anderson.

I have only just got your note, and am very sorry that I am now engaged for tomorrow. Russell on Wednesday told me that you were going to feed at Greenwich on Sunday, & when he hinted that I might possibly get an invite, I told him I should be happy under those circumstances to go with you. But not having heard I this morning made an engagement with my brother—which I cannot now escape. I find your note was written on Thursday, but it was unfortunately addressed to the Club— I do hope you will understand all this, & believe me I should have been most delighted. I thought the thing had gone off as I had not heard.

A few friends will dine with me at Richmond on Monday 13 at 7 pm Star & Garter— Will you come?

Address to me
Waltham Cross.

Yours always
Anthy Trollope

To Frederic Chapman

MS Parrish Collection.

June 10. 1864.   WALTHAM HOUSE, WALTHAM CROSS.
My dear Chapman.

I send up number 9—corrected—with a copy for Mr Brown—and I also send enclosed the subjects for the illustrations.

I find I could let Miss Taylor[8] have copies of Numbers 7, 8, 9 and 10— if you can not get them—only in this case, let me know.

[7] Perhaps Joseph Anderson, a fellow member of the Garrick Club.

[8] Trollope dismissed Browne and had the second half of *Can You Forgive Her?* illustrated by a Miss E. Taylor of St. Leonards, an amateur artist of whom nothing is known. (See *Illustrators*, pp. 96–101; see also Trollope to Smith, 12 August 1864.) From the first, Trollope had been dissatisfied with Browne's work. Millais wrote (in a letter to his wife after only one number of the novel had appeared): "Hablot Brown [*sic*] is illustrating [Trollope's] new serial. Chapman is publishing it, and [Trollope] is not pleased with the illustrating, and proposed to me to take it off his hands, but I

Did you ever register Orley Farm and Rachel Ray with reference to
the Foreign rights— If not pray do so. Have you done anything towards
finding out whether either have been pirated? Did you not say that some
one had asked to purchase the right to translate Orley Farm?[9]

Pray answer these questions.

Yours always
Anthony Trollope

To Mrs. Trollope[1]
MS Bodleian. B 237.

June 21. 1864.   WALTHAM HOUSE, WALTHAM CROSS.
My dear Mrs. Trollope
    Here you have my brother and self.[2] You will perceive that my brother
is pitching into me. He always did.

Yours very sincerely
Anthony Trollope

To Mr. and Mrs. Charles Buxton[3]
MS Parrish Collection.

June 21. 1864   WALTHAM HOUSE, WALTHAM CROSS.
Mr Anthony Trollope
presents his compliments to Mr. and Mrs. Charles Buxton and much
regrets that a previous engagement will prevent his accepting their invitation for Friday next—

---

declined. Messrs. C. and H. gave him so much more for his novel that they wished
to save on the illustrations, and now Trollope is desirous of foregoing his extra price
to have it done by me." (J. G. Millais, *The Life and Letters of Sir John Everett Millais*,
I, 379.) Browne's strained relations with Trollope, together with his dismay at having
been let go by Dickens, are reflected in a letter Browne wrote in February or March
1864: "Marcus [Stone] is no doubt to do Dickens [*Our Mutual Friend*]. . . . Dickens
probably thinks a new hand would give his old puppets a fresh look, or perhaps he
does not like my illustrating Trollope neck-and-neck with him—though, by Jingo, he
need fear no rivalry *there*! Confound all authors and publishers. say I. There is no
pleasing one or t'other." (Frederic G. Kitton, *Dickens and His Illustrators* [1899], p.
113.)
    [9] See Trollope to Charpentier, 10 July 1864.
    [1] Probably Mrs. Mary Trollope.
    [2] Trollope enclosed a photograph of himself and T. A. Trollope.
    [3] Probably Charles Buxton (1823–71), liberal politician and son of the great anti-
slavery leader Sir Thomas Fowell Buxton, and his wife Emily Mary Buxton, née Holland. A hunting enthusiast, Buxton later became a close friend of Trollope.

Thomas Adolphus Trollope and Anthony Trollope

To G. H. Lewes

MS Yale. B 238; *George Eliot Letters*, VIII, 319.

June 26—1864.   WALTHAM HOUSE, WALTHAM CROSS.
My dear Lewes.

There never was better criticism than that on Greek tragic art in the two first pages of your chapter—called Iphigenia,—and I make you my compliments.[4] I had felt it all before, but could not have expressed it. Of course I speak of the Greek; not of the German which is to me a book altogether sealed. But not so true are you to truth in your rhapsody as to dead bones. "But—dead bones for dead bones—," &c &c, page 287. You know you are only warming an idea. The history of mans mind must have in it more of poetry than the history of man's body,—even tho we throw you in the elephant's.[5]

Yours ever
Anthy Trollope

I tried to see you the other day. Heavens,—what pens and ink you do keep in your dining room!!! My kindest regards to your wife. I will if it be possible see you before long.

To George Smith

MS John Murray. Excerpt, *Commentary*, pp. 256–57; B 239.

July 1—1864.
Friday   WALTHAM HOUSE, WALTHAM CROSS.
My dear Smith.

I got your letter this morning too late to allow of my answering it, so that you should get my letter before you left town. We have people staying with us,—a housefull;—and I cannot therefore get away, as I should so much have liked to have done, to meet Mrs. Gaskell.[6] If I were to ride

---

[4] In his *Life of Goethe* Lewes discussed Goethe's *Iphigenie auf Tauris*, contending (in the passage admired by Trollope) that Greek tragedy was concerned with the darkest passions and "the current of those passions for ever kept in agitation"; critics who thought "repose" the characteristic of tragedy had been misled by the movement of Greek drama, which was "necessarily large, slow, simple."

[5] In a passage on Goethe's scientific studies, Lewes mentioned Goethe's "inexhaustible pleasure" in an elephant's skull, and commented: "Men confined to their libraries, whose thoughts scarcely venture beyond the circle of literature, have spoken with sarcasm, and with pity, of this waste of time. But—dead bones for dead bones— there is as much poetry in the study of an elephant's skull, as in the study of those skeletons of the past—history and classics. All depends upon the mind of the student; to one man a few old bones will awaken thoughts as far-reaching and sublime as those which the fragments of the past awaken in the historical mind."

[6] Elizabeth Cleghorn Gaskell (1810–65), the novelist. Mrs. Gaskell had established a friendly relationship with T. A. Trollope during a visit to Florence in 1863, and she was an admirer of Anthony's works. When *Framley Parsonage* was appearing in

over on Monday should I have any chance of finding her & Mrs. Smith at home. I mean about 5 pm. I could then get back to my people by dinner time.

Laurence[7] seemed to think the black ground of the frame too dark; but I dare say he is wrong. *Pray do not have it altered.* I thought it very nice. I came upon it accidentally in his room when I came from the frame makers.

Such a week as I have had in sitting! Only that he is personally such a nice fellow, & has so much to say for himself, I should have been worn out. I have been six times, or seven I think,—& am to go again. He compliments me by telling me that I am a subject very difficult to draw. He has taken infinite pains with it. Of course I myself am no judge of what he has done.

Yours always
Anthony Trollope

To George Smith

MS John Murray. *Commentary*, p. 257; B 240.

July 6. 1864   WALTHAM HOUSE, WALTHAM CROSS.
My dear Smith.

This morning we hung Thackeray up in our library,[8] and we are *very much* obliged to you for the present,—not only in that it is in itself so valuable, but more especially because it is one so suited to our feelings. To-day we go into the Garrick Club,[9] and have an initiatory dinner at which as Chairman I shall propose his memory. I heard yesterday from Shirley B[1] that the Dean of Westminster has consented to put up a

---

the *Cornhill*, she wrote to George Smith: "I wish Mr. Trollope would go on writing Framley Parsonage for ever. I don't see any reason why it should ever come to an end, and every one I know is always dreading the *last* number." (J. A. V. Chapple and Arthur Pollard, eds., *The Letters of Mrs. Gaskell* [Manchester, 1966], p. 602.) Much to Trollope's regret, he was never able to meet Mrs. Gaskell (see Trollope to Smith, 15 November 1865).

[7] Samuel Laurence (1812–84), the distinguished portrait painter. George Smith arranged for Laurence to draw various Victorian authors, including Trollope. Three versions of his chalk portrait of Trollope exist: one in the Parrish Collection, one in the collection of Gordon N. Ray, and one in the National Portrait Gallery.

[8] A chalk drawing by Samuel Laurence, now in the collection of Gordon N. Ray. Another version is in the National Portrait Gallery.

[9] The Garrick Club was moving to its new premises on Garrick Street.

[1] Charles William Shirley Brooks (1816–74), miscellaneous writer; since 1851 on the staff of *Punch*, which he edited, 1870–74. On 4 July Brooks wrote to Trollope: "The Dean [A. P. Stanley, Dean of Westminster] permits me to advertise his assent to a Memorial, which I proposed to him as a compromise, thus leaving its nature open, and the advertisements are in the printers' hands." (MS Taylor Collection.) In the event, a bust of Thackeray by Marochetti was installed in Westminster Abbey. Thackeray's older daughter, later Lady Ritchie, was never satisfied with the likeness, and arranged for it to be altered (by H. Wehner) in 1900. After the alterations she wrote

memorial (whether bust or statue is not yet decided) & the subscription list is now opened. I have been nervous about this lest the time should slip away. The next thing will be to have a perfect edition of his works,— for which we must look to you.[2]

I hope it will not be long before you come & see the portrait.

Yours always
very truly
Anthony Trollope

To John Tilley
MS General Post Office, London.

July 8th. 1864   Waltham Cross
Sir

I trust that I may be allowed to remonstrate against the answer given in your letter of 21st. April last to an application for encrease of Salary made by the Surveyors on the 8th. of that month. I should have done this sooner had I not been led to believe that there would soon be a general meeting of the Surveyors at which I proposed to discuss the answer which we had received. There has however been no such meeting, and as no general rejoinder to your reply to us can well be arranged by the Surveyors as a body without such a meeting I assume to myself, as I believe I am justified in doing, the right to remonstrate against the Secretary's letter as sent to me personally.

I do not remember to have seen, since I have been in the public service, so little satisfactory a reply to any representation from such a body of official servants as the Surveyors are,—or one so calculated to give offence. We are at first told that the Postmaster General refrains from giving any opinion whether our Salaries,—or the Salaries of other officers,— are sufficient or insufficient. As to the sufficiency of the Salaries of other officers, I do not know that we have raised any question unless by comparing our own to theirs; but if I at all understand my position in the public service, I have a right to demand that the sufficiency or insufficiency of the remuneration paid to me shall be considered on any reasonable and respectful application. I am a public servant of 30 years standing, and have never before either separately or jointly with others, requested a reconsideration of my Salary;—and I am aggrieved that I should now have received such an answer. I have served under the Secre-

---

a friend: "I went to the Abbey to-day . . . and thought with true gratitude as I took my seat by the *familiar* father once more and not that strange travestie." (Henry Sayre Van Duzer, *A Thackeray Library* [New York, 1919], p. 3.)

[2] Smith bought up Thackeray's copyrights and over the next two decades brought out five complete editions of his works, including the 24-volume Edition de Luxe (1879).

Trollope. Chalk portrait by Samuel Laurence, 1864.

W. M. Thackeray. Portrait by Samuel Laurence, 1864.

taryships of Sir F. Freeling,[3] Colonel Maberly,[4] and Sir Rowland Hill, and I feel assured that no application from the whole corps of Surveyors would have been answered in so studiously offensive a manner[5] by either of those gentlemen.

The Secretary's letter of 21st. April then denies the allegation made by the Surveyors that the Salaries of the Staff Officers in London had been supplemented by special allowances because those Salaries had been thought insufficient, and goes on to state that those special allowances had been granted for special services rendered in each case by the gentleman to whom they were granted. As in my endeavour to enforce my own application with reference to my own Salary I must compare it with that given to other officers, I have no alternative but to demur to this statement; and, tho' I do so unwillingly, I must quote instances.

It happens that at the beginning of this year, before Sir Rowland Hills resignation, additional annual allowances, supplementary Salaries, were paid to nearly all the Staff Officers in London. The two Assistant Secretaries received them. The Receiver and accountant General received such payment. The Superintendents of the circulation and of the Mail Office received them; and the head of the Packet Service branch received such payment. Indeed I believe all the Staff Officers did so with the exception of the chief clerk in the Secretary's office whose regular Salary had been lately encreased. I am aware that in all these cases special services were alleged,—but I am not aware, nor as far as I know is any gentleman in the department aware, that special services had been rendered,—except by Mr Scudamore, the late Receiver and Accountant General, whose great services on the part of the Crown have been altogether exceptional. It will of course be understood that I am not at all denying the official merits of any of the gentlemen in question. No doubt they have all done their duty well. No doubt their pay was insufficient. No doubt they deserved all they got. But I have never even heard of the special services that they have achieved,—over and above the work done in their regular official capacities, the performance of which the Postmaster General had a right to expect from them. I will, however, confine myself to the highest of the functionaries so paid, and will venture to insist that the two assistant Secretaries were never called upon to perform special services. With regard to the one of whose work I have known the most,—I mean Mr Tilley, I do not think that he will for a moment assert,—otherwise than with the general latitude of loose of-

---

[3] Sir Francis Freeling (1764–1836), Secretary of the Post Office when Trollope entered the service in 1834. See *Autobiography*, pp. 30, 35, 44.

[4] See Maberly to the Postmaster General, 29 July 1841.

[5] The words "studiously offensive a manner" are underscored in pencil, presumably by Tilley.

ficial phraseology, that he, as assistant Secretary, performed any special services. He did his work that was not special in a way that by the consent of all of us deserved the reward that it has received; and, no doubt, before that supplemental allowance was awarded to him, he was paid insufficiently for the ordinary work of his office. That was felt to be the case. But I would now ask him to go beyond his official phraseology and to declare verbally to Lord Stanley whether his opinion of the matter is not the same as my own.

It is said to us in the Secretary's letter of the 21st. April that these additional allowances were personal to the men and would not be continued. If I am correctly informed the PostmrGeneral has already recommended to the Treasury a greatly encreased scale for the two assistant Secretaries, thereby shewing his Lordship's opinion, and that he at any rate has thought the amount previously paid for nominally special services to be in fact due from the Crown for the ordinary duties of the officers in question.

The Surveyors of the department, whose duties are now, at any rate, as onerous as they ever were, are the only officers whose incomes have been lessened during my service in the department. Mr. Tilley was a Surveyor. Will he kindly state the amount of his official income during the period of his Surveyorship? It was greater, I fancy, than the official income of the then Assistant Secretary. He in time became assistant Secretary,—and by a scale proposed by him the incomes of the Surveyors were reduced, while, on his behalf, the income of the Assistant Secretaryship was encreased. I find no fault with the encrease thus given to him,— nor with the second encrease which he received,—nor with the third, the special-service encrease which he enjoyed; but I maintain that this was given because it was felt that the rate of remuneration paid to the Staff Officers was not sufficient for their positions in accordance with the encreased expense of living, and I maintain that we Surveyors are now entitled to similar consideration. When Mr Tilley's Salary had been raised to, I think, £1000, and that of the Head of the London departments was £800, ours was £700. The incomes of Mr Tilley and of his colleague were then raised to, I think, £1100; those of the Heads of the Departments were encreased by £100—or £200 each; and I submit that we were, and that we are, entitled to the same regard. The Surveyors, however, are absent from London. The feeling which the personal presence of the individuals has created in the favour of the London offices has not been felt in our favour, and we have gone to the wall.

I believe no gentleman in the service,—always excepting Mr Scudamore,—has a better right to put forward a claim for special services than I have. I have worked for the department successfully in various parts of the world, altogether out of my own sphere, and under circumstances that were special. But I have made no such claim and do not make any now.[6] I know that such payments are in every way objectionable. They lead to endless heartburns and jealousies. They are given,—and must be ever given when given,—in a spirit of partisanship, and they are unjust alike to the department and to the public. When they become general, as they have done with us, officers are taught to believe that they should work assiduously, not for their Salaries, but with the hope of payment beyond their Salaries,—till, at last, the man who has no special service allowance is felt by others and feels himself to be an inferior man. These allowances create the bitterest personal feelings in the breasts of those who are excluded. At the beginning of this year out of the seven Gentlemen in the London office next under the Secretary, six held special incomes for alleged special services!

I think that as an old, and I believe I may say meritorious, officer of the Crown, I have a right to ask the Postmaster General to reconsider the matter of these special payments, and to readjust the Salaries of the Surveyors in accordance with the amounts actually paid to other officers. And I also think that I am justified in asking his Lordship to recommend the newly appointed Secretary to be more considerate of the feelings of those officers among whom he passed his official life, till he received his promotion.

> I am Sir,
> Your most obedient Servant
> Anthony Trollope

The Secretary
General Post Office

John Tilley to Lord Stanley

MS General Post Office, London.

9. July 1864
My dear Lord.

I send to your Lordship for perusal before submitting it to you officially this most intemperate letter from Mr Trollope in reply to the Circular letter (Copy enclosed) addressed to the Surveyors in the terms of the Minute of the 18th. April.

> Yours truly
> J Tilley

The Lord Stanley of Alderley, Dover Street.

[6] Post Office records show that after this dispute individual surveyors requested additional payments for "special services," but that Trollope made no such request. In the *Autobiography* Trollope added a footnote (p. 163): "During the period of my service in the Post Office I did very much special work for which I never asked any remuneration,—and never received any, though payments for special services were common in the department at that time."

To M. Charpentier
MS Parrish Collection.

July 10 1864.   WALTHAM HOUSE, WALTHAM CROSS.

J'ai reçu de M. Charpentier libraire, editeur à Paris, et directeur de la revue Nationale, la somme de quinze cent francs, pour le droit exclusif que je lui cède de traduire en Français mes ouvrages *Orley Farm* et *Rachel Ray*.[7]

Anthony Trollope

John Tilley to Trollope
MS (draft) General Post Office, London.

[13 July 1864]

I have laid before the PMG yr. letter dated the 8 Inst in reply to the Circular letter which was addressed to the English Surveyors on the 21st. of April last conveying to them His Lordships decision upon their application for an increase of salary.

His Lordship desires me to say that that letter is in strict conformity to the Minute which was drawn up by his direction after a personal discussion of the subject and that so far from justifying the language which you have permitted yourself to use it appears to him to contain no one word which is fairly open to objection.

His Lship is at a loss to understand why you should come forward alone to question a circular letter which was addressed to yourself as only one of a body. He can only conclude that none of your colleagues felt aggrieved or if they did that no one else could be found to put his signature to a document ⟨so improperly worded as⟩ such as that which you have forwarded.

Be that as it may Lord Stanley, passing by the numerous inaccuracies in your letter desires me to express his regret at its tone and at the temper which you have displayed and to say that you have adduced no reasons which appear to him to call for a reconsideration of his decision.[8]

To Frederic Chapman
MS Pierpont Morgan Library. SB 241.

July 14–64   WALTHAM HOUSE, WALTHAM CROSS.

My dear Chapman.

I dont know the gentleman who wrote the enclosed;—but I promised my aunt Mrs. Milton[9] who does know him well, that you would have

---

[7] *La Ferme d'Orley* was serialized in the *Revue Nationale,* from March 1865 through August 1866; this followed the serialization of the *Bertrams,* which had concluded in October 1864. *L'Heritage des Belton* appeared from January through July 1867.

[8] At the bottom of this draft appears "App[rove]d. S[tanley]."

[9] Perhaps the widow of Trollope's uncle Henry Milton.

Mrs. McQuoids[1] MS read & an answer given without delay. She has published two or three novels with Geo. Smith; but he will not come up to the lady's mark in reference to money. He I believe offers £150—she, I believe, wants £250.

Perhaps you can see your way to come to terms with her. I have you understand no authority for proposing a price to you.

Yours always
A. T.

To George Smith

MS John Murray. SB 242.

July 16. 1864 Greenbank. Grasmere. Windermere.
My dear Smith.

You will see by my address that we are down among the lakes, and that I cannot dine with you on the 25th. I see its to be gentlemen, but whatever you do, don't smoke.

I'm here, by no means having a holyday,—but working harder than I ever worked before,—making up for the time that I was being drawn. I did not tell you I think, that my wife liked the portrait *very much indeed*. She seemed to have a fuller respect for me when she had seen it than ever before.

Yours always
A. T.

To Christopher Hodgson

MS Parrish Collection.

July 17—1864 Greenbank. Windermere.
My dear Hodgson.

Many thanks. My letters all come very nicely now. This place is quiet; and pretty, and the house comfortable. But it is difficult to get nice walks. We shall stay a week or ten days, & then perhaps move.

Yours always
Any Trollope

To Lord Stanley

MS General Post Office, London.

July 18. 1864 Greenbank Windermere
My Lord.

I hope you will not take it amiss that I address your Lordship personally with reference to an application for encrease of Salary made by

---

[1] Mrs. Katherine Sarah Macquoid (1824–1917), prolific minor novelist.

the Surveyors, and to a correspondence which has since taken place on the same subject between the Secretary & myself.

In the first place I must beg you to believe that I am not actuated by any desire to be either obtrusive or insubordinate. I am now an old servant of the Crown, and can refer to my services for a great many years to prove that such is not my nature.[2] I have endeavoured to pull well with the men at work with me, both above and below, and can boast that I have always obeyed the orders given me to the best of my ability. But I think that it is due to me in return for such service that I should be heard when I complain,—especially as I have not been prone to complaints,—and that any serious allegation made by me should meet with consideration.

Mr Tilley states in his letter to me of the 13th. Inst, written doubtless by your Lordships direction, that you are at a loss to understand why I should come forward to answer a Circular addressed to the Surveyors as a body. I did so because I chose to run a risk in which I could not ask them to join me. A Civil Servant no doubt runs a risk when he calls in question the discretion of his superior officers as I have done. But a course which may be imprudent, need not therefore be improper. The course I have now taken may perhaps be imprudent, and I have therefore asked no others to join me;—but I feel assured that it is not improper.

My complaint is this. The Salaries of the Staff officers of the department were fixed some years ago,—including those of the Assistant Secretaries, the heads of the London Departments, the Surveyors, and, perhaps I should add the Senior clerks in the Secretary's office. Since that the official incomes of, as I think, all these officers,—with the exception of the Surveyors,—have been raised. I maintain that this was in fact done because the Salaries as existing were not found to be adequate, in accordance with rising incomes elsewhere. This has probably never been stated officially,—but such has, I believe doubtless, been the moving tho' not recognised cause of such encreases. But, as regards all the officers above the Surveyors, the encrease has been made by allowances for, so called, special services. Now, my Lord, if you will accurately look into this matter you will find that there have been no really special services,— except in the case of Mr Scudamore. Certainly there were no special services performed by the Assistant Secretaries. Of course this has created discontent,—as does the whole system of special allowances. And as the

---

[2] At this point Tilley penciled in "qy" (query). Trollope of course knew that all correspondence addressed to the Postmaster General would be read by Tilley. Rowland Hill, in retirement, noted in his journal in November 1864: "I must own that I am not very sorry to learn that the conspirators against me are now quarrelling as to the division of the spoil. There has, I learn, been a fearful passage of arms between Trollope and Tilley—Trollope, of course, being the aggressor." (MS General Post Office, London.)

regular Salaries of those whom I have named below the Surveyors have also been encreased, the Surveyors of course feel themselves to be hardly used.

Such being the case they made an application which I think was temperate, and for which their standing in the service must be allowed to have demanded consideration. But in answer to it they were told that your Lordship refrained from offering an opinion whether their Salaries were or were not sufficient, and that the revision of them was not a step which you were prepared to take! I am sure your Lordship must admit that this was not satisfactory.

It was exactly the way in which Oliver was treated when he came forward on behalf of the Charity boys to ask for more;—and I own that I thought Mr Tilley was very like Bumble in the style of the answer he gave us.[3]

I am aware that I am laying myself open to rebuke from your Lordship for addressing myself directly to you in this matter;—but I trust that you will take what I have said without offence. I wish to give none; but I do wish to obtain that thoughtful consideration of our case which I know that we have a right to expect.[4]

I have the honor to be
Your Lordship's
Most obedient Servant
Anthony Trollope

The Lord Stanley of Alderley

To ?[5]

MS Parrish Collection.

July 27—1864   Grasmere—Windermere

*   *   *

agree with you; but still am unwilling to go on in my way without listening to what some friend may say to me. My feeling is that a man should fight to the last if he feels himself to be right. I shall not however

*   *   *

Yours always
Anthony Trollope

[3] *Oliver Twist*, chap. ii.

[4] In response to this letter, Tilley wrote to Stanley on 19 July: "I submit Mr. Trollope be informed that your Lordship has nothing to add to the communication addressed to him of the 13th. Instant." Tilley's note is endorsed "App[roved] S[tanley]" and "Mr. Trollope 'informed' 20th. July 1864." (MS General Post Office, London.) On 14 February 1865 Trollope was asked by the Postmaster General (at Tilley's urging) whether he wished to undertake a postal mission to the East, and on 20 June 1866 he was offered the position of Metropolitan Surveyor (see Trollope to Tilley, 31 July 1866). Trollope declined both offers, which may have been attempts to mollify him.

[5] The contents of this fragment suggest that it was written to a Post Office colleague, perhaps a fellow surveyor.

To Altisidora Annesley

MS Parrish Collection.

July 27–1864

Greenbank. Grassmere
Windermere

My dear Miss Annesley—

When I saw you the other day you gave me half a promise that you and your younger sister[6] would come to us for a few days in the early part of August— Since that we have been down here among the lakes, but we shall be home on the 3rd. Will you and your sister come to us on the 5th., Friday, and stay till the next Wednesday. My wife who is sitting opposite to me, and who has just come back nearly dead from the mountains feels conscience-stricken, thinking that she ought to write this letter. But I have told her that you will credit me when I assure you that it is written by me as her Secretary. She much hopes that she may have the pleasure of seeing you.

Fancy a confederate army within four miles of Baltimore, and then within seven of Washington.[7]

If you write this week address to the written direction on the top of my letter. Pray give my wifes compliments to your sister and tell her that she trusts she may see [her] at Waltham.

Yours very faithfully
Anthony Trollope

To George Smith

B 243 (Sadleir's transcript). Excerpt, *Commentary*, p. 274.

12 August 1864

*   *   *

I think you would possibly find no worse illustrator than H. Browne; and I think he is almost as bad in one kind as in another. He will take no pains to ascertain the thing to be illustrated. I cannot think that his work can add any value at all to any book.

I am having the ten last numbers of Can You Forgive Her illustrated by a lady. She has as yet done two drawings on wood. They are both excellent, and the cutter says that they will come out very well. She has £5: 5:– a drawing for them. Why not employ her? She is a Miss Taylor of St. Leonards.

[6] Probably Augusta Arthur Constantia Annesley (?1826–92), whom Trollope mistakenly assumed to be younger than Altisidora.

[7] Early in July a large force of Confederate troops invaded Maryland, destroying a part of the Baltimore and Ohio Railway and defeating the Federal force that attempted to arrest their progress. On 12 July fighting took place within sight of Washington.

Illustration for *Can You Forgive Her?*, by H. K. Browne

But of course the question is one for you to settle yourself. As for myself I can never express satisfaction at being illustrated in any way by H. Browne.[8]

If you are going to bring out a cheap edition of The Small House, of course I should prefer the 5/– shape very much; as all those which Chapman has are in that form.[9]

* * *

To Owen Grant

MS Parrish Collection. B 244.

August 14. 1864.   WALTHAM HOUSE, WALTHAM CROSS.
My dear Owen.

The other day Kate wrote to me asking me about Charlie—& expressing a hope that he would by this time have made such an improvement as to justify his friends in putting him forward for another nomination. I was then away in Westmoreland, but immediately on my return I went to the Post office & enquired about him.

I do not find the account satisfactory. You know that he is employed on task work, and it seems that he does not earn above 4/ a day. The average of those employed as he is employed is nearer 6/. This comes partly from extreme slowness,—& partly from errors in his work. I fear he would be rejected if he were sent up again for competition at present— He has time enough for the next six months or more;—but unless he can work harder than he does at present, he will not do any good in the Post office. I found that the men are well disposed to him, but they think he is idle.

I tell you this because I can not tell Kate so much. I can not bring myself to give her bad tidings of her boy. I shall tell her that I have written to you, & that it is clearly not expedient that another nomination should be procured for him quite immediately.

I send this to your office. No doubt you are out of town but it will be sent after you.

Yours always
Anthony Trollope

[8] Apparently Smith had suggested Browne as illustrator for *The Claverings*. Though accepting Trollope's verdict on Browne, Smith declined to employ Miss Taylor and had the novel illustrated by another hand (see Trollope to Smith, 31 March 1865).

[9] Smith brought out a cheap edition at six shillings (1864).

To George Smith

MS John Murray. Excerpt, *Commentary*, pp. 257–58; B 245.

Freshwater
10. October 1864   Isle of Wight
My dear Smith.

I suppose you are back from your Italian wanderings, & I write a line to thank you—in my wifes name chiefly,—but also in my own, for your gracious present to us of myself—done to the life, in a wonderfully vigorous manner. When I look at the portrait I find myself to be a wonderfully solid old fellow. The picture is certainly a very good picture & my wife declares it to be very like,—& not a bit more solid than the original. For your munificence we both thank you very heartily, and hope you and your wife will soon come to see it—& the other—in their places.

My brother says you would not go & stay with him after all. No doubt you feared that with the aid of some Italian bravo and dagger he would compel you to accept an unlimited number of articles for the Cornhill. I shall be very anxious to hear your account. I have heard that you did nurse maid to Bice[1] up at the convent.

Yours always faithfully
Anthony Trollope

That stupid Mrs. MacQuoid has written to me to ask to dedicate her novel to me.[2] I have written to decline, as I hate such trash. But she writes simply from Stanley place. What postman can be supposed to know where Stanley place is? Some of your people will know. Will you have the address completed? I enclose the letter.

I also send a Devonshire Mss—& a letter from me, which you will find not to be very pressing.

To George Smith

SB 246 (Sadleir's transcript).

4 November 1864   Waltham Cross
Trollope wants to write eight or nine pages for Smith in reply to the Archbishop of York and to a leader in *The Times*.[3]

---

[1] Beatrice Trollope.

[2] Mrs. Macquoid's *By the Sea*, published by Smith in January 1865 (1864 on the title page), carried no dedication.

[3] William Thomson (1819–90), Archbishop of York from 1862, had inveighed against the immorality of fiction and especially "sensational stories" in an address to the Huddersfield Church Institute. *The Times* reported the speech in full (2 November 1864, p. 9), and then on the next day published a leading article endorsing Thomson's views (3 November 1864, pp. 8–9). Trollope was predictably indignant, not least because the *Record*'s 1863 attack on *Good Words* (which labeled Trollope as "this year's chief sensation writer") was still very fresh in his memory (see Macleod to Trollope, 11 June 1863). *The Times*, however, had second thoughts: one day after

To George Smith

SB 247 (Sadleir's transcript).

6 November 1864

Smith apparently disapproved of the idea of the article, and Trollope agreed to drop it. His object was to answer the attack made on sensationalists by showing that all modern English novels present life decently and do little or no harm; that, indeed, they do good, taking poetry's place in cultivating the imagination; that they advocate those lessons of life which mammas teach, or ought to teach, to their daughters.

To George Smith

MS John Murray. SB 248.

November 24. 64.   WALTHAM HOUSE, WALTHAM CROSS.

My dear Smith.

At our meeting yesterday I took the liberty,—as we were looking up our money,—of putting your name down for £10 – 10/ to the Thackeray monument. Will you indemnify me?

Yours always

Geo Smith Esq   Anthony Trollope

To E. F. S. Pigott[4]

MS Parrish Collection.

November 24. 1864.   WALTHAM HOUSE, WALTHAM CROSS.

My dear Pigott.

Will you come down to us on Saturday December 3rd.—& stay till Monday—or if the exigencies of the press be too imperative we will let you go on Sunday after dinner.

Yours always

Anthony Trollope

---

endorsing Thomson's views, it reversed itself by publishing a leading article defending the recreational value of fiction (4 November 1864, p. 6). Though *The Times*'s volte-face may have helped to persuade Trollope not to write a rejoinder (see next letter), it did not cause him to forget Thomson's speech. In his lecture "On English Prose Fiction as a Rational Amusement," Trollope later wryly noted: "A bishop gets up now and then to lecture against novels;—as I am now getting up to lecture in their defence." (*Four Lectures*, p. 95.)

[4] Edward Frederick Smyth Pigott (1824–95), lawyer and journalist; member of the staff of the *Daily News*; examiner of plays in Lord Chamberlain's Department, 1874–95.

To Mr. Freeling[5]

MS University of Virginia.

November 24. 64   WALTHAM HOUSE, WALTHAM CROSS.
My dear Freeling.
Will you come down here on Saturday Decr. 3—and stay till Monday.
We shall have a few friends.
Trains leave Shoreditch at 4.5 pm or 5.10 pm which are, either
of them in time. There is a morning train up at 10—getting to London
at 10.35—& another at 9 am if the exigencies of your office are severe.

Yours faithfully
Anthony Trollope

To George Smith

SB 249 (Sadleir's transcript).

4 December 1864
Smith had apparently renewed the suggestion of an article on fiction, for now
Trollope begs off on grounds of inadequate time.

To George Smith

MS Bodleian.

December 13. 1864   Ipswich.
My dear Smith.
It shall be as you say about the story—i e, to commence in the January
number for 1866.[6]
Shall I be greedy if I ask you to pay for it on delivery? When you re-
quired an expansive period for the commencement of the publication,
(—I then having proposed to have it ready for 1 Jany 1865—)—you ex-
pressed your willingness to pay for it on delivery. But if you think that
this alteration alters the circumstances in respect to the date of payment,
I shall not take it amiss.

Yours always
Anthony Trollope

address Waltham as usual.

---

[5] Perhaps Francis Henry Freeling, senior clerk, second class, in the Post Office (probably a relative of Sir Francis Freeling, under whose aegis Trollope entered the Post
Office in 1834).
[6] *The Claverings* appeared in the *Cornhill* from February 1866 through May 1867,
although the agreement for this work, dated 13 November 1863, called for serialization to begin in January 1865 (MS Bodleian).

To Miss E. Taylor

MS Parrish Collection.

December 13. 1864.   Ipswich.
My dear Miss Taylor.

I have just got your note. I shall be in town tomorrow for a part of the day, but so busy that I doubt whether I can get to Bruton Street. Could you meet me at Chapmans 193 Piccadilly at a quarter to 5. I would then have the subjects of 2 more numbers for you. If you can do so, write me a line to that effect addressed to me at the Literary Fund Chambers Adelphi Terrace— I go up to London to attend a Committee meeting there, & shall be there till 4 . 30.

Yours very truly
Anthony Trollope

To Miss E. Taylor

MS Taylor Collection.

December 14. 1864   ROYAL LITERARY FUND
My dear Miss Taylor

I am sorry not to see you, as I specially wanted to see you about the future numbers. I had no possibility of getting up to you.

I intended to propose to you to select your own subjects—letting me know what you select before you go to work. As to the numbers which you now have in hands, pray take the single figure you propose.

I now send you two numbers further. I have marked on them some subjects, but have done so as hints—& wish you to use your own judgement.

very faithfully yours
Anthony Trollope

To G. H. Lewes

MS Yale. B 250; *George Eliot Letters*, VIII, 327.

24 December 1864.   WALTHAM HOUSE, WALTHAM CROSS.
My dear Lewes

I cannot deny that I am disappointed and grieved by your letter;[7] but you are not to suppose that I shall either find fault with you or argue

---

[7] Lewes had declined the editorship of the newly planned *Fortnightly Review*. In her journal for 15 December, George Eliot wrote: "Last week Mr. Trollope and Mr. F. Chapman dined with us and there was talk of a new periodical of which it is possible G. may be the editor." In his journal for 25 December, G. H. Lewes wrote: "Yesterday I received a charming letter from Trollope who I feared would be very much disgusted with me for having withdrawn from the editorship of a new Fortnightly

with you. I know well how these things go, and do not think that a man is open to censure because he changes his views. I am not one of those who suppose that a mans mind should be subject to no hesitations,—to no vacillating influences. Men who are strong enough never to be so subject are distasteful to me. Haud ignarus dubitationis, dubitantibus succurrere disco.[8] So much I say to quell any fear that you may have that I should condemn you,—believing that you would not willingly be condemned by one who regards you as well as I do.

But having said this I must go on to declare that I greatly regret your defection. I have felt the necessity of the aid of some one who would know what he was about in arranging the work of such a venture as we propose; and I have also felt,—more strongly perhaps than I can explain to you,—that to make the affairs comfortable to myself, the person selected for the above described purpose should be one with whom I could hold close friendly intercourse. I do not care to put myself at the beck of any one whom I do not know, or whom, when known, I may not like.

I would recommend you, for your own sake, to come to the meeting on Thursday. It would, I think, be better that you should state your own withdrawal, than that I should do so for you. As to that, however, you can make up your mind and let me know your intention.

Yours always faithfully
Anthony Trollope

Give all kind remembrances of the season to your wife. I feel that I ought to congratulate her upon your decision.

To George Smith
MS Bodleian. SB 251.

Decr. 31. 1864   WALTHAM HOUSE, WALTHAM CROSS.
My dear Smith.
My novel "Harry Clavering"[1] is finished—and will be in your hands on Saturday—this day week. I shall take a week to re-read it. I tell you

---

Review which he wanted me to take and which I had accepted rather imprudently, seduced by the prospect of a good income and pleasant work. But my fears lest it should be too much for my health, and disturb our domestic habits, have made me resign." (*George Eliot Letters*, IV, 169, 172.) Lewes, however, eventually accepted the editorship. For a discussion of the founding of the *Fortnightly Review* and Trollope's part in this, see Walter E. Houghton, ed., *The Wellesley Index to Victorian Periodicals* (Toronto, 1972), II, 173–83; and *Autobiography*, pp. 189–96.

[8] Trollope has substituted "doubt" and "doubters" in Virgil's *Non ignara mali miseris succurrere disco*: "Not ignorant of misery do I learn to befriend the unhappy" (*Aeneid*, I, 630).

[1] This title was discarded in favor of *The Claverings*.

this in obedience to your intimation regarding the little quid pro quo—as to which I am grateful for your liberal readiness of purse.

How about the Evening?[2] The fortnightly is still hanging dubious. I will see you before long & we will tell our respective stories.

Yours always
A. T.

1865

To George Smith

MS John Murray. SB 253.

9 Jan 1865   GARRICK CLUB
My dear Smith.

I have put your name down[3]—& Sir C Taylor[4] will support it— I did not ask him to second you;—but he will no doubt if you wish. You had however better write to W Collins.

Dont forget to tell me what you think of that Mss. I suppose it would not suit you to publish it in the Magazine.

Yours always
Anty Trollope

[2] Smith was planning the *Pall Mall Gazette*, an evening newspaper that began publication on 7 February 1865 (the title came from a journal in Thackeray's *Pendennis*). Trollope contributed to the paper from the start, and for three or four years considered himself a member of the staff. Frederick Greenwood was the editor, but Smith (as the proprietor and publisher) performed many of the editorial functions. All Trollope's correspondence about his work for the paper was with Smith: see Trollope to Smith, 18 January 1865, n. 5. See also Bradford Booth, "Trollope and the *Pall Mall Gazette,*" *NCF*, 4 (June and September 1949), 51–69, 137–58.

[3] Trollope proposed Smith for the Garrick Club on 9 January; he was elected on 1 April.

[4] Sir Charles Taylor (1817–76), a sportsman and a close Garrick Club friend of Trollope. Trollope described Taylor as "our king at the Garrick Club. . . . He gave the best dinners of my time. . . . A man rough of tongue, brusque in manners, odious to those who dislike him, somewhat inclined to tyranny, he is the prince of friends, honest as the sun, and as open-handed as Charity itself." (*Autobiography*, p. 150.) Edmund Yates noted that this characterization was as appropriate for Trollope as for Taylor (*Edmund Yates: His Recollections and Experiences* [1884], I, 237).

To George Smith[5]

Bibliography, p. 231.

18 January 1865
Trollope sends a column on the self-defense issued by W. D. Christie, late
minister at Rio, for the *Pall Mall Gazette*.[6]

To George Smith

Bibliography, p. 231.

26 January 1865[7]
For the *Pall Mall Gazette* Trollope offers to review James Anthony Froude's
Elizabeth[8] in 2½ columns and sends a review of the *Public Schools Calendar*.[9]

[5] Sadleir prints 28 notes from letters that Trollope wrote to Smith proposing or
discussing articles for the *Pall Mall Gazette* (*Bibliography*, pp. 231–33). These notes
are reprinted here as letter summaries, except in the handful of cases where the original letters have been preserved. The correspondence indicates the extent of Trollope's involvement with the newspaper.

[6] In "Notes on the Brazilian Question" (*Pall Mall Gazette*, 11 February 1865, pp.
6–7), Trollope reviewed the recently published *Notes on Brazilian Questions* by W. D.
Christie, husband of Trollope's old friend Mary Christie, née Grant. The pamphlet
was Christie's defense of his conduct as Minister to Brazil in the period 1859–63, when
his insistence on Brazil's treaty obligations to end the slave trade, combined with his
pressing of doubtful claims for the compensation of British subjects, brought about a
severing of diplomatic relations. (Christie was recalled and retired on pension.) Although convinced of Christie's honesty and patriotism, Trollope was sharply critical
of a diplomat who had shown himself "thin-skinned, sore, and often savage" and
whose dealings with the Brazilians had been characterized by "British arrogance."
Trollope thought that Christie's failings could be documented in Christie's own
pamphlet and that the pamphlet was both damaging to Christie and embarrassing
to the British government. This is certainly the review that Trollope described in his
Autobiography (pp. 201–2) as being a "great sorrow" for him to write. Christie is not
named, but the pamphlet is described as a vindication of the author's conduct in the
public service, and the author's wife is spoken of as being as "dear to me as if she
were my own sister." According to Trollope, he was persuaded against his better
judgment to undertake the review by improper pressure from Christie, and he admitted "emphasizing much more strongly than was necessary the opinion which I
had formed of his indiscretion,—as will often be the case when a man has a pen in
his hand." There followed "a breaking off of intercourse between loving friends,"
until Mary Christie eventually brought about a reconciliation. (Sadleir [*Commentary*,
p. 261] mistakenly supposed Lord Westbury to be the subject of this passage in the
Autobiography.)

[7] Sadleir printed two separate notes for this date, but they are probably from the
same letter.

[8] The first two volumes of Froude's *The Reign of Elizabeth* (vols. VII and VIII of
his *History*). Smith apparently declined Trollope's offer. It will be recalled that
remarks in Charles Kingsley's review of these two volumes led to J. H. Newman's
writing *Apologia Pro Vita Sua*.

[9] "The Public Schools Calendar for 1865," *Pall Mall Gazette*, 2 March 1865, p. 6.

To ?

MS Parrish Collection.

Jan 30. 1865.   WALTHAM HOUSE, WALTHAM CROSS.
My dear Madam.

Mrs. Trollope tells me that you wish me to take Bobby Synge[1] to the Charter House for his examination on Wednesday Feb 8. If you cannot have this done otherwise without inconvenience to yourself I will endeavour to arrange it; but as I should not on other account be in London, and as I shall have friends here, I would avoid it if I could do so,—*without putting you to inconvenience.*

> Believe me to be
> Dear Madam
>   very faithfully yours
>   Anthony Trollope

I shall perhaps have a line from you on the subject if you wish me to take Bobby on the day named.

To Henry Taylor

MS Bodleian.

Feb 3. 65   WALTHAM HOUSE, WALTHAM CROSS.
My dear Mr Taylor.

I am much obliged by your letter,—and by your present. I have written to Mr. Chapman desiring him to send it to me, and hope I may live to get you to put your name in it.[2] You have many strong admirers among lovers of English poetry, but few stronger, and certainly none of an earlier date than myself. The oracles whose words were the rarest have ever been valued the most, and you have been one of those rare-speaking oracles, who have been satisfied to put the care and work of years into a few pages. That daring of reticence is a noble courage,—of which the faith of old days gave us many examples; but which in these times of *occupet extremum scabies*,[3] is very scarce. But I feel assured that in your instance it will meet its full reward,—however late that may

---

[1] Robert Follett Synge (1853–1920), later Sir Robert, the son of Trollope's friend W. W. F. Synge. He entered Charterhouse in 1865. According to Muriel Rose Trollope, Trollope's granddaughter, young Synge and his brother spent their holidays at Waltham House ("What I Was Told," *Trollopian*, 2 [March 1948], 233). Synge was appointed to the Foreign Office in 1884 and became Deputy Marshal of Ceremonies in 1902.

[2] Taylor's three-volume *Poetical Works* (1864), which Trollope reviewed enthusiastically in the *Fortnightly*, 1 (1 June 1865), 129–46. See Trollope to Lewes, 9 August 1860, n. 6.

[3] "The devil take the hindmost," the cry of the modern poet who writes too much and studies too little (Horace, *Ars Poetica*, l. 417).

come. I do hope it may be in your own days, for that last infirmity of noble minds[4] always seeks it's [*sic*] gratification,—and the more absolutely mute is the desire, the keener is its edge.

very faithfully yours
Anthony Trollope

To Miss E. Taylor
MS Parrish Collection. SB 254.

Feb 7—1865.   WALTHAM HOUSE, WALTHAM CROSS.
My dear Miss Taylor.

I yesterday saw Chapman. He says that no drawings of yours are in his hands—or have been. It seems that those you have sent must have gone to the woodcutters—& have been used by them to assist them. Such at least I presume to be the case. I need not say how glad Mrs. Trollope would have been to keep the one you intended for her had we been able to rescue it.

I saw the two on the wood now in his hands, & like them both much.

Yours always
Anthony Trollope

To the Secretary of the Athenaeum
MS Parrish Collection.

Feb—10—1865   WALTHAM HOUSE, WALTHAM CROSS.
Dear Sir.

The enclosed has no doubt been sent to me in error. I find by my banker's book that my subscription to the Athenaeum was paid on 2 January.

If my name has been put up as a defaulter be good enough to erase it;—and also let me have a line to say that the matter is all right.

Yours truly

The Secretary   Anthony Trollope
Athenaeum.

To ?
MS Gordon N. Ray.

Feb 11—65   WALTHAM HOUSE, WALTHAM CROSS.
Sir.

I know Mr. Geo Smith (of Smith & Elder) very well, & I find him to be a liberal man. But he like all publishers likes to be certain of his wares

---

[4] *Lycidas,* l. 71.

before he pays his money. I hardly know how to advise you as to terms. You do not tell me the length of the story; nor have I any idea of it's [*sic*] nature. Nor do I know whether money is the first or only the second object with you. As a rule I think that a beginner should be content to get something like £30 a volume for the ordinary novel volume;—but then I do not know how far you rank yourself as a beginner. I can only assure [you] that I wrote very many volumes before I got as much.

Your faithful Servant
Anthony Trollope

To George Smith

MS Bodleian.

March 6th. [1865]   WALTHAM HOUSE, WALTHAM CROSS.
Dear Smith.

Last night, I sent you, according to promise, the Man who hunts & does not jump.[5] That, if you publish it tomorrow, I do not expect back for correction.

Now, with this, I send the hunting parson.[6] You may perhaps give me time to correct that.

Yours always
A. T.

To George Smith

Commentary, p. 259. SB 255.

12 March 1865   Waltham Cross

*   *   *

I send back the proof of "The Master of Hounds"[7] and I send a paper on "How to Ride to Hounds."[8] That shall be the last of the set, and I don't think I'll write another word about hunting. I had given you credit for ordering the "Sportswoman's" letter.[9]

*   *   *

[5] "The Man Who Hunts and Never Jumps," *Pall Mall Gazette*, 7 March 1865, pp. 9–10.

[6] "The Hunting Parson," *Pall Mall Gazette*, 11 March 1865, p. 4. These and other hunting essays (eight in all) were published in the *Pall Mall Gazette* during February and March 1865; they were reprinted in book form as *Hunting Sketches* (1865).

[7] *Pall Mall Gazette*, 15 March 1865, pp. 4–5.

[8] *Pall Mall Gazette*, 20 March 1865, pp. 3–4.

[9] On 9 March the *Pall Mall Gazette* (p. 4) carried a letter signed "A Sportswoman"; this took issue with two mock-serious letters from "Paterfamilias" (25 February, p. 3, and 6 March, p. 3) that had attacked Trollope's "The Lady Who Rides to Hounds" (17 February, p. 3). In fact, Trollope had already contested (28 February, p. 3) Paterfamilias's three arguments against young ladies hunting, insisting that "Anonyma" (i.e., the courtesan) was not to be met with in the field, that accidents were rare, and

To George Smith

Bibliography, p. 232.

12 March 1865[1]
For the *Pall Mall Gazette*, Trollope promises an American letter[2] and sends a paper on Lord Brougham.[3]

To George Smith

Commentary, p. 259. SB 256.

15 March 1865

*　　　*　　　*

Will you kindly ask your assistants in Salisbury Street[4] *not* to alter my MS.? Let them send back or omit to use any paper that is unsatisfactory, and I will not even ask the reason. But don't let one be altered.

*　　　*　　　*

To John [? Tilley]

MS New York University.

18 March 1865.　　　　　　　　WALTHAM HOUSE, WALTHAM CROSS.
My dear John.
It is astonishing how much I hear about parsons & ladies hunting. There was a letter about each in the Pall Mall today,—that about the

---

that women who knew the sport did not "flurry themselves into such figures" as Paterfamilias described (soiled and perspiring, or with noses bloodied and swollen). Paterfamilias was probably Matthew James Higgins, a regular contributor to the *Pall Mall Gazette*, and the "Sportswoman" was probably another member of the *Pall Mall Gazette* staff. See also Trollope to ? Tilley, 18 March 1865.

[1] Sadleir prints two separate notes for this date, but they are probably from the same letter; in fact, they may even have been taken from the preceding letter.

[2] "The American Conflict," *Pall Mall Gazette*, 16 March 1864, p. 4 (signed by Trollope). This immediately followed Trollope's letter "Honesty in Statesmanship," on the late Duc de Morny (signed "An Englishman"). The *Pall Mall Gazette* had printed two earlier letters on America signed by Trollope (7 February 1865 and 27 February 1865).

[3] "The Accusations Against Lord Brougham," *Pall Mall Gazette*, 20 March 1865, p. 3 (signed "An Englishman"). Leonard Edmunds was said to have paid over £200 a year to Brougham and another £100 to Brougham's brother for a Patent Office appointment (see Trollope to Smith, 27 June 1865). Trollope decried "the credit which these charges against a great man seem to have received," and expressed confidence that there would be an explanation honorable to Brougham. The *Pall Mall Gazette*'s leader of 20 March agreed with Trollope. In 1870 Trollope was called on to assist in preparing Brougham's memoirs for publication: see Trollope to Brougham, 9 July 1870.

[4] The *Pall Mall Gazette* was printed by John Kellett Sharpe, 14 Salisbury Street, Strand.

parsons being from Fitzjames Stephen.[5] I am going to do a concluding article about them both.[6] Tell Mr Joyce[7] with my kind regards that I know I shall see him out yet & going ahead of me in a style that will leave me hopeless of emulation.

Yours always
Anty Trollope

To George Smith
Bibliography, p. 232.

18 March 1865
Trollope promises a paper on bankrupts for the *Pall Mall Gazette.*[8]

To George Smith
Bibliography, p. 232.

19 March 1865
Trollope sends his paper on clerks and usurers.[9]

[5] James Fitzjames Stephen (1829–94), later Sir James, renowned judge; author of important works on English law; a principal contributor to the *Pall Mall Gazette* and a regular contributor to the *Cornhill.* In the letter referred to here, "Why Should Not Parsons Hunt" (signed "Homo Sum"), Stephen took issue with Trollope for coming down regretfully against parsons hunting (in "The Hunting Parson," *Pall Mall Gazette*, 11 March 1865, p. 4). The other letter, "Ladies in the Hunting Field" (signed "Thalestris"), supported Trollope's position in favor of allowing women to hunt.

[6] No such article has been traced. It is unlikely that Trollope wrote the *Pall Mall Gazette* leader of 24 March (pp. 1–2) entitled "Pros and Cons as to Hunting Ladies and Hunting Parsons," since the leader contended that it might be well if parsons were permitted to enjoy the hunt. The leader concluded that "Thalestris" was right and that modest young ladies who hunt for the love of the sport should not be discouraged: "As the number of Dianas increases, the idea of impropriety will die away."

[7] Probably Francis Hayward Joyce (d. 1906), Vicar of Harrow from 1862 to 1897, and brother of Herbert Joyce, who worked for the Post Office. Joyce may have been the clergyman whom Trollope consulted with reference to *The Vicar of Bullhampton* (see Trollope to Joyce, 16 September 1868).

[8] "Usurers and Clerks in Public Offices," *Pall Mall Gazette*, 23 March 1865, p. 2. In the article Trollope warmly supported the Postmaster General for having at least temporarily reversed the rule that made liable to dismissal a Post Office clerk who got into trouble with moneylenders: like other people, clerks should be able to seek relief through the Bankruptcy Court without risking their jobs. Trollope urged the Crown to make the new ruling permanent, citing the difficulty of living on £100 a year. The article clearly drew on Trollope's own experience: see *Autobiography*, chap. iii (especially pp. 48–50).

[9] At about this time Trollope may also have sent Smith his letter on Napoleon III's *History of Julius Caesar*, "As to the Need of Caesars" (signed "An Englishman"), since this appeared in the *Pall Mall Gazette* on the same day as his paper on clerks and usurers (23 March 1865).

To George Smith

Bibliography, p. 232.

19 March 1865

Trollope suggests a series of "Imaginary Meditations" for the *Pall Mall Gazette*, proposing:

Napoleon on death of Morny.
Garibaldi at Capua.
Limola[1] on his re-election.
Rev. Mr. ———— on his nomination to
Bishopric of ————.

To George Smith

Bibliography, p. 232.

20 March 1865

Trollope apparently submits to an immediate rejection of the idea for a series of "Imaginary Meditations," but will try a paper on "The Emperor."[2]

To George Smith

Bibliography, p. 232.

26 March 1865

Trollope sends Smith his paper "The Emperor."

To George Smith

Bibliography, p. 232.

27 March 1865

Trollope has sent letters on America[3] and Napoleon for the *Pall Mall Gazette*. He sends an indignant "Englishman" letter[4] and promises a fifth and last letter on America.[5]

---

[1] Almost certainly Sadleir's misreading of Lincoln, who was reelected by a landslide in 1864.

[2] "Napoleon on the Death of Morny," *Pall Mall Gazette*, 31 March 1865, pp. 5–6, the only "Imaginary Meditation" that Smith allowed.

[3] "The American Conflict," *Pall Mall Gazette*, 30 March 1865, pp. 3–4 (signed by Trollope).

[4] "What Is a Job?," *Pall Mall Gazette*, 28 March 1865, p. 4 (signed "An Englishman"). This concerned the Lord Westbury scandal (see Trollope to Smith, 27 June 1865).

[5] "The American Conflict," *Pall Mall Gazette*, 6 April 1865, pp. 3–4 (signed by Trollope).

To Herman Merivale

MS Parrish Collection.

March 30. 1865   WALTHAM HOUSE, WALTHAM CROSS.
My dear Merivale.

You may have seen the advertised prospectus of a new fortnightly review which it is proposed to commence on May 1st.[6]—something on the
plan of the Revue des deux mondes. It will be edited by George Lewes,
and I am interested in it as part proprietor and contributor. Will you
join us, and do some work for us? We shall have fiction, original essays,
elaborate (or I should perhaps better say studied,) criticism, a chronicle
of the political doings of the day, and occasionally notices on art and
science. We purpose having 9 or 10 articles in each number, the numbers
containing each 128 pages of letterpress. Let me know if you think you
can help us.[7]

> Yours always
> Anthony Trollope

We begin with a capital of £8000 which is all taken up.

To George Smith

SB 257 (Sadleir's transcript).

31 March 1865   Waltham Cross

Trollope announces the arrival of a consignment of 12,000 cigars. How many
does Smith want?

To George Smith

MS Bodleian. Excerpt, *Commentary*, p. 259; excerpt, B 258.

March 31. 1865.   WALTHAM HOUSE, WALTHAM CROSS.
My dear Smith.

The drawing which I return is very spirited, pretty & good. The horse
is faulty. He is too long— Look at the quarters behind the girls seat. And
your artist has made the usual mistake of supposing that a horse goes at
his fence in the full stride of his gallop. He does not do this, but gathers
himself for his jump exactly as a man does. This horse could only have
gone through the paling,—could not possibly have jumped it.

Still I would get the man—(if a man) to do it, merely hinting to him
these points.[8]

[6] The first number of the *Fortnightly Review* appeared on 15 May.
[7] Merivale became a contributor.
[8] Smith was seeking an illustrator for *The Claverings*. The artist to whose work
Trollope gave qualified approval here was evidently not given the commission, since
Mary Ellen Edwards seems to have been chosen at the last minute (see Trollope to
Smith, 21 December 1865).

If you want any reviews done, or works of general literature, poetry, history—or what not, let me try a new hand for you. I told you of it when I saw you, & now write this as a reminder. You shall not be bound to take the work.

Yours always
A. T.

To George Smith
MS John Murray. SB 259.

April 3. 1865.   WALTHAM HOUSE, WALTHAM CROSS.
My dear Smith.

I wrote you a line hurriedly this afternoon,—and now write another almost in as great a hurry before I go to bed, saying that if you can join us at dinner at the Garrick on Wednesday at 7 pm you will find Billy Russell, Charles Taylor, Frank Fladgate[9] & myself ready to welcome you; —in assistance towards which Taylor has bespoken up from his country quarters a young sucking pig. At any rate, whether sucking pig be or be not to your taste come & join us, & we will be very jolly.

Yours always
Anthony Trollope

To George Smith
Bibliography, p. 232.

11 April 1865
Trollope has sent last night a letter about Prévost-Paradol for the *Pall Mall Gazette*.[1]

To George Smith
Bibliography, p. 232.

14 April 1865
Trollope sends an article on the St. Albans Raiders for the *Pall Mall Gazette*.[2]

[9] Frank Fladgate (1799–1892), barrister; member of the Committee of the Garrick and a special friend of Thackeray.

[1] "The Election of M. Prevost-Paradol," *Pall Mall Gazette*, 12 April 1865, pp. 3–4 (signed "An Englishman"). In the letter Trollope expressed delight that Prévost-Paradol had been elected to the French Academy despite his opposition to the Emperor's government.

[2] "The St. Albans Raiders," *Pall Mall Gazette*, 17 April 1865, pp. 10–11. In the article Trollope criticized a Canadian court for not detaining Confederate guerrillas who had escaped to Canada after robbing a bank and killing a bystander in St. Albans, Vermont.

To Lord Houghton

MS Trinity College, Cambridge.

April 15–1865   WALTHAM HOUSE, WALTHAM CROSS.
My dear Lord Houghton.

I heard yesterday of the death of my brothers wife[3] at Florence, and am to-day starting for Italy—to him. Will you therefore kindly excuse me for putting aside your invitation for the 27.

Yours always
Anthony Trollope

To H. B. Williams[4]

MS Gordon N. Ray.

May 1. 1865.   WALTHAM HOUSE, WALTHAM CROSS.
My dear Williams.

When in Italy with my brother the other day I saw a letter from you to him in which you said you would be in London early in May. I shall indeed be delighted to see you if I could get you down here for a spell. I do not remember whether you gave any dates. Just at present one finds one's time more cut up by compulsory engagements than at any other period of the year—, but if you will tell me your spare days I will do my best to manage it. I shall be at home next Sunday—but you parson like, will probably not leave home till the Monday. Also on the next Saturday & Sunday I shall be at home.

Yours always faithfully
Anthony Trollope

We are from 30 to 40 minutes from the Shoreditch Station. Our station is Waltham, & 5 minutes brings you to my house.

To George Smith

B 260 (Sadleir's transcript). *Commentary*, pp. 259–60.

5 May 1865

*   *   *

I went to a May meeting today at 11 am. punctual, and would not go to another to be made Editor of the Pall Mall Gazette! You do not know

---

[3] Theodosia Garrow Trollope, long in ill health, died on 13 April 1865. Her death occasioned a renewal of the old and irresponsible rumors about Beatrice Trollope's paternity; see Edward C. McAleer, ed., *Dearest Isa: Robert Browning's Letters to Isabella Blagden* (Austin, Texas, 1951), pp. 277, 279–81.

[4] The letter is endorsed "Autograph from Revd. H. B. Williams." This was probably Henry Blackstone Williams (?1813–79), Fellow of New College, 1837–45; Fellow of Winchester College, 1847–79; Rector of Bradford Peverell, Dorchester, 1850–79.

what you have asked. Go to one yourself and try. You sit four hours and listen to six sermons;—and the sermons are to me (—and would be to you,)—of such a nature that tho' they are in their nature odious and so tedious that human nature cannot listen to them, still they do not fall into a category at which you would wish to throw your ridicule.

I will tomorrow morning write you an article (a Zulu at a May meeting), for which the materials arranged themselves not unhappily; but I *can do no more.*[5] Suicide would intervene after the third or fourth, or I should give myself up to the police as the murderer of Mr. . . .[6]

In short I cannot bring myself to go through another May meeting— even tho' the object be to comply with your wishes.

I had thought perhaps my boy Harry might have done the attendance for me, but he,—having accompanied me today,—found so ready a resource in somnolence, that to him a May meeting would simply mean sleep for the future.

*   *   *

To George Smith
MS John Murray. B 261.

9. May. 1865.   73 St. Georges Square
My dear Smith.

I hope I shall not offend you tho' I fear I may run some risk of annoying you by my present letter.

I am obliged [to] return the enclosed cheque as I cannot consent to be paid the rate of two guineas and a half for articles about the length of a leader in the Times.

I know that on reading this your first feeling will be that I should be the last man to stand out for higher pay than you are disposed to give. But that is not what I do. If you will think of it I am sure you will perceive that tho' I may well afford to give you any little aid in my power from friendship, I cannot afford to work as a professional man at wages which I should be ashamed to acknowledge.

I can easily understand,—and do understand,—that the sort of work I may do for you is not of value to you at all equal to that which others

---

[5] Smith had asked Trollope to write an account of the May Meetings at Exeter Hall. Attracting large and generally evangelical audiences, these meetings were held annually to arouse and sustain support for many of England's leading religious and charitable societies. Trollope attended the anniversary of the London Society for Promoting Christianity Amongst the Jews, a prominent evangelical agency founded in 1808 and exclusively Anglican since 1815. Adopting the stance of a foreign observer, he entitled his description "The Zulu in London" (*Pall Mall Gazette*, 10 May 1865, pp. 3–4). The article is reprinted in Ruth apRoberts, ed., *Clergymen of the Church of England* (Leicester, 1974), pp. 51–60. For a sympathetic account of the meeting that Trollope attended, see the *Record*, 8 May 1865, p. 3.

[6] Sadleir omitted the name, presumably because it was illegible.

furnish who are more capable of supplying the wants of a daily newspaper; but that simply shews that a daily newspaper is not in my line.

I am so fond of the P. M. G,[7]—and so greatly admire your energy and skill and I may say genius in the matter—that I really dislike doing or saying anything which may terminate my connexion with it. If you will let me think that I may from time to time send you a letter,—all for love, I shall be delighted; and I pray you to accept those lately inserted in that light. Should you, on thinking over the matter, wish for three or four papers about tourists in the autumn, I will do them for you at the price you paid for the hunting sketches, which was I think 4 guineas a column. Or it may well be that you can get these done better by a younger hand at a lesser cost.

Pray tell me that you appreciate my motives, and that there is to be no ill will between us. I want you to understand that I can write for you without a view to income, but I cannot accept wages which if acknowledged would lower my position in my profession.[8]

Yours always faithfully
Anthony Trollope

To Mr. A. W. Bennett[9]

MS Parrish Collection.

May 10. 1865.   WALTHAM HOUSE, WALTHAM CROSS.
Sir.

I am obliged to express my regret that the very little time that I have in London will prevent my sitting to Mr E. Edwards[1] for my photograph.

Your obd. Servant
Anthony Trollope

Mr A. Bennett
5 Bishop's Gate Street
Without

To George Smith

MS John Murray. SB 262.

May 11. 1865   Waltham Cross.
My dear Smith.

I am much obliged by the kindness of your note, & am quite satisfied that we understand each other, & each feel that there is no ground for complaint against the other.

---

[7] *Pall Mall Gazette.*

[8] See Trollope to Smith, 11 May 1865.

[9] Alfred William Bennett (1833–1902), botanist; in business as a bookseller and publisher at 5 Bishopsgate Street Without from 1858 until 1868, when he became a lecturer in botany.

[1] Ernest Edwards, Photographer, 20 Baker Street.

Send me back the cheque & I will pay it into my bankers in the usual way. That will be the easiest way of getting over that little difficulty.[2]

Yours always faithfully
Anthony Trollope

To Lord Houghton

MS Trinity College, Cambridge.

12 May 1865   WALTHAM HOUSE, WALTHAM CROSS.

My dear Lord Houghton

I shall be very happy to dine with you on Friday, this day week.

Yours sincerely
Anthony Trollope

To George Smith

B 263 (Sadleir's transcript).

16 May 1865

*　　　*　　　*

I saw of course the notice in the P. M. G., but had not, and have not, seen the Saturday.[3]

I cannot but think such personal notices, in which the criticism is all on the man and nothing on the matter, to be in very bad taste.

*　　　*　　　*

To George Smith

SB 926 (Sadleir's transcript).

[? May 1865]   Waltham

*　　　*　　　*

Why attack the P.O. What does your writer really know against it? Let him give me instances and I will see them properly noticed. I hope you will publish the letter I send you. Surely unjust and sweeping attacks made, without cause, must be bad.[4]

*　　　*　　　*

[2] Trollope's account books list his income from the *Pall Mall Gazette* as follows: 1865, £234 14s. 6d.; 1866, £97 2s. 6d.; 1868, £7 17s. 6d. (Parrish Collection).

[3] Trollope had written a letter to the *Pall Mall Gazette* on the death of Abraham Lincoln (5 May 1865, p. 4). Just over a week later the *Saturday Review*, in an article entitled "Mistaken Estimates of Self," commented that Trollope's "whole letter is an extraordinary illustration of the way in which a charming novelist may flounder about in platitudes and almost penny-a-lining commonplaces when he turns political philosopher" (13 May 1865, pp. 563–64). Two days later the *Pall Mall Gazette* replied, commenting that it was no wonder the *Saturday Review* preferred unsigned articles since one of their writers had been "discoursing for months past" on the theme that the South would never surrender; by contrast, Trollope had long supported the Northern cause (15 May 1865, pp. 9–10).

[4] Trollope is probably referring to an "Occasional Note" in the *Pall Mall Gazette* of 15 May 1865, p. 9, about Post Office savings banks. The writer argued that even

To G. H. Lewes

MS Yale. B 264; *George Eliot Letters*, VIII, 340–41.

30 May 1865   Glasgow
My dear Lewes.

As to putting Belton E.[5] first in No. 3, do just as you please.[6] I have a strong opinion against putting the novel always first as it indicates an idea that it is our staple;—which indicates the further idea that the remainder is padding.[7] Were I Editor I think I should always give the novel a distinctive place just before the Chronique.[8] But that is a matter of small, or no, moment.

My revises were returned 4 days since,—& the non return up to then was not my fault. Indeed I had not asked for revises. But they were sent, and sent without the original proofs, and were therefore useless. I wrote for the original sheets and then returned the revises.

Touching the signing[9] I have been so driven by official work that I have not put a pen to it. But I will. I am not *at all*[1] anxious as to the number in which it may appear. Indeed it would be too late now for the third. Fourth or fifth will do as well. It shall be with you in about a week.

Who is to do your chronique? If you are in a difficulty I *will attempt it*. Only, could not the pages be less pressed? It is closer than we at first intended. Poor Billy![2] Why did he give up?

I have got, just got, No. 2 & have only read your article.[3] It is beautiful, but, oh, so cruel. You are as hard almost as Carlyle;—without the salve which one has for Carlyle's blows, in the feeling that they are all struck

---

before the establishment of savings banks the "inadequacy of the Post Office machinery to the immense correspondence of the country had long been notorious"; the result of the extra burden of maintaining savings banks was that "the delivery of letters is every day growing more uncertain and unsatisfactory. Complaints are unattended to. Country postmasters act the part of little tyrants without reprimand of any kind, and letter-carriers are guilty with impunity of the grossest irregularities." No letter or article in defense of the Post Office appeared in the paper.

[5] By an agreement dated 5 April 1865 Trollope was to receive £800 for the serialization of *The Belton Estate* in the *Fortnightly*. The novel began in the first number of the new periodical, published on 15 May 1865, and ran through 1 January 1866. For the book issue, Chapman & Hall paid £700 for all rights to the first 2,000 copies, with half copyright reverting to Trollope thereafter. See also Trollope to Virtue & Co., 24 January 1867, n. 4.

[6] Lewes varied the arrangement of articles; *The Belton Estate* appeared first in four of its sixteen installments (nos. 5, 6, 11, and 15).

[7] See Trollope to Smith, 26 January 1861.

[8] A section on "Public Affairs" that appeared near the end of each number.

[9] "On Anonymous Literature," *Fortnightly*, 1 (1 July 1865), 491–98.

[1] Underlined twice.

[2] Almost certainly William Howard Russell.

[3] "The Principles of Success in Literature, Chapter II: The Principle of Vision," *Fortnightly*, 1 (1 June 1865), 185–96.

in the dark, & may probably, after all, not be deserved.[4] But it is very beautiful. Your style leaves nothing to be desired.

Enjoying myself! revising a post office with 300 men, the work and wages of all of whom are to be fixed on one's own responsibility! Come & try it, & then go back to the delicious ease & perfect freedom of your Editors chair!

Yours always
Any Trollope

To G. H. Lewes

MS Yale. B 265; *George Eliot Letters*, VIII, 342.

June 1. 1865   Glasgow
My dear Lewes.

Beesly's[5] paper on Catiline is admirable.[6] It is written by a man leaning on his pen with delight, which leaning always gives a life to the work. But he writes too much like an advocate with a side to defend, to be perfectly convincing. I still believe that Cicero was more of a patriot than Catiline. That both were false and both cruel is to be assumed,— for they were Romans of that false & cruel time that began with Sulla and ended—when there was no longer spirit enough in Rome either for falsehood or cruelty. That Cicero was constitutionally a coward,—tho he knew how to die,—& Catiline a man of nerve was little to the credit or discredit of either,—as little as having strong arms or long legs. Had Beesly been more historic & less enthusiastic he would have told us that Cicero, who was so loud against Verres, was at any rate honest in his own province,—(a very rare virtue) and that he sought nothing from his countrymen at home beyond the objects of a fair ambition, & was therefore entitled to deal heavily with a demagogue.[7]

That he lied,—is as I have said a matter of course because he was a

---

[4] Trollope may have been thinking about Carlyle since he was about to publish a review of Ruskin's *Sesame and Lilies* (1865) in which he urged Ruskin to leave preaching to Carlyle, who, "almost as a prophet," has denounced Englishmen in such a fashion that "we are ready to pardon the abuse he showers on us, on account of the good that we know he has done us" (*Fortnightly*, 1 [15 July 1865], 633–35). Carlyle's private reaction is recorded in a letter to his wife. Ruskin's *Sesame and Lilies*, he wrote, "must be a pretty little thing. Trollope, in reviewing it with considerable insolence stupidity and vulgarity, produces little specimens far beyond any Trollope sphere of speculation. A distylish little pug, that Trollope; irredeemably imbedded in commonplace, and grown fat upon it, and prosperous to an unwholesome degree. Don't *you* return his love; nasty gritty creature, with no eye for 'the Beautiful the' etc.,—and awfully 'interesting to himself' he be." (Trudy Bliss, ed., *Thomas Carlyle: Letters to His Wife* [1953], p. 381.)

[5] Edward Spencer Beesly (1831–1915), philosopher and educator; an authority on Comte.

[6] "Catiline as a Party Leader," *Fortnightly*, 1 (1 June 1865), 167–84.

[7] Trollope later discussed this point in his *The Life of Cicero* (1880), chap. ix.

Roman; and equally a matter of course that he lied successfully, because he was gifted with the use of words.

I however, am myself so given to rebellion in politics that I am delighted to see and hear any Catiline defended, and any Cicero attacked.

I am glad you have no difficulty about the chronique.

Yours ever
A. T.

Tom immersed in a lawsuit with a Russian—(in Florence!) which is like to keep him there all the summer,—as to the sale or non sale of his house!!!

To George Smith
MS Parrish Collection. SB 266.

June 3—1865 Glasgow
My dear Smith.

Alas—alas. I am out on P. O. business & shall not be back till three days after your dinner. I regret this infinitely because your dinners are always jolly, but the more (very much) because I gather from the address of the card that it is to be essentially a P. M. G. dinner. I will be with you in the spirit.

Two thoroughly well educated Scotchmen, not knowing each other, have told me that they thought the PMG the best paper they ever knew.

Yours always faithfully
Anthony Trollope

To Beatrice Trollope[8]
MS Robert A. Cecil. B 267.

8 June 1865. Belfast.
Dearest Bice.

I got a letter yesterday from Mrs. Lark, who was a great friend of your mama's, in which she said that she wanted to see you in London. She goes away on the 16th. June. I was obliged to tell her that you would not be back so soon.

Your great aunt Mrs. Clyde,—my mothers sister,—who is a very old woman living in Exeter has sent you a present of ten guineas. We must have a great consultation between you, and aunt Rose, and papa, and Barney,[9] and all the other wise people, as to what you had better buy.

---

[8] After Theodosia Trollope's death (in Florence), Trollope brought her daughter, Bice, back to Waltham; he also arranged for Frances Eleanor Ternan to instruct her in music (see Trollope to Thomas Adolphus Trollope, 19 January 1868).

[9] Barney was the Irish groom who had been with Trollope since Trollope's days at Banagher. Trollope paid Barney £5 a year extra for waking him up every morning

What do you say to a new cow? Or perhaps ten guinea's worth of chocolate bonbons? In the mean time you must write a pretty letter to Aunt Mary (that is her name) for the present, & send it to me to send on.

Remember me most kindly to Mr. & Mrs. Fell.

Your own affectionate uncle

T

(for Toney)

To Mrs. Anderson

MS University of Michigan. SB 268.

June. 14—1865.
Wednesday   WALTHAM HOUSE, WALTHAM CROSS.
My dear Mrs. Anderson.

I received your letter in Dublin, and got home yesterday.

My wife says that calling is very unsatisfactory, especially as she does not know how she could get up to town this week—having only returned home last night, and wishes me therefore to ask you & Dr. Anderson to come down here on Saturday instead & stay till Monday. There is a very nice train at 4–5 pm. which leaves Shoreditch and reaches Waltham without stopping. You would then be in time to get a drive before dinner.

We should be very glad to see you on Friday if you can not come on Saturday—but should prefer the Saturday—as you would then of course stay over Sunday. Pray talk Dr. Anderson over to this arrangement.

Yours always faithfully

Anthony Trollope

To R. S. Smyth[1]

R. S. Smyth, "The Provincial Service Fifty Years Ago," *St. Martin's-le-Grand*, 13 (October 1903), 375–76. B 269.

June 21st. 1865   WALTHAM HOUSE, WALTHAM CROSS.
My dear Sir,—

That which is unsatisfactory to you in the nature of your position and prospects at Belfast, is owing to the fact that you find yourself to be pos-

---

so that he would be at his writing table at 5:30 A.M.: "During all those years at Waltham Cross he never was once late with the coffee which it was his duty to bring me. I do not know that I ought not to feel that I owe more to him than to any one else for the success I have had." (*Autobiography*, p. 271.) Muriel Rose Trollope, Trollope's granddaughter, gives Barney's surname as FitzPatrick ("What I Was Told," *Trollopian*, 2 [March 1948], 230); James Pope Hennessy gives it as MacIntyre (*Anthony Trollope* [Boston, 1971], p. 75).

[1] R. S. Smyth had served under Trollope while Trollope was Surveyor for the Northern District of Ireland. Smyth wrote that Trollope "was held out to the

sessed of better qualities for business than you had, when younger, given yourself credit for possessing, and not by any means to the inferiority of pay or rank which you have in the Belfast Post Office. If you will remember what were your expectations when you joined the Office some ten years since, you will find that this is so. Had you at that time been assured of the senior clerkship, with a prospect of an increase to the then rate of senior clerks' pay, you would have thought the place sufficiently alluring. That is now your position, and you are dissatisfied, not because you think that that is bad, but because you think higher of yourself. Such a condition is very common with men of energy, and such men must then decide whether they will begin the world again by placing themselves where a higher career may be open to them (in which there is always risk), or whether they will accept the moderate and sure advantages which they already possess. It may well be that you can do better for yourself, as you are still young, by finding service elsewhere; but I think you should endeavour, if you remain where you are, to teach yourself not to regard the service with dissatisfaction. That you will always do your work well I am sure, but it will be much for your own comfort if you can make yourself believe that the service in which you are has not been bad or hard to you.

> Very faithfully yours,
> Anthony Trollope

To George Smith

Commentary, p. 261. SB 270.

June 27 1865

* * *

I have sent to the P.M.G. office a letter about Lord Westbury[2]—which I hope you may find yourself able to use.

* * *

---

juniors in the service as a terror, and my early experience of him was not calculated to remove such an impression." However, when postal duties brought Trollope to Belfast in June 1865, Smyth took the opportunity to discuss his prospects, and Trollope "entered into the matter in a very friendly, almost a fatherly way," taking the line he does in this letter.

[2] Richard Bethell (1800–1873), 1st Baron Westbury; Lord Chancellor, 1861–65. After it had been discovered that Leonard Edmunds, Clerk to the Commissioner of Patents, had misused public funds, Westbury allowed Edmunds to resign and then appointed his own son and a relative of his wife to the positions that Edmunds had held. Trollope wrote three articles of increasing vehemence on the celebrated affair for the *Pall Mall Gazette*: "What Is a Job?," 28 March 1865, p. 4; "Lord Westbury and Mr. Edmunds," 8 May 1865, pp. 3–4; and "The Lord Chancellor," 28 June 1865, p. 4 ("nothing short of the removal of the Lord Chancellor from his office ought to satisfy the feeling of the country"). On 5 July, after a censure by the House of Commons, Westbury resigned.

To George Smith

B 271 (Sadleir's transcript). Excerpt, *Commentary*, p. 261.

29 June 1865

*   *   *

I only got your letter about the horse (altho' dated 27th) as also your other about that inferior animal the Lord Chancellor, this morning. Touching the horse, as we are going over to you tomorrow Barney shall ride him over and he can come back with us. He is quite right; but he has been having tares for the last three weeks, and is somewhat soft.—

Touching Lord Westbury his fault (in my judgement) has been this,—that he has taught himself to think that intellect would do without moral conduct in English public life. He certainly ought to go, as no one can doubt that he has disgraced his position.

*   *   *

To George Smith

MS John Murray. SB 272.

July 10. 1865.   WALTHAM HOUSE, WALTHAM CROSS.

My dear Smith

I am just beginning my Tourists sketches thinking you may want them when you have done the elections.

I think of the nine following headings, which however may be probably changed a little as the papers get themselves written.

Yours always
Anthony Trollope
(See other side)

I. The man who travels alone
II. The unprotected female tourist.
III The art tourist.
IV The family that goes abroad because it's the thing to do.
V The united Englishmen who travel for fun
VI The tourist in search of knowledge
VII. The Alpine club man—(won't I?)
VIII Tourists who enjoy their work
IX Tourists who hate their work[3]

---

[3] Except for "Tourists who enjoy their work," all the sketches were published in the *Pall Mall Gazette*; they appeared irregularly from 3 August to 6 September 1865. ("Tourists who hate their work," however, was published as "Tourists Who Don't Like Their Travels.") Chapman & Hall issued the sketches in book form as *Travelling Sketches* (1866).

To Samuel Laurence

MS Parrish Collection. SB 274 (misdated).

July 12—1865   Waltham Cross
My dear Laurence.

A young lady in whom I am interested and who is trying hard to earn something for her family has paid £3.3. to a firm in Wells street, to learn the art of copying lithographs,—on an understanding that she was then to be employed by them. She went thro her lessons and then they gave her some drawings to copy. She sent them in and they have been returned with the simple intimation that they are not good enough. The people are

E. Fuller & Co
42 Wells Street—

and I write to you, because you being so near to them, can let me know whether they are trustworthy people, and whether this poor girl—(a Miss Hughes, of 12 Alfred Place, Camden Town,) has any real chance of employment from them. They would know you & perhaps you would not mind asking them,—i e if they are respectable.

Yours always sincerely
Anthony Trollope

To William Dean Howells[4]

MS Harvard. SB 273.

July 13. 1865.   Chelmsford
Dear Sir.

I got your letter this morning, having been some days away from home. I hardly know when I may be in town. Could you come to my house on Saturday, or Sunday? We can give you a bed. On Saturday Mrs. Trollope will not be at home but I shall be there with a friend— Mrs. Trollope will be home on Sunday.

You must go to the Shoreditch Station and take a ticket for Waltham. The station is very near my house. The 5.10 pm train on Saturday

---

[4] William Dean Howells (1837–1920), distinguished American author and critic; at this time, at the beginning of his literary career. Howells had served as the American Consul at Venice from 1861 to 1865, and he had stopped off in London on his return home to find a publisher for his *Venetian Life*. Mildred Howells said of the visit mentioned in this letter: "Anthony Trollope, in response to the letter of introduction asked Howells to his house, but scarcely spoke to him while he was there; and he offered him none of the hoped-for help, or advice, as to English publishers, that the young American was too proud to mention." (Mildred Howells, ed., *Life in Letters of William Dean Howells* [Garden City, New York, 1928], I, 93). Howells strongly disliked Trollope, but later came to consider him as second only to Jane Austen among English novelists and as "one of the finest of artists as well as the most Philistine of men" (William Dean Howells, *My Literary Passions* [New York, 1895], p. 247).

would bring you to dinner. The guide book will shew you the Sunday trains.

Address to Waltham Cross.

Yours faithfully

Anthony Trollope

To W. W. F. Synge

MS Parrish Collection.

July 15—1865
Sunday.[5] WALTHAM HOUSE, WALTHAM CROSS.
My dear old fellow.

I got home here yesterday–& got your note this morning. I saw yesterday in the papers that you were back. When can you come here? I shall be in town on Wednesday, & shall be at the Garrick where I would dine with you at 6.30—if you would—& you could come down with me by the 8.30 train?—or else we would come down by 5.10 pm train together—only let me know what are your plans. For ought I know you may be dancing attendance on the Queen, from morning to night—[6]

Best love from my wife.

Yours always

A. T.

To George Smith

Bibliography, p. 232.

25 July 1865

Trollope sends a letter to the *Pall Mall Gazette* in reply to an article about Public Servants.[7]

---

[5] Sunday was 16 July.

[6] Synge, Commissioner and Consul General to the Sandwich Islands since December 1861, had been ordered by the British Government to escort the widowed Queen Emma of Hawaii on her voyage to England. The arrival of the R.M.S. *Tasmania* at Southampton on 13 July, with the queen and her suite on board, was announced in *The Times* of 14 July, and a fuller report (probably that seen by Trollope) appeared the next day (*The Times*, 14 July 1865, p. 9; 15 July 1865, p. 6).

[7] "The Civil Service Commissioners," *Pall Mall Gazette*, 27 July 1865, pp. 3–4 (signed "A Civil Servant of Thirty Years' Standing"), in reply to "On the Hiring of Public Servants," *Pall Mall Gazette*, 24 July 1865, p. 1. Trollope condemned secret inquiries by the Commissioners into candidates' characters. The article met with the approval of John Tilley, who sent a copy to the Postmaster General.

To Messrs. Carpenter & Westley[8]

MS Parrish Collection.

31. July 1865   WALTHAM HOUSE, WALTHAM CROSS.
Gentlemen.
I beg to enclose your bill with cheque for the amount.
Your obt Servant
Messrs. Carpenter & Westley   Anthony Trollope

To George Smith

MS Bodleian.

[July or August 1865]   WALTHAM HOUSE, WALTHAM CROSS.
My dear Smith.
Thanks for the liberal cheque.
I'll do the two Travellers, & let you have them before long—i e in a day or two.
Yours always
A. T.

To George Smith

MS Bodleian. Excerpt, Hamer, p. 213.

August 4—1865   WALTHAM HOUSE, WALTHAM CROSS.
My dear Smith.
Do whatever you please about my novel. Do not feel yourself at all compelled to encrease the bulk of the amount in the Feb & March numbers, because you begin in February; but do it just as you please.[9]
The enclosed is very good,—but it would hardly do to call yourself the Twaddler.
Yours always
Any Trollope

To Norman Macleod

MS Taylor Collection. SB 275.

August 10 65   WALTHAM HOUSE, WALTHAM CROSS.
My dear Macleod
Will you come down to us on Saturday & stay till Monday. 5.10 pm train from Shoreditch brings you in time for dinner at 6 (then eaten to

[8] Carpenter & Westley, Opticians, 24 Regent Street.
[9] *The Claverings*, originally intended for publication in January 1865, had been rescheduled for January 1866 (see Trollope to Smith, 13 December 1864), and Smith was probably embarrassed about another month's delay.

get a cigar in the garden afterwards). My house is 10 minutes walk from the Station and a porter brings up your bag. Likely I may be coming by the same train myself. My brother will be with me.

Thine

Any Trollope

What about Miss Anna Drury's Manuscript?[10]

To George Smith

MS Bodleian.

20 Aug. 1865   WALTHAM HOUSE, WALTHAM CROSS.
My dear Smith.

Would you kindly let me have a copy of the Small House of Allington, and send for me to Chapman,—the one vol edition. I wish to have it sent with some other books to a friend in America.

Yours always

Anthony Trollope

To George Smith

MS John Murray. B 276.

Augt. 24. 1865   WALTHAM HOUSE, WALTHAM CROSS.
My dear Smith.

I am almost ashamed to trouble you again about the S. H. of A., having made such a mull of it before;—but there is being made to me a proposition by C. & H. (with reference as I fancy to a further proposition to them from Smith[11] of the Strand) to purchase from me for a term of years my copyright in certain novels i e 10 or 11 in number. If I did not make any further arrangement with you about the S.H., I should naturally include it in the lump with the others, fixing my price accordingly. You will understand that I by no means want to take it away from your hands;—but perhaps you would tell me whether at the end of your time for selling—i e in next spring,—you would make me any & what offer.

Yours always

Geo. Smith Esq   Anthony Trollope

[10] *Good Words* did not serialize *The Brothers* (1865), *The Three Half-Crowns* (1866), or any other novel by Miss Drury, though it did publish her "The Story of a London Fog" in November 1867.

[11] William Henry Smith (1825–91), head of the firm that had become England's leading wholesale newsagent; later a prominent Tory politician. In 1848 Smith introduced railway bookstores, which became enormously popular and over which he gained a virtual monopoly. He also developed a large circulating library that, together with Mudie's Lending Library, did much to shape Victorian tastes in reading.

To James Hutton[1]

MS Parrish Collection. B 277.

Sept. 7. 65.   WALTHAM HOUSE, WALTHAM CROSS.
My dear Mr Hutton.

I greatly regret your decision,—as regards ourselves. For yourself, of course I can say nothing further.

The Mss you sent me I have left for Lewes as he will now be here in a day or two—and I am not interfering in his work more than has been necessary in his absence. It could not have appeared in the next number.

It shall certainly either be used or returned.

Yours most faithfully
Anthony Trollope

To George Smith

MS John Murray. B 278.

September 7. 1865.   WALTHAM HOUSE, WALTHAM CROSS.
My dear Smith.

I told you the other day that W. H. Smith was, (or was going to be,) in treaty with C & H. for my copyrights, & that C & H. intended to treat for a royalty on each copy printed. F. C.[2] now tells me that no such proposal has been made, but that W. H. Smith has suggested that I sd. name a price for the sale of my copyrights. This I have not done,—and do not think that I am disposed to do it.

Would you be disposed to buy them?— You will understand that my object is not immediate money, but a desire to make what I can of the property, and to put them into good hands—

Of the following—I have the half copyrights, to be disposed of at once.

The Macdermots.	
The O'Kellys.	
Dr. Thorne.	originally 3 volumes.
The Bertrams.	
Castle Richmond.	

West Indies.	1 octavo
North America.	2 "
Tales of all Countries.	originally
Rachel Ray.	two.

---

[1] James Hutton (1818–93), miscellaneous writer; contributed a review of William Edward's *Reminiscences of a Bengal Civilian* to the *Fortnightly*, 6 (1 October 1866), 510–12.

[2] Frederic Chapman.

The North America has been reprinted in two smaller volumes;—all the others in one.

Miss Mackenzie³—2 volumes
      has never yet been reprinted.

Orley Farm
   and
Can You Forgive Her

have never been reprinted. The first would be sold say in twelve months time; the other in two years, so as to allow time for selling the present 20/ editions.

Belton Estate—2 volumes
to be sold within a year after it has come out, which will be on 1 Jany next.

Chapman holds all these copyrights with me, and he is aware that I am going to write to you. If you can make me an offer I can deal with him.⁴

The other copyrights of books written by me are those of
   The Three Clerks—owned in entirety by Bentley—
And of The Warden & Barchester Towers, owned between myself & Longman,—as to which I would do anything to assist you, if you wished to get them.

Yours always faithfully
Anthony Trollope

To George Smith

SB 279 (Sadleir's transcript).

13 September 1865

Trollope sends Smith an itinerary of a month's trip through Germany and Austria. His son Fred is about to leave for Melbourne.⁵ Can Smith furnish him with any suitable letters of introduction?

---

³ *Miss Mackenzie* (for which Trollope received £1,200) was written in 1864 and published by Chapman & Hall in February 1865.

⁴ Negotiations over these copyrights dragged on for some time. See Trollope to Smith, 2 November 1865 and 19 May 1866.

⁵ Trollope and his wife permitted Frederic, then on the eve of turning 18, to go to Australia on the proviso that he return to England when he was 21, before deciding to settle permanently in the colony. Fred returned to England in 1868, then emigrated to Australia in the spring of 1869; see *Autobiography*, p. 326. For Fred's later career, see Frederic Trollope to Trollope, 3 January 1877.

To ?[6]

MS Columbia. B 280.

31. Oct. 1865   WALTHAM HOUSE, WALTHAM CROSS.
Sir.

I found your letter of Sept 30 on my return yesterday from the continent. My absence from home has been the reason of my not earlier noticing and answering it.

I must in the first place beg you to believe that I do not write without thinking very much of what may be the effects of what I write,—and that I do my work with a most anxious wish & with much effort that what I produce may at least not do harm. Were I to believe that any young persons could be led into evil ways by what I have published I should be very unhappy.

The subject of adultery is one very difficult of discussion. You have probably found it so in preaching. It is a sin against which you are called on to inveigh, (—and I also as I think of my own work,)—but as to which it is difficult to speak because of the incidents to adultery which are not only sinful, but immodest & in some degrees indecent. Of theft, lying, & murder you can speak openly to young & old, but against adultery or fornication you must caution those who are most in danger with baited [*sic*] breath. That I think is the cause of your letter to me.

But the bible does not scruple to speak to us of adultery as openly as of other sins. You do not leave out the seventh Commandment. The young girl for whom I or you are so tender is not ignorant of the sin;—and, as I think, it would not be well that she should be ignorant of it.

The education of our daughters is a subject on which at present many of us Englishmen differ greatly. Thinking as I do that ignorance is not innocence I do not avoid, as you would wish me to do, the mention of things which are to me more shocking in their facts than in their names. I do not think that any girl can be injured by reading the character whose thoughts I have endeavoured to describe in the novel to which you have alluded. It is not probable that I shall carry you with me, but I may perhaps succeed in inducing you to believe that I do not write in the manner of which you complain without thought or without a principle.

Your very faithful Servant
Anthony Trollope

Allow me to assure you that I accept as a very great compliment any criticism on my work from a man such as you—

[6] Trollope explained, in reference to the relationship between Lady Glencora and Burgo Fitzgerald in *Can You Forgive Her?*, that "there came to me a letter from a distinguished dignitary of our Church, a man whom all men honoured, treating me with severity for what I was doing." The letter printed here is Trollope's reply. He added that the clergyman's "rejoinder was full of grace, and enabled him to avoid

To George Smith

MS John Murray. SB 281.

November 2—1865   WALTHAM HOUSE, WALTHAM CROSS.
My dear Smith.

I have discussed the matter with Fred Chapman and I now enclose a statement of the nature of the copyrights to be sold and of the price. Of course you will understand that tho' I have affixed a price to each copyright, the offer is made for the whole. The two last novels, Orley Farm and Can You Forgive her are much longer than the others—each being in fact a 5 volume novel. And they are the most popular & have never been issued in a cheap form. I hope the enclosed will give you what information you will require.[7]

           very faithfully
Geo Smith Esq   Anthony Trollope

To George Smith

MS Parrish Collection. B 282.

November 15. 1865.   WALTHAM HOUSE, WALTHAM CROSS.
My dear Smith.

We have been most grieved to hear of the death of Mrs. Gaskell. I do not know how often I was to have met her at your house, and yet never did so. I regret it greatly now. It seems that she must [have] gone quite suddenly. It will have shocked you greatly,—and your wife.

Are you going to print the clerical papers?[8] I have not gone on with them till I found what you were doing; but should do so if I get the proofs from your office.

           Yours always
Geo Smith Esq   Anthony Trollope

Had Mrs. Gaskell finished her story for you?[9]

---

the annoyance of argumentation without abandoning his cause. He said that the subject was so much too long for letters that he hoped I would go and stay a week with him in the country." (*Autobiography*, pp. 182–83.)

    [7] The enclosure has not survived. Smith declined to buy the copyrights; see Trollope to Smith, 19 May 1866.

    [8] Trollope's ten essays on clergymen were published at intervals in the *Pall Mall Gazette* from 20 November 1865 to 25 January 1866; they were issued in volume form by Chapman & Hall as *Clergymen of the Church of England* (1866).

    [9] The last number of Mrs. Gaskell's *Wives and Daughters*, published in the *Cornhill* in January 1866, left the novel incomplete, but by very little.

To J. M. Moir[1]

MS Parrish Collection. SB 283.

Novr. 17. 1865.   WALTHAM HOUSE, WALTHAM CROSS.
Sir.
I shall be most happy to see my name on the list of your stewards.
I will be present at your dinner & support my friend Dr. McCleod on Thursday week next if it be possible, but I fear I shall be obliged to be absent from London on official business.[2]

                                              very faithfully
J M Moir Esq   Anthony Trollope

To George Smith

SB 211 (Sadleir's transcript).

25 November 1865[3]   Waltham Cross
Trollope prefers February or March for beginning *The Claverings.* "Nevertheless, as you know, I always submit in all things."

To George Smith

MS Parrish Collection. SB 284.

Decr. 3. 1865.   WALTHAM HOUSE, WALTHAM CROSS.
My dear Smith.
I have today sent three of the Clerical sketches to 14 Salisbury Street Strand—

                                              Yours always
                                              Anthony Trollope

I hope you wrote—or will write to my brother.

[1] John Macrae Moir (1827–81), journalist; first editor of *People's Magazine*, 1867; one of the compilers of *Men of the Time*; Secretary of London's Scottish Hospital.

[2] The dinner, which marked the Scottish Hospital's 201st anniversary, was held on 30 November 1865, with Norman Macleod in the chair. Trollope attended the dinner and proposed the toast to Macleod. (Macleod's speech was interrupted once or twice by hecklers, probably ultra-evangelicals angry about Macleod's lax views on the Sabbath. This issue soon brought Trollope into print on Macleod's behalf: see Trollope to Smith, 3 February 1866.)

[3] Dated 25 November 1863 in Booth, but the content clearly indicates 1865.

Sir Edward Bulwer Lytton[4] to Trollope

MS Taylor Collection. Taylor, "Letters," p. 7.

Queens Hotel
Decr. 12 1865   Torquay
Sir,

I have long wished to convey to you some intimation of the very great pleasure of your Novels has given me [*sic*]. But I have been hitherto deterred partly by the hope that I might ere this have had the good fortune to make your personal acquaintance, partly by the fear that such intruded praise to an author so successful might be considered rather an impertinence than a compliment.

However, being just fresh from "Miss Mackenzie," I really cannot resist telling you how warmly I admire the conception and execution of the character to which you give that name. It is full of the most delicate beauty.

For that & other favours of the same kind

Believe me yours obliged
E Bulwer Lytton

To Sir Edward Bulwer Lytton

MS Hertfordshire Record Office.

December 20. 1865   WALTHAM HOUSE, WALTHAM CROSS.
Sir.

Your letter of the 12th Instant has gratified me very much. Laudari a laudato[5] is ever the greatest pleasure, and to receive and to possess such a letter as yours from the Author of Pelham will always be to me a source of pride. Our earliest treasures are always our dearest. Pelham was the first of your works that I knew, and I read it at an age which enabled me to submit myself to its influence, as I could not do now to any work of fiction.[6]

I hope that I may yet have the honour and pleasure of making your acquaintance some day.

Yours very faithfully
and much obliged
Anthony Trollope

---

[4] Edward George Bulwer Lytton (1803–73), later Baron Lytton of Knebworth, the novelist.

[5] "To be praised by the praised," Cicero, *Fam.*, V, xii, 7.

[6] Trollope's praise of Bulwer Lytton's fiction, though circumspect, is less than frank. An entry of 19 December 1840 in Trollope's commonplace book speaks of "how wrong [Bulwer] is in his ideas on life & human nature—how false his philosophy is, & to what little purpose he has worked his brain"; "his novels are calculated to

To Chapman & Hall

MS Parrish Collection. B 285.

December 20. 1865   Waltham Cross.
Gentlemen.

With reference to the conversation I had with you to day regarding the republication in America of my work, the Belton Estate, by Messrs. Lippincott of Philadelphia, I must beg you to understand that I am altogether averse to the measure which you propose to adopt in placing early sheets, or rather entirely printed early copies, in the hands of Messrs. Lippincott for publication in America.

I must remind you that you have no legal power to do that which you propose to do, as, in my contract with you in reference to the work in question, I have expressly kept the foreign rights in my own hands. When the book is published by you, and has found its way to the United States, it will of course be open to any American publisher to republish it, and it is open to you to sell to any firm, in the States or elsewhere, any copies of the book as published by you. But it is not within your rights to sell unpublished matter of mine to any one, or to place in the hands of any publisher, at any time, volumes printed at your expense, but bearing on the title page the name of an American firm of publishers.

I must therefore request that you will not send out to the Messrs. Lippincott any copies of the work so prepared, and that you will not place in their hands any copies whatever of the work, till it has been published here.

I request also that you will be good enough to let me know that the copies prepared with the title page I saw today, bearing Messrs. Lippincotts name as publishers, will not be sent to the United States.[7]

> I am Gentlemen,
> Your most obedient Servant

Messrs. Chapman & Hall   Anthony Trollope
193 Piccadilly

---

injure a very young man" because his heroes are "perfectly unnatural" (Appendix A). See also *Autobiography*, pp. 249–51, for an unflattering assessment of Bulwer's fiction.

[7] Trollope's protest was apparently disregarded: Lippincott's first edition has an English imprint on the reverse side of the title page and on the last page (B). Chapman & Hall also angered Trollope by publishing *The Belton Estate*, which was clearly intended as a two-volume novel, in three volumes. Trollope endorsed his schedule of returns "Surreptitiously printed in three volumes" (MS Bodleian). For Trollope's resistance to attempts of a similar kind by other publishers, see Trollope to Strahan, 10 March 1867, and Trollope to Macmillan, 18 October 1870.

To George Smith

Sadleir's transcript, Pickering & Chatto, London. SB 286.

Dec. 21. 1865. Waltham.

* * *

I have no doubt that you will do the best in your power as to the illustrations. The book illustrated by Mrs. Edwards[8] has not yet reached me, but as time presses I answer your note at once. I fear I cannot be in town tomorrow or Saturday. I would suggest that the subject for the illustration should be the entrance into the little parish church of Clavering of Lord Ongar with Julia Brabazon as his bride.

Page 24. "A puir feckless thing, tottering along like" That should be the legend to the picture.

If a vignette be required, as I judge to be your intention, I would propose the two figures of Harry Clavering and Julia Brabazon, where the former stops the latter at the garden gate. Page 1.[9]

* * *

To Lord Houghton

MS Trinity College, Cambridge.

26. Decr. 1865. WALTHAM HOUSE, WALTHAM CROSS.
My dear Lord Houghton

Mrs. Trollope & myself will be most happy to go to you on Tuesday 16. January—if you will allow this instead of the Monday, & stay till Friday morning.[1] I have at present on hand a roving enquiry as to wages (incidental to rinderpest) much more engrossing than any chapters, and perhaps may be able to find out that everybody is starving in Yorkshire.[2]

very faithfully yours
Anthony Trollope

[8] Mary Ellen Edwards (1839–1908), "M. E. E.," a popular illustrator who supplied the drawings for *The Claverings*. See *Illustrators*, pp. 103–13.

[9] Trollope's suggestions for the first number of *The Claverings* (*Cornhill*, February 1866) were followed. For the book edition, the illustration chosen here was used as frontispiece, but the vignettes were omitted throughout.

[1] Among Lord Houghton's other guests at Fryston in January 1866 was Lady Rose Sophia Mary Fane (1834–1921), daughter of the 11th Earl of Westmorland. An intelligent girl with a wide knowledge of public affairs and a love of literature and the arts, Lady Rose wrote a full account of the house party to her mother. "I wish I had never seen Mr. Trollope," she said of her first meeting with the novelist; "I think he is detestable—vulgar, noisy & domineering—a mixture of Dickens vulgarity & Mr. Burtons selfsufficiency—as unlike his books as possible." But she found Rose Trollope "a quiet sort of woman & wd. be well enough only she has perfectly white hair which is coiffé en cheveux [i.e., bareheaded]—in the most fashionable way with (last night) a little rose stuck in it wh: looks most absurd." (Weigall MSS, Kent County Archives.)

[2] An 1865 outbreak of rinderpest, or cattle plague, caused thousands of cattle to

THE
CORNHILL MAGAZINE.

FEBRUARY, 1866.

The Claverings

by *F. . . . . . .*

CHAPTER I.

JULIA BRABAZON.

THE gardens of Clavering Park were removed some three hundred yards from the large, square, sombre-looking stone mansion which was the country-house of Sir Hugh Clavering, the eleventh baronet of that name; and in these gardens, which had but little of beauty to recommend them, I will introduce my readers to two of the personages with whom I wish to make them acquainted in the following story. It was now the end of August, and the parterres, beds, and bits of lawn were dry, disfigured, and almost ugly, from the effects of a long drought. In gardens to which care and labour are given abundantly, flower-beds will be pretty, and grass will be green, let the weather be what it may; but care and labour were but scantily bestowed on the Clavering Gardens, and everything was yellow, adust, harsh, and dry. Over the burnt turf towards a gate

7.

"A VERY PRETTY LITTLE COTTAGE ALONG LIKE—"

Illustration for *The Claverings*, by M. E. Edwards

To Miss Cleveland[3]

MS Parrish Collection.

December 27. 1865
My dear Miss Cleveland

What am I to think of myself when on the above date I sit down to answer your letter of 30 Sept.? And yet—I was so glad to get it,—as was my wife to have a note from your mother. We have by no means forgotten that passage in the Arabia[4] when your party and ours were so pleasantly contiguous,—nor the times when we met again in Massachussetts. I wish I could think such meetings might be renewed;—but how are we to think so, when you come to England & do not make us out? We accuse you of sin against a friendship which we thought to exist,—and then pardon you, hoping that the pardon may have followed repentance as all pardon should.

Touching your late wars & present politics, I cannot, even to you, but say a word, as I do to all Americans to whom I write. Your triumph has been a great triumph to me,—& a triumph to a very large party in England who think as I think. Americans are mistaken who suppose that here in England there exists anything approaching to a general feeling against the cause of their government. You have here as much sympathy as any one people has a right to expect from another; and this sympathy, where it does exist, is very warm. As regards myself, my anxiety for your success could not have been greater had I been myself an American. It has been complete and I, who have ventured to prophesy a little on the matter, have been triumphant.

You ask me after Lily Dale, your namesake.[5] I can assure you that if she ever should marry any one in print, it would be John Eames. No other marriage would be possible to her in accordance with the poetical justice of romance. But I think there will be no marriage for her in print. As far as she has gone she has been successful to me her literary father, and it is ill meddling with such successes when they have been achieved. And why should a novelist do so, seeing that a new story is much the easier task of the two.[6]

---

be slaughtered. Farmers and landowners suffered heavy losses, and this led to a depression of agricultural wages at a time when the prices of meat and milk were naturally high.

[3] Perhaps Eliza Callahan Cleveland (*b.* 1839), daughter of the widowed Mrs. S. P. Cleveland. (Mrs. Cleveland was a close friend of Charles Eliot Norton.)

[4] Trollope and his wife had left Liverpool for Boston aboard the *Arabia* on 24 August 1861.

[5] Trollope may indeed have named Lily Dale after Miss Cleveland: he began writing *The Small House at Allington* in April 1862, immediately on his return from the United States.

[6] Trollope did reopen the Lily Dale and Johnny Eames romance; in fact, he began writing *The Last Chronicle of Barset* the very next month (in January 1866).

I have made a mess of my sheets of paper in this note,[7]—as you will have found out. I hope it will not prevent you from accepting it. Pray accept my kindest regards & give the same to your mother. When you come hither again we hope your engagements will allow you to come to us.

Believe me dear Miss Cleveland
                                   Most sincerely Yours
                                   Anthony Trollope

To John [? Tilley]
MS Parrish Collection. B 287.

31. Decr. 65.   WALTHAM HOUSE, WALTHAM CROSS.
Dear John
   I have told the publishers to send you a copy of a good book, called Belton Estate, which will improve your mind, and the minds of your children if you and they will attend to it.
   Ever so many happy new years to you all.
                                        Thine A. T.

1866

To W. W. F. Synge
MS Parrish Collection.

2 Jany 65 [1866]   WALTHAM HOUSE, WALTHAM CROSS.
My dear Synge
   I only just now settled where I should be on Wednesday, & could not therefore write before.
   I shall be at the Garrick, & shall dine there,—but must leave the club to go down to Chelmsford at 7.45. If it would suit you to dine with me at 6.30 pm, leave word at the club by 4 pm.
   Come to me on Saturday 27 January? Pray do. The Bells will be here. You must come before you go, if only to abuse Lord Clarendon.[8]
                                        Thine always
                                        A. T.

---

[7] The upper right-hand corner of the first page is torn away.
[8] George William Frederick Villiers (1800–1870), 4th Earl of Clarendon; statesman. Since Villiers served as Foreign Secretary in 1853–58, 1865–66, and 1868–70, he was Synge's chief at the time of this letter.

To George Smith

MS Bodleian. Excerpt, Hamer, p. 214.

Jan 2. 1866.   WALTHAM HOUSE, WALTHAM CROSS.
My dear Smith.

Thanks about Mrs. Pollock.[9] You will have understood from Mr Enoch that I do not at all want any change in the pages of the Cornhill. I had thought that the heading had run thro' the pages in the S. H of All.[1]

Would [you] like next year to bring out a novel in separate numbers, (20) after the manner of Orley Farm? If so, would you wish me to propose terms or would you propose them?[2]

I should ask the same sum that Chapman gave me for Can You Forgive Her. But he buys only half the remainder of the copyright, which is an arrangement you do not like,—and are quite right in disliking.

You will answer this quite at your leisure.

I want to do two more clerical sketches—10 in all—if that will not be too many.

Always yours
Anthony Trollope

To George Smith

Bibliography, p. 232.

4 January 1866

Trollope asks for a comment to be printed in the *Pall Mall Gazette* on Conway's article in the *Fortnightly* about the American war.[3]

---

[9] Juliet Creed Pollock (*d.* 1899), subsequently a contributor to *St. Paul's Magazine.* Trollope was a good friend of Mrs. Pollock and her husband, William Frederick Pollock (1815–88), later Sir William, a barrister and from 1874 to 1886 the Queen's Remembrancer. Trollope was also a neighbor of the Pollocks from 1873, when he moved to Montagu Square. W. F. Pollock's *Personal Remembrances* (1887) makes frequent mention of Trollope.

[1] Trollope refers to *The Claverings.* As with *The Small House at Allington,* the title of the novel was printed at the top of each page.

[2] Trollope began writing *The Last Chronicle of Barset* on 21 January 1866. Negotiations with Smith for this work can be followed in a number of subsequent letters (Smith to Trollope, 3 February 1866, 6 February 1866, 24 February 1866, and 26 February 1866; and Trollope to Smith, 3 February 1866, 6 February 1866, and 25 February 1866). These letters clearly illustrate the difficulties of serial publication. See also Mary Hamer, "Working Diary for *The Last Chronicle of Barset,*" *TLS,* 24 December 1971, p. 1606.

[3] "England and the United States," *Pall Mall Gazette,* 8 January 1866, pp. 2–3 (signed by Trollope); in response to Moncure D. Conway's "America, France, and England," *Fortnightly,* 3 (1 January 1866), 442–59.

To George Smith

MS Bodleian.

Jany 4. 66   Chelmsford
Dear Smith.

Do not mind sending the proof of the travelling sketches. The reader will look to it.

I am very sorry to hear you are so unwell. You want a holyday.

Yours always
Anthony Trollope

You should go out with the Brighton harriers once a week.

To ?

MS Parrish Collection.

January 22—1866   WALTHAM HOUSE, WALTHAM CROSS.
My dear Sir.

I shall be most happy to take the chair at the dinner to be given to my old friend Mr Bokenham.[4]

Thursday the 8th. will suit me very well.

Perhaps I shall hear then,—or earlier if need be,—what is the nature of the testimonial proposed to be given. I shall be most happy to subscribe but shall be glad to know what amounts of subscriptions will be needed.

Yours very faithfully
Anthony Trollope

Perhaps you will let me know as soon as you conveniently can whether I may regard Thursday 8th. as the day fixed.

To George Smith

Bibliography, p. 232.

30 January 1866

Trollope offers articles on Church endowments and Church patronage for the *Pall Mall Gazette*.[5]

---

[4] William Bokenham, a Post Office employee since 1820 and the Controller of the Circulation Office. The dinner was given on Friday, 9 February, at the London Coffee House, Ludgate Hill. Trollope gave a speech, which *The Times* described as "admirable" (10 February 1866, p. 12).

[5] See Smith to Trollope, 3 February 1866.

To George Frick

MS Brown University.

2. Feb. 1866   WALTHAM HOUSE, WALTHAM CROSS.

Dear Sir

Will you let me know as soon as you conveniently can where we are to dine on Friday next, & at what hour.

Yours faithfully

Geo. Frick Esq   Anthony Trollope

To George Smith

Bibliography, p. 232.

3 February 1866

Trollope asks for the urgent insertion of a note in the *Pall Mall Gazette*.[6]

George Smith to Trollope

MS Bodleian.

Feby 3rd. 1866   45, PALL MALL. S.W.

My dear Trollope

We have three Church articles under weigh and we shall presently have our space filled with Political articles; I am therefore afraid of asking you for more Church articles at present—

I have been considering your kind proposal of a serial. We do not know what may happen before twelve months have passed; a new sixpenny periodical or a sixpenny serial would leave us very little hope of success with a shilling serial and we are afraid to arrange for one so long in advance. What we would be glad to do would be to agree to pay you £3000 for the right to print any number of copies in one form, to be decided on by us, of a Book of the size of twenty numbers of "Orley Farm." The copyright and profit of any future editions in a different form from the first to be equally divided between you and S E & Co.

Believe me

Yours sincerely

Anthony Trollope Esq   G Smith

---

[6] "Mr. Anthony Trollope and the 'Saturday Review,' " *Pall Mall Gazette*, 5 February 1866, p. 3 (signed by Trollope). In "An Amateur Theologian," 3 February 1866, pp. 131–33, the *Saturday Review* had objected strongly to Trollope's article "The Fourth Commandment," *Fortnightly Review*, 3 (15 January 1866), 529–38, which had commended Norman Macleod's strictures against Scottish sabbatarians. In the *Pall Mall Gazette* letter, Trollope charged that the *Saturday Review* had "no special fault to find with my remarks,—always excepting the great vice of a novelist choosing to make remarks." (The *Saturday Review*'s title, "An Amateur Theologian," was probably an allusion to the *Pall Mall Gazette*'s celebrated "Amateur Casual": see Trollope to Smith, 25 February 1866.)

To George Smith
MS Bodleian. B 288.

3. February. 1866.   WALTHAM HOUSE, WALTHAM CROSS.
My dear Smith.

I do not think that I have any objection to make to the terms you propose about my new novel. I should wish there to be an understanding as to the period of publication,—viz that it shall all appear in the course of 1867, & 1868;—also as to the payment, which you will probably not object to make by instalments of £150 a month from 1 January 1867 to 1 August 1868,—on condition of course that so much of the MS is in your hands. I purpose finishing it by next Christmas. I will see you tomorrow for a moment at about 3.30 pm if you can spare the time.

                                          Yours always
Geo Smith Esq   Anthony Trollope

George Smith to Trollope
MS Bodleian.

Feby 6th. 1866   45, PALL MALL. S.W.
My dear Trollope

Enclosed is the little agreement.[7] I have put it so that if we like the Book may run to 30 Numbers. This is not in exact accordance with what was said today but quite in conformity with the spirit of our arrangement I think— If you think that having to deliver the 1st. No in June will make any difference to you the agreement must be altered, but I suppose it will suit you quite as well to deliver the first portion in June as later.

                                          Yours sincerely
Anthony Trollope Esq   G Smith

To George Smith
MS (Trollope's copy) Bodleian. B 289.

6 Feb 1866   WALTHAM HOUSE, WALTHAM CROSS.
My dear Smith.

I quite agree as to the enclosed and send a copy signed by myself— I return the original that you may insert the change of date, 1866—for 1865 inserted in error.

But it is essential, in reference to the proposed 30 numbers, to be prepared for such a division if it be contemplated. It would not be practicable to divide 20 numbers into 30 equal parts, unless the work be specially done with this intent. I commonly divide a number of 32 pages (such as the numbers of "Orley Farm") into 4 chapters each. If you

---

[7] The terms were those offered by Smith in his letter to Trollope of 3 February.

wish the work to be so arranged as to run either to 20 or to 30 numbers, I must work each of the 20 numbers by 6 chapters, taking care that the chapters run so equally, two and two, as to make each four into one equal part or each 6 into one equal part— There will be some trouble in this, but having a mechanical mind I think I can do it. If you wish it I will do so. Had you made up your mind for the sixpenny venture I could of course do the work more easily and more pleasantly.

You will understand that I wish to suit your views altogether; but that it is necessary that you should say—Write it in 20 parts or in 30 parts— or in parts to suit either number. And you will also understand that if your mind be made up either to 30 or to 20, you need not put my mechanical genius to work.

To Mr. Gibbon
MS Parrish Collection. SB 290.

12. Feb 66
Sunday   Cambridge
My dear Mr Gibbon.

Thursday will do very well, and I am much obliged to you and Mr Stoner for coming. There is a train leaves Shoreditch at 5.10 pm. which will bring you to Waltham Cross in good time for dinner. I will have an old one-eyed Irishman to meet you. I am sorry that you should stay with me so short a time the first time I have you under my roof—

very affectionately yours
Anthony Trollope

To Mrs. Harriet Knower
MS Parrish Collection.

Feb 18. 66.   WALTHAM HOUSE, WALTHAM CROSS.
My dear Mrs. Knower.

Shall I ever again be forgiven? I have your last note before me now,— and Mary's dear kind letter;—have had them constantly before me, always meaning to write. And I can only plead that I work harder than most men, and have fewer half hours at my own disposal. I always mean to write letters when evening comes, but at evening I am tired and hate the sight of a pen.[8]

We were so glad to have Mary's photograph! It is now hung in our bed room among others of people whom we love well;—and I wish yours

---

[8] Years later Trollope contradicted these sentiments, saying that he was a prompt correspondent (Trollope to Knower, 30 September 1874). See also Trollope to Christie, 29 February 1864.

were there also. Mary wrote as tho she had on her mind some idea that something might bring her over here. I wish it would—and you with her. I often think of the one evening when you sat on our lawn and complained that I scolded you.

I hardly know what to think of the position of the two Countries. It seems to me that Mr. Seward says everything he can say to drive us into ill will. Surely of all statesmen he is the most insolent! And what is to be gained by it? War with the States would be very dreadful to us;—but it would be as bad to you? Whether you came off first or second best, your commerce would be about ruined, and your debt would be doubled! I have all thro been very true to American interests, but the tone of your despatches to England riles me sadly.[9] However, I thoroughly believe that it will lead to nothing.

Here we are in terrible distress about the rinderpest,—of which plague among the cattle we do not at all know how to rid ourselves. The effect for the present is not as bad as the future prospect. Meat is plentiful now, because men kill their herds to prevent the incidence of the disease;—but this time next year we shall have nothing but foreign beef steaks to comfort us.

Our second trouble is the Fenianism which you hatch for us in New York. But we do not care so much about that, as we are able to keep the Fenians down. Hitherto the poor Fenians have had by far the worst of it.[10]

Pray forgive me for being so long silent, & pray write again. Rose sends her kindest love to you & Mary—as do I also.

Your affectionate friend
Anthony Trollope

[9] Through William Henry Seward (1801–72), the Secretary of State, the American government repeatedly claimed that the British building and manning of ships that became Confederate cruisers (notably the *Alabama* and *Shenandoah*, which had preyed very successfully on Northern shipping) was a violation of neutrality. The recently published correspondence between the British and American governments, especially Seward's dispatch of 30 November 1865, "riled" many Englishmen. The *Saturday Review* (17 February 1866, p. 188) described the dispatch as "couched in language as offensive to the English Government as anything could be that should not be wholly inconsistent with the maintenance of friendly relations," and held that the British Foreign Secretary "took the wisest course in declining to enter into arguments and examine assertions put forward in so uncourteous a manner." In 1871 Britain agreed to pay damages to be set by arbitrators, and in 1872 $15,500,000 was awarded. In *North America* Trollope had frequently criticized Seward, especially for his truculent attitude toward England and his policy of publishing his sometimes arrogant dispatches.

[10] The Fenian movement was founded simultaneously in New York and Dublin in 1858 for the purpose of achieving Irish independence through armed uprising. The British had moved against the Fenians in 1865 and 1866, putting down several small uprisings and suspending the Habeas Corpus Act in Ireland. But Fenianism continued an important force in Ireland, and many Fenians supported Home Rule, the Land League, and the activities of Parnell, all of which Trollope strongly opposed, most pointedly in his unfinished last novel, *The Landleaguers* (1883).

George Smith to Trollope

MS Bodleian.

Feby 24th. 1866   45, PALL MALL. S.W.

My dear Trollope

My man has not yet come to London, but I will decide on numbers equal of 20 pages of "Orley Farm" and chance it—

Would you mind putting Frederick Greenwood's[11] name down at the Garrick as a Gentleman of the Literary Profession his address is Hornsey? I will second him and I hope it will be all right. I don't think he has many enemies.

Yours sincerely

Anthony Trollope Esqre   G Smith

To George Smith

SB 291 (Sadleir's transcript).

25 February 1866

*   *   *

[Trollope will write *The Last Chronicle* in 30 numbers of 21 pages each.] I will put down Greenwood's name tomorrow,[12]—simply saying "Literature" as his profession. Pity it isn't his brother as I should have had such pleasure in entering his as a "casual."[1]

*   *   *

[11] Frederick Greenwood (1830–1909), journalist and editor. Greenwood had suggested the idea of the *Pall Mall Gazette* to Smith, and was its editor from 1865 to 1880. He was also connected with the *Cornhill*: along with G. H. Lewes and E. D. Cook, he had taken over editing the magazine when Thackeray left in 1862, and from 1864 to 1868 he was in name the sole editor, although Smith continued to do much of the editorial work.

[12] Trollope proposed Greenwood for the Garrick Club on 3 March, and Greenwood was elected on 21 April.

[1] James Greenwood, Frederick's brother, had posed as a homeless pauper and had spent a bitterly cold night in the open shed used to house "casuals" at the Lambeth Workhouse. His account of the experience, "A Night in a Casual Ward," *Pall Mall Gazette*, 12, 13, and 15 January 1866 (signed "An Amateur Casual"), roused widespread concern. Trollope noted that the author's anonymity increased the articles' effect: "I was more than once assured that Lord Houghton was the man. I heard it asserted also that I myself had been the hero." He added that the articles "had done more to establish the sale of the journal than all the legal lore of Stephen, or the polemical power of Higgins, or the critical acumen of Lewes." (*Autobiography*, p. 200.)

George Smith to Trollope
MS Bodleian.

February 26th. 1866   45, PALL MALL. S.W.
My dear Trollope
It does not much matter whether the story be divided into 30 or 32 nos and if you find the former number more convenient let it be so. My notion was that if we had 32 numbers we might publish the Book at 18/ —charging 1/. to the public (about 8d. to the Booksellers) for binding each volume, whereas if we have 30 nos we must make the price 17/— which is an odd sort of price— Then as to time if we published it in monthly parts we might have given two double parts at the end and so completed the publication in 30 months— But I have an idea of weekly parts and then the whole publication would be completed in 32 weeks.[2]
Many thanks for your kindness to F. G. and to

Anthony Trollope Esqre

Yours sincerely
G Smith

To W. H. Gregory[3]
MS Berg Collection.

March. 6. 1866.   WALTHAM HOUSE, WALTHAM CROSS.
My dear Gregory
I thought it better to write a line to F. Lawley before proposing him at the Garrick, and he has written to me, declining for the present,—alleging various reasons.
As I told you that I would put his name down I write to explain why I do not do so—

Yours always
Anthony Trollope

[2] This was in fact the manner of publication finally settled upon: *The Last Chronicle of Barset* appeared in 32 sixpenny parts issued weekly from 1 December 1866 to 6 July 1867. The first volume of the book issue was published in March 1867, and the second volume in July 1867.

[3] William Henry Gregory (1817–92), later Sir William; MP for Galway, 1857–71; Governor of Ceylon, 1871–77. Gregory had been at Harrow with Trollope, but he and Trollope did not become friends until Trollope was stationed in Ireland (where he was a frequent visitor at Coole Park, Gregory's country home in Galway). Gregory later wrote movingly of Trollope: see Lady Gregory, ed., *Sir William Gregory, K.C.M.G.: An Autobiography* (1894), pp. 35–38.

To Mrs. J. E. Millais

MS Pierpont Morgan Library.

March 7. 66   WALTHAM HOUSE, WALTHAM CROSS.

My dear Mrs. Millais

Mrs. Trollope & I will be very happy to dine with you on Friday. On the Wednesday she goes one way & I another. I dine with Mr Phillips at Sydenham & that looks very like the Cosmopolitan afterwards. I acknowledge with all my heart that your drawing room is more comfortable & prettier, & more engaging; but really the Cosmopolitan is warm, if it be nothing else.

Yours always truly
Anthony Trollope

To ?

MS Parrish Collection. B 292.

March 8. 66   WALTHAM HOUSE, WALTHAM CROSS.

Sir.

The house which I had chiefly in my minds eye when I described Mr. Thornes house in Barchester Towers was a place called, I think, Montacute House,[4] belonging to Mr Phelips—not far from Yeovil in Somersetshire. But the house was not in all respects such as I described;—and indeed in some respects was very different. Ullathorne, if I remember,— (for I have not the book by me,)—was described as standing with two parlors, one at right angles to the other.[5] Montacute house is straight.

But for colour of stone, irregularity of design falling into and creating lines of architectural beauty, and for general picturesque forms of stone work without such magnificence as that of Longleat[6] or Hatfield,[7] Montacute House is the best example I know in England.

Your obt Servant
Anthony Trollope

[4] Montacute House was an Elizabethan mansion built for Sir Edward Phelips; construction probably began ca. 1590.

[5] *Barchester Towers*, chap. xxii.

[6] Longleat (near Warminster in Wiltshire), the seat of the Marquess of Bath, was begun in 1568, the earlier house having been largely destroyed in a fire the previous year.

[7] Hatfield House (near St. Albans in Hertfordshire), the property of the Marquess of Salisbury, was chiefly Jacobean in construction. In *The New Zealander*, Trollope suggested that Hatfield, Longleat, and Montacute were neglected masterpieces (chap. xii). In *Doctor Thorne*, he compared Greshambury House to Longleat and Hatfield (chap. i).

To George Smith

MS John Murray. *Commentary*, p. 268; B 293.

9 March 66.　　　　　　　　　　　WALTHAM HOUSE, WALTHAM CROSS.
My dear Smith—
　　If you like to publish NB in the C. H. M.[8] for £300 you shall do so. If you like to publish 1500 for £300 you shall do so. If you like to buy the copyright for £500—(undertaking not to disclose the name without my permission,) you shall do so.

Yours always
A. T.

To Robert Browning[9]

MS Library of Congress. B 294.

9 March 1866　　　　　　　　　　　　　　　GARRICK CLUB
My dear Browning.
　　Our dinner is at St. James hotel, Piccadilly, Francatelli's,[1] at 7—PM on Wednesday next. Do come to us. Your coming will not be taken, nor is our wish for you to come, intended as in any way, binding you to anything more on our behalf than the light of your face on our little dinner. Not but that we are *most anxious* for your stouter assistance if at any time you can give it to us. I think we shall have a nice dinner.[2]

Yours always
Anthony Trollope

---

[8] *Nina Balatka*, here offered to Smith for the *Cornhill Magazine*, was a novel Trollope had determined to publish anonymously. Trollope said of *Nina Balatka* and its companion volume *Linda Tressel*: "I determined . . . to begin a course of novels anonymously, in order that I might see whether I could succeed in obtaining a second identity. . . . Both [novels] were written immediately after visits to the towns in which the scenes are laid,—Prague, namely, and Nuremberg. Of course I had endeavoured to change not only my manner of language, but my manner of storytelling also. . . . English life in them there was none. There was more of romance proper than had been usual with me. And I made an attempt at local colouring, at descriptions of scenes and places, which has not been usual with me. In all this I am confident that I was in a measure successful. . . . I know that the stories are good, but they missed the object with which they had been written." (*Autobiography*, pp. 204–6.) See Trollope to Smith, 21 March 1866.

[9] Browning probably met Trollope as a result of his friendship with T. A. Trollope (see *What I Remember*, chap. xxix). William Allingham's diary for 26 May 1868 reads: "Lunch at Browning's. Talk runs chiefly on his forthcoming new Poem in many thousand lines [*The Ring and the Book*]. . . . He has told the story over and over again to various friends; offered it to A. Trollope to turn into a novel, but Trollope couldn't manage it; then R. B. thought, 'why not take it myself?' " (H. Allingham and D. Radford, eds., *William Allingham: A Diary* [1907], p. 180.)

[1] Charles Elmé Francatelli (1805–76) was chef and manager at the St. James Hotel; earlier, he had been chef at the Reform Club.

[2] On 19 February Browning wrote to Isa Blagden: "A. Trollope has invited me to

To Cholmondeley Pennell[3]

MS Parrish Collection. SB 295.

11 March 1866. WALTHAM HOUSE, WALTHAM CROSS.

Mr A Trollope presents his compliments to Mr C. Pennell. On Wednesday next Mr Trollope will be at the Athenaeum at 10 AM, if it will suit Mr Pennell to call at the Club at that hour.

To ?[4]

MS Parrish Collection. B 296.

March. 12. 1866 WALTHAM HOUSE, WALTHAM CROSS.

My dear Sir

If it be not too late, let the words scandala magnata be altered to scandals.

I have made search, and I believe after all I am wrong about the word magnatum. I cannot quite explain to you, all my reasons for having supposed myself to be right.

Yours always
(in a penitential spirit)
Anthony Trollope

To George Smith

Commentary, p. 268. SB 297.

21 March 1866

*   *   *

All right about N. B.[5] Would you kindly send her back—to Waltham? She won't mind travelling alone. Whether I shall put her by, or try an-

---

a dinner of the Proprietors and Staff of the Fortnightly Review,—I don't know why—for I never gave them a line in my life. Their review or Magazine is very good and respectable, but hardly successful I should fear, as a speculation. The 'Pall Mall,' which was in a sorry condition, is now in high vogue,—so do things alter." (Edward C. McAleer, ed., *Dearest Isa: Robert Browning's Letters to Isabella Blagden* [Austin, Texas, 1951], pp. 230–31.) Browning replied to Trollope on 10 March: "I hardly know whether it is necessary to repeat that I *will* dine with you all and be most happy to do so, next Wednesday—as I said so at first; but 'plus non vitiat,—' they hold in law matters. You are all too kind and generous—and I have nothing but the gratitude for that to give in return." (MS Taylor Collection.)

[3] Henry Cholmondeley Pennell (1837–1915), Inspector of Sea Fisheries, 1866–75; author of books on sports and natural history. Trollope's account books (Parrish Collection) show that he dined with Pennell on the evening of 13 March.

[4] Perhaps Frederick Enoch, who was seeing *Clergymen of the Church of England* through the press (Smith, Elder printed the book for Chapman & Hall).

[5] Smith had declined *Nina Balatka*.

other venture with her I don't quite know.⁶ At any rate you are too much the gent to claim acquaintance if you meet her in the street.

*   *   *

To Lord Houghton
MS Trinity College, Cambridge.

21. March. 1866.   WALTHAM HOUSE, WALTHAM CROSS.
My dear Lord Houghton.

Will you dine with us of the Fortnightly on Wednesday 11. April at 7. I will let you know the locus in quo if you will kindly say that you will come.

very faithfully yours
Anthony Trollope

Alexander Strahan to Trollope
MS Bodleian.

3d. April 1866
Anthony Trollope Esq   148 STRAND, LONDON, W.C.
Dear Sir,

I have much pleasure in sending you the accompanying cheque at Dr. Macleods request. And while I am writing about the *Garrick* let me say that I should like very well to become a member. If you think me worthy of admission I will be much obliged by your proposing me. And I feel pretty sure that Dr. Macleod or Mr. Dallas or Charles Reade will do any seconding that is needed. But if you don't think I would be a desirable member (as very likely I would not be) please let the matter drop and forgive me for suggesting it.⁷

I do not know if you have ever seen *The Argosy*. I was the projector of it and I have now become the publisher and proprietor. Hitherto it has not done well, but it must do well yet for it is very good and very cheap.⁸ I mean to make a cabinet question of it, as they say in the House of Commons, and to stand or fall by its success. By and by I will take leave to put myself into communication with you for a regular three-volume story. Meantime let me ask you to give me a short sketch of say ten or

---

⁶ See Blackwood to Trollope, 14 April 1866.

⁷ Trollope did not propose Strahan; nor did Strahan ever become a member of the Garrick Club.

⁸ *The Argosy* was initially announced by Sampson Low in November 1865, but it was transferred to Strahan at the last moment. By December 1866 it was in such difficulty as to be "cheaply purchasable," and early in 1867 it was in fact bought by Mrs. Henry Wood (*Commentary*, p. 278). See Virtue to Trollope, 15 November 1866.

twelve pages, and I will gladly pay you your own terms. And if you could kindly favour me with this by the 16th. or 17th. inst it would be in time for the May No. which completes the first Volume.[9]
A single line of reply at your convenience will much oblige

Yours very truly
A. Strahan

John Blackwood[1] to Trollope
MS Bodleian Library. B 298.

April 14/66   Edinburgh
My dear Sir
  It gives me very great pleasure to receive your letter to Mr. Langford[2] & to see the frank way in which you accept the remarks I ventured to make on Nina Balatka.
  I accept at once the alteration you propose in the terms I offered and

[9] Trollope endorsed this letter "Agreed to write four stories, for the Argosy at £60 each. 13 pages each story / 6 April 1866." Three stories by Trollope appeared in *The Argosy*: "Father Giles of Ballymoy" (May 1866); "Lotta Schmidt" (July 1866); and "The Misfortunes of Frederick Pickering" (September 1866). These were reprinted in *Lotta Schmidt* (1867).
  [1] John Blackwood (1818–79), from 1852 head of the well-known Edinburgh publishing house founded by his father, William Blackwood; editor of *Blackwood's Magazine*, 1845–79; publisher of George Eliot's works. Blackwood and Trollope became very good friends.
  [2] Joseph Munt Langford (1809–84), dramatic critic and head of the London branch of Blackwoods; a Garrick Club acquaintance of Trollope. After Smith rejected *Nina Balatka*, Trollope evidently spoke to Langford. The manuscript was then sent on to Blackwood, who wrote on 10 April a long critique to Langford: "I have read Nina Balatka . . . & still am much puzzled what to say. The story shows the hand of the accomplished artist throughout & nothing could be more masterly than the way in which the opening sentence at once arrests the readers attention. Ninas warm frank outpouring of her love is a most beautiful piece of painting but as the story goes on one cannot sympathise with her in her love for her cold suspicious Jew." After considerable negative criticism, Blackwood continued: "Mr. Trollope has so skilfully thrown a perfectly foreign Prague atmosphere about all his characters so perfectly un English that there is the sort of air of hardness about the story that one feels in reading a translation. The great merit of the Tale seems to me the clearness with which it stands out. There is an individuality about it which will make any one who reads it remember it. Whether this is sufficient to make it really popular & stand out from the ruck as the work of an anonymous author is a doubtful point. My own feeling is that it would not produce such an effect in the Magazine or sell to such an extent afterwards as to make it wise for me to offer a large sum for the copyright. . . . The secret I would keep strictly & as there is nothing in the Tale to recall the popular painter of Englishwomen in the drawing room & on the Lawn I do not think he would be detected. . . . You can convey this letter to Mr. Trollope & whatever may be the result of the negociation I wish him to understand how much I feel gratified, by his confidence in me a personal stranger to him & also by his desire to have a tale of his in the old Magazine." (MS Bodleian).

accordingly agree to give you £250—for the appearance of the story in the Magazine and £200—for the remainder of the Copyright.

I agree with you that Nina herself is very much of a real character and there is a great charm & purity in the way she pours forth her love. This made me all the more savage at the Jew when he tried to disgrace such a mistress by making her purloin her fathers key & it was quite a relief to me when I found you got her out of the scrape which you do most ingeniously.

I am overdone with serials in the Magazine at present and I hope you will not care if I postpone the start of Nina for a month or two. Indeed it would not be a good plan to begin the story at a time when I have no doubt my readers think I have too many papers in parts going on already.

I intend to be in London about the middle of May when I look forward with much interest to making your personal acquaintance.

Hoping that the correspondence we have now entered into may prove a pleasant & advantageous one to us both

Believe me dear Sir
Yours very truly
John Blackwood

Anthony Trollope Esq

To George Smith

Bibliography, p. 232.

20 April 1866[3]
Trollope sends an article on Ladies' Bazaars for the *Pall Mall Gazette*.[4]

To W. H. Russell

MS Taylor Collection.

1 May. 1866   WALTHAM HOUSE, WALTHAM CROSS.

Take notice.
to wit.
On Wednesday 9 May the Fortnightly dine at Star & Garter Richmond at 6.30 pm—instead of Willis at 7. pm. on which occasion and at which place, & *at the said hour* let Dr. W. H. Russell appear in the flesh before us—or worse will ensue.

Anthony Trollope

[3] Misdated 1865 by Sadleir.
[4] "Bazaars for Charity," *Pall Mall Gazette*, 21 April 1866, p. 12.

To Frederic Chapman

MS Parrish Collection. B 299.

May. 11. 1866.   Conway[5]

My dear Chapman.

I made attempts to see you on Monday, Wednesday & Thursday, but failed. I therefore went to W H Smith on Thursday morning,—as you will probably have learned from him. It was necessary to explain that two of the novels, Orley Farm and Can You Forgive Her can not well be brought out in one volume each and that they should be republished in two—at 6/ each. I told him also that my price for my half copyrights was £2650— When I made them up, I found that this was the sum to which they would come. I suppose you would let me have your half for the same. I shall be back home by the end of next week.

Very faithfully yours
Anthony Trollope

To W. J. Godby

MS Parrish Collection.

[? May 1866][6]   Capel Curig[7]

My dear Godby.

I have just got your note & you will have gotten mine.

We cannot be in Shrewsbury till the evening tomorrow; but as we shall dine at Pentre-Voelas,[8] I will walk up to you directly I get in.

Yours always
Any Trollope

To Octavian Blewitt

MS Royal Literary Fund.

11 May 1866   WALTHAM HOUSE, WALTHAM CROSS.

My dear Mr Blewitt.

I particularly wanted to see you and much regret that I failed in getting to the meeting on Wednesday.

Would it be possible to do anything further for Mrs. Coulson?[9] *She is literally pennyless.* Mrs. Bell wants me to bring it forward, and I know well how terrible is the necessity. But it is useless doing so, if the case

---

[5] A town in Caernarvonshire, Wales.

[6] Probably this date, when Trollope and Rose were in the north of Wales.

[7] A village in Caernarvon, in the north of Wales; tourist center for people ascending Snowdon.

[8] A village in Denbigh, in the north of Wales.

[9] A slip of the pen for "Coulton."

would not admit of a favourable reception. Her own literary merits are not great— Her private merits in taking on herself the burden of the family of her brother, who, as you know, himself did considerable literary work, were very great indeed. Her case is most cruelly hard. Will you tell me what you think.

Yours always faithfully
Anthony Trollope

If I thought the fund would give her £25—I would bring her case forward.[1]

To George Smith

MS John Murray. B 300.

Private

May 19. 1866.   WALTHAM HOUSE, WALTHAM CROSS.
My dear Smith.

I was at your place today, and finding you out of town I made an appointment with Enoch for seeing you at ½ past 2 on Monday,—which appointment I will keep. I want to see you again about my copyrights. I have a dislike to suggesting to you again to buy them, but the circumstances are altered,—as I will explain,—and I think we are intimate enough for me to ask you to tell me, without fuss and in the way of friendship, whether it would suit you to have them.

Chapman wishes to part with them & to realise what he can get for them, and W. H. Smith has offered to buy the bulk of them, (I will tell you which when I see you) for £3000,—or to hire them all at a certain rate for 5 years. I will not sell my half of them he wishes to buy for £1500, but have no objection to let them for the 5 years. But Chapman is willing to take the £1500 for his half,—and has told me that if I can make any bargain for the whole which will give me what I want for my half, he will take that sum for his share. Perhaps this may enable us to deal. Could you consider it again & let me know what you can give? I send you the list. Those that have an L. before them are electrotyped, & you would have the stereos.[2] The stock in hand at cost price of all but the two first, (Can You Forgive Her & Orley Farm) would come to £230—which wd. go to Chapman. As regards those two he proposes that the purchaser should give him 3/6 a copy for what he has. The books are in two

---

[1] This was Trollope's second intercession on Sophia Coulton's behalf (see Trollope to the Committee of the Royal Literary Society, 2 November 1863). In addition to the initial grant of £50 in November 1863, Mrs. Coulton received £50 in January 1865 and £25 in July 1867. No grant, however, resulted from this letter.

[2] Trollope is using the terms "stereos" and "electros" interchangeably. In the stereotype process, plates were cast from plaster molds; in the newer electrotype process, plates were made by depositing copper electrolytically on a wax mold, then backing the copper with lead.

volumes, cost price 20/– and £95 should be paid for the plates of the two, & the stereos of Orley Farm. The plates of Orley Farm are by Millais. This will make them come very much cheaper than when I wrote before. I will take £2300 for my share. The whole price therefore would be £3800. I have been away in Wales, & the thing has been delayed, & we must give Smith an answer. Therefore I trouble you with this letter. Keep the list till I see you on Monday.[3]

Yours always faithfully
Anthony Trollope

To Herman Merivale

MS Parrish Collection.

THE FORTNIGHTLY REVIEW,

May 23–1866 OFFICE—193, PICCADILLY.[4]

My dear Merivale.

I have directed the publishers to send you the new volume of Essays on International policy by Harrison & five others,—all Oxford men I think. You will know their names. The book I think will receive considerable notice— Will you do us an article on it for the Fortnightly.[5]

Yours always
Anthony Trollope

To Richard Bentley

MS Parrish Collection. SB 301.

June 9. 1866. WALTHAM HOUSE, WALTHAM CROSS.

Dear Sir.

Would you oblige me by giving me a copy of the cheap edit of the Three Clerks.[6] If you can do so, send it to my address at Chapman & Halls.

Yours always

R Bentley Esq Anthony Trollope

---

[3] Smith again declined. On 4 June 1866 Trollope sold his half share of the fourteen copyrights to W. H. Smith for £2,000, payment due on 1 October 1866. The books continued to be issued under the imprint of Chapman & Hall.

[4] While Lewes was abroad in June and July, Trollope served as editor of the *Fortnightly*.

[5] E. Lyulph Stanley, not Merivale, reviewed *International Policy: Essays on the Foreign Relations of England* (1866) in the *Fortnightly*, 5 (15 July 1866), 636–40. The authors were Richard Congreve, Frederic Harrison, E. S. Beesly, E. H. Pember, J. H. Bridges, Charles A. Cookson, and Henry Dix Hutton. The Preface announced that the contributors were applying the principles of positivism to international policy.

[6] Probably the six-shilling 1865 edition, No. 10 in the series Bentley's Favourite Novels.

To Lord Houghton

MS Trinity College, Cambridge.

June 20—1866   WALTHAM HOUSE, WALTHAM CROSS.
My dear Lord Houghton.
Would you look at the enclosed,—which has been sent to me by a
Southern Gentleman. The letters are for sale & my friend (who, as regards his own word, is to be believed) enquires of me whether they
would be saleable here. If the letters are trustworthy, how should they
be dealt with, with a view to sale? And do you think them genuine,
judging from the internal evidence?[7]

Yours always
Anthony Trollope

To George Smith

SB 302 (Sadleir's transcript).

24 June 1866
Trollope suggests a title for the novel subsequently published as *The Last
Chronicle of Barset*: "The Story of a Cheque for £20, and of the Mischief Which
It Did." Its short title would be: "A Cheque for £20."

To George Smith

SB 303 (Sadleir's transcript).

24 June 1866

                    *   *   *
Use the enclosed or not as you like.[8] There is no doubt as to the truth.
It was the Bishop of Oxford,[9] and he gave the living which fell vacant
the other day,—Myddleton I think,—which had been held for fifty years
by a scamp, a son of old Bishop Tomlin,[1] to his own youngest son,—just
in orders. I have a word or two to say to you about curates and church
preferment some day.
                    *   *   *

[7] These letters have not been traced.
[8] An article for the *Pall Mall Gazette*, evidently not published.
[9] Samuel Wilberforce (1805–73). His son Ernest Roland Wilberforce (1840–1907)
was given the living of Middleton Stoney.
[1] Sir George Pretyman Tomline (1750–1827), Bishop of Lincoln and Dean of St.
Paul's from 1787; Bishop of Winchester, 1820–27. The son was Richard Pretyman
(1792–1866). He and his brother George Thomas Pretyman each held at least six
ecclesiastical offices, from which they derived enormous incomes (B).

To Lady Amberley[2]
MS Parrish Collection. SB 305.

July 6—1866.   WALTHAM HOUSE, WALTHAM CROSS.
My dear Lady Amberley
   I am afraid I cannot manage to get to you on Tuesday as I dine out and doubt whether I can get away in time. If I can I will. I shall be most happy to join your party on Saturday i.e. 14. If I do not manage to see you before you will perhaps kindly tell me of your whereabouts.
                          very faithfully yours
                          Anthony Trollope

To Octavian Blewitt
MS Parrish Collection. SB 304.

July 6. 1866   ATHENAEUM CLUB
My dear Mr. Blewitt.
   I do not think I would *as yet* rewrite the Memorial for hon Lady Wraxall,[3]—because of the signatures. I think it will be well that I should ask Lord Stanhope[4] on Wednesday if he will put it into Lord Derbys[5] hands.

                          Yours always
                          Any Trollope

To ?
MS Parrish Collection.

July 8—1866.   WALTHAM HOUSE, WALTHAM CROSS.
My dear Sir.
   I should have answered your letter sooner,—but that of all letters it is the most difficult to answer. The quantity of tales which are written and which find their way into the hands of all concerned in the trade of writing novels,—the authors especially,—is so great that one does not

   [2] "Kate," Lady Amberley (1842–74), wife of Viscount Amberley, the son and heir of Lord John Russell. Lady Amberley, like her mother Lady Stanley, was a political hostess, though of a more radical persuasion. Trollope was her guest at least four times. For Trollope's attendance at Lady Stanley's parties, see Trollope to Lady Stanley, 25 February 1874.
   [3] Trollope was attempting to arrange a pension for Mary Anne Wraxall (*d.* 1882), widow of Sir Frederic Charles Lascelles Wraxall (1828–65).
   [4] Philip Henry Stanhope (1805–75), 5th Earl Stanhope, historian; President of the Royal Literary Fund from 1863 until his death. The Fund had recently given Lady Wraxall a grant of £50.
   [5] Edward George Geoffrey Smith Stanley (1799–1869), 14th Earl of Derby, statesman; at this time, serving as Prime Minister for the third time.

know what answer to make to such an application as yours. The lady of whom you speak could not get a magazine here to print a first novel. They never, I think, do so. First novels appear I believe always by themselves, in volumes; and as often as not the writer pays the publisher a part of the expence of printing them. Chapman & Hall are my publishers, and if your friend chooses to send her Mss to them, they will have it read. If they think the merit great they will publish it, but they will not pay for a first book. Nor will they publish it, unless they are told the merit is considerable. I regret that it is out of my power to say more than this.

My mother whom you knew is dead, & both my sisters, and my brother Henry.[6] Hervieu[7] still lives, & is I think in London. But I never see him.

Yours very truly
Anthony Trollope

To George Smith

Bibliography, p. 232.

15 July 1866
Trollope sends a letter about Lord John Russell for the *Pall Mall Gazette*.[8]

To George Smith

MS John Murray. SB 306.

July 21—1866   WALTHAM HOUSE, WALTHAM CROSS.
My dear Smith.

I send a note in my own name about the curates incomes question,[9]— to which you adverted the other day; feeling strongly that I am in the right. If you like it print it. If you do not, burn it. I am very keen about it, but I should not open the controversy elsewhere.

Yours always
Anty Trollope

[6] Henry Trollope (1811–34).

[7] Auguste Hervieu; see Trollope to Thomas Adolphus Trollope, 25 May 1839, n. 4.

[8] "What It Is to Be a Statesman," *Pall Mall Gazette*, 18 July 1866, pp. 3–4 (signed "An Englishman"). In the article Trollope attacked the *Saturday Review* for its abuse of Russell, who had recently resigned as Prime Minister because of ill health.

[9] Trollope's *Clergymen of the Church of England* had drawn Anglican criticism, most notably from Henry Alford, Dean of Canterbury and editor of the *Contemporary Review*, who had attacked Trollope's book as amateur and had questioned the accuracy of Trollope's remarks about curates' incomes (*Contemporary Review*, 2 [June 1866], 240–62). Trollope called this notice "the most ill-natured review that was ever written upon any work of mine" (*Autobiography*, p. 201). The Anglican *Guardian* had also attacked Trollope on the subject of curates' incomes, though it subsequently printed a letter in Trollope's defense from an impoverished curate (6 June 1866, p. 602; 18 July 1866, p. 748). Though the *Pall Mall Gazette* had just cited the curate's letter as a vindication of Trollope (20 July 1866, p. 9), Trollope went on to hammer

To [? H. A. Bright][1]

MS University of Liverpool.

July 28. 1866   WALTHAM HOUSE, WALTHAM CROSS.

My dear Sir.

If you would kindly have the cigars forwarded to me—to the care of
Messrs. Chapman & Hall
193 Piccadilly.
I would be much obliged to you. Perhaps your clerk would clear them
and let me know what I should remit. Then I would send you, (or him)
a cheque for the amount.

William Synge writes in very bad spirits,—saying that Cuba is so expensive that he can hardly manage to live there; but I hope that things
will get better with him after a while.

faithfully yours
Anthony Trollope

To John Tilley

MS Parrish Collection.

POST OFFICE

July 31 66   Vere Street[2]

My dear John.

Touching the appointments of the Postmasters, I want you to reconsider the expediency of offering the appointments to the Assistant Controllers generally before they are offered to the men who have been at
the offices. The only two men concerned will be Smith & Salisbury.

---

home his own defense in the signed letter that is the subject of this note to Smith
("Curates' Incomes," *Pall Mall Gazette*, 24 July 1866, pp. 3–4). For a full account of this
issue, see Ruth apRoberts, ed., *Clergymen of the Church of England*, pp. 38–49.

[1] Almost certainly Henry Arthur Bright (1830–84), merchant and author, since
payment for the cigars was made to his family firm in Liverpool (Trollope to Messrs.
Gibbs, Bright & Co., 6 August 1866). See also Trollope to Bright, 24 April 1871.

[2] Trollope had recently been asked to reorganize the postal system of London by
changing eight of its ten postal districts into "post towns," each with its own postmaster. His temporary headquarters were at Vere Street. A postal worker recalled:
"I was detailed for duty there when the change took place, and I remember Anthony
Trollope superintended the arrangements for constituting Postal London in so many
separate towns. His method of attacking work was rather odd, and I have seen him
slogging away at papers at a stand-up desk, with his handkerchief stuffed into his
mouth, and his hair on end, as though he could barely contain himself. He struck
me as being rather a fierce-looking man, and a remark which he made to a postmaster
on one occasion did not appear to me to savour either of courtesy or kindness. The
poor fellow, who had probably seen thirty years' service, and who was wedded to the
old system of working the districts, was fretting terribly at the prospect of becoming
a postmaster and of being left to his own resources, so to speak, when Trollope turned
round on him with the remark: 'Why don't you pay an old woman sixpence a week
to fret for you?'" (R. W. J., "Early Post Office Days," *St. Martin's-le-Grand*, 6 [July
1896], 295.)

Smith would gain nothing by the change beyond the quicker rise to
£500. His salary is now I think £450, and he goes up to £500.

Salisbury, who is perhaps the best man on the whole that we have (and
who has 8 children) only goes up to £450, and thus the office which he
would get, if Smith were not in his way, would be a rise of £50 for life
to him. I would not thus plead for him where [*sic*] I not sure that he
would be much the better Postmaster. Smith is too old to come in well
upon new work,—and new work of a difficult kind. He has never had
anything to do with the management of Letter Carriers. Salisbury knows
it all completely. And I think that the fact that men have been so long
at such work does give them a sort of claim.

Yours always
Anthony Trollope

To George Eliot

MS Parrish Collection. B 307; *George Eliot Letters*, VIII, 381–82.

August 3 1866.   WALTHAM HOUSE, WALTHAM CROSS.
My dear Mrs. Lewes.

I must welcome you home with a word of thanks for Felix Holt which
I received from Mr. Blackwood as a present from you.

I hope you are gratified by the reception which it has obtained. I know
how disdainful you are of ordinary eulogium,—being perhaps led on to
be somewhat more so than your own nature would make you by the
severity of G. H. L. But in spite of him and of his severity, and of your
own disdain whether natural or acquired, the unrivalled success of Felix
Holt must have touched you. For, as far as I can make an estimate of
such things, I think its success is unrivalled.[3]

For myself I think it has more elaborated thought in it, and that it is
in that way a greater work, than anything you have done before. With
the character of Mr. Lyon I am perfectly satisfied, loving all his words
dearly. Felix is very great as the result of an admirably conceived plan
of a character. With Esther I feel sometimes inclined to quarrel because
she seems to doubt, after she knows that she loves the man. Mrs. Tran-
some is excellent and great. Mrs. Holt is very good,—tho not equal to
Mrs. Poyser[4] as being perhaps less like what I have seen with these eyes
of the flesh & heard with these ears. As to story Adam Bede is still my
favorite. For picturesque word painting Romola stands first. To me the
great glory of Felix Holt is the fulness of thought which has been bestowed on it.

My kindest regards to the Master. If he wants any of the new batch of
8000 cigars which I have just got over from Cuba let him tell me at once

[3] John Blackwood told Lewes, "I do not know that I ever saw a Novel received
with a more universal acclaim than Felix." (*George Eliot Letters*, IV, 289.)
[4] In *Adam Bede*.

how many. I called on Thursday and heard from cook some feeble excuse about the weather. The summer winds had detained you!!

Yours always most heartily
Anthony Trollope

George Eliot to Trollope

MS (copy in Muriel Rose Trollope's hand) Parrish Collection. *George Eliot Letters*, IV, 296.

The Priory
North Road
Aug. 5 1866   Regents Park
My dear Mr. Trollope

All goodness in the world bless you! First, for being what you are. Next, for the regard I think you bear towards that (to me) best of men, my dear husband. And after those two chief things, for the Goodness both in word and act towards me in particular. That is the answer that I at once made inwardly on reading your letter, so I write it down now without addition. The Little Man hopes to see you & speak to you on that tender subject, the Cigars, on Wednesday, perhaps at one?

Always yours in affectionate friendship
M. E. Lewes

To George Smith

MS John Murray. B 308.

August 5. 1866
My dear Smith.

I am very sorry to hear what you say about your wife. I hope you do not mean anything serious. Let me have a line to tell me.

About the money, put it down for 1 Jany. I shall not want it sooner and shall think that very good pay.

I need hardly say how glad I am to hear that you like what you have seen of the story.[5] When I have worked to order the only criticism for which I care much is the criticism of the buyer who has trusted me so far as to purchase what he has not seen.

Millais was talking to me about certain illustrations. I said—(after certain other things had been said)—"You know you will not do any more." He replied—"If you like it I'll do another of yours."

He is in Scotland. Shall I write and ask him?

I thought you had said that you wanted cigars— So many people ask me that I forget who is a candidate & who is not.

Yours always
Anthony Trollope

[5] *The Last Chronicle of Barset.*

To J. E. Millais

J. G. Millais, *The Life and Letters of Sir John Everett Millais*, I, 284.

August 6th. 1866   WALTHAM HOUSE, WALTHAM CROSS.

My Dear Millais—

I have written (nearly finished) a story in thirty-two numbers, which is to come out weekly. The first number is to appear some time in October. Smith publishes it, and proposes that there shall be one illustration to every number, with small vignettes to the chapter headings. Will you do them? You said a word to me the other day, which was to the effect that you would perhaps lend your hand to another story of mine. Many of the characters (indeed, most of them) are people you already know well—Mr. Crawley, Mr. Harding, Lily Dale, Crosbie, John Eam[e]s, and Lady Lufton. George Smith is very anxious that you should consent, and you may imagine that I am equally so. If you can do it, the sheets shall be sent to you as soon as they are printed, and copies of your own illustrations should be sent to refresh your memory.... Let me have a line.[6]

Yours always
Anthony Trollope

To Messrs. Gibbs, Bright & Co.

MS Parrish Collection.

August 6—1866   Waltham Cross

Gentlemen.

I enclose cheque for £31.7.9 and beg to thank you for your trouble in reference to the cigars.

Yours very truly

Messrs Gibbs Bright & Co   Anthony Trollope
Liverpool

To George Smith

MS Bodleian. Excerpt, Hamer, p. 213.

August 12—1866.   WALTHAM HOUSE, WALTHAM CROSS.

My dear Smith.

I wonder whether a slight alteration can be made in the proof of the Feb. No. of the Claverings. I did not get a revise of that number.

---

[6] Millais answered on 7 August: "I am just on the point of starting for the North, and I don't like to decide in a hurry. If it had been 2 drawings a month I would have said yes at once, but this weekly business is a problem in the middle of painting.... Let me have a day or two & the advice of my wife & I will send you a definite answer." (MS John Murray.) See Trollope to Millais, 20 August 1866.

Page 24. First line of last paragraph, after the words "as we shall see Doodles no more" I wish to insert (—or almost no more,—)—for there is in fact a glimpse of Doodles in the last page. If you will give this note over to Mr Enoch I do not doubt but what he will put it right.[7]

I hope your wife is getting all right again.

Yours always
Anthony Trollope

To John Blackwood

MS Parrish Collection. B 309.

August 17. 66   WALTHAM HOUSE, WALTHAM CROSS.

My dear Blackwood.

I send back Chap 8—corrected. Do just as you like about the divisions. I have no doubt your judgement in such matters is at the least as good as mine. It is easy to have too little of a story, & *very easy* to have too much. I do not know whether you have suggested to yourself any time for bringing out the whole. I see that 8 chapters are just half, and if you thought of bringing out the volume in January, you would probably make the story run six numbers in the magazine.[8]

But, as I said before, use your own judgement altogether in this. I will promise to be satisfied.

Your friend in the country is very clever.[9] But I find that appreciation of particular style is as peculiar a gift as appreciation of peculiar music, or as the power of remembering faces. Some men who are always reading never acquire it. Some excellent critics do not hit it at all. Whereas other men, who do not even think themselves to be critical, unconsciously recognize all the little twists and niceties of individual style. I hope you explained to your clever friend that as far as this matter went he had proved himself to be no where!

Yours always
Anthony Trollope

Mr. & Mrs. Felix Holt[1] have returned blooming like two garden peonies. I may be away from September 12—to end of October. I merely mention this as to proofs.

---

[7] The alteration was made (chap. xxxix).

[8] *Nina Balatka* ran in *Blackwood's Magazine* for seven months, from July 1866 through January 1867.

[9] Someone had quickly recognized the anonymous *Nina Balatka* as Trollope's.

[1] G. H. Lewes and George Eliot.

To J. E. Millais

MS Parrish Collection. B 310.

August 20. 1866   WALTHAM HOUSE, WALTHAM CROSS.
My dear Millais
    A thousand thanks for the "grice,"[2] which have been most welcome.
I hope you are having good sport. I do envy you fellows— But then I
think that my good time is coming in the winter.
    But how about the Illustrations. You promised me a further answer.
Do *do* them! They wont take you above half an hour each.[3]
                                    Yours always
                                    Anty Trollope

I am obliged to send this to your house in town unless I were to address
it simply
            Grouseland.

To [? W. L. Clay][4]

B. Altman & Co. advertisement, *New York Times*, 18 February 1979, p. 46.

20 August 1866   Waltham House, Waltham Cross.
    Trollope writes concerning a conference. "I take very great interest in the
subject of International Copyright." If unable to attend, he will draw up and
send a short paper on the subject.

To [? Charles] Rea[5]

MS Parrish Collection.

August 22—1866   Waltham Cross
My dear Mr. Rea
    Neither Seymour[6] nor Morrison[7] came to our meeting today. I read
your letter. We carried a proposition to make the review a monthly

[2] A facetious plural of "grouse."
[3] Millais had given up illustration on a regular basis by this time, and refused. In
the following year, however, he agreed to illustrate *Phineas Finn* to help Trollope
launch *St. Paul's Magazine*.
[4] Probably the Reverend Walter L. Clay (1833–75), Secretary of the National Association for the Promotion of Social Science. Trollope's letter concerns the Association's
annual meeting: see Trollope to ?, 13 September 1866.
[5] Probably Charles Rea, a Post Office official who twice acted as Trollope's deputy
when Trollope was on leave from England's Eastern District. On Trollope's resignation in 1867, Rea became the district's surveyor.
[6] Henry Danby Seymour (1820–77), MP for Poole, 1850–68; one of the original proprietors of the *Fortnightly Review*.
[7] James Augustus Cotter Morison (1832–88), biographer; one of the original proprietors of the *Fortnightly*.

periodical on & from 1 January[8]—and we have named a day in October for another meeting in which we will discuss the name and other details. It is essential that we should settle something & therefore I hope we may not again go back from what we have done. Otherwise I should think it would be better that some of us should buy the periodical from the others. I fear however that the outsiders among us will not come forward to meet us in any such proposition.[9]

very truly yours
Anthony Trollope

To John Blackwood

MS Parrish Collection. B 311.

September 7. 1866. WALTHAM HOUSE, WALTHAM CROSS.
My dear Blackwood
I send back the sheets corrected, and I think I never saw cleaner proofs go back.

Touching the breaks I cannot find that the requirements of the story make any difference. In the October month you can put 3 chapters (VIII–IX–& X) making 21 pages, or 2 chapters making 14. It must depend on your desire to finish the story in six or seven numbers. You will see that there will not be enough for eight. If you like to finish the story with the end of the year, there will be three chapters for each number. In that case you must let me have Chapter XIII to correct by the end of the month, as, I shall be in Italy from 1. to 31 October.

For myself I like Nina better in print than in Mss, but the man comes out too black. I think I'll make him give her a diamond necklace in the last chapter.

To shew in what doubt critics may be as to authorship;—The Times critic held me out that ODowd was by Bulwer,[1]—he, probably having got some inkling of dead knowledge, & then unconsciously forming his critical opinion thereby.

With kind regards to your wife,
Yours always
A. T.

[8] The *Fortnightly* became a monthly in November 1866.

[9] Towards the end of 1866, the original company, its resources exhausted, sold the review to Chapman & Hall "for a trifle" (*Autobiography*, p. 190). For the change in editors about this time, see Trollope to Lewes, 9 November 1866.

[1] Charles Lever's 25-part series "Cornelius O'Dowd upon Men and Women," which appeared in *Blackwood's* between February 1864 and August 1866. This series was followed by a 42-part series entitled simply "Cornelius O'Dowd," which appeared between September 1866 and March 1872.

To George Smith

SB 312 (Sadleir's transcript).

11 September 1866

Trollope asks Smith to send copies of *Framley Parsonage* and *The Small House* to Mr. Thomas[2] so that he "should see the personages as Millais has made them."

To ?

MS Parrish Collection. SB 313.

Sept. 13—1866   WALTHAM HOUSE, WALTHAM CROSS.

Sir.

I ought have answered sooner your kind letter of the 1st. Instant, but I could not do so till circumstances would enable me to say positively whether I could attend this years annual Social Science gathering at Manchester. I told Mr Clay that my doing so was uncertain. I now find that I must go to my brother in Italy, for which purpose I shall leave England on the 1st. October. Will you therefore give my kindest compliments and thanks to Mr. and Mrs. Edmund Grindly and tell them how much I regret that I cannot have the pleasure of accepting their hospitality. I should have sent this answer to them before could I have sooner known my own plans.

I will write to Mr. Clay respecting the matter of International copyright—[3]

yours very faithfully
Anthony Trollope

[2] George Housman Thomas (1824–68), painter and illustrator; commissioned by Queen Victoria to paint pictures depicting the leading events of her reign. Thomas illustrated *The Last Chronicle*. See *Illustrators*, pp. 114–23.

[3] Trollope wrote a paper entitled "On the Best Means of Extending and Securing an International Law of Copyright," which was printed in George W. Hastings, ed., *Transactions of the National Association for the Promotion of Social Science, 1866* (1867), pp. 119–25. The paper was read at the congress, and reported at length in the *Athenaeum* of 13 October 1866 (pp. 467–68), with the comment that "to literary men and to readers interested in literature, there was no paper . . . of greater interest."

To George Smith

MS Bodleian. Excerpt, Hamer, p. 215.

Sept 21—1866. Glengarriffe.[4]

My dear Smith.

I have determined to keep the name as it is printed. The Last of the Chronicles of Barset.[5]

I send back the six numbers.

Yours always
A. T.

Such weather!!

To Mr. Hill

MS Parrish Collection. SB 314.

27—Oct—1866. Paris—

My dear Mr Hill

I found your note waiting me here on my arrival in Paris from Italy this morning. I much regret that engagements at home will prevent my having the pleasure of accepting your kind invitation for Thursday.

Yours very truly
Anthony Trollope

To G. H. Lewes

MS Yale. B 315; *George Eliot Letters*, VIII, 387–88.

November 9. 1866

My dear Lewes.

I wrote to you last night an official letter at the request of the Committee; but I cannot let you part from us without saying with more of personal feeling than I could put into that letter how sorry I am that it should be so.[6] I hate the breaking of pleasant relations; and am distrustful as to new relations. I have felt however for some time that it must be so; and that you would not hang on to us much longer. I have felt also that your time was too valuable to be frittered away in reading Mss, and in writing civil,—or even uncivil—notes.

---

[4] Glengariff is a seaside village on Bantry Bay, Co. Cork.

[5] Trollope had previously discarded the title "The Story of a Cheque for Twenty Pounds and of the Mischief Which It Did." He subsequently altered the title that he insisted upon here, probably at Smith's urging.

[6] Lewes had resigned as editor of the *Fortnightly*.

Only two propositions as to the editing are before us. 1st. to ask Mr. John Morley[7] to undertake it. 2d. that I should do it for 6 months, without Salary, keeping Mr. Dennis[8] with perhaps a somewhat encreased Salary. No doubt a permanent arrangement will be best, & the second plan has little in it of advantage either for me or for the Review. But it is supported by the desire which many of us have to keep the employment for Mr. Dennis as long as it can be kept; and also by a feeling that we hardly know enough of Mr. Morley. This latter may be overcome by better information; and I shall be very glad if you will tell me your opinion. Do you think that Mr. Morley is competent for the work? And do you believe that his opinions as to politics and literature are of a nature to support those views which we have endeavoured to maintain? If I found that the Review had drifted into the hands of a literary hack who simply followed out his task without any honesty of purpose, I should wash my hands of it.

When you want a new pair of boots it is pretty nearly enough for you to know that you are going to a good bootmaker. But this going to an Editor is a very different thing. A man may be a most accomplished Editor,—able at all periodical-editing work,—and yet to you or to me so antipathetic as to make it impossible that the two should work together. You will understand what I mean when I say that should I find I dont like the nose on our new Editors face, I must simply drop the Review; and that therefore I cannot but be very anxious.

Let me know what you think about Morley.[9]

Give my kindest regards to your wife.

Yours always

Address Waltham Cross   Any Trollope
I am to see Mr. Morley on Tuesday.

---

[7] John Morley (1838–1923), later Viscount Morley of Blackburn, the distinguished man of letters and liberal statesman.

[8] John Dennis, critic and miscellaneous writer; subeditor of the *Fortnightly*.

[9] The appointment went to Morley, and during his tenure as editor (1867–82), the *Fortnightly* became England's foremost journal of liberal opinion. Trollope wrote: "Mr. John Morley has done the work with admirable patience, zeal, and capacity. Of course he has got around him a set of contributors whose modes of thought are what we may call much advanced; he being 'much advanced' himself, could not work with other aids. The periodical has a peculiar tone of its own; but it holds its own with ability." (*Autobiography*, p. 194.)

To [? Alexander] Macmillan[1]

MS Parrish Collection.

9 Nov. 1866.   WALTHAM HOUSE, WALTHAM CROSS.
My dear Mr Macmillan.

I am very sorry to say that I am engaged on next Friday. I know Mr Clark[2] intimately & should have been very glad to have met him.

Yours always
Anthony Trollope

To George Smith

MS Bodleian. *Commentary*, p. 273; SB 316.

November 11−1866   WALTHAM HOUSE, WALTHAM CROSS.
My dear Smith.

I send back the proof with the lettering. It is always well if possible to select a subject for which the lettering can be taken from the dialogue. Because this cannot be done as to No. 1, the lettering is poor. As to Nos. 2 & 4—it is all right. In No. 3, the scene is sufficiently distinct to dispense with the rule. The best figure is that of Miss Prettyman in No. 2. Grace is not good. She has fat cheeks, & is not Grace Crawley. Crawley before the magistrates is very good. So is the bishop. Mrs. Proudie is not quite my Mrs. Proudie.[3]

Say £40 for the German translation.

Your letter found me only last night.

Yours always
Anthony Trollope

[1] Probably Alexander Macmillan (1818–96), head of the publishing firm of Macmillan and Co., which he and his brother Daniel (1813–57) had founded.

[2] William George Clark (1821–78), Public Orator at Cambridge, 1857–70; one of the editors of *The Cambridge Shakespeare*.

[3] Trollope refers to Thomas's illustrations and their legends for *The Last Chronicle*: "Mr. and Mrs. Crawley" (chap. i); " 'I love you as though you were my own,' said the Schoolmistress" (chap. vi); "Mr. Crawley before the Magistrates" (chap. viii); and " 'A convicted thief!' repeated Mrs. Proudie" (chap. xi).

"A Convicted Thief," repeated Mrs. Proudie.

Illustration for *The Last Chronicle of Barset*, by G. H. Thomas

James Virtue[4] to Trollope
MS Bodleian.

Nov 15th. 1866   VIRTUE & CO. LONDON E.C.
My dear Sir,

Upon further consideration I am inclined to think that instead of purchasing the "Argosy," perhaps it would be better to start an entirely new Magazine. A new Volume of the Argosy commences Decr. 1—you could not possibly mature any new arrangements before that time and we should then be committed to a new Volume, and you would be held responsible by the public, for a tale or tales that you did not select and that you had but little time to examine.

What say you to a new Magazine to be started say—Jany 1, to be edited by you and so announced.

Editors salary to be £*1000* p annum, this to include all Editorial Expenditure.

All arrangements with contributors to be made by you entirely, upon such terms as we may agree upon together, but the management of the literary portion and Illustrations must be entirely in your hands.

Your own writings would of course be paid for, same as if you wrote for any other Magazine.

I should propose to get up a Magazine similar in appearance to the Argosy, but upon better paper and with more pages,—but if you feel inclined to entertain the idea we can discuss the details, if we can first agree upon main principles such as Editor's salary and the like.

I am sure there is room for a good Magazine, under your management, it will be hard if we cannot hold our own against such as "Belgravia" and "Temple Bar."

                              I am, dear Sir,
                              Very truly yours
Anthony Trollope Esq   James Virtue
Waltham Cross

[4] James Sprent Virtue (1829–92), an important and successful printer; manager of the family business from 1855; also a publisher, specializing in art books. In 1866 he lent £10,000 to Alexander Strahan & Co., whose periodicals he printed, and when Strahan could not meet his repayments Virtue considered taking over Strahan's *Argosy* in order to recoup part of his loss. This letter marks his decision to offer Trollope the editorship of a new magazine (eventually named *St. Paul's Magazine*) instead of the *Argosy*. Virtue already knew Trollope since he was the printer (and possibly one of the proprietors) of the *Fortnightly*. See Patricia Thomas Srebrnik, "Trollope, James Virtue, and *Saint Paul's Magazine*," forthcoming in the Trollope centenary issue of *Nineteenth-Century Fiction*. Virtue was at least partially responsible for the well-known "Spy" cartoon of Trollope that appeared in *Vanity Fair* on 5 April 1873. Sir Leslie Ward told how Virtue invited him to his house, where he (Ward) and Trollope took a walk: "The famous novelist was not in the least conscious of my eagle eye, and imagining I should let him down gently, Mr. Virtue did not warn him, luckily for me, for I had an excellent subject. When the caricature appeared, Trollope was furious, and naturally did not hesitate to give poor Virtue a 'blowing-up.' " (Sir Leslie Ward, *Forty Years of 'Spy'* [1915], pp. 104–5.)

James Virtue to Trollope

MS Bodleian.

Novr. 16th. 1866   VIRTUE & CO. LONDON E.C.

My dear Sir,

I am sorry that I am engaged for tomorrow— I have to leave town at 2 o'clock, and cannot be back before Monday morning— I have to go to Brighton on Monday Evening—but otherwise I will meet you where and when you please, make your own appointment for day or evening and I am at your service.

My ideas are as yet very crude.—I have no definite plan, as so much depends upon our understanding together and what your ideas may be as well as mine.

Briefly—I should say—Pay the Contributors well to get good talent.

If our Magazine made 128 pages I should think an average of 20/. a page ought to do, but this must so much depend upon prices paid by other magazines, and the ability of the writers that it is difficult to name a definite sum.

Certainly Illustrate, with two full page Illustrations, and perhaps a few others in the body of the Magazine, but we should not commence with this probably.

About the novel to commence with—I have nothing whatever in contemplation for this, my experience lies so little in that way that I fear I should have to look to you entirely for the Literature— Is there no possibility of arranging even for a short one of your own. But perhaps when you have thought over the matter more fully—you would lay out roughly your plan for the whole Magazine and then we might determine which portion should be illustrated & such like.

I should have no objection to guarantee the arrangement for two years but concerning this we had better talk when we meet, as I apprehend that if by any mischance the enterprise failed to get a sufficient circulation and that if, contrary to my expectations, it did not turn out a success, it might be advisable for both of us to consider the propriety of working a dead horse, and whether we had not better stop before the expiration of two years,—but if you hold to this as an important item I should have no great objection as I am not likely to abandon it unless under some very unexpected & extraordinary circumstances which in all probability would affect Editor as well as proprietors, and that they would then have no difficulty in arranging what should best be done.

The above may give you a rough idea of what we contemplated—but is of course subject to modification.

I calculate that a sale of 25,000 would pay,—but I certainly expect a far higher circulation.

I am, dear Sir,
Truly yours
James Virtue

A. Trollope Esq.

To Frances Power Cobbe[5]

MS Huntington Library.

18—November 1866   WALTHAM HOUSE, WALTHAM CROSS.
My dear Miss Cobbe.

I beg your pardon. I had thought you had written about the Cornhill,—as many persons take me to be the Editor of that periodical.

I should think that a paper from you would be welcome to the Editor of the Fortnightly. His address is

John Morley Esq
193 Piccadilly.

If you like to send to him any paper I will speak to him on the subject.[6]

Yours very faithfully
Anthony Trollope

To Mr. Barker

MS McGill University.

Nov 24th. [1866]
Saturday   WALTHAM HOUSE, WALTHAM CROSS.
Mr. & Mrs. Anthony Trollope request the pleasure of Mr. Barker's company to dinner on Tuesday next—at 6.30 pm—

John Morley to Trollope

MS Princeton.

Nov. 28/66.
Wednesday.   18 Old Burlington Street.
My dear Mr. Trollope.

I have had placed in my hands a poem by Mr. Swinburne[7]—in my own judgment a most exquisite composition, and without any of those unfortunate characteristics with wh. Mr. Swinburne's name is at the present moment connected.[8] It wd. occupy 8 pages of the *Review*. We shd. have to give him 20 guineas for it. Will the Board[9] authorise me to offer

---

[5] Frances Power Cobbe (1822–1904), philanthropist, feminist, and miscellaneous writer. While staying with Isa Blagden in Florence, Miss Cobbe became a friend of T. A. Trollope.

[6] Miss Cobbe published "What Is Progress, and Are We Progressing?" in the *Fortnightly*, 7 (March 1867), 357–70.

[7] "Child's Song in Winter," *Fortnightly*, 7 (1 January 1867), 19–26.

[8] A reference to the controversy surrounding the publication of Swinburne's *Poems and Ballads* in April 1866. Morley was in fact one of Swinburne's critics, having castigated Swinburne (despite finding much to praise in the work) for "tuning his lyre in a sty" (*Saturday Review*, 4 August 1866), and Morley's notice was among those that caused the publisher, Moxon, to withdraw the volume from circulation. See F. W. Hirst, *Early Life and Letters of John Morley* (1927), II, 68.

[9] Trollope served as chairman of the *Fortnightly*'s finance board.

this price? Under all the circumstances, considering first the real beauty of the poem, and second, the usefulness of it as an attractive advertisement, I hope that you will consent to my offering somewhat more than the usual fee.

May I ask you to be good enough to submit this to the consideration of the Board?

Believe me, dear Mr. Trollope,
Your's very truly,
John Morley

Anthony Trollope, Esq.

To Frederic Chapman

MS Pierpont Morgan Library. SB 317.

2 Decr. 1866   Waltham X
My dear Chapman.

I have told Mr Morley that he may give the 20 guineas. I hope I am right.

Yours always
A. T.

To Charles Lever[1]

MS Taylor Collection.

2. December 1866.   WALTHAM HOUSE, WALTHAM CROSS.
My dear Lever

I have not seen Smith, who has been absorbed for the last week, in his case with the quack doctor,—(who has just got a farthing damages)[2]—but I am assured by his manager that the arrangement with you is made.[3] I hope this is so, and that it is satisfactory.

Yours always
Anthy Trollope

[1] Charles Lever (1806–72), the novelist. Trollope wrote of "my dear old friend Charles Lever. . . . Of all the men I have encountered, he was the surest fund of drollery." (*Autobiography*, p. 251.)

[2] The result of a libel action brought by an American quack doctor, Robert Hunter, against the *Pall Mall Gazette* for its article "Imposters and Dupes," published on 10 November 1865, while a charge of rape against Hunter was still being investigated. There was ample evidence that Hunter had made false claims in his advertisements.

[3] Probably for the serialization of Lever's *The Bramleighs of Bishop's Folly* in the *Cornhill* from June 1867 through October 1868.

James Virtue to Trollope
MS Bodleian.

Decr. 13th. 1866   VIRTUE & CO. LONDON E.C.
My dear Sir,
I have quite decided to start the new Magazine, but before making our final arrangements I should like to have your opinion about the time for publication.
I have thought much lately, about the advisability of postponing our publication until a later time of the year than we contemplated. If we publish upon either April 1 or May 1, of next year—I fear that the Paris Exhibition may interfere a little with our chance of success upon the one side, and upon the other we should have the advantage of your having finished your tale in the Cornhill, and you could then commence in ours without clashing— Under these circumstances I am rather inclined to suggest postponement until after the summer and to commence either January 1. 1868—or perhaps a month or two earlier—but before I think anything about this I should like to have your opinion first, so as not to clash with your arrangements.

         I am, my dear Sir,
         Very truly yours
Anthony Trollope Esq   James Virtue
Waltham.

To James Virtue
MS (Trollope's copy) Bodleian.

14. December 1866.   WALTHAM HOUSE, WALTHAM CROSS.
My dear Mr Virtue.
I have been thinking a great deal about the Magazine & am sure you are right in your intention of postponing it. I could not begin a story before 1. July, and I look on that as a bad time for commencing. But I should much prefer 1—October 1867. to 1 Jany 1868. If we commenced 1 Oct. I should give all the intervening time to preparing a story for the magazine, and doing other work for it. If it were postponed longer, I could hardly afford this, and must take some other work in hand. ⟨You will understand this.⟩
I have thought of two names
"The Monthly Westminster,"
"The Monthly Liberal"—
I think my own name "Trollopes Monthly" would be objectionable, because it means nothing when the connexion between the magazine & the Editor has been dissolved.
I would propose to have every month a political article,—one month on foreign politics and one month on home politics. I would have but

very little reviewing;—*or none*. None, unless on some very rare occasion.

I would begin a novel myself, & would propose to carry it thro 20 numbers,—as was done with the Small House of Allington—in the Cornhill.

Would you think well to have a second novel, of course written on cheaper terms? Even so it will cost more than ordinary matter, but not much more—perhaps 25/ a page instead of 20/. It makes the work of getting the number out much easier, and saves sometimes the necessity of using indifferent matter.

I think that during the Session I would endeavour to explain in a few pages what Parliament is doing.

I think I understood you to say that you did not object to my proposition that our mutual engagement should be made for two Years certain at £1000 per ann:—to include all expense of editing; not of original matter supplied by the Editor.

My terms for a novel to run thro 20 numbers—(24 pages a number) the same length as Small House of Allington will be £3200 for the entire copyright.—The length of such a novel is 4 ordinary volumes.

You will probably let me know how far you agree with my views, in order that I may get to work, if we are of one mind.

Perhaps I may see you on Wednesday at the Fortnightly meeting.

Yours faithfully

Anthony Trollope

To ?
MS Parrish Collection.

Decr. 16. 1866

I have explained to the writer that I am not Editor of the Cornhill, & that I have sent this on to the Editor.

Anthy Trollope

To Thomas Adolphus Trollope
MS Parrish Collection. SB 318.

December 24—1866.   WALTHAM HOUSE, WALTHAM CROSS.

My dear Tom.

This will be handed to you by my friend Mr. W. G. Clark—Public orator at Cambridge, & late tutor at Trinity. He is now going to Florence, and I wish for both your sakes that you should be acquainted.

Yours always

Anthony Trollope

To Miss Weston

MS Parrish Collection. SB 319.

Decr. 27—1866.   WALTHAM HOUSE, WALTHAM CROSS.
My dear Miss Weston.
You paid me the compliment of saying that you would accept the enclosed. I dare say you have forgotten it;—but I like to keep my promises.

very faithfully yours
Anthony Trollope

To Edward Walford[4]

MS Parrish Collection.

28. Decr. 1866   WALTHAM HOUSE, WALTHAM CROSS.
Dear Sir
Other engagements forbid me to accept the offer kindly made by me to you [*sic*] with reference to the Gentleman's Magazine.

very faithfully yours

E. Walford Esq   Anthony Trollope

To Lord Houghton

T. Wemyss Reid, *The Life, Letters, and Friendships of Richard Monckton Milnes, First Lord Houghton* (1911), II, 155–56. B 320.

[1866]   WALTHAM HOUSE, WALTHAM CROSS.
My dear Lord Houghton.
I send you a copy of "The Warden," which Wm. Longman assures me is the last of the First Edit. There were, I think, only 750 printed,[5] and they have been over ten years in hand. But I regard the book with affection, as I made £9 2s. 6d. by the first year's sale, having previously written and published for ten years without any such golden results. Since then, I have improved even upon that.

Yours always faithfully
Anthony Trollope

---

[4] Edward Walford (1823–97), compiler and antiquarian; subeditor of *Once a Week*, 1859–65; editor of *Once a Week*, 1865–66; editor of *Gentleman's Magazine*, 1866–68.
[5] Longman had printed 1,000 copies; for the full sales record, see *Bibliography*, p. 262.

1867

To John Blackwood

MS National Library of Scotland. B 321.

Jany. 1. 1866 [1867]   WALTHAM HOUSE, WALTHAM CROSS.
My dear Blackwood.

All the good wishes of the season to you and your wife.

Thanks for the money for which I send a receipt. Send me the volumes when they are out.[6] I trust you may do well with them, & that we may have a further bit of business some day. Touching the weekly, the period of its coming out was Smiths idea & not my own, & frightened me when I first heard of it. How far it answers I do not know. It is his own speculation, & he is a man of such pride of constancy that I should not dare to propose to him any change. He will never complain to me, being in that respect made of the same stuff as yourself. As regards the workmanship of the story I believe it to be as good as anything I have done. A weekly novel should perhaps have at least an attempt at murder in every number. I never get beyond giving my people an attack of fever or a broken leg.

Many thanks for continuing to me the Magazine. I hope we may see you & Mrs. Blackwood in the Spring.

Always yours
Anthony Trollope

To John Dennis

MS Parrish Collection.

January 1. 1866 [1867]   WALTHAM HOUSE, WALTHAM CROSS.
My dear Dennis.

I return to you Mr Morley's note which I regard not only as arrogant, but insolent in its tone as coming from one literary man to another in your present joint positions. I can only conceive that it was written in a moment in which his amour propre was wounded. I will not now pledge myself to anything, as I am obliged to write immediately on receipt of your letter; but my impression is that unless Mr. Morley will withdraw it, I shall withdraw altogether from the Review.

Between you and him as to your position as Sub Editor it is impossible that anyone should interfere; because the arrangement between you is altogether of a private nature. But it is undoubtedly the case that the

[6] *Nina Balatka* was published in two volumes in late January 1867.

Company would have lessened their offer to him by £100, per an; and offered you £100 as notice to quit had it not been understood that Mr Morley intended to avail himself of your services in the event of the higher sum being offered to him.

I can hardly conceive that he can as yet have had time to judge of your qualifications in subediting.[7] Indeed it is impossible that he should have had time. But had he so judged and condemned you on his judgement, he should so have expressed himself and not have thrown you over on a point entirely personal to his own feelings.

I would propose that I should speak to him,—but will see you first. I will be at Chapmans on Wednesday at 2;—in the shop. Or will you come to me at the Athenaeum at ¼ before 2? That will be better— Write me a line to the Athenaeum.

Yours very truly
Anthony Trollope

Bring Mr Morley's note.

To [? J. A.] Hardcastle[8]
MS Parrish Collection. SB 322.

Jany 8—1867   Wisbeach
My dear Hardcastle.

I should have liked to accept your invitation for Thursday of all things, (exclusive of the ball)—but tho' I shall be at Painters Hall[9] on Friday, I cannot manage to get to you.

very faithfully yours
Anthony Trollope

To Charles Mortlock[1]
MS Parrish Collection.

Janry. 10th. 1867   WALTHAM HOUSE, WALTHAM CROSS.
Sir.

I will write to Harleston about the loss of time of the Denton Messenger,—and to Scole to ascertain whether there is any impediment to the making up of your bag there. But, (—in the latter alternative,)—you would have to pay £1.1/– to the Postr of Scole, & £2.2/ to the Con-

---

[7] For G. H. Lewes's high opinion of Dennis as a subeditor, see *George Eliot Letters*, VIII, 375.

[8] Probably Joseph Alfred Hardcastle (1815–99), MP for Bury St. Edmunds.

[9] Painters' Hall, 9 Little Trinity Lane, the Hall of the Painters and Stainers Company, one of the City of London Livery Companies (granted its charters in 1467 and 1561). The company were pioneers in the movement for technical education.

[1] Charles Mortlock, of the Lodge, Denton (East Norfolk).

tractor for the Mail Cart, who is not under an obligation to carry private bags *except on receipt of that additional payment*.[2]

Yours very faithfully
Anthony Trollope
Surveyor, G.P.O.

C. Mortlock Esq
Denton Lodge

James Virtue to Trollope

MS Bodleian.

Jany 14th. 1867   VIRTUE & CO. LONDON E.C.
My dear Sir,

Shall we have a regular formal Agreement for our understanding together, or shall it be put in the form of correspondence—if the former I will give the particulars to my Solicitor and he shall send you a rough draft as soon as it is prepared— I shall be quite content with letters only, stating the terms and accepting them on both sides—but perhaps you would prefer a more formal document and I have no possible objection, if such be your wish.

We shall meet, on Wednesday, I presume.

Very truly yours
James Virtue

Anthony Trollope Esq.

To James Virtue

MS (Trollope's copy) Bodleian.

Jan 14. 1867.
My dear Mr Virtue—

I do not think we shall want any lawyers work between us. I have never found the need of any yet with a publisher.

I would propose that you should write a note to me, accepting my proposal to edit your magazine for two years certain from 1 Oct 1867 at the rate of £1000 a year as salary for all editorial work (not including original matter) and that I should write you a note accepting your offer of those terms for that work.

Touching the novel there should be between us a memorandum of an agreement as to the terms, of which I enclose you a copy— I do not know whether I should have stated your own name, or the name of a firm—& if of a firm, whether I have named the firm right. If you agree to the memorandum, you should send me a signed copy & I will send you a signed copy—

I shall be at 193 Piccadilly on Wednesday when I shall hope to see you.

A. T.

[2] Mortlock wanted his mail to be sorted at Scole and sent directly to the Lodge; normally, mail for the Harleston area went by cart from Scole to Harleston, where it was then sorted and despatched to the surrounding villages, including Denton.

To Virtue & Co.

MS (Trollope's copy) Bodleian.

Jan 24 1867   Athenaeum Club.

Gentleman.

Referring to your letter of 21st. Inst, I beg to say that I accede to the terms named therein for the editing of a magazine to be published by you, and to be commenced on 1 Oct 1867.[3]

A. T.

Messrs. Virtue & Co

To Virtue & Co.

MS (Trollope's copy) Bodleian. B 323.

January 24. 1867

Gentlemen

I beg to say that I agree to the terms for the sale of a novel by me to you—contained in your letter of the 21st. Inst.

Viz. That the novel shall consist of not less than 480 pages—(such pages as those of the Cornhill Magazine).

That it shall be supplied to you not later than the end of September next.

That it shall be published in your magazine in continuous monthly parts to begin 1st. Oct, and that the entire copyright for that and subsequent publication shall be your own.

That you shall pay me for the copyright £3200 in monthly instalments of £160 per month—on acct from 15 October next.[4]

I am
Gentlemen
your most obedient Servant

Messrs Virtue & Co.   Anthony Trollope
294 City Road

[3] Virtue agreed to pay Trollope £1000 per annum: "This arrangement to continue for two years, so that if we do not continue the Magazine, we agree still to pay you £2000 during two years." Virtue also agreed to pay "a further sum of Seventy Five Pounds, for [a subeditor's] services during three months prior to day of publication, but after that time you will pay all expenses of Sub Editing." In a postscript, Virtue added: "Such articles as you contribute to the Magazine are to be paid for at same rate, as it is intended to pay other Contributors, viz 20/. pr page—during the first twelve months, after that it will be subject to future arrangement between us." (MS Bodleian.) Trollope asked Robert Bell to be subeditor; see Bell to Trollope, 24 January 1867.

[4] This agreement is for *Phineas Finn*, serialized in *St. Paul's* from October 1867 (the magazine's first number) through May 1869. The sum of £3,200 was the highest price that Trollope commanded outright for a work of fiction (Virtue paid the same price for *He Knew He Was Right*, which was issued in weekly and monthly parts from 17 October 1868 through 22 May 1869). In overall terms, however, Trollope received more for *Can You Forgive Her?* (£3,525, which included half profits on copies over

Robert Bell to Trollope

MS Bodleian.

Jany. 24th. [1867]
Thursday   14. YORK STREET. PORTMAN SQUARE, W.
My dear friend
    I found your letter on my return from Ramsgate.
    Your proposition[5] is liberal & thoroughly satisfactory. I have but one misgiving, the state of my health. After having made a partial recovery at Ramsgate, I fell back into a relapse, & am now in the hands of Dr. Garrod again.
    These successive illnesses harrass & fret me, &, should they continue must seriously interfere with my power of work.
    This is my case. Nothing would give me greater pleasure than to be associated with you in any literary work, & on the other hand, nothing could be more humiliating to me than to find that I was not doing my share of the work adequately. Think of this.[6] You see I write by the hand of my dear wife.

                              Ever yours
                              Robert Bell

To Sir Charles Taylor

MS Parrish Collection. B 324.

January 26. 1867   WALTHAM HOUSE, WALTHAM CROSS.
My dear Taylor.
    The difficulty of the position of Mme Blaze de Bury[7] as a novelist consists in this—that having many years ago made a reputation, she has not

---

10,000); and in unit terms, he received more for *The Claverings*. Unit terms are particularly important because Trollope conceived of and sold his fiction in units. The £2,800 that he was paid for the three-unit *Claverings* represented £933 per unit, whereas the £3,200 that he was paid for the four-unit *Phineas Finn* represented only £800 per unit; and in unit terms the payments that he received for the five-unit *Can You Forgive Her?* and the five-unit *He Knew He Was Right* were even smaller. From this perspective, the £1,757 that Trollope received for the two-unit *Belton Estate* represented his second highest rate of return.

    [5] To serve as Trollope's subeditor for *St. Paul's* at the salary of £250 per annum (to be paid out of Trollope's £1,000 per annum).

    [6] Bell soon died; see Trollope to Smith, 12 April 1867. Trollope enlisted the journalist Edward James Stephen Dicey (1832–1911) as subeditor on the same terms. A frequent contributor to *St. Paul's*, Dicey went on to serve as editor of the *Observer* from 1870 to 1879.

    [7] Marie Pauline Rose Blaze de Bury (1813–94), née Stuart. The hostess of a leading Paris salon, Mme Blaze de Bury contributed to the *Revue des Deux Mondes* and *Blackwood's*, and wrote novels under the pseudonym Hamilton Murray. In a letter to his wife, John Blackwood called her "a sort of masculine female political *intrigante*

maintained it. It is, I should say, over 15 years since M. Vernon came out.[8]

Has she the pluck to stand the chance of failure,—or rather of failing which is not exactly the same thing. If so let her write her novel entire & send it over to you. I would have it read,—or read it; and no doubt could get it sold if it was liked. She must not however expect a long price, as she would come out almost as a new novelist.

There is no novelist in the Cornhill. Geo Smith makes his bargains from time to time with one writer after another, as he finds it expedient. He buys the novels unwritten, but generally with the proviso that tho he is to be bound to pay the specified price, he is not to be bound to use the novel in the magazine unless he likes it.

I fear your friend is likely to be disappointed in her desire to sell a novel from a sample. Had she been writing novels for the last 10—or 5— or even 3 years, continuously, she could probably sell one without any sample; but I fear the publisher would not regard her past successes.[9]

I shall be in town and at the Club on Wednesday,—perhaps you will delay your answer till you have seen me.[1]

Yours always
Anthony Trollope

To Tom Taylor

MS University of Texas. SB 325.

8 Feb—1867   WALTHAM HOUSE, WALTHAM CROSS.
My dear Taylor.

Thanks for Browning & C Kingsley. I have written to Elliott & Fry[2] asking them whether next Thursday will suit for a sitting. I am glad you and yours like the new venture.[3] As for The Claverings, it seems to be so long since I wrote it that I have forgotten all about it.[4]

Yours always
Anthony Trollope

(an awfully clever woman)" (Porter, p. 121). T. A. Trollope, who knew her in Paris in 1840, remembered her as "one of my most charming friends of those days" (*What I Remember*, p. 324).

[8] *Mildred Vernon: A Tale of Parisian Life in the Last Days of the Monarchy* (1848).

[9] Interestingly, Trollope published Mme Blaze de Bury's novel himself: *All for Greed* appeared in *St. Paul's* from October 1867 through May 1868.

[1] Taylor forwarded Trollope's letter to Mme Blaze de Bury with a note saying, "I send you a letter from Anthony Trollope, to whom I wrote on your subject. I am sure his is the best opinion going." (MS Parrish Collection.)

[2] Elliot & Fry, Photographers, 55 Baker Street.

[3] Perhaps a reference to *The Last Chronicle of Barset*, published weekly from 1 December 1866.

[4] Trollope finished writing *The Claverings* on 31 December 1864. In February 1867 it was still appearing in the *Cornhill*.

Trollope. Engraving after a photograph by Elliot & Fry.

To John Tilley

MS New York University.

Feb 8—1867

My dear John.

I dont understand from your note whether the audit office strictures are to come to me, or whether I am to express any opinion in the first place. If so, consider it expressed & let them come. Joking apart I shall be very glad to see what your friend says.

Well; yes— I think I may say that pardon has been conceded.

Yours always

A. T.

To Thomas Adolphus Trollope

MS Parrish Collection.

25 Feb. 1867

My dear Tom.

The enclosed is from James Virtue who is to be the proprietor & publisher of our new magazine. Can you enable me to answer his question.[5]

Yours always affec

Anthony Trollope

To Charles Burney

MS Gordon N. Ray.

March 6. 1867   WALTHAM HOUSE, WALTHAM CROSS.

My dear Burney

I ought to have answered your note sooner. I thought however that something would turn up about the vacancy. Today I have heard from your Mr Post & he wants to be allowed to hold the office together with a public house. This he cannot do, & I have so told him.

All these appointments are made by parliamentary not official schedule, and as you are now on the warm side of the wall, (tho I dont think it can be very warm) you can doubtless manage the appointment thro Ducane.[6]

The first time I am near you I will come & look you up.

Yours always

Anthony Trollope

[5] Both T. A. Trollope and Frances Eleanor Trollope became contributors to *St. Paul's*.

[6] Charles Du Cane (1825–89), later Sir Charles, at this time MP for North Essex; Civil Lord of the Admiralty, 1866–68; Governor of Tasmania, 1869–74. Du Cane lived at Great Braxted Park, Witham, and by this date Burney was Rector of Wickham Bishops, Witham.

Alexander Strahan to Trollope
MS Bodleian.

7th. March 1867
Anthony Trollope Esq   56, LUDGATE HILL
Dear Sir,

I have much pleasure in herewith sending you the first budget of proofs of your book.[7]

Finding it would make 2 Vols of fair novel size I thought it as well to make 2 of it. This will enable me to spend a good deal more in advertising it and making it more widely known. And if I make a little more profit to myself I am sure you will not object.

I hope a happy *saleable* title has suggested itself to your mind.[8] A good deal depends upon this even with the best authors.

If not inconvenient for you, you will please return some of the proofs by Monday, as the sooner the book is published now the better. And if the title was settled we could begin to advertise at once, which would be an advantage.

Yours very truly,
A. Strahan.

To Alexander Strahan
MS (Trollope's copy) Bodleian. *Bibliography*, p. 288; B 327.

March 10—1867—
My dear Mr. Strahan.

On my return home yesterday I found your letter of the 7th., and I regret to say that I cannot allow the tales in your hands to be published in two volumes— I must ask you to understand that I altogether refuse my sanction to such an arrangement—

I have always endeavored to give good measure to the public— The pages, as you propose to publish them, are so thin and desolated, and contain such a poor rill of type meandering thro' a desert of margin,[9] as to make me ashamed of the idea of putting my name to the book— The stories were sold to you as one volume and you cannot by any argument be presumed to have the right of making it into two without my sanction to the change— Your intention is to publish the book as an ordinary two volume novel for I presume 20/– There is enough for a fair sized vol to be sold at cost price 10/6—

[7] A collection of short stories, all but two of which had been published in Strahan's magazines, *Good Words* and *The Argosy.*
[8] Trollope had originally intended to call the collection "Tales of All Countries. Third Series," but it was published as *Lotta Schmidt and Other Stories.*
[9] *The School for Scandal* (I.i): "A beautiful quarto page, where a neat rivulet of text shall meander through a meadow of margin."

I enclose a page of one of the former series, and ask you to compare it with the pages, which I return, from your own printers—

I am grieved that the expense of second printing should be thrown upon you. Tho' I have not been in any way the cause of this, I will share the expense of this printing with you on condition that you break up the type and print the stories afresh—

A. T.

To Lady Amberley

MS Parrish Collection. SB 328.

11. March [1867]
Monday   WALTHAM HOUSE, WALTHAM CROSS.
My dear Lady Amberley

I shall be in the Gallery of the House on ˣTuesday afternoon, & shall be delighted to go to you in the evening.

very truly yours
Anthony Trollope

ˣtomorrow

Your letter dated 7—has just reached me.

To [? Standen]

MS Parrish Collection.

March 25. 1867   WALTHAM HOUSE, WALTHAM CROSS.
Dear Sir.

The enclosed will explain itself. If the 4000 cigars are with you,—(or when they reach you)—will you let me know how I can get them. Or perhaps you would send them for me to

Chapman & Hall
publishers
193—Piccadilly.

If you will kindly let me know what I owe for duty &c &c. I will pay the amount to you or to any other person.

very faithfully

[? Standen] Esq   Anthony Trollope

To Lady Amberley

MS Parrish Collection. SB 329.

March 29—1867   WALTHAM HOUSE, WALTHAM CROSS.
My dear Lady Amberley.

I was very sorry to hear from Arthur Russell[10] that Lord Russell had lost a friend. I shall be very happy to dine with you on Tuesday 9th. You do not say your hour. If I am in town, (or can be) on Tuesday 2—I will come to you.

Yours always
Anthony Trollope

To [? Mrs. Frances Elliot][1]

MS Parrish Collection. B 330.

March 29. 1867   WALTHAM HOUSE, WALTHAM CROSS.
My dear friend.

I wrote you a horrid scrawl yesterday, having just received a petition from Strahan for some means of giving illustrations of the Martyr churches.[2] I doubt it cannot be done.

Have there not been other "Representative Women" so called? I have some such notion—but whether it is only so because of the "Representative Men," or whether it be a fact, I cannot say. If it be no fact I would make it a fact by doing a lot of them. I liked both those you sent me, but the lady the best. I may say I generally prefer ladies.

Apollonius of Tyana has been done very well lately, by one McCall,

[10] Arthur Russell (1825–92), nephew of Lord John Russell, whose secretary he had been, 1849–54. Trollope mentioned Russell as a Cosmopolitan Club friend (*Autobiography*, p. 160).

[1] Very probably Frances Minto Elliot (1820–98), née Dickinson, prolific writer on the social history of Italy, Spain, and France; author of *The Diary of an Idle Woman in Italy* (1871). Her second husband was Gilbert Elliot (1800–1891), the Dean of Bristol, whose family connection with the Earl of Minto led her to adopt (very irregularly) the name Minto. Mrs. Elliot had a wide circle of literary acquaintance, including Dickens. Her entry in Frances Hays's *Women of the Day* (1885) claimed that "in Trollope's 'Autobiography,' . . . there is a most touching allusion to their friendship" (p. 64), but the passage cited is the one that referred to Kate Field without naming her (all early editions of the *Autobiography* omitted the word "American" from the description). Mrs. Elliot contributed to Trollope's magazine, and the reference here may be to "Madame Tallien: A Biographical Sketch," *St. Paul's*, 1 (January 1868), 455–65, or to "Madame de Sevigné," *St. Paul's*, 2 (June 1868), 319–27. On 8 March 1877, Frances Eleanor Trollope wrote to Bice: "Mrs. Dean of Bristol Elliot . . . declares she has *not* quarrelled with your Uncle. This will be a severe blow to poor Anthony should he ever hear of it." (MS Robert A. Cecil.)

[2] No article referring to Rome's Martyr churches appeared in Strahan's *Good Words* or *Argosy* in 1867.

(I think) in the Fortnightly.[3] Of Julian the world is very ignorant. But I always regarded his apostacy as good old fashioned conservatism. We Xtians have always been so very bitter mouthed against those who have left us or would not come to us. My wife will read the MS. She has not as yet, because I have hardly been at home since I was with you. I write now from the town post.

Yours always
A. T.

John Blackwood to Joseph Langford
Porter, pp. 361–62.

April 3, 1867   Edinburgh.

* * *

I am pleased to hear of Trollope's disposition for further relations. When you see him give him my compliments, ar̗ say I am quite inclined. "Author of 'Nina Balatka' " may become a very convenient *nom de plume*, especially for such a very prolific writer as our friend. The anxiety about the authorship shows that the book is telling although not selling. I have a note from Oliphant[4] to-day saying, "I am much questioned as to the authorship of 'Nina Balatka'; is it Trollope?" I have replied that the authorship is a secret,[5] and playfully suggest that if he is further pestered on the subject he should hint that it is by Disraeli!

* * *

To F. I. Scudamore
MS Parrish Collection.

5 Ap—67   WALTHAM HOUSE, WALTHAM CROSS.

My dear Scudamore—

Walter Molesworth[6]—the writer of the enclosed is an old friend of mine. Could you tell me the circumstances of the case, so that I could answer him, & pardon me the trouble I am asking you to take.

Yours always
(in English—French or German)
Anty Trollope

---

[3] W. M. W. Call, "Apollonius of Tyana," *Fortnightly*, 2 (15 September 1865), 488–503.

[4] Laurence Oliphant's note is in the Parrish Collection.

[5] An unsigned review in the *Spectator*, 40 (23 March 1867), 329–30, almost certainly by Richard Holt Hutton, began: "If criticism be not a delusion from the very bottom, this pleasant little story is written by Mr. Anthony Trollope." (Smalley, pp. 268–69.) Trollope remarked that Hutton showed "more sagacity than good-nature" in saying this, but went on to call him "the most observant, and generally the most eulogistic" of his critics (*Autobiography*, p. 205).

[6] Walter Molesworth: see Trollope to Merivale, 21 December 1856, n. 7.

To the President and Council of the Royal Academy
MS University of Michigan.

April 8. 1867   WALTHAM HOUSE, WALTHAM CROSS.
Mr. Anthony Trollope presents his compliments to the President and Council of the Royal Academy, and will have much pleasure in accepting their kind invitation for 4 May.[7]

To Lady Amberley
MS Parrish Collection. SB 909.

                Garlants Hotel. Suffolk Street.
[April 1867]   Pall Mall.
Dear Lady Amberley.
    I was very sorry I could not be in town last Tuesday. Would you kindly let me know what is your hour for dinner.[8]
                        Yours very truly
                        Anthony Trollope

To F. I. Scudamore
MS Parrish Collection.

April 9. 1867.   POST OFFICE
Dear Scudamore.
    Many thanks for the papers about poor Meyer. Could you send me back Molesworths letter, as I have not his address. He is a Devonshire man, & is only in London for a few days. I have not looked at the papers yet.
                        Yours always
                        Anthy Trollope

---

    [7] To attend the Anniversary Dinner of the Royal Academy prior to the public opening of the annual Summer Exhibition. Trollope not only attended the dinner but answered the final toast ("to the Interests of Literature").
    [8] Trollope attended Lady Amberley's Tuesday "at home" on 9 April. Lady Amberley gave the following account in her diary: "We had a little dinner of Huxley, Anthony Trollope[,] Lady Russell, and Mr. Knatchbul [sic] Hugesson whom Amberley brought home fr. the H. of C. Dinner was very pleasant, Ly R. enjoyed it very much and was pleased to make acquaintance with Trollope and Huxley. A and I thought T's voice too loud, he rather drowned Huxley's pleasant quiet voice which was certainly better worth hearing." (Bertrand and Patricia Russell, eds., *The Amberley Papers: The Letters and Diaries of Lord and Lady Amberley* [1937], II, 27.)

To George Smith

MS John Murray. B 331.

April 12. 1867   WALTHAM HOUSE, WALTHAM CROSS.
My dear Smith
You know probably that dear old Robert Bell died this morning. I send a notice of him which I hope you may find yourself justified in inserting in the P.M.G. tomorrow.[9] He was a very manly fellow. I loved him well. And I should be sorry that he should pass away without a word of record.

                         Yours always
Geo Smith Esq   Anthony Trollope

To Edmund Routledge[1]

MS Parrish Collection. SB 332.

April 13–1867   WALTHAM HOUSE, WALTHAM CROSS.
Dear Sir
I fear I shall be too busy all thro' the autumn and to the end of the year to do anything for your new magazine.[2]

                      Yours faithfully
E Routledge Esq   Anthony Trollope

To John Dennis

MS Parrish Collection. B 333.

April 15. 1867   WALTHAM HOUSE, WALTHAM CROSS.
My dear Dennis.
Do not forget to return the lecture, as I have no other copy.[3] I find that committees appreciate best a mode of arrangement in regard to lectures, which I have twice suggested. I offer to give a radical lecture, or to subscribe £10— They always take the £10—saying that the radical lecture is too much for their strength.

Bell will be buried at Kensall Green as I understand on Thursday. I shall be there certainly.

He edited the Home News for India & Australia for the Messrs. Grind-

---

[9] "Mr. Robert Bell," *Pall Mall Gazette*, 13 April 1867, p. 2. Trollope's theme was the professional literary man: literature was Bell's sole means of earning a livelihood throughout an honorable career that lasted for more than forty years.

[1] Edmund Routledge (1843–99), second son of the publisher George Routledge.

[2] Routledge's new magazine, *Broadway*, appeared in September 1867.

[3] Perhaps "Higher Education of Women," reprinted in *Four Lectures* (1938).

lay.[4] But of the circumstances I know nothing, nor do I know anything of the Messrs. Grindlay. I have not the slightest idea who will succeed him.

Yours always faithfully
Anthony Trollope

To James Virtue

MS Parrish Collection. SB 334.

April 19. 1867   WALTHAM HOUSE, WALTHAM CROSS.
My dear Virtue.
   I send the cover of the Orley Farm.
   The wording would be

Whitehall Magazine
Edited by
Anthony Trollope.
With Illustrations
By
J. E. Millais

Picture of Whitehall Gate

London
Virtue & Co. City Road

It should be a little bigger than the enclosed.[5]

Yours always
A. T.

---

[4] *Home News for India*, a weekly, published 1847–98; *Home News for Australia*, a monthly, published 1853–98.
   [5] The title "Whitehall Magazine" was discarded, as were several earlier possibilities, including "The Monthly Westminster" and "The Monthly Liberal" (see Trollope to Virtue, 14 December 1866). The names all reflect the distinctly political emphasis that Trollope wished to give the magazine.

To John Murray[6]

MS Parrish Collection. B 335.

9. May. 1867 ATHENAEUM CLUB
My dear Sir.

I presume that you knew something of the late Robert Bell, from your connexion with the Corporation of the Literary Fund. A memorial is to be presented to Lord Derby by Lord Stanhope asking for a pension for his widow, and it now lies at the office of the Literary Fund, 4, Adelphi Terrace. The Memorial contains the circumstances of the case. Will you call at the office and sign it.

Yours very faithfully
John Murray Esq Anthony Trollope

To Wilkie Collins

MS Parrish Collection. SB 336.

9 May. 1867 ATHENAEUM CLUB
My dear Collins

Will you sign a memorial on behalf of the widow of the late Robert Bell, which is to be presented by Lord Stanhope to Earl Derby? Poor Bell worked hard at letters for over 50 years.

The memorial is lying at No. 4—Adelphi Terrace, Strand, the rooms of the Literary Fund. Ask for Mr. Blewitt.

Yours always
faithfully
Anthony Trollope

Charles Dickens to Trollope

MS Taylor Collection. Taylor, "Letters," p. 7.

Ninth May 1867 GAD'S HILL PLACE,
Thursday HIGHAM BY ROCHESTER, KENT.
My dear Trollope,

The instant I got your letter at my office, I of course went over to the Adelphi Terrace and signed the Memorial. I had heard with much satisfaction that poor Mrs. Bell had found a friend in you, for I knew she could have no stauncher or truer friend.

Faithfully Yours Always
Anthony Trollope Esquire. Charles Dickens

[6] John Murray (1808–92), prominent publisher; son and successor of the John Murray who had published one of Mrs. Trollope's works.

To Fred[7]

MS Parrish Collection.

11. May 1867   WALTHAM HOUSE, WALTHAM CROSS.
My dear Fred.
Your Wednesday is the dinner of the Literary Fund. I must be there—
and you ought to be there instead of entertaining W. Melville[8] & others
at the Garrick. All the same I wish I could be with you.

Yours always
Any Trollope

To Octavian Blewitt

MS Parrish Collection.

15 May. 1867   WALTHAM HOUSE, WALTHAM CROSS.
My dear Mr Blewitt
I am very sorry to say that I cannot do the speech,[9] as the toast will not
come on till late and I am pledged to my wife to go out with her at 10—
You will find plenty quite ready—let Bagehot[1] or Dicey or Morley give
the toast, & Doyle[2] answer it. Thanks for what you say of the Memorial.
I shall see you tomorrow.

Yours always
Anthony Trollope

[7] "Fred" is unidentified, but is probably the same Fred to whom Trollope apparently
wrote later in the year (given here as Trollope's last letter for 1867).

[8] George John Whyte-Melville (1821–78), minor novelist and sportsman; the hunting scenes in his novels were much admired.

[9] At the Royal Literary Fund's Anniversary Dinner, to be held that evening.

[1] Walter Bagehot (1826–77), the distinguished economist, journalist, and man of
letters.

[2] Sir Francis Hastings Charles Doyle (1810–88), poet; Professor of Poetry at Oxford,
1867–77. Doyle in fact proposed the toast (to "Imaginative Literature and Mr. Anthony Trollope"), and Trollope answered it. Earlier, Earl Stanhope, President of the
Fund, had expressed his pleasure at Trollope's practice of having characters reap-
pear in subsequent novels, an "invention, attended with most successful results, of
which, as far as I know, the original merit belongs to M. de Balzac." Trollope said: "I
am quite sure that the response to this toast might have been much better given by
Sir Francis Doyle. . . . I think that where . . . Poetry and Fiction have been brought
together . . . the more noble one [poetry] should have had the latter word. . . . For myself, I can only speak of fiction, and I should be happy, after what has been said by
the President of the Society, to drink long life to M. de Balzac. I am told that he was
the man who invented that style of fiction in which I have attempted to work. I assure any young men around me who may be desirous of following the same steps that
they cannot possibly find any style easier. The carrying on of a character from one
book to another is very pleasant to the author; but I am not sure that all readers will
participate in that pleasure." (Royal Literary Fund's *Annual Report* for 1867, pp.
28–29.)

To ?[3]

MS Parrish Collection.

May 15. 1867   Waltham Cross
Dear Sir.
I send you with many thanks a cheque for £12 – 0 – 8 charges on the cigars.

Yours always faithfully
Anthony Trollope

To John Dennis

MS UCLA.

May 18–1867.   WALTHAM HOUSE, WALTHAM CROSS.
My dear Dennis.
I fear I shall not be at the next Fortnightly meeting. But were I there, what could I do? In fact nobody will ever do anything. My own idea is that there is really nothing to be done. I do not specially dislike Morley, but I do not care for his style of work, & cannot interest myself in the thing.

Yours always
Anthy Trollope

To George Smith

SB 337 (Sadleir's transcript).

[31 May 1867]

*   *   *

No dedication and no preface. It is all nonsense. I never wrote a preface and never dedicated a book.[4]

*   *   *

To Lady Western[5]

MS Parrish Collection. SB 338.

[3 June 1867][6]   Clovelly. Devonshire.
My dear Lady Western.
I got the card which you so kindly sent me to the Athenaeum, and answered it the same day, saying how sorry I was that I should be down

---

[3] Probably the recipient of Trollope's letter of 25 March 1867 (? Standen).

[4] Smith had evidently suggested a dedication and preface for *The Last Chronicle of Barset*. Despite Trollope's scorn for prefaces, however, he soon wrote one to defend the prominent part given to a "fallen woman" in *The Vicar of Bullhampton* (this appeared in the novel's first book edition, published in April 1870).

[5] Lady Western, wife of Sir Thomas Burch Western (1795–1873), MP for North Essex.

[6] Dated from postmark.

here for a few days just at the time you named. I cannot conceive how my letter failed. I think I wrote it at another club, the Garrick.

I am very sorry that I am absent from town on your day.

most faithfully
Anthony Trollope

To Frederic Chapman

MS Parrish Collection. B 339.

June 13. 1867   WALTHAM HOUSE, WALTHAM CROSS.
My dear Chapman.

I wanted to see you yesterday to ask you to assist me in getting Bell's books down to me here. I have bought the lot. I am told there are nearly 4,000.[7] Could you not put me in the way of getting them down here. I should like to have this done early next week. I will call on you tomorrow evening about 5. I have another subject on which I wish to speak to you.

Yours always
Any Trollope

To John Blackwood

MS Taylor Collection.

June. 13. 1867   WALTHAM HOUSE, WALTHAM CROSS.
My dear Blackwood.

I have just got your card. Is Mrs. Blackwood with you? Will you come and dine & sleep on Monday July 1? And will your wife do so also if she be with you.

Yours always
Anthony Trollope

To ?

MS University College London.

June—15—1867   WALTHAM HOUSE, WALTHAM CROSS.
Dear Sir.

Many thanks for your kind letter, which, alas, is all too late, as the entire work[8] was written & printed, before the first number came out. I

---

[7] Bell's library had been put up for auction by his impoverished widow, but Trollope went to the executors, had the auction arrangements canceled, and bought the entire library at a price above market value. "We all know," he said, "the difference in value between buying and selling of books." (Escott, p. 307.) On Trollope's own library, see Trollope to Henry Merivale Trollope, 23 July 1880.

[8] *The Last Chronicle.*

have never been able to correct such errors as those pointed out [by] you kindly, because I always complete my story before the first printing is published, & the printer, taking advantage of this, prints in advance.

I forget now how I got over the final difficulty of discharging Crawley, —not having the sheets by me, & the whole thing being with me a task long over & almost forgotten. The first great lapse of examining the wife was very great.[9] But I console myself with thinking that a novelist, in dealing as he must do, almost necessarily, with many affairs of life, with many professions & with various trades may be excused, perhaps, the blunders if his pictures are generally true. Not to be false in sentiment, not [to] be untrue to nature, not to be dull, not to be grandiloquent, not to be injurious in his teaching, not to be immoral in his pictures,—these I think should be his attempts. Do not suppose that I think myself to have been successful in all, or always in any. But I explain my views hoping that my explanation may be held as an excuse in some sort for manifold errors on technical points.[1]

With thanks for your care now and on a former occasion I am
Yours faithfully
Anthony Trollope

To George MacDonald[2]

MS Parrish Collection.

June 27—1867   WALTHAM HOUSE, WALTHAM CROSS.
My dear Mr Macdonald

I have written to the Post Office about your nephew— If I hear anything, I will write to you again. I am never there myself. My work is altogether away from the General Post Office;—in the provinces.
Yours very faithfully
Any Trollope

[9] Probably a reference to chap. i.

[1] In *Phineas Finn*, completed shortly before this date, Trollope had commented somewhat ironically on the problem of accuracy: "The poor fictionist very frequently finds himself to have been wrong in his description of things in general, and is told so roughly by the critics, and tenderly by the friends of his bosom. . . . He catches salmon in October; or shoots his partridges in March. . . . He opens the opera-houses before Easter, and makes Parliament sit on a Wednesday evening. And then those terrible meshes of the Law! How is a fictionist, in these excited days, to create the needed biting interest without legal difficulties; and how again is he to steer his little bark clear of so many rocks . . . ?" (Chap. xxix.) See also Trollope to Pollock, 8 January 1874.

[2] George MacDonald (1824–1905), popular Scottish poet and novelist; best known today for his fantasies for children, such as *At the Back of the North Wind* (1871).

To Octavian Blewitt

MS Royal Literary Fund.

July 9—1867³   ATHENAEUM CLUB
My dear Mr Blewitt.

I ought to have sent you this back before. There is nothing so distressing as this arranging of the nonsensical words which one has spoken at these meetings. I have however on this occasion re-written a word or two about dear old Robert Bell.⁴

Yours always
Anthony Trollope

I shall be up on Wednesday.

To John Blackwood

MS National Library of Scotland. Excerpt, Parker, p. 58; B 340.

July 10. 1867   WALTHAM HOUSE, WALTHAM CROSS.
My dear Blackwood.

I sent you the novel by this days post, registered, to the same address as this letter. I sent it a few days earlier than I said because I do not quite know when you will want to use it; and I shall be abroad from July 17 to August 20th. When shall you want to have the first number corrected? If for the September number, which is not probable perhaps, you must either let me have the sheets before I go, or send them to Mrs. Trollope to bring after me. She does not start till the 21st. If the story will not be used till October I can correct the sheets after my return. Touching the name, I find that "Linda Tressel" is the most suitable, as you will say when you read it. The other however is not unsuitable, and you can take your choice. Do *not* take the two.

Let me have a line to acknowledge receipt of the novel.⁵

Yours always
Anthony Trollope

³ The date is scrawled in evident haste at the top of the letter; perhaps the letter was written on Monday, 8 July, since Trollope speaks of being up on Wednesday rather than "tomorrow."

⁴ At the Royal Literary Fund's Anniversary Dinner on 15 May, Trollope said of Bell: "It may be that many of our guests here assembled will only have known him as one of the eminent literary men of the age . . . but workers at the purposes of the Literary Fund will know that we have lost one who can hardly be replaced." (Royal Literary Fund's *Annual Report* for 1867, p. 29.)

⁵ On 16 July Blackwood replied, offering £450 for the copyright of *Linda Tressel* (the same amount that he had given for *Nina Balatka*). Blackwood added: "On looking into the matter I was disappointed to find that we had not sold 500 copies of Nina which is a great shame & a heavy loss but I trust that the well earned reputation [that] could not help Nina herself will help Linda." (MS Bodleian.) Since this story was also to be published anonymously, Blackwood probably believed that enough people knew

To A. H. Layard[6]

MS British Library. B 341.

ATHENAEUM CLUB

July 15. 1867   Address, Waltham Cross.
My dear Mr. Layard.
Thanks for the kindness of your letter.
After what you have said I will look elsewhere for papers on home politics, as we should certainly wish to have the subject treated consecutively—& not less than every other month. I feel though that I cannot press the matter on you.
I hope in every other month also to have an article on foreign politics —and these articles would not necessarily be written by one & the same person. Could you, do you think, write such an article for me for the November number.[7]

Yours very sincerely
Anthony Trollope

To John Blackwood

MS National Library of Scotland.

July 18—1867.   WALTHAM HOUSE, WALTHAM CROSS.
My dear Blackwood.
Many thanks for your letter. I will accept your offer for £450. I am just off,—and shall be back by August 20, which will be in time for correcting the[8] proof. I hope the venture may succeed.

Yours always
Anthony Trollope

---

of the secret to make it an open one. But, like *Nina Balatka, Linda Tressel* had poor sales. The novel was serialized in *Blackwood's* from October 1867 through May 1868, and published in two volumes in May 1868.

[6] Austen Henry Layard (1817–94), later Sir Austen, distinguished archaeologist (the excavator of Nineveh) and statesman. In *The New Zealander* (written in 1855–56, but not published until 1972), Trollope had abused Layard (under the name "Hevenin") for his attacks on the conduct of the Crimean War.

[7] Layard was unable to meet the November deadline, but supplied an article for the following month: "England's Place in Europe," *St. Paul's*, 1 (December 1867), 275–91.

[8] Letter cut here; remainder in another hand.

To Messrs. Parks & Barnet

MS Parrish Collection.

July 18. 1867   WALTHAM HOUSE, WALTHAM CROSS.
Gentlemen.

I am very sorry to say that I must be away from England on July 27, the day you name.

very faithfully yours
Messrs. Parks & Barnet   Anthony Trollope

To L. Valentine[9]

MS Parrish Collection.

16. August. 1867   Geneva.
Sir.

Your letter of the 12 July has only just reached me on my travels,—owing to erroneous address. I fear that my hands are too full to enable me to write a story for your magazine. I am however grateful to you for the kind offer made to me.

Yours faithfully
L. Valentine Esq   Anthony Trollope

To Miss Dunlop

MS Parrish Collection. SB 343.

22. Augt. 1867   WALTHAM HOUSE, WALTHAM CROSS.
My dear Miss Dunlop.

I need hardly say with how much pleasure!—only that my big brother is getting so much the best of me in this photograph.[1]

Yours most sincerely
Anthony Trollope

To Mr. Smith

MS Parrish Collection.

Augt 22—1867   WALTHAM HOUSE, WALTHAM CROSS.
My dear Mr Smith

On my return home yesterday from the Engadine,[2] I got your kind letter asking me to dine at Richmond on the 20th.—too late, alas. I do not doubt the party was a pleasant one. Many thanks for thinking of me.

Yours very truly
Anthony Trollope

[9] Just possibly Mrs. Laura Valentine (*d.* 1899), editor of annuals and compilations, who may have signed herself "L. Valentine."
[1] See Trollope to Mrs. Trollope, 21 June 1864.
[2] The Engadine Valley, Switzerland.

To J. E. Millais

MS Parrish Collection.

ATHENAEUM CLUB

August 22. 1867   address Waltham Cross

My dear Millais

Are you as yet out of town? I came back yesterday having had such a scorching in Italy!

Virtue wishes me to speak to you about planning a cover or wrapper for the new Magazine, which is to be called the "*St. Pauls.*" Can you do it, & if so at once? He is very anxious that you should.[3]

Yours always

Anthony Trollope

When will your illustrations be ready.

To John Blackwood

MS National Library of Scotland. SB 344.

2 Sept 1867   WALTHAM HOUSE, WALTHAM CROSS.

My dear Blackwood

I write a line to say that I am home, whenever you may wish to send me proofs.

Yours always

A. T.

John Blackwood to Trollope

MS (copy) National Library of Scotland.

Strathtyrum[4]

Sept 13th. 1867   St Andrews

My dear Trollope

I enclose proof of the first part of "Linda Tressel" of which I intended that more should have been put into type but by some blunder it has not been done.

I have read the whole story & I am very sorry to say that I fear you have made a blunder and so have I.—

There is no adequate motive for Madame Staubachs conduct & her persistence becomes irritatingly wearisome.

You have really no right to say that it was the Calvinistic old jades *virtues* that caused poor Linda's sufferings.

I hope devoutly that I may turn out wrong in my opinion but the

[3] The vignette of St. Paul's Cathedral on the cover of the new magazine is unsigned, but it may well be by Millais.

[4] Blackwood's country home near St. Andrews Golf Course.

No. 3. DECEMBER, 1867. Price 1s

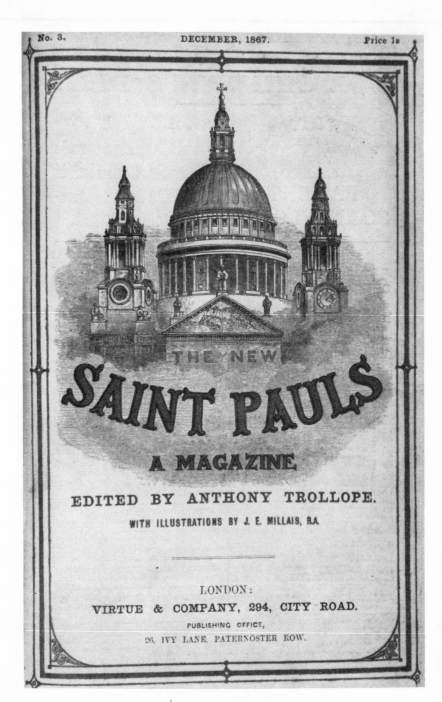

THE NEW

SAINT PAULS

A MAGAZINE

EDITED BY ANTHONY TROLLOPE.

WITH ILLUSTRATIONS BY J. E. MILLAIS, R.A.

LONDON:

VIRTUE & COMPANY, 294, CITY ROAD.

PUBLISHING OFFICE,

26, IVY LANE, PATERNOSTER ROW.

St. Paul's Magazine

provoking sameness of each step in the story weighed very heavily upon me as I read.

Still I shall pray that I am mistaken & that the literary merit of the story will carry it through.

Herr Molk is a capital sketch and Linda herself is excellent if she had a man to give her heart to. Ludovic is too much of a myth except in that frantic kissing scene. The descriptions throughout are vivid & good & I daresay the want of somebody like a man is the main defect.

When Linda denounces Peter as a ——— beast do you mean that she called him a damned beast? I am sure she was justified.

Altho' Madame Staubach only wearies me it is possible that the blessed newspaper critics may call her A Creation & so I shall conclude by wishing her all success. Tell Mrs. Trollope that it is a comfort to me to think that she liked the story.

I hope you had a good time abroad & have returned in great power for your work which is always heavier than that of most men.

always yours truly

Anthony Trollope Esq John Blackwood

To John Blackwood

MS National Library of Scotland. *Commentary*, p. 270; Parker, p. 58; B 345.

September 16. 1867   WALTHAM HOUSE, WALTHAM CROSS.
My dear Blackwood.

I will return the proof today or tomorrow; but I write a line at once to say that you are quite at liberty to give up the story if you do not mind the expense of having put it into type. Do not consider yourself to be in the least bound by your offer;—only let me have the MS back at once without going to the printers. What has been with them must of course be recopied.

Let me have a line from you at once,—and feel quite sure that your returning it to me will moult no feather between you & me.[5]

Yours always faithfully
Anthy Trollope

To ?

Maggs Catalogue 421 (Spring 1922). SB 346.

18 September 1867

Trollope writes a woman who wishes to submit a manuscript novel to *St. Paul's Magazine* that he has one novel appearing and two to follow.

[5] Blackwood's reply has not been traced, but he obviously renewed his determination to publish *Linda Tressel*. See Trollope to Blackwood, 19 September 1867.

To John Blackwood

MS Parrish Collection.

Sept 19–67.   Waltham X
My dear Blackwood.

We will hope our best for the fate of L. T.

It is hardly possible for a novelist who depends more on character than on incident for his interest always to make the chief personages of his stories pleasant acquaintances. His object is to shew what is the effect of such and such qualities on the happiness of those on whom they act; and in doing this he can hardly contrive that a nice young man should always be there to be married to the nice young woman. It may be so now & again; but not always— Scott & his followers, who deal with incidents chiefly,—from the taking of a castle of Torquilstone down to the elopement of a lady with her groom,—have of course always been able at their pleasure to have a Rowena ready for their Ivanhoe,—or a Polly Jones for their Jack Smith as the case may be. Do not suppose that I am turning up my nose at stories of action, which I regard as of far away the highest class if written with the requisite power,—but am simply describing the difference between the work of such workers and my own. I wanted to shew how religion, if misunderstood, may play the very Devil in a house;—and as regards the "Devil" part I have succeeded according to your own description. If however the household be uninteresting I have failed. I cannot admit that I am bound always to have a pleasant young man. Pleasant young men are not so common. Of a certain age, I admit they are to be found!

Yours always
A. T.

To R. S. Oldham[6]

MS Parrish Collection. SB 347.

Sept 22. 1867.   WALTHAM HOUSE, WALTHAM CROSS.
My dear Oldham.

I send the enclosed in re Tommie. I wrote a long preachment to your wife the other day, & therefore will be concise with you to day. I suppose you are back in the land of cakes.[7]

Yours always
with much love
Any Trollope

[6] Richard Samuel Oldham (1823–1914), Rector of St. Mary's Episcopal Church, Glasgow; Dean of Glasgow, 1877–78. In its obituary on Oldham, *The Times* claimed that "in his early days in Glasgow, disguised and accompanied by Anthony Trollope, he visited the worst slums of the city. As a result of this he established day and Sunday schools and mission chapels which flourish to this day." (26 June 1914, p. 10.)

[7] Scotland.

To James Grant[8]

MS Parrish Collection.

OFFICE OF THE ST. PAULS MAGAZINE,
Septr. 25. 1867   294, CITY ROAD, LONDON.
Sir.

As we are already provided with novels—having two in print—and another ready, I fear it would be of no use for me to ask you to send your Mss. I beg however to thank you kindly for the offer.

Yours faithfully
James Grant Esq   Anthony Trollope
   26 Danube Street
   Edinburgh

To John Blackwood

MS National Library of Scotland. SB 349 (misdated).

3—Oct 1867   WALTHAM HOUSE, WALTHAM CROSS.
Dear Blackwood

Many thanks for the £225. I suppose a receipt when the transaction is completed will satisfy you and the C. of Ex.[9]

Yours always
Anthony Trollope

To A. H. Layard

MS British Library. B 348.

Oct 5—1867   WALTHAM HOUSE, WALTHAM CROSS.
My dear Mr. Layard.

I write not knowing at all where you are. In your last note you spoke of an article which you wd write for us,—not for the November number, but for the one to follow. I have consequently arranged for two articles on home politics for our two first numbers, (—of which you may perhaps have seen the first,)—and shall be glad, if it suits you, to have yours for the December number. If so it should be with me quite early in November. You probably know that the magazine-mongers insist on having these periodicals out some days before the end of the month;—and that in order to fit the articles any one intended for special publication in a particular month should be early.

Yours always
Anthony Trollope

---

[8] James Grant (1822–87), prolific novelist and miscellaneous writer; ardent advocate of Scottish rights.

[9] Chancellor of the Exchequer, a joking reference to Blackwood's accountant.

John Tilley to Trollope

MS (copy in a Post Office clerk's hand) Parrish Collection. *Autobiography*, pp. 280–81.

Oct. 9. 1867.   General Post Office
Sir,

I have received your letter of the 3rd. instant in which you tender your resignation as Surveyor in the Post Office Service[1] and state as your reason for this step that you have adopted another profession the exigencies of which have become so great as to make you feel that you cannot give to the duties of the Post Office that amount of attention which you consider the Postmaster General has a right to expect.

You have for many years ranked among the most conspicuous servants of the Post Office which on several occasions when you have been employed on large and difficult matters has reaped much benefit from the great abilities which you have been able to place at its disposal; and, in mentioning this I have been especially glad to record that, notwithstanding the many calls upon your time, you have never permitted your other avocations to interfere with your Post Office work, which has always been faithfully, and, indeed energetically performed.[2]

In accepting your resignation, which he does with much regret, the Duke of Montrose[3] desires me to convey to you his own sense of the value of your services and to state how alive he is to the loss which will be sustained by the Department in which you have long been an ornament and where your place will be with difficulty supplied.[4]

I am,
Sir,
Your obedient Servant,

Anthony Trollope Esqre.   J Tilley

[1] Trollope's letter of resignation has not been traced. In the *Autobiography*, however, he printed Tilley's reply because, despite its "official flummery," it "may be taken as evidence that I did not allow my literary enterprises to interfere with my official work" (p. 281).

[2] At this point in the *Autobiography* Trollope inserted a parenthesis: "There was a touch of irony in this word 'energetically,' but still it did not displease me."

[3] James Graham (1799–1874), 4th Duke of Montrose; Postmaster General, 1866–68.

[4] Trollope replied immediately, and on 10 October Tilley forwarded the reply to the Duke, adding "You will be glad to see that Mr. Trollope is pleased with his letter." (MS General Post Office, London.) By resigning, Trollope forfeited any claim to a pension. Had he worked until age 60 (another eight years), he would have been eligible for an annual pension of about £500.

To John Blackwood
MS National Library of Scotland. SB 350.

Oct 11—1867   WALTHAM HOUSE, WALTHAM CROSS.
My dear B.
I have had no second number of L. T. to correct.
Yours always
A. T.

To ?[5]
MS Taylor Collection.

October 14. 1867   WALTHAM HOUSE, WALTHAM CROSS.
My dear old fellow.
It is time. I sent in my resignation a week ago,—and I shall be a free man on 31 October as far as the Post Office goes. I should have written a line to you, to say that it was all over and that we were no longer in the same boat. But I do not see why there is the slightest reason why that should make any difference in our old friendship—which is so old that nothing ought to break or stop it now. I am quite as willing as ever I was to lend you a razor and a pair of stockings, and shall be quite as determined to insist on having them back *some day*.

The chaps in the GPO are going to give me a dinner on the 31st. I suppose you couldn't come up—and take a part, & hear the speechifying, and help to make a row. We should be delighted to give you a bed as long as you liked,—and your wife half of it, if she could come. Tell her so with my love. Harry, who is now a Cornet of mounted Yeomanry & is with his regiment, shall have your message. I had to go up to London on Saturday to send him *dress spurs*.[6]
Yours always
Most affectionately
Anthony Trollope

To M. E. Grant Duff[7]
B 351.

                                OFFICE OF THE ST. PAULS MAGAZINE,
17 October 1867   294, CITY ROAD, LONDON.
Dear Sir.
You may perhaps have seen the first number of the Saint Paul's Magazine, which is being edited by myself. If so you will have noticed that it

---

[5] Apparently a colleague in the Post Office; perhaps a surveyor.
[6] "*Spurs*" is underlined twice.
[7] Mountstuart Elphinstone Grant Duff (1829–1906), later Sir Mountstuart, MP for

is our object to make the magazine a vehicle for political articles on the Liberal side. I am not at liberty to mention the names of those who are already writing for us, but I believe you would find the matter such as you would approve in point of feeling and line of argument.

I trouble you now to ask you whether you would give us occasionally the advantage of your assistance in reference to foreign politics. If you could do so we should much like to have an article from you on the present condition of Prussia with regard to France for the number to be published in November.[8] In this case your MS should be with us by the 7th* of this month, in order to give you time to revise your own proofs. The length should be 12 or 14 pages. Should this not be within your power I am sure you will excuse my troubling you.

Yours faithfully
Anthony Trollope
address:—Waltham House,

M. E. Grant Duff, Esq., M.P.   Waltham Cross.

* i.e. by 7th November to be ready for publication by 24th or 25th of that month.

To Charles Kent[9]

MS Huntington Library. B 351a.

October 18th. 1867.   WALTHAM HOUSE, WALTHAM CROSS.
Sir.

I shall be most happy to be one of the Stewards at the dinner proposed to be given to Mr Dickens on Saturday November 2—& will certainly make one of the party on that occasion.[1]

Your faithful Servant
Anthony Trollope

Elgin Burghs. A recognized authority on foreign policy (his *Studies of European Politics* had appeared in 1866), Grant Duff was appointed Undersecretary of State for India in Gladstone's 1868 ministry.

[8] Grant Duff did not write the article. A year later Adam Gielgud contributed "Prussia, Germany, and France," *St. Paul's*, 3 (November 1868), 147–62.

[9] William Charles Mark Kent (1823–1902), proprietor and editor of the *Sun*, 1853–71; close friend of Dickens.

[1] The dinner, held on 2 November 1867 at Freemasons' Hall, honored Dickens on the eve of his departure for a reading tour in the United States. Trollope answered the toast to literature, a field in which Dickens was "a great chieftain"; most of Trollope's speech, however, was devoted to challenging Carlyle's debunking of fiction. (Charles Kent, *The Dickens Dinner* [1867], pp. 23–25.)

To W. H. Gregory

R. G. Gregory's transcript. B 352.

OFFICE OF THE ST. PAULS MAGAZINE,
294, CITY ROAD, LONDON.

Oct. 21. 1867—

My dear Gregory.

F. Lawley has mentioned to me that he has had some communication with you about an article which he thinks you might write about poor Lord Dunkellin,[2] who as I hear from him was a close friend of yours. I have no doubt if you have the necessary papers at command you could make a charming paper on the subject. If you like to do this we shall be delighted to take it from you. We are as liberal as others in our payment & will not cut down your little honorarium. Let me have a line to say if you can do it, & if so at about what length. It should be about 12 pages. If intended for the December number it should be with me by December 7.

Yours always
Anthony Trollope

To A. H. Layard

MS British Library. B 353.

OFFICE OF THE ST. PAULS MAGAZINE,
294, CITY ROAD, LONDON.

October 21 1867

My dear Layard.

Thanks for your note. It seems now almost sure that the Emperor will find himself driven to send troops to Italy.[3] If so, he will surely have committed the worst blunder. You ask for a late date;—but we are forced to be very early in type. You will of course choose to correct your own proof. The whole thing has to be stereotyped— And they will insist on having the magazine ready for distribution by the 24th. Will you let me name the 10th. as the last available day.

I will bear in mind what you say about not mentioning your name. Not but what these things always get out.

Yours faithfully
Anthony Trollope

[2] Ulick Canning de Burgh (1827–67), Lord Dunkellin; military secretary to Lord Canning when Canning was Governor-General of India; Liberal MP for Co. Galway, 1865–67. Gregory did not write the article but described Dunkellin in his *Autobiography* (1894).

[3] On 28 October 1867 the French fleet arrived off Civita Vecchia; two days later Napoleon III's troops entered Rome to counter movements by Garibaldi against the Papal States.

To Christopher Hodgson

MS D. R. Bentham.

Oct 21. 1867.   Waltham Cross.
My dear Hodgson.

I am very much gratified by your most friendly note. I am delighted to hear that we shall meet on the 31st.[4]—but hope that may not be the last by many a time.

It is not so much that the office is no long[er] worth my while, as you say, as that other things have grown upon [me] so fast that I feel myself beginning to neglect the office and I am sure you will acknowledge that when that is the case it had better be given up.

Yours always
Most heartily
Anthony Trollope

To [? A. G.] Marten[5]

MS Bodleian. SB 354.

October 22—1867   WALTHAM HOUSE, WALTHAM CROSS.
My dear Mr Marten.

I know no other person whose name is on the enclosed list but yours. Who is the lady, & should she be assisted? The letter reads like that of a person in the begging letter trade.[6] I think you will excuse this trouble.

Yours faithfully
Anthony Trollope

To [? Mrs. Frances Elliot][7]

MS Parrish Collection. B 355.

Oct 23. 67   WALTHAM HOUSE, WALTHAM CROSS.
My dear friend.

I could not possibly have come to Brighton before Oct 31, when I am clear of the Post Office—and now I do not like, (indeed at present cannot)

---

[4] According to the *Spectator*, nearly one hundred people were present at the Albion Tavern for the farewell dinner given to Trollope on his retirement from the Post Office. F. I. Scudamore, who was in the chair, made "an amusing and entertaining speech on the difficulties with which Mr. Trollope had had to contend in gaining such a place in literature, without ever neglecting his duties in a very hardworked service. . . . Mr. Trollope in returning thanks for the toast of his health professed melancholy at bidding adieu to the Post Office." (*Spectator*, 2 November 1867, p. 1219.)

[5] Possibly Alfred George Marten (1830–1910), later Sir Alfred, barrister; MP for Cambridge Borough, 1874–80.

[6] Doubtless a request for aid from the Royal Literary Fund.

[7] References to "the dean" and the Dickens Dinner make it almost certain that the addressee was Mrs. Elliot (whose husband, the Dean of Bristol, served as a steward at the dinner). For the Dickens Dinner, see Trollope to Kent, 18 October 1867.

get out of this dinner to Dickens. I am very sorry that it should turn out so,—& of course did not anticipate that it would be so when we were talking over the matter at the hotel. I thought you wd. have stayed there longer.

If you leave Brighton on Monday 4th. would you come here that day? We have no cook, ours having gone blind, but it doesnt seem to make much difference. Let us have a line to say whether you & Cecil[8] will come?

About Dickens' dinner the dean should write to Charles Kent, (whom I do not know & never heard of till I got the enclosed). This will tell him all I can tell. You & he know that I am not specially in that set, but having been asked I did not like to refuse.

Yours always
A. T.

To [? Charles Kent]

MS New York University.

Oct 26. 67   WALTHAM HOUSE, WALTHAM CROSS.

Dear Sir

Please send me a ticket for Mr Dickens' dinner for myself.

very faithfully
Anthony Trollope

To ?

MS Parrish Collection. B 356.

October 27. 1867   Cambridge

Dear Madam.

I wish I could say anything that might encourage you; but I cannot advise you to take the offer of Messrs S & O.[9] I feel certain if you do so that the publication of the book will not bring profit to you. What you will do is to ask your friends to subscribe,—which they may probably do to the number of the 40 copies. But they will feel that they are subscribing for you,—while they will in truth be subscribing for Messrs S & O.

Should you finally determine to publish, I shall be happy to put my name down for a copy.

very faithfully yours
Anty Trollope

---

[8] Perhaps one of the four daughters of Mrs. Elliot's first marriage.

[9] Saunders, Otley & Co., London publishers.

To A. Benthall[1]

MS Parrish Collection. SB 357.

Oct 30—1867   WALTHAM HOUSE, WALTHAM CROSS.
My dear Benthall
    I'll write to Mr Howes. His cantankerousness can't hurt me. I shall be very happy to shake hands with you tomorrow.

Yours always
Anty Trollope

To Mrs. Anna Steele[2]

MS Parrish Collection. Bradhurst, p. 260; B 358.

October 30. 67   WALTHAM HOUSE, WALTHAM CROSS.
My dear Mrs. Steele
    Regarding you as a wicked rival who are springing up to take the bread out of my mouth, and who have just committed the sin of having four columns in the Times,[3] I wonder how you can have so cruel a heart as to write to me at all. For you must be sure that I hate you. Nevertheless I shall be most delighted to go to Belhus,[4] if only to shew you with what an outward shew of equanimity I can bear your triumphs.
    But, I am sorry to say I am engaged all next week,—having promised to go to Brighton on Tuesday. Any day after Sunday the 17, I should be most happy.
    I would congratulate you heartily on your success, which I regard as very great, were I not sure that you would not believe a word that I said.

Yours very faithfully
Anthony Trollope

---

[1] A. Benthall of the Post Office; Principal Clerk for Home Mails, 1854–68; Assistant Undersecretary, 1868.

[2] Anna Caroline Steele (d. 1914), daughter of the Reverend Sir John Page Wood and his wife Emma (see Trollope to ?, 17 October 1868). Mrs. Steele returned to Rivenhall, her family home near Witham in Essex, almost immediately after her marriage in 1858. The Woods were great friends of Trollope, who often hunted with them from Rivenhall (see Trollope to Wood, 24 December 1872). In 1865 Anna and her mother had pseudonymously published a book of poems, *Ephemera*, with line drawings by Lady Wood.

[3] *The Times* (28 October 1367, p. 9) carried a lengthy review of Mrs. Steele's novel *Gardenhurst*, calling it a promising first novel. In fact, it was the most successful of her novels, running to several cheap editions. *Gardenhurst* was dedicated to Mrs. Steele's youngest sister, Mrs. Katharine O'Shea, who later became notorious for her liaison with Parnell.

[4] Belhus, near Rainham in Essex, was the country seat of Sir Thomas Barrett Lennard (1826–1919) and his wife Emma (d. 1916), who was a sister of Mrs. Steele.

To Mrs. Cecilia Meetkerke

MS Parrish Collection. B 360 (misdated).

Novr. 1. 1867   WALTHAM HOUSE, WALTHAM CROSS.
My dear Mrs. Meetkerke.

I must be at Brighton on Saturday or I would have been most happy.

If any changes were made in the poem[5] that were wrong, you are responsible for certainly not a word was changed after the proof was sent to you. You could have objected then,—& it would not have been too late.

Yours always
Most sincerely
A. T.

To ?

MS Parrish Collection.

Novr. 4. 1867   294, City Road.
Sir.

I have read your article on ozone, & return it, not at all as condemning or expressing an opinion that it is defective; but finding it to be more fit for a scientific journal than for the Saint Pauls. I, in truth, am altogether unable to say whether your account of ozone is correct or incorrect,—is well told or ill told. I believe it to be correct & very worthy of publication, but I do not feel justified in publishing a paper which is by its nature altogether beyond my own powers of criticism. I am, Sir,

Your very obt Servant
Anthony Trollope

To A. H. Layard

MS British Library. B 359.

              OFFICE OF THE ST. PAULS MAGAZINE,
November 7. 1867   294, CITY ROAD, LONDON.
My dear Layard.

I send you your article[6] in type— I have read it with very thorough satisfaction. I do not quite think as you do as to the future of Prussia, but I am quite aware that you have better grounds for thinking than I have.

At Page 15, line 6, would you object to softening the scorn conveyed

---

[5] "Secrets," *St. Paul's*, 1 (November 1867), 172.
[6] "England's Place in Europe," *St. Paul's*, 1 (December 1867), 275–91. See Trollope to Layard, 15 July 1867 and ? December 1867.

in the "limited capacity."— I hardly think such expression, well as it may be deserved, tends to conviction.

And in the last line of the article would you object to soften the assured threat of destruction held out against the "Tory" order & class. I think you hardly mean it to yourself. It is somewhat antagonistic to what you have already said, and is certainly antagonistic to what you feel.[7]

You will see that you run to 17 pages,—with a space for insertion of 20 or 25 lines if you please.

I have therefore arranged that your article *shall* take 17 pages.

Again thanking you & assuring you that I like the paper very much I am

> Most faithfully
> Anthony Trollope

You must put a name to the article. I shall be here on Saturday, & may perhaps get it back then corrected.

To A. H. Layard

MS British Library. SB 361.

OFFICE OF THE ST. PAULS MAGAZINE,
November. 9 1867   294, CITY ROAD, LONDON.
My dear Layard.

Your revise will go down to you in duplicate by this post, (Saturday.) Send back the correct revise to the publishers
> Virtue & Co.
> 294 City Road

Marked "for the St. Pauls."

I shall see you no doubt in London during the Short Session coming & I will say a word to you about the Eastern Article.[8]

> Yours always
> Anthony Trollope

Virtue & Co. to Trollope

MS Bodleian.

November 15 1867   VIRTUE & CO. LONDON E.C.
Dear Sir

We accept your offer & terms viz To write a novel same length as Chronicles of Barset. We to purchase copyright for three thousand two hundred pounds. The novel to be brought out in 32 weekly parts in

[7] Layard softened both expressions.
[8] See Trollope to Layard, 3 April 1868.

consecutive weeks, the first week to be any day we may choose between July 1. 1868 & Oct 15. 1868.[9] We to pay £100 per week on days of publication.

> We remain Dear Sir
> Very truly yours
> Virtue & Co

A Trollope Esqre.

To Charles Lever

MS Taylor Collection.

Novr. 19. 1867   294 City Road
My dear Lever.

I ought to have written to you immediately on receipt of your Mss[1] which came to hand properly, but I thought to have postponed doing so till I sent you the proof. I sent the Mss to the printer at once, but find it [*sic*] today that it is not yet in print. It will be so on Thursday. Do you care to correct your own proofs,—or may I do so for you? I find that the paper is over long for one article being 19 pages. Is it divisable [*sic*] into two, and may I divide it? Ten pages is *not at all* an insufficient length, though 12 or perhaps 14 is not too long. But we do not like so much as 19. Perhaps you could lengthen the matter so as to make 20. It is now I find 18½— I have not read it,—preferring type to your exceedingly beautiful but somewhat minute fist.

> Yours always
> Anthony Trollope

To ?[2]

MS Glamorgan Record Office.

Nov. 19. 67
Dear Sir.

I never knew the exact incident described with Mrs. Dobbs Broughton,[3] but I have seen many instances of similar mental occupation during periods of what would be supposed to be mental prostration. It fell

[9] *He Knew He Was Right*, published in sixpenny weekly parts from 17 October 1868 through 22 May 1869, and in parallel two-shilling monthly parts from November 1868. The book edition was issued in two volumes in May 1869 by Strahan, to whom Virtue had transferred the copyright.

[1] Perhaps a reference to the first section of Lever's three-part short fiction "Paul Gosslett's Confessions in Love, Law, and the Civil Service," *St. Paul's*, 1 (February 1868), 582–99. Lever was also the author of a brief article in the same issue entitled "On Human Lignites," pp. 560–63.

[2] Perhaps Henry Austin Bruce (1815–95), later 1st Baron Aberdare, a prominent politician (since this letter is from a collection of letters largely to him).

[3] In *The Last Chronicle*, chap. lxiv.

to my lot once to have to tell a lady who was going out to be married,
(—she and I being in the same ship,)—that news had met us that her intended husband was dead. I left her seated on the floor of a small ladies'
cabin, & she at once asked to have a large trunk brought to her. In the
course of an hour I found her packing & unpacking the trunk, putting
the new wedding clothing at the bottom & bringing the old things, now
suitable for her use, to the top. And so she employed herself during the
entire day.[4]

Yours faithfully
Anthony Trollope

To [? W. H.] Smith

MS Parrish Collection.

November 23. 1867.   WALTHAM HOUSE, WALTHAM CROSS.
My dear Mr Smith.

Would it suit you to call at the Athenaeum at 3.30. PM on Wednesday. I shall be at work there. But if this time is inconvenient, I will call
on you at that hour in the Strand.

Yours always
Anthony Trollope

To ?

MS Parrish Collection.

30. Nov. 1867.   WALTHAM HOUSE, WALTHAM CROSS.
Sir.

On receipt of your last letter I wrote to you to say that I could give no
decided answer to your question, but that I had no present intention of
standing for one of the boroughs in question.[5] That letter was returned
to me through the Post Office with an intimation that no such person
was known at the address. Now that I look at your name I think I may
have read it wrong;—if so I beg to be excused.

Your faithful Servant
Anthony Trollope

[4] Trollope used this incident as the basis for his short story "The Journey to Panama," first published in *Victoria Regia* (1861) and reprinted in *Lotta Schmidt* (1867).

[5] On Trollope's long-cherished ambition to sit in Parliament, see *Autobiography*,
chap. xvi.

To A. H. Layard

MS British Library. B 362.

November 30 1867   WALTHAM HOUSE, WALTHAM CROSS.
My dear Layard.

I see by the debate on the Great Beke case[6] that you are out of town for 10 days. Perhaps that may be as mendacious as some other things;— but as I had hoped to have seen you, & suppose you are now gone, it may be as well to write you a line. Will you like to write for us the article of which you spoke, so as to be in my hand Feb 9—for the number to be published on Feb 25th?—or would you write on any other subject of foreign affairs? You shall take the East: Question if you like;—but of course, as you know, we are all of us a little afraid of you on that steed. But you shant be baulked; after the very excellent paper you have given us.

Could I get you to come to us here for a couple days during the next month? Do you hunt?

                           Yours always
A H Layard Esq   Anthony Trollope

To A. H. Layard

MS British Library. B 363.

Dec 5. 1867.   WALTHAM HOUSE, WALTHAM CROSS.
My dear Layard.

I had no intention of letting you off, but did not write before, as one has to make various arrangements.

As you can not write your East: article in time for publication in

---

[6] The "Great Beke case" arose during parliamentary debates to appropriate funds for the Abyssinian Expedition, undertaken in 1868 to rescue British subjects long held captive by Emperor Theodore. This costly expedition was not popular, however, and opponents blamed the situation on the previous government, especially on Lord John Russell, Liberal Foreign Secretary, and on Russell's junior minister, Layard. The criticism of Layard depended largely on the contentions of Charles Tilstone Beke (1800–1874), the Abyssinian explorer, who insisted that Layard had mishandled negotiations with Theodore by sending out an emissary of disreputable character. In the House of Commons debate of 26 November, Layard indignantly rebutted this accusation and went on to assert that Beke's intervention in the 1864 negotiations had had a very mischievous effect. Layard left London on 29 November, the day Beke was defended, but on his return apologized for using unparliamentary language. See *Hansard*, 3d series, 190 (26 November, 29 November, and 6 December 1867), 259, 266–71, 421–26, 667–75. A full account of the events leading up to the successful expedition is given in Darrell Bates's *The Abyssinian Difficulty* (Oxford, 1979). Layard and Beke had already been involved in an exchange of letters in the *Pall Mall Gazette* (26 February 1867, pp. 4–5, 27 February 1867, p. 3, and 8 March 1867, pp. 4–5).

February, will you let me have it for publication in April?—say by April 3—or 4th.[7] I will then keep the space for it— My purpose is to alternate articles on Home & Foreign questions.

Yours always
Anty Trollope

To Max Schlesinger[8]

MS Parrish Collection.

Decr. 5. 1867   WALTHAM HOUSE, WALTHAM CROSS.
My dear Mr Schlesinger.

You will have seen perhaps the article in the December number of Saint Pauls[9] which took the place which yours would have had, had you been able to write it for us. That which is about to come out in the January number will be by my brother, on the present Italian question.[1] In the February number we shall have a paper on home politics.[2] Will you write the article for our March number,—on the then state of Prussia,—and let me have it by February 3—or 4th?[3] I trouble you now, so that there may be plenty of time.

Yours always faithfully
Anthony Trollope

To ?

MS Parrish Collection.

5 Decr. 1867.   WALTHAM HOUSE, WALTHAM CROSS.
Dear Sir.

I beg to thank you for the kind compliment conveyed in your letter of the 5th. Instant. You do not name a day for your festival, and I fear I shall be in the country for the greater part of January. But for that I should have been proud to be one of your Stewards. I should be happy to see my name on the list, and would attend if I were near London on the day.

Yours faithfully
Anthony Trollope

---

[7] Layard's two-part article appeared in June and July; see Trollope to Layard, 3 April 1868.

[8] Maximilian Schlesinger (1822–81), author of a two-part article on Bismarck in the *Fortnightly*, 5 (1 July and 15 July 1866), 385–405, 600–623.

[9] A. H. Layard, "England's Place in Europe," *St. Paul's*, 1 (December 1867), 275–91.

[1] T. A. Trollope, "The New Member of the European Family," *St. Paul's*, 1 (January 1868), 402–18.

[2] Trollope wrote the article himself: "Whom Shall We Make Leader of the New House of Commons?," *St. Paul's*, 1 (February 1868), 531–45.

[3] Schlesinger did not write the article.

To James Virtue

MS Parrish Collection. SB 364 (misdated).

Decr 6. 1867.   WALTHAM HOUSE, WALTHAM CROSS.
My dear Mr Virtue.

My throat is again so bad that I really do not dare to come out tonight. I should have to come down by a 12 night train, and this would be very imprudent.

I am thoroughly sorry for this as I had quite thought that I should have met all your men tonight, and I should greatly have liked to do so, as we are now joined together. But I must ask you to explain this for me. Pray make it understood that if I were well, or if the weather were a little less inclement, I would certainly be there.

> Yours always
> Anthony Trollope

To George Smith

Sadleir's transcript, Pickering & Chatto, London.

Dec. 7. 1867

*   *   *

I should like to see my novels touching Barchester published in a series, and it has been suggested to me that this should be done now. You will know better than any one else whether this would be feasible. They consist of the following:

The Warden.
Barchester Towers.
Dr. Thorne (not absolutely essential to this series.)
Framley Parsonage.
The Small House.
The Last Chronicle.

The last three are yours with the exception of some remainder of interest which I have in The Last Chronicle and Dr. Thorne (which, as I have said, is not essential though it should be included) is the property of W. Smith, but might probably be purchased from him at a small sum. Longman have a half copyright arrangement with me for the two first, The Warden and Barchester Towers—which he expresses himself unwilling to relinquish, but for which he does not, of late, account for any profits. Do you think we might arrange the publication, and would it be worth your while to go into it?[4]

*   *   *

---

[4] See Trollope to Smith, 13 December 1867.

To William Allingham[5]

MS Taylor Collection. SB 365.

OFFICE OF THE ST. PAULS MAGAZINE,
294, CITY ROAD, LONDON.

Decr. 10 1867

Dear Sir.

I hope you will not object to our omitting the line containing a dedication of your little poem on Squire Curtis.[6] It is unusual, and I think ugly in a magazine.

Yours faithfully
Anthony Trollope

Would you like your initials at the end?

John Blackwood to Trollope

MS (copy) National Library of Scotland.

11th. Decr. 1867   Edinburgh
My dear Trollope

Along with this I send proof of Parts 4 & 5 of Linda which I have just read with very great pleasure.

I still have slightly the feeling of impatience at the story which frightened me at first but there is more variety than I thought & there is strong individual human character very happily painted. The views too of the fanatical old woman in favouring Linda with so many stripes in this world to save her from eternal brimstone in the next, come out much more clearly in type than in a hurried perusal of the M.S.—as does also the character of Linda with the haunting dread of brimstone which her early education had planted in her mind. Herr Molk is good & does exactly what was to have been expected of him. There is something very comical in the artful way that the pious Staubach lets poor innocent Linda go to consult him.

I wish Tetchens vulgar sordid character had been brought out more, as a sort of comic foil to the gravity of the story of Linda's persecutions.

As far as I can judge the public seem to be liking the story.

I have read Phineas Finn & think it very good. The picture of the House on the night of a great division is excellent.

I hope Mrs Trollope & you are well &

always yours truly
Anthony Trollope Esq   John Blackwood

[5] William Allingham (1824–89), poet; editor of *Fraser's Magazine*, 1874–79.
[6] "The Ballad of Squire Curtis," *St. Paul's*, 2 (April 1868), 77–78. The poem is signed "W. A.," and was reprinted in Allingham's *Songs, Ballads, and Stories* (1877).

To Thomas Hood[7]

MS Victoria University of Wellington. *N&Q*, n.s. 17 (January 1970), 17.

OFFICE OF THE ST. PAULS MAGAZINE,
December 12. 1867   294, CITY ROAD, LONDON.
Dear Sir.

I send a proof of your poem. Dicey will have spoken to you about the last line, which is somewhat awkward—& hardly expresses plainly as a last line should the point you have in view.[8]

Yours truly
Anthony Trollope

To George Smith

Sadleir's transcript, Pickering & Chatto, London.

Dec. 13. 1867.

*   *   *

I did not mean to urge any immediate new edition, but to arrange for such edition as might be expedient when the proper time should come. Of course the cheaper work should not come out as long as the sale of the present edition of The Last Chronicle is a reasonable sale.

My idea was that you should buy my interests in the books and arrange with Longmans—so that the whole venture should be your own. If you thought this feasible I would see you about it some day. No doubt the set of books includes those which are the most popular that I have written, and I should be pleased to see them brought out in a uniform set. You at present own so much the larger proportion of the copyright, that no one but you could do it.[9]

*   *   *

To John Blackwood

MS National Library of Scotland.

Decr. 14—1867
Saturday.   WALTHAM HOUSE, WALTHAM CROSS.
My dear Blackwood.

I sent back Part IV of L. T. yesterday—& send part V. today. I am glad you warm to my two poor women. I purposely avoided making Tetchen

---

[7] Thomas Hood (1835–74), journalist, humorist, and poet; son of the well-known poet Thomas Hood; editor of *Fun*.

[8] The final line of Hood's "Weary November," *St. Paul's*, 1 (January 1868), 436, remained strangely incongruous.

[9] Smith apparently declined to act, and it was many years before Trollope arranged with Chapman & Hall for the eight-volume Chronicles of Barsetshire (1878–79); see Trollope to Chapman, 6 March 1878.

more of a character, as in so short a story I wished to concentrate the interest— But I am aware that it want some element of softness or of humour.

Yours always faithfully
Anthony Trollope

To ?[1]

MS Parrish Collection.

23. December 1867   WALTHAM HOUSE, WALTHAM CROSS.
Dear Sir.

I have read with much attention & interest your paper on our War Department, and have had much doubt as to publication or non publication. But, at last, I conclude that from its nature the paper is more fitted to make its way as a Report made officially than as a magazine article. I do not think it would be attractive enough, appearing in that guise, to create a wide observation. It is in itself a very wide & apparently well-considered official Report. But I do not think it has that sharpness (often prejudicial to justice) which would charm the readers of a magazine.

Yours very faithfully
Anthony Trollope

To Austin Dobson[2]

MS University of London Library. SB 366.

OFFICE OF THE ST. PAULS MAGAZINE,
December 24 1867   294, CITY ROAD, LONDON.
Dear Sir.

Your *very pretty* lines of La Belle Marquise[3] have gone to the printer. You shall have a slip for correction. It may be some little time before they are used, but I am much obliged to you for them.

Yours faithfully
Anthony Trollope

[1] The addressee of this letter (and of Trollope to ?, 29 December 1867) may have been Henry Brackenbury: see Trollope to Brackenbury, 2 March 1868.

[2] Henry Austin Dobson (1840–1921), poet, biographer, and man of letters; author of the Fielding, Richardson, and Fanny Burney volumes in Macmillan's English Men of Letters series. Dobson became Trollope's leading contributor of verse for *St. Paul's*. Sadleir noted that Dobson was "in effect 'discovered' by Trollope as a poet and greatly helped" (*Commentary*, p. 296).

[3] "Une Marquise: A Rhymed Monologue in the Louvre," *St. Paul's*, 1 (March 1868), 709–11.

To Sir Henry Thompson⁴

MS Parrish Collection.

December 26. 1867   WALTHAM HOUSE, WALTHAM CROSS.

My dear Sir Henry Thompson

Your card, dated per envelope 21 Inst, addressed to the Garrick, has only just reached me! If I am not too late I shall be most happy to dine with you on 4th. January.

Yours always
Anthony Trollope

To ?

MS Parrish Collection.

29 Decr. 67   WALTHAM HOUSE, WALTHAM CROSS.

Dear Sir.

I shall be happy to read any paper you may send to me.

It was not that your article was not pregnant. But it was in my opinion an official report;—and a very good official report,—rather than a magazine paper. There is always that difficulty in the way of a man cognizant of official matter when he essays to write for the public on any such subject. The thing produced is more likely too good than too bad, but it lacks the general interest which an Editor is bound to seek for the papers he inserts.

faithfully yours
Any Trollope

⁴ Sir Henry Thompson (1820–1904), later 1st Baronet, distinguished physician; surgeon to Queen Victoria. On the evening of 13 January 1874, Trollope was one of sixteen prominent people who met at the Thompson's home and signed the following document, which brought into existence the Cremation Society of England: "We, the undersigned, disapprove the present custom of burying the dead, and we desire to substitute some mode which shall rapidly resolve the body into its component elements, by a process which cannot offend the living, and shall render the remains perfectly innocuous. Until some better method is devised we desire to adopt that usually known as Cremation." (MS Cremation Society of Great Britain.) Other signatories included Shirley Brooks, J. E. Millais, John Tenniel, and T. Spencer Wells. Thompson, first Chairman and President of the Society, took up the crusade, and cremation became legal in 1884. David Skilton has noted the relevance of the cremation issue in Trollope's futuristic novel about euthanasia: see *"The Fixed Period*: Anthony Trollope's Novel of 1980," *Studies in the Literary Imagination*, 6 (Fall 1973), 46–48.

To F. J. Furnivall[5]

MS Huntington Library.

December 29 [?1867][6]   WALTHAM HOUSE, WALTHAM CROSS.
Dear Sir.

Many thanks for your note. The only periodical with which I am now concerned is the Saint Paul's magazine,—and we have determined not to review at all,—thinking it a work that should not be taken in hand unless it can be done with a thorough staff & undivided care.

Yours always
faithfully
Anthy Trollope

To A. H. Layard

MS Desmond Corcoran.

[? December 1867]   ATHENAEUM CLUB
My dear Layard

Many thanks for the slips. I have heard the article[7] most highly spoken of in various places,—and, better still, most sharply abused in Tory haunts. For such a paper adverse party criticism, if it be long and full, is more valuable than any praise. Not to be noticed at all is the evil.

I count upon you at present for a paper to be supplied early in March, for the April Number— Is that right?

Yours always
Any Trollope

To Mrs. Annie Thomas Cudlip[8]

MS Huntington Library.

                                    Office of St. Pauls Magazine
[?1867]   294. City Road.
My dear Mrs. Cudlip.

I shall be delighted to read anything that you would send me. I know your novels, but I can not ask you to send me a novel, as we are already

---

[5] Frederick James Furnivall (1825–1910), scholar and editor; Secretary of the Philological Society, 1862–1910; editor of the Society's projected dictionary, which eventually became, under James Murray, the OED; founder of the Early English Text Society (1864), Chaucer Society (1868), Browning Society (1881), and Shelley Society (1886).

[6] Watermark 1867.

[7] "England's Place in Europe," *St. Paul's*, 1 (December 1867), 275–91; see Trollope to Layard, 15 July 1867 and 7 November 1867.

[8] Annie Hall Thomas Cudlip (1838–1918), prolific minor novelist. Trollope accepted a story of hers for *St. Paul's*; see Trollope to Cudlip, 6 March 1868.

full. I can assure you that I shall be very glad to use any thing of yours if it would suit us. If it should not, I will restore it.

Yours faithfully
Anthony Trollope

To Fred[9]

MS Parrish Collection.

[?1867][1]   WALTHAM HOUSE, WALTHAM CROSS.
My dear Fred

The information that you have sent me about the French Church is just what I want.[2] How can you and I be sufficiently thankful that we are not Curés in France; or,—if you will think of it,—we might have been Vicaires! Sometimes when facts are brought under my nose shewing the real difference between the modes of life in England & France I am astounded by the wealth of this Country. Think of a *senior class* Treasury clerk with something about £200 a year: with that as his *maximum*[3]!!!

Yours always
Anthony Trollope

1868

To Mr. Watts

MS Parrish Collection.

Jan 4. 1868   WALTHAM HOUSE, WALTHAM CROSS.
My dear Watts.

I will be at Peterborough station by the train leaving London at 5.0. PM on Monday. Do not mind your brougham. I will get a fly.

Yours always
Any Trollope

I will leave the horses to follow.

―――――

It is raining this moment.

[9] See Trollope to Fred, 11 May 1867.
[1] Watermark 1867.
[2] This four-page memorandum contains information about government pay for French priests: "Cures of 3rd. class [are paid] 900 fr or £36 a year / 'premier vicaires' or 1st assistants in parishes where there are less than 5000 inhabitants are paid 350 fr. [or] £14 a year." (MS University of Illinois.)
[3] Underlined twice.

To E. S. Dallas[4]

MS (Trollope's copy) Bodleian. B 397 (misdated).

Jany 5—1868
My dear Dallas

A novel such as The Claverings—i e a novel in 3 volumes would run through 32 numbers of Once a Week giving 7 pages a week. A novel such as the Small House or Phineas Finn, i e equal in amount to 4 volumes would give 9 pages for 32 weeks. I should not care to spread a story into a greater number of divisions.

My price for the former would be £2800—for the latter £3200; for the copyright. These are the prices which I got for the Claverings and for Phineas Finn— I should ask two thirds of these prices for the publication in the periodical alone,—specifying in such case that I should be enabled to publish the whole simultaneously a full month before the termination of the whole. Otherwise I should find the property cruelly lessened by the power of the libraries to let out the whole in the copies of your periodical.

I would commence the publication in the first week of May 1869. My purpose wd be not to publish any novel along side of it for the first six months. I would not bind myself to the letter of this arrangement, but I should keep to it in the spirit.

Yours ever
A. T.

To Mrs. W. F. Pollock

MS Parrish Collection. SB 367.

Jany 12—68   Stilton[5]
My dear Mrs. Pollock

I am out of town, but I hear that your Mss[6] is at the office. Many thanks. I have directed that it be put into type, & I will send you the proof. I hear from home that I am to have the pleasure of being with you on Friday week.

Yours always
Sincerely
Anthony Trollope

---

[4] Eneas Sweetland Dallas (1828–79), editor of *Once a Week*; staff writer for *The Times*; Garrick Club friend of Trollope. This letter began the troubled publishing history of *The Vicar of Bullhampton*. See *Autobiography*, pp. 326–28, and *Commentary*, pp. 304–7. See also Trollope to Bradbury & Evans, 3 February 1868, and Dallas to Trollope, 21 January 1869 and 22 March 1869.

[5] A small town in Huntingdonshire, about 70 miles north of London.

[6] "Fashion in Poetry," *St. Paul's*, 1 (March 1868), 693–708.

To A. H. Layard

MS Desmond Corcoran.

Janry 14. 1868.   WALTHAM HOUSE, WALTHAM CROSS.
My dear Layard.

Do I understand that I expect your article for the April number,—to be with me by March 5—or 6—or for the May number, to be with me by April 5—or 6. I should *much prefer* the former.

Yours always

Anthony Trollope

A H Layard Esq MP.

To Charles Buxton

MS Parrish Collection.

Casewick

Stamford[7]

January. 17 1868
My dear Buxton.

Your kind note of the 14th. has only just reached me here. I shall be delighted to go over to you and dine on Monday,—if I am not now too late,—and if my wife will come to bring her with me. I think we can manage to get back the same evening. I will write again when I get home, which will be to night.

The lecture begins at eight.[8] Shall we say six to be with you.

If however my not answering you sooner has changed your plans do not scruple to say so.

Yours always

Anthy Trollope

To Thomas Adolphus Trollope

MS Dr. Chester W. Topp.

Jany 19. 1868
Sunday—   WALTHAM HOUSE, WALTHAM CROSS.
My dear Tom.

I am sorry to have to tell you that Bice has got the mumps. She was a little unwell yesterday evening, & this morning Rose sent for the doctor. He has just told us that such is the case.

She is of course uneasy, but is not at present suffering. He says that she will be worse before she is better; but that it is not a complaint to cause fear. It will retard her going back to school for some time, as it is

---

[7] Casewick, near Stamford in Lincolnshire, was the seat of Sir John Trollope.

[8] Trollope gave his lecture "Politics as a Study for Common People" at Stratford, in east London, on 20 January 1868 (the lecture that he had given at Leeds in 1864).

slow, very infectious, & so weakening as to require counter-strengthening afterwards. I or Rose will let you hear from time to time.

The doctor says, (but I should first tell you that I told him of our correspondence on the subject)—that she is a child requiring a full diet— firstly from certain innate weaknesses (i e that she is not of nature robust) and secondly because her intellect is more active than is usual at her age. He has ordered her while ill to have two glasses of wine daily— An[d] this you will take for what it is worth in your judgement. I need not tell you that she will have all care while she is ill. At this moment she is quite jolly. An hour ago she was down in the mouth.

Love to Fanny.[9]

Yours always
A. T.

To Messrs. Bradbury & Evans
MS (Trollope's copy) Bodleian. B 368.

Feb 3. 1868
Gentlemen.

Thanks for your letter of Feb 1, respecting the proposed novel for next year.[1] It is my intention that it shall be in your hands before 1 May 69— so that its publication will be commenced at that date. Of course it is understood that it is intended for your periodical, Once a Week.[2]

very faithfully yours,
Messrs Bradbury Evans   Anthony Trollope

[9] Frances Eleanor Trollope (?1834–1913), whom T. A. Trollope had married in Paris in October 1866 (Anthony acting as one of the witnesses); the sister of Dickens's mistress Ellen Ternan (see Trollope to Robinson, 6 June 1878). Trollope and his wife had known Frances Eleanor Ternan for some time, and, after Theodosia Trollope's death, seem to have arranged the match: "My brother, who had assisted in the negotiation that brought Miss Ternan to Florence [as governess to Bice], when I told him of my engagement, said, 'Yes, of course! I knew you would.' And I did." (T. A. Trollope, *What I Remember* [1889], III, 41.)

[1] Bradbury & Evans agreed to Trollope's terms, £2,800 for absolute copyright in a novel the length of *The Claverings*. *The Vicar of Bullhampton*, however, turned out to be a little short, and the price was reduced to £2,500.

[2] Two days later, E. S. Dallas, the editor of *Once a Week*, wrote to Trollope: "Please to make the novel run for 32 numbers—at an average of seven pages each number. . . . Mind I expect a stunner." (MS Bodleian.)

To John Blackwood

MS National Library of Scotland.

Feb 13. 68.   WALTHAM HOUSE, WALTHAM CROSS.
My dear Blackwood.

I have sent off the needed Part of L. T. to Edinburgh tonight— The other I will send back tomorrow.

I go to Hastings with my wife tomorrow—via Brighton—2–pm train— from London Bridge—& might possibly see you. I shall be back on Monday & will come & see you.

Yours always
A. T.

To Charles Buxton

MS Parrish Collection.

20 Feb. 1868   WALTHAM HOUSE, WALTHAM CROSS.
My dear Buxton.

Thanks for your letter. I think I see the difficulties of the position. I will make it my business to see you early in next week when I shall have thought over the whole matter & will then speak to you openly on the subject.[3]

Yours very faithfully
Anthony Trollope

We had such an awfully bad day at Skreens[4] today.

To Frederick Locker

MS Harvard. SB 369.

OFFICE OF THE ST. PAULS MAGAZINE,
Febry. 24. 1868   294, CITY ROAD, LONDON.
My dear Mr Locker.

Thanks. I'll send you a proof as soon as its printed.[5]

Yours obliged
Anthy Trollope

We don't print names, but will print the F. L.

---

[3] Perhaps the subject was Trollope's standing for Parliament, a cause in which Buxton interested himself (see *Autobiography*, p. 297).

[4] A reference to hunting at Skreens, near Roxwell, Essex.

[5] "A Nice Correspondent!," *St. Paul's*, 2 (June 1868), 328–29; signed "F. L."

To Andrew Mitchell[6]

MS Parrish Collection.

Feb 25—1868   WALTHAM HOUSE, WALTHAM CROSS.
My dear Mitchell.

My transgressions,—are ever before me,—as are also the printed documents of the G. C. demanding their little bill. I send a M. O. which will make it all right for a time.

Yours ever
Anthony Trollope

To John Tilley

MS General Post Office, London.

29. Feb. 1868   Waltham Cross
Sir

Referring to your letter of the 26th. Instant I beg to say that I shall be very happy to undertake the service which the Postmaster General proposes to entrust to me, and I request that his Grace may be assured that I will use my best exertions towards carrying out his instructions with accuracy.

I shall be ready to start for New York in the Cunard Steamer of the 11th. April next.[7]

I am
Sir,
Your most obedient Servant

John Tilley Esqre   Anthony Trollope

[6] Perhaps Andrew Mitchell, of the law firm Mitchell, Allardyce, and Mitchell, 160 West George St., Glasgow. The envelope is addressed to Mitchell, at the Gaiter's Club, Glasgow (see Trollope to Burns, 12 July 1878, n. 4).

[7] The British Post Office had given the required twelve months' notice that it would terminate the existing postal convention with the United States, and Trollope's task was to negotiate a new convention. On 12 December 1867 Tilley had written to the Postmaster General: "It will be necessary to send a strong man, and I think of proposing to you to ask Mr. Trollope to undertake the revision as we shall get the benefit not only of his ability but of his personal popularity with the Americans. I know of no one else who would do the work so well." (MS General Post Office, London.) The hope was that the Americans would agree to join the British in sending mails only through the ports of Queenstown (Co. Cork) and Liverpool, using Cunard mail packets (with regular sailings three times a week), and that they would bear part of the cost of sorting on board. See Trollope to Tilley, 1 May 1868, 18 May 1868, 3 July 1868, and 7 July 1868, and Trollope to Thomas Adolphus Trollope, 1 August 1868.

To Henry Brackenbury[8]

MS Parrish Collection. SB 370.

March 2—1868   WALTHAM HOUSE, WALTHAM CROSS.
My dear Brackenbury.
I send the note. Trevelyan's[9] Number is either 6. or 8. I think 6. But you would probably find him any Monday, Tuesday, Thursday or Friday at the House between 4. & 7.

> Yours always
> Anthy Trollope

To Henry Brackenbury

Henry Brackenbury, *Some Memories of My Spare Time* (Edinburgh, 1909), p. 49.

*   *   *

[?1868]
Do not be too severe on Governments. Having known something of Government work for very many years, my conviction is that as a rule our public men do their work as well as their very peculiar circumstances in subjection to a representative Government allow them to do. I do not think our public men are niggards or are disposed to be mean by disposition.

*   *   *

[8] Henry Brackenbury (1837–1914), later Sir Henry, military man and eventually a general; writer on military subjects; Professor of Military History at Woolwich, 1868. Brackenbury contributed several articles to *St. Paul's*.

[9] George Otto Trevelyan (1838–1928), later 2d Baronet, eminent historian, man of letters, and statesman; MP for Tynemouth, 1865–68; MP for the Scottish Border Burghs, 1868–86. The son of the diplomat and statesman Sir Charles Edward Trevelyan (1807–86), George Otto went to India in 1862 as his father's private secretary and began contributing articles in letter form to *Macmillan's Magazine* under the title "The Competition Wallah." The articles were published as a book in 1864, and their vivid account of Anglo-Indian life made Trevelyan's name in London literary circles. Trevelyan was a prominent advocate of army reform and helped bring about the abolition of the purchase system. Both he and his father were impressed by Brackenbury's articles in *St. Paul's*, and he wrote to Trollope asking the author's name. Trollope forwarded the letter to Brackenbury, with the endorsement: "Is there any objection to 'giving you up' to Competition wallah and father?" (Henry Brackenbury, *Some Memories of My Spare Time* [Edinburgh, 1909], pp. 52–53.) A decade earlier, Trollope had caricatured Sir Charles Trevelyan as Sir Gregory Hardlines in *The Three Clerks* (because of Trevelyan's introduction of competitive examinations in the Civil Service in 1853, a system that Trollope opposed all his life). Later, however, Trollope and Sir Charles became close friends (see *Autobiography*, pp. 111–12).

To J. S. Muspratt[1]
MS Parrish Collection.

3 March 1868.   WALTHAM HOUSE, WALTHAM CROSS.

[Photograph attached]
Anthony Trollope

To Dr. Muspratt with Mr A Trollopes compliments.
I have nothing larger in the way of a photograph by me.

To Mrs. Annie Thomas Cudlip
MS Parrish Collection.

                                 OFFICE OF THE ST. PAULS MAGAZINE,
March 6th. 1868   294, CITY ROAD, LONDON.
My dear Mrs. Cudlip.
Your story "For a Year" is in print, and a corrected proof will be sent
to you for authors corrections. But we cannot use it unless you will
kindly consent to make a considerable change in the event or ending of
the tale; and I must trust to your kindness not to be angry with me for
pointing this out. Although the change will be total as regards the event
of the tale, it will not make any change necessary in the work till the
beginning of the 16th. page, and we will give you up to 18 pages in
which to complete it.

You make the girl die of poison administered by herself because she
fears the mans treachery, and then you knock the man over the head in
a Railway carriage. I think that in this you miss all our sympathy for a
very prettily drawn girl. And your finale wounds all our ideas of probability, as the event of the accident would certainly have been made
known up at the house.

Let the man become a traitor the second time,—failing in his bridal
engagement either from madness, or any cause you who have created the
character may feel to be most consonant with it. Then let the girl die,—
not by poison,—but in the struggle which she makes to support her
misery.[2]

I must again ask you to pardon me, & will freely acknowledge that if
my counsel is distasteful to you, you may doubtless use your story in
another magazine. You will have the kindness to let me have an answer

---

[1] Dr. James Sheridan Muspratt (1821–71), chemist; founder of the Liverpool College of Chemistry, a private institution for training chemists, 1848. Trollope, who
had prepared a one-inch photograph of himself for autograph seekers, attached one
to this note.

[2] "For a Year," *St. Paul's*, 2 (June 1868), 257–73. Mrs. Cudlip revised her story precisely as Trollope suggested.

as to which you will do because, as you will see, the type is put up and should be discharged if not used.

The proof will be with you in a couple of days.

Yours very truly
Anthony Trollope

To Austin Dobson

MS University of London Library. Alban Dobson, *Austin Dobson: Some Notes* (1928), p. 78; B 371.

OFFICE OF THE ST. PAULS MAGAZINE,
March 7th. 1868   294, CITY ROAD, LONDON.

Dear Sir.

I return your poems, though I like them much, especially that of the dying knight, because, as it seems to me, they are not sufficiently clear in their expressions for the general readers of a magazine. The general reader would have no idea for instance. Why "There is no bird in any last years nest."[3] Nor would the "alien ire" be at all understood.

I think it indispensable that poetry for a magazine should be so clearly intelligible that ill-constructed, uneducated, but perhaps intelligent, minds, can comprehend it. I hope you will forgive me, if you do not agree with me.

Yours faithfully
Anthy Trollope

To Lord Houghton

MS Trinity College, Cambridge.

March 8. 1868   WALTHAM HOUSE, WALTHAM CROSS.

My dear Lord Houghton.

I am going to America (to endeavour to make a postal convention) on April 11, & I want to get myself presented at Court before I go. The Prince has a Levee on Tuesday 17th. Would you kindly present me.[4]

If you can do this, I believe you should send to me a note to this effect that I may have it at the Lord Chamberlain's office. I do not know whether you are in town, but if not I believe that your assent without your actual presence would suffice.

Yours very faithfully
Anthony Trollope

---

[3] The refrain from "The Dying of Tanneguy du Bois," published in the June number of *Under the Crown* and reprinted in *Vignettes in Rhyme* (1873).

[4] Trollope was one of some 250 people presented at this Levée, held at St. James's Palace; however, he was presented by Lord Stanhope, not by Lord Houghton. Presentations to the Prince of Wales were equivalent to presentations to the Queen.

To A. H. Layard

MS Parrish Collection.

March 15. 68.   WALTHAM HOUSE, WALTHAM CROSS.
My dear Layard.

May I calculate on having your article on Eastern Europe by April 3—
or 4? And can you say what will be the length?

We have an article on Panslavism[5] in the April number, of which I
will send you a copy, as it may be well you should see it. It will not, I
think, at all interfere with you.

Yours always
Anty Trollope

To George Smith

MS John Murray. B 372.

March 20. 1868.   WALTHAM HOUSE, WALTHAM CROSS.
My dear Smith.

I have read Bosworth's pamphlet carefully.[6] It seems to me that he has,
in his warfare against you, fallen into three great faults. He has published a statement saying that with you your word is not as good as your
bond; he has applied the term "Rattening" to your mode of trade, (the
meaning of which word we all know), and he has published an advertisement in the Athenaeum respecting one of your publications in terms
which are wilfully false in their signification. If you answer him at all,
you should do so I think on these headings.

I do not know how far he may be right in saying that his order for the
copies of the Queens Book[7] could have been enforced, had the value of
the books ordered been under £10;—but no doubt you could shew that
you had no intention to recede from any contract made by you;—and
that his statement imputing to you dishonest motives is baseless. It
would be very easy to shew that the peculiarly objectionable word "Rattening" has been used with a malicious object, and that there is not the
slightest ground on which any man,—let his opinion on the subject of
the sale be what it may,—can impute fairly to you, or other publishers
acting with you, any of those modes of action which have been called
Rattening.

---

[5] "The Panslavist Revival in Eastern Europe," *St. Paul's*, 2 (April 1868), 18–33.

[6] Thomas Bosworth (?1823–99), a London bookseller and small publisher, had attacked Smith in a pamphlet entitled *On 'Rattening' in the Book-Trade* (1868). ("Rattening" means destroying an employer's machinery; here, it referred to interfering in
normal trade practices.) Bosworth had been selling at cost books called for by name
at his counter, making his profit on deliveries and on a service charge for his clerks'
time and advice. The big publishing houses moved against him. (B.)

[7] Arthur Helps, ed., *Leaves from the Journal of Our Life in the Highlands*, published on 10 January 1868, and then in a cheaper "People's Edition" on 16 March
1868.

As to the advertisement, which is so worded as to appear to emanate from the publisher & proprietor of the work in question, there can be no doubt of the falseness of the intention of the advertiser.[8]

Touching the question itself, I am disposed to think that you are right in refusing the sale of your books to men reselling on the terms and in the mode in vogue with Mr. Bosworth. I think I could use strong if not conclusive arguments to shew that the public would in the end suffer if the regular Retail bookseller were put out of the trade by the underselling of such as Mr. Bosworth. But this at any rate is clear. That as long as you & other publishers confine yourselves to legal steps—(such as selling when you please and refusing to sell when you please)—such attacks as those made in this pamphlet are libellous in spirit if not in law.

I think I should get this put forth in a newspaper article, if I were you. It would be easily argued in a column and a half or two columns.

Yours always
A. T.

To ?

MS Taylor Collection.

20 March 1868.   WALTHAM HOUSE, WALTHAM CROSS.
Dear Sir.

Will you kindly complete the address for me of the lady to whom the enclosed alludes, & send the note on by post. Mr. Geo Smith gave me the address to day but I have mislaid it.

Yours truly
Anthony Trollope

To A. H. Layard

MS Parrish Collection.

March 26—1868   WALTHAM HOUSE, WALTHAM CROSS.
My dear Layard.

Your article has just reached me, and on casting it I find that it would make about 25 pages. Of course this is a rough estimate. It would be very much preferable to have it in one paper. Men become sick of a subject as to which they have to look for a sequel. I will therefore have it all printed and get you to reduce it to 20 pages. I am sorry to give you this trouble; but I am sure that that will be better than splitting it.

Of course the paper on Pan Slavism was written by a Pole.[9]

Yours always
Any Trollope

---

[8] The advertisement has not been traced.
[9] Adam Jerzy Konstanty Gielgud (1834–1920).

To Sir John Trollope

National Register of Archives Report, 6115, p. 52.

[? April 1868]
   Trollope writes about an umbrella and Lord Kesteven's peerage,[1] and announces his departure for America to make a postal convention.

To John Blackwood

MS National Library of Scotland.

1. April 1868.   WALTHAM HOUSE, WALTHAM CROSS.
My dear Blackwood.
   I start for America on 10th. Instant, and am making some arrangements about money— Am I not right in supposing that you will pay me £225 on or about 1st. May—and may I calculate upon your having the kindness to cause that sum to be paid to my account at that date—at the Union Bank of London, Princes Street, Mansion House?
                                            very faithfully yours
John Blackwood Esq   Anthony Trollope

John Blackwood to Trollope

MS (copy) National Library of Scotland. Excerpt, Porter, p. 362.

April 3/68   Edinburgh
My dear Trollope
   It was on my mind to write to ask the name of your banker & in accordance with your note I shall pay the £225. to your credit with the Union Bank Princes St. Mansion House on the 4th. of May. I hear a good many complaints that Linda is an aggravating story but she excites much interest & there is no question about the skill with which her sad tale is told. She is I think more talked of than Nina & will I hope find a wider audience than her predecessor but the sale of novels is not in a satisfactory state & I suspect we would require to smoke a great many cigars together before we could [hit] upon the best mode of improving matters. I hope your *post* official expedition to America will form a pleasant & satisfactory one. Remember your promise that Mrs. T & you shd. come & pay us a visit whenever it suits you. My wife sends her best remembrances to you both & believe me.
                                            Always yours truly
Anthony Trollope Esq   John Blackwood

---

[1] On 14 April 1868 Sir John Trollope was raised to the peerage with the title Baron Kesteven of Casewick.

To A. H. Layard

MS Parrish Collection.

3. Ap. 68.   ATHENAEUM CLUB
My dear Layard.

I have only this moment got your paper from the printer. You will see that it makes 28 pages. I propose that you shall divide it into two articles—about 14 each. (use your own discretion here)— But to enable us to use it in this form we must postpone it for the numbers of June—& July.[2] Will you let me have a line to say whether this will suit you— I start for New York on Good Friday. Let me have the paper back from you as *early as you can in the week* addressed to me at Waltham Cross.

Yours ever
Anty Trollope

To A. H. Layard

MS Parrish Collection.

Exeter.
Address
Ap. 5. 1868   WALTHAM HOUSE, WALTHAM CROSS.
My dear Layard.

I send the second proof of your paper as you ask me to do. I think you should divide it either at the 13, or the 18 page, where I have marked the margin— The latter would perhaps be the better, but in that case you must insert some few words to bring the first division to a conclusion, and some few further words to commence the second division.

I shall be at Waltham Cross up to Friday morning, after that, address to the Editor, 294—City Road. E. Dicey will see that your wishes are carried out.

I go to America to make a postal convention, not to make money by reading.[3] I fear I shall bring back a very small bag.

Yours always
Anthony Trollope

[2] "What Is the Eastern Question?," *St. Paul's*, 2 (June 1868), 274–91; "How to Settle the Eastern Question," *St. Paul's*, 2 (July 1868), 403–15.

[3] Doubtless an allusion to Dickens, who was in America giving his enormously successful series of readings. When Trollope arrived in New York on 22 April, Dickens was on the point of sailing for home. Dickens wrote to James T. Fields of his "amazement" at seeing Trollope "come aboard in the mail tender just before we started! He had come out in the Scotia just in time to dash off again in said tender to shake hands with me, knowing me to be aboard here. It was most heartily done." (Walter Dexter, ed., *The Letters of Charles Dickens* [1938], III, 645.) Dickens's liking for Trollope is further evidenced in a letter of 6 May 1869 to T. A. Trollope: "I saw your brother Anthony at the Athenaeum not long ago, who was in the act of reading a letter from you. He is a perfect cordial to me, whenever and wherever I see him, as the heartiest and best of fellows." (MS Free Library of Philadelphia.)

To John Blackwood

MS National Library of Scotland.

April 6. 1868   WALTHAM HOUSE, WALTHAM CROSS.

My dear Blackwood

Many thanks for your note.

Touching the mode of publication & sale of novels, I have a strong conception that publishers must make a change in their mode of business, and must eschew the half guinea volume system;—and I am led to this opinion by observing that the public have unconsciously learned to expect that the best novels of the day are to be obtained by them in a different form. They think,—without thinking,—that they will get the best novels in the magazines, and that novels which have been published in magazines, should appear not in 3 vols.—but in one or two.

And for novels which appear with illustrations at 20/—(in 2 vol)—there is a sale among private people, whereas for those published in 3 vol at 31. 6d. there is none. It must however be remembered that the 2 volume novel at 20/ is a much longer work than the 3 vol at 31–6d. All the details respecting this I should much like to discuss with you. I find no difficulty whatever in selling a novel for £3,000: (—Let this be private)— But I cannot tell how the publisher gets back his money.

I and my wife will be delighted in paying you a visit in the late autumn if you can receive us then. I start now—at once.

Yours very faithfully
Anthony Trollope

To Austin Dobson

MS University of London Library.

6 Ap 68   WALTHAM HOUSE, WALTHAM CROSS.

Dear Sir.

I enclose slip for correction.[4] I would query the 2 last lines of the Third Stanza— "and the blue

In a word—" It is a somewhat unfinished expression of what you mean.

—also Stanza V

"As I heard—" when you use the word heard in the sense of "listened"—without an aim above expressed or understood. also the pseudo word—"abeat"

"Just to feel your pulses beat" might satisfy you.

Pray pardon this,— The verses shall go forward unaltered if you wish it.

Yours most faithfully
Any Trollope

[4] For Dobson's poem "Avice," *St. Paul's*, 2 (July 1868), 416–17. Dobson did not follow Trollope's suggestions for changes in the poem.

To J. M. Williams

MS New York University.

9—April 1868   WALTHAM HOUSE, WALTHAM CROSS.
Sir.

I regret that these were omitted in my former letter of this date—

I am Sir
Your faithful Servant
J. M Williams Esq   Anty Trollope

To John Tilley

MS General Post Office, London.

1 May 1868   Washington
Sir.

I beg to inform you that on reaching this place on the 24 Ultimo I waited on Mr. Randall the Postmaster General of the United States,[5] and that at his request I furnished him with a statement shewing the reasons which have induced the Postmaster General to close the existing convention and setting forth the propositions for a new convention which it is hoped may be made in conformity with the instructions which I have received. Mr. Randall then promised to give the matter his immediate attention;—alleging, however, that the present circumstances of the United States Government were very adverse to the immediate settlement of such a question.

I have seen Mr. Randall again today and he has told me that it is impossible for him to go into the matter till the question of the impeachment of the President of the United States be decided.[6] Should the President be convicted Mr. Randall would, as he informs me, at once resign. Under such circumstances it is not unnatural that he should decline to enter upon such a matter as a new postal convention,—particularly as it would be necessary that he should consult with Committees of the Senate and of the House of Representatives, which at the present moment it is impossible to convene.

Should the President be acquitted Mr. Randall assures me that the measure shall be taken in hand at once. Should there be a conviction, I must await the appointment of a new Poster General, before any steps can be taken.

I have the honour to be,
Sir,
Your most obedient Servant
John Tilley Esq   Anthony Trollope

[5] Alexander W. Randall (1819–72).

[6] President Andrew Johnson had been impeached on 25 February, and his trial began on 13 March. See Trollope to Tilley, 18 May 1868.

To ?

MS Parrish Collection.

1 May 1868　　　　　　　　　　　　　　　　　　　　Washington.
Dear Sir.
　I have great pleasure in annexing my signature below in two forms.[7]
　　　　　　　　　　　　　　　　Yours faithfully
　　　　　　　　　　　　　　　　Anthony Trollope

Mrs. Annie Fields[8] to Kate Field

MS Boston Public Library.

May 8th. 1868　　　　　　　　148. CHARLES STREET, BOSTON.
Dear Kate,
. . . Mr. Trollope is here expressing in no mild or measured terms his
disgust for Washington and Impeachment.
　　　　　　　　　　　　　　　　　Truly yours
　　　　　　　　　　　　　　　　　A. F.

To Mrs. Upham[9]

MS Parrish Collection.

[? 12 May 1868][1]　　　　　　　　　　　　　3 Temple Place
Tuesday　　　　　　　　　　　　　　　　　　Boston.
Mr Anthony Trollope presents his compliments to Mrs. Upham and
begs to express his regret that he is obliged to leave Boston on Friday.
Had he remained he would have had the greatest pleasure in accepting
Mrs. Upham's invitation and in meeting Madame [?]Parissas then.

---

　[7] Trollope attached a small photograph.
　[8] Annie Fields (1834–1915), née Adams, miscellaneous writer; wife of the publisher
James T. Fields. On 18 May she wrote again to Kate Field: "We had a very pleasant
visit from good whole-souled Mr. Trollope. A few such men redeemed Nineveh. He
always seems the soul of honesty." (MS Boston Public Library.)
　[9] Probably Mrs. T. Baxter Upham, a friend of James T. Fields and the wife of a
noted Boston musicologist.
　[1] Trollope's account books (Parrish Collection) indicate that he left Boston for
Washington on Friday, 15 May.

To George Smith

B 373 (Sadleir's transcript) and *Bibliography*, p. 233.

16 May 1868[2]   New York

*   *   *

[From New York, Trollope sends a "third letter" about America for the *Pall Mall Gazette*.[3]] I wrote a ballad yesterday on N. Y. Womanhood, intending to send it you.[4] But it is spiteful, and I will only shew it you when I get home.

*   *   *

To George Smith

Bibliography, p. 233.

17 May 1868[5]
From Washington Trollope sends a letter for the *Pall Mall Gazette* about the trial of two seamen. He promises two more letters, one on Congress and the Executive, the other on Reconstruction.[6]

To John Tilley

MS General Post Office, London.

May 18. 1868   Washington
My dear John.
The vote on the last article of impeachment was given on Saturday,[7] and the Post Genl here with his senior clerk[8] have given up the whole of this day, Monday, to me. I cannot therefore grumble at them for delay, but I am sorry to say that I do not see my way to a new Convention. In truth the whole desire of this office is exactly contrary to our desires, and is in conformity with the terms of the lately made & now expiring convention. They wish, and as I fancy, intend to send mails by any ships which may be available on any day, and are intent on upon [*sic*] doing this on the cheapest rate at which they can get such mails taken. Their public is more patient than ours, and they are less driven than are we in

---

[2] Sadleir mistakenly gives 16 March instead of 16 May for the portion of the letter in brackets. B 373 is almost certainly part of the same letter.

[3] Not traced.

[4] Not traced.

[5] Sadleir printed two separate notes for 17 March (actually 17 May), but they are probably from the same letter.

[6] None of these three letters has been traced.

[7] On 16 May President Johnson was acquitted on the crucial eleventh article of impeachment by a margin of one vote. Another one-vote margin acquitted him on the other two key articles on 26 May.

[8] Joseph H. Blackfan, Superintendent of Foreign Mails.

the matters of quickness and punctuality. I fear that they will not be got to bend themselves to three days, (and three days only), or to bend themselves to any special mode of payment that shall be in unison with ours. "Do you do as you like, and let us do as we like." That is their argument; and that, they say—no doubt with truth—, was our argument also when the last convention was a making. They acknowledge that the dropping through of any convention will be a misfortune, but it is not a misfortune they much fear, because their people are so patient. Book post will be discontinued, registration will be discontinued, closed forward mails will be discontinued, but they do not fear to face the public or Congress on these points. But they do fear to withdraw their support from the German lines of boats,—in which no doubt influential individuals are interested.

You will understand that I have reported before I have received a promised written communication from the P.M.G.—in order to save time. No telegram that I could send would be of any avail. That written communication I will send when I get it. But you can I think in the mean time send me instructions based on the report I now forward to you. You can indeed send me a telegram which shall decide all. If you are resolved that there shall be no mails regularly paid for under convention except three weekly between Lpool & New York viā Queenstown—you can say so. In that case no convention can be made. Of course I shall again do my best when I have received the written proposition of the PMG;—but it will be useless for me to remain here, if nothing can be done.[9]

I think I have made the points intelligible in this note—if not in my report.

Yours always
Anthy Trollope

To Kate Field

MS Boston Public Library. B 374.

May 19 68   Washington
My dear Kate,

I send the enclosed from my brother,—hoping that you will be able to understand them. What a very wicked woman Mrs. P.[1] seems to be! I returned here through N.Y. the other day without stopping an hour; and I heard the verdict of acquittal given on Saturday. I hope you like the

---

[9] Tilley tried repeatedly to persuade the Treasury to allow Trollope to make a treaty on whatever terms he could, urging on 27 June: "Might I ask you . . . to come to a decision as to the American postal convention. . . . Trollope went out to please me at some inconvenience to himself and he is most anxious to get back." Finally, on 1 July, Tilley was able to telegram Trollope: "Make Treaty on the best terms you can." (MSS General Post Office, London.)

[1] Probably Mrs. Theodore Parker. See Trollope to Field, 3 June 1868.

way in which your party interfered to stop the judgment in the middle when they found that it was going against their wishes. I thought it disgraceful.

Yours affectionately

A. T.

To Kate Field

MS Boston Public Library. *Commentary*, pp. 283–84; B 375.

24 May 1868 Washington
Dear Kate.

I got your letter on my return to W. from Richmond,[2] whither I have been to look after memorials of Davis[3] & Lee[4] and the other great heroes of the Secession. The Mss. of which your letter speaks has not reached me. The printed story, "Love and War"[5] (which I return as you may want it), I have read. It has two faults. It wants a plot, and is too egoistic. Touching the second fault first, it is always dangerous to write from the point of "I." The reader is unconsciously taught to feel that the writer is glorifying himself, and rebels against the self praise. Or otherwise the "I" is pretentiously humble, and offends from exactly the other point of view. In telling a tale it is, I think, always well to sink the personal pronoun. The old way, "Once upon a time," with slight modifications, is the best way of telling a story.

Now as to the plot;—it is there that you fail and are like to fail. In "Love and War" there is absolutely no plot,—no contrived arrangement of incidents by which interest is excited. You simply say that a girl was unhappy in such & such circumstances, and was helped by such and such (improbable) virtues & intelligences. You must work more out of your imagination than this before you can be a story-teller for the public. And I think you could do it. In spite of Dogberry, the thing is to be done by cudgelling.[6] But you must exercise your mind upon it, and not sit down simply to write the details of a picture which is conveyed to you, not by your imagination, but by your sympathies. Both sympathy and imagination must be at work,—and must work in unison,—before you can attract.

Your narration as regards language and ease of diction is excellent. I am sure that you can write without difficulty, but I am nearly equally sure that you must train your mind to work, before you can deal with

[2] Capital of Virginia and seat of the Confederate government during the Civil War.
[3] Jefferson Davis (1808–89), President of the Confederacy.
[4] Robert E. Lee (1807–70), leader of the Confederate army.
[5] "Love and War" was first published in *The Public Spirit* and then reprinted in *The Springfield Republican* (4 January 1868).
[6] "God hath blessed you with a good name; to be a well-favour'd man is the gift of fortune; but to write and read comes by nature." (*Much Ado About Nothing*, III.iii. 13–16.)

combinations of incidents. And yet I fully believe that it is in you to do it.

If I give you pain, pray excuse me. I would so fain see you step out & become one of the profession in which women can work at par along side of men. You have already learned so much of the art,—and then you are so young.

Most affectionately yours
A. T.

The end of your story should have been the beginning.

I will tell you of the last scene of the impeachment when it is over.

To George Smith

Bibliography, p. 233.

27 May 1868

From Washington, Trollope sends a letter for the *Pall Mall Gazette*.[7] He promises another on the relation of Great Britain with the United States.[8]

To Kate Field

MS Boston Public Library. *Commentary*, pp. 284–85; B 376.

May 28. 1868.   Washington.
My dear Kate.

I have read your MS. & return it. Of course, as it is a fragment, I cannot tell how far the plot might be successful. It is much more pretentious than the printed story, and is for that reason worse;—but I should say of it that the author ought to be able to write a good story.

As a rule young writers,—(I speak, of course, as [? of] writers of fiction,) —should be very chary of giving vent to their own feelings on what I may call public matters. If you are writing an essay, you have to convey of course your own ideas and convictions, to another mind. You will of course desire to do so in fiction also, and may ultimately do so (when your audience is made) more successfully than by essay writing. But your first object must be to charm and not to teach. You should avoid the "I" not only in the absolute expressed form of the pronoun, but even in regard to the reader's appreciation of your motives. Your reader should not be made to think that *you* are trying to teach, or to preach, or to convince. Teach, and preach, and convince if you can;—but first learn the art of doing so without seeming to do it. We are very jealous of

---

[7] "An English View of the President's Impeachment," *Pall Mall Gazette*, 15 June 1868, p. 10. The heading reads: "An able correspondent, familiar to our readers under the signature of 'An Englishman,' sends us under date May 27, the following letter from the United States, where he is at present on a visit."

[8] "American Affairs," *Pall Mall Gazette*, 11 July 1868, pp. 10–11. The heading reads: "The following letter is from a well-known English author, now on a visit to the United States."

preachers. We admit them at certain hours & places for certain reasons. We take up a story for recreation, and the mind, desirous of recreation, revolts from being entertained with a sermon. Your story about the Artist[9] is intended to convey your teaching as to what Americans and Americanesses should have done during the war. You will hardly win your way in that fashion. Tell some simple plot or story of more or less involved, but still common life, adventure, and try first to tell that in such form that idle minds may find some gentle sentiment & recreation in your work. Afterwards, when you have learned the knack of story telling, go on to greater objects.

There's a sermon for you.

Yours ever aff
A. T.

To Kate Field

MS Boston Public Library. *Commentary*, pp. 285–86; B 377.

3. June 1868   [Washington]
My dear Kate.

I hope you have not blown up Mrs. T. Parker[1] very badly; for if she says the money was paid to Chapman, it probably was so paid; and Chapman is the very man to forget to mention it. Indeed he never does mention anything. However I only did as I was told.

I don't seem to care much about Planchette,[2] however I am mild and submit to be taken to Planchettes and Hume's[3] and Dotens;[4] (What was the name of the Boston preaching and poetising woman?) I should like of all things to see a ghost, and if one would come and have it out with me on the square I think it would add vastly to my interest in life. Undoubtedly one would prefer half an hour with Washington or Hamilton

[9] Not traced.

[1] Mrs. Theodore Parker (*d.* 1880), widow of the well-known liberal Boston preacher, who had died in 1860. Mrs. Parker had reimbursed T. A. Trollope for some small expenditure by leaving money with the publisher Frederic Chapman. But Chapman neglected to forward the money, and Tom, having forgotten the arrangement, mentioned the trifling debt to Kate Field, who mentioned it to Mrs. Parker. Kate sent Mrs. Parker's reply to Anthony in Washington, who sent it on to Tom, and on 27 July Tom wrote to Kate begging that she convey apologies for his absentmindedness. (MSS Boston Public Library.)

[2] A planchette is a writing device used to record messages during a séance. Kate Field was just publishing a little book entitled *Planchette's Diary*.

[3] Daniel Dunglas Home (1833–86), Scottish-American spiritualist who had created a sensation in England in the mid-1850's and was the original for Browning's "Mr. Sludge, 'The Medium.'" According to his wife's notes, Trollope attended one of Home's séances at Ealing in 1855 (MS University of Illinois); Trollope's brother did the same, and described the séance in some detail (*What I Remember*, pp. 260–62).

[4] Lizzie Doten, the spiritualist poet and short-story writer. See Trollope to Field, 4 January 1862.

to any amount of intercourse with even Butler[5] or Charles Sumner. But when tables rap, and boards write, and dead young women come and tickle my knee under a big table, I find the manifestation to be unworthy of the previous grand ceremony of death. Your visitor from above or below should be majestical, should stalk in all panoplied from head to foot[6]—at least with a white sheet, and should not condescend to catechetical and alphabetical puzzles.

I enclose a note for your great friend Mr. Elliott.[7] He writes (apparently) from No. 44 Bible Bower. But as I cannot believe that there is as yet in New York any so near approach to the Elysian Fields, I think it better to send my note to you, than to trust it so addressed to the post. I do not know when I shall be in N.Y. I wont say that I might not be there tomorrow. This place is so awful to me, that I doubt whether I can stand it much longer. To make matters worse a democratic Senator who is stone deaf and who lives in the same house with me, has proposed to dine with me every day! I refused three times but he did not hear me, and ordered that our dinners should be served together. I had not the courage to fight it any further, and can see no alternative but to run away.

If you are going out of town, let me know when you go, and whither. I have half a mind to take a run to Niagara for the sake of getting cool in the spray.

Address as below if you write again.

Yours always
A. T.
Wormley I Street
Washington

To Mrs. Harriet Knower

MS Parrish Collection.

[? 7 June 1868][8]
My dear friend.
Do not wait for me this morning, as I am very late.

Yours ever
A. T.

Sunday

[5] Benjamin Franklin Butler (1818–93), the congressman who led the campaign to impeach Andrew Johnson.

[6] See *Hamlet*, I.i.143–44 and I.ii.227.

[7] Charles Wyllys Elliott (1817–83), author of works on miscellaneous subjects, including the history of New England.

[8] The envelope, addressed to Mrs. Knower, 36 W. 20 Street, New York, is postmarked Washington, D.C., June, but the date is blurred. Trollope's account books (Parrish Collection) indicate that he traveled from Washington to New York on

To Kate Field

MS Boston Public Library. *Commentary*, pp. 286–87; B 378 (misdated).

18 June. 1868 Washington

Dear Kate.

I got a telegram on yesterday (Wednesday) morning which took me away from N.Y. at 10—instead of 12—& so I do not know whether that horrid little Silenus sent the photographs[1] or no— I guess he didn't. At any rate he was bound to send them before & I hope he may be drowned in Burgundy and that his deputy with the dirty sleeves will photograph him in his last gasp,—piteously. If they ever reach you, tell me whether they are good for any thing. I should like one of you standing up, facing full front, with your hat. I think it would have your natural look, & you cant conceive how little I shall think of the detrimental skirt of which our Silenus complained. I have got letters from England, & such letters. My wife says in reference to her projected journey over here—"Don't I wish I may get it." Had I told her not to come, woman-like she would have been here by the first boat. However, she is quite right, as Washington wd. kill her. For myself I shall write my epitaph before I go to bed tonight.

> Washington has slain this man,
> By politics and heat together.
> +Sumner alone he might have stood,
> But not the Summer weather.
> +very doubtful.

My letters tell me that I should have received a telegram from England before I got them, which will enable,—(or have enabled me) really to begin my work. But no telegram has come. As I must remain, I shall run for the V.–Presidency on the strictest Democratic ticket— which I take to be repudiation of the debt and return to slavery. I shall pass the next two months in reading Mr. Elliott's various Mss,[2] which have arrived in a chest.

Yours ever
A. T.

Sunday, 7 June. (The account books also indicate that during his earlier visit to the States he met with Mary Knower on 13 September 1861 at Newport and with Mrs. Knower on 10 March 1862 at New York.)

[1] The photographer may have been Napoleon Sarony, of 630 Broadway, whose photographs of Trollope from about this date survive. (Silenus was a drunken satyr, the foster father and attendant of Bacchus.)

[2] Among the manuscripts was that of the novel *Wind and Whirlwind*, which was published later the same year. See Trollope to Field, 8 July 1868.

To Rhoda Broughton[3]

Commentary, pp. 344–45. B 379.

28 June 1868.　　　　　　　　　　　　　　　　　　Washington.
Dear Madam.

I have just read your novel *Not Wisely but too Well* and wish to tell you how much it has pleased me. I should not write you on such a matter if I were not also a novelist and one much interested in the general virtues and vices, shortcomings and excellences of my brethren. Some months since I was told by a friend,—a lady whom I know to be a good critic,—that *Cometh Up as a Flower* was a book that I ought to read; that your later published novel was also very clever, though not equal to the one which was earlier given to the public. This lady, who is an intimate friend of mine, told me either that she knew you or that some mutual friend created an interest on her behalf in your writings. I do not often read novels, but I did the other day, here in America, purchase, and have since read, the one I have named. I must tell you also that I have heard that your stories were written in a strain not becoming a woman young as you are—not indeed becoming any woman. I tell you this without reserve, as doubtless the same report must have reached your ears.

In the story which I have read there is not a word that I would not have had written by my sister, or my daughter—if I had one. I do not understand the critics who, when there is so much that is foul abroad, can settle down with claws and beaks on a tale which teaches a wholesome lesson without an impure picture or a faulty expression. I will not say that your story is perfect. Having been probably ten times as many years at the work as you have, I think, were I with you, I could point out faults here and there against nature. You fall into the common faults of the young, making that which is prosaic in life too prosaic, and that which is poetic, too poetic. The fault here is of exaggeration. But I read your tale with intense interest. I wept over it, and formed my wishes on it, and came to the conclusion that there had come up another sister among us, of whose name we should be proud.[4]

　　　　　　　　　　　　　　　　　　Yours with much admiration
　　　　　　　　　　　　　　　　　　Anthony Trollope

[3] Rhoda Broughton (1840–1920), a talented minor novelist who outlived her reputation for audacity. " 'I began life as Zola,' she once remarked; 'I finish it as Miss Yonge.' " (*The Times*, 7 June 1920, p. 17.) *Not Wisely but too Well* and *Cometh Up as a Flower* were both published in 1867.

[4] According to Sadleir, this generous and encouraging letter saved Miss Broughton "from a mood of sullen defiance *vis-à-vis* her critics" and renewed her self confidence. Nevertheless, in October 1876 she wrote to George Bentley: "Frederick Locker told me how Ouida abuses my books . . . and how Anthony Trollope says I might have done something if I had taken pains. But then he never praises any writer except Thackeray, at least I never heard him." (Michael Sadleir, *Things Past* [1944], p. 90.)

To John Tilley

MS General Post Office, London.

3. July. 1868   Washington
My dear Tilley.

I had better perhaps say a few words in explanation of the report
which I send home to day. The views of the PMG here have no doubt altered since I last discussed the matter of the convention with him, which
means in fact that certain members of Congress have coerced him. I enclose two extracts from newpapers[5] which go to shew that efforts are
being made here to get up a transatlantic American line to sail from
N. Y. to Liverpool,—and it is the intention to subsidise this line by allowing to it the whole postage on the letters it shall convey—i e the first
12 cents for each single letter. Mr Randall now professes himself to be
very strongly in favour of this line. I do not think such was his opinion
a month ago.

The proposed revision of Article No. 2. was drawn out by me at
the Post Office here, and Mr Blackfan the chief clerk, who is the man
who really understands the question as it regards mail accommodation,
thought that by its adoption we might still get to a convention. Mr.
Randall however would not have it.

Indeed, if I am to put any trust in what he says as to his own determination, he intends to insist on Article No. 2. as it stands in the present
convention. I do not know whether you would have acceded to my proposed Art. 2—, (which after all would not have been satisfactory for it
left us in the predicament of saying first that we would do a thing and
then that we would do it, but only at a certain price—)—but I do not
see how we are to concede further than that, unless we agree to maintain
the existing convention with an alteration or two as to rates on newspapers &c.

There can be no doubt I think that the motive power in all this is
the influence of certain members of Congress who know and care nothing for the transit of mails, but who do know and care a great deal about
certain Companies.

Yours always
Anthony Trollope

[5] The article from the Washington *Morning Chronicle* of 2 July complained that
the "wiseacre who controls the British Postal Department" canceled the old convention "in the interest of a subsidized line of steamers" (Cunard), proposing that all
mails be carried both ways on British vessels (General Post Office, London).

To John Tilley

MS General Post Office, London.

July 7. 1868   Washington.
My dear John.

The PMG here is away at present at the Democratic convention at N. York;—but I hope I have now concluded the convention with Blackfan, who is the only man here who really understands it. After getting your telegram authorizing me to relinquish Art 2. (which I hope you understood to be a direct departure from your previous telegram bidding me arrange for the three despatches to & from Queenstown;—for of course if each country is to be at liberty to send what mails it may please as authorized by Art 11, there can be no positive obligation for these routes viâ Queenstown) I went to work and drafted new clauses for the new Convention, in reference to all those articles which had to be altered. I enclose on a slip the Art. which I propose to be No. 1 of the Detailed regulations. I cannot positively say that even this will be acceded to,—as of course they allege here, that the very gist of the convention as arranged in 66—is contained in Art 11— which gives each nation the duty of selecting its own mode of despatching Mails. But I think I shall obtain this, which indeed means little or nothing—and is little more than a verbal adherance to our scheme.

Moreover they desire to bind me to a reduction of letter postage at the end of another year. This of course I decline, but have consented to a clause saying that the rates shall be reconsidered at the end of 12 months. They also want me to allow book parcels up to two ounces to pass as newspapers. If they insist on this I shall telegraph. They also want a clause to admit prices current as newspapers. I shall endeavour to leave this to be concluded by correspondence. If not, shall telegraph.

I suppose this will be my last letter. If I can settle, as I hope, tomorrow, I shall telegraph to say that I come home on the 15th. This will give you the power to stop me, but I do pray you may not use it.

I cannot but feel that they have had the whip hand of us altogether,— in this respect;—that if all convention was stopped between the two countries by our being unable to settle on the terms of a new convention, the onus of the national inconvenience would fall on us in having disturbed an arrangement, and not on them. This I have no doubt you also have felt. We shall have settled the rates and fines, and shall have got them to acknowledge the superiority of the Queenstown route (if they will do so) and that will be all.[6]

Yours ever
Any Trollope

[6] The convention that Trollope arranged was substantially the same as the one it replaced and thus, from the viewpoint of the British authorities, a relative failure, though no one blamed Trollope. The Queenstown route was one of three mentioned

To Kate Field

MS Boston Public Library. *Commentary*, pp. 287–89; B 380.

July 8. 1868.   Washington
My dear Kate.

I have put off answering your note of the 2nd till I could say certainly what my movements would be,—but even now I can say nothing of the kind. The Post Genl is away, electing a democratic candidate for the White House, and consequently I am still in suspense. Oh, Lord what a night I spent,—the last as ever was,—among the mosquitoes, trying to burn them with a candle inside the net! I could not get at one, but was more successful with the netting. I didn't have a wink of sleep, and another such a night will put me into a fever hospital.

I still hope to leave here in time for the boat home on this day week. As I do not know where you are or where Mrs. Homans is, I do not think I shall go on to Boston at all. If I had a day or two I would either run to Niagara or to Lake George. I am killed by the heat, and want to get out of a town. If you'll go down close to the sea, & near enough for me to get at you, I would then go to you.

I dont quite understand about the photographs but I'll do as you bid me, pay the bill, (including the drink) and send you one of the two. I have got your section framed down to the mere hat and eyes and nose. It is all I have of you except a smudged (but originally very pretty) portrait taken from a picture.

Thanks for the account of myself taken from the 2 papers,[7] which describes me as being like a minie ball with gloves on. If I saw the writer I should be apt to go off and let him know that I never wear gloves. What fools people are. I saw in some paper an account of you amidst other strong-minded women—Janet L. Tozer, Annie B. Slocum, Martha M. Mumpus, Violet Q. Fitzpopam &c.[8] I observed that every one except you had an intermediate initial— I really think that with a view to the feel-

---

in the Detailed Regulations, but other stipulations made it clear that neither country was bound to this route.

[7] The Boston *Daily Evening Transcript* described Trollope as follows (16 June 1868, p. 2): "He is a strange looking person. His head is shaped like a minnie ball, with the point rounded down a little, like the half of a lemon cut transversely in two. It is small, almost sharp at the top, and bald, increasing in size until it reaches his neck. His complexion and general bearing are much like Dickens's. His body is large and well preserved. He dresses like a gentleman and not like a fop, but he squeezes his small, well-shaped hand into a very small pair of colored kids. He 'wears a cane,' as all Englishmen do." Four days later another item appeared in the same paper (20 June 1868, p. 2): "Anthony Trollope, the brother of Thomas Adolphus, remarked to a friend in this country, 'I cannot understand why my novels are reprinted in the United States while Tom's are not, for his are better than mine, especially his Italian ones.'" (B.)

[8] Facetious names.

ings of the country you should insert one. It is manifestly necessary to success. Kate X. Field would do very well.

Of course I will do what you ask me about the proofs of the Dickens paper.[9] You must send them to the Brevoort House. If you could have got Dickens to do it for you in London it would have been better.[1]

What do you think your friend Elliott has proposed? That I should have his novel[2] published in England with my name on the Title page,—and with any slight alterations in the vol. which I might be pleased to make!!! That I call cool—and peculiarly honest,—& so clever too, as no two people were ever more unlike each other in language, manner, thought, and style of narrative.

Give my kindest love to your mother. The same to yourself dear Kate—if I do not see you again,—with a kiss that shall be semi-paternal—one third brotherly, and as regards the small remainder, as loving as you please.

A. T.

To Kate Field

MS Boston Public Library. *Commentary*, pp. 289–90; B 381.

13 July. 1868 Monday   Brevoort House N.Y.
My dear Kate.

Here I am, and I start for England on Wednesday. Last night, I came from Washington. To night I go to Boston. Tuesday night I come back here. I shall therefore be within 12 miles of you but shall not see you. I could not possibly get back to you, as you will see from the above programme. I shall be at the Parker House at Boston, but shall spend the morning & probably the day with the Homans at 4 Temple Place. I wish I could have seen your dear old face once more, (before the gray hairs come, or the wings which you will wear in heaven)—but I do not see how it is to be—

I have got the photographs, & have paid for them—$11.50. I wish I could have paid for yours at the same time.

---

[9] Trollope is referring to an English edition of Kate Field's *Pen Photographs of Charles Dickens's Readings* (1868), a short book written in February 1868 and based on Dickens's public readings in New York in January 1868. Kate Field was later presented to Dickens after a Boston reading, apparently in early April, and she recorded in her diary that Dickens "said he was delighted to make my acquaintance." She also noted that "Dickens praises my 'Photographs' very warmly." (Lilian Whiting, *Kate Field: A Record*, pp. 175–78, 181–82.)

[1] Dickens had proposed that Kate Field send advance sheets of her book to Chapman & Hall for simultaneous publication in England. This was not done, and Dickens later said that it was too late for republication in England. See Trollope to Field, 30 September 1868.

[2] Charles Wyllys Elliott's *Wind and Whirlwind* (1868) was published under the pseudonym Thom White.

The letter from Theodore P's widow I sent to Tom, (not to you). I could do nothing else with it. If Tom be not a fool he will let the thing pass as an account settled. I will do as you bid me about the Dickens papers if I get hold of them. On Wednesday morning if they be not here I will send for them. I think I will ask D. to speak to C & H—or at least consult him.

Your friend who lives in the Bible hotel[3] has written me a most polite letter to say that my answer to him was just what he expected.

Touching the story for the Saint Pauls,[4]—remember that it is to go into one number and be not more than from 14 to 16 pages—each page 520 words. I say this because Tom writes to ask me whether you are not going to write a longer kind of story. I should have no room now for a longer story. Address.

> A. Trollope Esq
> 294, City Road
> London.

Touching the black phantom, I hope he has winged his way to distant worlds. He did not hurt me,—but a man is tough in these matters. It vexed you and teased my wife.

God bless you dear,—I wish I thought I might see your clever laughing eyes again before the days of the spectacles;—but I suppose not. My love to your mother.

> Yours always
> A. T.

To George Smith

MS Bodleian. Excerpt, Hamer, p. 213.

28 July 1868   WALTHAM HOUSE, WALTHAM CROSS.
My dear Smith.

I have told the writer of the enclosed that the copyright of the Claverings belongs to you, & that you wd. send him an answer. If it came within your way I should be glad the Claverings should appear translated in the paper in question.

> Yours always
> A. T.

[3] Charles Wyllys Elliott.
[4] On 6 June Trollope had suggested that Kate Field write a story for his magazine. She was flattered, and planned to try, but no story of hers appeared in *St. Paul's*. Her diary for 1868 indicates that she met Trollope at least four times during May and June (see Lilian Whiting, *Kate Field: A Record*, p. 183).

To Thomas Adolphus Trollope

MS Parrish Collection. B 382 (misdated).

August 1—1868.   WALTHAM HOUSE, WALTHAM CROSS.
My dear Tom.

I got home here at 12 on Monday night after a most disagreeable trip to America,—so much so that I do not intend to go on any more ambassadorial business. However I made the treaty, have been duly thanked by the P.M.G. and no doubt will be duly paid.[5]

⟨[?]Touching Bice . . .⟩[6]

I hope ⟨she⟩ Bice is getting strong again. Somebody told me that she saw her at Geo Smiths, & that she looked well.

Touching your articles, Vieusseux comes out in the next number, Parini will appear about 3 or 4 afterwards—Goldoni in its turn,—similarly.[7] It does not do to bring such subjects on too rapidly. I wrote to you about Fanny's first number.[8] I have not yet read the second, as I have been very busy; but I will do so very shortly.[9]

My love to Fanny. I send this as directed to Salzburgh.

Yours always affect.

Anthony Trollope

To Edward Robert Bulwer Lytton[1]

MS Hertfordshire Record Office.

August 1 1868   WALTHAM HOUSE, WALTHAM CROSS.
My dear Lytton.

I spoke to you when at Knebworth as to writing a novel (or short-tale[)] in verse for the Saint Pauls. I dont know whether you thought of it since.

[5] Tilley had written Trollope on 30 July: "I am desired by His Grace [the Duke of Montrose] to convey to you his thanks for the services you have rendered, and at the same time to state that, although you have not succeeded in inducing the United States Post Office to agree to such favourable terms as this Department hoped to obtain, he is satisfied no exertions on your part were spared to obtain the end in view." (MS [initialed draft] General Post Office, London.) Trollope was paid five guineas per day for 111 days (£582 15s), plus passage and other expenses.

[6] The next nine lines are scored through and indecipherable.

[7] "Giampietro Vieusseux, the Florentine Bookseller," *St. Paul's*, 2 (September 1868), 727–35; "Parnini: and Milan in the Latter Half of the Eighteenth Century," *St. Paul's*, 3 (November 1868), 214–29; and "Goldoni: and Life in Italy a Hundred and Twenty Years Since," *St. Paul's*, 4 (July 1869), 482–97.

[8] Frances Eleanor Trollope's novel *The Sacristan's Household*, which was serialized in *St. Paul's* from July 1868 through June 1869.

[9] The next five lines (a new paragraph) are scored through and indecipherable.

[1] Edward Robert Bulwer Lytton (1831–91), later 1st Earl of Lytton, statesman and poet; son of the novelist. (Lytton published his early poetry under the pseudonym Owen Meredith.)

I now write to ask whether you would write for me a story in verse for a Christmas number. It should fill about *16* pages, and we should have it by the middle of October. Virtue would give you £35 for the use of it (i e 16 pages), leaving the copyright in your hands. Our purpose is to publish 5 or 6 tales together, all by well known hands. I should write one. It wd. be brought out sometime in November. Pray do if you can, & let me have a line to say. If you can do it, you can fix the length,—but must let me know beforehand as others must of course be made to fit.[2]

I have just returned from Washington where I have spent a most odious summer.

Yours always faithfully
Anthy Trollope

The tale should have some bearing on Xmas, more or less remote—

To Austin Dobson

MS University of London Library.

August 1—1868   WALTHAM HOUSE, WALTHAM CROSS.
Dear Sir.

If you [have] any short piece of poetry that would suit us for two or three pages, I should be glad of it for the *September* number. If so let me know *at once*.

Yours always
Any Trollope

To Miss Elmore[3]

MS Parrish Collection.

1. August 1868.   WALTHAM HOUSE, WALTHAM CROSS.
My dear Miss Elmore.

I am so glad I met you among the pictures as I had very stupidly blundered over your signature. Below you have me—not quite as large as life.[4]

Very truly yours
Anthony Trollope

---

[2] Lytton did not write anything for *St. Paul's*; moreover, the special Christmas number was not issued.

[3] Perhaps the daughter of the painter Alfred Elmore.

[4] A small photograph was attached.

To George MacDonald

MS Parrish Collection.

August 3. 1868.   WALTHAM HOUSE, WALTHAM CROSS.
My dear Mr Macdonald.
We are thinking of bringing out an extra Christmas number of the
Saint Paul's Magazine. Would you try your hand at a Christmas story
for us? It should fill about 20 pages of the magazine, and should of
course have some slight Christmas adaption. You should let me have it
if possible by the end of September or quite early in October, as I should
have to make a story of my own fit to the length of the others, & the number must be brought out in November.[5] If you could do this Messrs
Virtue would give you £25 for the use of the tale, leaving the copyright
in your hand, to be used, say after 12 months, as you might please.
                                        very faithfully
                                        Anthony Trollope

To George MacDonald

MS Parrish Collection.

August. 7. 1868   ATHENAEUM CLUB
My dear Mr Macdonald
Let it not be sensible;—but weird rather, and of a Christmas-ghostly
flavour, if such be possible. I don't know whether Pudding and Hades
can be brought together;—but if any man can do it, you can.
                                        Yours always
                                        Anthony Trollope

To Austin Dobson

MS University of London Library.

August 7. 1868   GARRICK CLUB
Dear Mr Dobson.
I send the proof of the one of your poems which suits us best just at
present.[6] I do not understand the heading, nor can I reconcile it to your
note— I presume the poem is not a translation. If not, why say that it is?
However I do not doubt but that you will put it right— If it be a translation,—or even an adaptation,—of course say so.[7] It is very pretty,—as is

[5] MacDonald's story, "Uncle Cornelius: His Story," appeared in *St. Paul's*, 3 (January 1869), 423–41.
[6] "A Song of Angiola in Heaven," *St. Paul's*, 2 (September 1868), 676–77.
[7] The poem was printed without any subtitle. The manuscript for this poem has
not been traced, but like its companion pieces it may have been submitted as one of
"The Songs of Niccolò Pescara, Knight of Forli." In reprinting his four Angiola

also the other Song of Angiola,[8] which I will keep by me if you please. The Landlady[9] is hardly good enough;—and yet it is good. The other I do not care so much for.

You will perhaps send in the proof as soon as you can. If you can post it early tomorrow, Saturday—addressed to me

Waltham House
Waltham Cross.

I shall get it before I start for Scotland on Monday morning.

I should be glad if I could see you when I come back.

Yours faithfully
Anthony Trollope

To Henry Taylor

MS Bodleian.

August 10. 1868   WALTHAM HOUSE, WALTHAM CROSS.
My dear Mr Taylor.

I have read your friends tale,[1] and will tell you as clearly as I can what I think of it. It has been written with the common idea that the person who can feel the details of a love story, and who has sufficient powers of creation to make out a new plan for such a story, can also write a novel. I think that this is a mistake, and that a certain amount of apprenticeship in the labour of writing so as to please a public is necessary. I have no doubt but that the author in this case could be taught,—or could teach herself,—to write a story that would be read; but this story lacks much that is needed. It has three faults,—and all these faults are the faults of a young untrained writer. The first and chief is that there is not enough of matter in it. The plot is made out and told; but there has not been on the part of the author a sufficient recognition of the fact that an author is bound to fill all his pages with matter that shall be interesting. Many authors do not do so. Perhaps but few do. But still such should be the writer's theory of his work,—and especially if the writer be a novelist.

Secondly—the persons who speak, do not speak naturally. This is a fault most natural to young authors; as the opposite virtue of natural

---

poems, Dobson said in a note that "it is perhaps scarcely necessary to state that [they] owe their form and existence to the beautiful renderings of the Early Italian Poets . . . by Mr. D. G. Rossetti, published in 1861." (*Vignettes in Rhyme* [1873], p. 220.)

[8] "A Song of Angiola on Earth," *St. Paul's*, 3 (February 1869), 592–93.

[9] "My Landlady" was published in the *Nautical Magazine* in December 1872 and reprinted in *Vignettes in Rhyme*.

[1] On 24 June Taylor sent Trollope the manuscript of a novel to consider for *St. Paul's*, adding, "the Authoress is very young & not at all sensitive, so that you need not think that you have any irksome office imposed upon you, if you shd. find it to be that of rejection." (MS University of Illinois.)

dialogue can come but from observation. The author however of prose dialogue, whether young or old, should always endeavour to test his (or her) own dialogue by the ear, and learn whether the words written sound like words spoken.

Thirdly,—the tale is broken by a divided sympathy. The author herself could not say of this tale which of her two young ladies is the one to whose interests and on whose behalf, she desires to bind her readers.

The story is a pretty story, and there is much in the telling of it, in spite of my hard & ill natured criticism which would make me think that the writer could write a good novel, if she would give much more time to the work, and teach herself to think that the work to be done is not so very easy. I will address the MS to you to the care of Chapman & Hall.

Yours most sincerely
Anthony Trollope

To E. S. Dallas

MS Parrish Collection. B 383.

STRATHTYRUM
ST. ANDREWS

22 August 1868

My dear Dallas.

Many thanks for the Clarissa.[2] I quite admit that you have improved the book greatly and that it ought to be read in its improved form;—but I do not think that even what you have done will make the novel popular. It is not in concord with the present and growing tastes of the country.

Nor do I think that Clarissa deserves all the praise you give to the work. Its pathos is so exquisite that probably we may be justified in saying that in that respect it excels all other novels. And it may perhaps be the case, that of all attributes to prose fiction, pathos is the most effective. But then Clarissa is to my idea so defective in most other respects as to be far from the first of English prose tales. The vehicle in which the narration is given is awkward and tedious,—so much so as to be to the majority of readers repulsive. The fact that the writing of such letters is impossible wounds one at every turn. The language used by the writers, is unnatural,—especially that used by Lovelace. Clarissa is unnaturally good. The other Harlowes unnaturally bad. Lovelace is a mixture such as no one ever met. And then the language of the writers, so different in their characters, is quite similar in style and unnatural throughout. I agree that for an intelligent reader the pathos carries all this down;— only that the reader must be patient as well as intelligent. The ways of the present age are effectually impatient.

---

[2] Dallas had just published a three-volume abridgment of Richardson's *Clarissa*. Trollope developed his criticisms of the novel in a lengthy review, "Clarissa," *St. Paul's*, 3 (November 1868), 163–72.

The French are infinitely more patient than we are; and then the pathos is as open to them as us;—not so the awkwardness of the language.

Yours always

Anthony Trollope

To Charles Lever

MS Taylor Collection.

OFFICE OF THE ST. PAULS MAGAZINE,

August 26 1868   294, CITY ROAD, LONDON.

My dear Lever

I am on the whole glad that you declined to do the Xmas story, as Virtue has at my solicitation given up the idea of the extra number, with which I was never much in line. I have desired them to send you the "Old Gradys"[3] for correction. I have corrected the "Man with the ——— ———," myself, the only correction being that I have changed the name, which, to one innocent as you, was no doubt innocent enough; but which to town-living people here in England, who have dirty minds, would have given rise to nasty suggestions touching dissenteric troubles. You must excuse the liberty. I have called it "The Adventurer."[4] If you are particular about it, & have a better name & will send it at once it will be in time.

You are a slanderer in saying that I would not answer & attend to any letter you might write— I have attended to all you have written with a most praiseworthy and philo-colleague punctuality. And then to go to dear Pigott for punctuality!

Yours ever

A. T.

To E. S. Dallas

MS Berg Collection. B 384.

Broadford[5]

Sept 1. 1868.   Skye.

My dear Dallas.

I return the article with thanks. The truth of the story was this:—I wrote a play over twenty years ago, which I called the "Noble Jilt." It was done before my novel writing days. This I sent to my old friend Bartley who was then manager at Covent Garden, and he returned it with a most heart-breaking letter,[6] saying that it had every fault incident

---

[3] Not traced.

[4] "Life Studies. No. III.—The Adventurer," *St. Paul's*, 3 (October 1868), 32–34.

[5] A village on the isle of Skye, the largest of the Hebrides.

[6] Bartley to Trollope, 18 June 1851.

to a play, & no virtue. It went away into darkness for some fifteen years, and then was brought out & turned into a novel. After all old Bartleys criticism, I believe it to be a good play.

I read that remonstrance from C. R. in the number of O. a W. that you gave me.[7] Do you not think that he was very wrong to write it? I think you were almost wrong to publish it. Why should he notice what was said in the Mask? If he be conscious of right in the matter, such a flap from the tale [*sic*] of so small a fish should not hurt him at all. Does he not know that men who are above the line must always bear little stings from men who are below,—and that there should be no flinching and in truth no suffering from such stings? Who is there, that has not been so attacked? But other men do not notice such attacks, and thus the attackers lose their object.

Touching the papers on sympathy[8] what you say is true, no doubt;—but it is a truth in words rather than in facts. The same idea as to sympathy is made very clear in the matter of patriotism. Patriotism is the virtue of a limited & confined sympathy. A truly cosmopolitan feeling is a much grander condition of mind. But you may preach for ever without being able to teach men that they should love all the world as well as their own country.

Yours always
Anthony Trollope

To [? F. H.] Joyce[9]
MS Taylor Collection.

16 Sep 1868.   WALTHAM HOUSE, WALTHAM CROSS.
My dear Mr Joyce.

I write to you on an ecclesiastical subject, though not with a high ecclesiastical purport. I am writing a novel. And in my story I have a very vexed question as to the building of a methodist chapel on a spot of "supposed" common ground immediately in front of the vicars gate;—a very hideous tabernacle and sickly Salem. I am sure you will feel the position. Now I will bring out at last that the spot of ground is glebe.

---

[7] "Fair Play and Foul Play," an article in the July number of *The Mask: A Humorous and Fantastic Review of the Month* (a periodical written and edited by Alfred Thompson and Leopold Lewis), had pointed out the similarities between the novel *Foul Play* (which had just been serialized in *Once a Week*) by Charles Reade and Dion Boucicault and *Le Portefeuille rouge* by Fournier and Meyer. Reade was provoked into replying in *Once a Week* ("Foul Play: The Sham Sample Swindle," 22 August 1868, pp. 151–55), and his reply was in turn held up to ridicule in the September number of the *Mask*.

[8] "The Critical Temper," *Once a Week*, 22 August 1868, pp. 146–48.

[9] Perhaps the Reverend Francis Hayward Joyce, Vicar of Harrow and brother of Herbert Joyce of the Post Office.

Can you tell me, you being a clerk very clerkly in such matters, where are usually deposited the actual title deeds, and *mapped* definitions of Glebe lands.[1]

Yours always faithfully
Anthony Trollope

To [? F. W.] Farrar[2]

MS Parrish Collection. B 385.

23–Sept. 1868   WALTHAM HOUSE, WALTHAM CROSS.

Mr Trollope presents his compliments to Mr Farrar. The MS was sent to Mr Farrar immediately on the receipt of Mr Lyttons letter,—which had been long in reaching Mr Trollope in consequence of his absence from home. If it have been received Mr Farrar will perhaps write a line to Mr Lytton to say so. If not, Mr Farrar will no doubt let Mr Trollope hear to that effect.

To J. E. Taylor[3]

MS Parrish Collection. SB 386.

OFFICE OF THE ST. PAULS MAGAZINE,
Sept 25 [23 or 24]. 1868[4]   294, CITY ROAD, LONDON.
Dear Sir.

I have been asked to forward to you the enclosed.

I am afraid of the subject of Darwin. I am myself so ignorant on it, that I should fear to be in the position of editing a paper on the subject—

Yours very truly
Anthony Trollope

[1] See *The Vicar of Bullhampton*, chap. lv.

[2] Very probably Robert Lytton's friend the Reverend Frederic William Farrar (1831–1903), Churchman and writer. Best known for *Eric; or, Little by Little* (1858), Farrar contributed to the *Fortnightly*, *Macmillan's*, and other periodicals. He was a master at Harrow from 1855 to 1870, and became Dean of Canterbury in 1895.

[3] John Ellor Taylor (1837–95), writer and lecturer on science; author of *Geological Essays* (1864) and *Half Hours at the Sea-Side* (1872).

[4] Envelope postmarked on 24 September.

To Amelia Edwards[5]

MS Parrish Collection. SB 387.

26 Sept 1868.   WALTHAM HOUSE, WALTHAM CROSS.
My dear Miss Edwards.

Our mutual friend Mrs. Elliot[6] has asked me to make your acquaintance,—which I should do with great pleasure to myself. I shall be in town on Thursday morning,—and should I call on you as early as 11 – am, should I find you at home & be able to see you? Perhaps you would address a line to me at the Athenaeum Club.

Most faithfully
Anthony Trollope

To Kate Field

MS Boston Public Library. *Commentary*, pp. 290–91; B 388.

30 Sept 1868   WALTHAM HOUSE, WALTHAM CROSS.
My dear Kate—

I have just got your letter. I thought you had one of the photographs. You had said something of taking one from the intoxicated little party. However I now enclose one as I understand from your letter that I am scolded for going away without leaving it.

And now about your Mss.—as to which I should doubtless have written with more alacrity had I had good news to send. I lost not a moment in applying to Dickens after my return home, but I found that he was opposed to the publication altogether;—and I also found, as I was sure would be the case, that without his cooperation the publication with any good results would be altogether impossible. You may take it for granted that he would not like it. I greatly grieve that you should have had so much fruitless labour in preparing the paper for publication here.[7]

On that Tuesday Mrs. Homans told me that she expected you. I had gathered that you were already too far from Boston to make it possible that you should be there. It was a melancholy day, as I felt quite sure that it would be my last day in America. But I was better pleased to spend it in Boston than elsewhere. Whether I shall ever see again you or her must depend on your coming here. I am becoming an infirm old man, too fat to travel so far.

[5] Amelia Ann Edwards (1831–92), née Blanford, novelist and Egyptologist. For Trollope's comments on *Debenham's Vow* (1870), one of her best-known works, see Trollope to Edwards, 9 December 1869.

[6] Frances Elliot.

[7] After Dickens's death, Kate Field published a revised edition of *Pen Photographs of Charles Dickens's Readings* (1871). She subsequently lectured widely on Dickens: the *Graphic* called her lecture of 12 April 1872 (at Willis's Rooms) a "decided success," commenting that "few can doubt the clearness of her insight, the acuteness of her criticism, and the beauty of the language in which she clothes her ideas" (13 April 1872, p. 339).

Let me have the story when it is ready. I will do the best I can with it—for indeed I would willingly see myself in some little way helping you in a profession which I regard as being the finest in the world.

God bless you—my kindest love to your mother—

> Most affectionately
> Yours
> A. T.

To G. H. Lewes

MS Yale. B 389; *George Eliot Letters*, VIII, 430.

Oct 3—1868   WALTHAM HOUSE, WALTHAM CROSS.

Dear Lewes.

Thanks. The paper[8] has not come to me, but has no doubt gone to the office. I will order a proof to be sent to you as soon as I get there. I have no doubt all good smokers will express their lasting gratitude in some substantial form;—a pyramid of cigar ashes—or a mausoleum for, long-delayed, future use, constructed of old pipe stems and tobacco stoppers. I will call up & discourse [upon] it, when I have read it.

In regard to the Spanish Gypsy[9] my regret is that the poet departed in portions of her work from the dramatic form. The departure would seem to imply,—which was certainly not the case,—that she had lacked power to say all her story in that which is certainly the most efficacious and I think the most perfect form of expression. I think too that the strictly dramatic portions of the poem are stronger than those in which she recedes to narrative,—as would be naturally the case.

Fedalma, Zarca & Juan are perfect. Sylva [*sic*], no doubt intentionally, is so much inferior as a creation to these, that the character, & words attributed to the character, are less striking.

> Yours always
> A. T.

To Austin Dobson

MS University of London Library. Excerpt, Alban Dobson, *Austin Dobson: Some Notes*, pp. 78–79; B 390.

8 Oct 1868   WALTHAM HOUSE, WALTHAM CROSS.

My dear Mr. Dobson.

Certainly we will have Boucher,[1]—which is admirable, & not a stanza too long. The feeling of it is excellent, & the execution generally very happy. There is no doubt about our having it.

---

[8] "The Dangers and Delights of Tobacco," *St. Paul's*, 3 (November 1868), 172–84.

[9] A dramatic poem by George Eliot, published in June 1868.

[1] "The Story of Rosina. An Incident in the Life of François Boucher," *St. Paul's*, 3 (January 1869), 460–66. Dobson accepted most of Trollope's suggestions, including the omission of the envoy.

Then of course come the less agreeable remarks, a criticism or two as to parts,—which however I will leave to your own judgement. 1st. I do not quite like the bit of Chaucer which the reader does not expect—& fails altogether to understand till the subsequent explanation comes.

2d. I dislike the word "weigh" in Stanza XVI—the simple change to "play" would be an improvement.

3d. Blessed as the blind &c—Stanza XXI— I may be stupid, but I see no idea in this. The blind, if they bless, bless without seeing. But the blind are not specially given to the conferring of blessings.

Stanza XXXII— "That only love *informs*"—is I think weak.

"Knew in her cheek a little colour burn" Stanza XXXIV—is certainly involved— & I think so much so as to be generally unintelligible.

But in regard to all these objections, I will give way to you if you object to them.

As to L'Envoy—I hope you will not object to omit it altogether. It adds nothing, as the story is told so plainly that the lesson wants no elucidation. And the reference to the Magazine is altogether objectionable. You will want to reprint this some day.

I return the Mss,—but will have it printed as soon as you have looked to these things.

I know I am sticking pins into you by my remarks;—but what is an Editor to do?

Yours always
A. T.

To ?

MS Parrish Collection. B 391.

Oct 17. 1868

I have been asked to express an opinion as to a novel by Lady Wood[2] called Sorrow by the Sea. I am informed that this novel has been suppressed by the Publishers and that payment of the stipulated price has been refused by them on the ground that the book is immoral and injurious in its tendency.[3] I have therefore read the novel in question.

I presume I am justified in supposing that the publishers found their denial of payment on a criticism on the book which appeared in the Athenaeum of May 2nd.[4] I have read that criticism, and I can under-

---

[2] Emma Caroline Wood (1802–79), née Michell, mother of Anna Steele (see Trollope to Steele, 30 October 1867). Lady Wood began her career as a professional novelist in 1866 to supplement her family's income after the death of her husband. She was a far more prolific writer than her daughter. Many of her novels were published by Chapman & Hall.

[3] *Sorrow on the Sea* was published by Tinsley.

[4] The review was thoroughly excoriating. It began by saying that " 'Sorrow on the Sea' is a very bad novel"; and it ended by saying that "the details of these volumes

stand that publishers should say that if that be just, they are bound to withhold the book from circulation; and that, so withholding it through fault of the author, they must decline to pay the stipulated price. Whether or no a jury would maintain them in such a course, if the criticism were justified by evidence, I am not lawyer enough to say;—but it is manifest that the burden of justifying the criticism must be on the publishers. It cannot be sufficient for them to say that this or that paper has condemned the book, and that therefore they will retreat from the bargain. If this were so no author could be safe.

I have no hesitation in saying that the criticism in question is manifestly unjust, unfair in its severity, and untrue both in its deductions and assertions. It begins with very heavy censure against the author, accusing her of having applauded the conduct of a certain lady of quality in that she caused her memoirs to be published in Peregrine Pickle.[5] What the author has done is to applaud the conduct of the lady in question, as narrated by Smollett, in that she resorted to strong exercise to deaden her sense of grief in periods of misfortune. It is hard to believe that the mistake on the part of the writer of the criticism has been accidental and not malicious. The whole article is very heavy in its censures, mentioning certain points in the authors tale & the manner of telling them; and then asserting that the bad parts of the book were too bad to be quoted by them.[6] As far as I have been able to form a judgement the reviewer has quoted the very worst in words or sentiments which were to be found in the book. It is then said in the last line of the criticism that there are passages in the book, which ought not to be produced in any language. In answer to this it must first be stated that that which is unfit for publication in one language, must be unfit for publication in any other. But the intention of the writer is to make English readers believe that the author of the novel, an English lady, has written in English that which would be held to be disgraceful even in the literature of countries which are less severe on such matters than are we in England. No evidence whatever is given in the article to support this statement.

I am of opinion that there is nothing in the book to justify the criticism, or the action taken on that criticism by the publisher. I do not think that the book is injurious to morals or likely to do evil. I conceive that there was no adequate cause for suppressing it, and I think that the

---

are literally unfit for presentation in any language." (*Athenaeum*, 2 May 1868, pp. 623–24.)

[5] "The Memoirs of a Lady of Quality," in *Peregrine Pickle*, chap. lxxxviii, a long narrative thought to be by Lady Vane, with revisions by Smollett.

[6] One of the objections to the novel was its treatment of baby-farming. Lady Wood's brother-in-law, Lord Hatherley, is said to have been so shocked by the novel that he bought up all available copies and had them burned (Joyce Marlow, *The Uncrowned Queen of Ireland: The Life of 'Kitty' O'Shea* [1975], p. 23).

452 October 1868

criticism in the Athenaeum to which I have alluded was manifestly unjust. I am willing, should there be occasion, to support the claim of the author of the book by public testimony to this effect.

Anthony Trollope

To Mrs. E. L. Youmans[7]
MS New York Historical Society. SB 392.

OFFICE OF THE ST. PAULS MAGAZINE,
October 20 1868   294, CITY ROAD, LONDON.
Dear Madam
I have just received your note of the 17th. I do not live in London, & cannot always say much beforehand when I shall be there. I think that I should certainly be found at the above address at 2.30 pm on Thursday next,—the day after tomorrow.

Yours faithfully
Anthony Trollope

To Mrs. W. F. Pollock
MS Parrish Collection.

October 29. 1868   GARRICK CLUB
My dear Mrs. Pollock
I grieve to say that for some days—or perhaps weeks to come I can do nothing so pleasant as have a chat with you. I go down tomorrow to canvas the free & independent electors of Beverley, which, (—only dont mention this as coming from me,)—I believe to be one of the most degraded boroughs in England.[8] As soon as ever I am free from my horribly disagreeable work I will come & see you.

The *Time* of Scorn in Othello,[9] I have never pretended to understand. It is one of those passages which I have never believed to be genuine.

Yours ever
truly
Anthony Trollope

[7] Catherine E. Youmans, née Newton, wife of the writer and editor Edward Livingston Youmans (1821–87), the leading American disciple of Herbert Spencer. Like her husband, Mrs. Youmans had literary talents.

[8] For Trollope's account of his attempt to be returned as MP for Beverley, see *Autobiography*, pp. 298–306. At about this time Dickens wrote to T. A. Trollope: "Anthony's ambition [to stand for Parliament] is inscrutable to me. Still, it is the ambition of many men; and the honester the man who entertains it, the better for the rest of us, I suppose." (*What I Remember*, p 362.)

[9] "But, alas! to make me / The fixed figure for the time of scorn / To point his slow and moving finger at." (IV.ii.52–53.)

To Lord Houghton

MS Trinity College, Cambridge.

October 31—1868.   WALTHAM HOUSE, WALTHAM CROSS.
My dear Lord Houghton.
   Very many thanks.
   I came up from Beverley today, & go down again on Tuesday, and then there comes that desperate work of canvassing,—than which no Life upon earth can be more absolute hell. If I can get to you on Saturday the 7th. I shall be delighted & will do so, & will give you timely notice during the week.

very faithfully yours
Anthony Trollope

I should be delighted to meet the Arch B———p of *York*.[1]

To Lord Houghton

MS Trinity College, Cambridge.

4 November 1868   Beverley
My dear Lord Houghton.
   I find that I shall be kept here so late on Saturday, & must be here again so early on Monday, that I am obliged to abandon the pleasure of seeing you & Lady Houghton at Fryston.[2]

very faithfully yours
Anthony Trollope

To Austin Dobson

MS University of London Library.

November 5. 1868.   Beverley.
Dear Sir
   I have written to the printers to send the proof of Rosina direct to you.

Yours faithfully
Anthony Trollope

I wish you much joy.

[1] Underlined twice. (The Archbishop of York was William Thomson; see Trollope to Smith, 4 November 1864.)
[2] Lord Houghton's country seat in Yorkshire.

To Amelia Edwards

MS National Library of Scotland. SB 393.

Nov. 18. 68　　　　　　　　　WALTHAM HOUSE, WALTHAM CROSS.
My dear Miss Edwards.

I send Mrs. E'[s] Mss. I will write a line to you before the end of the week saying when I will be in town in the course of next week.

Yours faithfully
Anthy Trollope

To Mrs. Anna Steele

B 429 (misdated).

21 Nov 69 [1868][3]　　　　　　WALTHAM HOUSE, WALTHAM CROSS.
My dear friend.

My back is not in the least broken,—except by my trot home to-day—I was out to-day & yesterday for the first time, and am like an old porter. But as for the election, I let that run like water off a ducks back. I have somewhat of a grievance as to South Essex,—as I offered to contest the division before the bill was passed, when the expense would not have been £2,000, and when A. J.[4] not only would not come forward but was most prominent in urging me to do so. But in politics I take all these things as Fate may send them. A walkover for the county was too good a thing for me to expect.[5] I shall have another fly at it somewhere some day, unless I feel myself to be growing too old.

What about your mothers book?[6] Why do you say not a word about it? When will it suit you to come to us?

Dont be a shrivelled leaf, before you have come to summers colour. At present you have but the green of spring struggling against the chills of infancy.

Yours always
A. T.

I want to make you *write* a novel in serial parts. I know all you have to say against it, & it is all nothing.

---

[3] Clearly written shortly after the Beverley election; Booth's "69" is probably a misreading.

[4] Andrew Johnston, first chairman of the Essex County Council; MP for South Essex, 1868–74.

[5] See *Autobiography*, p. 297.

[6] Probably a reference to *Sorrow on the Sea*: see Trollope to ?, 17 October 1868.

To Amelia Edwards

MS Parrish Collection.

Sunday. 22 Nov. 1868   WALTHAM HOUSE, WALTHAM CROSS.
My dear Miss Edwards.

I regret my mistake about Mrs. Elliots Mss. I now send the other.

Should I find you at home at 4. PM on Tuesday? If so I will call at that hour. I would then take back the other Mss.

Yours always faithfully
Anthony Trollope

To Austin Dobson

MS University of London Library.

Novr. 26 1868   WALTHAM HOUSE, WALTHAM CROSS.
My dear Mr Dobson.

There is time,—and the change[7] can be made if you please. But I like the first reading much the best. I left the proof for stereotype this morning for the Xmas number, but can change it if you will reply at once. And I will do so if you demand it— But I much prefer the original.

I have read the poem now 4 times, & like it very much. It has the true ring of mixed irony & pastoral, & is very pretty.

Yours ever
A. T.

To Henry Taylor

MS Parrish Collection.

27. November 1868   WALTHAM HOUSE, WALTHAM CROSS.
My dear Mr Taylor.

Thanks for your kind note of the 16th.

My hard work begins in November,—and then hunting also begins, which with me is a second class of hard work,—so that I seldom stray away from town till the spring or summer comes again. Indeed the autumn months are those in which alone I premeditate absences.

I will not, however, let the winter pass by without taking so far advantage of your kindness as to make a mid day descent upon you some Sunday at East Sheen.[8]

very faithfully yours
Anthony Trollope

[7] In "The Story of Rosina."
[8] Henry Taylor lived at Uplands, East Sheen, Surrey.

To Mrs. Cecilia Meetkerke

MS Fitzwilliam Museum. SB 394.

2 Decr. 1868.   WALTHAM HOUSE, WALTHAM CROSS.
My dear Mrs. Meetkerke.

Alas me, I am so driven about just now, that I hardly get time to have a days hunting anywhere. I have to be down at Bolton in Lancashire on Sunday;—and must be in London on the Friday. I have just been beaten standing for Beverley, and am now going to petition.[9]

Yours always faithfully
Anthony Trollope

To Austin Dobson

Sotheby Catalogue for 17 December 1974, lot 366.

3 December 1868

Trollope writes about the publication of verses by Dobson in *St. Paul's*.

To H. B. Wheatley[1]

MS Parrish Collection. SB 395.

December 4—1868   WALTHAM HOUSE, WALTHAM CROSS.
Dear Sir.

I enclose £2 – 2/ for the E. E. T. S.—that being my subscription for this year and for 1869.

faithfully yours
H B Wheatley Esq   Anthony Trollope

To James Virtue

MS Parrish Collection.

Private

December 14. 1868   WALTHAM HOUSE, WALTHAM CROSS.
My dear Mr Virtue.

We spoke the other day as to the mode of providing a novel for the Saint Pauls a little ahead; and it is as well that you should know how we stand.

Phineas Finn will be concluded in the number for May next—having

---

[9] See Trollope to Collier, 19 August 1869.

[1] Henry Benjamin Wheatley (1838–1917), writer, Pepys scholar; first Honorary Secretary of Early English Text Society. In *The Vicar of Bullhampton*, the sickly, scholarly Gregory Marrable was "engaged in revising and editing a very long and altogether unreadable old English chronicle in rhyme, for publication by one of those learned societies which are rife in London" (chap. xliv).

then run—through 20 numbers. Sacristans Household[2] will be concluded in June next—having then run through 12 numbers.

Mrs. Oliphant's novel[3] is to be commenced in the June number—& will run through 16—so as to be completed in October 1870.

I hope to have a story from Hamilton Aidé,[4] which will be cheap,—to run from July to December 1869—filling up for that six months the space now occupied by the Sacristans Household.

Of course the last 7 months of 1869 will thus be much cheaper to you than the previous 20 months.

It will then be necessary to begin 1870 with another novel to run along side of Mrs. Oliphant's.

As I should not as a matter [of] course go on at once with a novel myself in the Saint Pauls on concluding Phineas Finn in May—I have made arrangements to publish one in Once a Week, which will be concluded within the year.[5]

I could begin one in Saint Pauls 1. January 1870; if you wish it. If you would prefer that I should apply to George Elliot, I will do so. I think she would charge you double what I should. No doubt it would be worth much more than mine. It will be for you to judge what it would be worth your while to give to her. Do not for a moment suppose that there will be any feeling of rivalry between her & me. I should like to do exactly what you think best. If there is to be any chance of getting her work, you must of course give her timely notice.

If you like to take another of mine, I will write one to run through 18 numbers, 22 pages a number, for £140 each number or £2520 for the whole. This would be a shorter story than the two you now have,—but would be a three *full* volume novel.[6] It would [be] the exact length of the one I have now finished for "Once a Week"—the price of which is £2800. I have

*   *   *

[2] *The Sacristan's Household*, by Frances Eleanor Trollope.

[3] *The Three Brothers*, by Margaret Oliphant Wilson Oliphant (1828–97), the Scottish novelist.

[4] Charles Hamilton Aïdé (1829–1906), minor novelist. No serial fiction by Aïdé appeared in *St. Paul's* during the months Trollope named. Trollope had previously published Aïdé's two-part story "A Struggle for Mastery" in *St. Paul's*, 2 (August and September 1868), 563–80, 686–705, for which Aïdé was paid £25.

[5] *The Vicar of Bullhampton*, though in the end the novel did not appear in *Once a Week* (see Trollope to Dallas, 5 January 1868).

[6] By an agreement dated 13 April 1869, Virtue agreed to Trollope's terms (£2,520 for absolute copyright in a new novel of eighteen installments). But Virtue, who was already having doubts about *St. Paul's*, added a rider: "We should like the privilege however of being free to use the tale in any other Magazine, in case we shall, in the mean time, make any new arrangements for St Paul's Magazine." (MS Bodleian.) By January 1870, when the novel (*Ralph the Heir*) was to appear, Virtue had transferred *St. Paul's* to Strahan, in whose business he owned a controlling interest (see Virtue to Trollope, 25 January 1870). Strahan published *Ralph the Heir* as a supplement to the moribund *St. Paul's* and simultaneously in separate sixpenny monthly parts, both issues running from January 1870 through July 1871. See *Bibliography*, pp. 298–99.

To ?
MS Parrish Collection. SB 396.

OFFICE OF THE ST. PAULS MAGAZINE,
17 Decr. 1868   294, CITY ROAD, LONDON.
Sir.
If you have the translation of Heine's tale by you, would you send it to me. We have never yet published a translation.[7]

Yours faithfully
with thanks
Anthony Trollope

1869

To Austin Dobson
MS University of London Library.

Jan. 5. 1869   Waltham Cross.
My dear Mr Dobson.
I knew you could make a very pretty poem of the Cephalus & Procris;[8] —but I think the cadence has not been done with enough of care— If I were you, I would remodel it— The rhythm is excellent.

Yours always
faithfully & obliged
Anty Trollope

To Messrs. Justerini & Brooks[9]
MS National Library of Scotland.

January 5—1869   WALTHAM HOUSE, WALTHAM CROSS.
Gentlemen.
I enclose bill with a cheque for the amount—£9—18/.

Your obedient Servant
Messrs Justerini & Brooks   Anthony Trollope

[7] No translation of Heine has been traced in *St. Paul's*.
[8] "The Death of Procris," *St. Paul's*, 4 (June 1869), 319–20.
[9] Justerini & Brooks, wine merchants; 2 Colonnade, Pall Mall, and Adelaide Street, Strand.

To Arthur Helps[1]

E. A. Helps, ed., *Correspondence of Sir Arthur Helps* (1917), p. 269. B 398.

Jan. 7. 1869.   GARRICK CLUB
My dear Mr. Helps.

I am very much obliged to you for your book[2] and your kind letter, which I have this moment received. When I have read it, which I will do at once, I will write to you again and tell you what I think about it—in very truth. I was surprised when I heard that you had descended into our arena, feeling that you had fought your battles on a nobler battlefield. With me, it often comes to me as a matter, I will not say of self-reproach but of regret, that I can express what I wish to express only by the mouths of people who are created—not that they may express themselves, but that they may amuse. You have gained your laurels after a more manly fashion.

Most faithfully
Anthony Trollope

To G. H. Lewes

MS Parrish Collection.

19 Jany 1869.   WALTHAM HOUSE, WALTHAM CROSS.
My dear Lewes

Your note came last night, & Mrs. Hill's[3] paper this morning. There never was an establishment so badly managed as the Post office since some one went out of it and some one went into it.

I have read Mrs. Hill's paper, and think that I should help neither her cause by inserting it,—nor the magazine. It is not that I do not respect her and her cause, or that she does not plead for it well; but that she is Utopian, and at the same time not so clear in the theory of her Utopia, as to make it probable that any thing should come of good from a suggestion so made in a magazine.

---

[1] Arthur Helps (1813–75), later Sir Arthur; Clerk of the Privy Council, 1860–75. Helps wrote widely and in many literary forms; he also edited and revised works by Queen Victoria.

[2] Helps's novel *Realmah* (1868); see Trollope to Helps, 26 January 1869.

[3] No article on the housing of the poor by Mrs. Caroline Hill (1809–1903) has been traced, so the reference is almost certainly to her daughter Octavia Hill (1838–1912), the influential housing reformer. (Another daughter, Gertrude, was married to Lewes's son Charles.) Miss Hill's housing scheme called for regular inspection by lady rent collectors as a means of encouraging tenant self-improvement, cleanliness, sobriety, etc. The paper submitted to Trollope may have been Miss Hill's "Organized Work among the Poor; Suggestions Founded on Four Years' Management of a London Court," *Macmillan's*, 20 (July 1869), 219–26, later reprinted in *Homes of the London Poor* (1875).

For myself I do not think that the evil which we see in this direction in London is more than is naturally incidental to so huge a city as London in the present condition of civilization. Education is the only cure, —not Utopian inspection—such a good man or woman may make in his own family or own Court. You cannot inspect people into Godliness, cleanliness, and good grub. I do think you may educate them to it, and we are doing so,—only education wont go as quick as population. Then comes in Malthus & all the rest of it.

For my own private sins, which are so to my loss, I have less to say. To tell such a one as you that a man neglects the company of such as you for the sake of hunting three days a week, would be to condemn oneself so utterly! If you will have me I will lunch with you on Thursday. Dont answer, unless you have to say you wont be there.

Yours always
Anty Trollope

E. S. Dallas to Trollope

MS Bodleian.

21 Jany 1869
My dear Trollope

I do not think that I arrogated to myself the right of breaking my engagements for I distinctly told you that if you held me to the letter of the bond between us as regards time I should certainly keep it. There was no "question of weeks or *months*" which I claimed to be at my own disposal. But I certainly was under the impression that a few *weeks* difference in the date of publication could make no difference to you. I am anxious to defend myself on this point because I was acting in the most perfect innocence. You have a perfect right to make your own arrangements, & I have no right to quarrel with them. But I do not think you have a right to pull me up for laxity for not understanding what is a novelty as it seems to me in the publishing business that an author should take it as a grievance that a novel for which he will be paid all the same however & whenever it is published should be delayed a month or six weeks. Messrs Bradbury & Evans have agreed to give you a very large sum for your novel. You know best how many publishers there are in London who would accede to such terms. They made no bones about it on my recommendation, & I thought it rather hard that you should charge us with breach of faith because we felt that in point of time we had a few weeks to come & go upon. Our engagement with you was made about a year ago. It is simply impossible in such a publication as ours to calculate to a day fifteen months beforehand when a story will commence. We could calculate to within a few weeks, & this we have done.

I am very glad to learn that you withdraw your objection to a short delay. We propose to begin the publication of the *Vicar of Bullhampton* in the first week of July.[4]

Yours truly
E S Dallas

To Octavian Blewitt

MS Royal Literary Fund.

25 Jan. 69   WALTHAM HOUSE, WALTHAM CROSS.
Dear Mr Blewitt

Reverdy Johnson[5] would be a very good man,—and is able to talk on any subject or on none without stint. But I would not ask him through an American,—such as Russell Sturgis[6] or Mr Peabody.[7] Lord Stanhope probably knows him,—or Lord Houghton. I know him,—but you will have no difficulty in finding access to him.

I fear I cannot get up tomorrow, but I will if I can.

Yours faithfully
O Blewitt Esq   Anthony Trollope

To Arthur Helps

MS Parrish Collection. B 399.

January 26. 1869.   WALTHAM HOUSE, WALTHAM CROSS.
My dear Mr Helps.

At last I have read Realmah. You can perhaps understand how a man may be so pressed, as to lack time from week to week to give a day to such a book.

I often tell my brother, who knows more than any man I know and who is [a] man desiring to communicate his knowledge and convictions, that he is too didactic, too anxious to teach, to write a good novel. I will not say the same to you, as yours is not a novel.[8] It is a most suggestive

---

[4] This difficulty was small compared to the one that followed (see Dallas to Trollope, 22 March 1869).

[5] Reverdy Johnson (1796–1876), American lawyer and diplomat; Minister to England, 1868–69. At the Royal Literary Fund's Anniversary Dinner on 5 May 1869, Johnson answered the toast to diplomats. Trollope answered the toast to English literature.

[6] Russell Sturgis (1805–87), Boston lawyer and merchant who had settled in England in 1849; senior partner in the financial house of Baring Bros. from 1873 until his retirement in 1882; friend of Thackeray and many other writers, English and American.

[7] George Peabody (1795–1869), American merchant, financier, and philanthropist who had settled in England; best known for his £500,000 gift for the construction of working-class housing in London.

[8] *Realmah* includes discussions by politicians on various issues of the day similar to those found in *Friends in Council* (several series, 1847–59), Helps's most successful work.

work, full of speculation and thought, doing just what Friends in Council did, only in another form. I will confess that in the volumes themselves I prefer Milverton & Ellesmere to Realmah, and can get more from them. In Realmah I am always trying to fathom a mystery, a double entendre, as to which I am not quite sure whether it exist or no, and which, at last, I think I perceive not to exist with the completeness which I first imagined. I looked even for a recondite meaning in every name, but did not find it.

The records of a presumed early civilization have always been very alluring. There is no form in which one's own political and social tenets can be put forward with more clearness, and in which satyre can be better conveyed without any personal sting. Utopia was a great attempt in this way. I do not know whether you know Helionde,[9]—which was far fetched. In Realmah, you have been very politic, very reasonable, very true,—& very readable. You will have conveyed your ideas to men of your own class; but, judging from the book only and knowing nothing of what may have been its fate as to readers of the magazine, I should doubt your hitting the mere devourers of novels. But that is what one wishes to do,—to force thoughts upon thoughtless men under the guise of amusement.

very faithfully yours
Anthony Trollope

There is at page 263—a proverb, with its interpretation,[1] which quite comes home to me after reading your book.

To Mrs. Anna Steele

B 400. Bradhurst, p. 188.

27 Jan. 69
Wednesday   WALTHAM HOUSE, WALTHAM CROSS.
My dear Mrs. Steele.

Of course we will come. Will you get 3 stalls for myself, wife and one of the boys— I send a guinea, hoping I dont intrude. You can, perhaps, send me the tickets.[2]

---

[9] Sydney Whiting, *Helionde; or, Adventures in the Sun* (1855). Whiting was a barrister with an active literary avocation (B).

[1] "Never believe a man when he talks about anything which he thoroughly understands." When someone objects that this is "the most impudent proverb I have ever heard," the speaker replies: "When a man understands anything very well, he generally has a special repute for it, and he speaks with an eye to that repute of his. Sir Arthur being an eminent man of letters, his *public* opinion of other men of letters is not worth that" (snapping his fingers). (II, 263.) Earlier in the book, one of the characters says of Lily Dale, "She is more to me than many a character I read of in history." (I, 26–27.)

[2] For a performance by the Belhus Dramatic Corps (the Barrett Lennards, the Woods, and some of their friends and neighbors), who put on amateur theatricals on

I don't care twopence about the lifeboat. I wish you could take the money to buy hunters for yourself and two brothers. Only Charley[3] mustn't ride home first when the fox is found.

Could we see you for a moment to settle when you would come to us in February. Come on a Tuesday—say Feb 16—hunt on Wednesday—would be the nicest. I'll mount you, & take you out, and find you in everything except whip & spurs,—including sherry, sandwiches, & small talk.

Yours always
Anthony Trollope

To Mrs. Anna Steele

B 401. Bradhurst, p. 188.

Jan 31. 1869.   WALTHAM HOUSE, WALTHAM CROSS.
My dear Mrs. Steele.

We will get our little place [? plan] in order by degrees. Won't your brother bring you on the Tuesday? Let me know. If that will suit you, I'll write to him. If you will not ride my sons mare—to which you would be very welcome,—you must send your own, not here which would be quite out of the way, but to Tylers Green, where my horses stand, where your horse should have the warmest stall and grass from the hand of fellowship. But you must stay the Wednesday night,—& your brother.

However we shall all be wiser about it when we know the meet for the 15th.

Yours always faithfully
Anthony Trollope

Thanks for the tickets.

To Henry Fawcett[4]

SB 402.

4 February 1869

Trollope will read Mrs. Fawcett's[5] paper on Fox,[6] but asks her to "remember that the impatience of ordinary magazine readers will not endure long articles."

---

behalf of charity. In this instance, the group used St. George's Theatre, Langham Place, to perform Anna Steele's *Under False Colours* and George Dance's farce *Petticoat Government* to raise money for a lifeboat society. *The Times* (11 February 1869, p. 8) found Mrs. Steele's melodrama "by no means devoid of merit" and praised the acting of both Mrs. Steele and Sir Thomas Barrett Lennard.

[3] Charles Page Wood (1836–1915), of Scrips, Kelvedon, Mrs. Steele's younger brother.

[4] Henry Fawcett (1833–84), Liberal MP for Brighton; Professor of Political Economy at Cambridge, 1863–84.

[5] Millicent Garrett Fawcett (1847–1929), later a leader in the women's suffrage movement.

[6] William Johnson Fox (1786–1864), Unitarian minister and author; Radical MP for Oldham, 1847–63.

To Henry Fawcett

MS Parrish Collection. SB 403.

Feb 11. 1869
My dear Mr Fawcett.

I am afraid that the memory of Mr. Fox has so far died out that we should hardly succeed in resuscitating it by the article you so kindly sent me. I return it by this post.

very faithfully yours
Anthony Trollope

H. Fawcett Esq
     M.P.

To Messrs. Lovejoy[7]

SB 404.

27 February 1869

Trollope denies ever receiving any such deed as that referred to by the Dean of Bristol.

To Alexander Macmillan

MS Parrish Collection.

March 5. 1869.   WALTHAM HOUSE, WALTHAM CROSS.
My dear Sir.

My story[8] is a common love story—but one that ends sadly. It is complete. It would run through eight of your numbers. I cannot say whether it would contrast or consort with Mrs. Craik's story,[9] as I have not read Mrs. Craik's story.

faithfully yours
Anthony Trollope

I saw Mr Phillips pictures at the Cosmopolitan the other night & was very much astonished at the immense amount of work which was there brought together. Much of it was admirable, but I doubt whether it was of a class to fetch high prices. By far the greater proportion was portraiture,—fancy portraiture I should believe the greater part, and I hardly think that is a class of pictures to fetch a high price from an artist of the day. I am sorry to hear so bad [an] account from you of the poor widow.[1]

[7] George Lovejoy (?1818–83), proprietor of a well-known bookstore and lending library at 117 London Street, Reading. This letter is evidently identical with B 326, which was taken from a misdated catalogue entry.

[8] *Sir Harry Hotspur of Humblethwaite*. The novel was serialized in *Macmillan's*, the monthly started by Alexander Macmillan in 1859.

[9] *A Brave Lady*, serialized in *Macmillan's* from June 1869 through April 1870, by the prolific minor novelist Dinah Maria Craik (1826–87), née Mulock.

[1] Henry Wyndham Phillips had died suddenly on 8 December 1868, at the age of 48.

To Alexander Macmillan

MS (Trollope's copy) Bodleian. B 405.

March 8. 69.

*   *   *

Thanks for your note.[2] I think that you and Mr. Grove[3] will like the story. You can have the Mss. when you please. It will be for you to make what arrangements you please in America,—the foreign copyright being yours.[4] Of course it must not be published in America before it is published here for all our sakes.

A. T.

I observe on reading your note that you say the story is to run about 14 or 16 of your pages. I dont know the length of your pages. It would run about 16 Cornhill pages,—i e something over that rather than under; but the pages have been written to that measure.

To George Smith

B 406 (Sadleir's transcript).

15 March 1869   Waltham Cross

*   *   *

I think I mentioned to you that I was thinking of extracting the material of a comedy from the story of The Last Chronicle of Barset. On commencing the absolute work I encounter an idea that as you have half the copyright of the novel I should have your permission. I don't quite know the law in that respect. But will you have the kindness to let me know whether you have any objection to my work. The name I have at present in my mind for the play is

Did He Steal It?[5]

*   *   *

[2] In a letter of the same date Macmillan had agreed to pay Trollope £750 for an eight-part novel. *Sir Harry Hotspur of Humblethwaite* ran in *Macmillan's* from May 1870 through December 1870. For the book issue, see Trollope to Macmillan, 18 October 1870.

[3] George Grove (1820–1900), later Sir George, editor of *Macmillan's*; subsequently compiler of the well-known *Dictionary of Music and Musicians* (1878–89).

[4] According to J. Henry Harper, Harper & Brothers paid £700 for the novel (*The House of Harper* [New York, 1912], p. 114).

[5] *Did He Steal It?: A Comedy in Three Acts* was privately printed by Virtue & Co. Trollope stated that he wrote the play at the invitation of a theater manager (very probably John Hollingshead; see Trollope to Hollingshead, 23 May 1869), who in turn rejected it (*Autobiography*, pp. 276–77).

E. S. Dallas to Trollope

MS Bodleian. *Commentary*, pp. 305–6.

22 March [1869]   GARRICK CLUB

My dear Trollope

We are in great perplexity about your novel,[6] & I write to ask you if you will agree to a proposal which will relieve us from this serious difficulty.

Messrs Bradbury Evans & Co bought Victor Hugos new story[7] in November last on the faith of a promise from the French publisher that it would be issued in January. It has been delayed however from week to week through the incessant corrections of the author, so that it cannot be published in Paris before the first week in April and we cannot begin to publish the translation in Once a Week before then. The result of this is that supposing we begin to publish Victor Hugo in the first week in April & begin to publish your novel in the first week in July, you & he will be running on side by side in Once a Week for three or four months. Now this is death to us. *Once a Week* consists of 24 pages of which 2 are devoted to advertisements and 2 to illustrations. Four from twenty four leaves twenty. An instalment of your novel added to an instalment of Victor Hugo will take up 15 or 16 pages leaving us from 4 to 5 pages for Table Talk, padding & correspondence which we proposed to begin when we begin V. Hugo. It is impossible to carry on in this fashion without increasing the size of Once a Week which is impossible without serious loss to us.

Under these circumstances we make the following proposition to you & beg that you will give it your favourable consideration. Bradbury & Evans propose to publish *The Vicar of Bullhampton* in the Gentleman's Magazine beginning the publication of it on the 1st. of May and running it on to the period at which it would have come to an end in *Once a Week*. If you will consent to this arrangement you will get us out of a very great difficulty. Do, like a good fellow, say that you agree. The *Gentlemans Magazine* is raised in character—is extremely well done—& will do you no discredit.

I fear this letter will not find you at home, & the publishers hope that you will permit them to announce the proposed arrangement in the forthcoming (April) number of the *Gentleman's Magazine* with which they go to press on Wednesday. If you could let me know your decision by letter or by telegraph on Wednesday morning you would do me and the publishers a great favour. I hope it will be yes. I am sorry to trouble you—but you will see the difficulty.[8]

Yours always truly
E S Dallas

6 *The Vicar of Bullhampton.*
7 *L'Homme Qui Rit.*
8 Trollope wrote of this "dolorous letter": "My disgust at this proposition was, I think, chiefly due to my dislike to Victor Hugo's latter novels, which I regard as pre-

To ?

MS Parrish Collection.

25 March 1869   294. City Road.
Dear Sir.

I regret to say that I cannot accept your very kind invitation as I had already accepted hospitality at Liverpool before I received your note.

very faithfully
Anthony Trollope

To Mr. Anderson

MS Parrish Collection. SB 407.

29 March 1869   WALTHAM HOUSE, WALTHAM CROSS.
My dear Anderson.

I know nothing of Kelly's projected return,—for I presume it to be projected by this time;—nor does his coadjutor Jem O Dowd,[9] who would know if anybody did— But he will soon turn up now.

Yours always
Anthony Trollope

James Virtue to Trollope

MS Bodleian.

Mch 30th. 1869   VIRTUE & CO. LONDON E.C.
My dear Mr. Trollope,

This time of the year is always bad for Artists work, in the way of book Illustrations—they only think of their Academy pictures and everything else is dismissed with scant attention— I shall see Stone[1] in a few days— but he has now so nearly finished the whole book that it will not perhaps be worth while to object strongly.

I am sorry to hear you progress so slowly.—this cold wind is enough

---

tentious and untrue to nature. To this perhaps was added some feeling of indignation that I should be asked to give way to a Frenchman. The Frenchman had broken his engagement. . . . And because of these laches on his part,—on the part of this sententious French Radical,—I was to be thrown over! . . . I would not come out in *The Gentleman's Magazine*, and as the Grinning Man could not be got out of the way, my novel was published in separate numbers." (*Autobiography*, p. 328.) *The Vicar of Bullhampton* appeared in eleven monthly parts (the first ten at one shilling, and the last, a double number, at half-a-crown) from July 1869 through May 1870. Trollope later published Mrs. Juliet Pollock's "M. Victor Hugo's England," *St. Paul's*, 4 (July 1869), 466–81, a lengthy and very critical commentary on *L'Homme Qui Rit*.

[9] Perhaps James Cornelius O'Dowd, barrister; formerly assistant editor of the *Globe*; member of the Garrick Club.

[1] Marcus Stone (1840–1921), historical and genre painter; illustrator of Dickens's *Our Mutual Friend*. Stone illustrated *He Knew He Was Right*. See *Illustrators*, pp. 124–39.

to take to bed for choice, but bed is not a good place to be tied down to.

We have decided to commence your new story[2] in St Pauls, on January 1, so please note this for your arrangements.—When next you come I will give you a formal acceptance of it stating price &c— I have been in Ireland for this last fortnight—and have had beautiful weather—very different from this.

very truly yours

Anthony Trollope Esq.   James Virtue

To the Editor of the *Daily Telegraph*

Daily Telegraph, 1 April 1869, p. 3. B 408.

March 31. 1868 [1869]

Sir—

Will you allow me to ask insertion in your columns for a few remarks which will be made with the fullest sincerity and in perfect good humour.

In a leading article of your impression of today[3] you charge me with having drawn portraits of the leading politicians of the time in a novel of mine lately published,—and you refer especially to a presumed portrait of Mr. Bright.

You say "Is it gentlemanlike to paint portraits thus?" "Is it right for any novelist to put into a novel of the day malignant little touches professing to lift the veil of private life and to depict a public man as he appears in private society or at his own fireside?"

Certainly it is neither gentlemanlike or right to do these things, and I protest that I have [not] done them. In the character of Mr. Turnbull to which allusion is made, I depicted Mr. Bright neither in his private or public character; and I cannot imagine how any likeness justifying such a charge against me can be found. The character that I have drawn has no resemblance to the chairman of the Board of Trade in person, in manners, in character, in mode of life, or even in the mode of expressing political opinion. It was my object to depict a turbulent demagogue;— but it was also my object so to draw the character that no likeness should be found in our own political circles for the character so drawn. I have been unlucky,—as the charge brought by you against me shows; but I protest that the ill-luck has not been the result of fault on my part. I intended neither portrait or caricature, and most assuredly I have produced neither.[4]

Your obedient servant

Anthony Trollope

[2] *Ralph the Heir.*

[3] *Daily Telegraph*, 31 March 1869, p. 4. The novel was *Phineas Finn*; other suggested identifications were Terrier/Derby, Daubeny/Disraeli, Mildmay/Russell, and Gresham/Gladstone.

[4] Trollope is being less than candid. For a discussion of his drawing on contemporary politicians in his fiction, see John Halperin, *Trollope and Politics* (1977), pp.

TREVELYAN AT CASALUNGA.

Illustration for *He Knew He Was Right*, by Marcus Stone

Mrs. Oliphant to Trollope

MS Gordon N. Ray.

[? March 1869]
Saturday   WINDSOR
Dear Mr. Trollope

I have been so much later than I intended to be, that I shall place my entire M.S. in your hands in a day or two[5]—the first time I am in town— It has cost me a sacrifice of my own purposes, but I daresay it is best in the end— The story is a little peculiar in construction— But however it will explain itself.

I am very sorry we are so soon to take leave of the engaging Phineas,[6] and cannot form the slightest idea what you are going to do with him— You would be amused if you could hear the hot discussions that go on in this quiet corner of the globe concerning the behaviour of Mr. Louis Trevelyan.[7]

I suppose I had best send my M.S. to Messrs. Virtue's place?—
                                        Truly yours
                                        M. O. W. Oliphant

To Amelia Edwards

MS Parrish Collection. SB 409.

2 April. 1869   WALTHAM HOUSE, WALTHAM CROSS.
My dear Miss Edwards.

I was very much gratified indeed by your kind letter. I should have written sooner but that as I was to be in town yesterday & the day before, I thought I should have been able to get to you, to call; but I was kept among the haunts of printers, publishers & the like, & could not do so— I hope I may have the pleasure of seeing you before long.
                                        Most faithfully
                                        Anthony Trollope

72–87; J. R. Dinwiddy, "Who's Who in Trollope's Political Novels," *NCF*, 22 (June 1967), 31–46; A. O. J. Cockshut, *Anthony Trollope* (1955), pp. 241–49; and R. W. Chapman, "Personal Names in Trollope's Political Novels," in *Essays Mainly on the Nineteenth Century* (1948), pp. 72–81. See also Trollope to Holmes, 15 June 1876.

[5] Mrs. Oliphant's novel *The Three Brothers*, which began serialization in *St. Paul's* in June 1869.

[6] The final installment of *Phineas Finn* appeared in May.

[7] The main character in *He Knew He Was Right*, which completed its serialization on 22 May.

To ?

MS (photocopy) UCLA. B 410 (misdated).

April 8. 69.   WALTHAM HOUSE, WALTHAM CROSS.
Madam
I am most happy to send you my autograph,—small as must be its value. I fear from the tone of your letter,—that you ask me for more than this,—for something written, an ode, sonnet, or some original matter. Unless I were to write you a novel in 3 volumes, (which is my only mode of performance) I should not know how to furnish you with this.

Your faithful Servant
Anthy Trollope

To Austin Dobson

MS University of London Library. Excerpt, *Commentary*, p. 297; excerpt, B 411.

18. Apr 1869   WALTHAM HOUSE, WALTHAM CROSS.
My dear Mr Dobson.
I have been very ill,—and have got into the back ground. Nevertheless I ought to have answered your last note sooner. I will use both your poems,—on the condition that you will ease a prejudice on my part by expunging the joke about Gibbons D & F.[8] It does not seem to me to [be] in harmony with the poem. I think the 6th. Stanza of the same poem is not quite clear. The whole is very pretty.
I do not like the birds[9] quite so well. The weakest verse is the Blackbird. I do not know whether you can improve it. I return the two. But my only insistance [*sic*] is in reference to the Decline & Fall.

Pray forgive me.
Yours always
A. T.

[8] "The Death of Procris" (see Trollope to Dobson, 5 January 1869) and "Ad Rosam," *St. Paul's*, 4 (July 1869), 428–30. The reference to Gibbon was expunged from "Ad Rosam" but restored when the poem was reprinted in *Vignettes in Rhyme*: "You snared me, Rose, with ribbons, / Your rose-mouth made me thrall, / Brief—briefer far than Gibbon's, / Was my 'Decline and Fall.' "
[9] "Love in Winter." The poem was published in *Good Words* in February 1871, and reprinted in *Vignettes in Rhyme*.

To J. E. Millais
MS Parrish Collection. SB 412.

20 Ap. 69   WALTHAM HOUSE, WALTHAM CROSS.
My dear Millais.
 I shall have very great pleasure in dining with the artists on May 8th.[10]
I suppose I am right in writing to you.

Yours ever
Any Trollope

To Alexander Macmillan
MS Colby College.

20 Ap. 1869   WALTHAM HOUSE, WALTHAM CROSS.
My dear Mr Macmillan.
 Did you get a note from me about an MS of Miss Anna Drury's? May
I send it you?

Yours sincerely
Anthony Trollope

To Alexander Macmillan
MS Columbia.

OFFICE OF THE ST. PAULS MAGAZINE,

22 Ap. 1869   294, CITY ROAD, LONDON.
My dear Mr Macmillan.
 I send you Miss Anna Drury's tale.[1]

Yours always
Any Trollope

To Mary Holmes[2]
MS Parrish Collection. B 413.

April 24–1869   WALTHAM HOUSE, WALTHAM CROSS.
My dear Miss Holmes.
 I am almost ashamed to answer your letter and I do not know that I
can do any good by doing so. When I got a letter from you ever so long

---

[10] The 54th Annual Festival of the Artists' General Benevolent Institution, held at
Willis's Rooms with Lord John Manners in the chair.

[1] Macmillan answered on 3 May 1869, declining the novel and saying that his
reader "was emphatic that though well written & having estimable qualities, its
chances of sale were not considerable" (MS British Library).

[2] Mary Holmes (?1815–78), who spent her life as a governess, worked hard at music
and literature but with little success. She was much given to writing to authors.

ago,—more than two years I think, I went to work to find whether I could do anything towards getting up the outside scene-work of a concert for you;—asking noblemen to lend their rooms and the like,—of all which I felt ashamed while I was making the attempt, and failed altogether at last. But in the failure months went by, and then I had not even an address at which to write to you to tell you that I had failed. You thought, no doubt, that I was cruel, and I thought that I had endeavoured to take a work in hand with which I ought never to have meddled.

And now I write simply to say that I am utterly powerless in the matter of music. I know well that it is not so much my absolute aid you require, as a touch of sympathy from somebody of whose sympathy you would be glad. But still, I, knowing that sympathy will make fat neither man nor woman would be so glad to help you if I knew how. But we all have our own circles, our own ways and fashions, and the paths to which our feet are familiar. My feet know nothing of musical paths. I can only wish you success, & promise you that I will come & call on you if you are settled in London.

> faithfully yours
> Anthony Trollope

To Mrs. J. E. Millais

MS Parrish Collection. SB 414.

1 May 1869.   WALTHAM HOUSE, WALTHAM CROSS.
My dear Mrs. Millais.

I have read Mr Anderson's paper about the gold diggings in Scotland. It is very well written; & interesting to those who will interest themselves about the subject,—but I fear that the subject would not be of sufficiently general value, to be of use to a magazine.

People however vary so greatly in their ideas, that it is very probable that either Mr Froude[3] for Frazers Magazine or Geo Smith for the Cornhill, would be glad to have it.[4]

> Most faithfully yours
> Anthony Trollope

Always a solitary, she found consolation in Catholicism, to which she was a staunch convert; she found especially rewarding her long correspondence with Newman. In 1852 she began exchanging letters with Thackeray, who befriended her and for a time confided in her. She came to London briefly as music mistress to his daughters. "But the charm that he found in her letters proved to be absent from her person. She had red hair and a red nose and sought anxiously to make a Catholic of him." (G. N. Ray, *Letters of W. M. Thackeray*, I, cxl.) Trollope's letters to Mary Holmes display more literary discussion of his own works than his letters to any other correspondent. Upon her death he wrote movingly of her (Trollope to Brackenbury, 3 October 1878).

[3] James Anthony Froude (1818–94), historian and man of letters; editor of *Fraser's Magazine*, 1860–74; Carlyle's literary executor and biographer.

[4] The article was not published in either magazine.

To Mary Holmes
MS Parrish Collection. SB 415.

3 May 69   WALTHAM HOUSE, WALTHAM CROSS.
My dear Miss Holmes
    Miss Thackeray[5] is in Italy.

                                                faithfully yours
                                                Anthony Trollope

To Frederic Chapman
MS Parrish Collection. SB 416.

May 8 1869   WALTHAM HOUSE, WALTHAM CROSS.
My dear Chapman.
    Thanks for sending me this part of a novel in type,—which I return.
    It is by far too diluted to be published in numbers. It could not be
divided into parts which would of themselves have any interest.
                                                Yours always
                                                Anthony Trollope

To Mrs. Annie Fields
MS Boston Public Library. SB 417.

May 18. 1869   Skipton.[6]
My dear Mrs. Fields.
    I write one line to say your letter has followed me into Yorkshire, and
about Yorkshire. I say this to explain my silence. We shall be back by
the middle of next week when I will not lose a day in trying to find you.
                                                Most faithfully yours
                                                Anthony Trollope

To John Hollingshead
Maggs Catalogue 386 (Christmas 1919). SB 418.

23 May 1869   Waltham Cross
    Trollope had undoubtedly received an unfavorable response from Hollings-
head on *Did He Steal It?* "I dont doubt about [? but] what you are right about
the play."

---

    [5] Anne Isabella Thackeray (1837–1919), later Lady Ritchie; Thackeray's eldest
daughter. A novelist in her own right, she drew moderate praise from Trollope (*Autobiography*, pp. 257–58).
    [6] A market town in Yorkshire.

To Alexander Macmillan

MS Parrish Collection.

25 June 1869   WALTHAM HOUSE, WALTHAM CROSS.
My dear Mr. Macmillan
    I want to see you for a few minutes. Shall I find you at or about 11.30 am on Monday next.

Yours always
Anthony Trollope

To Miss Harrison[7]

MS Parrish Collection.

26 June 1869   WALTHAM HOUSE, WALTHAM CROSS.
My dear Miss Harrison.
    I send you your story[8] printed in two parts for correction. The first is in 18 pages, which I will get you to reduce to 16, by lessening the dialogue on the pages I have marked with pencil. The dialogues are somewhat too long to be borne by so short a story. No. 2 should be reduced to 15 pages. It is now 15 and a half. I do not think you will find any difficulty in this. I wish you to correct the pages and to send them back to me here as soon as you can. We shall use them very soon;—and shall pay you for them.

Yours faithfully
Anthony Trollope

To Austin Dobson

MS University of London Library.

July 1. 1869   GARRICK CLUB
My dear Mr Dobson
    I have just found at Strahan's house that the cheque for the June number had not been sent to you. The reason given was that they did not know your address, I having simply written your name on the list. There has been a change of office though none really of management or ownership.[9]
    If you do not get a cheque in a day or [two] let me know.

Yours always
Anthony Trollope

---

   [7] Probably Agnes T. Harrison (?1839–1925), who contributed articles to *Macmillan's* and published a novel, *Martin's Vineyard* (1872). She later married Sir John Macdonell.
   [8] "Olivia's Favour: A Tale of Hallowe'en," *St. Paul's*, 4 (August and September 1869), 625–40, 749–62.
   [9] In May 1869 Virtue transferred *St. Paul's* to Strahan, whose business he in effect owned. See Virtue to Trollope, 25 January 1870.

To Amelia Edwards
MS Somerville College, Oxford.

July 20. [1869]
Tuesday   WALTHAM HOUSE, WALTHAM CROSS.
My dear Miss Edwards.

Would you do me & my wife the pleasure of coming to us next Saturday and staying till Monday morning. I am aware, as is my wife painfully, that duty would strictly require her to call on you first; but as she
lives down here, and as she is averse to going up to London, especially in
this hot weather, she thinks that perhaps, you will consent to waive the
strict law.

Yours very faithfully
Anthony Trollope

Millais will be with us. I dont know that any body else will be here.

To [? Charles] Burney
MS Taylor Collection.

July 22. 1869   GARRICK CLUB
My dear Burney.

I have been looking about among my papers for a letter of Dickens
and can find none. I will bear it mind and send you any one that comes
to hand. It is not often that I chance to hear from him, but such things
do occur now & then.

We thought Porter[10] looking very well in spite of his lameness, which
certainly increases with him. But his courage, in regard to that as to all
other things is wonderful. He was very Irish, and very fierce about the
Bill.[1] But so no doubt are you also. The truth is that if you parsons do
not quickly suit yourselves in some fashion to a voluntary system, by
which payment shall in some degree be apportioned to work done, there
will not be a crust left among you;—not because your endowments will
be taken, but because your endowments will not suffice to give you the
crust. It is coming to that already, & you had better look to it.

yours always
Anthony Trollope

[10] Perhaps one of the clergymen sons or grandsons of John Porter, Bishop of Clogher,
Ireland, 1798–1819.
[1] For the disestablishment of the Irish Church, the chief concern of Parliament in
1869. The Act received Royal Assent on 26 July.

To W. D. Gardiner[2]

MS Parrish Collection.

July 26 [27]. 1869
Tuesday   WALTHAM HOUSE, WALTHAM CROSS.
Sir.
    I shall be at Messrs. Virtue's printing house—294 City Road, at 11.
am on Thursday, and shall be happy to see you there, if it will suit you
to call.

Yours faithfully
Anthony Trollope

Or I shall be at the Athenaeum club the same morning at 10. am.

W D Gardiner Esq

To Frederic Chapman

MS Parrish Collection.

OFFICE OF THE ST. PAULS MAGAZINE,
August 9 1869   294, CITY ROAD, LONDON.
My dear Mr Chapman.
    I could at once sell to Mr Appleton[3] a tale[4] in one volume, divided into
8 numbers, for magazine publication in America for £700.

Yours truly
F Chapman Esq   Anthony Trollope

To Frederic Chapman

MS (Trollope's copy) Bodleian. B 419.

10 August 1869.   BEAUPORT,[5] BATTLE.
Dear Chapman.
    If you do anything about my tale with that American publisher do
not you let him have the right of publishing it in his Magazine for less
than £500—as I do not think you can make more than £200 out of a one
volume novel. If he should take it on these terms, which I doubt, you
shall republish it for £200 to me, on the understanding that I am to

---

[2] William Dundas Gardiner (1830–1900), barrister; Examiner to the Inns of Court,
1869.
    [3] William Henry Appleton (1814–99), head of the American publishing house that
he and his father had founded.
    [4] *The Golden Lion of Granpere.*
    [5] A village near the small town of Battle, close to Hastings, Sussex. Beauport was
the home of Trollope's friend Sir Charles Taylor.

have the first £200 out of the profits;—so that you shall not lose by it, nor be called on for your money before you have received it.[6]

Yours ever

A. T.

I will not ask you to pay £200 to me till you have made it out of the profits; so that you shall be at no loss.

The copyright will be mine.

To W. H. Bradbury[7]

MS *Punch* Office.

August 12—1869   WALTHAM HOUSE, WALTHAM CROSS.
Dear Sir.

I beg to acknowledge yours of 10th. with cheque for £250, and to thank you for the remittance.

faithfully yours

W H Bradbury Esq   Anthony Trollope

To G. H. Lewes

MS Yale. B 420; *George Eliot Letters*, VIII, 464.

August 13—1869   WALTHAM HOUSE, WALTHAM CROSS.
My dear Lewes.

Your news about your boy is very bad.[8] I can only tell you how strongly I feel for you.

I do admire Horne[9] as a poet,—that is I think highly of his Orion;—but I do not know of what nature is his prose, or how the man who wrote Orion in 1839 (or thereabouts) would write now in 1869. Nor am I specially wedded to serial articles (to use an abominable word). Readers of magazines skip them when on dry subjects. Seebohm's[1] did answer

---

[6] The scheme with Appleton came to nothing. Trollope subsequently tried to sell *The Golden Lion* to Blackwood; see Trollope to Blackwood, 20 February 1871.

[7] William Hardwick Bradbury (1830–92), second son of William Bradbury and a partner in the publishing house of Bradbury & Evans. The remittance acknowledged in the letter was for *The Vicar of Bullhampton*.

[8] Thornton Arnott Lewes (1844–69) was suffering from tuberculosis of the spine; he died on 19 October.

[9] Richard Henry (Hengist) Horne (1803–84), miscellaneous writer; author of the popular epic poem *Orion* (1843); Commissioner for Crown Lands in Australia, 1852–69. Horne published two articles in *St. Paul's* in 1873, long after Trollope had left the magazine.

[1] Frederic Seebohm (1833–1912), historian of Anglo-Saxon and medieval England. Seebohm was a frequent contributor to the *Fortnightly*; Trollope is probably referring to his seven-part "The Oxford Reformers of 1498," which appeared from May through October 1866.

with you,—but then they were very good. Bell's[2] did not. But they were very bad. If he has ought written & will send it to me, I will read it;—but I will not pledge myself.

And now I have a piece of news for you of the domestic kind which will surprise you. My eldest boy Harry has gone into partnership with Chapman. I pay £10000—(of course this is private)—and he has a third of the business.[3] I have had an immense deal of trouble in arranging it, and will tell you details when we meet. It is a fine business which has been awfully ill used by want of sufficient work and sufficient capital.

Do not let me intrude on you;—but if you are disengaged and Thornie is not too ill, I will come up to you next week some evening. My wife is away,—in Paris,—or rather goes tonight. I go with her, but return. Address Athenaeum Club.

Yours always affectionately
A. T.

To W. H. Bradbury

MS *Punch* Office.

16. August 1869.   WALTHAM HOUSE, WALTHAM CROSS.
Dear Sir.

Looking back at the revises of Bullhampton it seems to me that the printers have fallen into some error as to the numbering of Chapters XXXIV–XXXV–XXXVI–which should have been XXXV–XXXVI–and XXXVII. The numbers were right in the Mss. Will you call attention to this.

I return for press chapters 46 to 52—being I think the 8th. of your numbers, and I send the original corrections with the press, as I wish to call the printer's attention to the fact that certain corrections of mine as to the initial of the word *vicarage* have been wilfully omitted. It is for me to say whether the word should be *V*icarage or *v*icarage; and I should be obliged if the printer would allow me to have my way.

I do not like to make this little complaint without acknowledging on the part of your printers, as I often have done on the part of others, how much I am indebted to them not only for carefulness but for a great amount of erudition,—without which I & other writers would be often in trouble. Let them, however, print *v*icarage for me.

Yours always
Anthony Trollope

[2] Robert Bell's three-part "Social Amusements under the Restoration," which the *Fortnightly* published in September and October 1865.

[3] Henry Trollope remained in partnership with Chapman for only three and a half years. Trollope commented: "[Henry] did not like it, nor do I think he made a very good publisher. At any rate he left the business with perhaps more pecuniary success than might have been expected from the short period of his labours, and has since taken himself to literature as a profession. Whether he will work at it so hard as his father, and write as many books, may be doubted." (*Autobiography*, p. 325.)

To John Blackwood

MS National Library of Scotland. B 421.

OFFICE OF THE ST. PAULS MAGAZINE,

August 19 1869   294, CITY ROAD, LONDON.

My dear Blackwood.

After your kindness on the subject I cannot but tell you that the partnership between Chapman & my son is completed;—i e they are now partners & I have paid the money. The exact extent of Chapman's capital is to be fixed on 31—Decr. 1869 by Bell & Langford with power of naming a referee. The deed of partnership exacts this. Langford has been most kind & useful.

Yours always
Anthy Trollope

To J. F. Collier

MS John Rylands Library.

August 19—69   WALTHAM HOUSE, WALTHAM CROSS.

Dear Sir.

Could you let me know as yet on what day my evidence will be taken at Beverley, as I am very anxious to make arrangements for joining my wife who is abroad,—as also with reference to my journey to Beverley, I cannot imagine that I have anything to tell the commissioners, which will be worth their hearing.[4]

Yours faithfully

J F Collier Esq   Anthony Trollope

To Mrs. Houstoun[5]

MS Parrish Collection.

August 24. 1869   GARRICK CLUB

My dear Mrs. Houstoun.

I have no doubt your Mss is all right—and I have now written to Strahans for it, but there would be no chance at all of an Mss so addressed reaching me. My name was not even in the address, and Strahan would naturally suppose that it was intended for the Good Words which is edited at his house.

[4] Trollope gave his evidence on 3 September 1869, at the Town Hall, Beverley. See *Parl. Papers 1870*, XXIX [c. 16], 210–11: Beverley Bribery Commission, Minutes of Evidence (Trollope). J. F. Collier has not been identified. In the end, Beverley was disfranchised; for Trollope's comments, see *Autobiography*, pp. 305–6.

[5] Matilda Charlotte Houstoun (?1815–92), née Jesse, prolific minor novelist. None of her work appeared in *St. Paul's*.

The Editors address for Saint Pauls is 193 Piccadilly as you will find stated in the magazine.

Yours faithfully
Anthony Trollope

To Mrs. Houstoun

MS Parrish Collection.

August 25. 69   WALTHAM HOUSE, WALTHAM CROSS.

My dear Mrs. Houstoun

This will explain itself. Send me the name of the story, which I have not got, and I do not doubt we shall find the Mss.

Yours faithfully
Anthony Trollope

To ?

MS Parrish Collection.

September 4. 1869   Waltham Cross

My dear Sir.

Your note of the 2 September has just reached me as I am on the point of starting for the continent. I shall be back on the 1 October. Perhaps you will by that time name what days in the last week of January will suit you, giving me the choice of one or two.[6]

Yours faithfully
Anthony Trollope

To Austin Dobson

MS University of London Library.

[2 October 1869][7]   WALTHAM HOUSE, WALTHAM CROSS.

My dear Mr Dobson

Thanks for the eclogue[8] which is very nice & has the pleasant ring. I wonder whether you could alter a word or two. "I to him excelling" hardly brings to this reader your meaning as rapidly as it should be given in such a piece—& "like the string emitting"—is to me also slightly defective.

Above the merry mouth—eyes are of course above the mouth. Is there any real meaning or description in the word;

---

[6] For Trollope's lecture tour of late January 1870.

[7] Dated from Trollope to Dobson, 4 October 1869.

[8] "An Autumn Idyll," *St. Paul's,* 5 (December 1869), 302–5. Dobson altered the poem as Trollope suggested.

⟨"the" I think should be omitted in the next line. Should not court coquetting be courtly. Both in rhythm and sense, I think so.⟩

"Misconstrue" is harsh for such playful lines. In either praise or blame is a thought tame.

In order that you may think whether you wd. wish to alter either of these I return the poem.

Yours truly
A. T.

To Alfred Austin[9]

MS University of Illinois. Excerpt, Alfred Austin, *Autobiography of Alfred Austin* (1911), II, 6; excerpt, B 422.

3 Oct 69 　　　　　　　　　WALTHAM HOUSE, WALTHAM CROSS.
My dear Austin.

I wish you and your wife could have come. I hope you will regard it as an engagement that you should do so as soon as you get back to England.

It seems that the "Vindication"[1] is having a considerable sale. I have not seen other remarks on it specially in the Press than those made in the Saturday, which contained a piece of blundering criticism, unlike the Saturday which, always nasty, is seldom stupid.[2]

I find both from the American Press, and from letters from correspondents, that Mrs. Stowe is much more hardly handled there than she is here. I still feel that no more outrageous piece of calumny,—in the real sense of the word, was ever published; or as, I think, with lower motives.

My kind regards to your wife. Hoping that you may thoroughly enjoy your winter I am yours always.

Anthony Trollope

[9] Alfred Austin (1835–1913), prolific minor poet and leader writer; named Poet Laureate in 1896. Austin and Trollope were good friends. Austin's *The Garden That I Love* (1894) is said to describe Trollope's last home, at Harting (B).

[1] *A Vindication of Lord Byron*, by Austin. This pamphlet was a reply to Harriet Beecher Stowe's "The True Story of Lady Byron's Life," published in the September numbers of the *Atlantic Monthly* and *Macmillan's*, which had accused Byron of incest with his half sister Augusta.

[2] The *Saturday Review* had discussed the Byron case three times (4 September 1869, pp. 311–14; 11 September 1869, pp. 343–44; and 25 September 1869, pp. 404–6); it accused Mrs. Stowe of a "scandalous breach of faith as regards Lady Byron, and of extremely bad taste" (p. 343), but concluded that the charge against Byron was likely to be true.

To Austin Dobson

MS University of London Library.

4 Oct 1869   WALTHAM HOUSE, WALTHAM CROSS.
My dear Mr Dobson.

Thinking since I wrote on Saturday of Jack & his brothers I have fancied that there was something perhaps a little abrupt in the way the songs of the competitors are commenced. Do you remember the
> Dicat Opuntiae Frater Megillae
> Quo beatus vulnere
> Quā pereat sagittā.[3]

Might not Jack add some paraphrased translation of that sort when offering the pipe.

Excuse my troubling you.

Yours always
A. T.

To John Blackwood

MS National Library of Scotland. Excerpt, Porter, p. 362; Parker, pp. 58–59; B 423.

Oct 13–69   WALTHAM HOUSE, WALTHAM CROSS.
My dear Blackwood.

Yes. I am going to lecture at Edinburgh but not till Friday the 28 January;—a long day, my Lord, and I shall be very happy to be your guest;[4] am indeed most thankful to you for asking me. Some learned pundit,—at least he was a doctor,—kindly offered to give me the "hospitality of the city," which, as it means a half-formed introduction to the pickled snakes and a visit to the public library & the like I viewed with horror and did not accept.

I lecture about novels,[5] and shall expect Mrs. Blackwood to go and hear me. I will not be so hard upon you, because you must know more about novels than I can tell you. Whether Mrs. Trollope will go with me I do not yet know. It is a long journey for a lady to make in the middle of the winter & that only for a day or two. I give the same lecture at Hull on the 24th. and at Glasgow on the 27th.

Harry is hard at work and comes home freighted with Mss. What he does with them I dont know; but I feel glad that I am not an author

---

[3] "And let Opuntian Megilla's brother tell us by what arrow he is fortunately stricken." (Horace, *Odes*, I, xxvii, 10–12.) Dobson did not incorporate these sentiments into his "Autumn Idyll."

[4] Trollope echoes the proverb "They take a long day that never pay."

[5] "On English Prose Fiction as a Rational Amusement," published in *Four Lectures* (1938).

publishing with Chapman & Hall as I fancy he goes to sleep over them with a pipe in his mouth.

Yours always
Any Trollope

To Austin Dobson

MS University of London Library.

Oct 22–69.　　　　　　　　　WALTHAM HOUSE, WALTHAM CROSS.
My dear Mr Dobson.

On our opening day we expressly declared that it was not our intention to review books,—making that declaration with the view of hindering publishers from sending in the new publications. Since that we have had articles on one or two books—, but more with the view of dealing with some special subject than with any idea to critical expression.

If you like to write an article on Albert Durer, founded on Mrs. Heatons book,[6] I will read it, & return it at once if I do not use it. You must understand that I never pledge myself beyond that— If you do so, do not let it exceed 12 pages.

Most faithfully yours
A T

I altered the line in the idyll as you desired.

To Austin Dobson

Austin Dobson, *The Drama of the Doctor's Window* (1872), pp. 20–21.
B 424.

Nov. 8. 1869.　　　　　　　　WALTHAM HOUSE, WALTHAM CROSS.
My dear Mr. Dobson,—

Here, as always (I mean in regard to your juveniles which I send back by the same post as this) I like your idea, and manner, and current of thought, and versification:—but think that you have omitted that for which you have taken credit when you say that "you do not think you can do more to the verses." I mean that you are somewhat too quick, and apt to send out your work without attaining the amount of verbal perfection at which you are aiming.

Such a poem as your "Pyramus and Thisbe"[7] should be as clear as

---

[6] *The History of the Life of Albert Dürer* (1870), by Mary Margaret Heaton. See Trollope to Dobson, 12 January 1870.

[7] After revision, "Pyramus and Thisbe" became the Prologue (rather than the first act) of "The Drama of the Doctor's Window," *St. Paul's*, 5 (February 1870), 557–61. (Dobson incorporated most of Trollope's suggestions.) Shortly after the poem was published, Richard Webster (later Lord Alverstone) claimed that it had been plagiarized from the work of a young woman. When Webster persisted in his mistaken claim,

running water. No one should have to pause a moment to look for interpretation. If it is not fit to be read aloud so as to catch the intellects of not very intellectual people, it does not answer its professed object. But I have found myself compelled to unravel passages. This I am sure you will acknowledge should not be. I will venture, at the risk of calling down curses, to point out a few words I would alter. "Desire for green" is surely left there because a clearer expression would take trouble to find. Why "emphatic *terra firma?*" "Sniffed" should be sniffing, but I don't insist upon that. "Ulysses' rest" is, I think, very far-fetched, and almost misses your point. "After," Part III., Scene I., you mean "then." "Wide, blue, and tired" I do not understand. I do not know with what they act. What is blue and tired? "Fled." The word should be in the other stanza;—would, only the rhythm is troublesome. "Spelled!" Spell and spellbound I know; but not spelled except in regard to orthography. "With" should, I think, be "while." "Cultured caution" is far-fetched, and "sought" in the same line should be "found."

In fact, could you not look over it again and alter where you yourself doubt. Your criticism will be better than mine; and allow me to ask you to remember that did I not like the piece much, I should not descend to such picking of holes—which is unpleasant work. Pray let me have it again.

Yours always
Ant Trollope

To Austin Dobson

The Drama of the Doctor's Window, p. 21. B 425.

Nov. 15. 1869.   WALTHAM HOUSE, WALTHAM CROSS.
My dear Sir,—

I have directed a proof of your "Pyramus and Thisbe" to be sent to you.

You were right to put out the *terra firma*. The expression should not, I think, be used unless there is some, however farfetched reason for calling that "terra" especially "firma."

Yours always
A. T.

Dobson privately published *The Drama of the Doctor's Window*, which provided a complete account, including the entire first draft of the poem and all pertinent correspondence. (A copy of this rare pamphlet is in the Dobson collection in the University of London Library.)

To Mrs. John Bent[8]

MS Parrish Collection. B 426.

Novr. 18—1869.   WALTHAM HOUSE, WALTHAM CROSS.
My dear Mrs. Bent.

I have received the book[9] and I have written to thank my aunt.[1] I think the book must have belonged to her grandmother,—for it bears the name

Mary Gresley
1740—

Now Mrs. Clyde's mother could have owned no book, & could not indeed have been alive in 1740.[2] I fancy it has come down to the fourth generation. Many thanks for the trouble you have taken.

My wife sends her kind regards to you and the Major & the girls—to which I add my own.

very sincerely yours
Anthony Trollope

To [? William Lethbridge][3]

SB 427.

19 November 1869

Trollope is engaged and cannot accept an invitation.

To Richard Bentley

MS Parrish Collection. SB 428.

20 Nov. 1869.   WALTHAM HOUSE, WALTHAM CROSS.
My dear Mr. Bentley

You are bringing out a life of my chief favourite among novelists, Jane Austen.[4] I intend to have it reviewed in the Saint Pauls. Will you kindly

---

[8] Elizabeth Bent (?1806–76), the wife of Trollope's second cousin Major John Bent.
[9] A commonplace book, now in the Brigham Young University Library.
[1] Mary Clyde, née Milton.
[2] Trollope wrote on the first page of the volume: "Mary Gresley . . . who was the mother of Mary Gresley who married the Revd William Milton—who was the mother of *Mary Milton afterwards Mrs Clyde* from whose hands this book came to me—Anthony Trollope—and also of Frances Milton afterwards Mrs Trollope who again was the mother of T Adolphus Trollope and of me—Anthony Trollope who am the father of Harry Trollope and Fred Trollope / A.T. Nov 19. 1869." Mary Gresley was not his aunt's and mother's grandmother, but probably their great aunt; their grandmother was Cecelia Gresley, née Leeson. Trollope had just used the name in the short story "Mary Gresley," *St. Paul's*, 5 (November 1869), 237–56; reprinted in *An Editor's Tales* (1870).
[3] Probably William Lethbridge (1825–1901), a partner in the firm of W. H. Smith (and not William Sethbridge, as in SB 427). After Smith entered Parliament in 1868, Lethbridge took over most of the work of the business.
[4] J. E. Austen-Leigh, *A Memoir of Jane Austen* (1870).

cause a copy to be sent to Mrs. Pollock 59 Montagu Square, as early as you can. She will do it for me.[5]

very faithfully yours
Anthony Trollope

To Francis Black[6]

MS Parrish Collection. SB 430.

24. Novr. 1869   WALTHAM HOUSE, WALTHAM CROSS.
Dear Sir.
Many thanks for your kind invitation dated the 24 Instant. I should have been most happy to accept it had I not been engaged for some time past to stay with my friend Mr Blackwood the one night that I shall be in Edinburgh.

very faithfully yours
Anthony Trollope

Francis Black Esq

To Mrs. Brookfield[7]

MS Parrish Collection. SB 431.

OFFICE OF THE ST. PAULS MAGAZINE,
294, CITY ROAD, LONDON.

December 3 1869
My dear Mrs. Brookfield.
We have already in hand—and indeed almost entirely in print novels up to July 1871— There is one of my own coming out on 1 Jany next,— or I should say beginning then,—which will be continued till that date, and we have others. In this position I am not, as you will see, able to take advantage of your kind offer.

most faithfully yours
Anthony Trollope

To Tom Taylor

MS University of Texas. SB 432.

7 Decr. 69   WALTHAM HOUSE, WALTHAM CROSS.
My dear Taylor.
The lady's paper had come to me and had alas! gone back before I had any means of connecting it with you, or with your request to me.
But I read so much of the paper as to be sure that it would not have

---

[5] Juliet Pollock, "Jane Austen," *St. Paul's,* 5 (March 1870), 631–43.

[6] Francis Black (1831–92), partner in the Edinburgh publishing firm founded by his father, Adam Black; President of the Edinburgh Booksellers' Association.

[7] Jane Octavia Brookfield (1821–96), née Elton; best remembered for her friendship with Thackeray. Mrs. Brookfield was a minor novelist; the work she was offering Trollope was probably *Influence* (1871).

suited us. In the first place the time has I think gone by for disquisitions on the special pictures hung in the last Exhibition. Such papers should appear while the pictures are still on the wall.

Secondly—on such a subject as that of Art Criticism, an Editor if he be not an art critic himself,—which I am not,—should hardly trust himself to any, but one of whose judgement he has reason to feel trustful.

Yours always
Anthony Trollope

To Austin Dobson

MS University of London Library. Alban Dobson, *Austin Dobson: Some Notes*, p. 79; B 433.

December 8. 1869   WALTHAM HOUSE, WALTHAM CROSS.
My dear Mr Dobson.

I lunched yesterday with my dear friends George Elliot and G H Lewes,—as to whom you will at any rate know who they are. I regard them as the two best critics of English poetry (or prose), whom I know. They were very loud in their praise of your Autumn Idyll, and George Elliot asked me to let the author know what she thought of it.

Yours very truly
Anthony Trollope

Alexander Strahan to Trollope

MS Bodleian.

8 Decr. 1869   56 LUDGATE HILL
Dear Mr Trollope,

... Mr. Fraser is to illustrate your story.[8]

We have much pleasure in agreeing to pay you £150 for the right to republish yr. *Editor's Tales*[9] in book form. ...

Yours very truly
A Strahan & Co

---

[8] *Ralph the Heir* was illustrated by Francis Arthur Fraser, a popular illustrator of the 1860's and 1870's. Fraser also illustrated Trollope's *The Golden Lion of Granpere* for *Good Words*.

[9] *An Editor's Tales*, published in June 1870, contained six stories published previously in *St. Paul's*. The volume is generally regarded as Trollope's best collection of short fiction.

To Amelia Edwards

MS Somerville College, Oxford.

December 9. 1869   WALTHAM HOUSE, WALTHAM CROSS.
My dear Miss Edwards.

Debenham's Vow[1] came all right, and the delay has been wholly mine. Experience has no doubt made you conversant with two ways of acknowledging books,—the instantaneously courteous way which does not involve reading, and the slower mode which comes after perusal. Now I wished to read Debenham's vow before I wrote, and—what with hunting three days a week, writing a novel of my own, concocting articles, and reading basketfulls of manuscript, I have only now read it. The man's character is admirably kept up, and is, as you no doubt intended, the pearl of the book. The singularity of the story to me is that so good a novel should hang so entirely on one character. Had I been writing it, I should have endeavoured to divide, and should probably have frittered away, the interest between him and Claudia.

All the American scenes are excellent and full of life. I fancy you and I should agree on that now old question of North and South,—honouring the pluck and patriotism of the South, but knowing that on all utilitarian grounds the North must have prevailed. In fact what you, per Debenham, said after the war, I said in its earliest period.

To my seeming the fault of the story,—for there always is a fault,—is in the want of sympathy with Debenham in jilting Juliet— I think you should have made the girl accede to the arrangement by some mutual terms with him. He not only throws her over, but does so without noticing her.

Many thanks to you for the book— Pray excuse my freedom. Though you have gone so far off, I hope we may see you here at Waltham before long.

I will write to Mrs. Elliot about her Sienese article.[2] At present there are conflicting orders about it.

Yours very faithfully
Anthony Trollope

To ?

MS Parrish Collection.

12. Decr. 1869   WALTHAM HOUSE, WALTHAM CROSS.
My dear Sir.

Many thanks for your note about the hunting article. The papers are taking the question up, but do not seem to have much to say about it.

[1] Miss Edwards's novel *Debenham's Vow* (1870) had just been released.
[2] Not traced.

There is a yea yea, nay nay, little essay on the matter in the Saturday of yesterday.[3]

I had seen Kingsleys sermon before. I am not sure that I think it very good. There is I think more of sound & euphony than of meaning in it. The question however is a long one.[4]

I expect to be down with Sir M. next month.

Yours very truly[5]

To G. H. Lewes

MS Yale. B 434; George Eliot Letters, VIII, 470.

Decr. 13. 1869   WALTHAM HOUSE, WALTHAM CROSS.
My dear Lewes.

What can I do for you about cigars? If you liked that one I left with you, (which I think very mild though perhaps a little large,) I can send you a hundred of them,—strictly commercial—4d. a piece. I have a large parcel of unopened cigars,—12 hundred,—of which you shall have a box on trial instead if you prefer them. They are of course 12 months younger. I think they are probably quite as good a cigar, but a little stronger. Would you like a box of each?

I write as I was led to believe you were getting short of baccy.

Yours always
Anthy Trollope

You said a word as to the impropriety of inferring God's intentions with created things, from the observed habits of the creatures. Is this not a fair mode of argument for our own guidance. We know that there have been men who think it wrong to eat flesh; but may we not argue that we are intended to eat flesh, by seeing that certain animals do so, who from their nature cannot act against the Creators intentions?

But you may [? have] the cigars
without answering
all this.

---

[3] Trollope had heatedly defended the morality of field sports in "Mr. Freeman on the Morality of Hunting," *Fortnightly,* 12 (1 December 1869), 616–25, written in reply to E. A. Freeman's "The Morality of Field Sports," *Fortnightly,* 12 (1 October 1869), 353–85. The *Saturday Review* article, "The Morality of Field-Sports," 11 December 1869, pp. 760–61, generally sided with Freeman, although it tried to be fair to Trollope. Freeman subsequently took his case to the columns of the *Daily Telegraph* (18 and 19 December 1869), where his comments elicited remarks from a number of correspondents, including Ruskin. (Ruskin's letter to the *Daily Telegraph,* which supported Freeman, is reprinted in E. T. Cook and Alexander Wedderburn, eds., *The Complete Works of John Ruskin* [1908], XXXIV, 498.) For Trollope's discussion of this debate, see *Autobiography,* pp. 194–96.

[4] Perhaps a reference to Charles Kingsley's sermon of 7 March 1869 on the need for the compulsory education of children; this was published as *God's Feast: A Sermon Preached for the Industrial School, Cambridge* (1869).

[5] Signature omitted.

To R. S. Oldham

MS Parrish Collection. B 435.

December. 18. 1869.   WALTHAM HOUSE, WALTHAM CROSS.
My dear Oldham.

I purpose being in Glasgow on the 25th. January—Tuesday—at some hour, viz as soon as I can get there from Hull,—(at which place I lecture on the Monday.) I have engaged myself to go to George Burns[6] on the Wednesday, & shall stay there Wednesday & Thursday. On Friday I go to Edinburgh. All this you will see leaves me my Tuesday evening in Glasgow, and I have so left in order that I might have an evening with you to discuss Test abolition,[7] Oecumenical Council,[8] Dr. Temple,[9] and the state of things generally. Shall you be prepared? At what hour I shall get to Glasgow I cannot learn without an amount of continued study of Bradshaw[1] for which I have neither strength nor mental ability. But it must be before the hours of discussion are gone. Let me have a line to say whether we can meet as proposed.

Yours always
Any Trollope

To John Blackwood

MS National Library of Scotland.

December 18—1869   WALTHAM HOUSE, WALTHAM CROSS.
My dear Blackwood.

Would you be disposed to consider a proposition for a novel from me, for your magazine, with my name of course, to be commenced about March, April, or May 1871. I am just now beginning the story, and, if I made any such engagement, should of course be guided as to its proportions by the requisitions of the periodical in which it was to appear.[2] A

---

[6] George Burns (1795–1890), later Sir George, one of the founders of the steamship company that became the Cunard Line.

[7] A reference to the remaining religious tests at Oxford and Cambridge, which were finally abolished in 1871. (The 1871 Act allowed nonconformists, who had been able to take degrees since the 1850's, to hold university fellowships and offices.) Efforts to secure this reform had failed in 1867, 1868, and 1869.

[8] The Vatican Council met in Rome, 1869–70.

[9] Frederick Temple (1821–1902), later Bishop of London and Archbishop of Canterbury, had recently been nominated by Gladstone to the see of Exeter. This appointment aroused considerable opposition because of Temple's liberalism (he had contributed to *Essays and Reviews*).

[1] *Bradshaw's Monthly Railway Guide*, published since 1841 by George Bradshaw, the map engraver and printer.

[2] On 4 December 1869 Trollope began writing *The Eustace Diamonds*. On 28 December, however, Blackwood declined the work, adding "I have various things in prospect which may be in progress at that distant date but I would hardly like to tie myself so long before." (MS [copy] National Library of Scotland.) On 12 February

novel of mine will appear in Saint Pauls in 1870–& will come to a close
in the first half of the following year.

Yours always faithfully
Anthony Trollope

1870

To John Blackwood
MS Parrish Collection. SB 436.

Jan. 10. 1869 [1870].   WALTHAM HOUSE, WALTHAM CROSS.
My dear Blackwood.

I purpose being in Edinburgh some time on Friday 28 Janur [*sic*] on
which day I lecture. At what hour I do not know;—probably at eight—
Will you give me an early dinner.

I then lecture at Birmingham on the Monday following. If I can get
from Edinburgh to Birmingham on the Monday—without any tremendous struggling, I will stay the Saturday and Sunday with you if you and
Mrs. Blackwood will keep me so long.

Yours always
Anthony Trollope

To Austin Dobson
MS University of London Library.

Jan. 12. 1870   WALTHAM HOUSE, WALTHAM CROSS.
My dear Mr Dobson.

I am sorry to return your Mss;—but the truth is that there is so very
little to tell about Albert Durer[3] that it is hard to make a long article
respecting him interesting to readers such as are those who take in shilling magazines. The paper I now return has been elaborated with great
care; but, after all, the result is very small. People will not care to contest, in their own minds, the question whether the wife was or was not a
shrew;—nor will they regard with favour the good things that were done
for him by the burghers at Antwerp.

1870 Trollope sold the novel to Chapman & Hall for £2,500, with serialization scheduled to begin in the *Fortnightly* in July 1871.

[3] See Trollope to Dobson, 22 October 1869.

I am sure you will understand me when I say that I am bound to get matter such as will find readers, not among the highest class of men & women,—but with that class by which a magazine is mainly supported.

Most faithfully
Yours
Anthony Trollope

To the Station Master, Peterborough

MS Parrish Collection. SB 437.

January 16. 1870
Sunday   Glatton.[4]
Sir.

Will you kindly have a horse box for me on Wednesday morning to take two horses from Peterborough to Saxby[5] by the 10.30 am train,—and to bring them back in the afternoon. I shall also want a box to take three horses from Peterborough to Harlow[6] by the Great Eastern line on Thursday.

Yours obediently
Anthony Trollope

I will take care that the horses are at Peterborough on Wednesday before 10. AM.

The Station Master
Peterborough

To E. W. B. Nicholson[7]

MS Parrish Collection. B 438.

OFFICE OF THE ST. PAULS MAGAZINE,
Jan. 22. 1870   294, CITY ROAD, LONDON.
Dear Sir.

I am constrained to return your poem, and am prohibited by your letter from giving any reason for doing so.

You propose prose articles on certain subjects named by yourself of very various shades of interest,—and add an offer to *write on any other*

---

[4] A village in Huntingdonshire.
[5] A village in Leicestershire.
[6] A town in Essex.
[7] Edward Williams Byron Nicholson (1849–1912), later the founder of the Library Association and Bodley's librarian. In 1870 Nicholson was still an undergraduate; he had published several poems, stories, and miscellanea; William Morris and Charles Kingsley had mildly encouraged him, and this may have made him overestimate his literary talents.

subject. You will perhaps believe me, and perhaps will not, when I say that I am led by the culture and intellect shewn in your poem to regret that you should not have a clearer insight into your powers. Such insight will no doubt come in time; but till it does come I fear you will have to suffer the sorrow of an unfulfilled ambition.

E. B. Nicholson Esq

Yours very faithfully
Anthony Trollope

To Octavian Blewitt

MS Royal Literary Fund.

Jan 22–70
My dear Mr Blewitt
   Will you kindly take notice of the appointment made on the other side.[8]

Yours always
Any Trollope

James Virtue to Trollope

MS Bodleian.

Jany 25th. 1870   VIRTUE & CO.
My dear Mr. Trollope,
   I hear from Messr Strahan today that they intend to write to you upon the subject of St Pauls intending to try the Editorship for themselves by way of economy—
   But I could not let this intimation be made without saying that, personally, I so much regret that St Pauls and you should part company— Our relationship together has been so genial & pleasant that I much regret that any change should have become necessary—but when we parted with the Magazine from our own charge here, we also parted from all control over it, as although I am largely interested in Strahan's business—I have always declined and intend to decline—any active share in its management.
   I know that all this will seem a little curious to you, and that I have the power of "control"—if I chose to exercise it—but there are many things that have to be taken into consideration by me, apart from any personal feeling that I may have, and I fancy that the contemplated change will not take you altogether by surprise, as I suggested some time since that it was then probable.
   It is hard work to make a property of this description remunerative,

---

[8] Trollope was writing on the back of a note from W. F. Pollock, like himself a treasurer of the Royal Literary Fund, agreeing to 3 February as a suitable date for auditing the Fund's books.

and how far it will be affected by the change it is impossible to predict, but I think we should both be glad if they can make it a success.[9]

I am, dear Mr. Trollope,
Very truly yours
James Virtue

Alexander Strahan to Trollope

MS Bodleian.

25th. Jany 1870   56, LUDGATE HILL.
Dear Mr. Trollope,

I have much pleasure in sending you the enclosed cheque.

While doing so I should like to take the opportunity of letting you know that we have been thinking—the Magazine not being a remunerative property, and you having kindly expressed your willingness to do whatever might be thought best in its interest—we have been thinking that perhaps "Saint Pauls" might be allowed to follow the example of "Blackwood" and "edit itself," that is put up with such editing as publishers can give.

I would never think of making this proposal were the Magazine in a flourishing state. As it is I feel sure you will approve of our motives, even if you cannot see your way to commend our practice.

Yours very sincerely
A. Strahan

To Mrs. John Blackwood[1]

MS National Library of Scotland.

[30 January 1870]
Sunday   Birmingham.
My dear Mrs. Blackwood.

I send a little song that I have written expressly that Lord Neaves[2] may sing it at your house. I know that he sings none but his own; but he may say that he wrote this.

---

[9] In May 1869 Virtue, having tried unsuccessfully to have Chapman take over *St. Paul's*, transferred the magazine to Strahan, whose business he largely owned. Strahan reduced the rate of pay to contributors but was unable to improve the finances, and in July 1870 Trollope was eased out of the editorship. In 1872 Strahan had to retire from the firm he had founded, but took with him *St. Paul's*. Henry S. King then took over the copyright, his imprint appearing in November. Strahan remained on as editor but failed to reverse the losses, and the magazine ceased publication with the March 1874 issue.

[1] Julia Blandford (*d.* 1899), youngest daughter of the Reverend Joseph Blandford, had married John Blackwood in 1854.

[2] Charles Neaves (1800–1876), Lord Neaves, a Scottish judge and prominent Edinburgh literary figure, was a regular contributor to *Blackwood's*. A humorist, he published many of his satires in *Songs and Verses, Social and Scientific* (1868).

I send under another cover a pair of gloves which I innocently took off your hall table. On looking at them I grew pale to find that they bore the "Generals" name! I feel like a poor Trojan who had unconsciously prigged³ the spear of Achilles. You must act Minerva, and shield me from the warrior's wrath.

I have got such a thorough-going sore throat that I do not in the least envy the lecture-going people of Birmingham tonight. Would I were safe at home.

Yours always
Most sincerely
Anthony Trollope

But that I feared the General too much I would have sent the gloves to *dear* Mrs. L——

John Blackwood to W. Lucas Collins⁴

MS (copy) National Library of Scotland.

Jan 31/70   45 George St. Edinburgh
My Dear Collins
    ... Anthony Trollope has been staying with me for the last few days & you would have been delighted as I was to hear how enthusiastic he was about your Iliad & the whole scheme. He says it is altogether a most happy idea & that he could not imagine anything done with more taste & skill than your Iliad. As he is about the most shrewd & practical man of letters going it was very cheering to hear him. He carried away a copy of the Odyssey with him & proposes to review the two at once.⁵ ...

Always yours truly
John Blackwood

Rev L. Collins

---

³ "Prig" is thieves' slang for steal.

⁴ William Lucas Collins (1817–87), Vicar of Kilsby from 1867 to 1873 and Rector of Lowick from 1873 to 1887, was the editor of Blackwood's Ancient Classics for English Readers series. Trollope and Collins became intimate friends. Of their first meeting, Collins wrote to Blackwood on 31 May 1870: "The Trollopes came on Thursday and left on Saturday. We like them very much,—him especially, he was so very pleasant to talk to, and at the same time so perfectly unassuming. What I like best in Mrs. T is her honest and hearty appreciation of her husband." (MS National Library of Scotland.)

⁵ "Ancient Classics for English Readers," *St. Paul's*, 5 (March 1870), 664–68. Trollope praised the series as a means of removing "very common and very dense ignorance" about great classical authors, asserting that the series should be of particular interest to the "educated lady." Of the two volumes of Homer under review, he commented that "the editor of the series has chosen the best plum for himself,—as a discreet editor should do," for Homer had a tale to tell. Trollope found the volumes "very pleasant reading;—as good as a novel we might say, that being a common expression, were it not that they are very much better than most novels." On 28 February Blackwood wrote to Collins: "With this I send a copy of St Pauls containing Trollopes review of the series. It is a pity he has not put his name to it but I did not like to ask him to do so." (MS [copy] National Library of Scotland.)

To ?

MS Parrish Collection.

1. Feb. 1870.   WALTHAM HOUSE, WALTHAM CROSS.
My dear Sir.

I hardly know how to help your friend in reference to the Post Office appointment which is desired.

Latterly I have asked for various *nominations* (not appointments) which have always been promised and have never led to any thing.

Your friend had I think better approach Lord Hartington[6] through some political friend.

very faithfully yours
Anthony Trollope

To Miss Bond

MS (photocopy) UCLA. SB 439.

3 Feb 70   WALTHAM HOUSE, WALTHAM CROSS.
My dear Miss Bond.

It was only late on Monday night at Birmingham after my lecture that I got your kind present and learned from your note that you were the artist who did the very beautiful drawings,—birds &c, Little Red Riding Hood & others which were in my hands some time since. I left Birmingham early on the following morning & was therefore unable to see you.

Pray accept my best thanks for your very pretty gift. I hope you are doing well with your art.

very faithfully yours
Anthony Trollope

To Charles Kent

MS Parrish Collection. B 440.

Feb 6. 1870   WALTHAM HOUSE, WALTHAM CROSS.
My dear Sir.

I have considered closely the matter which we discussed the other day in Piccadilly and I feel myself obliged to decline your kind offer with reference to the Sun newspaper. I should be troubling you too much with affairs which are simply my own were I to give you the various reasons which make me feel myself bound to abandon the project, but I may as well state to you candidly that in carrying out the scheme I

[6] Spencer Compton Cavendish (1833–1908), Marquess of Hartington and later 8th Duke of Devonshire, was Postmaster General at this date.

should find myself under an obligation of giving more personal unpaid labour than I could afford to supply.[7]

very faithfully yours
Anthony Trollope

To Austin Dobson

MS University of London Library.

13. Feb—1870.   WALTHAM HOUSE, WALTHAM CROSS.

My dear Mr Dobson.

Thanks for the little poems. I have still to trouble you by asking for a few altered words. The imperious necessity of such work is that the wording of it should be happy;—and when you choose Horace as your guide the necessity becomes more binding than ever.

In "Outward bound"[8] I do not like "stiffened neck"—why? It is at least far-fetched & hard to understand.

"Shew"—for declare is not happy.

"Calm as Adams Peak." Here I am in the dark. What is Adam's Peak?

The Martiis caelebs[9] is less close to the Ode & so far less enjoyable,—but perhaps our readers will hardly find that out.

"Without the choking" does not recommend itself to me. One sees the meaning but it is far fetched & ugly.

Chill is a bad epithet for locks.

Whoever, even in fiction, had said he was slender? Slender dont stand for young unless there has been some former allusion to obesity as its reverse.

Excuse all this carping & let me have them back.

I am glad you have sent them. After the June number of this year, I give up the conduct of the magazine. I hope I may leave you as a legacy to my successors,[1] but I shall be glad to finish with your little pieces. No contributor who has worked with me has given me more pleasure than yourself.

very faithfully
Anthony Trollope

---

[7] Kent was trying to restore the fortunes of the *Sun*, a London evening paper that he owned and edited. The task proved impossible, however, and the *Sun* ceased publication in February 1871. Nothing is known about the "scheme" discussed in this letter.

[8] "Outward Bound," *St. Paul's*, 6 (June 1870), 290–91, was based on Horace, *Odes*, III, vii. Dobson removed the words to which Trollope objected.

[9] "A Gage D'Amour," *St. Paul's*, 6 (May 1870), 179–80, a poem based on Horace, *Odes*, III, viii, which begins "Martiis caelebs . . ." Dobson removed the words "without the choking," but let the rest of the poem stand as submitted.

[1] Dobson continued to be a regular contributor to *St. Paul's* until it ceased publication in 1874.

To ?

MS Parrish Collection.

Feb 13—70
Sunday   WALTHAM HOUSE, WALTHAM CROSS.
My dear Doctor.

Would you come and see me some time tomorrow Monday. I shall be at home till after lunch.

Yours ever
Any Trollope

To ?

MS Parrish Collection.

OFFICE OF THE ST. PAULS MAGAZINE,
Feb 14 1870   294, CITY ROAD, LONDON.
Sir.

I should be very glad to see your paper on the old Romances.[2] I should however tell you, before I ask you to send it to me, that I shall [not] continue to edit the Saint Pauls Magazine after June next, and that I fear I am full up to that time.

If your paper appeared suitable I would leave it as a legacy to my successor, but I could not of course be answerable for what my successor might do with it.

faithfully yours
Anthony Trollope

To ?

MS Parrish Collection. SB 441.

19 Feb 70   WALTHAM HOUSE, WALTHAM CROSS.
My dear[3]

Mr Galloway—of the firm of Morgan & Galloway,—the writer of the enclosed printed memorandum is a friend of mine, and a very upright man. The case which he gives in detail,—and in which the grievance has no doubt come from the want of bribes administered to the Peruvian authorities, seems [to] be one of great hardship, as to which British protection should be given. Have you time to look at it?

Yours always
Anthy Trollope

---

[2] No such article appeared in *St. Paul's.*
[3] The name of the addressee, evidently a government official, has been obliterated by a water stain.

To R. Dudley Baxter[4]

Mary D. Baxter, *In Memoriam: R. Dudley Baxter, M.A.* (1878), pp. 61–62.

February 19. 1870.   WALTHAM HOUSE, WALTHAM CROSS.

Dear Sir.

Allow me to thank you for your interesting pamphlet.[5] I differ from you somewhat, not only in politics generally, but in your definition of parties. To my idea, the great difference between Conservatives and Liberals (and I take these two names as the best I know to mark the two great political parties of the time) consists in this, that the Liberals think it to be for the welfare of the people and the good of the country that distances should be reduced and gradually annihilated. The Conservative thinks it to be for the good of each that he should maintain the great "distance" or degree of difference which divides the Duke from the labourer, while the Liberal conceives that the more that difference is contracted the better it will be for both parties. In venturing on this definition, I ascribe no inferior motives or superior patriotism to one than to the other. But, as I think, such has been the difference of ideas on this great subject since men divided themselves into parties. It was as plainly marked in the days of Caesar and Pompey as it is now; as plain indeed in the earlier days of the Greek republics; as plainly, probably, if we knew the facts, among still earlier ages. And it seems to me that the one party is almost as necessary as the other. Accumulating wealth will re-create the distances almost as fast as they are dissolved by popular energy.

I apologize for the length of my note, and am,

Yours faithfully

R. Dudley Baxter Esq   Anthony Trollope

To Charles Buxton

MS Parrish Collection.

23 Feb. 70   WALTHAM HOUSE, WALTHAM CROSS.

My dear Buxton.

I shall be very happy to join you on Saturday the 5th. at 7. PM.

Yours always

Anthony Trollope

What weather! It is now just a fortnight since I have been on a horse.

---

[4] Robert Dudley Baxter (1827–75), economist and political writer.
[5] *English Parties and Conservatism* (1870).

To Octavian Blewitt

MS Berg Collection. B 442.

24 Feb. 1870   WALTHAM HOUSE, WALTHAM CROSS.
My dear Mr. Blewitt.

I have this moment got your MS. & hasten to explain to you that I give up the editorship of the Saint Paul's Magazine in June next, and that I am almost full up to that date. I doubt whether I have room for so long an article. I will read it and then will write again;—but I write at once to assure you that any thing coming from you to me would be treated with the utmost respect. If I cannot use it myself, I may perhaps leave it as a legacy to Strahan's people.[6] I will tell you all about it, however, before long.

Pray believe me that it gives me great pleasure to see you employed at such work again.

Yours always faithfully
Anthony Trollope

To John Blackwood

MS National Library of Scotland. Parker, p. 59; B 443.

March 6. 1870   WALTHAM HOUSE, WALTHAM CROSS.
My dear Blackwood

I should have been happy to have read Miss Hasell's[7] paper on Browning,[8]—whom I regard as a very great poet,—were it not for that decision on the part of the proprietors of Saint Pauls magazine which I communicated to you. I cannot answer for what the magazine may see fit to do when it edits itself,—as does another periodical that we know of.[9]

I have matter to last me up to the end of my reign,—& more I fear than I can use. I fear to leave Mss to Strahans tender mercies, knowing that

---

[6] An article by Blewitt, "Bricks and Mortar Charities," appeared in *St. Paul's*, 6 (May 1870), 161–68. This may have been a shortened version of the one referred to in this letter. Another article by Blewitt, "Suburban Houses," appeared in *St. Paul's*, 7 (March 1871), 516–24.

[7] Elizabeth Julia Hasell (1830–87), miscellaneous writer. Miss Hasell had been a contributor to *Blackwood's* and the *Quarterly Review* since 1858.

[8] Blackwood had declined Miss Hasell's article and given her a letter of recommendation (3 March 1870) to Trollope: "I cannot remember what side you take [on Browning] but if you wish a favourable estimate of him in the St. Pauls I am pretty certain that you will not find any where a more elaborate or better written piece of Criticism than this by Miss Hasell." (MS [copy] National Library of Scotland.) The article was eventually accepted and published in two parts: "Browning's Poems.—The Ring and the Book," *St. Paul's*, 7 (December 1870 and January 1871), 257–76, 377–97.

[9] *Blackwood's Magazine*.

John Blackwood. Portrait by John Watson Gordon.

he has already on hand many tons of contributions which, if not accepted, are not rejected.

I have written to Miss Hasel [*sic*] explaining this as well as I can.

Yours always
Anthy Trollope

To John Blackwood

MS National Library of Scotland. Excerpt, *Commentary*, p. 308; Parker, p. 59; B 444.

OFFICE OF THE ST. PAULS MAGAZINE,
294, CITY ROAD, LONDON.

March 10. 1870   Address Waltham Cross

My dear Blackwood.

Since I got home from my lecturing expedition I have been at work on the Caesar,[1]—and find it very hard work. However I have done the first and longest of the two Commentaries. Before I attack the other, I should like to know what you & Mr. Collins think of the one I have done. Caesars remaining work is so clearly divided into two parts, that there will be no difficulty in this. The whole, if completed, will make a volume about the length of the Iliad;—(I mean of course Mr. Collins' Iliad). Would you let me send you the 7 chapters done, and then would you let me know what you think of it. There will be also an introductory chapter, (nearly done already,) but I will not send that as it cannot be completed till the second Commentary has been taken in hand.—I do not like, myself, sending a half completed work; but the job is so very stiff a one, and so much subsidiary reading is necessary, that I would spare myself six week[s] labour on the second Commentary if, as may be probable, you or Mr. Collins do not like what I have done. If you approve of that I will go to work again with a will.

Shall I send MS to you or to him? If to him give me the address.

Yours always faithfully
Anthony Trollope

To John Blackwood

MS National Library of Scotland. Parker, p. 59; B 445.

March 14. 1870   WALTHAM HOUSE, WALTHAM CROSS.

My dear Blackwood.

I send the Mss of the Caesar in two parcels. You will understand, and will make Mr Collins understand, that there is to be an introductory

---

[1] After expressing "very strong admiration" for the *Iliad* and the *Odyssey* in Blackwood's Ancient Classics for English Readers series, Trollope was asked by Blackwood to supply a volume for the series himself: "Whereupon I offered to say what might be said to the readers of English on the Commentaries of Caesar." (*Autobiography*, p. 338.) Trollope's *Commentaries of Caesar* was published in June 1870.

chapter,—which is indeed three parts done, but which I cannot complete until I have re-read the De Bell. Civ.

I am exceeding glad that you will print it before reading it, because, though parts have been rewritten thrice, the whole has not been re-copied, and the Mss, though very good copy for printers, is a little too much interlined for comfortable reading.

Yours always
Anthony Trollope

To Mrs. Annie Thomas Cudlip

MS Parrish Collection.

OFFICE OF THE ST. PAULS MAGAZINE,

March 14. 1870   294, CITY ROAD, LONDON.

My dear Mrs. Cudlip.

I will explain to you exactly how the St. Pauls is situated. I give up the Editorship in June. Till that time I have on hand more fiction, and indeed more matter of every kind, than I can use. Were I to keep your story now I could only hand it over to Mr. Strahan, (of the firm of Strahan & Co 56 Ludgate Hill) by whom, or under whom, I believe the magazine will be managed when I leave it. I should then be responsible for its publication though I could not ensure it. Indeed I fear I should be only adding to a vast mass of such matter already in Mr Strahans hands.

Under these circumstances it is better for me to return you your Mss so that you may send it to Mr. Strahan if you choose to do so. Your name is no doubt quite familiar to him.

very faithfully yours
Anthony Trollope

John Blackwood to Trollope

MS (copy) National Library of Scotland.

45 George Street
Edinburgh

March 28/70

My dear Trollope

Along with this I send proof of the seven chapters of your Caesar which I have just read with very great pleasure. You have I think hit it off capitally & with the introductory chapter & the remaining books the picture of the ruthless Missionary of Civilization will I expect be very perfect. In my recollection of him I had not thought him so cruel but I daresay he looked upon our ancestors & the others as barely human.

If I were to suggest anything I would say quote some more of his own terse sayings as nearly in his own words as they can be rendered & if possible a battle-piece or two. You & Collins however will know better than I, how bits of translation would fit into your pleasant flowing narrative.

Instead of the paragraph referring to the 8th. book would it not be better to put in a sentence or two saying that all went on swimmingly for Caesar during these two years so as to make the story complete for our readers.

On my proof which I send to Collins I have hardly made any marks but I have asked him to write to you with all suggestions that may occur to him. I would have written to you through him but I send direct instead to save time as too much time has already been lost by the Printers. The Printers excuse is that "the Type was locked up" a reason for delay which your son will I daresay have heard by this time.

I feel so satisfied that Collins will in the main agree in admiration for your work that I have no hesitation in saying go ahead even before you hear from him if your hands are free.

Always yours truly
John Blackwood

Anthony Trollope Esq

To John Blackwood

MS National Library of Scotland. Excerpt, *Commentary*, p. 308; Parker, p. 60; B 466.

March 29. 70   WALTHAM HOUSE, WALTHAM CROSS.

My dear Blackwood

I am very pleased that you are satisfied with my little endeavour.

According to the way in which that which is printed goes there will be about 150 pages of your printing when the whole is done;—or something more, if anything be added to the first part.

I will do as you suggest in adding a few short scraps of Caesar's own words translated. As to battle pieces I tried it— I found that any intelligible description of any one battle would be an addition which the volume would hardly bear. You can hardly guess how great was the necessity for condensation. A reader never sees this. I am bound to give some analysis of the seven books, and was driven to measure myself by lines at last;—to get the thing said in the pages I had allowed myself.

As to that last book written by Hirtius Pansa[2] I will own to you I have never read it. It never used to be printed with the Commentaries when I was young: nor is it now in the edition which I chiefly used. I will however, see what I can do to make the finale of the first Commentary seem less bald.

Yours always
Anthony Trollope

[2] Book VIII of the *Gallic Wars* was written by Aulus Hirtius. Trollope seems to have conflated this name with that of Caius Vibius Pansa, who, like Hirtius, was a consul after Caesar's assassination.

To Mrs. Houstoun

MS Parrish Collection.

April 5—1870. WALTHAM HOUSE, WALTHAM CROSS.
My dear Mrs. Houstoun

I am sorry to say that I am no longer in power (or rather shall not be after June next) in regard to the Saint Pauls Magazine, and cannot therefore avail myself of your offer or of that of others. After June 1st. I give up the magazine, and any application respecting it should be made direct to Mr A. Strahan of the firm of Messrs. Strahan & Co publishers of Ludgate Hill, by whom,—as I understand,—the magazine will be managed when I leave it.

very faithfully yours
Anthony Trollope

To W. Lucas Collins

MS National Library of Scotland. Excerpt, *Commentary*, p. 309; excerpt, Parker, p. 60; B 447.

April 6. 1870 WALTHAM HOUSE, WALTHAM CROSS.
My dear Sir.

I am very glad that you like the Caesar.[3]

Blackwood sent me but one copy of the printed sheets which I returned with certain additions as asked by him,—so that I have no copy by me. I have not even a manuscript. I did add certain translations of small paragraphs which seemed to be telling,—fearing however to add much as I find the difficulty to be chiefly in reducing the matter on hand to a proper compas [sic].

The printers errors I corrected, i e those noted by you—such [as] "finer" to "fewer," "suffeing" to "suffering" and various others. As to the phrases which strike you as too colloquial—"thick as blackberries" &c, you will, I do not doubt, understand the spirit in which they are used. The intention is to create that feeling of lightness which is produced by the handling of serious matters with light words, & which is almost needed in such a work. I would not admit slang, but such phrases as may be held to be admissible in ordinarily easy conversation do not seem to me to be objectionable. "As fast [as] he could lay leg to ground" seems a fair colloquial translation for "quam magnis itineribus." But let the phrases go if they displease you.

---

[3] On 5 April Collins wrote to Blackwood: "I have written to Trollope to tell him how much I like his work, and to beg him to finish it. I have pointed out, as modestly as I knew how, some few points where I think he might improve it, but mere trifles. He fails here and there—as would be very natural in the case of one who does not profess critical scholarship—in accuracy of translation." (MS National Library of Scotland.)

Does Caesar use the word ligatos? I do not find it. I speak of his anger against the Veneti in the third book. He calls the officers whom P Crassus had sent "legatos,"—and afterwards speaks with horror of the breach of the "Ius legatorum,"—and he says that they were "in vincula conjectos"—which answers the purpose of your argument just as well.[4] But to a modern reader the joke is in the assumption by Caesar that all tribes, let them be ever so barbarous, must have understood the Roman feeling—and also in this, that when it served his purpose to imprison German ambassadors he did not scruple to do it. The passage you quote from Cicero might be supported by the words which Horace put into the mouth of Regulus. "Qui lora, restrictis lacertis, Sensit iners timuitque mortem."[5]

I thought I had translated all the Latin phrases. It can easily be done.

I do not know Lewin's books. My books have been Long's Caesar, Merivale's Roman Empire, Napoleon[6] & Plutarch. The less one allows oneself to be tempted into would-be learned disquisitions the better I think in such a work.

I quite agree with what you say as to criticism. I am keenly alive to the gratification and discomfort it may produce and acknowledge

*　　*　　*

To John Blackwood

MS National Library of Scotland. SB 448.

April 7—1870　　　　　　WALTHAM HOUSE, WALTHAM CROSS.
My dear Blackwood.

Send me a copy of the Caesar, as far as it is printed—either corrected or uncorrected, does not matter. I have no copy by me to work with.

Yours ever
A. T.

[4] It appears that Collins supposed, wrongly, that Caesar used the word *ligatos* (bound together) in describing the imprisonment of the legates, a breach of the legates' privilege as ambassadors of Rome (*ius legatorum*); Trollope tells him that the phrase used for "imprisoned" was *in vincula conjectos*.

[5] "Who has felt the thongs tighten on his pinioned wrists and, fearing death, had yet done nothing about it?" (Horace, *Odes*, III, v, 35–36.)

[6] Thomas Lewin, *The Invasion of Britain by Julius Caesar* (1859); George Long, probably his Latin edition of Caesar's *Commentaries* (1861); Charles Merivale, *History of the Romans under the Empire* (1850–64); and Napoleon III, *Histoire de Jules César* (1865–66). Trollope described how he worked for three months: "I began by reading through the Commentaries twice, which I did without any assistance either by translation or English notes. . . . After reading what my author had left behind him, I fell into the reading of what others had written about him, in Latin, in English, and even in French,—for I went through much of that most futile book by the late Emperor of the French. I do not know that for a short period I ever worked harder." (*Autobiography*, p. 338.)

To Mrs. Houstoun

MS Parrish Collection.

April 15. 1870   WALTHAM HOUSE, WALTHAM CROSS.
My dear Mrs. Houstoun.

   I think I explained to you before the circumstances of the Magazine.
I have however read your article, which I now return. I hardly think it
would be suited for the periodical as I fancy that we disagree in so
many points in the matter of Irish politics and Irish social affairs.[7]

                              very faithfully yours
                              Anthony Trollope

To Kate Field

MS Boston Public Library. *Commentary*, pp. 291–92; B 449.

April 15. 1870   ATHENAEUM CLUB
Dear Kate.

   I am not a grumbler, and you are very—impertinent. All the same I am
delighted to think that you should have made $8000—and I congratu-
late you with all my heart. I am sure of this; that in whatever way you
earn money, it will be both honest and honourable, that the money will
represent hard work mental culture and much thought; and that as you
have never been depressed by poverty, so will you never be puffed up by
your wealth.

   You write as though I should find fault with your lecturing.[8] I am not
in the least disposed to do so. I think writing nicer for either man or
woman;—but that perhaps comes from the fact that I am better paid for
writing than for lecturing. I like your account of yourself,—with your
handsome dress, looking as well as you can, and doing your work col-
loquially. I have no doubt you look very well. You could do that when
you were not handsomely dressed,—and I should like to hear you lecture
amazingly. Only I should want to go home to summer [? supper] with
you afterwards & be allowed to express my opinion freely. But in truth I
am not patient under lectures, and much prefer lecturing myself,—as
I dare say you do also.

   [7] Trollope himself had written four articles on Irish matters for *St. Paul's*: "The
Irish Church Debate," 2 (May 1868), 147–60; "The Irish Church Bill in the Lords,"
4 (August 1869), 540–55; "What Does Ireland Want?" 5 (December 1869), 286–301; and
"Mr. Gladstone's Irish Land Bill," 5 (March 1870), 620–30.
   [8] Lyceum lecturing offered Kate Field the opportunity to earn enough money to
support herself and her mother. She gave her first lecture, the highly successful
"Women in the Lyceum," in March 1869, and during the following two years lectured
in cities and towns throughout America. Her appearance and voice contributed
greatly to her success: William Lloyd Garrison remarked that "it was worth an admission fee to see Kate Field on the platform" (Lilian Whiting, *Kate Field: A Record*,
p. 223).

As for your lecturing here, I do not doubt you would have very large audiences;—but they do not pay well. £10 a lecture is about the mark if you can fill a large room—600 or 700—for our rooms are not so large as yours,—and our lectures are chiefly given to audiences who do not pay for tickets, but pay by the year. So that the managing committees cannot afford to pay much. I had a word to say the other day about fiction, and I lectured in four places, receiving £15 in two and £10 in two. All of which information may I hope be useful to you soon, as I should so greatly delight in having you here.

I don't in the least understand why you fly out against me as to matrimony,—or as to what I have said on that subject in regard to you. I have said and say again that I wish you would marry. But I have never advised you to marry a man for whom you did not care. You tell me I don't know you. I think I do,—as to character & mind. As to *all* the details of your life of course I do not. You may at this moment be most violently in love with some impossible hero, and I know nothing about it. What I have meant to say in the way of council [*sic*] is this;—that you should not so bind yourself to an idea of personal independence, as to allow that feeling to operate in your mind against the idea of marriage. I think that it does so, and has done so;—not that I have any notion of any individual sent about his business on those grounds, but that I think such to be the tendency of your mind. As I think that, at any rate in middle life, married people have a better time than old bachelors and spinsters, I do not like that tendency in you. Now I think that is all very straightforward and decorous, and I don't know why I am to be flown at.

I never said you were like W. Petrie.[9] I said that that young woman did not entertain a single opinion on public matters which you could repudiate,—and that she was only absurd in her mode of expressing them— However we'll drop W. P. now.

I have given up, or rather am now just giving up my magazine, and therefore have no longer any power in that line. But in truth I myself hate Fechter as an actor, and I think the people here are sick of him. To me he was never a pleasant actor.[1]

I would tell you all about the magazine but that I am at the end of my letter. Our chief news is that early next year we go out to Australia to

[9] Wallachia Petrie, the "Republican Browning," introduced in chap. lv of *He Knew He Was Right.*

[1] Charles Albert Fechter (1824–79), the celebrated actor of the French and English stage. Fechter had recently gone to America, where he continued his acting career and where he remained until his death. Kate Field had obviously offered an article on Fechter for *St. Paul's*; she was a great admirer of Fechter and later in the year published two articles on him, "Charles Albert Fechter: A Biographical Sketch," *Atlantic Monthly*, 26 (September 1870), 285–307, and "Fechter as Hamlet," *Atlantic Monthly*, 26 (November 1870), 558–70. Her book *Charles Albert Fechter* appeared in 1882. For Trollope's dislike of Fechter's style, see also Trollope to Lewes, 1 November 1875.

see a son of ours who is settled there. I hope to induce my wife to return via San Francisco—With kindest love to your mother.

Very affectionately yours,

A. T.

To John Blackwood

MS National Library of Scotland. Excerpt, Porter, p. 363; excerpt, *Commentary*, p. 309; excerpt, Parker, p. 60; B 450.

16 April 1870   WALTHAM HOUSE, WALTHAM CROSS.
My dear Blackwood.

I think I can promise that the remainder of the MS shall be in your hands by May 1. I have done the two first books of the Civil War, and have nearly finished the introduction. It has been a tough bit of work; but I have enjoyed it amazingly, and am very much obliged to you for having suggested it. It has been a change to the spinning of novels, and has enabled me to surround myself for three months with books & almost to think myself a scholar.

I sent back the revise you sent me to Collins, with further corrections as suggested by him, and think that I incorporated nearly all (I may perhaps say all,)—that was proposed either by you or him. He I presume will send those sheets on to you.

I find from the Herodotus how very much depends on the touch of the man who does it. For the Herodotus is certainly not equal to the Homer; though it no doubt leaves the conviction that the man who did it understood his author.[2]

very faithfully yours

Anthony Trollope

We have a blaze of summer here all at once!

To Lord Houghton

MS Trinity College, Cambridge.

April 22. 1870   WALTHAM HOUSE, WALTHAM CROSS.
My dear Lord Houghton.

Will you dine with me at the Garrick Club at 7.30 on Wednesday 4—May.

Yours always

Anthony Trollope

---

[2] Trollope was obviously disappointed by George C. Swayne's treatment of Herodotus in Blackwood's Ancient Classics series: his review of Collins's Homer volumes (see Blackwood to Collins, 31 January 1870) shows that he was particularly looking forward to the volume on Herodotus as affording "scope for a narrative."

Lord Houghton

To Lord Houghton

MS Trinity College, Cambridge. T. Wemyss Reid, *The Life, Letters, and Friendships of Richard Monckton Milnes* (1911), II, 224–25; B 451.

April 22. 1870   WALTHAM HOUSE, WALTHAM CROSS.

My dear Lord Houghton

I hardly gather from your letter whether you think that an offer made in 1848 (if the fact of the offer be genuine and the offer equally so) supplies an answer to the question that was in dispute between us—[3] Were we not discussing an affair of the day?

But I was clearly wrong in this, that I did not limit my assertion by any stipulation as to the solvency of the offerer. I might offer you half a million for Fryston, and you would thereby be justified in saying that so much money had been offered for that property. But if you were thinking of selling Fryston my offer would have no weight with you, because you would know that the half million was not forthcoming.

Twelve years ago—(not to talk of twenty-two)—novels were worth almost double what they are now—but I think that no novel has ever been sold for £10000—and no novel would be worth it except by Dickens, —whose prices, by the bye, are much more moderate.

However if you think I have lost my bet I will pay it with a happy heart— I hope you will dine with me on May 4.

Yours always

Anthony Trollope

To Edmund Routledge

MS University College, London. F. A. Mumby, *The House of Routledge, 1834–1934* (1934), pp. 112–13; B 452.

April 22—1870.   WALTHAM HOUSE, WALTHAM CROSS.

My dear Sir.

I could not undertake to make the story more than 20 of your pages. That was the length I mentioned when I had the pleasure of seeing you. I have never been willing to bind myself to any publisher not to do other work than what I may undertake to do for him. Indeed I have never done it, and will not do so now. I do not think that there is any prob-

---

[3] The dispute was occasioned by speculation about what Disraeli had been paid by Thomas Longman for *Lothair* (published on 2 May 1870), his first novel since *Tancred* (1847). In fact, Disraeli had been paid £1,000 outright, with royalties to begin after 2,000 copies, and he was also to derive income from the sale of any subsequent rights for foreign or English editions. (Under this arrangement he received over £7,500 for the novel by the end of 1876.) Houghton had maintained that in 1868 (Trollope's "1848" arose from a misunderstanding) E. S. Dallas had offered Disraeli £10,000 outright for a novel to be written as soon as he left office. Trollope then bet Houghton £10 that no publisher would offer such a sum. For the sequel, see Trollope to Houghton, 19 May 1870.

ability of my writing another Christmas story, but I should prefer to be free. As I told you, the entire copyright would be yours. I would not specifically bind myself to a day for the delivery. I am a punctual workman, and should be anxious to accommodate any publisher for whom I worked— I do not doubt the story would be ready by the time named.

The day of payment would be indifferent—

As I have been obliged to decline so many of your stipulations I shall suppose the matter is off unless I hear again.

very faithfully yours
Anthony Trollope

E. Routledge Esq

To Edmund Routledge

MS University College, London. Mumby, *House of Routledge*, pp. 113–14; B 453.

April 23—1870.   WALTHAM HOUSE, WALTHAM CROSS.
Dear Sir.

I enclose the agreement signed and suppose you will send me a duplicate. There is no probability that I shall write another Christmas story as I have very much work on hand,—and stories do not come as thick as blackberries. But I fear mine for you will not exceed the 20 pages, as your pages are long and I have always found that a short story does not require above 18 or 20 pages to tell itself. You shall however have full measure, & I will endeavour to give it you by the first week in August.[4]

Yours faithfully
Anthony Trollope

To Charles Kent

MS Parrish Collection.

April 24. 1870   WALTHAM HOUSE, WALTHAM CROSS.
My dear Mr Kent.

Allow me to thank you for the present of your volume of poetry,[5] for which I am very much obliged.

Yours faithfully
Anthony Trollope

C Kent Esq

[4] "Christmas Day at Kirkby Cottage," *Routledge's Christmas Annual* for 1870. Trollope received £100 for the story.

[5] Probably *Poems: A New Edition* (1870), Kent's first collected edition.

John Blackwood to Trollope

MS (copy) National Library of Scotland.

April 26/70   45 George St.
                                                         Edinr.
My dear Trollope

Your M.S. arrived safely today. I was so anxious about the introduction to Caesar that I read the M.S. at once and I am most happy to say that I think it is very good indeed. The summing up at the end of the Introduction is particularly effective. The point is put indeed I may say the fact is stated with a simple beauty that is very fine.

It strikes me that you might have done better to give the leading facts of Caesar's life more distinctly in sequence as most people either do not know anything or have pretty well forgotten everything but it is impossible to judge of this until one reads the whole consecutively.

The M.S. is all in Printing Office, with orders to look sharp and will soon be sent to you in proofs according to your instructions.

I am delighted with your promptitude and punctuality.

You seem to have felt with Caesar as Scott did with that Brobdignag Chap. The Emperor Nap.[6]

                                     Always yours truly
                                     John Blackwood

To [? William] Blackwood[7]

MS National Library of Scotland. SB 463.

[? May 1870]   WALTHAM HOUSE, WALTHAM CROSS.
My dear Mr Blackwood

I have just got your letter & proofs which I will attend to down in Yorkshire tomorrow.

In the meantime could the following alterations be made.

        Marne for Maine p 35
        central for eastern p. 67
        copper for brass—p. 77
        higher for bigger p. 95

I send the identical pages as possibly the numbering may now be altered.

                                     Yours very truly
                                     Anthony Trollope

[6] A reference to the number of books Trollope used. Scott, in his "On the Materials Necessary for his 'Life of Napoleon,'" says: "But my house I must swap / With some Brobdignag chap, / Ere I grapple, God bless me! / With Emperor Nap."

[7] The formality of the salutation and the initialed note to this letter ("All in time & attended to. WB.") indicate that it was addressed to William Blackwood.

To Alfred Austin

MS Parrish Collection. B 454.

May 2—1870 WALTHAM HOUSE, WALTHAM CROSS.
My dear Austin.

I have read the satyre.[8] As to the spirit shewn in it, the authors capacity for versification,—and for poetry also as shewn in one or two pieces,—and all those points which depend on the use of language, there can I think be no doubt. The frequent alliteration offends me somewhat, but offends but slightly.

As to the stuff of the satyre, its truth or absence of truth,—or what we may better call its justification by the state of things or want of such justification,—you and I differ so much about the condition of mankind generally, that we should hardly agree. Of satyre such as is yours,—unmixed satyre,—satyre written solely with the object of censuring faults in the world presumed by the satyrist to be so grievous as to oppress the virtues,—I doubt the use, and generally doubt the truth. The age of which you write I believe to have been better than preceeding [sic] ages, and the class of women which you represent to be bad, I believe to be good. There are exceptions; bad, heartless, worldly women,—& always have been. And of such the doings are more visible than are the doings of the gracious. But that, (which must always be the case,) hardly justifies general satyre. I have known very many men who have believed women of their own class to be bad and deserving of satyre;—but they have always excepted their own mothers, sisters, wives and daughters.

You will say that this is a judgement against all satyre; and I think it is a judgement against all satyric writings written only as such. I do not believe that such writings have ever done good, or have left other impress than that of the cynic disposition, and power, of the writer. I doubt whether Juvenal ever aided at all in the suppression of vice;—but Horace, who was not a satyrist by profession, & who is playful and even good-natured in his very satyres, did probably teach men to be less absurd in their manner of writing, of speaking, and of eating than they would have been without him. Byron as a satirist was wholly powerless on vice, simply leaving the impression that he, a man gifted with strong powers of description, had to avenge himself upon a world that had injured him. And satyre runs ever into exaggeration, leaving the conviction that not justice but revenge, is desired. The exaggeration probably may come from no such feeling, but from the natural tendency of the writer to seek ever for strong and still stronger modes of expression; till at last all truth is lost in the charm of heaping epithet on epithet and

[8] Austin's *The Season: A Satire* (1861), of which a revised edition had appeared in 1869 with a Preface asserting that the follies attacked in 1861 had increased in the intervening years. The object of Austin's satire was the London Season as a marriage market, where "smiling matrons are appraisers sly," who "each base cheapening buyer having chid, / Knock down their daughters to the noblest bid."

figure on figure;—as the eater loses the flavour of his meat through the multiplied uses of sauces and pepper.

So much as to satyre in general. In judging you as a satyrist I feel my-self called on to say that you are too prone to throw forward your own person;—and in this satyre you do so on what I regard as the weakest ground an author can take to stand upon;—namely your youth.[9] Youth is an immense advantage because it has itself, and has maturity before it also. Maturity has nothing better to look to. But, for all work, maturity must be better than work[? youth]; and is so much better that it may be doubted whether youth is justified in making public its work by any other consideration than that of the doubt whether maturity may come. But youth, I think, should never claim special strength as its own. I al-together deny your implied assertion that youth should speak truth aloud, because age is prone to falsehood. As seen by my experience age is truer than youth, juster, clearer, more merciful, less selfish, and in-finitely more capable of teaching the lessons which satyre is intended to convey. In common parlance, no doubt, we hear of the generosity of youth,—of its noble impulses, and the like. But I think we only hear of this because such qualities, when seen in the young, are more striking,—by reason of their comparative rarity—than when found in the old. And selfishness in the old is specially noticed—because it specially disgusts. We hardly expect the young to be other than selfish.

You will justify the repeated allusion to yourself, as a special person in your satyre, by the example of Horace. But in Horace's days literary men were so few in number that one who had made a name for himself was justified in the use of the "I"—by the absurdity of ignoring it; as with us is a Prime Minister, or a chief Justice, or an Archbishop. And Horace was already Horace when he wrote his satyres. And, moreover, he was goodnatured,—almost I may say a trifler,—in his satyres; and the "Videar nimis acer"[1] is less ambitious than are you when you declare that "To conflict called you abdicate your ease."

There is my Sermo—and I hope you will not think that I have carried it beyond the bounds of friendship.

Yours always most sincerely
Anthony Trollope

I may assert that I should not have written so to one of whose great in-tellectual capacity I was not convinced.

---

[9] In one passage, for instance, Austin contended that although satirists from Horace on have amused rather than mended the times, "I claim the precious privilege of youth, / Never to speak except to speak the truth." Trollope's criticism may have re-minded Austin uncomfortably of the dismissive review in the *Athenaeum* (20 April 1861, p. 528), which said that the youthful author had not the art, experience, or wisdom necessary for satire, and left the reader disgusted with the writer rather than the scenes he described. The review so irritated Austin that he published a reply.

[1] Trollope refers to the line "There are some critics to whom it seems I am too savage in my satire." (Horace, *Satires*, II, i, 1.)

To Alexander Macmillan

MS British Library.

May 2—1870. WALTHAM HOUSE, WALTHAM CROSS.
My dear Mr Macmillan.
I am sorry to say that I am engaged next Friday.
Yours very truly
Anthony Trollope

To John Blackwood

MS Taylor Collection. Excerpt, *Commentary*, pp. 309–10; excerpt, B 455.

May 7. 1870 ATHENAEUM CLUB
My dear Blackwood.
I send down the whole work corrected,—having as I think complied with every suggestion made both by you and by Collins. I must see a revise, because there are notes &c added;—but I will not keep it above a day, if you can let me have it next week. Let them send to me the copy also with my corrections, i e, the one I now send.

It is a dear little book to me,[2]—and there is one other thing to be said about the little dear. I think the 1st. of June is your birthday.[3] At any rate we'll make it so for this year, and you will accept it as a little present.
Yours always
Anthony Trollope

John Blackwood to Trollope

MS (copy) National Library of Scotland. Porter, p. 364.

45 George Street.
Edinr.
May 9/70
My dear Trollope
I am truly gratified and touched by the very handsome manner in which you have presented me with the copyright of the Caesar.

It affects me as a great personal compliment & mark of regard never to be forgotten.

I did look this gift horse most carefully in the mouth and I can speak to its merits. My anxiety about it was double as I felt that if I did not think your adventure into this new field not only a success but a most decided one, I was bound to tell you my opinion.

---

[2] "Proud of his achievement in so new a line, Trollope, an old friend of our family, at once sent a copy to my uncle, the Dean [Charles Merivale], who replied with placid brevity: 'Thank you for your comic History of Caesar.' Trollope wept." (H. C. Merivale, *Bar, Stage, and Platform* [1902], p. 96.) See *Autobiography*, pp. 339–40, where this incident is told but Merivale's name withheld.

[3] John Blackwood was in fact born on 7 December 1818.

I carried your letter home to my wife & I need not say how warmly she enters into my feelings of gratification. She had been rather low last week, her own favourite horse Sunbeam having died of inflamation & your letter was quite a fillip to her. She feels very sure of your sympathy in her grief about [the] horse. . . .

Always yours truly

Anthony Trollope Esq. John Blackwood

To W. Lucas Collins

MS Parrish Collection.

May 10. 1870   WALTHAM HOUSE, WALTHAM CROSS.
My dear Mr. Collins.

We will come on Thursday 26—and will arrive at the Rugby Station[4] from Leicester at 4.50 pm. I am sorry to say that, coming on that line, we cannot use the Crick Station.[5]

very faithfully yours
Anthony Trollope

To ?

MS (photocopy) UCLA. SB 456.

OFFICE OF THE ST. PAULS MAGAZINE,

May 11 1870   294, CITY ROAD, LONDON.
Dear Sir.

I send to you today for correction your brothers article on It Ghelmez[6] —with the Mss. As it is to appear in our next number, will you kindly correct it at once and send it to me addressed to
Waltham Cross.

Yours faithfully
Anthony Trollope

To John Blackwood

MS National Library of Scotland. B 457.

May. 12—1870   WALTHAM HOUSE, WALTHAM CROSS.
My dear Blackwood.

I send back the revise, as I hope for the last time. I have added to the note to page 158, and if I could see a proof of that I should like it.

Your printer has made two most unnecessary blunders. At pages 87—

---

[4] The great midlands railway junction, 30 miles east of Birmingham.

[5] The village of Crick is only one mile from Kilsby, where Collins lived; Rugby is five miles.

[6] "It Ghelmez," *St. Paul's*, 6 (June 1870), 304–12. The author of this article, about a village in Turkey, has not been identified.

and 130 he has omitted two half pages, and has added pages numbered 87x—and 130x; but by doing so he has upset altogether the headings of the subsequent pages.

As regards the first I had proposed, as you will see to leave out the story of Pulfius and Varenus, so as to bring in the half page;—either to do that or to add a line to the 12 preceeding [*sic*] pages. But in doing that I had not known that there would be a second error of the same kind.

As it is I must leave it to you to arrange.

Will you allow Langford to send me 25 copies for friends of my own.

Yours always most faithfully

Anthony Trollope

We shall be back in town at any rate by the end of May, i e 28th. May. I write a line to your wife about poor Sunbeam.

To Mary Chapman[7]

MS Parrish Collection. SB 458.

May 15. 1870   WALTHAM HOUSE, WALTHAM CROSS.

My dear Miss Chapman.

I must plead a reason for not acceding to your request which Mr Brown could not use— I am giving up the St. Paul's Magazine. After the coming number it will be managed by an Editor whom you can address at Messrs. Strahan's

56 Ludgate Hill.

I believe Mr Strahan will do it himself.

Yours faithfully

Anthony Trollope

To [? William] Blackwood

MS Mrs. C. L. Mock.

Bolton Bridge[8]

Yorkshire.

May 16 1870

My dear Mr Blackwood

I now return the last sheets of the Caesar to you revised and I do not know that I require to see any of them again. I am sorry that I have been so troublesome.

most faithfully yours

Anthony Trollope

---

[7] Mary Francis Chapman (1838–84), minor novelist (under the pseudonym J. C. Ayrton). No contribution by her to *St. Paul's* has been traced.

[8] Trollope used the ruins of Bolton Priory and the "Strid," the narrowing of the channel of the Wharfe two miles above the Priory, as a setting in *Lady Anna*; see Trollope to Steele, 25 May 1870.

To Lord Houghton

MS Trinity College Cambridge. T. Wemyss Reid, *The Life, Letters, and Friendships of Richard Monckton Milnes*, II, 225–26; B 459 (incomplete).

19 May. 1870   Bolton Bridge
My dear Lord Houghton.

We will have no compromise and as I do [not] in the least doubt the truth of every word you say I enclose a cheque for £10.

But my conviction is not in the least altered, and I look upon the offer, (which it seems was made two years ago, not for Lothair but for some other novel not then known to be written,—in fact for a novel to be written—) to be of the same worth as would be an offer from me to you of half a million for your property at Fryston. Whether you might wish to sell Fryston or not, you would disregard an offer coming from a man who clearly could not pay the sum offered.

Two years ago Dallas was editing the paper called Once a Week;—and, as it happened, I sold a novel, through him, to the proprietors of that paper just at that time, for publication in the paper. My price was not exorbitant:—i e it was exactly at the rate I was being paid for the article from other sources. I found that he was running a muck among novelists, offering to buy this and that, buying indeed this & that, and in the mean while the paper had to be disposed of as worthless. It was sold I believe for all but nothing. My bargain had been made bona fide with the proprietors, and my novel was written for them. But I was obliged to assent to another mode of publication, and to abate my price.[9] Therefore I regard an offer made by Dallas as no genuine offer,—even though his offer were for Lothair.

And again;—I know pretty well the value of these articles in the market, and I think that I know that no novel would be worth £10,000 to a publisher by any author,—no house could afford to give such a sum.[1] Dickens' last novel, (which I do not hesitate to say is worth three times the value of Lothair in a simply pecuniary view) has been sold for a considerably less sum,—not indeed the entire copyright, but the immediate publication, and half copyright afterwards.[2] I have heard you

[9] In fact, Trollope's manuscript for *The Vicar of Bullhampton* had been somewhat short, and the reduction in payment from £2,800 to £2,500 was by mutual consent. The change from publication in *Once a Week* to publication in part issue was against Trollope's wishes: see Trollope to Dallas, 5 January 1868, and Dallas to Trollope, 22 March 1869.

[1] George Smith offered George Eliot £10,000 for *Romola*, but the figure was reduced to £7,000 when she insisted on twelve-part rather than sixteen-part serialization in the *Cornhill*. Dickens, who did not sell his copyrights outright but entered into complicated profit-sharing arrangements with his publishers, made more than £10,000 from various works. (He made nearly £11,000, for example, from the sale of the parts and first volume publication of *Bleak House*, and somewhat more from *Little Dorrit*.) In 1880 Longman gave Disraeli £10,000 for the entire copyright of *Endymion*.

[2] Dickens's agreement with Chapman & Hall for *The Mystery of Edwin Drood* called for £7,500 plus half profits for all sales beyond 25,000 copies.

quote, as to other works, sums reputed to be given, but which were fabulous. For a novel published as Lothair is published, and sure of a large circulation, a publisher could afford to give an author about 10/ a copy for all copies sold by him at the cost price,—nominally 31. 6d., for which he gets about 17/6. The other 7/6 would pay the cost, the advertising, and give the publisher a small profit. Clay[3] told me the other day that 6000 copies had been sold—That would make £3000 for the author. And the market has been so glutted with the work that the publisher cannot hope to sell above another 1000. Where could he possibly recoup himself for an expenditure of £10,000?[4]

I do, however, believe that Dallas made the offer two years since.

Yours always
Anthony Trollope

My object the other night was to explain to you that Dallas at the time was acting under a foolishly erroneous idea of achieving popularity for the paper he was editing.

To Austin Dobson

MS University of London Library. Excerpt, Commentary, p. 297; B 460.

Bolton Bridge
address

21 May 1870   WALTHAM HOUSE, WALTHAM CROSS.
My dear Mr. Dobson.

I will do as you desire with your poem[5] which I have read with much pleasure. I cannot as yet miss [? dismiss] the old habit and would ask you whether "overgrow" in the second line satisfies you in the sense in which you use it—you mean—overlay. Again "look" in the first line on page 3 hardly pleases me;—or the phrase lower down of "arousing the quiet." We disturb the quiet and arouse the echo— To say that a hounds "yell" would not, as a term in venery, be accepted by hunting men, may be hypercritical. Pray excuse me, and if you will return the Mss with or without alteration I will hand it over to Mr. Strahan with some very few others when in the course of next month I give up the seals.

And now I will descend from poetry to prose. In my endeavour to establish the Saint Pauls on what I considered to be a good literary footing, I insisted on myself naming the remuneration to be paid. It has not been very great, but it has been fairly good. The object now is to make

[3] Probably a member of the Clay family, well-known London printers.

[4] T. Wemyss Reid said that the exact sum offered to Disraeli was known to Houghton, "a fact which did not prevent Mr. Trollope from insisting that it was impossible that any such sum could have been paid" (*Life, Letters, and Friendships of Richard Monckton Milnes*, II, 224).

[5] "A Gentleman of the Old School," *St. Paul's*, 6 (July 1870), 367–69. Dobson made the changes Trollope suggested.

the magazine pay. What may be the result of that resolve to contributors in the way of remuneration will never be known to me after June. I fear it may not be altogether satisfactory.

I cannot refrain from saying how much gratification I have had during the last two years and a half in meeting with two or three contributors whom I have not known before,—(in your case have not even yet known in the flesh) and as to whom I have felt that they would grace our literature hereafter. But I must own to a corresponding vexation of spirit when I have found that literary work which I have known to be good, has not made that mark, under my editorship, which I have known that it has deserved. As to your poems I have heard great praise from some few whose praise is really worth having,—from a man or two and also a woman or two, who in speaking of poetry speak of that which they understand; but I have been disappointed at finding, as regards yourself and others, that good work has not been more widely recognized.

But it is perhaps well for literature that good work should not attain its recognition easily, and that perseverance at the back of it should be needed. I am sure that you will succeed if you persevere.

My Caesar will be a little thing,—but it has been a great delight to me to do it, as giving a break to the constant writing of prose fiction and taking me back to the old books which I read when I was young.

very faithfully yours
Anthony Trollope

To Mrs. Anna Steele

B 461.

May 25–70   Bolton Bridge
My dear Mrs. Steele.

One word in answer to your nice note, though it be on a subject very difficult to speak of.[6]

Of course one's sympathies are with the fathers and mothers & brothers,—and should be so; but not the less should one have mercy on the most terrible sufferers of this age;—on a class who suffer heavier punishment in proportion to their fault than any other, and who often have come to their ineffable misery almost without fault at all.

It would be quite against the grain with me to represent such a woman as interesting, charming, fit for diamonds, and a thing to be adored.

The whole Formosa business[7] was to my thinking detestably false. But

---

[6] The subject is Carry Brattle, the "fallen woman" of *The Vicar of Bullhampton*; see Trollope's Preface to the novel and *Autobiography*, pp. 329–35.

[7] Formosa is the prostitute in Dion Boucicault's play of the same title. The play caused a furore when it was presented at the Drury Lane Theatre; see Trollope's article "Formosa," *St. Paul's*, 5 (October 1869), 75–80, where Trollope insisted that young women and wives were not so ignorant of life as to be contaminated by seeing a

Austin Dobson. Chalk drawing by A. N. Fairfield, 1874.

a poor creature may fall,—as we call it—and yet be worth redeeming. Fathers & mothers will forgive anything in a son, debauchery, gambling, lying—even the worst dishonesty & fraud—but the "fallen" daughter is too often regarded as an outcast for whom no hope can be entertained. Excuse all this enthusiasm, and believe me

Yours always
A. T.

This is the prettiest spot in England.[8] We have been here ten days & go homewards tomorrow. I hope Lady Lennard is not ill again by your hurry to go to Brighton.[9]

To Austin Dobson

MS University of London Library. B 462.

29 May 70   WALTHAM HOUSE, WALTHAM CROSS.
My dear Mr. Dobson.

I have just read Leisure's epitaph[1] aloud to my wife and family—and we are charmed with it. It is very good indeed. Should Strahan, (who maybe is not given to the Muses,) hesitate, shall I try it elsewhere?

Yours
A. T.

To Mrs. Anna Steele

B 464.

June 6—1870   WALTHAM HOUSE, WALTHAM CROSS.
My dear Mrs. Steele

Thanks for your kind letter. I have not seen the article in *The Times*,[2] —nor had I heard of it till I got your note— It was, I find, in the Supplement, which in this house usually gets thrust away, and so it escaped notice. I shall not care to search it up now.

Not that, as a rule, I am indifferent to criticism on my own work. I

---

stage depiction of a prostitute, and that stage depictions of prostitutes were only objectionable if the prostitutes were depicted as admirable.

[8] In *Lady Anna* (chap. xv) Trollope wrote of Bolton Bridge: "No more luxuriant pasture, no richer foliage, no brighter water, no more picturesque arrangement of the freaks of nature, aided by the art and taste of man, is to be found, perhaps, in England."

[9] The Barrett Lennards had a house in Brighton.

[1] Dobson's poem "A Gentleman of the Old School" carried an epigraph from George Eliot: "Leisure is gone . . . fine old Leisure."

[2] An unsigned notice of *The Vicar of Bullhampton* (*The Times*, 3 June 1870, p. 4) called the book monotonous: "It is a nice, easy, safe reading book for old ladies and young ladies . . . but we do not think that either in construction or development this novel will add much to Mr. Anthony Trollope's reputation."

fancy that I am too anxious, like other authors, to see what others say about me. But now, as I know it to be hard, I will pass it by.

But I do profess so much in my own behalf;—that I never ask who has criticised me, and that I am above animosity against those who blame, as I am above gratitude to those who praise me. Whatever may be the motive of the critic, I presume that it has been that which alone can be honest—that namely of giving a just judgement. If it be so, the writer who gives it can deserve neither thanks or blame from me. I am sure the matter should be so regarded.

Do not, however, suppose that I profess myself to be indifferent. I know, as well as any man, or woman, the value of a favourable review in the Times.

Yours lovingly
A. T.

To Austin Dobson

MS University of London Library. B 465.

June 15—1870   GARRICK CLUB
My dear Mr. Dobson.

The last day of my rule over the magazine has been deferred for a month,—and I am inserting your poem, which is I think almost the best we have had. I am going out of town for a few days, but I hope to make your acquaintance when I return.

Yours always
Any Trollope

To Octavian Blewitt

MS Royal Literary Fund. SB 466.

June 28—70   WALTHAM HOUSE, WALTHAM CROSS.
My dear Mr Blewitt.

I have been applied to very earnestly in regard to the case of Mrs. Mark Lemon.[3] As I shall be at the Committee it will be needless that I should write. Shirley Brooks who knows all her circumstances intimately has written or will write as to the necessity of her case. Will any other testimony to that effect will [sic] be required? I should think not.

Yours very faithfully
Anthony Trollope

If any second letter as [to] the condition of the family be necessary— will you write a line to Shirley Brooks to that effect. His address is 6. Kent Terrace. Regents Park.

---

[3] Helen Lemon, widow of Mark Lemon (1809–70), the editor of *Punch* from 1841 to 1870. After Lemon's death on 23 May, he was found to be heavily in debt, owing partly to unsuccessful speculations. The Literary Fund gave Mrs. Lemon a grant of £100.

To John Blackwood

MS National Library of Scotland. Excerpt, Parker, p. 60; B 467.

June 30—1870   ATHENAEUM CLUB
My dear Blackwood

I yesterday met W. G. Clark, and was speaking to him about the Ancient Classics. He is, I think I may say, undoubtedly, the first Aristophanic scholar of the day,—and is certainly of all men the one most connected at present with the name of Aristophanes. He is moreover in every respect well qualified to do what you would want to have done with the Greek comedian. He was tutor at Trinity and public orator at Cambridge till he resigned those offices,—and is well known to all literary men.

He said yesterday that he would much like to do the work.[4] I had sent him the Caesar. If I would send you or Collins to apply to him you had better address him as W. G. Clark Esq
                                    Trinity
                                    Cambridge,
—for though he is in orders, he is struggling to get out of them.[5]
                                    Yours faithfully
                                    Anthony Trollope

To Lord Brougham[6]

MS National Library of Scotland.

July 9. 1870   WALTHAM HOUSE, WALTHAM CROSS.
My dear Lord Brougham.

Sir Charles Taylor[7] has sent me a letter from you referring to the publication of your late brother's[8] correspondence, as to which, if it will suit you, I would propose to call on you at Crawley's hotel on Wednesday next at 2. PM.

I would very strongly advise you not to accept Longmans offer of 2/3s. of profit. The payment made by a publisher for such a work should be by a royalty on all copies sold; or by a lump sum. The former method would I think be the fairest for all parties.

On all other points I will defer speaking till I shall meet your Lordship.

---

[4] W. Lucas Collins, editor of the series, prepared the volume on Aristophanes (1872).

[5] This was made possible by the Clerical Disabilities Act, passed in 1870.

[6] William Brougham (1795–1886), 2d Baron Brougham and Vaux. With this letter began Trollope's very considerable involvement with the publication by Blackwood of *The Life and Times of Lord Brougham* (1871).

[7] William Brougham had married Taylor's sister Emily Frances in 1834.

[8] Henry Peter Brougham (1778–1868), 1st Baron Brougham and Vaux, the distinguished jurist and political leader; one of the founders of the *Edinburgh Review* and later one of the founders of University College, London; effective advocate of the 1832 Reform Bill and other social and judicial reforms.

If Wednesday will not suit you, I will call on Tuesday. But I shall be in town on Wednesday, but not so on Tuesday unless you wish it.

very faithfully

Yours Anthony Trollope

I find that I could not be in Albemarle Street on Tuesday at 2,—but would at 12. noon. I should prefer the Wednesday.

To John Blackwood

MS National Library of Scotland. Excerpt, Parker, p. 61; B 468.

Sept 8. 1870 Brougham Hall

My dear Blackwood.

I have been here for the last three days reading the MS of the first Vol of Lord Brougham's autobiography,—having undertaken the task with the view of suggesting to the present Lord Brougham any steps that might be well taken towards preparing the work for publication; and I now write to you at his request as it appears that there is an intention that you shall publish the book.

It is intended that there should be three volumes. It may be a question whether it should not be compressed into two. I have only seen the first, —which it is intended to publish before the other two. That such a work will excite considerable interest there can be no doubt. In the first volume there is very much of interest;—especially in regard to the establishment of the Edinbro' Review, and Brougham's early correspondence with Lord Grey. But the whole matter, as it now exists, is unconnected, confused, very incomplete, and altogether unchronological. It is also full of errors,—from ignorance on the part of copiers.

I have given it as my opinion to Lord Brougham that he must do one of two things;—he must either consent to put forth a bad book to the public, which will be confused and incomplete,—explaining in a short preface from himself that the somewhat heterogeneous mass of matter is given to the public in that shape, because it was so left by Lord Brougham,—excusing, (without absolute acknowledgement of fault,) the shortcomings of the work by the fact that it was arranged when the author was past 80 years old;—or else he must put the whole of the Mss into the hands of some competent Editor, with full editorial power, so that the errors may be corrected, and the confusion reduced from the present Chaos to fair literary order. I have told him that if he intends to do this he must consult with his publisher as to such Editor, and that he cannot expect to procure such work without liberal payment. I am far from saying that he could certainly get such work even for liberal payment.

In regard to the Mss which I have read I have advised the present Lord Brougham to omit a long journal of a tour in Sweden, which for various reasons I think ill adapted for such a work as is intended. If this be omitted I doubt whether the MS now apportioned for the 1st. volume would suffice.[9]

The matter as handed to me was continuous. I have divided it into chapters, and have prepared headings for the chapters.[1] But I have done this rather as shewing what is needed, than as supplying the actual words which should be used for the headings. Even should it be thought well to publish the book without any Editor, (and Lord Broughams feeling rather lies in that direction,) there would be needed a not small amount of correction, as to which the care of an instructed person would be required. You will find that this is so, when you look yourself at the MS.

I myself think that for the reputation of the late Lord Brougham, for the comfort of the present owner of the MS, & for the sake of the public who will read the book, the whole work should be regularly edited.

I have told Lord Brougham that you would no doubt write to him after receiving the letter from me. He will then see you, taking the MS of the first vol to Edinburgh with him, if it shall appear by your letter to him that you wish to see it with the view of publishing it.

Most faithfully yours
Anthony Trollope

To Lord Brougham

MS National Library of Scotland.

Sept 11. 1870.   WALTHAM HOUSE, WALTHAM CROSS.
My dear Lord Brougham.

I have written and now enclose the sort of preface which I should put to the work, were I you, *and were I determined to publish the book without an Editor.* It is still my own opinion that you should confide the whole work to some able man. You have to think of your brother's reputation as regards this special work. Such a preface as I have suggested may,—or may not,—be held as a valid excuse for the moment. But, hereafter, Lord Brougham's Autobiography will be known among the biographical literature of his country as a good book or as a bad book, in accordance with its intrinsic merits, and will not be judged by the light of any apology. As it now stands it is too confused to satisfy future readers, and would I fear find only that immediate circulation which anything coming from your brothers hand would be sure to command.

Tell Lady Brougham with my regards that I had a very pleasant journey as far as Stafford when I lost Lady F. She was treated most ignominiously and shamefully,—was put into a carriage from which she

[9] The journal of the Swedish tour was not omitted (*The Life and Times of Lord Brougham*, I, chap. iii).
[1] The work has lengthy chapter summaries and some short chapter headings; these may be by Trollope.

was obliged to change at Stafford; and when I was carried out of that station she was left with her maid on the platform struggling with an immense mass of cloaks, rugs, dressing cases, baskets, umbrellas, bags, and shawls which no porter could be got so much as to look at;—and in a state of mental agony as to her heavier luggage which I sincerely hope did *not* come on to London. We were an hour late then— I only hope she be not at Stafford still with nothing but baskets and umbrellas.

Yours always
faithfully
Anthony Trollope

John Blackwood to Trollope

MS National Library of Scotland.

STRATHTYRUM
ST. ANDREWS

Septr. 11/70
My dear Trollope

Many thanks for your very clear statement of the condition in which you find the M.S. of the first volume of Lord Broughams Memoirs. From what you say I have no doubt the present Lord's best plan will be to put the whole materials into the hands of a responsible editor.

It is not probable that the book could afford to pay for an Editor whose time is as valuable as yours & I do not suppose it would suit your plans to undertake the task.

The man who occurs to me as most likely to suit is John Hill Burton[2] the historian. . . .

always yours truly
John Blackwood

Anthony Trollope Esq

To Lord Brougham

MS National Library of Scotland.

Sept 16—70   WALTHAM HOUSE, WALTHAM CROSS.
My dear Lord Brougham.

Very many thanks indeed for the trouble you have taken. I fear it must have been a great labour to you. My astonishment is that the work for so long a time was carried on by so few hands.

---

[2] John Hill Burton (1809–81), historian of Scotland; author of biographies and books on law and economics; a regular contributor to *Blackwood's*. The plan to enlist Burton's services was adopted. Blackwood wrote to Brougham on 29 September that he had sent the manuscript to Burton, who "was most anxious as I knew he would be to lend any assistance he could privately but would not have his name known as Editor in a case where he could not have full power" (MS National Library of Scotland). See Trollope to Brougham, 12 October 1870.

I hope that you and Blackwood may soon agree as to what shall be done about the opus magnum.

> very faithfully yours
> Anthony Trollope

To George Smith

SB 469 (Sadleir's transcript).

28 September 1870

Trollope insists that the title page of *The Struggles of Brown, Jones, and Robinson,* now first being published in (authorized) book form, shall carry the legend: "Reprinted from the Cornhill of 1862." "It must, of course, appear as a reprint."[3]

To John Morley

MS Parrish Collection.

4 Oct. 70   Waltham Cross
My dear Morley.

Clark who was Public orator at Cambridge is to be with us next Saturday & Sunday. Will you come to meet him.

> Yours ever A. T.
> Anty Trollope

If my success were equal to my energy I should be a great man.

To Mrs. Anna Steele

SB 470.

7 October 1870   Waltham Cross

Trollope thanks Mrs. Steele for some favor unnamed, mentions his four hunters, and adds, "I am so sick of the war![4] Are not you? And I hate the French,—and ever did. But I wish now that they could be spared further suffering." He concludes with a postscript about *Sir Harry Hotspur*: "Humblethwaite is too gloomy and wretched."

[3] Smith acquiesced, but omitted the reference to 1862.
[4] The Franco-Prussian War had broken out on 19 July.

To Lord Brougham

MS National Library of Scotland.

7. October 1870   WALTHAM HOUSE, WALTHAM CROSS.

My dear Lord Brougham.

I think you will do quite right in taking the joint advice of Mr. Burton and Mr. Blackwood. The former is a man of great attainment and literary capacity, and the latter thoroughly understands his business as a publisher.

I think that the suggestion as made by Mr. Burton will work precisely the same effect on the book itself as that proposed by me. But, in accordance with his plan, this will be done without the appearance of any other name on the title page than that of your brother. When the book comes into the hands of the critics, of course the notes and general arrangements of the book,—which will visibly not have been your brothers work,—will become liable to remark. It will be said that the book has either been well handled or ill handled;—but that it should have been handled will have been a necessity and that it has been handled will be a notorious and manifest fact. I think that for the sake of all concerned it is better that there should be no secret as to who has had the doing of such work;—and I think that the critics are less likely to be abusive if the name of the doer is given; and that the man himself is more likely in such case to be careful. In point of fact he will be the Editor,—must have discretion as to altering and correcting errors, and omitting repetitions or contradictions. I think the name should be given. But I am quite ready to acknowledge that my opinion in such a matter should not have weight enough with you to stand against Mr. Burtons who is to undertake the work,—backed as it is by your own and Blackwoods.

As to the mode of publication,—a volume at a time or three volumes together,—I think you should be guided altogether by Blackwood.

very faithfully yours
Anthony Trollope

To ?

MS Parrish Collection.

10. Oct. 1870   WALTHAM HOUSE, WALTHAM CROSS.

My dear Sir.

The telegram to me about the November lecturing did not in the least signify. I am only sorry that I could not do as your friends asked me.

Thanks for the card. Your friends have done for me more than my Godfathers ever did. They had me christened Anthony,—the men of

Leeds[5] have added Moore. It sounds very well, and I feel myself rather flattered. But I dont know where they got the name for me. I shall be most happy to accept your kind offer of hospitality, and will present myself at your house some time on the 17th. of January next.

very faithfully yours

Anthony Trollope

To Lord Brougham
MS National Library of Scotland.

October 12. 1870.   Waltham Cross

My dear Lord Brougham.

I have enquired at the Post Office and they say there that the post to Cannes is at present open, and as far as they know, safe. Our Indian Mails still go through France, though they are, I believe, prepared to adopt another route at a days warning. I should fear that you and Lady Brougham will hardly get to Cannes in November.[6]

Touching the book, of course if Mr. Burton will set to work and do the book, adding or curtailing what has to be added or curtailed, you can then judge whether his name should or should not appear. I own I still think it should do so, if the work done amounts to anything considerable. You may possibly find a word less significant than that of Editor—though I hardly know what that word would be.[7]

Yours always faithfully

Anthony Trollope

To Alexander Macmillan
MS Parrish Collection. B 471.

18. October 1870   WALTHAM HOUSE, WALTHAM CROSS.

My dear Mr Macmillan.

I am sorry that any thing to do with my tale should be less advantageous to you than you had expected. But the fact is that as one pound of tea wont make two by any variance in packing the article,—so neither

---

[5] On 17 January 1871 Trollope gave his lecture "On English Prose Fiction as a Rational Amusement" to the Leeds Philosophical and Literary Society.

[6] The 1st Lord Brougham had built a chateau at Cannes, where he spent part of each year. The war did disrupt mail service via Paris to Marseilles, and from 1871 onward mail to India went to Brindisi and thence direct to Alexandria.

[7] When the *Life and Times of Lord Brougham* was published, Burton's assistance was not acknowledged. Brougham printed his brother's instructions that, apart from corrections of dates or proper names, the narrative was to be printed as he had written it and that no editor was to be employed. Those directions, he noted, had been "scrupulously obeyed." The book's notorious inaccuracies demonstrate that Burton's assistance did not amount to "editing."

will a one-volumed tale make two volumes. You will say that in one case the quantity is fixed, and in the other not. But in regard to the latter article the quantity is too well and too nearly fixed to admit of such violent stretching. The real pound may be, and often is, lessened by an ounce in the packing;—but to make two pounds out of one is more than can be done even in Marlbro Street. I am quite sure that you agree with me.[8]

You tell me that the trials of authors have their mitigations. I have had none to complain of, but what have come from a dull brain and relaxed application.

Yours always faithfully
Anthony Trollope

To Lord Brougham

MS National Library of Scotland.

November 14. 1870.   Waltham Cross.
My dear Lord Brougham.

I think that Blackwood's offer to you is less beneficial than it should be.

I am of opinion that he should pay you a royalty of not less than 5/– a volume.

In your place I should make to him a counter offer as follows.

The publisher to publish not less than 2,000 copies at first, and to pay a royalty of 5/– on each volume published.

The publisher to settle the price, and to publish as many as he pleases at that price and sell them, within a period of 3 years.

The publisher to have any profit to be made out of American or other publications during that time.

The effect (or effects) would be,—that you would receive £500 down on the publication of each volume, and 5/ for each volume published (or printed) beyond the 2000.

---

[8] Macmillan, who had purchased both serial and book rights to *Sir Harry Hotspur of Humblethwaite* (see Trollope to Macmillan, 8 March 1869), sold the book rights for the first edition to Hurst & Blackett for £300, the copyright to revert to him after nine months. Trollope's objection to publishing the story in two volumes must have been made about a week previous to this letter, for on 13 October Henry Blackett wrote to Macmillan "to say our printers have nearly one volume of 'Sir Harry Hotspur' already in type, and it will of course be attended with considerable expense to cancel it; the work forms Two Volumes, of the same size as the last story issued by us (a volume of which I send herewith) so that I can hardly see how Mr. Trollope should maintain his objection to the publication; if however he still objects, I must relinquish the work into your hands, tho' I appreciate your liberality in proposing to waive a portion of the sum agreed upon if we print it in a single volume." (MS British Library.) Apparently, part of the eventual solution was for Macmillan to arrange to have the book printed for Hurst & Blackett by Clay. See also *Bibliography*, pp. 119–20.

That the publisher could not publish a cheap edition without your sanction.

That you would limit the term to 3 years.

And that in return for these concessions you would give up the American market to the publisher.

My experience tells me that in the hands of a private individual the American market is worth little or nothing. The publisher should manipulate it, and can do so with much greater advantage.

You should be very careful to know what you are to pay to Mr. Burton.

I certainly think that not less than 2000 copies should be printed as a commencement.

Yours very faithfully
Anthony Trollope

To Lord Brougham

MS National Library of Scotland.

24 November 1870.   Waltham Cross
My dear Lord Brougham.

I still think that Blackwoods offer to you is not sufficient. If you be not so far implicated in the transaction already as to be unable to withdraw I should decline, were I you, to give him the book for less than £500 a volume for 2000 copies and 5/ a volume for all copies beyond the 2000.

I explained to you my connexion with the house of Chapman & Hall; and am now not at all anxious to persuade you to transfer the publishing from Blackwood to them; but Chapman & Hall would give you the terms I have named—of course in dealing on such terms with either Blackwood or Chapman you would concede the foreign rights.

I hope you have come to explicit terms with Mr. Burton. Of course I cannot know how far you are bound to Blackwood by your employment of Mr. Burtons services through Blackwoods agency.

I think that in writing to Blackwood you should refrain from questioning the detailed expenditure as suggested by him, confining yourself to your own demand.[9]

Yours very truly
Anthony Trollope

[9] On 26 November Blackwood wrote to Brougham, accepting his "modifications" and agreeing to pay "£400 for the first 2,000 of Volume one of the Memoir . . . [and] 5/– per copy on every copy we sell beyond the 2,000 while the selling price continues at 16/." (MS [copy] National Library of Scotland.)

To Lord Brougham

MS National Library of Scotland.

Nov. 30. 1870   Waltham Cross.
My dear Lord Brougham.

I am very glad you have got to the end of your trouble as to a publisher. Blackwood will do the work very well for you.

It is always well in such agreements to name some term, as otherwise
a publisher would have the power of preventing you from making some
other agreement—perhaps as to a cheaper edition,—with another house.
And he might act as a dog in the manger, refusing to bring out such
cheaper edition himself on any reasonable terms, and not allowing you
to do so with any other firm. Therefore it is expedient to name a term.
If there be any copies left at the end of the term you would be bound to
buy them at *cost* price before making a further agreement; but as the
publisher would have no profit on such transaction he would not have
any large amount. And of course reasonable time would be allowed by
you, even over the 3 years, for their disposal. But the term if settled en-
ables you to hinder the publisher from insisting on his right of sale, as
against any other right, after the work in the first form has ceased to be
profitable to you as the owner of the copyright.

very faithfully
Yours
Anthony Trollope

To Charles Kent

MS Parrish Collection. B 472.

December 22—1870   GARRICK CLUB
My dear Mr. Kent.

Many thanks for your kind letter,—which should have been answered
sooner but that the copy of the paper which you sent me went astray and
I had to procure it. Such praise as yours is always most pleasant to an
author[1]— I only hope it may have been deserved. I am always most
doubtful about my work;—and in some moods am altogether beyond
doubt.

Most faithfully yours
Anthony Trollope

---

[1] In a review of *Sir Harry Hotspur*, Kent had written: "It is not only a brilliant
example of Anthony Trollope's powers as a novelist, but is in a very striking manner
a radiant specimen of English imaginative literature." Kent went on to admire Trollope's "consummate delicacy" in handling his material in such a way that even "the
redoubtable Mr. Podsnap" would find nothing "to bring a blush to the cheek of a
young person." (*Sun*, 15 December 1870, p. 2.)